ROBUSTNESS

ROBUSTNESS

LARS PETER HANSEN

THOMAS J. SARGENT

PRINCETON UNIVERSITY PRESS   PRINCETON AND OXFORD

In the United Kingdom: Princeton University Press
3 Market Place, Woodstock, Oxfordshire, OX20 1SY

Library of Congress Control Number: 2007927641
ISBN-13: 978-0-691-11442-2 (cloth)

British Library Cataloging-in-Publication Data are available

The publisher would like to acknowledge the authors of this volume
for providing the camera-ready copy from which this book was
printed. The authors composed this book in Computer Modern
using TEX and the TEXsis 2.18 macros.

Printed on acid-free paper. ∞

press.princeton.edu

Printed in the United States of America

10   9   8   7   6   5   4   3   2   1

In memory of our friend Sherwin Rosen

Contents

Preface   xv

Acknowledgments   xvii

Part I: Motivation and main ideas

1. Introduction   3

Generations of control theory. Control theory and rational expectations. Misspecification and rational expectations. Our extensions of robust control theory. Discounting. Representation of worst-case shock. Multiple agent settings. Explicitly stochastic interpretations. Calibrating fear of misspecification. Robust filtering and estimation. Robust control theory, shock serial correlations, and rational expectations. Entropy in specification analysis. Acknowledging misspecification. Why entropy? Why max-min? Is max-min too cautious? Aren't you just picking a plausible prior? Why not learn the correct specification? Is the set of perturbed models too limited? Is robust control theory positive or normative? Other lessons. Topics and organization.

2. Basic ideas and methods   25

Introduction. Approximating models. Dynamic programming without model misspecification. Measuring model misspecification with entropy. Two robust control problems. Modified certainty equivalence principle. Robust linear regulator. More general misspecifications. A simple algorithm. Interpretation of the simple algorithm. Robustness and discounting in a permanent income model. The LQ permanent income model. Solution when $\sigma = 0$. Linear regulator for permanent income model. Effects on consumption of concern about misspecification. Observational equivalence of quantities but not continuation values. Distorted endowment process. A Stackelberg formulation for representing misspecification. Concluding remarks. Matlab programs.

3. A stochastic formulation   53

Introduction. Shock distributions. Martingale representations of distortions. A digression on entropy. A stochastic robust control problem. A recursive formulation. Verifying the solution. A value function bound. Large deviation interpretation of $\mathcal{R}$. Choosing the control law. Linear-quadratic model. Relative entropy and normal distributions. Value function adjustment for the LQ model.

Part II: Standard control and filtering

4. Linear control theory   67

Introduction. Control problems. Deterministic regulator. Augmented regulator problem. Discounted stochastic regulator problem. Solving the deterministic linear regulator problem. Nonsingular A_{yy}. Singular A_{yy}. Continuous-time systems. Computational techniques for solving Riccati equations. Schur algorithm. Digression: solving DGE models with distortions. Doubling algorithm. Initialization from a positive definite matrix. Application to continuous time. Matrix sign algorithm. Solving the augmented regulator problem. Computational techniques for solving Sylvester equations. The Hessenberg-Schur algorithm. Doubling algorithm. Conclusion.

5. The Kalman filter   103

Introduction. Review of Kalman filter and preview of main result. Muth's problem. The dual to Muth's filtering problem. The filtering problem. Sequence version of primal and dual problems. Sequence version of Kalman filtering problem. Sequence version of dual problem. Digression: reversing the direction of time. Recursive version of dual problem. Recursive version of Kalman filtering problem. Concluding remarks.

Part III: Robust control

6. Static multiplier and constraint games   119

Introduction. Phillips curve example. The government's problem. Robustness of robust decisions. Basic setup with a correct model. The constraint game with $b = 0$. Multiplier game with $b = 0$. The model with $b \neq 0$. Probabilistic formulation ($b = 0$). Gaussian perturbations. Letting the minimizing agent choose random perturbations when $b = 0$. Constraint and multiplier preferences. Concluding remarks. Rational expectations equilibrium.

7. Time domain games for attaining robustness 139

Alternative time domain formulations. The setting. Two Stackelberg games. Two Markov perfect equilibria. Markov perfect equilibrium: definition. Markov perfect equilibria: value functions. Useful recursions. Computing a Markov perfect equilibrium: the recursion. Step one: distorting the covariance matrix. Step two: distorting the mean. Another Markov perfect equilibrium and a Bellman-Isaacs condition. Taking inventory. Markov perfect equilibrium of infinite horizon game. Recursive representations of Stackelberg games. Markov perfect equilibria as candidate Stackelberg equilibria. Maximizing player chooses first. Minimizing player chooses first. Bayesian interpretation of robust decision rule. Relation between multiplier and constraint Stackelberg problems. Dynamic consistency. Miscellaneous details. Checking for the breakdown point. Policy improvement algorithm. Concluding remarks. Details of a proof of Theorem 7.7.1. Certainty equivalence. Useful formulas. A single Riccati equation. Robustness bound. A pure forecasting problem. Completing the square.

8. Frequency domain games and criteria for robustness 173

Robustness in the frequency domain. Stackelberg game in time domain. Fourier transforms. Stackelberg constraint game in frequency domain. Version 1: H_2 criterion. Version 2: the H_∞ criterion. Stackelberg multiplier game in frequency domain. A multiplier problem. Robustness bound. Breakdown point reconsidered. Computing the worst-case misspecification. Three examples of frequency response smoothing. Example 1. Example 2. Example 3. Entropy is the indirect utility function of the multiplier game. Meaning of entropy. Risk aversion across frequencies. Concluding remarks. Infimization of H_∞. A dual prediction problem. Proofs of three lemmas. Duality. Evaluating a given control law. When $\theta = \theta_F$. Failure of entropy condition. Proof of Theorem 8.8.2. Stochastic interpretation of H_2. Stochastic counterpart.

9. Calibrating misspecification fears with detection error probabilities 213

Introduction. Entropy and detection error probabilities. The context-specific nature of θ. Approximating and distorting models. Detection error probabilities. Details. Likelihood ratio under the approximating model. Likelihood ratio under the distorted model. The detection error probability. Breakdown point examples revisited. Ball's model. Concluding remarks.

10. A permanent income model   223

Introduction. A robust permanent income theory. Solution when $\sigma = 0$. The $\sigma = 0$ benchmark case. Observational equivalence for quantities of $\sigma = 0$ and $\sigma \neq 0$. Observational equivalence: intuition. Observational equivalence: formal argument. Precautionary savings interpretation. Observational equivalence and distorted expectations. Distorted endowment process. Another view of precautionary savings. Frequency domain representation. Detection error probabilities. Robustness of decision rules. Concluding remarks. Parameter values. Another observational equivalence result.

Part IV: Multi-agent problems

11. Competitive equilibria without robustness   253

Introduction. Pricing risky claims. Types of competitive equilibria. Information, preferences, and technology. Information. Preferences. Technology. Planning problem. Imposing stability. Arrow-Debreu. The price system at time 0. The household. The firm. Competitive equilibrium with time-0 trading. Equilibrium computation. Shadow prices. Recursive representation of time 0 prices. Recursive representation of household's problem. Units of prices and reopening markets. Sequential markets with Arrow securities. Arrow securities. The household's problem in the sequential equilibrium. The firm. Recursive competitive equilibrium. Asset pricing in a nutshell. Partial equilibrium interpretation. Concluding remarks.

12. Competitive equilibria with robustness   271

Introduction. A pure endowment economy. The planning problem. Household problem. A robust planning problem. Max-min representation of household problem. Sequence problem of maximizing player. Digression about computing μ_0^w. Sequence problem of minimizing player. A decentralization with Arrow securities. A robust consumer trading Arrow securities. The inner problem. The outer problem. A Bayesian planning problem. Practical remarks. A model of occupational choice and pay. A one-occupation model. Equilibrium with no concern about robustness. Numerical example of Ryoo-Rosen model. Two asset pricing strategies. Pricing from the robust planning problem. Pricing from the ex post Bayesian planning problem. Concluding remarks. Decentralization of partial equilibrium. Solving Ryoo and Rosen's model by hand.

13. Asset pricing 295

Introduction. Approximating and distorted models. Asset pricing without robustness. Asset pricing with robustness. Adjustment of stochastic discount factor for fear of model misspecification. Reopening markets. Pricing single-period payoffs. Calibrated market prices of model uncertainty. Concluding remarks.

14. Risk sensitivity, model uncertainty, and asset pricing 307

Introduction. Organization. Equity premium and risk-free rate puzzles. Shocks and consumption plans. Recursive preferences. Stochastic discount factor for risk-sensitive preferences. Risk-sensitive preferences let Tallarini attain the Hansen-Jagannathan bounds. Reinterpretation of the utility recursion. Using martingales to represent probability distortions. Recursive representations of distortions. Ambiguity averse multiplier preferences. Observational equivalence? Yes and no. Worst-case random walk and trend stationary models. Market prices of risk and model uncertainty. Calibrating γ using detection error probabilities. Recasting Tallarini's graph. Concluding remarks. Value function and worst-case process. The value function. The distortion. An alternative computation. The trend stationary model.

15. Markov perfect equilibria with robustness 327

Introduction. Markov perfect equilibria with robustness. Explanation of x_{it+1}, x_t notation. Computational algorithm: iterating on stacked Bellman equations. Bayesian interpretation and belief heterogeneity. Heterogeneous worst-case beliefs. Concluding remarks.

16. Robustness in forward-looking models 333

Introduction. Related literature. The robust Stackelberg problem. Multiplier version of the robust Stackelberg problem. Solving the robust Stackelberg problem. Step 1: Solve a robust linear regulator. Step 2: Use the stabilizing properties of shadow price Py_t. Step 3: Convert implementation multipliers into state variables. Law of motion under robust Ramsey plan. A monopolist with a competitive fringe. The approximating and distorted models. The problem of a firm in the competitive fringe. Changes of measure. Euler equation for λ^q under the approximating model. Euler equation for λ^q under the monopolist's perturbed model. The monopolist's transition equations. The monopolist's problem. Computing the volatility loading on λ_t^q. Timing subtlety. An iterative algorithm. Recursive representation of a competitive firm's problem. Multipliers. Cross-checking the solution for u_t, w_{t+1}. Numerical example. Concluding remarks. Invariant subspace method. The Riccati equation. Another Bellman equation.

Part V: Robust estimation and filtering

17. Robust filtering with commitment   359

Alternative formulations. A linear regulator. A static robust estimation problem. A digression on distorted conditional expectations. A dynamic robust estimation problem. Many-period filtering problem. Duality of robust filtering and control. Matlab programs. The worst-case model. Law of motion for the state reconstruction error. The worst-case model associated with a time-invariant K. A deterministic control problem for the worst-case mean. A Bayesian interpretation. Robustifying a problem of Muth. Reconstructing the ordinary Kalman filter. Illustrations. Another example. A forward-looking perspective. Relation to a formulation from control theory literature. The next chapter. Dual to evil agent's problem.

18. Robust filtering without commitment   383

Introduction. A recursive control and filtering problem. The decision maker's approximating model. Two sources of statistical perturbation. Two operators. The $\mathbf{T}^1$ operator. The $\mathbf{T}^2$ operator. Two sources of fragility. A recursive formulation for control and estimation. A certainty equivalent shortcut. Computing the $\mathbf{T}^1$ operator. Worst-case distribution for $z - \check{z}$ is $\mathcal{N}(u, \Gamma(\Delta))$. Worst-case signal distribution. Examples. Concluding remarks. Worst-case signal distribution.

Part VI: Extensions

19. Alternative approaches   403

Introduction. More structured model uncertainty. Model averaging. A shortcut. Probabilistic sophistication. Time inconsistency. Continuation entropy. Disarming the entropy constraint. Rectangularity can be taken too far.

References   413

Index   427

Author Index 431

Matlab Index 435

Preface

A good decision rule for us has been, "if Peter Whittle wrote it, read it." Whittle's book, *Prediction and Regulation by Linear Least Squares Methods* (originally published in 1963, revised and reprinted in 1983), taught early builders and users of rational expectations econometrics, including us, the classical time series techniques that are perfect for putting the idea of rational expectations to work. When we became aware of Whittle's 1990 book, *Risk Sensitive Control*, and later his 1996 book, *Optimal Control: Basics and Beyond*, we eagerly worked through them. These and other books on robust control theory, such as Başar and Bernhard's 1995 $H^\infty - Optimal\ Control$ *and Related Minimax Design Problems: A Dynamic Game Approach*, provide tools for approaching the 'soft' but important question of how to make decisions when you don't fully trust your model.

Work on robust control theory opens up the possibility of rigorously analyzing how agents should cope with fear of model misspecification. While Whittle mentioned a few economic examples, the methods that he and other authors of robust and risk-sensitive control theories had developed were designed mainly for types of problems that differ significantly from economic problems. Therefore, we soon recognized that we would have to modify and extend aspects of risk-sensitive and robust control methods if we were to apply them to economic problems. That is why we started the research that underlies this book. We do not claim to have attained a general theory of how to make economic decisions in the face of model misspecification, but only to have begun to study this difficult and important problem that has concerned every researcher who has estimated and tried to validate a rational expectations model, every central banker who has knowingly used dubious models to guide his monetary policy decisions, and every macroeconomist whose specification doubts have made him regard formal estimation as wrongheaded and who has instead "calibrated" the parameters of a complete, but admittedly highly stylized, model.

Acknowledgments

For criticisms of previous drafts and stimulating discussions of many issues we thank Fernando Alvarez, Francisco Barillas, Marco Bassetto, Luca Benati, Dirk Bergemann, V.V. Chari, Eugene Chiu, Richard Dennis, Jack Y. Favilukis, Anastasios Karantounias, Kenneth Kasa, Patrick Kehoe, Junghoon Lee, Francesco Lippi, Pascal Maenhout, Ricardo Mayer, Anna Orlik, Joseph Pearlman, Tomasz Piskorski, Mark Salmon, Christopher Sims, Jose Scheinkman, Martin Schneider, Tomasz Strzalecki, Joseph Teicher, Aaron Tornell, François Velde, Peter von zur Muehlen, Neng Wang, Yong Wang, Pierre-Oliver Weil, and Noah Williams. We especially thank Anna Orlik for reading and criticizing the entire manuscript. We also owe a special thanks to François Velde for extraordinary help with typesetting and design problems. We thank Evan Anderson and Ellen McGrattan for allowing us to use many of the ideas in our joint paper in chapter 4. In addition to providing comments, Francisco Barillas, Christian Matthes, Ricardo Mayer, Tomasz Piskorski, Yong Shin, Stijn Van Nieuwerburgh, Chao D. Wei, and Mark Wright helped with the computations. We thank the National Science foundation for separate grants that have supported our research. Sargent thanks William Berkley for several useful conversations about risk and uncertainty. Our editors at Princeton University Press, Dale Cotton, Seth Ditchik, and Peter Dougherty provided encouragement and valuable suggestions about style and presentation. We thank Carolyn Sargent for suggesting the image on the cover. We thank John Doyle, an artist as well as a manufacturer of robust control theory, for letting us reproduce figure 1.1.1. His menacing image of a robust control theorist brandishing θ reminds us why Arthur Goldberger and Robert E. Lucas, Jr., warned us to beware of theorists bearing free parameters. Our aim is to convince readers that the parameter θ provides a practical way to confront concerns about model misspecification that applied economists encounter daily. It is tempting to make the agents in our models fear misspecification too and to study the outcomes it induces. This book is about how to do that.

Part I
Motivation and main ideas

Chapter 1
Introduction

Knowledge would be fatal, it is the uncertainty that charms one. A mist makes things beautiful.
— *Oscar Wilde, The Picture of Dorian Gray, 1891*

1.1. Generations of control theory

Figure 1.1.1 reproduces John Doyle's cartoon about developments in optimal control theory since World War II.[1] Two scientists in the upper panels use different mathematical methods to devise control laws and estimators. The person on the left uses classical methods (Euler equations, z-transforms, lag operators) and the one on the right uses modern recursive methods (Bellman equations, Kalman filters). The scientists in the top panels completely trust their models of the transition dynamics. The, shall we say, gentleman in the lower panel shares the objectives of his predecessors from the 50s, 60s, and 70s, but regards his model as an approximation to an unknown and unspecified model that he thinks actually generates the data. He seeks decision rules and estimators that work over a nondenumerable set of models near his approximating model. The H_∞ in his postmodern tattoo and the θ on his staff are alternative ways to express doubts about his approximating model by measuring the discrepancy of the true data generating mechanism from his approximating model. As we shall learn in later chapters, the parameter θ is interpretable as a penalty on a measure of discrepancy (entropy) between his approximating model and the model that actually generates the data. The H_∞ refers to the limit of his objective function as the penalty parameter θ approaches a "break down point" that bounds the set of alternative models against which the decision maker can attain a robust decision rule.

1.2. Control theory and rational expectations

Classical and modern control theory supplied perfect tools for applying Muth's (1961) concept of rational expectations to a variety of problems in dynamic economics. A significant reason that rational expectations initially diffused slowly after Muth's (1961) paper is that in 1961 few economists knew the tools lampooned in the top panel of figure 1.1.1. Rational expectations took

---

[1] John Doyle consented to let us reproduce this drawing, which appears in Zhou, Doyle, and Glover (1996). We changed Doyle's notation by making θ (Doyle's μ) the free parameter carried by the post-modern control theorist.

Figure 1.1.1: A pictorial history of control theory (courtesy of John Doyle). Beware of a theorist bearing a free parameter, θ.

hold in the 1970s only after a new generation of macroeconomists had learned those tools. Ever since, macroeconomists and rational expectations econometricians have gathered inspiration and ideas from classical and recursive control theory.[2]

When macroeconomists were beginning to apply classical and modern control and estimation theory in the late 1970s, control theorists and applied mathematicians were seeking ways to relax the assumption that the decision maker trusts his model. They sought new control and estimation methods to improve adverse outcomes that came from applying classical and modern control theory to a variety of engineering and physical problems. They thought that model misspecification explained why actual outcomes were sometimes much worse than control theory had promised and therefore sought decision rules and estimators that acknowledged model misspecification. That is how robust control and estimation theory came to be.

---

[2] See Stokey and Lucas with Prescott (1989), Ljungqvist and Sargent (2004), and Hansen and Sargent (1991) for many examples.

1.3. Misspecification and rational expectations

To say that model misspecification is as much of a problem in economics as it is in physics and engineering is an understatement. This book borrows, adapts, and extends tools from the literature on robust control and estimation to model decision makers who regard their models as approximations. We assume that a decision maker has created an approximating model by a specification search that we do not model. The decision maker believes that data will come from[3] an unknown member of a *set* of unspecified models near his approximating model.[4] Concern about model misspecification induces a decision maker to want decision rules that work over that set of nearby models.

If they lived inside rational expectations models, decision makers would not have to worry about model misspecification. They *should* trust their model because subjective and objective probability distributions (i.e., models) coincide. Rational expectations theorizing removes agents' personal models as elements of the model.[5]

Although the artificial agents within a rational expectations model trust the model, a model's author often doubts it, especially when calibrating it or after performing specification tests. There are several good reasons for wanting to extend rational expectations models to acknowledge fear of model misspecification.[6] First, doing so accepts Muth's (1961) idea of putting econometricians and the agents being modeled on the same footing: because econometricians face specification doubts, the agents inside the model might too.[7] Second, in various contexts, rational expectations models underpredict prices

---

[3] Or, in the case of the robust filtering problems posed in chapter 17, *have* come from.

[4] We say "unspecified" because of how these models are formed as statistical perturbations to the decision maker's approximating model.

[5] In a rational expectations model, each agent's model (i.e., his subjective joint probability distribution over exogenous and endogenous variables) is determined by the equilibrium. It is not something to be specified by the model builder. Its early advocates in econometrics emphasized the empirical power that followed from the fact that the rational expectations hypothesis eliminates all free parameters associated with people's beliefs. For example, see Hansen and Sargent (1980) and Sargent (1981).

[6] In chapter 16, we explore several mappings, the fixed points of which restrict a robust decision maker's approximating model. As is usually the case with rational expectations models, we are silent about the process by which an agent arrives at an approximating model. A qualification to the claim that rational expectations models do not describe the process by which agents form their models comes from the literature on adaptive learning. There, agents who use recursive least squares learning schemes eventually come to know enough to behave as they should in a self-confirming equilibrium. Early examples of such work are Bray (1982), Marcet and Sargent (1989), and Woodford (1990). See Evans and Honkapohja (2001) for new results.

[7] This argument might offend someone with a preference against justifying modeling assumptions on behavioral grounds.

of risk from asset market data. For example, relative to standard rational expectations models, actual asset markets seem to assign prices to macroeconomic risks that are too high. The equity premium puzzle is one manifestation of this mispricing.[8] Agents' caution in responding to concerns about model misspecification can raise prices assigned to macroeconomic risks and lead to reinterpreting them as compensation for bearing model uncertainty instead of risks with known probability distributions. This reason for studying robust decisions is positive and is to be judged by how it helps explain market data. A third reason for studying the robustness of decision rules to model misspecification is normative. A long tradition dating back to Friedman (1953), Bailey (1971), Brainard (1967), and Sims (1971, 1972) advocates framing macroeconomic policy rules and interpreting econometric findings in light of doubts about model specification, though how those doubts have been formalized in practice has varied.[9]

1.4. Our extensions of robust control theory

Among ways we adapt and extend robust control theory so that it can be applied to economic problems, six important ones are discounting; a reinterpretation of the "worst-case shock process"; extensions to several multi-agent settings; stochastic interpretations of perturbations to models; a way of calibrating plausible fears of model misspecification as measured by the parameter θ in figure 1.1.1; and formulations of robust estimation and filtering problems.

1.4.1. Discounting

Most presentations of robustness in control theory treat undiscounted problems, and the few formulations of discounting that do appear differ from the way economists would set things up.[10] In this book, we formulate discounted problems that preserve the recursive structure of decision problems that macroeconomists and other applied economists use so widely.

---

[8] A related finding is that rational expectations models impute low costs to business cycles. See Hansen, Sargent, and Tallarini (1999), Tallarini (2000), and Alvarez and Jermann (2004). Barillas, Hansen, and Sargent (2007) argue that Tallarini's and Alvarez and Jermann's measures of the costs of reducing aggregate fluctuations are flawed if what they measure as a market price of risk is instead interpreted as a market price of model uncertainty.

[9] We suspect that his doubts about having a properly specified macroeconomic model explains why, when he formulated comprehensive proposals for the conduct of monetary and fiscal policy, Friedman (1953, 1959) did not use a formal Bayesian expected utility framework, like the one he had used in Friedman and Savage (1948).

[10] Compare the formulations in Whittle (1990) and Hansen and Sargent (1995).

1.4.2. Representation of worst-case shock

As we shall see, in existing formulations of robust control theory, shocks that represent misspecification are allowed to feed back on endogenous state variables that are influenced by the decision maker, an outcome that in some contexts appears to confront the decision maker with peculiar incentives to manipulate future values of some of those shocks by adjusting his current decisions. Some economists[11] have questioned the plausibility of the notion that the decision maker is concerned about *any* misspecifications that can be represented in terms of shocks that feed back on state variables under his partial control. In chapter 7, we use the "Big K, little k trick" from the literature on recursive competitive equilibria to reformulate misspecification perturbations to an approximating model as exogenous processes that cannot be influenced by the decision maker. As we illustrate in the analysis of the permanent income model of chapter 10, this reinterpretation of the worst-case shock process is useful in a variety of economic models.

1.4.3. Multiple agent settings

In formulations from the control theory literature, the decision maker's model of the state transition dynamics is a primitive part of (i.e., an exogenous input into) the statement of the problem. In multi-agent dynamic economic problems, it is not. Instead, parts of the decision maker's transition law governing endogenous state variables, such as aggregate capital stocks, are affected by other agents' choices and therefore are equilibrium outcomes. In this book, we describe ways of formulating the decision maker's approximating model when he and possibly other decision makers are concerned about model misspecification, perhaps to differing extents. We impose a common approximating model on all decision makers, but allow them to express different degrees of mistrust of that model and to have different objectives. As we explain in chapters 12, 15, and 16, this is a methodologically conservative approach that adapts the concept of a Nash equilibrium to incorporate concerns about robustness. The hypothesis of a common approximating model preserves much of the discipline of rational expectations, while the hypothesis that agents have different interests and different concerns about robustness implies a precise sense in which *ex post* they behave as if they had different models. We thereby attain a disciplined way of modeling apparent heterogeneity of beliefs.[12]

---

[11] For example, Christopher Sims expressed this view to us.

[12] Brock and deFontnouvelle (2000) describe a related approach to modeling heterogeneity of beliefs.

1.4.4. Explicitly stochastic interpretations

Much of this book is about linear-quadratic problems for which a convenient certainty equivalence result described in chapter 2 permits easy transitions between nonstochastic and stochastic versions of a problem. Chapter 3 describes the relationship between stochastic and nonstochastic setups.

1.4.5. Calibrating fear of misspecification

Rational expectations models presume that decision makers know the correct model, a probability distribution over sequences of outcomes. One way to justify this assumption is to appeal to adaptive theories of learning that endow agents with very long histories of data and allow a Law of Large Numbers to do its work.[13] But after observing a short time series, a statistical learning process will typically leave agents undecided among members of a set of models, perhaps indexed by parameters that the data have not yet pinned down well. This observation is the starting point for the way that we use detection error probabilities to discipline the amount of model uncertainty that a decision maker fears after having studied a data set of length T.

1.4.6. Robust filtering and estimation

Chapter 17 describes a formulation of some robust filtering problems that closely resemble problems in the robust control literature. This formulation is interesting in its own right, both economically and mathematically. For one thing, it has the useful property of being the dual of a robust control problem. However, as we discuss in detail in chapter 17, this problem builds in a peculiar form of commitment to model distortions that had been chosen earlier but that one may not want to consider when making current decisions. For that reason, in chapter 18, we describe a class of robust filtering and estimation problems without commitment to those prior distortions. Here the decision maker carries along the density of the hidden states given the past signal history computed under the approximating model, then considers hypothetical changes in this density and in the state and signal dynamics looking forward.

---

[13] For example, see work summarized by Fudenberg and Levine (1998), Evans and Honkapohja (2001), and Sargent (1999a). The justification is incomplete because economies where agents use adaptive learning schemes typically converge to self-confirming equilibria, not necessarily to full rational expectations equilibria. They may fail to converge to rational expectations equilibria because histories can contain an insufficient number of observations about off-equilibrium-path events for a Law of Large Numbers to be capable of eradicating erroneous beliefs. See Cho and Sargent (2007) for a brief introduction to self-confirming equilibria and Sargent (1999a) for a macroeconomic application.

1.5. Robust control theory, shock serial correlations, and rational expectations

Ordinary optimal control theory assumes that decision makers know a transition law linking the motion of state variables to controls. The optimization problem associates a distinct decision rule with each specification of shock processes. Many aspects of rational expectations models stem from this association.[14] For example, the Lucas critique (1976) is an application of the finding that, under rational expectations, decision rules are functionals of the serial correlations of shocks. Rational expectations econometrics achieves parameter identification by exploiting the structure of the function that maps shock serial correlation properties to decision rules.[15]

Robust control theory alters the mapping from shock temporal properties to decision rules by treating the decision maker's model as an approximation and seeking a *single* rule to use for a *set* of vaguely specified alternative models expressed in terms of distortions to the shock processes in the approximating model. Because they are allowed to feed back arbitrarily on the history of the states, such distortions can represent misspecified dynamics.

As emphasized by Hansen and Sargent (1980, 1981, 1991), the econometric content of the rational expectations hypothesis is a set of cross-equation restrictions that cause decision rules to be functions of parameters that characterize the stochastic processes impinging on agents' constraints. A concern for model misspecification alters these cross-equation restrictions by inspiring the robust decision maker to act as if he had beliefs that seem to *twist* or *slant* probabilities in ways designed to make his decision rule less fragile to misspecification. Formulas presented in chapters 2 and 7 imply that the Hansen-Sargent (1980, 1981) formulas for those cross-equation restrictions also describe the behavior of the robust decision maker, provided that we use appropriately *slanted* laws of motion in the Hansen-Sargent (1980) forecasting formulas. This finding shows how robust control theory adds a concern about misspecification in a way that preserves the econometric discipline imposed by rational expectations econometrics.

1.6. Entropy in specification analysis

The statistical and econometric literatures on model misspecification supply tools for measuring discrepancies between models and for thinking about decision making in the presence of model misspecification.

---

[14] Stokey and Lucas with Prescott (1989) is a standard reference on using control theory to construct dynamic models in macroeconomics.

[15] See Hansen and Sargent (1980, 1981, 1991).

Where y^* denotes next period's state vector, let the data truly come from a Markov process with one step transition density $f(y^*|y)$ that we assume has invariant distribution $\mu(y)$. Let the econometrician's model be $f_\alpha(y^*|y)$ where $\alpha \in A$ and A is a compact set of values for a parameter vector α. If there is no $\alpha \in A$ such that $f_\alpha = f$, we say that the econometrician's model is *misspecified*. Assume that the econometrician estimates α by maximum likelihood. Under some regularity conditions, the maximum likelihood estimator $\hat{\alpha}_o$ converges in large samples to [16]

$$\text{plim } \hat{\alpha}_o = \text{argmin}_{\alpha \in A} \int I(f_\alpha, f)(y) \, d\mu(y) \qquad (1.6.1)$$

where $I(f_\alpha, f)(y)$ is the conditional relative entropy of model f with respect to model f_α, defined as the expected value of the logarithm of the likelihood ratio evaluated with respect to the true conditional density $f(y^*|y)$

$$I(f_\alpha, f)(y) = \int \log\left(\frac{f(y^*|y)}{f_\alpha(y^*|y)}\right) f(y^*|y) \, dy^*. \qquad (1.6.2)$$

It can be shown that $I(f_\alpha, f)(y) \geq 0$. Figure 1.6.1 depicts how the probability limit $\hat{\alpha}_o$ of the estimator of the parameters of a misspecified model makes $I(f_\alpha, f) = \int I(f_\alpha, f)(y) d\mu(y)$ as small as possible. When the model is misspecified, the minimized value of $I(f_\alpha, f)$ is positive.

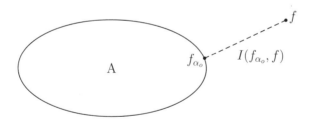

Figure 1.6.1: Econometric specification analysis. Suppose that the data generating mechanism is f and that the econometrician fits a parametric class of models $f_\alpha \in A$ to the data and that $f \notin A$. Maximum likelihood estimates of α eventually select the misspecified model f_{α_o} that is closest to f as measured by entropy $I(f_\alpha, f)$.

Sims (1993) and Hansen and Sargent (1993) have used this framework to deduce the consequences of various types of misspecification for estimates of

---

[16] Versions of this result occur in White (1982, 1994), Vuong (1989), Sims (1993), Hansen and Sargent (1993), and Gelman, Carlin, Stern, and Rubin (1995).

parameters of dynamic stochastic models.[17] For example, they studied the consequences of using seasonally adjusted data to estimate models populated by decision makers who actually base their decisions on seasonally unadjusted data.

1.7. Acknowledging misspecification

To study decision making in the presence of model misspecification, we turn the analysis of section 1.6 on its head by taking f_{α_o} as a given approximating model and surrounding it with a set of unknown possible data generating processes, one unknown element of which is the true process f. See figure 1.7.1. Because he doesn't know f, a decision maker bases his decisions on the only explicitly specified model available, namely, the misspecified f_{α_o}. We are silent about the process through which the decision maker discovered his approximating model $f_{\alpha_o}(y^*|y)$.[18] We also take for granted the decision maker's parameter estimates α_o.[19] We impute some doubts about his model to the decision maker. In particular, the decision maker suspects that the data are actually generated by another model $f(y^*|y)$ with relative entropy $I(f_{\alpha_o}, f)(y)$. The decision maker thinks that his model is a good approximation in the sense that $I(f_{\alpha_o}, f)(y)$ is not too large, and wants to make decisions that will be good when $f \neq f_{\alpha_o}$. We endow the decision maker with a discount factor β and construct the following intertemporal measure of model misspecification:[20]

$$\mathcal{I}(f_{\alpha_o}, f) = E_f \sum_{t=0}^{\infty} \beta^t I(f_{\alpha_o}, f)(y_t)$$

where E_f is the mathematical expectation evaluated with respect to the distribution f. Our decision maker confronts model misspecification by seeking a decision rule that will work well across a set of models for which $\mathcal{I}(f_{\alpha_o}, f) \leq \eta_0$, where η_0 measures the set of models F surrounding his approximating model f_α. Figure 1.7.1 portrays the decision maker's view of the world. The decision maker wants a single decision rule that is reliable for *all* models f in the set displayed in figure 1.7.1.[21] This book describes how he

---

[17] Also see Vuong (1989).

[18] See Kreps (1988, chapter 11) for an interesting discussion of the problem of model discovery.

[19] In chapter 9, we entertain the hypothesis that the decision maker has estimated his model by maximum likelihood using a data set of length T and use Bayesian detection error probabilities to guide the choice of a set of models against which he wants to be robust.

[20] Hansen and Sargent (2005b, 2007a) provide an extensive discussion of reasons for adopting this measure of model misspecification.

[21] 'Reliable' means good enough, but not necessary optimal, for each member of a set of

can form such a robust decision rule by solving a Bellman equation that tells him how to maximize his intertemporal objective over decision rules when a hypothetical malevolent nature minimizes that same objective by choosing a model f.[22] That is, we use a max-min decision rule. Positing a malevolent nature is just a device that the decision maker uses to perform a systematic analysis of the fragility of alternative decision rules and to construct a lower bound on the performance that can be attained by using them. A decision maker who is concerned about robustness naturally seeks to construct bounds on the performance of potential decision rules, and the malevolent agent helps the decision maker do that.

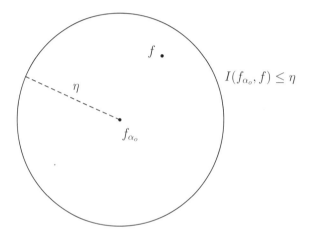

Figure 1.7.1: Robust decision making: A decision maker with model f_{α_o} suspects that the data are actually generated by a nearby model f, where $I(f_{\alpha_o}, f) \le \eta$.

1.8. Why entropy?

To assess the robustness of a decision rule to misspecification of an approximating model requires a way to measure just how good an approximation that model is. In this book, we use the relative entropy to measure discrepancies between models. Of course, relative entropy is not the only way we

---

models. The Lucas critique, or dynamic programming, tells us that it is impossible to find a single decision rule that is *optimal* for all f in this set. Note how the one-to-one mapping from transition laws f to decision rules that is emphasized in the Lucas critique depends on the decision maker knowing the model f. We shall provide a Bayesian interpretation of a robust decision rule by noting that, *ex post*, the max-min decision rule is optimal for *some* model within the set of models.

[22] See Milnor (1951, 1954) for an early formal use of the fiction of a malevolent agent.

could measure discrepancies between alternative probability distributions.[23] But in using relative entropy, we follow a substantial body of work in applied mathematics that reaps benefits from entropy in terms of tractability and interpretability. In particular, using entropy to measure model discrepancies enables us to appeal to the following outcomes:

1. In the general nonlinear case, using entropy to measure model discrepancies means that concerns about model misspecification can be represented in terms of a continuation value function that emerges as the indirect utility function after minimizing the decision maker's continuation value with respect to the transition density, subject to a penalty on the size of conditional entropy. That indirect utility function implies a tractable "risk-sensitivity" adjustment to continuation values in Bellman equations. In particular, we can represent a concern about robustness by replacing $E_t V(x_{t+1})$ in a Bellman equation with $-\theta \log E_t \left(\exp \left(\frac{-V(x_{t+1})}{\theta} \right) \right)$, where $\theta > \underline{\theta} > 0$ is a parameter that measures the decision maker's concern about robustness to misspecification. (We shall relate the lower bound $\underline{\theta}$ to H_∞ control theory in chapter 8.) The simple $\log E_t \exp$ form of this adjustment follows from the decision to measure model discrepancy in terms of entropy.

2. In problems with quadratic objective functions and linear transition laws, using relative entropy to measure model misspecification leads to a simple adjustment to the ordinary linear-quadratic dynamic programming problem. Suppose that the transition law for the state vector in the approximating model is $x_{t+1} = A x_t + B u_t + C \epsilon_{t+1}$, where ϵ_{t+1} is an i.i.d. Gaussian vector process with mean 0 and identity covariance. Using relative entropy to measure discrepancies in transition laws implies a worst-case model that perturbs the distribution of ϵ_{t+1} by enhancing its covariance matrix and appending a mean vector w_{t+1} that depends on date t information. Value functions remain quadratic and the distribution associated with the perturbed model remains normal. Because a form of certainty equivalence prevails,[24] it is sufficient to keep track of the mean distortion when solving the control problem. This mean distortion contributes $.5 w_{t+1} \cdot w_{t+1}$ to the relative entropy discrepancy between the approximating model and the alternative model. As a consequence, a term $\theta w'_{t+1} w_{t+1}$ is appended to the one-period return function when computing the robust control and a worst-case conditional mean.

---

[23] Bergemann and Schlag (2005) use Prohorov distance rather than entropy to define the set of probability models against which decision makers seek robustness.

[24] See page 33.

3. As we shall see in chapter 9, entropy connects to a statistical theory for discriminating one model from another. The theory of large deviations mentioned in chapter 3 links statistical discrimination to a risk-sensitivity adjustment.[25]

1.9. Why max-min?

We answer this question by posing three other questions.

1. What does it mean for a decision rule to be robust? A robust decision rule performs well under the variety of probability models depicted in figure 1.7.1. How might one go about investigating the implications of alternative models for payoffs under a given decision rule? A good way to do this is to compute a lower bound on value functions by assessing the *worst* performance of a given decision rule over a range of alternative models. This makes max-min a useful tool for searching for a robust decision rule.

2. Instead of max-min, why not simply ask the decision maker to put a prior distribution over the set of alternative models depicted in figure 1.7.1? Such a prior would, in effect, have us form a new model – a so-called hypermodel – and thereby eliminate concerns about the misspecification of *that* model. Forming a hypermodel would allow the decision maker to proceed with business as usual, albeit with what may be a more complex model and a computationally more demanding control problem. We agree that this "model averaging" approach is a good way to address some well-structured forms of model uncertainty. Indeed, in chapter 18 we shall use model averaging and Bayesian updating when we study problems that call for combined estimation and control. But the set of alternative models can be so vast that it is beyond the capacity of a decision maker to conjure up a unique well behaved prior. And even when he can, a decision maker might also want decisions to be robust to *whatever* prior he could imagine over this set of models.

   More is at issue than the choice of the prior distribution to assign to distinct well specified models. The specification errors that we fear might be more complex than can be represented with a simple model averaging approach. It is reasonable to take the view that each of the distinct models being averaged is itself an approximation. The decision maker might lack precise ideas about how to describe the alternative specifications that worry him and about how to form prior distributions over

---

[25] Anderson, Hansen, and Sargent (2003) extensively exploit these connections.

them. Perhaps he can't articulate the misspecifications that he fears, or perhaps the set of alternative models is too big to comprehend.[26]

Our answer to this second question naturally leads to a reconsideration of the standard justification for being a Bayesian.

3. "Why be a Bayesian?" Savage (1954) gave an authoritative answer by describing axioms that imply that a rational person can express all of his uncertainty in terms of a unique prior. However, Schmeidler (1989) and Gilboa and Schmeidler (1989) altered one of Savage's axioms to produce a model of what it means to be a rational decision maker that differs from Savage's Bayesian model. Gilboa and Schmeidler's rational decision maker has multiple priors and behaves as a max-min expected utility decision maker: the decision maker *maximizes* and assumes that nature chooses a probability to *minimize* his expected utility. We are free to appeal to Gilboa and Schmeidler's axioms to rationalize the form of max-min expected utility decision making embedded in the robust control theories that we study in this book.[27]

1.10. Is max-min too cautious?

Our doubts are traitors, And make us lose the good we oft might win, By fearing to attempt.
— *William Shakespeare, Measure for Measure, act 1 scene 4*

Our use of the detection error probabilities of chapter 9 to restrict the penalty parameter θ in figure 1.1.1 protects us against the objection that the max-min expected utility theory embedded in robust control theory is too cautious because, by acting as if he believed the worst-case model, the decision maker puts too much weight on a "very unlikely" scenario.[28] We choose θ so that the entropy ball that surrounds the decision maker's approximating model in

---

[26] See Sims (1971) and Diaconis and Freedman (1986) for arguments that forming an appropriate prior is difficult when the space of submodels and the dimensions of parameter spaces are very large.

[27] Hansen and Sargent (2001) and Hansen, Sargent, Turmuhambetova, and Williams (2006) describe how stochastic formulations of robust control "constraint problems" can be viewed in terms of Gilboa and Schmeidler's max-min expected utility model. Interesting theoretical work on model ambiguity not explicitly connected to robust control theory includes Dow and Werlang (1994), Ghirardato and Marinacci (2002), Ghirardato, Maccheroni, and Marinacci (2004), Ghirardato, Maccheroni, Marinacci, and Siniscalchi (2003), and Rigotti and Shannon (2003, 2005), and Strzalecki (2007).

[28] Bewley (1986, 1987, 1988), Dubra, Maccheroni, and Ok (2004), Rigotti and Shannon (2005), and Lopomo, Rigotti, and Shannon (2004) use an alternative to the max-min expected utility model but still one in which the decision maker experiences ambiguity about models. In their settings, incomplete preferences are expressed in terms of model ambiguity

figure 1.7.1 has the property that the perturbed models on and inside the ball are difficult to distinguish statistically from the approximating model with the amount of data at hand. This way of calibrating θ makes the likelihood function for the decision maker's worst-case model fit the available data almost as well as his approximating model. Moreover, by inspecting the implied worst-case model, we can evaluate whether the decision maker is focusing on scenarios that appear to be too extreme.

1.11. Aren't you just picking a plausible prior?

By interchanging the order in which we maximize and minimize, chapter 7 describes an *ex post* Bayesian interpretation of a robust decision rule.[29] Friendly critics have responded to this finding by recommending that we view robust control as simply a way to select a plausible prior in an otherwise standard Bayesian analysis.[30] Furthermore, one can regard our chapter 9 detection error probability calculations as a way to guarantee that the prior is plausible in light of the historical data record at the disposal of the decision maker.

We have no objection to this argument in principle, but warn the reader that issues closely related to the Lucas (1976) critique mean that it has to be handled with care, as in any subjectivist approach. Imagine a policy intervention that alters a component of a decision maker's approximating model for, e.g., a tax rate, while leaving other components unaltered. In general, *all* equations of the decision maker's worst-case transition law that emerge from the max-min decision process will vary with such interventions. The dependence of other parts of the decision maker's worst-case model on subcomponents of the transition law for the approximating model that embody the policy experiment reflects the context-specific nature of the decision maker's worst-case model. Therefore, parts of the *ex post* worst-case "prior" that describe the evolution of variables *not* directly affected by the policy experiment will depend on the policy experiment. The sense in which robust control is just a way to pick a plausible prior is subtle.

Another challenge related to the Lucas critique pertains when we apply robust control without availing ourselves of the *ex post* Bayesian interpreta-

---

and there is a status quo allocation that plays a special role in shaping how the decision maker ranks outcomes. Some advocates of this incomplete preferences approach say that they like it partly because it avoids what they say is an undue pessimism that characterizes the max-min expected utility model. See Fudenberg and Levine (1995) for how max-min can be used to attain an interesting convergence result for adaptive learning.

[29] We introduce this argument because it provides a sense in which our robust decision rules are admissible in the statistical decision theoretic sense of being undominated.

[30] Christopher A. Sims has made this argument on several occasions.

tion. Throughout this book, whenever we consider changes in the economic environment, we imitate rational expectations policy analysis by imputing common approximating models, one before the policy change, the other after, to all agents in the model and the econometrician (e.g., see chapter 14). It is natural to doubt whether decision makers would fully trust their statistical models after such policy changes.

1.12. Why not learn the correct specification?

For much of this book, but not all, we attribute an enduring fear of misspecification to our decision maker. Wouldn't it be more realistic to assume that the decision maker learns to detect and discard bad specifications as data accrue?

One good answer to this question is related to some of the points made in section 1.9. In chapter 9, we suggest calibrating the free parameter θ borne by the "gentleman" in the bottom panel of figure 1.1.1 so that, even with nondogmatic priors, it would take long time series to distinguish among the alternative specifications about which the decision maker is concerned. Because our decision maker discounts the future, he cannot avoid facing up to his model specification doubts simply by waiting for enough data.[31] Thus, one answer is that, relative to his discount factor, it would take a long time for him to learn not to fear model misspecification.

However, we agree that it is wise to think hard about what types of misspecification fears you can expect learning to dispel in a timely way, and which types you cannot. But what are good ways to learn when you distrust your model? Chapters 17 and 18 are devoted to these issues.[32] We present alternative formulations of robust estimation and filtering problems and suggest ways to learn in the context of distrusted approximating models. Our approach allows us to distinguish types of model misspecification fears that a decision maker can eventually escape by learning from types that he cannot.[33]

---

[31] As we shall see, one reason that it takes a very long data set to discriminate between the models that concern the decision maker is that often they closely approximate each other at high frequencies and differ mostly at very low frequencies. Chapter 8 studies robustness from the viewpoint of the frequency domain.

[32] Also see Hansen and Sargent (2005b, 2007a, 2007b).

[33] Epstein and Schneider (2006) also make this distinction. In the empirical model of Hansen and Sargent (2007b), a representative consumer's learning within the sample period reduces his doubts about the distribution of some unknown parameters, but does little to diminish his doubts about the distribution over difficult to distinguish submodels, one of which confronts him with long-run risk in the growth rate of consumption.

1.13.   Is the set of perturbed models too limited?

Parts of this book are devoted to analyzing situations in which the decision maker's approximating model and the statistical perturbations to it that bother him all take the form of the stochastic linear evolution

$$x_{t+1} = Ax_t + Bu_t + C\left(\epsilon_{t+1} + w_{t+1}\right) \tag{1.13.1}$$

where x_t is a state vector, u_t a control vector, ϵ_{t+1} an i.i.d. Gaussian shock with mean 0 and covariance I, and w_{t+1} is a vector of perturbations to the mean of ϵ_{t+1}. Under the approximating model, $w_{t+1} = 0$, whereas under perturbed models, w_{t+1} is allowed to be nonzero and to feed back on the history of past x_t's.

Some critics have voiced the complaint that this class of perturbations excludes types of misspecified dynamics that ought to concern a decision maker, such as unknown parameter values, misspecfication of higher moments of the ϵ_{t+1} distribution, and various kinds of "structured uncertainty." We think that this complaint is misplaced for the following reasons:

1. For the problems with quadratic objective functions and approximating models like (1.13.1) with $w_{t+1} = 0$, restricting ourselves to perturbations of the form (1.13.1) turns out not to be as restrictive as it might at first seem. In chapters 3 and 7, we permit a much wider class of alternative models that we formulate as absolutely continuous perturbations to the transition density of state variables. We show that when the decision maker's objective function is quadratic and his approximating model is linear with Gaussian ϵ_{t+1}, then he chooses a worst-case model that is of the form (1.13.1) with a C that is usually only slightly larger and a w_{t+1} that is a linear function of x_t. We shall explain why he makes little or no error by ignoring possible misspecification of the volatility matrix C.

2. In section 19.2 of chapter 19, we show how more structured kinds of uncertainty can be accommodated by slightly reinterpreting the decision maker's objective function.

3. When the approximating model is a linear state evolution equation with Gaussian disturbances and the objective function is quadratic, worst case distributions are also jointly Gaussian. However, making the approximating model be non-Gaussian and non-linear or making the objective function be not quadratic leads to non-Gaussian worst-case joint probability distributions, as chapter 3 indicates. Fortunately, by extending the methods of chapters 17 and 18, as Hansen and Sargent (2005, 2007a) do, we know how to model robust decision makers who learn about non-linear

models with non-Gaussian shock distributions while making decisions. The biggest hurdles in carrying out quantitative analyses like these are computational. Most of the problems studied in this book are designed to be easy computationally by staying within a linear-quadratic-Gaussian setting. But numerical methods allow us to tackle analogous problems outside the LQG setting.[34]

1.14. Is robust control theory positive or normative?

Robust control and estimation theory has both normative and positive economic applications. In some contexts, we take our answer to question (2) in the preceding section to justify a positive statement about how people *actually* behave. For example, we use this interpretation when we apply robust control and estimation theory to study asset pricing puzzles by constructing a robust representative consumer whose marginal evaluations determine market prices of risk (see Hansen, Sargent, and Tallarini (1999), Hansen, Sargent, and Wang (2002), and chapter 13).

Monetary policy authorities and other decision makers find themselves in situations where their desire to be cautious with respect to fears of model misspecification would inspire them to use robust control and estimation techniques.[35] Normative uses of robust control theory occur often in engineering.

1.15. Other lessons

Our research program of refining typical rational expectations models to attribute specification doubts to the agents inside of them has broadened our own understanding of rational expectations models themselves. Struggling with the ideas in this book has taught us much about the structure of recursive models of economic equilibria,[36] the relationship between control and estimation problems, and Bayesian interpretations of decision rules in dynamic rational expectations models. We shall use the macroeconomist's Big K, little k trick with a vengeance.

The 1950s-1960s control and estimation theories lampooned in the top panel of figure 1.1.1 have contributed enormously to the task of constructing dynamic equilibrium models in macroeconomics and other areas of applied economic dynamics. We expect that the robust control theories represented

---

[34] See Cogley, Colacito, Hansen, and Sargent (2007) for an example.

[35] Blinder (1998) expresses doubts about model misspecification that he had when he was vice chairman of the Federal Reserve System and how he coped with them.

[36] For example, see chapter 12.

in the bottom panel of that figure will also bring many benefits that we cannot anticipate.

1.16. Topics and organization

This monograph displays alternative ways to express and respond to a decision maker's doubts about model specification. We study both control and estimation (or filtering) problems, and both single- and multiple-agent settings. As already mentioned, we adapt and extend results from the robust control literature in two important ways. First, unlike the control literature, which focuses on undiscounted problems, we formulate discounted problems. Incorporating discounting involves substantial work, especially in chapter 8, and requires paying special attention to initial conditions. Second, we analyze three types of economic environments with multiple decision makers who are concerned about model misspecification: (1) a competitive equilibrium with complete markets in history-date contingent claims and a representative agent who fears model misspecification (chapters 12 and 13); (2) a Markov perfect equilibrium of a dynamic game with multiple decision makers who fear model misspecification (chapter 15); and (3) a Stackelberg or Ramsey problem in which the leader fears model misspecification (chapter 16). Thinking about model misspecification in these environments requires that we introduce an equilibrium concept that extends rational expectations. We stay mostly, but not exclusively, within a linear-quadratic framework, in which a pervasive certainty equivalence principle allows a nonstochastic presentation of most of the control and filtering theory.

This book is organized as follows. Chapter 2 summarizes a set of practical results at a relatively nontechnical level. A message of this chapter is that although sophisticated arguments from chapters 7 and 8 are needed fully to justify the techniques of robust control, the techniques themselves are as easy to apply as the ordinary dynamic programming techniques that are now widely used throughout macroeconomics and applied general equilibrium theory. Chapter 2 uses linear-quadratic dynamic problems to convey this message, but the message applies more generally, as we shall illustrate in chapter 3. Chapter 3 tells how the key ideas about robustness generalize to models that are not linear quadratic.

Chapters 4 and 5 are about optimal control and filtering when the decision maker trusts his model. These chapters contain a variety of useful results for characterizing the linear dynamic systems that are widely used in macroeconomics. Chapter 4 sets forth important principles by summarizing results about the classic optimal linear regulator problem. This chapter builds on the survey by Anderson, Hansen, McGrattan, and Sargent (1996) and culminates in a description of invariant subspace methods for solving linear optimal control and filtering problems and also for solving dynamic linear equilibrium models. Later chapters apply these methods to various problems: to compute robust decision rules as solutions of two-player zero-sum games; to compute robust filters via another two-player zero-sum game; and to compute equilibria of robust Stackelberg or Ramsey problems in macroeconomics. Chapter 5 emphasizes that the Kalman filter is the *dual* (in a sense familiar to economists from their use of Lagrange multipliers) of the basic linear-quadratic dynamic programming problem of chapter 4 and sets the stage for a related duality result for a robust filtering problem to be presented in chapter 17.

The remaining chapters are about making wise decisions when a decision maker distrusts his model. Within a one-period setting, chapter 6 introduces two-player zero-sum games as a way to induce robust decisions. Although the forms of model misspecifications considered in this chapter are very simple relative to those considered in subsequent chapters, the static setting of chapter 6 is a good one for addressing some important conceptual issues. In particular, in this chapter we state multiplier and constraint problems, two different two-player zero-sum games that induce robust decision rules. We use the Lagrange multiplier theorem to connect the problems.

Chapters 7 and 8 extend and modify results in the control literature to formulate robust control problems with discounted quadratic objective functions and linear transition laws. Chapter 7 represents things in the time domain, while chapter 8 works in the frequency domain. Incorporating discounting requires carefully restating the control problems used to induce robust decision rules. Chapters 7 and 8 describe two ways to alter the discounted linear quadratic optimal control problem in a way to induce robust decision rules: (1) to form one of several two-player zero-sum games in which nature chooses from a set of models in a way that makes the decision maker want robust decision rules; and (2) to adjust the continuation value function in the dynamic program in a way that encodes the decision maker's preference for a robust rule. The continuation value that works comes from the minimization piece of one of the two-player zero-sum games in (1). In category (1), we present a detailed account of several two-player zero-sum games with different timing protocols, each of which induces a robust decision rule. As an extension of category (2), we present three specifications of preferences that express concerns about model misspecification. Two of them are expressed in the frequency domain: the H_∞ and entropy criteria. The entropy objective function summarizes model specification doubts with a single parameter. That parameter relates to a Lagrange multiplier in a two-player zero-sum constraint game, and also to the *risk-sensitivity* parameter of Jacobson (1973) and Whittle (1990), as modified for discounting by Hansen and Sargent (1995).

Chapters 7 and 8 show how robustness is induced by using max-min strategies: the decision maker maximizes while nature minimizes over a set of models that are close to the approximating model. There are alternative timing protocols in terms of which a two-player zero-sum game can be cast. A main finding of chapter 7 is that zero-sum games that make a variety of different timing protocols share outcomes and representations of equilibrium strategies. This important result lets us use recursive methods to compute our robust rules and also facilitates computing equilibria in multiple-agent economics.

Arthur Goldberger and Robert E. Lucas, Jr., warned applied economists to beware of theorists bearing free parameters (see figure 1.1.1). Relative to settings in which decision makers completely trust their models, the multiplier and constraint problems of chapters 7 and 8 each bring one new free parameter that expresses a concern about model misspecification, θ for the multiplier problem and η for the constraint problem. Each of these parameters measures sets of models near the approximating model against which the decision maker seeks a robust rule. Chapter 9 proposes a way to calibrate these parameters by using the statistical theory for discriminating models.[37] We apply this theory in chapters 10 and 14.

Chapter 10 uses the permanent income model of consumption as a laboratory for illustrating some of the concepts from chapters 7 and 8. Because he prefers smooth consumption paths, the permanent income consumer's savings are designed to attenuate the effects of income fluctuations on his consumption. A robust consumer engages in a kind of precautionary savings because he suspects error in the specification of the income process. We will also use the model of chapter 10 as a laboratory for asset pricing in chapter 13. But first, chapters 11 and 12 describe how to decentralize the solution of a planning problem with a competitive equilibrium. Chapter 11 sets out a class of dynamic economies and describes two decentralizations, one with trading of history-date contingent commodities once and for all at time zero, another with sequential trading of one-period Arrow securities. In that sequential setting, we give a recursive representation of equilibrium prices. Chapter 11 describes a setting where the representative agent has no concern about model misspecification, while chapter 12 extends the characterizations of chapter 11 to situations where the representative decision maker fears model misspecification.

Chapter 13 builds on the chapter 12 results to show how fear of model

---

[37] See Anderson, Hansen, and Sargent (2003).

misspecification affects asset pricing. We show how, from the vantage point of the approximating model, a concern for robustness induces a multiplicative adjustment to the stochastic discount factor. The adjustment measures the representative consumer's fear that the approximating model is misspecified. The adjustment for robustness resembles ones that financial economists use to construct risk neutral probability measures for pricing assets. We describe the basic theory within a class of linear quadratic general equilibrium models and then a calibrated version of the permanent income model of chapter 10. A remarkable observational equivalence result identifies a locus of pairs of discount factors and robustness multipliers, all of which imply identical real allocations.[38] Nevertheless, prices of risky assets vary substantially across these pairs. In chapter 14, we revisit some quantitative findings of Tallarini (2000) and reinterpret asset pricing patterns that he imputed to very high risk aversion in terms of a plausible fear of model misspecification. We measure a plausible fear of misspecification by using the detection error probabilities introduced in chapter 9.

Chapters 15 and 16 describe two more settings with multiple decision makers and introduce an equilibrium concept that extends rational expectations in what we think is a natural way. In a rational expectations equilibrium, all decision makers completely trust a common model. Important aspects of that common model, those governing endogenous state variables, are equilibrium outcomes. The source of the powerful cross-equation restrictions that are the hallmark of rational expectations econometrics is that decision makers share a common model and that this model governs the data.[39] To preserve that empirical power in an equilibrium with multiple decision makers who fear model misspecification, we impose that all decision makers share a common approximating model.[40] The model components that describe endogenous state variables are equilibrium outcomes that depend on agents' robust decision making processes, i.e., on the solutions to their max-min problems.

Chapter 15 describes how to implement this equilibrium concept in the context of a two-player dynamic game in which the players share a common

---

[38] This result establishes a precise sense in which, so far as real quantities are concerned, increased fear of model misspecficiation acts just like *reduced* discounting of the future, so that its effects on real quantities can be offset by *increasing* the rate at which future payoffs are discounted.

[39] The restriction that they share a common model is the feature that makes free parameters governing expectations disappear. This is what legitimizes a law of large numbers that underlies rational expectations econometrics.

[40] In the empirical applications of Hansen, Sargent, and Tallarini (1999) and Anderson, Hansen, and Sargent (2003), we also maintain the second aspect of rational expectations modeling, namely, that the decision makers' approximating model actually *does* generate the data.

approximating model and each player makes robust decisions by solving a two-player zero-sum game, taking the approximating model as given. We show how to compute the approximating model by solving pairs of robust versions of the Bellman equations and first-order conditions for the two decision makers. While the equilibrium imposes a common approximating model, the worst-case models of the two decision makers differ because their objectives differ. In this sense, the model produces endogenous *ex post* heterogeneity of beliefs.

In chapter 16, we alter the timing protocol to study a control problem, called a Ramsey problem, where a leader wants optimally to control followers who are forecasting the leader's controls. We describe how to compute a robust Stackelberg policy when the Stackelberg leader can commit to a rule. We accomplish that by using a robust version of the optimal linear regulator or else one of the invariant subspace methods of chapter 4.

Chapter 17 extends the analysis of filtering from chapter 5 by describing a robust filtering problem that is dual to the control problem of chapter 7.[41] This recursive filtering problem requires that a time t decision maker must respect distortions to the distribution of the hidden state that he inherits from past decision makers. As a consequence, in this problem, bygones are not bygones:[42] the decision makers concerns about *past* returns affect his estimate of the current value of a hidden state vector.

Chapter 18 uses a different criterion than chapter 17 and finds a different robust filter. We think that the chapter 18 filter is the appropriate one for many problems and give some examples. The different filters that emerge from chapters 17 and 18 illustrate how robust decision rules are 'context specific' in the sense that they depend on the common objective function in the two-player zero-sum game that is used to induce a robust decision rule. This theme will run through this book.

Chapter 19 concludes by confronting some of the confining aspects of our work, some criticisms that we have heard, and opportunities for further progress.

---

[41] We originally found this problem by stating and solving a conjugate problem of a kind familiar to economists through duality theory. By faithfully following where duality leads, we discovered a filtering problem that is peculiar (but not necessarily uninteresting) from an economic standpoint. A sketch of this argument is presented in appendix A of chapter 17.

[42] But see the epigraph from William Stanley Jevons quoted at the start of chapter 18.

Chapter 2
Basic ideas and methods

There are two different drives toward exactitude that will never attain complete fulfillment, one because "natural" languages always say something more than formalized languages can – natural languages always involve a certain amount of noise that impinges on the essentiality of the information – and the other because, in representing the density and continuity of the world around us, language is revealed as defective and fragmentary, always saying something less with respect to the sum of what can be experienced.
— Italo Calvino, Six Memos for the Next Millennium, 1996

2.1. Introduction

A model maps a sequence of decisions into a sequence of outcomes. Standard control theory tells a decision maker how to make optimal decisions when his model is correct. Robust control theory tells him how to make good decisions when his model approximates a correct one. This chapter summarizes methods for computing robust decision rules when the decision maker's criterion function is quadratic and his approximating model is linear.[1] After describing possible misspecifications as a set of perturbations to an approximating model, we modify the Bellman equation and the Riccati equation associated with the standard linear-quadratic dynamic programming problem to incorporate concerns about misspecification of the transition law. The adjustments to the Bellman equation have alternative representations, each of which has practical uses in contexts that we exploit extensively in subsequent chapters. This chapter concentrates mainly on single-agent decision theory, but chapters 11, 15, and 16 extend the theory to environments with multiple decision makers, all of whom are concerned about model misspecification. In the process, we describe equilibrium concepts that extend the notion of a rational expectations equilibrium to situations in which decision makers have different amounts of confidence in a common approximating model.[2] Chapter 3

---

[1] Later chapters provide technical details that justify assertions made in this chapter.

[2] Chapter 11 discusses competitive equilibria in representative agent economies; chapter 15 injects motives for robustness into Markov perfect equilibria for two-player dynamic games; and chapter 16 studies Stackelberg and Ramsey problems. In Ramsey problems, a government chooses among competitive equilibria of a dynamic economy. A Ramsey problem too ends up looking like a single-agent problem, the single agent being a benevolent government that faces a peculiar set of constraints that represent competitive equilibrium allocations.

studies models with more general return and transition functions and shows that many of the insights of this chapter apply beyond the linear-quadratic setting. The LQ setting is computationally tractable, but also reveals most of the conceptual issues that apply with more general functional forms.

2.2. Approximating models

We begin with the single-agent linear-quadratic problem. Let y_t be a state vector and u_t a vector of controls. A decision maker's model takes the form of a linear state transition law

$$y_{t+1} = Ay_t + Bu_t + C\check{\epsilon}_{t+1}, \qquad (2.2.1)$$

where $\{\check{\epsilon}_t\}$ is an i.i.d. Gaussian vector process with mean 0 and identity contemporaneous covariance matrix. The decision maker thinks that $(2.2.1)$ approximates another model that governs the data but that he cannot specify. How should we represent the notion that $(2.2.1)$ is misspecified? The i.i.d. random process $\check{\epsilon}_{t+1}$ can represent only a very limited class of approximation errors and in particular cannot depict such examples of misspecified *dynamics* as are represented in models with nonlinear and time-dependent feedback of y_{t+1} on past states. To represent dynamic misspecification,[3] we surround $(2.2.1)$ with a set of alternative models of the form

$$y_{t+1} = Ay_t + Bu_t + C\left(\epsilon_{t+1} + w_{t+1}\right), \qquad (2.2.2)$$

where $\{\epsilon_t\}$ is another i.i.d. Gaussian process with mean zero and identity covariance matrix and w_{t+1} is a vector process that can feed back in a possibly nonlinear way on the history of y

$$w_{t+1} = g_t\left(y_t, y_{t-1}, \ldots\right), \qquad (2.2.3)$$

where $\{g_t\}$ is a sequence of measurable functions. When $(2.2.2)$ generates the data, it is as though the errors $\check{\epsilon}_{t+1}$ in model $(2.2.1)$ were conditionally distributed as $\mathcal{N}(w_{t+1}, I)$ rather than as $\mathcal{N}(0, I)$. Thus, we capture the idea

---

[3] In chapters 3 and 6, we allow a broader class of misspecifications. Chapter 3 represents the approximating model as a Markov transition density and considers misspecifications that twist probabilities over future states. When the approximating model is Gaussian, many results of this chapter survive even though $(2.2.2)$ ignores an additional adjustment to the innovation covariance matrix of the shock in the distorted model that turns out not to affect the distortion to the conditional mean of the shock. In many applications, the adjustment to the covariance matrix is quantitatively insignificant. It vanishes in the case of continuous time. See Anderson, Hansen, and Sargent (2003) and Hansen, Sargent, Turmuhambetova, and Williams (2006).

that the approximating model (2.2.1) is misspecified by allowing the conditional mean of the shock vector in the model (2.2.2) that actually generates the data to feed back arbitrarily on the history of the state. To express the idea that model (2.2.1) is a *good* approximation when (2.2.2) generates the data, we restrain the approximation errors by

$$E_0 \sum_{t=0}^{\infty} \beta^{t+1} w'_{t+1} w_{t+1} \leq \eta_0, \qquad (2.2.4)$$

where E_t denotes mathematical expectation evaluated with model (2.2.2) and conditioned on $y^t = [y_t, \ldots, y_0]$. In section 2.3, chapter 3, and chapter 9, we shall interpret the left side of (2.2.4) as a statistical measure of the discrepancy between the distorted and approximating models.

The alternative models differ from the approximating model by having shock processes whose conditional means are not zero and that can feed back in potentially complicated ways on the history of the state. Notice that our specification leaves the conditional volatility of the shock, as parameterized by C, unchanged. We adopt this specification for computational convenience. We show in chapter 3 the useful result that our calculations for a worst-case conditional mean w_{t+1} remain unaltered when we also allow conditional volatilities C to differ in the approximating and perturbed models.

The decision maker believes that the data are generated by a model of the form (2.2.2) with some *unknown* process w_t satisfying (2.2.4).[4] The decision maker forsakes learning to improve his specification because η_0 is so small that statistically it is difficult to distinguish model (2.2.2) from (2.2.1) using a time series $\{y_t\}_{t=1}^T$ of moderate size T, an idea that we develop in chapter 9.[5]

The decision maker's distrust of his model (2.2.1) makes him want good decisions over a set of models (2.2.2) satisfying (2.2.4). Such decisions are said to be robust to misspecification of the approximating model.

We compute robust decision rules by solving one of several distinct but related two-player zero-sum games: a maximizing decision maker chooses controls $\{u_t\}$ and a minimizing (also known as a "malevolent" or "evil") agent chooses model distortions $\{w_{t+1}\}$. The games share common players, actions, and payoffs, but assume different timing protocols. Nevertheless, as we show in chapters 7 and 8, equilibrium outcomes and decision rules for the games

---

[4] See chapter 3 for a specification of the approximating model as a joint probability density over an infinite sequence of y_ts and misspecifications that are represented as alternative joint probability densities.

[5] However, see chapter 18 and Hansen and Sargent (2005b, 2007a) for ways to include robust forms of learning.

coincide, a consequence of the zero-sum feature of all of the games.[6] This makes the games easy to solve. Computing robust decision rules comes down to solving Bellman equations for dynamic programming problems that are very similar to equations routinely used today throughout macroeconomics and applied economic dynamics. Before later chapters assemble the results needed to substantiate these claims, this chapter quickly summarizes how to compute robust decision rules with standard methods.

We begin with the ordinary linear-quadratic dynamic programming problem without model misspecification, called the optimal linear regulator. Then we describe how robust decision rules can be computed by solving another optimal linear regulator problem.

2.2.1. *Dynamic programming without model misspecification*

The standard dynamic programming problem assumes that the transition law is correct.[7] Let the one-period loss function be $r(y, u) = -(y'Qy + u'Ru)$ where the matrices Q and R are symmetric and together with A and B in $(2.2.1)$ satisfy some stabilizability and detectability assumptions set forth in chapter 4. The *optimal linear regulator problem* is

$$-y_0 P y_0 - p = \max_{\{u_t\}_{t=0}^{\infty}} E_0 \sum_{t=0}^{\infty} \beta^t r(y_t, u_t), \quad 0 < \beta < 1, \qquad (2.2.5)$$

where the maximization is subject to $(2.2.1)$, y_0 is given, E denotes the mathematical expectation operator evaluated with respect to the distribution of $\check{\epsilon}$, and E_0 denotes the mathematical expectation conditional on time 0 information, namely, the state y_0. Letting y^* denote next period's value of y, the linear constraints and quadratic objective function in $(2.2.5)$, $(2.2.1)$ imply the Bellman equation

$$-y'Py - p = \max_u E\left[r(y, u) - \beta y^{*\prime} P y^* - \beta p\right] \Big| y, \qquad (2.2.6)$$

where the maximization is subject to

$$y^* = Ay + Bu + C\check{\epsilon}, \qquad (2.2.7)$$

where $\check{\epsilon}$ is a random vector with mean zero and identity variance matrix.

Subject to assumptions about A, B, R, Q, β to be described in chapter 4, some salient facts about the optimal linear regulator are the following:

---

[6] The zero-sum feature perfectly misaligns the preferences of the two players and thereby renders timing protocols irrelevant. See chapter 7 for details.

[7] Many technical results and computational methods for the linear quadratic problem without concerns about robustness are catalogued in chapter 4.

1. *The Riccati equation.* The matrix P in the value function is a fixed point of a matrix Riccati equation:

$$P = Q + \beta A'PA - \beta^2 A'PB\left(R + \beta B'PB\right)^{-1} B'PA. \qquad (2.2.8)$$

The optimal decision rule is $u_t = -Fy_t$ where

$$F = \beta\left(R + \beta B'PB\right)^{-1} B'PA. \qquad (2.2.9)$$

We can find the appropriate fixed point P and solve problem $(2.2.5)$, $(2.2.1)$ by iterating to convergence on the Riccati equation $(2.2.8)$ starting from initial value $P_0 = 0$.

2. *Certainty equivalence.* In the Bellman equation $(2.2.6)$, the scalar $p = \frac{\beta}{1-\beta}\text{trace}PCC'$. The volatility matrix C influences the value function through p, but not through P. It follows from $(2.2.8)$, $(2.2.9)$ that the optimal decision rule F is independent of the volatility matrix C. In $(2.2.1)$, we have normalized C by setting $E\check{\epsilon}_t\check{\epsilon}_t' = I$. Therefore, the matrix C determines the covariance matrix CC' of random shocks impinging on the system. The finding that F is independent of the volatility matrix C is known as the certainty equivalence principle: the same decision rule $u_t = -Fy_t$ emerges from stochastic $(C \neq 0)$ and nonstochastic $(C = 0)$ versions of the problem. This kind of certainty equivalence fails to describe problems that express a concern for model misspecification; but another useful kind of certainty equivalence does. See page 33.

3. *Shadow prices.* Since the value function is $-y_0'Py_0 - p$, the vector of shadow prices of the initial state is $-2Py_0$. Form a Lagrangian for $(2.2.1)$, $(2.2.5)$ and let the vector $-2\beta^{t+1}\mu_{t+1}$ be Lagrange multipliers on the time t version of $(2.2.1)$. First-order conditions for a saddle point of the Lagrangian can be rearranged to form a first-order vector difference equation in (y_t, μ_t). The optimal policy solves this difference equation subject to an initial condition for y_0 and a transversality or detectability condition $E_0 \sum_{t=0}^{\infty} \beta^t r(y_t, u_t) > -\infty$. In chapter 4, we show that subject to these boundary conditions, the vector difference equation consisting of the first-order conditions is solved by setting $\mu_t = Py_t$, where P solves the Riccati equation $(2.2.8)$.

2.3. Measuring model misspecification with entropy

We use entropy to measure model misspecification. To interpret our measure of entropy, we state a modified certainty equivalence principle for linear quadratic models. Although we use a statistical interpretation of entropy, by appealing to the modified certainty equivalence result to be stated on page 33, we shall be able to drop randomness from the model but still retain a measure of model misspecification that takes the form of entropy.

Let the approximating model again be (2.2.1) and let the distorted model be (2.2.2). The approximating model asserts that $w_{t+1} = 0$. For convenience, we analyze the consequences of a fixed decision rule and assume that $u_t = -Fy_t$. Let $A_o = A - BF$ and write the approximating model as

$$y_{t+1} = A_o y_t + C\check{\epsilon}_{t+1} \tag{2.3.1}$$

and a distorted model as[8]

$$y_{t+1} = A_o y_t + C\left(\epsilon_{t+1} + w_{t+1}\right). \tag{2.3.2}$$

The approximating model (2.3.1) asserts that $\check{\epsilon}_{t+1} = (C'C)^{-1}C'(y_{t+1} - A_o y_t)$. When the distorted model generates the data, $y_{t+1} - A_o y_t = C\check{\epsilon}_{t+1} = C(\epsilon_{t+1} + w_{t+1})$, which implies that the disturbances under the approximating model appear to be

$$\check{\epsilon}_{t+1} = \epsilon_{t+1} + w_{t+1}, \tag{2.3.3}$$

so that misspecification manifests itself in a distortion to the conditional mean of innovations to the state evolution equation.

How close is the approximating model to the model that actually governs the data? To measure the statistical discrepancy between the two models of the transition from y to y^*, we use conditional relative entropy defined as

$$I\left(f_o, f\right)(y) = \int \log\left(\frac{f\left(y^*|y\right)}{f_o\left(y^*|y\right)}\right) f\left(y^*|y\right) dy^*,$$

where f_o denotes the one-step transition density associated with the approximating model and f is a transition density obtained by distorting the approximating model.[9]

---

[8] Chapter 3 allows a larger set of perturbations to the approximating model and gives an appropriate definition of entropy.

[9] Define the likelihood ratio $m(f(y^*|y)) = \frac{f(y^*|y)}{f_0(y^*|y)}$. Then notice that

$$I\left(f_o, f\right)(y) = \int \left(m \log m\right) f_o\left(y^*|y\right) dy^* = E_{f_o}\left[m \log m|y\right],$$

where the subscript f_o means integration with respect to the approximating model f_o. Hansen and Sargent (2005b, 2007a) exploit such representations of entropy. See chapter 3.

In the present setting, the transition density for the approximating model is

$$f_o(y^*|y) \sim \mathcal{N}(Ay + Bu, CC'),$$

while the transition density for the distorted model is[10]

$$f(y^*|y) \sim \mathcal{N}(Ay + Bu + Cw, CC'),$$

where both u and w are measurable functions of y^t. In subsection 3.11 of chapter 3, we verify that the expected log-likelihood is

$$I(w_{t+1}) = .5w'_{t+1}w_{t+1}. \tag{2.3.4}$$

In chapter 9, we describe how measures like (2.3.4) govern the distribution of test statistics for discriminating among models. In chapter 13, we show how the log-likelihood ratio also plays an important role in pricing risky securities under an approximating model when a representative agent is concerned about model misspecification.

As an intertemporal measure of the size of model misspecification, we take

$$R(w) = 2E_0 \sum_{t=0}^{\infty} \beta^{t+1} I(w_{t+1}), \tag{2.3.5}$$

where the mathematical expectation conditioned on y_0 is evaluated with respect to the distorted model (2.3.2). Then we impose constraint (2.2.4) on the set of models or, equivalently,

$$R(w) \leq \eta_0. \tag{2.3.6}$$

In the next section, we construct decision rules that work well over a set of models that satisfy (2.3.6). Such robust rules can be obtained by finding the best response for a maximizing player in the equilibrium of a two-player zero-sum game.

---

[10] For a continuous-time diffusion, Hansen, Sargent, Turmuhambetova, and Williams (2006) describe how the assumption that the distorted model is difficult to distinguish statistically from the approximating model means that it can be said to be absolutely continuous over finite intervals with respect to the approximating model. They show that this implies that the perturbations must then assume a continuous-time version of the form imposed here (i.e., they can alter the drift but not the volatility of the diffusion).

2.4. Two robust control problems

This section states two robust control problems: a constraint problem and a multiplier problem. The two problems differ in how they treat constraint (2.3.6). Under appropriate conditions, the two problems have identical solutions. The multiplier problem is a robust version of a stochastic optimal linear regulator. A certainty equivalence principle allows us to compute the optimal decision rule for the multiplier problem by solving a corresponding nonstochastic optimal linear regulator problem.

We state the

Constraint problem: Given η_0 satisfying $\bar{\eta} > \eta_0 \geq 0$, a constraint problem is

$$\max_{\{u_t\}_{t=0}^{\infty}} \min_{\{w_{t+1}\}_{t=0}^{\infty}} E_0 \sum_{t=0}^{\infty} \beta^t r(y_t, u_t) \qquad (2.4.1)$$

where the extremization[11] is subject to the distorted model (2.2.2) and the entropy constraint (2.3.6), and where E_0, the mathematical expectation conditioned on y_0, is evaluated with respect to the distorted model (2.2.2). Here $\bar{\eta}$ measures the largest set of perturbations against which it is possible to seek robustness.

Next we state the

Multiplier problem: Given $\theta \in (\underline{\theta}, +\infty]$, a multiplier problem is

$$\max_{\{u_t\}_{t=0}^{\infty}} \min_{\{w_{t+1}\}_{t=0}^{\infty}} E_0 \sum_{t=0}^{\infty} \beta^t \left\{ r(y_t, u_t) + \beta\theta w_{t+1}' w_{t+1} \right\} \qquad (2.4.2)$$

where the extremization is subject to the distorted model (2.2.2) and the mathematical expectation is also evaluated with respect to that model.

In the max-min problem, $\theta \in (\underline{\theta}, +\infty]$ is a penalty parameter restraining the minimizing choice of the w_{t+1} sequence. The lower bound $\underline{\theta}$ is a so-called breakdown point beyond which it is fruitless to seek more robustness because the minimizing agent is sufficiently unconstrained that he can push the criterion function to $-\infty$ despite the best response of the maximizing agent. Formula (8.4.8) for $\underline{\theta}$ shows how the value of $\underline{\theta}$ depends on the return function, the discount factor, and the transition law. Tests for whether $\theta > \underline{\theta}$ are presented in formula (7.9.1) and in chapter 8, especially section 8.7. We shall discuss the lower bound $\underline{\theta}$ and an associated upper bound $\bar{\eta}$ extensively in chapter 8.

---

[11] Following Whittle (1990), extremization means joint maximization and minimization. It is a useful term for describing saddle-point problems.

Chapters 7 and 8 state conditions on θ and η_0 under which the two problems have identical solutions, namely, decision rules $u_t = -Fy_t$ and $w_{t+1} = Ky_t$. Chapter 7 establishes many useful facts about distinct versions of the multiplier problem that employ alternative timing protocols[12] and that justify solving the multiplier problem recursively. Let $-y_0'Py_0-p$ be the value of problem (2.4.2). It satisfies the Bellman equation[13]

$$-y'Py - p = \max_u \min_w E\left\{r\left(y, u\right) + \theta\beta w'w - \beta y^{*\prime}Py^* - \beta p\right\} \qquad (2.4.3)$$

where the extremization is subject to

$$y^* = Ay + Bu + C\left(\epsilon + w\right) \qquad (2.4.4)$$

where $*$ denotes next period's value, and $\epsilon \sim \mathcal{N}(0, I)$. As a tool to explore the fragility of his decision rule, in (2.4.3) the decision maker pretends that a malevolent nature chooses a feedback rule for a model misspecification process w.

In summary, to represent the idea that model (2.2.1) is an approximation, the robust version of the linear regulator replaces the single model (2.2.1) with the set of models (2.2.2) that satisfy (2.2.4). Before describing how robust decision rules emerge from the two-player zero-sum game (2.4.2), we mention a kind of certainty equivalence that applies to the multiplier problem.

2.4.1. Modified certainty equivalence principle

On page 29, we stated a certainty equivalence principle that applies to the linear quadratic dynamic programming problem without concern for model misspecification. It fails to hold when there is concern about model misspecification. But another certainty equivalence principle allows us to work with a non-stochastic version of (2.4.3), i.e., one in which $\epsilon_{t+1} \equiv 0$ in (2.4.4). In particular, it can be verified directly that precisely the same Riccati equations and the same decision rules for u_t and for w_{t+1} emerge from solving the random version of the Bellman equation (2.4.3) as would from a version that sets $\epsilon_{t+1} \equiv 0$. This fact allows us to drop ϵ_{t+1} from the state-transition

---

[12] For example, one timing protocol has the maximizing u player first commit at time 0 to an entire sequence, after which the minimizing w player commits to a sequence. Another timing protocol reverses the order of choices. Other timing protocols have each player choose sequentially.

[13] In chapter 7, we show that the multiplier and constraint problems are both recursive, but that they have different state variables and different Bellman equations. Nevertheless, they lead to identical decision rules for u_t.

equation and p from the value function $-y'Py - p$, without affecting formulas for the decision rules.[14] Nevertheless, inspection of the Bellman equation and the formula for the decision rule for u_t show that the volatility matrix C *does* affect the decision rule. Therefore, the version of the certainty equivalence principle stated on page 29 — that the decision rule is independent of the volatility matrix — does not hold when there are concerns about model misspecification. This is interesting because of how a desire for robustness creates an avenue for the noise statistics embedded in the volatility matrix C to impinge on decisions even with quadratic preferences and linear transition laws.[15] This effect is featured in the precautionary savings model of chapter 10, a simple version of which we shall sketch in section 2.8.

2.5. Robust linear regulator

The modified certainty equivalence principle lets us attain robust decision rules by positing the nonstochastic law of motion

$$y_{t+1} = Ay_t + Bu_t + Cw_{t+1} \qquad (2.5.1)$$

with y_0 given, where the w process is constrained by the nonstochastic counterpart to (2.2.4). By working with this nonstochastic law of motion, we obtain the robust decision rule for the stochastic problem in which (2.5.1) is replaced by (2.2.2). The approximating model assumes that $w_{t+1} \equiv 0$. Even though randomness has been eliminated, the volatility matrix C affects the robust decision rule because it influences how the specification errors w_{t+1} feed back on the state.

To induce a robust decision rule for u_t, we solve the nonstochastic version of the multiplier problem:

$$\max_{\{u_t\}} \min_{\{w_{t+1}\}} \sum_{t=0}^{\infty} \beta^t \left[r\left(y_t, u_t \right) + \theta \beta w'_{t+1} w_{t+1} \right] \qquad (2.5.2)$$

where the extremization is subject to (2.5.1) and y_0 is given. Let $-y'_0 Py_0$ be the value of (2.5.2). It satisfies the Bellman equation[16]

$$-y'Py = \max_u \min_w \{ r\left(y, u \right) + \theta \beta w'w - \beta y^{*'} Py^* \} \qquad (2.5.3)$$

---

[14] The certainty equivalence principle stated here shares with the one on page 29 the facts that P can be computed before p; it diverges from the certainty equivalence principle without robustness on page 29 because now P and therefore F both depend on the volatility matrix C. See Hansen and Sargent (2005a) for a longer discussion of certainty equivalence in robust control problems.

[15] The dependence of the decision rule on the volatility matrix is an aspect that attracted researchers like Jacobson (1973) and Whittle (1990) to risk-sensitive preferences (see chapter 3).

[16] Notice how this is a special case of (2.4.3) with $p = 0$. The modified certainty equivalence principle implies that the same matrix P solves (2.5.3) and (2.4.3).

where the extremization is subject to the *distorted* model

$$y^* = Ay + Bu + Cw. \tag{2.5.4}$$

In $(2.5.3)$, a malevolent nature chooses a feedback rule for a model-misspecification process w. The minimization problem in $(2.5.3)$ induces an operator $\mathcal{D}(P)$ defined by[17]

$$-y^{*\prime}\mathcal{D}\left(P\right)y^* = -\left(x'A' + u'B'\right)\mathcal{D}\left(P\right)\left(Ax + Bu\right) = \min_{w}\left\{\theta w'w - y^{*\prime}Py^*\right\} \tag{2.5.5}$$

where the minimization is subject to the transition law $y^* = Ay + Bu + Cw$. From the minimization problem on the right of $(2.5.5)$, it follows that[18]

$$\mathcal{D}\left(P\right) = P + \theta^{-1}PC\left(I - \theta^{-1}C'PC\right)^{-1}C'P. \tag{2.5.6}$$

The Bellman equation $(2.5.3)$ can then be represented as

$$-y'Py = \max_{u}\left\{r\left(y, u\right) - \beta y^{*\prime}\mathcal{D}\left(P\right)y^*\right\} \tag{2.5.7}$$

where now the maximization is subject to the *approximating* model $y^* = Ay + Bu$ and concern for misspecification is reflected in our having replaced P with $\mathcal{D}(P)$ in the continuation value function. Notice the use of the approximating model as the transition law in the Bellman equation $(2.5.7)$ instead of the distorted model that is used in $(2.5.3)$, $(2.5.4)$. The reason for the alteration in transition laws is that Bellman equation $(2.5.7)$ encodes the activities of the minimizing agent within the operator $\mathcal{D}$ that distorts the continuation value function.[19]

Define $T(P)$ to be the operator associated with the right side of the ordinary Bellman equation $(2.2.6)$ that we described in $(2.2.8)$:

$$T\left(P\right) = Q + \beta A'PA - \beta^2 A'PB\left(R + \beta B'PB\right)^{-1}B'PA. \tag{2.5.8}$$

Then according to $(2.5.7)$, P can be computed by iterating to convergence on the composite operator $T \circ \mathcal{D}$ and the robust decision rule can be computed by $u = -Fy$, where

$$F = \beta\left(R + \beta B'\mathcal{D}\left(P\right)B\right)^{-1}B'\mathcal{D}\left(P\right)A. \tag{2.5.9}$$

---

[17] See page 168, item 1, for more details.

[18] Before computing $\mathcal{D}$ in formula $(2.5.5)$, we always check whether the matrix being inverted on the right side of $(2.5.6)$ is positive definite. This amounts to a check that θ exceeds the "breakdown point" $\underline{\theta}$.

[19] The form of $(2.5.7)$ links this formulation of robustness to the recursive form of Jacobson's (1973) risk-sensitivity criterion proposed by Hansen and Sargent (1995), as we shall elaborate on in chapter 3.

The worst-case shock obeys the decision rule $w = Ky$, where

$$K = \theta^{-1} \left(I - \theta^{-1} C' PC \right)^{-1} C' P \left(A - BF \right). \qquad (2.5.10)$$

Several comments about the solution of $(2.5.3)$ are in order.

1. *Interpreting the solution.* The solution of problem $(2.5.2)$, $(2.5.1)$ has a recursive representation in terms of a pair of feedback rules

$$u_t = -Fy_t \qquad (2.5.11a)$$

$$w_{t+1} = Ky_t. \qquad (2.5.11b)$$

Here $u_t = -Fy_t$ is the robust decision rule for the control u_t, while $w_{t+1} = Ky_t$ describes a worst-case shock. This worst-case shock induces a distorted transition law

$$y_{t+1} = (A + CK) y_t + Bu_t. \qquad (2.5.12)$$

After having discovered $(2.5.12)$, we can regard the decision maker as devising a robust decision rule by choosing a sequence $\{u_t\}$ to maximize

$$-\sum_{t=0}^{\infty} \beta^t \left[y_t' Q y_t + u_t' R u_t \right]$$

subject to $(2.5.12)$. However, as noted above, the decision maker believes that the data are actually generated by a model with an *unknown* process $w_{t+1} = \tilde{w}_{t+1} \neq 0$. It is just that by planning against the worst-case process $w_{t+1} = Ky_t$, he designs a robust decision rule that performs well under a set of models. The worst-case transition law is endogenous and depends on $\theta, \beta, Q, R, A, B$, and C. Equation $(2.5.12)$ incorporates how the distortion w feeds back on the state vector y; it permits w to feed back on *endogenous* components of the state, meaning that the decision maker indirectly influences future values of w through his decision rule. Allowing the distortion to depend on endogenous state variables in this way may or may not be a useful way to think about model misspecification. How useful it is depends on whether allowing w_{t+1} to feed back on endogenous components of the state vector captures plausible specifications that concern the decision maker. But there is an alternative interpretation that excludes feedback of w on endogenous state variables, which we take up next.

2. *Reinterpreting the worst-case model.* We shall sometimes find it useful to reinterpret the solution of the robust linear regulator problem $(2.5.1)$,

(2.5.2) so that the decision maker believes that the distortions w do *not* depend on those endogenous components of the state vector whose motion his decisions affect. In particular, in chapter 7, we show that the robust decision rule $u_t = -Fy_t$ solves the ordinary linear regulator problem

$$\max_{\{u_t\}} \sum_{t=0}^{\infty} \beta^t r\left(y_t, u_t\right) \qquad (2.5.13)$$

subject to the distorted transition law

$$y_{t+1} = Ay_t + Bu_t + Cw_{t+1} \qquad (2.5.14a)$$

$$w_{t+1} = KY_t \qquad (2.5.14b)$$

$$Y_{t+1} = A^*Y_t \qquad (2.5.14c)$$

where $A^* = A - BF + CK$, where (F, K) solve problem $(2.5.2)$, $(2.5.1)$, and where we impose the initial condition $Y_0 = y_0$. In $(2.5.14)$, the maximizing player views Y_t as an exogenous state vector that propels the distortion w_{t+1} that twists the law of motion for state vector y_t. This is a version of the macroeconomist's Big K, little k trick, where Y plays the role of Big K. The solution of $(2.5.13)$, $(2.5.14)$ has the outcome that $Y_t = y_t \; \forall t \geq 0$.[20] Chapters 7 and 8 show how formulation $(2.5.13)$, $(2.5.14)$ emerges from a version of the multiplier problem that imposes a timing protocol in which the minimizing agent at time 0 commits to an entire sequence of distortions $\{w_{t+1}\}_{t=0}^{\infty}$ and in which it is best for the minimizing agent to make w_{t+1} obey $(2.5.14b)$, $(2.5.14c)$. As we shall see in chapter 8, this formulation helps us interpret frequency domain criteria for inducing robust decision rules. In addition, the transition law $(2.5.14)$ rationalizes a Bayesian interpretation of the robust decision maker's behavior by identifying a particular belief about the shocks for which the maximizing player's decision rule is *optimal*, a belief that is distorted relative to the approximating model.[21] This observation is reminiscent of some ideas of Fellner.

3. *Relation to Fellner (1965).* In the introduction to *Probability and Profit*, William Fellner wrote:

---

[20] In contrast to formulation $(2.5.1)$, $(2.5.2)$, in problem $(2.5.13)$, $(2.5.14)$ the maximizing agent does not believe that his decisions can influence the future position of the distortion w. Depending on the types of perturbations to the approximating model that the maximizing agent wants to protect against, we might actually prefer interpretation $(2.5.1)$, $(2.5.2)$ in some applications.

[21] A decision rule is said to have a Bayesian interpretation if it is undominated in the sense of being optimal for some model. See Robert (2001, pp. 74-77) and Blackwell and Girschik (1954).

"... the central problems of decision theory may be described as semiprobabilistic views. By this I mean to say that in my opinion the directly observable weights which reasonable and consistent individuals attach to specific types of prospects are not necessarily the genuine (undistorted) subjective probabilities of the prospects, although these *decision weights* of consistently acting individuals do bear an understandable relation to probabilities ... the directly observable decision weights (expectation weights) which these decision makers attach to alternative monetary prospects need not be universally on par with probabilities attached to head-or-tails events but may in cases be derived from such probabilities by "slanting" or "distortion." Slanting expresses an allowance for the instability and controversial character of some types of probability judgment; the extent of the slanting may even depend on the magnitude of the prize which is at stake when a prospect is being weighted."

Robust control theory embodies some of Fellner's ideas. Thus, the "decision weights" implied by the "slanted" transition law (2.5.14) differ from the "subjective probabilities" implied by the approximating model (2.2.1). The distortion, or slanting, is context-specific because K depends on the parameters β, R, Q of the discounted return function.

4. *Robustness bound.* The minimizing player in the two-player game assists the maximizing player by helping him construct a useful bound on the performance of his decision rule. Let $A_F = A - BF$ for a fixed F in a feedback rule $u = -Fy$. In chapter 7 on page 170, we show that equation (2.5.7) implies that

$$- (A_F y + C w)' P (A_F y + C w) \geq -y' A_F' \mathcal{D} (P) A_F y - \theta w' w. \quad (2.5.15)$$

The quadratic form in y on the right side is a conservative estimate of the continuation value of the state y^* *under the approximating model* $y^* = A_F y$.[22] Inequality (2.5.15) says that the continuation value *under a distorted model* is at least as great as a conservative estimate of the continuation value *under the approximating model*, minus θ times the measure of model misspecification $w' w$. The parameter θ influences the conservative-adjustment operator $\mathcal{D}$ and also determines the rate at which the bound deteriorates with misspecification. Lowering θ lowers the rate at which the bound deteriorates with misspecification. Thus, (2.5.15) provides a sense in which lower values of θ provide more conservative estimates of continuation utility and therefore more robust guides to decision making.

---

[22] That is, when $w = 0$, $-(A_F y)' \mathcal{D}(P) A_F y$ understates the continuation value.

5. *Alternative games with identical outcomes.* The game (2.5.2) summarized by the Bellman equation (2.5.3) is one of several two-player zero-sum games with identical lists of players, actions, and payoffs, but different timing protocols. Chapter 7 describes the relationships among these games and the remarkable fact that they have identical outcomes. The analysis of chapter 7 justifies using recursive methods to solve all of the games. That chapter also discusses senses in which the decision maker's preferences are dynamically consistent.

6. *Approximating and worst-case models.* The behavior of the state under the robust decision rule *and* the worst-case model can be represented by

$$y_{t+1} = Ay_t - BFy_t + CKy_t. \qquad (2.5.16)$$

However, the decision maker does not really believe that the worst-case shock process will prevail. He uses $w_{t+1} = Ky_t$ to slant the transition law as a way to help construct a rule that will be robust against a range of *other* w_{t+1} processes that represent unknown departures from his approximating model. We occasionally want to evaluate the performance of the robust decision rule under other models. In particular, we often want to evaluate the robust decision rule when the approximating model governs the data (so that the decision maker's fears of model misspecification are actually unfounded). With the robust decision rule and the approximating model, the law of motion is

$$y_{t+1} = (A - BF)y_t. \qquad (2.5.17)$$

We obtain (2.5.17) from (2.5.16) by replacing the worst-case shock Ky_t with zero. Notice that although we set $K = 0$ in (2.5.16) to get (2.5.17), F in (2.5.16) embodies a best response to K, and thereby reflects the agent's "pessimistic" forecasts of future values of the state. We call (2.5.17) the approximating model under the robust decision rule and we call (2.5.16) the worst-case or distorted model under the robust decision rule.[23] In chapters 13 and 14, we use stochastic versions of both the approximating model (2.5.17) and the distorted model (2.5.16) to express alternative formulas for the prices of risky assets when consumers fear model misspecification.

7. *Lower bound on θ and H_∞ control.* Starting from $\theta = +\infty$, lowering θ increases the fear of misspecification by lowering the shadow price on the

---

[23] The model with randomness adds $C\epsilon_{t+1}$ to the right side of (2.5.17).

norm of the control of the minimizing player. We shall see in chapter 8 that there is a lower bound for θ. This lower bound is associated with the *largest* set of alternative models, as measured by entropy, against which it is feasible to seek a robust rule: for values of θ below this bound, the minimizing agent is penalized so little that he finds it possible to choose a distortion that sends the criterion function to $-\infty$. Control theorists are interested in the cutoff value of θ because it is affiliated with a rule that is robust to the biggest allowable set of misspecifications. We describe the associated H_∞ control theory in chapter 8. However, the applications that we are interested in usually call for values of θ that exceed the cutoff value by far. We explain why in chapter 9, where we use detection error probabilities to discipline the setting for θ.

8. *Risk-sensitive preferences.* It is a useful fact that we can ignore doubts about model specification and instead adjust attitudes toward risk in a way that implies the decision rule and value function that come from the two-player zero-sum game (2.5.2). In particular, the decision rule $u_t = -Fy_t$ that solves the robust control problem also solves a stochastic infinite-horizon discounted control problem in which the decision maker has no concern about model misspecification but instead adjusts continuation values to express an additional aversion to risk. The risk adjustment is a special case of one that Epstein and Zin (1989) used to formulate their recursive specification of utility and is governed by a parameter $\sigma < 0$. If we set $\sigma = -\theta^{-1}$ from the robust control problem, we recover the same decision rule for the two problems.

The risk-sensitive decision maker trusts that the law of motion for the state is

$$y_{t+1} = Ay_t + Bu_t + C\epsilon_{t+1} \qquad (2.5.18)$$

where $\{\epsilon_{t+1}\}$ is a sequence of i.i.d. Gaussian random vectors with mean zero and identity covariance matrix. The utility index of the decision maker is defined recursively as the fixed point of recursions on

$$U_t = r(y_t, u_t) + \beta \mathcal{R}_t(U_{t+1}) \qquad (2.5.19)$$

where

$$\mathcal{R}_t(U_{t+1}) = \frac{2}{\sigma} \log E \left[\exp \left(\frac{\sigma U_{t+1}}{2} \right) \Big| y^t \right] \qquad (2.5.20)$$

and where $\sigma \leq 0$ is the risk-sensitivity parameter. When $\sigma = 0$, an application of l'Hospital's rule shows that $\mathcal{R}_t$ becomes the ordinary conditional expectation operator $E(\cdot | y^t)$. When $\sigma < 0$, $\mathcal{R}_t$ puts an additional adjustment for risk into the assessment of continuation values.

For a quadratic $r(y, u)$, the Bellman equation for Hansen and Sargent's (1995) risk-sensitive control problem is

$$-y'Py - \hat{p} = \max_u \left\{ r(y, u) + \beta \mathcal{R} \left(-y^{*\prime} Py^* - \hat{p} \right) \right\}, \quad (2.5.21)$$

where the maximization is subject to $y^* = Ay + Bu + C\epsilon$ and ϵ is a Gaussian vector with mean zero and identity covariance matrix.

Using a result from Jacobson (1973), it can be shown that

$$\mathcal{R} \left(-y^{*\prime} Py^* - \hat{p} \right) = -(Ay + Bu)' \mathcal{D}(P)(Ay + Bu) - p(P, \hat{p}) \quad (2.5.22)$$

where $\mathcal{D}$ is the same operator defined in $(2.5.6)$ with $\theta = -\sigma^{-1}$, and the operator p is defined by

$$p(P, \hat{p}) = \hat{p} - \sigma^{-1} \log \det (I + \sigma C' P C). \quad (2.5.23)$$

Consequently, the Bellman equation for the infinite-horizon discounted risk-sensitive control problem can be expressed as

$$-y'Py - \hat{p} = \max_u \{ r(y, u) - \beta (Ay + Bu)' \mathcal{D}(P)(Ay + Bu) - \beta p(P, \hat{p}) \}.$$
$$(2.5.24)$$

Evidently, the fixed point P satisfies $P = T \circ \mathcal{D}(P)$, and therefore it is the same P that appears in the Bellman equation $(2.4.3)$ for the robust control problem. The constant $\hat{p}$ that solves $(2.5.24)$ differs from p in $(2.4.3)$, but since they depend only on P and not on p or $\hat{p}$, the decision rules are the same for the two problems. For more discussion of these points, see chapter 3.

2.6. More general misspecifications

Thus far, we have permitted the decision maker to seek robustness against misspecifications that occur only as a distortion w_{t+1} to the conditional mean of the innovation to the state y_{t+1}. When the approximating model has the Gaussian form $(2.2.1)$, this is less restrictive than it may at first appear. In chapter 3, we allow a more general class of misspecifications to the linear Gaussian model $(2.2.1)$, but nevertheless find that important parts of the preceding results survive when return functions are quadratic and the transition law implied by the approximating model is linear. For convenience, express the approximating model $(2.2.1)$ in the compact notation

$$f_o(y^* | y) \sim \mathcal{N}(Ay + Bu, CC'),$$

which portrays the conditional distribution of next period's state as Gaussian with mean $Ay + Bu$ and covariance matrix CC'. Let $f(y^*|y)$ be an arbitrary alternative conditional distribution that puts positive probability on the same events as the approximating model f_o. The conditional entropy of model f relative to the approximating model f_o is

$$I\left(f_o, f\right)(y) = \int \log\left(\frac{f\left(y^*|y\right)}{f_o\left(y^*|y\right)}\right) f\left(y^*|y\right) d\,y^*.$$

Entropy $I(f_o, f)(y)$ is thus the conditional expectation of the log-likelihood ratio evaluated with respect to the distorted model f. A multiplier robust control problem is associated with the following Bellman equation:

$$-y'Py - p = \max_u \min_f E\left\{r\left(y, u\right) + 2\theta\beta I\left(f_o, f\right)(y) - \beta y^{*\prime} Py^* - \beta p\right\}. \quad (2.6.1)$$

Let $\sigma = -\theta^{-1}$ and consider the inner minimization problem, assuming that $u = -Fy$. In chapter 3, we shall show that the extremizing f is the Gaussian distribution

$$f\left(y^*|y\right) \sim \mathcal{N}\left(Ay - BFy + CKy, \hat{C}\hat{C}'\right) \quad (2.6.2)$$

where (F, K) are the same matrices appearing in (2.5.11),

$$\hat{C}\hat{C}' = C\left(I + \sigma C'PC\right)^{-1}C', \quad (2.6.3)$$

and P is the *same* P that appears in the solution of the Bellman equation for the deterministic multiplier robust control problem (2.5.3). Equation (2.6.2) assures us that when we allow the minimizing player to choose a general misspecification $f(y^*|y)$, he chooses a Gaussian distribution with the *same* mean distortion as when we let him distort only the mean of a Gaussian conditional distribution. However, formula (2.6.3) shows that the minimizing agent would also distort the covariance matrix of the innovations, if given a chance.[24]

The upshot of these findings is that when the conditional distribution $f(y^*|y)$ for the approximating model is Gaussian, even if we actually were to permit general misspecifications $f(y^*|y)$, we could compute the worst-case f by solving a deterministic multiplier robust control problem for P, F, K, and then use P to compute the appropriate adjustment to the covariance matrix (2.6.3). In chapter 13, we use some of these ideas to price assets under alternative assumptions about the set of models against which decision makers seek robustness.

---

[24] In a diffusion setting in continuous time, the minimizing agent chooses not to distort the volatility matrix because it is infinitely costly in terms of entropy. See Hansen, Sargent, Turmuhambetova, and Williams (2006) and Anderson, Hansen, and Sargent (2003).

2.7. A simple algorithm

Chapter 7 discusses alternative algorithms for solving (2.5.3) and relationships among them. This section describes perhaps the simplest algorithm, an adapted ordinary optimal linear regulator. Chapters 7 and 8 describe necessary technical conditions, including restrictions on the magnitude of the multiplier parameter θ.[25]

Application of the ordinary optimal linear regulator can be justified by noting that the Riccati equation for the optimal linear regulator emerges from first-order conditions alone, and that the first-order conditions for extremizing (i.e., finding the saddle point by simultaneously minimizing with respect to w and maximizing with respect to u) the right side of (2.5.3) match those for an ordinary (non-robust) optimal linear regulator with joint control process $\{u_t, w_{t+1}\}$. This insight allows us to solve (2.5.3) by forming an appropriate optimal linear regulator.

Thus, put the Bellman equation (2.5.3) into a more compact form by defining

$$\tilde{B} = [\, B \quad C \,] \tag{2.7.1a}$$

$$\tilde{R} = \begin{bmatrix} R & 0 \\ 0 & -\beta\theta I \end{bmatrix} \tag{2.7.1b}$$

$$\tilde{u}_t = \begin{bmatrix} u_t \\ w_{t+1} \end{bmatrix}. \tag{2.7.1c}$$

Let ext denote extremization – maximization with respect to u, minimization with respect to w. The Bellman equation can be written as

$$-y'Py = \text{ext}_{\tilde{u}} \left\{ -y'Qy - \tilde{u}'\tilde{R}\tilde{u} - \beta y^{*\prime}Py^* \right\} \tag{2.7.2}$$

where the extremization is subject to

$$y^* = Ay + \tilde{B}\tilde{u}. \tag{2.7.3}$$

The first-order conditions for problem (2.7.2), (2.7.3) imply the matrix Riccati equation

$$P = Q + \beta A'PA - \beta^2 A'P\tilde{B}\left(\tilde{R} + \beta\tilde{B}'P\tilde{B}\right)^{-1}\tilde{B}'PA \tag{2.7.4}$$

and the formula for $\tilde{F}$ in the decision rule $\tilde{u}_t = -\tilde{F}y_t$

$$\tilde{F} = \beta\left(\tilde{R} + \beta\tilde{B}'P\tilde{B}\right)^{-1}\tilde{B}'PA. \tag{2.7.5}$$

---

[25] The Matlab program `olrprobust.m` described in the appendix implements this algorithm; `doublex9.m` implements a doubling algorithm of the kind described in chapter 4 and Hansen and Sargent (2008); please note that `doublex9.m` solves a *minimum* problem and that $-\theta^{-1} \equiv \sigma < 0$ connotes a fear of model misspecification.

Partitioning $\tilde{F}$, we have

$$u_t = -Fy_t \qquad\qquad (2.7.6a)$$

$$w_{t+1} = Ky_t. \qquad\qquad (2.7.6b)$$

The decision rule $u_t = -Fy_t$ is the robust rule. As mentioned above, $w_{t+1} = Ky_t$ provides the θ-constrained worst-case specification error. We can solve the Bellman equation by iterating to convergence on the Riccati equation (2.7.4), or by using one of the faster computational methods described in chapter 4.

2.7.1. Interpretation of the simple algorithm

The adjusted Riccati equation (2.7.4) is an augmented version of the Riccati equation (2.2.8) that is associated with the ordinary optimal linear regulator. The right side of equation (2.7.4) defines one step on the composite operator $T \circ D$ where T and D are defined in (2.5.8) and (2.5.5).[26] Hansen and Sargent's (1995) discounted version of the risk-sensitive preferences of Jacobson (1973) and Whittle (1990) also uses the D operator.

2.8. Robustness and discounting in a permanent income model

This section illustrates aspects of robust control theory in the context of a linear-quadratic version of a simple permanent income model.[27] In the basic permanent income model, a consumer applies a single marginal propensity to consume to the sum of his financial wealth and his human wealth, where human wealth is defined as the expected present value of his labor (or endowment) income discounted at the same risk-free rate of return that he earns on his financial assets. Without a concern about robustness, the consumer has no doubts about the probability model used to form the conditional expectation of discounted future labor income. Instead, we assume that the consumer doubts that model and therefore forms forecasts of future income by using a conditional probability distribution that is twisted or slanted relative to his approximating model for his endowment. Otherwise, the consumer behaves as an ordinary permanent income consumer.

---

[26] This can be verified by unstacking the matrices in (2.7.4). See page 170 in chapter 7.

[27] See Sargent (1987) and Hansen, Roberds, and Sargent (1991) for accounts of the connection between the permanent income consumer and Barro's (1979) model of tax smoothing. See Aiyagari, Marcet, Sargent, and Seppälä (2002) for a deeper exploration of the connections.

His slanting of conditional probabilities leads the consumer to engage in a form of precautionary savings that under the approximating model for his endowment process tilts his consumption profile toward the future relative to what it would be without a concern about misspecification of that process. Indeed, so far as his consumption and savings program is concerned, activating a concern about robustness is equivalent with making the consumer more patient. However, that is not the end of the story. Chapter 13 shows that attributing a concern about robustness to a representative consumer has different effects on asset prices than are associated with varying his discount factor.

2.8.1. The LQ permanent income model

In Hall's (1978) linear-quadratic permanent income model, a consumer receives an exogenous endowment $\{d_t\}$ and wants to allocate it between consumption c_t and savings k_t to maximize

$$-E_0 \sum_{t=0}^{\infty} \beta^t (c_t - b)^2, \beta \in (0, 1).$$ (2.8.1)

We simplify the problem by assuming that the endowment is a first-order autoregression. Thus, the household faces the state transition laws

$$k_t + c_t = Rk_{t-1} + d_t$$ (2.8.2a)

$$d_{t+1} = \mu_d (1 - \rho) + \rho d_t + c_d (\epsilon_{t+1} + w_{t+1}),$$ (2.8.2b)

where $R > 1$ is a time-invariant gross rate of return on financial assets k_{t-1} held at the end of period $t - 1$, and $|\rho| < 1$ describes the persistence of his endowment. In (2.8.2b), w_{t+1} is a distortion to the mean of the endowment that represents possible model misspecification. We use $\sigma = -\theta^{-1}$ to parameterize the consumer's desire for robustness. Soon we'll confirm how easily this problem maps into the robust linear regulator. But first we'll use classical methods to elicit some useful properties of the consumer's decisions when $\sigma = 0$.

2.8.2. Solution when $\sigma = 0$

We first solve the household's problem *without* a concern about robustness by setting $\theta^{-1} \equiv \sigma = 0$. Define the marginal utility of consumption as $\mu_{ct} = b - c_t$. The household's Euler equation is

$$E_t \mu_{c,t+1} = (\beta R)^{-1} \mu_{ct},$$ (2.8.3)

where E_t is the mathematical expectation operator conditioned on date t information. Treating $(2.8.2a)$ as a difference equation in k_t, solving it forward in time, and taking conditional expectations on both sides gives

$$k_{t-1} = \sum_{j=0}^{\infty} R^{-(j+1)} E_t \left(c_{t+j} - d_{t+j} \right). \qquad (2.8.4)$$

Solving $(2.8.3)$ and $(2.8.4)$ and using $\mu_{ct} = b - c_t$ implies

$$\mu_{ct} = -\left(1 - R^{-2} \beta^{-1} \right) \left(R k_{t-1} + E_t \sum_{j=0}^{\infty} R^{-j} \left(d_{t+j} - b \right) \right). \qquad (2.8.5)$$

Equations $(2.8.3)$ and $(2.8.5)$ can be used to deduce the following representation for μ_{ct}

$$\mu_{c,t+1} = (\beta R)^{-1} \mu_{c,t} + \nu \epsilon_{t+1}. \qquad (2.8.6)$$

We provide a formula for the scalar ν in $(2.8.11)$ below.

Given an initial condition $\mu_{c,0}$, equation $(2.8.6)$ describes the consumer's optimal behavior; $\mu_{c,0}$ can be determined by solving $(2.8.5)$ at $t = 0$. It is easy to use $(2.8.5)$ to deduce an optimal consumption rule of the form

$$c_t = g y_t$$

where g is a vector conformable to the pertinent state vector y. In the case $\beta R = 1$ that was analyzed by Hall (1978), $(2.8.6)$ implies that the marginal utility of consumption μ_{ct} is a martingale under the approximating model, which because $\mu_{ct} = b - c_t$ in turn implies that consumption itself is a martingale.

2.8.3. Linear regulator for permanent income model

This problem is readily mapped into a linear regulator in which the marginal utility of consumption $b - c_t$ is the control. Express the transition law for k_t as

$$k_t = R k_{t-1} + d_t - b - (c_t - b).$$

Define the state as $y_t' = \begin{bmatrix} 1 & k_{t-1} & d_t \end{bmatrix}'$ and the control as $u_t = \mu_{ct} \equiv (b - c_t)$ and express the state transition law as $y_{t+1} = A y_t + B u_t + C(\epsilon_{t+1} + w_{t+1})$ or

$$\begin{bmatrix} 1 \\ k_t \\ d_{t+1} \end{bmatrix} = \begin{bmatrix} 1 & 0 & 0 \\ -b & R & 1 \\ (1-\rho)\mu_d & 0 & \rho \end{bmatrix} \begin{bmatrix} 1 \\ k_{t-1} \\ d_t \end{bmatrix} + \begin{bmatrix} 0 \\ 1 \\ 0 \end{bmatrix} (b - c_t) + \begin{bmatrix} 0 \\ 0 \\ c_d \end{bmatrix} (\epsilon_{t+1} + w_{t+1}). \qquad (2.8.7)$$

This equation defines the triple (A, B, C) associated with a robust linear regulator. For the objective function, (2.8.1) implies that we should let $r(y, u) = -y'Ry - u'Qu$ where $R = 0_{3 \times 3}$ and $Q = 1$.

We can obtain a robust rule by using the robust linear regulator and setting $\sigma < 0$. The solution of the robust linear regulator problem is a linear decision rule for the control μ_{ct}

$$\mu_{ct} = -Fy_t. \tag{2.8.8}$$

Under the approximating model, the law of motion of the state is then

$$y_{t+1} = (A - BF) y_t + C\epsilon_{t+1}. \tag{2.8.9}$$

Equations (2.8.8) and (2.8.9) imply that

$$\mu_{c,t+1} = -F (A - BF) y_t - FC\epsilon_{t+1}. \tag{2.8.10}$$

Comparing (2.8.10) and (2.8.6) shows that $-F(A - BF) = -(\beta R)^{-1}F$ and

$$\nu = -FC, \tag{2.8.11}$$

which is the promised formula for ν.

2.8.4. Effects on consumption of concern about misspecification

To understand the effects on consumption of a concern about robustness, we use as a benchmark Hall's assumption that $\beta R = 1$ and no concern about robustness ($\sigma = 0$). In that case, the multiplier μ_{ct} and consumption c_t are both driftless random walks. To be concrete, we set parameters to be consistent with ones calibrated from post-World War II U.S. time series by Hansen, Sargent, and Tallarini (1999) for a more general permanent income model. HST set $\beta = .9971$ and fit a two-factor model for the endowment process; each factor is a second-order autoregression. To simplify that specification, we replace this estimated two-factor endowment process with the population first-order autoregression one would obtain if that two-factor model actually generated the data. That is, we use the population moments implied by Hansen, Sargent, and Tallarini's (HST's) estimated endowment process to fit the first-order autoregressive process (2.8.2b) with $w_{t+1} \equiv 0$. Ignoring constant terms, we obtain the endowment process $d_{t+1} = .9992d_t + 5.5819\epsilon_{t+1}$ where ϵ_{t+1} is an i.i.d. scalar process with mean zero and unit variance.[28] We use $\hat{\beta}$ to denote HST's value of $\beta = .9971$. Throughout, we suppose that $R = \hat{\beta}^{-1}$.

We now consider three cases.

---

[28] We computed ρ, c_d by calculating autocovariances implied by HST's specification, then used them to calculate the implied population first-order autoregressive representation.

- The $\beta R = 1, \sigma = 0$ case studied by Hall (1978). With $\beta = \hat{\beta}$, we compute that the marginal utility of consumption follows the law of motion

$$\mu_{c,t+1} = \mu_{c,t} + 4.3825\epsilon_{t+1} \tag{2.8.12}$$

  where we compute the coefficient 4.3825 on ϵ_{t+1} by noting that it equals $-FC$ by formula (2.8.11).

- A version of Hall's $\beta R = 1$ specification with a concern about misspecification. Retaining $\hat{\beta} R = 1$, we activate a concern about robustness by setting $\sigma = \hat{\sigma} = -2E^{-7}$.[29] We now compute that[30]

$$\mu_{c,t+1} = .9976\mu_{c,t} + 8.0473\epsilon_{t+1}. \tag{2.8.13}$$

  When $b - c_t > 0$, this equation implies that $E_t(b - c_{t+1}) = .9976(b - c_t) < (b - c_t)$, which in turn implies that $E_t c_{t+1} > c_t$. Thus, the effect of activating a concern about robustness is to put upward drift into the consumption profile, a manifestation of a type of "precautionary savings" that comes from the consumer's fear of misspecification of the endowment process.

- A case that raises the discount factor relative to the $\beta R = 1$ benchmark prevailing in Hall's model but withholds a concern about robustness. In particular, while we set $\sigma = 0$ we increase β to $\tilde{\beta} = .9995$. Remarkably, with $(\sigma, \beta) = (0, \tilde{\beta})$, we compute that $\mu_{c,t+1}$ obeys exactly (2.8.13).[31] Thus, starting from $(\sigma, \beta) = (0, \hat{\beta})$, insofar as the effects on consumption and saving are concerned, activating a concern about robustness by lowering σ while keeping β constant is evidently equivalent to keeping $\sigma = 0$ but *increasing* the discount factor to a particular $\tilde{\beta} > \hat{\beta}$.

These numerical examples illustrate what is true more generally, namely, that in the permanent income model an increased concern about robustness has effects on (c_t, k_{t+1}) that operate exactly like an increase in the discount factor β. In chapter 10, we extend these numerical examples analytically

---

[29] We discuss how to calibrate σ in chapters 9, 10, 13, and 14.

[30] We can confirm this formula computationally as follows. Use `doublex9` to solve the robust optimal linear regulator and compute representations $\mu_{c,t} = -Fy_t$ and compare it to the term $F(A-BF)y_t$ on the right side of (2.8.10) to discover that $F(A-BF) = .9976F$, i.e., the coefficients are proportional with .9976 being the factor of proportionality.

[31] We discover this computationally using the method of the previous footnote.

within a broader class of permanent income models. In particular, let $\alpha^2 = \nu'\nu$ and suppose that instead of the particular pair $(\hat{\sigma}, \hat{\beta})$, where $(\hat{\sigma} < 0)$, we use the pair $(0, \tilde{\beta})$, where $\tilde{\beta}$ satisfies

$$
\tilde{\beta}(\sigma) = \frac{\hat{\beta}\left(1 + \hat{\beta}\right)}{2\left(1 + \sigma\alpha^2\right)}\left[1 + \sqrt{1 - 4\hat{\beta}\frac{1 + \sigma\alpha^2}{\left(1 + \hat{\beta}\right)^2}}\,\right]. \tag{2.8.14}
$$

Then the laws of motion for $\mu_{c,t}$, and therefore the decision rules for c_t, are identical across these two specifications of concerns about robustness. We establish formula $(2.8.14)$ in appendix B of chapter 10.

2.8.5. *Observational equivalence of quantities but not continuation values*

We have seen that, holding other parameters constant, there exists a locus of (σ, β) pairs that imply the same consumption-savings programs. It can be verified that the P matrices appearing in the quadratic forms in the value function are identical for the $(\hat{\sigma}, \hat{\beta})$ and $(0, \tilde{\beta})$ problems. However, in terms of their implications for pricing claims on risky future payoffs, it is significant that the $\mathcal{D}(P)$ matrices differ across such (σ, β) pairs. For the $(0, \tilde{\beta})$ pair, $P = \mathcal{D}(P)$. However, when $\sigma < 0$, $\mathcal{D}(P)$ differs from P. As we shall see in chapter 13, when we interpret $(2.8.1)$, $(2.8.2)$ as a planning problem, $\mathcal{D}(P)$ encodes the shadow prices that can be converted into competitive equilibrium state-date prices that can then be used to price uncertain claims on future consumption. Thus, although the $(\hat{\sigma}, \hat{\beta})$ and $(0, \tilde{\beta})$ parameter pairs imply identical savings and consumption plans, they imply different valuations of risky future consumption payoffs. In chapter 13, we use this fact to study how a concern about robustness influences the theoretical value of the market price of macroeconomic risk and the equity premium.

2.8.6. *Distorted endowment process*

On page 36, we described a particular distorted transition law associated with the worst-case shocks $w_{t+1} = Ky_t$. If the decision maker solves an ordinary dynamic programming program without a concern about misspecification but substitutes the distorted transition law for the one given by his approximating model, he attains a robust decision rule. Thus, when $\sigma < 0$, instead of facing the transition law $(2.8.7)$ that prevails under the approximating model, the household would use the distorted transition law [32]

$$\begin{bmatrix} y_{t+1} \\ Y_{t+1} \end{bmatrix} = \begin{bmatrix} A & CK \\ 0 & (A - BF + CK) \end{bmatrix} \begin{bmatrix} y_t \\ Y_t \end{bmatrix} + \begin{bmatrix} B \\ 0 \end{bmatrix} \mu_{ct} + \begin{bmatrix} C \\ C \end{bmatrix} \epsilon_{t+1}. \quad (2.8.15)$$

For our numerical example with $\sigma = -2E - 7$, we would have $A - BF + CK =$

$$\begin{bmatrix} 1.0000 & 0 & 0 \\ 15.0528 & 0.9976 & -0.4417 \\ -0.0558 & 0.0000 & 1.0016 \end{bmatrix} \text{ and } CK = \begin{bmatrix} 0 & 0 & 0 \\ 0 & 0 & 0 \\ -0.0558 & 0.0000 & 0.0024 \end{bmatrix}.$$

Notice the pattern of zeros in CK, which shows that the distortion to the law of motion of the state affects only the component d_t of the state y. The components Y of the state are information variables that account for the dynamics in the misspecification imputed by the worst-case shock w. In chapter 10, we shall analyze the behavior of the endowment process under the distorted model $(2.8.15)$.

It is useful to consider our observational equivalence result in light of the distorted law of motion $(2.8.15)$. Let $\hat{E}_t$ denote a conditional expectation with respect to the distorted transition law $(2.8.15)$ for the endowment shock and let E_t denote the expectation with respect to the approximating model. Then the observational equivalence of the pairs $(\hat{\sigma}, \hat{\beta})$ and $(0, \tilde{\beta})$ means that the following two versions of $(2.8.5)$ imply the same μ_{ct} processes:

$$\mu_{ct} = -\left(1 - R^{-2}\hat{\beta}^{-1}\right)\left(Rk_{t-1} + \hat{E}_t \sum_{j=0}^{\infty} R^{-j}\left(d_{t+j} - b\right)\right)$$

and

$$\mu_{ct} = -\left(1 - R^{-2}\tilde{\beta}^{-1}\right)\left(Rk_{t-1} + E_t \sum_{j=0}^{\infty} R^{-j}\left(d_{t+j} - b\right)\right).$$

For both of these expressions to be true, the effect on $\hat{E}$ of setting σ less than zero must be offset by the effect of raising β from $\hat{\beta}$ to $\tilde{\beta}$.

2.8.7. A Stackelberg formulation for representing misspecification

In chapters 7 and 8, we show the equivalence of outcomes under different timing protocols for the two-player zero-sum games. In appendix B of chapter 10, we shall use a Stackelberg game to establish the observational equivalence for consumption-savings plans of $(0, \tilde{\beta})$ and $(\hat{\sigma}, \hat{\beta})$ pairs. The minimizing player's problem in the Stackelberg game can be represented as

$$\min_{\{w_{t+1}\}} -\sum_{t=0}^{\infty} \hat{\beta}^t \left\{ \mu_{ct}^2 + \hat{\beta}\sigma^{-1} w_{t+1}^2 \right\} \quad (2.8.16)$$

---

[32] This is not a minimal state representation because we have not eliminated the constant from the Y component of the state.

subject to

$$\mu_{c,t+1} = \left(\tilde{\beta}R\right)^{-1} \mu_{c,t} + \nu w_{t+1}. \tag{2.8.17}$$

Equation (2.8.17) is the consumption Euler equation of the maximizing player. Under the Stackelberg timing, the minimizing player commits to a sequence $\{w_{t+1}\}_{t=0}^{\infty}$ that the maximizing player takes as given. The minimizing player determines that sequence by solving (2.8.16), (2.8.17). The worst-case shock that emerges from this problem satisfies $w_{t+1} = k\mu_{ct}$ and is identical to the worst-case shock $w_{t+1} = Ky_t$ that emerges from the robust linear regulator for the consumption problem.

2.9. Concluding remarks

The discounted dynamic programming problem for quadratic returns and a linear transition function is called the optimal linear regulator problem. This problem is widely used throughout macroeconomics and applied dynamics. For linear-quadratic problems, robust decision rules can be constructed by thoughtfully using the optimal linear regulator. The optimal linear regulator has other uses too. In chapters 5, 17, and 18 we describe filtering problems. Via the concept of duality explained there, the linear regulator can also be used to solve such filtering problems, including those where the decision maker wants estimates that are robust to model misspecification.

Chapter 3 introduces a stochastic version of robust control problems and describes how they link to the non-stochastic problems of the present chapter. Chapters 4 and 5 then prepare the way for deeper studies of robust control and filtering problems by reviewing the foundations of ordinary (i.e., non-robust) control and filtering theory. In these two chapters, we shall encounter tools that will serve us well when we move on to construct robust decision rules and filters.

A. Matlab programs

A robust optimal linear regulator is defined by the system matrices Q, R, A, B, C, the discount factor β, and the risk-sensitivity parameter $\sigma \equiv -\theta^{-1}$. The Matlab program olrprobust.m implements the algorithm of section 2.7 by calling the optimal linear regulator program olrp.m. The program olrprobust solves a *minimum* problem, so that $\sigma < 0$ corresponds to a concern about robustness and R and Q should be more or less positive definite, where we say more or less because of the some detectability qualifications explained in chapter 4. Call the program olrprobust as follows:

```
[F,K,P,Pt]=olrprobust(beta,A,B,C,Q,R,sig);
```

The objects returned by `olrprobust` determine the decision rule $u_t = -F y_t$, the distortion $w_{t+1} = K y_t$, the quadratic form in the value function $-y' P y$, and the distorted continuation value function $-y^{*\prime}(Pt)y^*$. The program `doublex9` implements the doubling algorithm described in chapter 4 and by Hansen and Sargent (2008, chapter 9). To compute the robust rule with a discounted objective function, one has to induce `doublex9` to solving a discounted problem by first setting $Ad = \sqrt{\beta} A, Bd = \sqrt{\beta} B$, calling `[F,Kd,P,Pt]=doublex9(Ad,Bd,C,Q,R,sig)`, then finally setting $K = Kd/\sqrt{\beta}$. The program `bayes4.m` uses both `olrprobust` and `doublex9` to compute robust decision rules and verifies that they give the same answers.

Chapter 3
A stochastic formulation

*When Shannon had invented his quantity and consulted von Neumann
on what to call it, von Neumann replied: 'Call it entropy. It is already in
use under that name and besides, it will give you a great edge in debates
because nobody knows what entropy is anyway.'*
— *Quoted by Georgii, "Probabilistic Aspects of Entropy," 2003*

3.1. Introduction

This book makes ample use of the finding that the stochastic structure of a
linear-quadratic-Gaussian robust control problem is a secondary concern because we can deduce robust decision rules by studying a related deterministic
problem.[1] This chapter describes this finding in some detail. We start with
a more general setting, then focus on the linear quadratic Gaussian case. We
begin with a stochastic specification of shocks in an approximating model
and describe misspecifications to that model in terms of perturbations to the
distribution of the shocks. In the special linear-quadratic-Gaussian setting,
formulas that solve the nonstochastic problem contain all of the information
needed to solve a corresponding stochastic problem.[2]

3.2. Shock distributions

Consider a sequence of i.i.d. Gaussian shocks $\{\epsilon_t\}$ that enter the transition
equation for an approximating model. The perturbed model alters the distribution of these shocks and, in particular, allows them to be temporally
dependent. Let $\epsilon^t = [\epsilon_t{}', \epsilon_{t-1}{}', \ldots, \epsilon_1{}']'$. Throughout, we will condition on
the initial state y_0.[3] The date t information available to the decision maker
is y_0 and ϵ^t.

---

[1] Some control theorists extend this insight beyond linear quadratic models and argue
that stochastic structures are artificial and that all shocks should be regarded as deterministic processes that represent misspecifications. Although this interesting point of view has
brought important insights, we don't embrace it. Instead, we strongly prefer to regard a
model as a stochastic process and misspecifications as perturbations to a salient stochastic
process that the decision maker takes as an approximating model.

[2] See Jacobson (1973).

[3] When some of the states are hidden from the decision maker, we would have to say
more, as we do in Hansen and Sargent (2005b, 2007a) and in chapters 17 and 18. In this
chapter, we will suppose that all of the state variables are observed.

3.3. Martingale representations of distortions

Following Hansen and Sargent (2005b, 2007a), we use martingales to represent distortions in the probabilities. This allows us to represent perturbed models by introducing some appropriately restricted multiplicative preference shocks into the original approximating model.

Let $\pi(\varepsilon)$ denote the multivariate standardized normal distribution, where ε is a dummy variable with the same dimension as the number of entries of the random vector ϵ_t. Let $\hat{\pi}(\varepsilon|\epsilon^t, y_0)$ denote an alternative density for ϵ_{t+1} conditioned on date t information. Form the likelihood ratio

$$m_{t+1} = \frac{\hat{\pi}\left(\epsilon_{t+1}|\epsilon^t, y_0\right)}{\pi\left(\epsilon_{t+1}\right)}.$$

Notice that

$$E\left(m_{t+1}|\epsilon^t, y_0\right) = \int \frac{\hat{\pi}\left(\varepsilon|\epsilon^t, y_0\right)}{\pi\left(\varepsilon\right)} \pi\left(\varepsilon\right) d\varepsilon = 1,$$

where integration is with respect to the Lebesgue measure over the Euclidean space with the same dimension as the number of entries of ϵ_t. Now set $M_0 = 1$ and recursively construct $\{M_t\}$

$$M_{t+1} = m_{t+1} M_t.$$

Solving this recursion gives

$$M_t = \prod_{j=1}^{t} m_j.$$

The random variable M_t is a function of ϵ^t and y_0 and evidently satisfies

$$E\left(M_{t+1}|\epsilon^t, y_0\right) = M_t.$$

Hence, M_t is a martingale relative to the sequence of information sets (sigma algebras) generated by the shocks. The random variable M_t is a ratio of joint densities of ϵ^t conditioned on y_0 and evaluated at the random vector ϵ^t. The numerator density $\hat{\Pi}_t$ is the alternative one that we shall use to compute expectations.

Now let $\phi(\epsilon^t, y_0)$ be a random variable that is a Borel measurable function of ϵ^t and y_0, where ε^t is a dummy variable with the same dimension as the random vector ϵ^t. The expectation of $\phi(\epsilon^t, y_0)$ under the $\hat{\pi}_t$ density can be computed as

$$\int \phi\left(\varepsilon^t, y_0\right) \hat{\Pi}_t\left(\varepsilon^t\right) d\varepsilon^t = E\left[M_t \phi\left(\epsilon^t, y_0\right)|y_0\right]$$

where integration is with respect to the Lebesgue measure over a Euclidean space with the same dimension as the random vector ϵ^t.

3.4. A digression on entropy

Define the *entropy* of the distortion associated with M_t as the expected log-likelihood ratio with respect to the distorted distribution, which can be expressed as $E(M_t \log M_t | y_0)$. The function $M_t \log M_t$ is convex in M_t and so lies above its linear approximation at the point $M_t = 1$. Thus,

$$M_t \log M_t \geq M_t - 1$$

because the derivative of $M_t \log M_t$ is $1 + \log M_t$ and equal to one for $M_t = 1$. Since $E(M_t | y_0) = 1$, it follows that

$$E(M_t \log M_t | y_0) \geq 0$$

and that $E(M_t \log M_t | y_0) = 0$ only when $M_t = 1$, in which case there is no probability distortion associated with M_t.

The factorization $M_t = \prod_{j=1}^{t} m_j$ implies the following decomposition of entropy:

$$E(M_t \log M_t | y_0) = \sum_{j=0}^{t-1} E \left[M_j E \left(m_{j+1} \log m_{j+1} | \epsilon^j, y_0 \right) | y_0 \right].$$

Here $E[m_{t+1} \log m_{t+1} | y^t]$ is the conditional relative entropy of a perturbation to the one-step transition density associated with the approximating model. Notice the absence of discounting on the right side. To get a recursive formulation of stochastic robust control that sustains an enduring concern about model misspecification, Hansen and Sargent (2007a) advocate using a discounted version of the object on the right side to penalize a malevolent player's choice of a sequence of increments $\{m_{t+1}\}$. Discounted entropy over an infinite horizon can be expressed as

$$(1 - \beta) \sum_{j=0}^{\infty} \beta^j E(M_j \log M_j | y_0) = \sum_{j=0}^{\infty} \beta^j E \left[M_j E \left(m_{j+1} \log m_{j+1} | \epsilon^j, y_0 \right) | y_0 \right],$$

where we have used a summation-by-parts formula. The right-hand side formula is particularly useful to us in recursive formulations of robust control problems in which we allow m_{t+1} to be chosen by a malevolent second agent at date t.

This formulation requires that the perturbed distributions $\hat{\Pi}_t$ be *absolutely continuous* with respect to the baseline distribution Π_t. This means that the perturbed distribution cannot assign positive probability to events constructed in terms of ϵ^t and y_0 that have probability measure zero under the distribution implied by the approximating model.

3.5. A stochastic robust control problem

We want a robust decision rule for an action u_t. Suppose that the state evolves according to

$$y_{t+1} = \varpi\left(y_t, u_t, \epsilon_{t+1}\right),$$

the time period t return function is $r(y_t, u_t)$, and y_0 is an initial condition. We require that a control process $\{u_t\}$ have its time t component u_t be a function of ϵ^t and y_0, so that y_t and $r(y_t, u_t)$ also become functions of ϵ^t and y_0.

To obtain a stochastic robust control problem that sustains an enduring concern about model misspecification, Hansen and Sargent (2007a) advocate using a two-player zero-sum game of the form

$$\max_{\{u_t\}} \min_{\{m_{t+1}\}} \sum_{t=0}^{\infty} E\left[\beta^t M_t \left\{r\left(y_t, u_t\right) + \alpha\beta E\left(m_{t+1}\log m_{t+1}|\epsilon^t, y_0\right)\right\}|y_0\right]$$

(3.5.1)

subject to

$$y_{t+1} = \varpi\left(y_t, u_t, \epsilon_{t+1}\right),$$
$$M_{t+1} = m_{t+1}M_t,$$

(3.5.2)

where $Em_{t+1}|\epsilon^t, y_0 = 1$. Here $\alpha \in [\underline{\alpha}, +\infty]$ is a penalty on the entropy associated with the m_{t+1} process. Soon we shall relate α to θ from chapter 2.

The two-person zero-sum game (3.5.1)-(3.5.2) has the player choosing processes for $\{u_t\}_{t=0}^{\infty}$, $\{m_{t+1}\}_{t=0}^{\infty}$ in a particular order. The dates on variables indicate informational constraints. We require that u_t be a function of ϵ^t and y_0 and m_{t+1} be a function of ϵ^{t+1} and y_0.

3.6. A recursive formulation

Chapter 7 describes technical conditions that allow us to alter timing protocols without affecting outcomes and thereby to formulate an equivalent game that is recursive. The recursive game makes u_t a function of the Markov state y_t and m_{t+1} a function of ϵ_{t+1} and the Markov state y_t, where m_{t+1} must have unit expectation.

To pose a recursive form of problem (3.5.1)-(3.5.2), we let the Markov state be the composite of M_t and y_t. We guess that the value function has the multiplicative form $W(M, y) = MV(y)$ and consider the Bellman equation

$$MV\left(y\right) = \max_{u} \min_{m(\varepsilon)} M\left\{r\left(y, u\right) + \beta \int \left(m\left(\varepsilon\right) V\left[\varpi\left(y, u, \varepsilon\right)\right]\right.\right.$$
$$\left.\left. + \alpha m\left(\varepsilon\right)\log m\left(\varepsilon\right)\right)\pi\left(\varepsilon\right)d\varepsilon\right\}$$

subject to the restriction that $\int m(\varepsilon)\pi(\varepsilon)d\varepsilon = 1$. The minimizing player chooses m as a function of ε so that m in effect is an infinite dimensional control vector.

The linear scaling of the value function by M allows us to consider the following problem that omits the state variable M:

$$V(y) = \max_{u} \min_{m(\varepsilon)} \left\{ r(y,u) + \beta \int \bigg(m(\varepsilon) V[\varpi(y,u,\varepsilon)] \right.$$
$$\left. + \alpha m(\varepsilon) \log m(\varepsilon) \bigg) \pi(\varepsilon) d\varepsilon \right\}$$

(3.6.1)

subject to $\int m(\varepsilon)\pi(\varepsilon)d\varepsilon = 1$. A consequence of our being able to omit M_t as a state variable is that the control laws for u and $m(\cdot)$ will depend on y, but not M.[4]

Consider the inner minimization problem

Problem A:

$$\mathcal{R}(V)(y,u) \equiv \min_{m(\varepsilon)} \int \bigg(m(\varepsilon) V[\varpi(y,u,\varepsilon)] + \alpha m(\varepsilon) \log m(\varepsilon) \bigg) \pi(\varepsilon) d\varepsilon$$

subject to $\int m(\varepsilon)\pi(\varepsilon) = 1$.

The objective is convex in m and the constraint is linear. The constraint $Em = 1$ restricts the average $m(\cdot)$ but leaves open how to allocate m over alternative values of ε. Although $m(\cdot)$ is infinite dimensional, it is easy to solve Problem A. Its solution is well known from the literature on relative entropy and large deviation theory.

The first-order conditions for minimization imply that

$$\log m(\epsilon) = \frac{-V[\varpi(y,u,\varepsilon)]}{\alpha} + \lambda$$

where λ is Lagrange multiplier chosen so that $\int m(\varepsilon)\pi(\varepsilon)d\varepsilon = 1$. Therefore,

$$m^*(\epsilon) = \frac{\exp\left(\frac{-V[\varpi(y,u,\epsilon)]}{\alpha}\right)}{\int \exp\left(\frac{-V[\varpi(y,u,\varepsilon)]}{\alpha}\right) \pi(\varepsilon) d\varepsilon}.$$

(3.6.2)

Furthermore, under the minimizing m^*,

$$\int \bigg(m^*(\varepsilon) V[\varpi(y,u,\epsilon)] + \alpha m^*(\varepsilon) \log m^*(\varepsilon) \bigg) \pi(\varepsilon) d\varepsilon$$
$$= -\alpha \log \left[\int \exp\left(\frac{-V[\varpi(y,u,\varepsilon)]}{\alpha}\right) \pi(\varepsilon) d\varepsilon \right]$$
$$= \mathcal{R}(V)(y,u).$$

This is the risk-sensitive recursion of Hansen and Sargent (1995).

---

[4] Our decision to use entropy to measure model discrepancies facilitates this outcome.

3.6.1. Verifying the solution

As a check on this calculation, write

$$\int m \log m\pi d\varepsilon = \int \frac{m}{m^*} \left(\log m - \log m^*\right) m^* \pi d\varepsilon + \int m \log m^* \pi d\varepsilon$$

$$\geq \int m \log m^* \pi d\varepsilon.$$

This inequality follows because the quantity

$$\int \frac{m}{m^*} \left(\log m - \log m^*\right) m^* \pi d\varepsilon$$

is a measure of the entropy of m relative to m^* and hence is nonnegative. Thus,

$$\int mV\left[\varpi\left(y, u, \cdot\right)\right] \pi d\varepsilon + \alpha \int m \log m\pi d\varepsilon \geq$$

$$\int mV\left[\varpi\left(y, u, \cdot\right)\right] \pi d\varepsilon - \int mV\left[\varpi\left(y, u, \cdot\right)\right] \pi d\varepsilon + \mathcal{R}\left(V\right)\left(y, u\right)$$

$$= \mathcal{R}\left(V\right)\left(y, u\right),$$

where we have substituted using formula (3.6.2) for m^*. This verifies that m^* is the minimizer in Problem A.

3.7. A value function bound

The random function m^* of ε tilts the density of the shock ε exponentially using the value function to determine the directions where the decision maker is most vulnerable. Since m^* depends on the state y_t, the resulting distorted density for the shocks can make the shocks temporally dependent and thereby represent misspecified dynamics. The form of the worst-case density depends on both the original density π and the shape of the value function V. When π is normal and V is quadratic, the distorted density is normal.

As a direct implication of Problem A, we obtain a bound on the distorted expectation of the value function as a function of relative entropy:

$$\int mV\left[\varpi\left(y, u, \cdot\right)\right] \pi\left(\varepsilon\right) d\varepsilon \geq \mathcal{R}\left(V\right)\left(y, u\right) - \alpha \int m \log m\pi\left(\varepsilon\right) d\varepsilon. \qquad (3.7.1)$$

The first term on the right depends on α but not on the alternative model as characterized by m. The second term is $-\alpha$ times entropy. Thus, inequality (3.7.1) justifies interpreting α as a *utility price of robustness*. The larger is the relative entropy, the larger is the downward adjustment in the relative entropy bound.

3.8. Large deviation interpretation of $\mathcal{R}$

We have interpreted Problem A in terms of a concern about robustness that is achieved by substituting the operator $\mathcal{R}$ for the conditional expectations operator in a corresponding Bellman equation without a concern for robustness. Let y^+ denote the state next period. In this section, we use ideas from the theory of large deviations to indicate how the operator $\mathcal{R}(V)(y, u)$ contains information about the left tail of the distribution of the continuation value $V(y^+)$ where the distribution of $y^+ = \varpi(y, u, \varepsilon)$ is induced by the density $\pi(\varepsilon)$ associated with the approximating model. Recall from Problem A that $\mathcal{R}$ depends on α and collapses to the conditional expectation operator as $\alpha \nearrow +\infty$. We shall show that $\mathcal{R}$ contains more information about the left tail of V as α is decreased. We gather this interpretation from an exponential inequality that bounds the (conditional) tail probabilities of the continuation value. This tail probability bound shows how $\mathcal{R}$ expresses a form of enhanced risk aversion that makes the decision maker care about more than just the conditional mean of the continuation value.

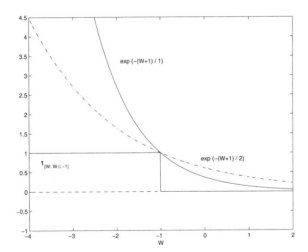

Figure 3.8.1: Ingredients of large deviation bounds: $\exp\left(\frac{-(W+r)}{\alpha}\right)$ and $\mathbf{1}_{\{W:W \leq -r\}}$ for $r = 1$ and two values of α: 1 and 2.

The tail probability bound is widely used in the theory of large deviation approximations.[5] It uses the inequality

$$\mathbf{1}_{\{V:V \leq -r\}} \leq \exp\left[\frac{-(V+r)}{\alpha}\right]$$

---

[5] For an informative survey, see Bucklew (1990).

depicted in figure 3.8.1, where $\mathbf{1}$ is the indicator function. This inequality holds for any real number r and any $\alpha > 0$. Then computing expectations conditioned on the current state vector y and control u yields

$$\text{Prob}\{V\left(y^+\right) \leq -r|y,u\} \leq E\left(\exp\left[-\frac{V\left(y^+\right)}{\alpha}\right]\bigg|y,u\right)\exp\left(-\frac{r}{\alpha}\right)$$

or

$$\text{Prob}\{V\left(y^+\right) \leq -r|y,u\} \leq \exp\left[-\frac{\mathcal{R}\left(V|y,u\right)}{\alpha}\right]\exp\left(-\frac{r}{\alpha}\right). \qquad (3.8.1)$$

Inequality $(3.8.1)$ bounds the tail probability on the left by an exponential in r. Thus, α determines a decay rate in the tail probabilities of the continuation value. Decreasing α increases the exponential rate at which the bound sends the tail probabilities to zero, thereby expressing how a lower α heightens concern about tail events. Associated with this rate is a scale factor

$$\int \exp\left(-\frac{V\left[\varpi\left(y,u,\varepsilon\right)\right]}{\alpha}\right)\pi\left(y,u,\varepsilon\right)d\varepsilon = \exp\left[-\frac{\mathcal{R}\left(V|y,u\right)}{\alpha}\right].$$

The adjustment to the value function determines the constant associated with the prespecified decay rate. For a fixed α, a larger value of $\mathcal{R}(V)(y,u)$ gives a smaller scale factor in the probability bound.

3.9. Choosing the control law

To construct a robust control law, solve the outer maximization problem of $(3.6.1)$

$$\max_u r\left(y,u\right) + \beta\mathcal{R}\left(V\right)\left(y,u\right).$$

Notice that we computed m as a function (y,u) before solving for u. It is often the case that we could compute m and u simultaneously as functions of y by in effect stacking first-order conditions instead of proceeding in sequence. This justifies an algorithm for the linear quadratic case that we describe in section 2.7 of chapter 2.

3.10. Linear-quadratic model

To connect the approach of this chapter to the nonstochastic formulations summarized in chapter 2, we turn to a linear quadratic setting with Gaussian disturbances. Consider the following evolution equation:

$$y^+ = Ay + Bu + C\varepsilon$$

where y^+ is the next period value of state vector. Consider a value function

$$V\left(y\right) = -\frac{1}{2}y'Py - \rho.$$

From our previous calculations, we know that

$$m^*\left(\varepsilon\right) \propto \exp\left[\frac{1}{2\alpha}\varepsilon'C'PC\varepsilon + \frac{1}{\alpha}\varepsilon'C'P\left(Ay + Bu\right)\right].$$

When π is a standard normal density, it follows that

$$\pi\left(\varepsilon\right)m^*\left(\varepsilon\right) \propto \exp\left[-\frac{1}{2}\varepsilon'\left(I - \frac{1}{\alpha}C'PC\right)\varepsilon\right.$$
$$\left. + \varepsilon'\left(I - \frac{1}{\alpha}C'PC\right)\left(\alpha I - C'PC\right)^{-1}C'P\left(Ay + Bu\right)\right],$$

where the proportionality coefficient is chosen so that the function of ε on the right-hand side integrates to unity. The right-hand side function can be recognized as being proportional to a normal density with covariance matrix $\left(I - \frac{1}{\alpha}C'PC\right)^{-1}$ and mean $\left(\alpha I - C'PC\right)^{-1}C'P(Ay + Bu)$. Evidently, the covariance matrix of the shock is enlarged. The altered mean for the shock implies that the distorted conditional mean for y^+ is

$$\left[I + C\left(\alpha I - C'PC\right)^{-1}C'P\right]\left(Ay + Bu\right).$$

These formulas for the distorted means of ε and y^+ agree with formulas that we derived from a deterministic problem in chapter 2.

3.11. Relative entropy and normal distributions

As we have just seen, the worst-case distribution will also be normal. As a consequence, we consider the corresponding measure of relative entropy for a normal distribution. This renders the following calculation interesting. Suppose that π is a multivariate standard normal distribution and that $\hat{\pi}$ is normal with mean w and nonsingular covariance Σ. We seek a formula for $\int(\log\hat{\pi}(\varepsilon) - \log\pi(\varepsilon))\hat{\pi}(\varepsilon)d\varepsilon$. First, note that the likelihood ratio is

$$\log\hat{\pi}\left(\varepsilon\right) - \log\pi\left(\varepsilon\right) = \frac{1}{2}\left[-\left(\varepsilon - w\right)'\Sigma^{-1}\left(\varepsilon - w\right) + \varepsilon'\varepsilon - \log\det\Sigma\right] \quad (3.11.1)$$

To compute relative entropy, we must evaluate expectations using a normal distribution with mean w and covariance Σ. Observe that

$$-\int\frac{1}{2}\left(\varepsilon - w\right)'\Sigma^{-1}\left(\varepsilon - w\right)\hat{\pi}\left(\varepsilon\right)d\varepsilon = \frac{1}{2}\mathrm{trace}\left(I\right).$$

Applying the identity $\varepsilon = w + (\varepsilon - w)$ gives

$$\frac{1}{2}\varepsilon'\varepsilon = \frac{1}{2}w'w + \frac{1}{2}(\varepsilon - w)'(\varepsilon - w) + w'(\varepsilon - w).$$

Taking expectations,

$$\frac{1}{2}\int \varepsilon'\varepsilon\hat{\pi}(\varepsilon)\,d\varepsilon = \frac{1}{2}w'w + \frac{1}{2}\text{trace}(\Sigma).$$

Combining terms gives

$$\int (\log \hat{\pi} - \log \pi)\,\hat{\pi}d\varepsilon = -\frac{1}{2}\log\det\Sigma + \frac{1}{2}w'w + \frac{1}{2}\text{trace}(\Sigma - I). \quad (3.11.2)$$

3.12.   Value function adjustment for the LQ model

Our adjustment to the value function is

$$\mathcal{R}(V)(y,u) = -\alpha \log\left[\int \exp\left(\frac{-V[\varpi(y,u,\varepsilon)]}{\alpha}\right)\pi(\varepsilon)\,d\varepsilon\right].$$

For linear quadratic problems, we have at our disposal a more explicit depiction of this adjustment. Recall that this adjustment is given by $\int V\hat{\pi}d\varepsilon + \alpha \int (\log \hat{\pi} - \log \pi)\hat{\pi}d\varepsilon$ for the $\hat{\pi}$ obtained as the solution to the minimization problem. As we have already shown, $\hat{\pi}$ is a normal density with mean $(\alpha I - C'PC)^{-1}C'P(Ay + Bu)$ and covariance matrix $\left(I - \frac{1}{\alpha}C'PC\right)^{-1}$. Using our earlier calculations of relative entropy (3.11.2), the adjustment to the linear-quadratic objective function, $-\frac{1}{2}y'Py - \rho$ is[6]

$$\mathcal{R}(V)(y,u) = -\frac{1}{2}(Ay+Bu)'\left[P + PC(\alpha I - C'PC)^{-1}C'P\right](Ay+Bu) - \rho$$
$$+ \frac{\alpha}{2}\text{trace}\left[\left(I - \frac{1}{\alpha}C'PC\right)^{-1} - I\right]$$
$$- \frac{\alpha}{2}\log\det\left(I - \frac{1}{\alpha}C'PC\right)^{-1}.$$

It is enough to work with a deterministic counterpart to this adjustment in the linear-quadratic case. For the purposes of computation, consider the following deterministic evolution for the state vector:

$$y^+ = Ay + Bu + Cw$$

---

[6] This expression motivates setting θ in chapter 2 equal to $\alpha/2$ in order to match up with the formulation in this chapter.

where we have replaced the stochastic shock by a distorted mean w. Since this is a deterministic evolution, covariance matrices do not come in play now. Solve the problem

$$\min_{w} -\frac{1}{2}\left(Ay + Bu + Cw\right)' P \left(Ay + Bu + Cw\right) + \frac{\alpha}{2}w'w.$$

In this problem, relative entropy is no longer well defined. Instead, we penalize the choice of the distortion w using only the contribution to relative entropy $(3.11.2)$ coming from the mean distortion. The solution for w is

$$w^* = \left(\alpha I - C'PC\right)^{-1} C'P \left(Ay + Bu\right).$$

This coincides with the mean distortion of the worst-case normal distribution described earlier. The minimized objective function is

$$-\frac{1}{2}\left(Ay + Bu\right)' \left[P + PC \left(\alpha I - C'PC\right)^{-1} C'P\right] \left(Ay + Bu\right),$$

which agrees with the contribution to the stochastic robust adjustment to the value function coming from the quadratic form in $(Ay + Bu)$. What is missing relative to the stochastic problem is the distorted covariance matrix for the worst-case normal distribution and the constant term in the adjusted value function. However, neither of these objects alters the computation of the robust decision rule for u as a function of the state vector y.

This trick underlies much of the analysis in the book. For the purposes of computing and characterizing the decision rules in the linear-quadratic model, we can focus exclusively on mean distortions and can abstract from covariance distortions. In the linear-quadratic case, the covariance distortion alters the value function only through the additive constant term. Using and refining the formulas in this chapter, we can deduce both the covariance matrix distortion and the constant adjustment. As we shall see, these ideas also apply when we turn to issues involving decentralization and welfare analysis.

Part II
Standard control and filtering

Chapter 4
Linear control theory

4.1. Introduction

This chapter analyzes the standard discounted linear-quadratic optimal control problem, called the optimal linear regulator. The robust decision maker to be described in later chapters adjusts this problem to reflect his doubts about the linear transition law. This chapter describes basic concepts of linear optimal control theory and efficient ways to compute solutions.[1] We describe methods that are faster than direct iterations on the Bellman equation (the Riccati equation) and are more reliable than solutions based on eigenvalue-eigenvector decompositions of the state-costate evolution equation.[2]

In later chapters, we use these techniques to formulate and solve various robust decision and estimation problems. Invariant subspace methods are key tools. In the present chapter, we show how they can be used to solve the Riccati equation that emerges from the Bellman equation for the linear regulator. In later chapters, we shall use invariant subspace methods in two important settings: (a) to compute robust decision rules and estimators in single-agent problems; and (b) to solve Ramsey problems in "forward-looking" macroeconomic models. Invariant subspace methods also provide efficient algorithms for analyzing and solving equilibria of rational expectations models that are formed by combining Euler equations and terminal conditions for a collection of decision makers with other equilibrium conditions and laws of motions for exogenous variables.

Section 4.2 decomposes the basic linear optimal control problem into subproblems that are more efficient to solve and describes classes of economic problems that give rise to such problems. Sections 4.3, 4.4, 4.5, and 4.6 describe recent algorithms for solving these sub-problems. Subsection 4.4.2 briefly describes how to use invariant subspace methods to solve or approximately solve dynamic general equilibrium models.

---

[1] Substantial parts of this chapter are based on Anderson, Hansen, McGrattan, and Sargent (1996).

[2] Our survey of these methods draws heavily on Anderson (1978), Gardiner and Laub (1986), Golub, Nash, and Van Loan (1979), Laub (1979, 1991), and Pappas, Laub, and Sandell (1980).

4.2. Control problems

In this section, we pose three optimal control problems. We begin with a problem close to the time-invariant deterministic optimal linear regulator problem. We label this the deterministic regulator problem. We then consider two progressively more general problems.

The first generalization introduces forcing sequences or "uncontrollable states" into the deterministic regulator problem. While this generalization is also a deterministic regulator problem, there are computational gains to exploiting the *a priori* knowledge that some components of the state vector are *uncontrollable*. We refer to this generalization as the augmented regulator problem. As we will see, a convenient first step for solving an augmented regulator problem is to solve a corresponding deterministic regulator problem in which the forcing sequence is "zeroed out." In other words, we obtain a piece of the solution to the augmented regulator problem by initially solving a problem with a smaller number of state variables.

The second generalization introduces, among other things, discounting and uncertainty into the augmented regulator problem. We refer to the resulting problem as the discounted stochastic regulator problem. Using well-known transformations of the state and control vectors, we show how to convert this problem into a corresponding undiscounted augmented regulator problem without uncertainty. Therefore, while our original problem is a discounted stochastic regulator problem, we solve it by first solving a deterministic regulator problem with a smaller number of state variables, then solving a corresponding augmented regulator problem, and finally using this latter solution to construct the solution to the original problem in the manner described below.

4.2.1. Deterministic regulator

The *deterministic regulator problem* is the following control problem. Choose a control sequence $\{v_t\}$ to maximize

$$-\sum_{t=0}^{\infty} \left(v_t{}'Rv_t + y_t{}'Q_{yy}y_t\right),$$

subject to

$$y_{t+1} = A_{yy}y_t + B_y v_t$$

$$\sum_{t=0}^{\infty} \left(|v_t|^2 + |y_t|^2\right) < \infty. \tag{4.2.1}$$

This control problem is a standard time-invariant, deterministic optimal linear regulator problem with one modification. We have added a stability condition, (4.2.1), that is absent in the usual formulation. This stability condition plays a central role in at least one important class of dynamic economic models: permanent income models. More will be said about these models later. In these models, the stability condition can be viewed as an infinite-horizon counterpart to a terminal condition on the capital stock.

Following the literature on the time-invariant optimal linear regulator problem, we impose the following:

Definition 4.2.1.   The pair (A_{yy}, B_y) is *stabilizable* if $y'B_y = 0$ and $y'A_{yy} = \lambda y'$ for some complex number λ and some complex vector y implies that $|\lambda| < 1$ or $y = 0$.

ASSUMPTION 1: (A_{yy}, B_y) is stabilizable.

Stabilizability is equivalent to the existence of a time-invariant control law that stabilizes the state (see Anderson and Moore, 1979, Appendix C). For our applications, it can often be verified by showing that a trivial control law, such as setting investment equal to zero, achieves this stability.

In solving this problem, we are primarily interested in specifications for which all of the state variables are "endogenous," and hence the following stronger restriction is met:

Definition 4.2.2.   The pair (A_{yy}, B_y) is *controllable* if $y'B_y = 0$ and $y'A_{yy} = \lambda y'$ for some complex number λ and some complex vector y implies that $y = 0$.

When (A_{yy}, B_y) is controllable, starting from an initialization of zero, the state vector can attain any arbitrary value in a finite number of time periods by an appropriate setting of the controls (see Anderson and Moore, 1979, Appendix C).[3] For this reason, we can think of a state vector sequence with evolution equation governed by a pair (A_{yy}, B_y) that is controllable as being an *endogenous* state vector sequence.

While Assumption 1 gives us a nonempty constraint set, it is still possible that the supremum of the objective is not attained. We assume the following:

ASSUMPTION 2: The matrix Q_{yy} is positive semidefinite, and the matrix R is positive definite.

---

[3] This is one of five equivalent characterizations of *reachability* given in Appendix C of Anderson and Moore (1979). However, many other control theorists take one of these characterizations as the definition of *controllability*. For instance, see Kwakernaak and Sivan (1972) and Caines (1988). We choose to follow this latter convention.

Among other things, this concavity assumption puts an upper bound of zero on the criterion function. Therefore, the supremum is finite (and nonpositive). We require that the supremum is attained.

ASSUMPTION 3: There exists a solution to the deterministic regulator problem for each initialization of y_0.

A commonly used sufficient condition in the control theory literature for there to exist a solution is *detectability*. Factor $Q_{yy} = D_y D_y'$.

Definition 4.2.3. The pair (A_{yy}, D_y) is *detectable* if $D_y' y = 0$ and $A_{yy} y = \lambda y$ for some complex number λ and some complex vector y implies that $|\lambda| < 1$ or $y = 0$.

When the pair (A_{yy}, D_y) is detectable, it is optimal to choose a control sequence that stabilizes the state vector. In this case, the solution to the control problem is the same with or without the stability constraint (4.2.1). However, as we mentioned previously, for permanent income models the stability constraint is essential for obtaining an interpretable solution to the problem. For these models, detectability is too strong a condition to impose. Chan, Goodwin, and Sin (1984) give a weaker sufficient condition for there to exist a solution (see (iii) of Theorem 3.10). In the context of a continuous-time formulation, Hansen, Heaton, and Sargent (1991) proposed a very similar sufficient condition for stabilizable systems based on a spectral representation of the deterministic regulator problem. Unfortunately, these conditions may be tedious to check in practice. Some of the solution algorithms we survey below could, in principle, be modified to detect a violation of Assumption 3.

A sufficient condition for convergence of one of the solution algorithms that we survey below is that the pair (A_{yy}, D_y) be *observable*:

Definition 4.2.4. The pair (A_{yy}, D_y) is *observable* if $D_y' y = 0$ and $A_{yy} y = \lambda y$ for some complex number λ and some complex vector y implies that $y = 0$.

Clearly, observability is stronger than detectability. Moreover, observability is guaranteed when the matrix Q_{yy} is nonsingular. When the pair (A_{yy}, D_y) is observable, the value function associated with the deterministic regulator problem is strictly concave in the state vector y (Caines and Mayne (1970, 1971)).

The solution to the deterministic regulator problem takes the form

$$v_t = -F_y y_t$$

for some feedback matrix F_y. The stability constraint $(4.2.1)$ guarantees that the eigenvalues of $A_{yy} - B_y F_y$ have absolute values that are strictly less than one because the state evolution equation when the optimal control is imposed is given by

$$y_{t+1} = (A_{yy} - B_y F_y)\, y_t.$$

4.2.2. Augmented regulator problem

The *augmented regulator problem* is the following control problem. Choose a control sequence $\{v_t\}$ to maximize

$$-\sum_{t=0}^{\infty} \left(v_t' R v_t + y_t' Q_{yy} y_t + 2 y_t' Q_{yz} z_t\right),$$

subject to

$$\begin{bmatrix} y_{t+1} \\ z_{t+1} \end{bmatrix} = \begin{bmatrix} A_{yy} & A_{yz} \\ 0 & A_{zz} \end{bmatrix} \begin{bmatrix} y_t \\ z_t \end{bmatrix} + \begin{bmatrix} B_y \\ 0 \end{bmatrix} v_t$$

$$\sum_{t=0}^{\infty} \left(|v_t|^2 + |y_t|^2\right) < \infty.$$

We have modified the optimal linear regulator problem by including the *exogenous* forcing sequence $\{z_t\}$. The presumption here is that this partitioning may occur naturally in the specification of the original control problem. Of course, as is well known in the control theory literature, we could always transform an original state vector into controllable and uncontrollable components. Constructing this transformation, however, can be difficult to do in a numerically reliable way. In the next section we will display a class of optimal resource allocation problems associated with dynamic economies for which z_t contains a vector of taste and technology shifters. By assumption, this component of the state vector cannot be influenced by a control vector such as the level of investment.

For the augmented regulator problem to be well posed, we require that the forcing sequence be stable:

ASSUMPTION 4: The eigenvalues of A_{zz} have absolute values that are strictly less than one.

The solution to the deterministic regulator problem gives us a piece of the solution to the augmented regulator problem. More precisely, the solution to the augmented problem is

$$v_t = -F_y y_t - F_z z_t,$$

where the matrix F_y is the same as in the solution to the regulator problem for which the forcing sequence $\{z_t\}$ is zeroed out. Consequently, our solution methods entail, first, computing F_y by solving a deterministic regulator problem of lower dimension and, then, computing F_z given F_y.

4.2.3. Discounted stochastic regulator problem

Let $\{\mathcal{F}_t : t = 0, 1, ...\}$ denote an increasing sequence of sigma algebras (information sets) defined on an underlying probability space. We presume the existence of a "building block" process of conditionally homoskedastic martingale differences $\{\epsilon_t : t = 1, 2, ...\}$, which obeys

ASSUMPTION 5: The process $\{\epsilon_t : t = 1, 2, ...\}$ satisfies
(i) $E(\epsilon_{t+1}|\mathcal{F}_t) = 0$;
(ii) $E(\epsilon_{t+1}\epsilon_{t+1}'|\mathcal{F}_t) = I$.

The *discounted stochastic regulator problem* is to choose a control process $\{u_t\}$, adapted to $\{\mathcal{F}_t\}$, to maximize

$$-E\left(\sum_{t=0}^{\infty} \beta^t \begin{bmatrix} u_t' & x_t' \end{bmatrix} \begin{bmatrix} R & W' \\ W & Q \end{bmatrix} \begin{bmatrix} u_t \\ x_t \end{bmatrix} \middle| \mathcal{F}_0\right),$$

subject to

$$x_{t+1} = Ax_t + Bu_t + C\epsilon_{t+1}$$

$$E\left(\sum_{t=0}^{\infty} \beta^t \left(|u_t|^2 + |x_t|^2\right) \middle| \mathcal{F}_0\right) < \infty.$$

The state vector x_t is taken to be the composite of the endogenous and exogenous state variables. Let $U_y = [I \ 0]$ be a matrix that selects the endogenous state vector $U_y x_t$ and $U_z = [0 \ I]$ be a matrix that selects the exogenous state vector $U_z x_t$ for an optimization problem with discounting. To justify our partitioning, the matrix A is restricted to satisfy $U_z A U_y' = 0$, and the matrix B is restricted to satisfy $U_z B = 0$. Notice that in addition to incorporating discounting and uncertainty, the discounted stochastic regulator includes cross-product terms between controls and states, captured with $u'W'x$, which are absent in the augmented control problem.

We now apply a standard trick for converting a discounted stochastic regulator problem to an augmented regulator problem. Using the well known certainty equivalence property of stochastic optimal linear regulator problems, we zero out the uncertainty without altering the optimal control law. That is, we are free to set the matrix C to zero and instead solve the resulting deterministic control problem. We eliminate discounting and cross-product terms between states and controls by using the transformations

$$y_t = \beta^{t/2} U_y x_t, \quad z_t = \beta^{t/2} U_z x_t, \quad v_t = \beta^{t/2} \left(u_t + R^{-1} W' x_t \right).$$

As it is evident from these formulas, we have absorbed the discounting directly into the construction of the transformed state and control vectors. In addition, the cross-product matrix W is folded into the construction of the transformed control vector. We are left with a version of the augmented regulator problem with the following matrices:

$$\begin{bmatrix} A_{yy} & A_{yz} \\ 0 & A_{zz} \end{bmatrix} = \beta^{1/2} \left(A - B R^{-1} W' \right), \quad B_y = \beta^{1/2} U_y B,$$

$$\begin{bmatrix} Q_{yy} & Q_{yz} \\ Q_{yz}{}' & Q_{zz} \end{bmatrix} = Q - W R^{-1} W'. \tag{4.2.2}$$

Assumptions 1 - 4 are imposed on the constructed matrices on the left-hand side of the equal signs in (4.2.2).

As before, write the solution to the augmented regulator problem as

$$v_t = -F_y y_t - F_z z_t.$$

Then the solution to the discounted stochastic regulator problem is

$$u_t = -F x_t,$$

where

$$F = \begin{bmatrix} F_y \\ F_z \end{bmatrix} + R^{-1} W'.$$

Also as before, the matrix F_y can be computed by solving the corresponding deterministic regulator problem with the forcing sequence "zeroed out." Subsequent sections will describe methods for computing F_y and F_z.

In macroeconomics, the *discounted stochastic regulator problem* is often obtained in the fashion of Kydland and Prescott (1982), who use it to replace a nonlinear-quadratic problem. Thus, consider the nonquadratic optimization problem: choose an adapted (to $\{\mathcal{F}_t\}$) control process $\{u_t\}$ to maximize

$$-E \left(\sum_{t=0}^{\infty} \beta^t r \left(u_t, x_t \right) \, \middle| \, \mathcal{F}_0 \right), \tag{4.2.3}$$

subject to

$$x_{t+1} = A x_t + B u_t + C \epsilon_{t+1}.$$

Here r is not required to be a quadratic function of u_t and x_t. When the associated constraints are nonlinear, sometimes we can substitute the nonlinear constraints into the criterion function to obtain a problem of the form of

(4.2.3). Kydland and Prescott simply replace the function r by a quadratic form in $[\,u_t'\ \ x_t'\,]'$ as required for the discounted stochastic regulator problem, where the quadratic function is designed to "approximate" r well near a particular value for the state vector.[4] In chapter 5, we describe a different approach where, by design, the initial optimal resource allocation problem can be directly converted into a discounted stochastic regulator problem.

4.3. Solving the deterministic linear regulator problem

In this section we describe ways to solve for the matrix F_y. Recall that this matrix has a double role. First, it gives the control law for a particular *deterministic regulator problem*. More importantly for us, it also gives a *piece* of the solution to the *discounted stochastic regulator problem*.

In describing methods for computing F_y, it is convenient to work with the state-costate equations associated with the Lagrangian

$$\mathcal{L} = -\sum_{t=0}^{\infty} \left[y_t' Q_{yy} y_t + v_t' R v_t + 2\mu_{t+1}' \left(A_{yy} y_t + B_y v_t - y_{t+1} \right) \right]. \qquad (4.3.1)$$

First-order necessary conditions for the maximization of $\mathcal{L}$ with respect to $\{v_t\}_{t=0}^{\infty}$ and $\{y_t\}_{t=0}^{\infty}$ are

$$v_t: \qquad R v_t + B_y' \mu_{t+1} = 0, \qquad t \geq 0 \qquad (4.3.2)$$

$$y_t: \qquad \mu_t = Q_{yy} y_t + A_{yy}' \mu_{t+1}, \qquad t \geq 0. \qquad (4.3.3)$$

To obtain a composite state-costate evolution equation, solve (4.3.2) for v_t, substitute the solution into the state evolution equation, and stack the resulting equation and (4.3.3) and write the state-costate evolution equation as

$$L \begin{bmatrix} y_{t+1} \\ \mu_{t+1} \end{bmatrix} = N \begin{bmatrix} y_t \\ \mu_t \end{bmatrix}, \qquad (4.3.4)$$

where

$$L \equiv \begin{bmatrix} I & B_y R^{-1} B_y' \\ 0 & A_{yy}' \end{bmatrix}, N \equiv \begin{bmatrix} A_{yy} & 0 \\ -Q_{yy} & I \end{bmatrix}.$$

---

[4] While Kydland and Prescott (1982) apply an ad hoc global approximation to r in which the range of approximation is adapted to the amount of underlying uncertainty, many later researchers have instead simply used a local Taylor series approximation around some "nonstochastic" steady state produced by shutting down all randomness in the model. Kydland and Prescott note that for the range of uncertainty they considered, the two methods gave similar answers. In forming the linear-quadratic problem, it is important to substitute the nonlinear constraints into the objective function before taking a Taylor series approximation.

For a continuous-time system the corresponding differential equation for states and costates is

$$\begin{bmatrix} Dy_t \\ D\mu_t \end{bmatrix} = H \begin{bmatrix} y_t \\ \mu_t \end{bmatrix}, \tag{4.3.5}$$

where

$$H \equiv \begin{bmatrix} A_{yy} & -B_y R^{-1} B'_y \\ -Q_{yy} & -A_{yy}' \end{bmatrix}, \tag{4.3.6}$$

which assembles the first-order conditions for the problem with criterion $-\int_0^\infty [y(t)' Q_{yy} y(t) + u(t)' R u(t)] dt$ and law of motion $Dy(t) = A_{yy} y(t) + B_y u(t)$, where D is the time-differentiation operator. We describe several methods for solving equations (4.3.4) and (4.3.5). Formally, we will devote most of our attention to the discrete-time system (4.3.4). As we will see, methods designed for solving the continuous-time system (4.3.5) can be adapted easily to solve the discrete-time system (4.3.4), and conversely.

We want the solution of (4.3.4) that stabilizes the state-costate vector sequence for any initialization y_0. Since we have transformed the state vector to eliminate discounting, we impose stability in the form of square summability:

$$\sum_{t=0}^\infty \left| \begin{bmatrix} y_t \\ \mu_t \end{bmatrix} \right|^2 < \infty, \tag{4.3.7}$$

for the discrete-time system (4.3.4). (We impose the analogous square integrability restriction on the continuous time system (4.3.5)).

One way to ascertain the solution to the deterministic regulator problem is to find an *initial* costate vector expressed as a function of the initial state vector y_0 that guarantees the stability of system (4.3.4) or (4.3.5). The initialization of the costate vector takes the form $\mu_0 = P_y y_0$ and is replicated over time. Substituting $P_y y_t$ for μ_t into (4.3.4), we find that

$$\begin{aligned} \left(I + B_y R^{-1} B_y' P_y \right) y_{t+1} &= A_{yy} y_t \\ A_{yy}' P_y y_{t+1} &= -Q_{yy} y_t + P_y y_t. \end{aligned} \tag{4.3.8}$$

Using a partitioned inverse formula, it is straightforward to verify that

$$\left(I + B_y R^{-1} B_y' P_y \right)^{-1} = I - B_y \left(R + B_y' P_y B_y \right)^{-1} B_y' P_y. \tag{4.3.9}$$

Solving the first equation in (4.3.8) for y_{t+1}

$$y_{t+1} = \left(A_{yy} - B_y F_y \right) y_t, \tag{4.3.10}$$

where

$$F_y \equiv \left(R + B_y' P_y B_y \right)^{-1} B_y' P_y A_{yy}. \tag{4.3.11}$$

Premultiplying $(4.3.10)$ by $A'_{yy}P_y$ gives

$$A'_{yy}P_y y_{t+1} = \left(A'_{yy}P_y A_{yy} - A'_{yy}P_y B_y F_y\right) y_t. \qquad (4.3.12)$$

For the right-hand side of equation $(4.3.12)$ to agree with the right-hand side of the second equation of $(4.3.8)$ for any initialization y_0, it must be that

$$
\begin{aligned}
P_y &= Q_{yy} + A'_{yy}P_y A_{yy} - A'_{yy}P_y B_y \left(R + B'_y P_y B_y\right)^{-1} B'_y P_y A_{yy} \\
&= Q_{yy} + \left(A_{yy} - B_y F_y\right)' P_y \left(A_{yy} - B_y F_y\right) + F_y' R F_y
\end{aligned}
, \qquad (4.3.13)
$$

which is the familiar *Riccati equation*. In other words, the matrix P_y used to set the initial condition on the costate vector is also a solution to the Riccati equation $(4.3.13)$. With this initialization, the costate relation $\mu_t = P_y y_t$ holds for all $t \geq 0$. Finally, it follows from $(4.3.10)$ that this state-costate solution is implemented by the control law $v_t = -F_y y_t$.

The remainder of this section is organized as follows. In the first subsection, we initially consider the case in which the matrix A_{yy} is nonsingular. While this case is studied for pedagogical simplicity, it is also of interest in its own right. In the second subsection, we then treat the more general case in which A_{yy} can be singular. As emphasized by Pappas, Laub, and Sandell (1980), singularity in A_{yy} occurs naturally in dynamic systems with delays. One of our example economies used in our numerical experiments has a singular matrix A_{yy}. Finally, in the third subsection we study the continuous-time counterpart to the deterministic regulator problem. We describe an alternative solution method and show how to convert a discrete-time regulator problem into a continuous-time regulator with the same relation between optimally chosen state and costate vectors. We defer the discussion of the numerical algorithms used for implementing these methods until the next section.

4.3.1. Nonsingular A_{yy}

When the matrix A_{yy} is nonsingular, we can solve $(4.3.4)$ for

$$\begin{bmatrix} y_{t+1} \\ \mu_{t+1} \end{bmatrix} = M \begin{bmatrix} y_t \\ \mu_t \end{bmatrix}, \qquad (4.3.14)$$

where

$$M \equiv L^{-1}N = \begin{bmatrix} A_{yy} + B_y R^{-1} B'_y A'_{yy}{}^{-1} Q_{yy} & -B_y R^{-1} B'_y A'_{yy}{}^{-1} \\ -A'_{yy}{}^{-1} Q_{yy} & A'_{yy}{}^{-1} \end{bmatrix}. \qquad (4.3.15)$$

We find the matrix P_y by locating the stable *invariant subspace* of the matrix M.

Definition 4.3.1. An *invariant subspace* of a matrix M is a linear space $\mathcal{C}$ of possibly complex vectors for which $M\mathcal{C} = \mathcal{C}$.

Invariant subspaces are constructed by taking linear combinations of eigenvectors of M. A *stable invariant subspace* is one for which the corresponding eigenvalues have absolute values less than one. To solve the model, we seek a matrix P_y such that $\begin{bmatrix} I \\ P_y \end{bmatrix} y$ is in the stable invariant subspace of M for every n dimensional vector y. We now elaborate on how to compute this subspace.

The matrix M has a particular structure that we can exploit in characterizing its eigenvalues. To represent this structure, we introduce a matrix J given by

$$J \equiv \begin{bmatrix} 0 & -I \\ I & 0 \end{bmatrix}.$$

Notice that $J^{-1} = J' = -J$.

Definition 4.3.2. A matrix M is *symplectic* if $MJM' = J$.

It is straightforward to verify that M given by (4.3.15) is symplectic. It follows that

$$M' = J^{-1}M^{-1}J. \qquad (4.3.16)$$

Therefore, the transpose of M is *similar* to its inverse. Recall that *similar* matrices define the same linear transformation but with respect to a different coordinate system. Thus, M' and M^{-1} share the same eigenvalues. For any matrix M, the eigenvalues of M^{-1} are the reciprocals of the eigenvalues of M, so it follows that the eigenvalues of a real symplectic matrix come in reciprocal pairs, and the number of stable eigenvalues cannot exceed the number of states n. However, merely requiring M to be symplectic permits there to be eigenvalues with absolute values *equal* to one, and so we will need an additional argument to show that there are exactly n stable eigenvalues.

To locate the stable invariant subspace of the symplectic matrix M, we follow Laub (1979) and (block) triangularize M:

$$V^{-1}MV = W$$

$$W = \begin{bmatrix} W_{11} & W_{12} \\ 0 & W_{22} \end{bmatrix}, \qquad (4.3.17)$$

where V is a nonsingular matrix. By construction, the matrices M and W are similar. The matrix partitions in (4.3.17) are built to coincide with the number of stable and unstable eigenvalues. In particular, the absolute values of the eigenvalues of W_{11} are stable.

A special case of this decomposition is an appropriately ordered Jordan decomposition of M as was used by Vaughan (1970) in developing an invariant subspace algorithm for computing P_y. Laub (1991) traces this solution strategy back to the 19th century and credits MacFarlane (1963) and Potter (1966) with introducing it to the control literature. As emphasized by Laub (1991), it is preferable to build algorithms based on other upper triangular decompositions that are more stable numerically. The Jordan decomposition is particularly problematic when the symplectic matrix M has eigenvalues with multiplicities greater than one (see also Golub and Wilkinson (1976)). In the next section, we describe alternative Schur decompositions that are more numerically reliable.

To use this triangularization to calculate P_y, apply V^{-1} to both sides of the state equation (4.3.14)

$$\check{y}_{t+1} = W\check{y}_t,$$

where

$$\check{y}_t = V^{-1} \begin{bmatrix} y_t \\ \mu_t \end{bmatrix}.$$

This transformation permits us to study asymptotic properties in terms of two smaller uncoupled subsystems. Partition $\check{y}_t$ into two blocks with dimensions given by the number of stable and unstable eigenvalues

$$\check{y}_t \equiv \begin{bmatrix} \check{y}_{1,t} \\ \check{y}_{2,t} \end{bmatrix}.$$

Then

$$\check{y}_{2,t+1} = W_{22}\check{y}_{2,t},$$

and the solution sequence $\{\check{y}_{2,t}\}$ fails to converge to zero unless it is initialized at zero. Setting $\check{y}_{2,0}$ at zero can be accomplished by an appropriate initialization of the costate vector, as we now verify.

Partition the matrices V and V^{-1} as

$$V = \begin{bmatrix} V_{11} & V_{12} \\ V_{21} & V_{22} \end{bmatrix}, V^{-1} = \begin{bmatrix} V^{11} & V^{12} \\ V^{21} & V^{22} \end{bmatrix}.$$

Since V is nonsingular and there exists a (stable) solution to the optimal control problem, we must have

$$V^{21}y_t + V^{22}\mu_t = 0. \tag{4.3.18}$$

The rank of the matrix $[\, V^{21} \quad V^{22} \,]$ equals the number of unstable eigenvalues of M, and thus the rank of its null space must equal the number of stable eigenvalues. For a solution to exist for every initialization $y_0 = y$, it follows from (4.3.18) that there must exist μ such that

$$V^{21}y + V^{22}\mu = 0.$$

Thus, the dimensionality of the null space of $[\, V^{21} \quad V^{22}\,]$ must also be at least n. Therefore, M has exactly n stable eigenvalues, and the matrix partition V^{22} is nonsingular. Solving (4.3.18) for μ_t gives

$$\mu_t = -\left(V^{22}\right)^{-1} V^{21} y_t.$$

Consequently, the matrix P_y used to initialize the costate vector is given by

$$P_y = -\left(V^{22}\right)^{-1} V^{21} = V_{21} V_{11}{}^{-1}, \qquad (4.3.19)$$

where the second equality follows from the fact that the rank of $\begin{bmatrix} V_{11} \\ V_{21} \end{bmatrix}$ is n, and

$$[\, V^{21} \quad V^{22}\,] \begin{bmatrix} V_{11} \\ V_{21} \end{bmatrix} = 0.$$

4.3.2. Singular A_{yy}

We now extend the solution method to accommodate singularity in A_{yy}. This method avoids inverting the L matrix in (4.3.4). Instead of locating the stable invariant subspace of M, a deflating subspace method finds the stable deflating subspace of the pencil $\lambda L - N$.

Definition 4.3.3. A *pencil* $\lambda L - N$ is the family of matrices $\{\lambda L - N\}$ indexed by the complex variable λ.

Definition 4.3.4. A *deflating subspace* of the pencil $\lambda L - N$ is a subspace $\mathcal{C}$ of complex vectors such that the dimension of $\mathcal{C}$ is at least as large as the dimension of the sum of the subspaces $L\mathcal{C}$ and $N\mathcal{C}$.

For the matrices L and N of equation (4.3.4), it can be verified that the intersection of their null spaces contains only the zero vector.[5] This ensures

---

[5] See Theorem 3 of Pappas, Laub, and Sandell (1980) for the case in which (A_{yy}, D_y) is detectable. As we noted previously, the restriction to a detectable system rules out some interesting economic models. More generally, nonexistence of a common nonzero vector in the null spaces of N and L can be shown by way of contradiction. Suppose there is a common nonzero vector in the null space. Then the matrix $(I + Q_{yy} B_y R^{-1} B_y')$ is singular. However, this singularity contradicts Theorem 1 of Kimura (1988).

us that a generalized eigenvalue problem is well posed. When a subspace $\mathcal{C}$ is deflating, there exists a vector y in $\mathcal{C}$ that solves the generalized eigenvalue problem

$$\lambda L y = N y$$

(see Theorem 2.1 in Stewart 1972). Implicitly, we are including the possibility of a solution with $\lambda = \infty$, which occurs when y is in the null space of L but not in the null space of N. As with the previous (invariant subspace) method, the deflating subspace of interest for solving the optimal control problem is the deflating subspace associated with the stable state-costate sequence. The stable deflating subspace is the subspace associated with the stable generalized eigenvectors (the eigenvectors associated with generalized eigenvalues with absolute values strictly less than one.) Hence, we solve the model by finding a matrix P_y such that $\begin{bmatrix} I \\ P_y \end{bmatrix} y$ is in the stable deflating subspace of the pencil $\lambda L - N$.

Recall that when A_{yy} is nonsingular, the matrix M is symplectic. More generally, system $(4.3.4)$ is associated with a symplectic pencil

Definition 4.3.5. A pencil $\lambda L - N$ is *symplectic* if $LJL' = NJN'$.

Pappas, Laub, and Sandell (1980, Theorem 4) show that the generalized eigenvalues of the symplectic pencil $(\lambda L - N)$ come in reciprocal pairs, just as the eigenvalues of M do when A_{yy} is nonsingular. Hence, we again have that the number of stable generalized eigenvalues is no greater than n. Furthermore, we can imitate our argument in the case in which A_{yy} is nonsingular to show that there are exactly n stable generalized eigenvalues.[6]

We triangularize the state-costate system $(4.3.4)$ using the solutions to the generalized eigenvalue problem. As in Theorem 2.1 of Stewart (1972), there exists a decomposition of the pencil $\lambda L - N$ such that

$$U L V = T = \begin{bmatrix} T_{11} & T_{12} \\ 0 & T_{22} \end{bmatrix}, \ U N V = W = \begin{bmatrix} W_{11} & W_{12} \\ 0 & W_{22} \end{bmatrix}, \qquad (4.3.20)$$

where U and V are unitary matrices and the matrix partitions have the same number, n, of elements as the number of entries in the state vector y_t. Premultiplication of the pencil $\lambda L - N$ by the nonsingular matrix U preserves the solutions to the generalized eigenvalue problem, and postmultiplication by V alters the generalized eigenvectors but not the eigenvalues. A consequence

---

[6] Theorems 3 and 4 of Pappas, Laub, and Sandell (1980) establish this result when the pair (A_{yy}, D_y) is detectable.

of the triangularization is that the solutions to the generalized eigenvalue problem for the original system are constructed directly from the solutions to the two smaller problems

$$\lambda T_{11} \tilde{y} = W_{11} \tilde{y}$$
$$\lambda T_{22} \tilde{y} = W_{22} \tilde{y}.$$

(4.3.21)

As with the invariant subspace method, we build the blocks of the triangularization so that the generalized eigenvalues of the first problem in (4.3.21) satisfy $|\lambda| < 1$, and for the second problem $|\lambda| > 1$. As a consequence, the span of the first n columns of V gives the vectors of the deflating subspace we seek. The span of the remaining n columns contains the problematic initializations of the state-costate vector for which the implied sequence of state-costate vectors diverges exponentially. In addition, it includes the span of the generalized eigenvectors associated with infinite eigenvalues. Imitating the solution method when A_{yy} is nonsingular, we initialize the costate vector as $\mu_t = P_y y_t$, where the matrix P_y is again given by (4.3.19).

To understand better the nature of this unstable subspace, recall that an eigenvector associated with an infinite eigenvalue is in the null space of T_{22}. Suppose the triangularization of L and N is built so that we can further partition the matrices

$$T_{22} = \begin{bmatrix} M_{11} & M_{12} \\ 0 & 0 \end{bmatrix}$$

$$W_{22} = \begin{bmatrix} O_{11} & O_{12} \\ 0 & O_{22} \end{bmatrix},$$

where the matrices M_{11} and O_{22} are nonsingular. Such a triangularization always exists. Consider solving the following equation recursively for a sequence $\{\tilde{y}_{t+1}\}$; for each t solve for $\tilde{y}_{t+1}$ given $\tilde{y}_t$ by using

$$T_{22} \tilde{y}_{t+1} = W_{22} \tilde{y}_t.$$

For this equation to have a solution, the second component of $\tilde{y}_t$ must be zero for all t because

$$O_{22} \tilde{y}_{t,2} = 0,$$

(4.3.22)

and O_{22} is nonsingular. In addition to eliminating the nonexistence problem, imposing this restriction also resolves the multiplicity problem. Note that the multiplicity problem for the triangular system is that for a given t, (4.3.22) does not restrict $\tilde{y}_{t+1,2}$. However, applying (4.3.22) at $t+1$ resolves the problem.

4.3.3. Continuous-time systems

To conclude this section, we consider solving continuous-time Hamiltonian systems of the form (4.3.5). The defining feature of a *Hamiltonian* matrix is

Definition 4.3.6. A matrix H is *Hamiltonian* if JH is symmetric.

The matrix H in (4.3.5), (4.3.6) clearly satisfies this property. It follows that

$$H' = -JHJ^{-1},$$

which in turn implies that the matrix H' is similar to $-H$. Consequently, the eigenvalues of a real Hamiltonian matrix come in pairs that are symmetric about the imaginary axis of the complex plane. The *stable* eigenvalues of a Hamiltonian matrix are those whose real parts are strictly negative. Similar arguments to those given above guarantee that there are exactly n stable eigenvalues of H. Therefore, (4.3.5) can be solved by using an invariant subspace method and its associated decomposition (4.3.17), provided that the classification of stable and unstable eigenvalues is modified appropriately.[7]

There is an alternative approach for solving a continuous-time Hamiltonian system. Given a Hamiltonian matrix H, another Hamiltonian matrix G is constructed with the same stable and unstable invariant subspaces. The matrix G is called the "sign" of the matrix H, and is defined as follows. Take the Jordan decomposition of H

$$H = V \begin{bmatrix} \Lambda_{11} & 0 \\ 0 & \Lambda_{22} \end{bmatrix} V^{-1},$$

where Λ_{11} is an upper triangular matrix with the eigenvalues of H that have strictly negative real parts on the diagonals, and Λ_{22} is an upper triangular matrix with the eigenvalues of H that have strictly positive real parts on the diagonals. Then

$$G = \text{sign}\,(H) \equiv V \begin{bmatrix} -I & 0 \\ 0 & I \end{bmatrix} V^{-1}.$$

Thus, the sign of a matrix is a new matrix with the same eigenvectors as the original matrix and with eigenvalues replaced by -1 or 1 depending on the signs of the real parts of the original eigenvalues.

---

[7] Deflating subspace methods are not needed for solving the class of continuous-time quadratic control problems considered here because we can form directly the Hamiltonian matrix and apply an invariant subspace method. However, as we have formulated it, the continuous-time problem does not permit systems with finite gestation lags in making investment goods productive or systems for which consumption services depend on only a finite interval of past consumptions.

The matrix P_y can be inferred directly from G. To see this, we use an insight from Roberts (1980). By construction, all of the stable eigenvalues of G are equal to -1. Consequently, the matrix P_y solves the eigenvalue problem

$$G \begin{bmatrix} I \\ P_y \end{bmatrix} y = - \begin{bmatrix} I \\ P_y \end{bmatrix} y$$

for any n dimensional vector y, and the matrix P_y solves the affine equation

$$G \begin{bmatrix} I \\ P_y \end{bmatrix} + \begin{bmatrix} I \\ P_y \end{bmatrix} = 0. \tag{4.3.23}$$

This method is implemented by finding fast ways to compute the "sign" of a matrix.

While the matrix sign method is directly applicable for solving continuous-time Hamiltonian systems, Hitz and Anderson (1972) and Gardiner and Laub (1986) show how to use it to locate deflating subspaces of discrete-time systems. Consider the generalized eigenvalue problem for the symplectic pencil

$$\lambda L y = N.$$

Then

$$(1 + \lambda) (L - N) y = (1 - \lambda) (L + N) y.$$

Since the only common vector in the null space of L and N is zero, we construct the solution to the eigenvalue problem

$$\delta y = (L - N)^{-1} (L + N) y,$$

where

$$\delta = \frac{1 + \lambda}{1 - \lambda}.$$

Consequently, the stability relations (4.2.1) carry over here as well, and we apply the matrix sign algorithm to $(L - N)^{-1}(L + N)$.

It also turns out that $(L - N)^{-1}(L + N)$ is a Hamiltonian matrix, which we can exploit in computation. To verify the Hamiltonian structure, note that

$$(L - N) J (L' + N') = LJL' - NJN' - NJL' + LJN'$$
$$= -NJL' + LJN'$$
$$= NJN' - LJL' - NJL' + LJN'$$
$$= - (L + N) J (L' - N'),$$

where we have used the fact that $\lambda L - N$ is a symplectic pencil. Therefore,

$$J (L - N)^{-1} (L + N) = (L' + N') (L' + N')^{-1} J (L - N)^{-1} (L + N)$$
$$= (L' + N') [- (L - N) J (L' + N')]^{-1} (L + N)$$
$$= (L' + N') [(L + N) J (L' - N')]^{-1} (L + N)$$
$$= (L' + N') (L' - N')^{-1} J',$$

which proves that $(L - N)^{-1}(L + N)$ is a Hamiltonian matrix.

In summary, by construction, the stable (unstable) invariant subspace of the Hamiltonian matrix $(L-N)^{-1}(L+N)$ coincides with the stable (unstable) deflating subspace of the symplectic pencil $\lambda L - N$. This coincidence permits us to compute the matrix P_y used for initializing the costate vector for the discrete-time system (4.3.4) by applying a matrix sign algorithm to $(L - N)^{-1}(L + N)$.

4.4. Computational techniques for solving Riccati equations

We consider three types of algorithms for computing P_y:

(1) Schur algorithm;
(2) doubling algorithm;
(3) matrix sign algorithm.

A Schur algorithm is based on locating a stable subspace using a *Schur decomposition* of the state-costate system. As we noted in the previous section, once a stable subspace is located, the relevant Riccati equation solution P_y is easily computed. There are two versions of a Schur decomposition, depending on whether the matrix A_{yy} is known to be nonsingular or not. A Schur decomposition gives a more reliable way of locating stable spaces than the familiar Jordan decomposition and its generalization for pencils.

A doubling algorithm is an iterative method for speeding up the dynamic programming Riccati equation iteration by *doubling* the number of time periods in each iteration.

Recall from our discussion in the previous section that the stable deflating subspace of the pencil $\{\lambda L - N\}$ coincides with the invariant subspace of the sign of the matrix $(L - N)^{-1}(L + N)$ associated with the eigenvalue -1. A matrix sign algorithm is an iterative method for computing the sign of $(L - N)^{-1}(L + N)$ from which we can recover P_y easily. See section 4.4.6 for details of the matrix sign algorithm.

4.4.1. Schur algorithm

Suppose the matrix A_{yy} is nonsingular. As noted, the matrix P_y can be found by locating the stable invariant subspace of the matrix M given in (4.3.15). In some of our numerical calculations, we use what is referred to as a *real* Schur decomposition of M to locate its invariant subspace.

Definition 4.4.1. The *real Schur decomposition* of a real matrix M is an orthogonal matrix $\hat{V}$ and a real upper block triangular matrix $\hat{W}$ such that

$$\hat{V}'M\hat{V} = \hat{W} = \begin{bmatrix} \hat{W}_{11} & \hat{W}_{12} & \ldots & \hat{W}_{1m} \\ 0 & \hat{W}_{22} & \ldots & \hat{W}_{2m} \\ \vdots & \ddots & \ddots & \vdots \\ 0 & \ldots & 0 & \hat{W}_{mm} \end{bmatrix}$$

where $\hat{W}_{ii}$ is either a scalar or a 2×2 matrix with complex conjugate eigenvalues.[8]

A real Schur decomposition is a computationally convenient version of the block triangular decomposition (4.3.17) used to compute P_y when A_{yy} is nonsingular. Golub and Van Loan (1989) describe how to compute the real Schur decomposition (in particular, see sections 7.4 and 7.5). Recall that the block triangular matrix W in (4.3.17) results from partitioning the eigenvalues into stable and unstable eigenvalues. Algorithms that compute the real Schur decomposition of a matrix typically do not partition the diagonal blocks of $\hat{W}$ according to stability. Instead, given an arbitrary real Schur decomposition $M = \hat{V}\hat{W}\hat{V}'$, one can use the approaches described in either Bai and Demmel (1993) or Stewart (1976) to construct a sequence of orthogonal transformations that reorder the diagonal blocks of $\hat{W}$, while updating $\hat{V}$ so that $M = \hat{V}\hat{W}\hat{V}'$ holds at every step.

In summary, the steps for implementing a Schur algorithm are

(1) form the matrix M in (4.3.15);
(2) form a real Schur decomposition of M where the first n columns of $\hat{V}$, written in a partitioned form as $[\hat{V}_{11}' \ \hat{V}_{21}']'$, are a basis for the stable invariant subspace of M;
(3) solve $P_y\hat{V}_{11} = \hat{V}_{21}$ for P_y.

We recommend computing the real Schur decomposition of M by using the LAPACK function DGEES; P_y in step (3) can be computed using the built-in Matlab operator / that solves a linear equation using Gaussian elimination with partial pivoting.

A deflating subspace method is required when A_{yy} is singular and likely to be more stable numerically when A_{yy} is nearly singular. To implement this approach in practice, we use an ordered real generalized Schur decomposition to find an appropriate triangularization of the state-costate dynamical system (see Van Dooren (1982)).

---

[8] There also exists a *complex Schur decomposition* of a real or complex matrix in which $\hat{V}$ is a unitary matrix and $\hat{W}$ is upper triangular.

Definition 4.4.2. A *generalized real Schur decomposition* of a real matrix pencil $\lambda L - N$ is a pair of orthogonal matrices $\hat{U}$ and $\hat{V}$, a real upper triangular matrix $\hat{T}$, and a real upper block triangular matrix $\hat{W}$, such that

$$\hat{U}L\hat{V} = \hat{T} = \begin{bmatrix} \hat{T}_{11} & \hat{T}_{12} & \cdots & \hat{T}_{1m} \\ 0 & \hat{T}_{22} & \cdots & \hat{T}_{2m} \\ \vdots & \ddots & \ddots & \vdots \\ 0 & \cdots & 0 & \hat{T}_{mm} \end{bmatrix}$$

$$\hat{U}N\hat{V} = \hat{W} = \begin{bmatrix} \hat{W}_{11} & \hat{W}_{12} & \cdots & \hat{W}_{1m} \\ 0 & \hat{W}_{22} & \cdots & \hat{W}_{2m} \\ \vdots & \ddots & \ddots & \vdots \\ 0 & \cdots & 0 & \hat{W}_{mm} \end{bmatrix},$$

where the pencil $\lambda \hat{T}_{ii} - \hat{W}_{ii}$ is either a 1×1 matrix pencil or a 2×2 matrix pencil with complex conjugate generalized eigenvalues.

As with the real Schur decomposition, we initially compute a generalized real Schur decomposition of $\lambda L - N$ without regard to whether the generalized eigenvalues are stable or not. We then reorder the diagonal blocks of $\hat{T}$ and $\hat{W}$ so that the generalized eigenvalues are partitioned in the manner required by (4.3.20). This partitioning can be done using the algorithms described in Van Dooren (1981, 1982) or in Kågström and Poromaa (1994).

Thus, the steps for implementing a generalized Schur algorithm are

(1) form the matrices L and N in (4.3.4);
(2) form a generalized real Schur decomposition of the pencil $\lambda L - N$ where the first n columns of $\hat{V}$, written in a partitioned form as $[\hat{V}'_{11} \quad \hat{V}'_{21}]'$, span the deflating subspace of the pencil $\lambda L - N$;
(3) solve $P_y \hat{V}_{11} = \hat{V}_{21}$ for P_y.

4.4.2. Digression: solving DGE models with distortions

Linear or log-linear approximations to the equilibrium conditions of dynamic general equilibrium (DGE) models take one of the forms

$$Ly_{t+1} = Ny_t + \tilde{G}z_t \tag{4.4.1}$$

or, if L is nonsingular,

$$y_{t+1} = My_t + Gz_t \tag{4.4.2}$$

where $M = L^{-1}N$ and z_t is a vector of forcing variables governed by a law of motion

$$z_{t+1} = A_{22}z_t, \tag{4.4.3}$$

where the eigenvalues of A_{22} are all less than or equal to unity in modulus. We shall consider the case in which L is nonsingular. We assume that the eigenvalues of M split into equal numbers of stable and unstable ones so that we can obtain a real Schur decomposition of $M = V^{-1}MV = W = \begin{bmatrix} W_{11} & W_{12} \\ 0 & W_{22} \end{bmatrix}$ where W_{11} is a stable matrix and W_{22} is an unstable matrix. The assumption that the eigenvalues split in this way is tantamount to assuming that there exists a unique stabilizing solution of (4.4.1).

Using $M = VWV^{-1}$ in (4.4.2) and premultiplying both sides by V^{-1} gives

$$V^{-1}y_{t+1} = WV^{-1}y_t + V^{-1}Gz_t \qquad (4.4.4)$$

or

$$y^*_{t+1} = Wy^*_t + G^*z_t \qquad (4.4.5)$$

where $y^*_t = V^{-1}y_t$ and $G^* = V^{-1}G$. Express (4.4.5) in terms of the uncoupled dynamic system

$$y^*_{1t+1} = W_{11}y^*_{1t} + W_{12}y^*_{2t} + G^*_1 z_t \qquad (4.4.6a)$$

$$y^*_{2t+1} = W_{22}y^*_{2t} + G^*_2 z_t. \qquad (4.4.6b)$$

Where $\tilde{L}$ is the lag operator, rewrite (4.4.6b) as $(I - W_{22}\tilde{L})y^*_{2t+1} = G^*_2 z_t$ or $-W_{22}\tilde{L}(I - W_{22}^{-1}\tilde{L}^{-1})y^*_{2t+1} = G^*_2 z_t$ or[8]

$$y^*_{2t} = -W_{22}^{-1}\left(I - W_{22}^{-1}\tilde{L}^{-1}\right)^{-1} G^*_2 z_t. \qquad (4.4.7)$$

Substituting this into (4.4.6a) and rearranging gives

$$y^*_{t+1} = W_{11}y^*_{1t} + \left[G^*_1 - W_{12}W_{22}^{-1}\left(I - W_{22}^{-1}\tilde{L}^{-1}\right)^{-1} G^*_2\right] z_t. \qquad (4.4.8)$$

Equations (4.4.7), (4.4.8) give the stabilizing solution for the uncoupled dynamic system cast in terms of y^*_t. To retrieve the original variables, we simply use $y_t = Vy^*_t$.

The very same solution would also be sustained as the solution of the stochastic system in which (4.4.3) is replaced by the stochastic law of motion

$$z_{t+1} = A_{22}z_t + Cw_{t+1} \qquad (4.4.9)$$

where w_{t+1} is a martingale difference sequence with identity covariance matrix, and where y_{t+1} on the left side of (4.4.1) and (4.4.2) is replaced by

---

[8] These formulas can be viewed as extensions to the vector case of formulas found in Sargent (1987, chapter IX).

$E[y_{t+1}|y_t, z^t]$, where here E is the mathematical expectation operator and z^t denotes the history of the z_s process up to and including t. Equations (4.4.7), (4.4.8) are also the heart of the solution that would obtain were we to assume that in a stochastic system the state z_t is not observed, but that noisy signals Y_t of the state z_t are observed. In that case, the solution is to replace z_t in (4.4.7), (4.4.8) with $E[z_t|Y^t]$. The projection $E[z_t|Y^t]$ can be computed recursively using the standard Kalman filtering formulas reported in chapter 5.

4.4.3. Doubling algorithm

Dynamic programming solves the infinite-horizon problem by backward induction, which leads to iterations on the Riccati equation (4.3.13). A doubling algorithm accelerates this approach. It preserves the idea of approximating the solution to the infinite-horizon problem by a sequence of finite-horizon problems, but instead of increasing the horizon by one time period in each iteration, the number of time periods gets *doubled*.

To see how this approach works, recall that the solution to the finite-horizon problem for periods $0, \ldots, (\tau - 1)$ can be viewed as a two-point boundary value problem where the initial state vector y_0 is set to some arbitrary vector y and the costate vector at the terminal date μ_τ is set to zero. Suppose for simplicity that A_{yy} is nonsingular. By iterating on relation (4.3.14), we find that

$$\hat{M} \begin{bmatrix} y_\tau \\ 0 \end{bmatrix} = \begin{bmatrix} y_0 \\ \mu_0 \end{bmatrix}, \tag{4.4.10}$$

where

$$\hat{M} \equiv M^{-\tau}.$$

To approximate the matrix P_y, we solve (4.4.10) for the initial costate vector μ_0 as a function of y_0. Partitioning $\hat{M}$ conformably to the state-costate partition, we see that

$$\hat{M}_{11} y_\tau = y_0, \qquad \hat{M}_{21} y_\tau = \mu_0.$$

Therefore, the implicit initialization of the costate vector is

$$\mu_0 = \hat{M}_{21} \left(\hat{M}_{11} \right)^{-1} y_0,$$

and our approximation for the matrix P_y is given by $\hat{M}_{21}(\hat{M}_{11})^{-1}$.

What is needed to implement this approach is a way to compute $\hat{M}$ when the horizon τ is large. Expanding the horizon one period at a time corresponds to multiplying the matrix M^{-1}, τ times in succession. However, when τ is chosen to be a power of 2, computations can be sped up by using

$$M^{-2^{k+1}} = \left(M^{-2^k}\right) M^{-2^k}. \tag{4.4.11}$$

As a consequence, when $\tau = 2^j$, the desired matrix can be computed in j iterations instead of 2^j iterations, which explains the name *doubling algorithm*.

Given that the matrix M^{-1} has unstable eigenvalues, direct iterations on $(4.4.11)$ can be very unreliable. Clearly, the sequence of matrices $\{M^{-2^k}\}$ diverges. One of the features of a doubling algorithm is to transform these computations into matrix iterations that converge. Another feature is that a doubling algorithm exploits the fact that the matrix M is symplectic. Symplectic matrices have several nice properties.[9] We have already seen that their eigenvalues come in reciprocal pairs. In addition, the product of symplectic matrices is symplectic, and the inverse of a symplectic matrix is symplectic. Moreover, for any symplectic matrix S, the matrices $S_{21}(S_{11})^{-1}$ and $(S_{11})^{-1}S_{12}$ are both symmetric and

$$\begin{aligned}
S_{22} &= (S'_{11})^{-1} + S_{21}(S_{11})^{-1}S_{12} \\
&= (S'_{11})^{-1} + S_{21}(S_{11})^{-1}S_{11}(S_{11})^{-1}S_{12}.
\end{aligned}$$

Therefore, a $(2n \times 2n)$ symplectic matrix can be represented in terms of the three $n \times n$ matrices $\alpha = (S_{11})^{-1}, \beta = (S_{11})^{-1}S_{12}, \gamma = S_{21}(S_{11})^{-1}$, the latter two of which are symmetric.

The doubling algorithm described by Anderson (1978) and Anderson and Moore (1979) exploits such a representation by using the following parameterization of M^{-2^k}

$$M^{-2^k} = \begin{bmatrix} (\alpha_k)^{-1} & (\alpha_k)^{-1}\beta_k \\ \gamma_k(\alpha_k)^{-1} & \alpha'_k + \gamma_k(\alpha_k)^{-1}\beta_k \end{bmatrix},$$

where the $n \times n$ matrices $\alpha_k, \beta_k, \gamma_k$ are given by the recursions

$$\begin{aligned}
\alpha_{k+1} &= \alpha_k(I + \beta_k\gamma_k)^{-1}\alpha_k \\
\beta_{k+1} &= \beta_k + \alpha_k(I + \beta_k\gamma_k)^{-1}\beta_k\alpha'_k \\
\gamma_{k+1} &= \gamma_k + \alpha'_k\gamma_k(I + \beta_k\gamma_k)^{-1}\alpha_k.
\end{aligned} \tag{4.4.12}$$

While this alternative parameterization introduces a matrix inverse into the recursions $(4.4.12)$ that is absent in $(4.4.11)$, the matrix $I + \beta_k\gamma_k$ being

---

[9] There is a variation of the Schur algorithm that exploits the symplectic structure of M. See pages 431-434 of Petkov, Christov, and Konstantinov (1991) for an overview of this algorithm.

inverted is only n dimensional. The nonsingularity of this matrix for all k is established in Kimura (1988). To initialize the doubling algorithm, we simply deduce the implicit parameterization of M^{-1} given in partitioned form by

$$M^{-1} = N^{-1}L = \begin{bmatrix} A_{yy}^{-1} & A_{yy}^{-1}B_y R^{-1}B_y' \\ Q_{yy}A_{yy}^{-1} & Q_{yy}A_{yy}^{-1}B_y R^{-1}B_y' + A_{yy}' \end{bmatrix}, \quad (4.4.13)$$

which leads to the initializations

$$\alpha_0 = A_{yy}, \quad \beta_0 = B_y R^{-1}B_y', \quad \gamma_0 = Q_{yy}.$$

While our derivation took the matrix A_{yy} to be nonsingular, Anderson (1978) argues that the doubling algorithm is more generally applicable.

A convenient feature of this parameterization is that there are known conditions under which the matrix sequences $\{\alpha_k\}, \{\beta_k\}, \{\gamma_k\}$ converge. When the pair (A_{yy}, D_y) is detectable, then the sequence $\{\gamma_k\}$ is nondecreasing and converges to the matrix P_y. (Here we are adopting the usual partial ordering for positive semidefinite matrices.) As noted by Kimura (1988, Theorem 5), under the same restrictions, the sequence $\{\beta_k\}$ is nondecreasing and converges to a positive semidefinite matrix P_y^* associated with a dual to the deterministic regulator problem.

The convergence of the $\{\alpha_k\}$ sequence is more problematic. Unfortunately, without simultaneous convergence of $\{\alpha_k\}$, it is not evident that iterations of the form given in (4.4.12) can be used as the basis of a numerical algorithm. If this latter sequence diverges, small numerical errors may get magnified, causing the resulting algorithm to be poorly behaved. Kimura (1988) provides some sufficient conditions for $\{\alpha_k\}$ to converge to a matrix of zeros. His sufficient conditions are used to guarantee that either P_y or P_y^* is nonsingular.

As we noted previously, a sufficient condition for P_y to be nonsingular is that the pair (A_{yy}, D_y) be observable. Sufficient conditions for the nonsingularity of the matrix P_y^* are that (i) (A_{yy}, B_y) is controllable; and (ii) (A_{yy}, D_y) is detectable (Kimura (1988)). Recall that controllability is often achieved by our a priori partitioning of the state vector into *endogenous* and *exogenous* components. Thus, for our purposes, the restrictions guaranteeing the nonsingularity of P_y^* may be of particular interest. Even so, detectability is too strong for some of our applications.

To apply a doubling algorithm more generally, we sometimes modify the control problem by adding small quadratic penalties to linear combinations of the states and controls. As long as these penalties are sufficient to guarantee that either P_y or P_y^* is nonsingular, we are assured of convergence of all three sequences. Of course, there is a danger that the penalty distorts the solution to the original control problem in a nontrivial way, which must be checked in practice.

4.4.4. Initialization from a positive definite matrix

Instead of adding small quadratic penalties to the objective function for each calendar date, we could add a terminal penalty to the finite horizon approximation to the control problem. From Chan, Goodwin, and Sin (1984), it is known that iterations on the Riccati difference equation converge to the unique stabilizing solution whenever the Riccati equation is initialized at a positive definite matrix.[10] Initializing the Riccati difference equation at a positive definite matrix is equivalent to imposing a terminal penalty that is a negative definite quadratic form in the state vector. We will now show how to initialize the doubling algorithm to impose a terminal penalty. This will permit us to compute P_y via a doubling algorithm for a richer class of control problems.

Consider first a finite time horizon problem with a quadratic penalty on the terminal state. We select this penalty so that the terminal multiplier $\mu_\tau = P_o y_\tau$ for some positive definite matrix P_o. Then equation (4.4.10) is altered to be

$$\hat{M} \begin{bmatrix} I \\ P_o \end{bmatrix} y_\tau = \begin{bmatrix} y_0 \\ \mu_0 \end{bmatrix}. \qquad (4.4.14)$$

Build a matrix K

$$K \equiv \begin{bmatrix} I & 0 \\ P_o & I \end{bmatrix}.$$

Then equation (4.4.14) can be rewritten as

$$K^{-1}\hat{M}KK^{-1}\begin{bmatrix} I \\ P_o \end{bmatrix} y_\tau = K^{-1}\begin{bmatrix} y_0 \\ \mu_0 \end{bmatrix}.$$

Equivalently,

$$M^* \begin{bmatrix} y_\tau \\ 0 \end{bmatrix} = \begin{bmatrix} y_0 \\ \mu_0 - P_o y_0 \end{bmatrix},$$

where

$$M^* = K^{-1}\hat{M}K.$$

Partitioning M^* consistently with the state-costate vector, the implicit initialization of the costate vector is now

$$\mu_0 = P_o y_0 + M^*_{12} (M^*_{11})^{-1} y_0,$$

---

[10] Here we are using the fact that the pair (A_{yy}, B_y) is stabilizable and that there exists a solution to the deterministic regulator problem when constraint (4.2.1) is imposed. The result follows from (i) and (iii) of Theorem 3.1 and Theorem 4.2 of Chan, Goodwin, and Sin (1984).

and our approximation for P_y is given by $M_{12}^*(M_{11}^*)^{-1} + P_o$.

We are now left with computing the matrix M^* when the horizon τ is very large. Notice that

$$M^* = \left(K^{-1}MK\right)^{-\tau}.$$

It is straightforward to verify that because M is symplectic, so is $K^{-1}MK$. This means that doubling algorithm (4.4.12) is applicable for computing $(K^{-1}MK)^{-2^k}$; however, the initializations must be altered. The new initializations can be deduced by looking at the implicit parameterization of the symplectic matrix $K^{-1}M^{-1}K$, and they are given by

$$
\begin{aligned}
\alpha_0 &= \left(I + B_y R^{-1} B_y' P_o\right)^{-1} A_{yy} \\
\beta_0 &= \left(I + B_y R^{-1} B_y' P_o\right)^{-1} B_y R^{-1} B_y' \qquad\qquad (4.4.15) \\
\gamma_0 &= Q_{yy} - P_o + A_{yy}' P_o \left(I + B_y R^{-1} B_y' P_o\right)^{-1} A_{yy}.
\end{aligned}
$$

Not surprisingly, the original initializations coincide with setting P_o to zero in (4.4.15).

There are two related advantages to these initializations over the previous ones. First, the sequence $\{\gamma_j\}$ converges to $P_y - P_o$ whenever P_o is positive definite. This follows from the Riccati difference equation convergence described previously and does not require that (A_{yy}, D_y) be detectable. Second, the sequence $\{\beta_j\}$ converges and satisfies the bounds

$$0 \le \beta_j \le (P_o)^{-1}$$

even when (A_{yy}, D_y) is not detectable.[11] Although we do not have a complete characterization of convergence of the resulting algorithm, all three matrix sequences (including $\{\alpha_j\}$) are guaranteed to converge with these alternative initializations if they converge with the original ones.

In summary, the steps for implementing the doubling algorithm are

---

[11] The convergence and bound can be established as follows. Let $\{\beta_j^*\}$ denote the sequence starting from the original initialization. Then it is straightforward to show that

$$\beta_j = \left(I + \beta_j^* P_o\right)^{-1} \beta_j^*.$$

Exploiting the nonsingularity of P_o, the following equivalent formula can be deduced:

$$\beta_j = (P_o)^{-1} - \left(P_o + P_o \beta_j^* P_o\right)^{-1}.$$

The reported bound follows immediately. The sequence $\{\beta_j^*\}$ is monotone increasing because it is a subsequence of Riccati difference equation iterations for a dual problem initialized at zero. Therefore, the sequence $\{\beta_j\}$ is also monotone increasing. Given the upper bound $(P_o)^{-1}$, this latter sequence must converge.

(1) initialize α_0, β_0, and γ_0 according to (4.4.15);
(2) iterate in accordance with (4.4.12);
(3) form P_y as the limit of $\{\gamma_k\} + P_o$.

4.4.5. Application to continuous time

As noted by Anderson (1978) and Kimura (1989), a doubling algorithm for a discrete-time symplectic system can be used to solve a continuous-time Hamiltonian system. Recall that in our discussion of solving control problems via a matrix sign algorithm, we showed how to covert a discrete-time symplectic system into a continuous-time Hamiltonian system. To apply a doubling algorithm, we want to "invert" this mapping, e.g., given a Hamiltonian matrix H, we construct a symplectic pencil with the same stable deflating subspace. The symplectic pencil associated with H is given by $\lambda(I + H) - (I - H)$. By adopting a very similar argument as before, we found it easy to show that the generalized eigenvectors for the constructed pencil coincide with the eigenvectors of the original Hamiltonian matrix H. Moreover, the classification of stable and unstable (generalized) eigenvalues is preserved.

4.4.6. Matrix sign algorithm

In section 4.3.3 we showed how to compute P_y from the sign of the Hamiltonian matrix for a continuous-time state-costate system. To compute P_y for a symplectic pencil $\lambda L - N$, we first form the Hamiltonian matrix

$$H = (L - N)^{-1} (L + N)$$

and then compute $\text{sign}(H)$. For this to be a viable solution method, we must be able to compute $\text{sign}(H)$ easily.

There are alternative matrix sign algorithms. An algorithm advocated by Roberts (1980) and Denman and Beavers (1976) is to average a matrix and its inverse

$$
\begin{aligned}
G_0 &= H \\
G_{k+1} &= G_k + (1/2)\left[(G_k)^{-1} - G_k\right], k = 0, 1, \ldots.
\end{aligned}
\tag{4.4.16}
$$

To speed up convergence, Gardiner and Laub (1986) suggest using the recursion

$$G_0 = H, \quad G_{k+1} = (1/2\epsilon_k)\left(G_k + \epsilon_k^2 G_k^{-1}\right),$$

where

$$\epsilon_k = |\det G_k|^{1/n}. \tag{4.4.17}$$

Bierman (1984) and Byers (1987) propose a further refinement, which exploits the fact that the matrix G_k is a Hamiltonian matrix for each k. Recall that if H is a Hamiltonian matrix, then JH is symmetric where

$$J = \begin{bmatrix} 0 & -I \\ I & 0 \end{bmatrix}.$$

Hence,

$$JG_{k+1} = \frac{1}{2\epsilon_k} \left(JG_k + \epsilon_k{}^2 JJG_k{}^{-1} J \right), \qquad (4.4.18)$$

where ϵ_k is either set to one as in the original sign algorithm or set via formula (4.4.17) using JG_k in place of G_k. Consequently, it suffices to compute the sequence of symmetric matrices $\{JG_k\}$ recursively via (4.4.18) starting from the initialization JH.[12]

In summary, the steps for implementing a matrix sign algorithm are

(1) form the matrices L and N in (4.3.4);
(2) compute the sign of $G = (L - N)^{-1}(L + N)$;
(3) compute P_y by solving the overdetermined system

$$\begin{bmatrix} G_{12} \\ G_{22} + I \end{bmatrix} P_y = - \begin{bmatrix} G_{11} + I \\ G_{21} \end{bmatrix} \qquad (4.4.19)$$

for P_y.

As noted in Anderson (1978), the original sign algorithm (4.4.16) also can be viewed as a doubling algorithm. Interpreted in this manner, it uses (at least implicitly) an alternative parameterization of the symplectic matrix M^{-1} to that used in the doubling algorithm (4.4.12). Both recursions entail inverting a matrix. While recursion (4.4.18) requires that a symmetric $(2n \times 2n)$ matrix be inverted in each iteration, the doubling algorithm (4.4.12) requires that a nonsymmetric $n \times n$ matrix be computed at each iteration.

4.5. Solving the augmented regulator problem

So far, we have shown how to compute the matrix F_y, which provides us with the optimal control law for the deterministic regulator problem. This matrix also gives us a piece of the solution to the augmented control problem and, hence, to the problem of interest, namely, the discounted stochastic regulator problem. The missing ingredient is the matrix F_z, where the optimal control law for the augmented regulator problem is given by $v_t = -F_y y_t - F_z z_t$.

---

[12] Kenney, Laub, and Papadopoulos (1993) and Lu and Lin (1993) discuss further improvements to the matrix sign algorithm.

In this section, we show that F_z can be calculated by solving a particular Sylvester equation.

We start by forming a Lagrangian modified to incorporate the exogenous state vector sequence $\{z_t\}$

$$\mathcal{L} = -\sum_{t=0}^{\infty}[y_t'Q_{yy}y_t + 2y_t'Q_{yz}z_t + v_t'Rv_t$$
$$+ 2\mu_{t+1}'\,(A_{yy}y_t + A_{yz}z_t + B_yv_t - y_{t+1})],$$

where the evolution of the forcing sequence is given by

$$z_{t+1} = A_{zz}z_t. \tag{4.5.1}$$

First-order necessary conditions for the maximization of $\mathcal{L}$ with respect to $\{v_t\}_{t=0}^{\infty}$ and $\{y_t\}_{t=0}^{\infty}$ are

$$v_t: \qquad Rv_t + B_y{}'\mu_{t+1} = 0, \qquad t \geq 0 \tag{4.5.2}$$

$$y_t: \qquad \mu_t = Q_{yy}y_t + Q_{yz}z_t + A_{yy}{}'\mu_{t+1}, \qquad t \geq 0. \tag{4.5.3}$$

Solve equation $(4.5.2)$ for v_t; substitute it into the state equation; and stack the resulting equation along with $(4.5.3)$ and $(4.5.1)$ as composite system

$$L^a \begin{bmatrix} y_{t+1} \\ \mu_{t+1} \\ z_{t+1} \end{bmatrix} = N^a \begin{bmatrix} y_t \\ \mu_t \\ z_t \end{bmatrix},$$

where

$$L^a \equiv \begin{bmatrix} I & B_yR^{-1}B_y' & 0 \\ 0 & A_{yy}{}' & 0 \\ 0 & 0 & I \end{bmatrix}, \qquad N^a \equiv \begin{bmatrix} A_{yy} & 0 & A_{yz} \\ -Q_{yy} & I & -Q_{yz} \\ 0 & 0 & A_{zz} \end{bmatrix}. \tag{4.5.4}$$

As with the deterministic regulator problem, the relevant solution is the one that stabilizes the state-costate vector for any initialization of y_0 and z_0. Hence, we seek a characterization of the multiplier μ_t of the form

$$\mu_t = P \begin{bmatrix} y_t \\ z_t \end{bmatrix},$$

such that the resulting composite sequence $[y_t'\ \ \mu_t'\ \ z_t']'$ is in the stable deflating subspace of the augmented pencil $\lambda L^a - N^a$. Assuming for the moment that a solution P exists, it must be the case that $P = [P_y\ \ P_z]$, where P_y is the Riccati equation solution that was characterized in section 4.3, and P_z is a matrix that has not yet been characterized. To see why this must be the case, note that the solution to the augmented regulator problem with $z_0 = 0$ coincides with the solution to the deterministic regulator problem. We showed that P_y is a matrix such that all vectors in the deflating subspace of the pencil $\lambda L - N$ can be represented as $[\,y' \quad y'P_y\,]'$. When the forcing sequence is initialized at zero, so that it remains there for all t, it must also be the case that $[\,y' \quad y'P_y \quad 0\,]'$ is in the stable deflating subspace of the augmented pencil $\lambda L^a - N^a$. This justifies our previous claim that the solution to the deterministic regulator problem is a piece of the solution to the augmented regulator problem.

To deduce the control law associated with the matrix P, we substitute P into (4.5.4), which yields

$$
L^a \begin{bmatrix} y_{t+1} \\ P_y y_{t+1} + P_z z_{t+1} \\ z_{t+1} \end{bmatrix} = N^a \begin{bmatrix} y_t \\ P_y y_t + P_z z_t \\ z_t \end{bmatrix}.
$$

Write the three equations in this composite system separately

$$
\begin{aligned}
\left(I + B_y R^{-1} B_y' P_y\right) y_{t+1} + B_y R^{-1} B_y' P_z z_{t+1} &= A_{yy} y_t + A_{yz} z_t \\
A_{yy}' P_y y_{t+1} + A_{yy}' P_z z_{t+1} &= \left(P_y - Q_{yy}\right) y_t + \left(P_z - Q_{yz}\right) z_t \\
z_{t+1} &= A_{zz} z_t.
\end{aligned}
$$

$$(4.5.5)$$

Substitute the last equation into the first and solve for y_{t+1}

$$
y_{t+1} = \left(I + B_y R^{-1} B_y' P_y\right)^{-1} \left[A_{yy} y_t + \left(A_{yz} - B_y R^{-1} B_y' P_z A_{zz}\right) z_t\right].
$$

It follows from relation (4.3.9) that this evolution equation for y_t can be rewritten as

$$
y_{t+1} = \left(A_{yy} - B_y F_y\right) y_t + \left(A_{yz} - B_y F_z\right) z_t, \tag{4.5.6}
$$

where F_y and F_z are given by

$$
F_y \equiv \left(R + B_y' P_y B_y\right)^{-1} B_y' P_y A_{yy}
$$

$$
F_z \equiv \left(R + B_y' P_y B_y\right)^{-1} B_y' \left(P_y A_{yz} + P_z A_{zz}\right). \tag{4.5.7}
$$

For the reasons given previously, our construction of F_y coincides with (4.3.11) used to represent the optimal control law for the deterministic regulator problem. Stability of the state vector sequence $\{y_t\}$ is guaranteed by evolution equation (4.5.6) because the matrix $A_{yy} - B_y F_y$ is the same matrix that appears in the state evolution equation for the deterministic regulator problem under the optimal control law. Since the solution to the deterministic regulator problem is stable by design, the eigenvalues of $A_{yy} - B_y F_y$ have absolute values that are strictly less than one. The optimal control law for the augmented regulator problem is given by

$$v_t = -F_y y_t - F_z z_t.$$

The matrix F_z can be computed using formula $(4.5.7)$ once we know P_z. We now show that P_z is the solution to a Sylvester equation. Premultiply $(4.5.6)$ by $A_{yy}{}'P_y$

$$A_{yy}{}'P_y y_{t+1} = A_{yy}{}'P_y (A_{yy} - B_y F_y) y_t + A_{yy}{}'P_y (A_{yz} - B_y F_z) z_t. \quad (4.5.8)$$

Using formula $(4.5.7)$, we rewrite the coefficient matrix on z_t as

$$A_{yy}{}'P_y (A_{yz} - B_y F_z) = (A_{yy} - B_y F_y)' (P_y A_{yz} + P_z A_{zz}) - A_{yy}{}'P_z A_{zz}.$$

To obtain an alternative formula for this coefficient, substitute the last equation of $(4.5.5)$ into the second equation and solve for $A_{yy}{}'P_y y_{t+1}$

$$A_{yy}{}'P_y y_{t+1} = \left(P_z - Q_{yz} - A_{yy}{}'P_z A_{zz}\right) z_t + (P_y - Q_{yy}) y_t. \quad (4.5.9)$$

Equating coefficients on z_t in $(4.5.8)$ and $(4.5.9)$ results in

$$(A_{yy} - B_y F_y)' (P_y A_{yz} + P_z A_{zz}) - A_{yy}{}'P_z A_{zz} = P_z - Q_{yz} - A_{yy}{}'P_z A_{zz}.$$

Rewriting this in the form of a Sylvester equation (in the unknown matrix P_z), we have that

$$P_z = Q_{yz} + (A_{yy} - B_y F_y)' P_y A_{yz} + (A_{yy} - B_y F_y)' P_z A_{zz}. \quad (4.5.10)$$

As already noted, the matrix $(A_{yy} - B_y F_y)$ has only stable eigenvalues. Also, we assumed that the matrix A_{zz} has only stable eigenvalues (Assumption 4). These restrictions are sufficient for there to exist a unique solution P_z to $(4.5.10)$. Up to now, our discussion proceeded under the presumption that there exists a matrix P, such that by setting $\mu_t = P \begin{bmatrix} y_t \\ z_t \end{bmatrix}$, we stabilize the state vector sequence. We can now work backwards using the (unique) solution to the Sylvester equation to show that indeed such a matrix P does exist.

4.6. Computational techniques for solving Sylvester equations

A Sylvester equation is represented by

$$M = W + SMT, \qquad (4.6.1)$$

where the matrices W, S, and T are specified in advance and M is the matrix to be computed. Consistent with (4.5.10), the matrices S and T have stable eigenvalues.[13]   The solution to a Sylvester equation can be depicted in a variety of ways. One is to vectorize (4.6.1) as

$$[I - T' \otimes S] \operatorname{vec}(M) = \operatorname{vec}(W), \qquad (4.6.2)$$

where vec$(\cdot)$ denotes stacks of the columns of a matrix argument. (To derive (4.6.2) from (4.6.1), use the identity $\operatorname{vec}(SMT) = [T' \otimes S]\operatorname{vec}(M)$.) Hence, vec$(M)$ is the solution to a linear equation system. Alternatively, M is given by the infinite sum

$$M = \sum_{j=0}^{\infty} S^j W T^j. \qquad (4.6.3)$$

This representation can be deduced by iterating on equation (4.6.1), starting from any initial matrix with the appropriate dimensions.

We consider two types of algorithms for computing M

(1) Hessenberg-Schur algorithm;
(2) doubling algorithm.

The Hessenberg-Schur algorithm uses a Schur decomposition of the matrix T to convert a single Sylvester equation to a collection of much smaller Sylvester equations, each of which can be vectorized as in (4.6.2). A Hessenberg decomposition of the matrix S is used further to simplify the calculations. The doubling algorithm is an iterative algorithm that approximates the infinite sum on the right-hand side of (4.6.3) by a finite sum. As with the doubling algorithm for solving a Riccati equation, the number of terms included in the finite sum approximation "doubles" at each iteration.

---

[13] We have recycled some of the notation used in previous sections.

4.6.1. The Hessenberg-Schur algorithm

As suggested by Bartels and Stewart (1972), one strategy for solving Sylvester equations entails block triangularizing the matrices T and/or S. We follow Golub, Nash, and Van Loan (1979) by forming a Schur decomposition of the matrix T: $V'TV = \hat{T}$, where V is an orthogonal matrix and $\hat{T}$ is upper block triangular with row and column blocks that are either one or two dimensional (see section 4.4.1 for a formal definition). Postmultiply Sylvester equation (4.6.1) by V and rewrite the equation as

$$\hat{M} = \hat{W} + \hat{S}\hat{M}\hat{T}, \qquad (4.6.4)$$

where $\hat{M} = MV$, $\hat{W} = WV$, and $\hat{S} = S$. Notice that (4.6.4) is in the form of a Sylvester equation in the matrix $\hat{M}$.

The block triangularity of $\hat{T}$ can now be exploited to reduce (4.6.4) into m smaller Sylvester equations, where m is the number of row and column blocks of $\hat{T}$. Write the matrix $\hat{T}$ in partitioned form as

$$\hat{T} = \begin{bmatrix} \hat{T}_{11} & \hat{T}_{12} & \cdots & \hat{T}_{1m} \\ 0 & \hat{T}_{22} & \cdots & \hat{T}_{2m} \\ \vdots & \ddots & \ddots & \vdots \\ 0 & \cdots & 0 & \hat{T}_{mm} \end{bmatrix}.$$

Use the column partition of W to partition $\hat{M}$ and $\hat{W}$, and let $\hat{M}_j$ and $\hat{W}_j$ denote the corresponding j^{th} partitions. Decompose Sylvester equation (4.6.4):

$$\hat{M}_1 = \hat{W}_1 + \hat{S}\hat{M}_1\hat{T}_{11} \qquad (4.6.5)$$

$$\hat{M}_j = \hat{W}_j + \hat{S}\sum_{k=1}^{j-1}\hat{M}_k\hat{T}_{kj} + \hat{S}\hat{M}_j\hat{T}_{jj}, \quad j = 2, ..., m. \qquad (4.6.6)$$

Notice that (4.6.5) is a Sylvester equation in $\hat{M}_1$ and that (4.6.6) is a Sylvester equation in $\hat{M}_j$ as long as the matrices $\hat{M}_k$ for $k = 1, 2, ..., j-1$ have already been computed. Thus, these m Sylvester equations can be solved sequentially as linear equations using vectorization (4.6.2).

An additional refinement advocated by Golub, Nash and Van Loan (1979) entails taking a Hessenberg decomposition of the matrix S.[14]

---

[14] Alternatively, we could take the Schur decomposition of S as proposed by Bartels and Stewart (1972).

Definition 4.6.1.   The *Hessenberg decomposition* of the square matrix S is an orthogonal matrix U and a matrix $\hat{S}$ that has all zeros below the first subdiagonal, such that $S = U\hat{S}U'$.

In addition to postmultiplying equation (4.6.1) by V, we now also premultiply this equation by U'. Equation (4.6.4) continues to hold with $\hat{M} = U'MV$, $\hat{W} = U'WV$, and $\hat{S} = U'SU$. This Sylvester equation can still be decomposed as in (4.6.5) and (4.6.6). With $\hat{S}$ in Hessenberg form, we can solve these latter Sylvester equations more efficiently using an equation solver designed for Hessenberg systems.[15]

In summary, the steps for implementing a Hessenberg-Schur algorithm for computing P_z are

(1) form the matrices $W = Q_{yz} + (A_{yy} - B_y F_y)' P_y A_{yz}$, $S = (A_{yy} - B_y F_y)'$, and $T = A_{zz}$;

(2) form a Hessenberg decomposition $S = U\hat{S}U'$ and a Schur decomposition $T = V\hat{T}V'$;

(3) compute the solution $\hat{M}$ to (4.6.5) and (4.6.6) and form $P_z = U\hat{M}V'$.

Since the Hessenberg decomposition of a matrix can be computed faster than the real Schur decomposition, one should always arrange the Sylvester equation so that the Hessenberg decomposition is taken of the matrix $(A_{yy} - B_y F_y)'$ or A_{zz}, whichever has more entries. The steps just described should be implemented if there are more elements in the vector y_t than z_t. If z_t has more elements, then the alternative Sylvester equation

$$P_z' = Q_{yz}' + A_{yz}' P_y (A_{yy} - B_y F_y) + A_{zz}' P_z' (A_{yy} - B_y F_y)'$$

should be solved for the matrix P_z'.[16]

---

[15] Interesting variations on the Hessenberg-Schur algorithm have been proposed by Hammarling (1982) and Gardiner *et al.* (1992).

[16] Anderson, Hansen, McGrattan, and Sargent (1996) formed the Hessenberg decomposition of a matrix using the Matlab subroutine HESS and the Schur decomposition of a matrix with SCHUR. We solved Hessenberg systems using the routines HSFA and HSSL, which are part of the package described in Gardiner, Wette, Laub, Amato, and Moler (1992). See pages 364–370 of Golub and Van Loan (1989) for how to compute the Hessenberg decomposition.

4.6.2. Doubling algorithm

The doubling algorithm for Sylvester equations iterates on

$$\alpha_{k+1} = \alpha_k \alpha_k$$
$$\beta_{k+1} = \beta_k \beta_k \qquad\qquad (4.6.7)$$
$$\gamma_{k+1} = \gamma_k + \alpha_k \gamma_k \beta_k$$

to convergence, where $\alpha_0 = S$, $\beta_0 = T$, and $\gamma_0 = W$. By repeated substitution, it can be shown that

$$\gamma_k = \sum_{j=0}^{2^k - 1} S^j W T^j.$$

In other words, each iteration doubles the number of terms in the sum.[17]

To use this doubling algorithm to compute P_z:

(1) initialize $\alpha_0 = (A_{yy} - B_y F_y)'$, $\beta_0 = A_{zz}$, and $\gamma_0 = Q_{yz} + (A_{yy} - B_y F_y)' P_y A_{yz}$;

(2) iterate in accordance to (4.6.7);

(3) form P_z as the limit of $\{\gamma_k\}$.

4.7. Conclusion

This chapter has focused on computational details for the optimal linear regulator. Many aspects of these calculations will recur in various settings below. Indeed, key ideas and formulas in all of the subsequent chapters of this book build directly or indirectly on results in this chapter. Thus, in chapter 5, we see how the Kalman filter emerges as the dual of the optimal linear regulator. Chapter 7 uses invariant subspace methods to prove the equivalence of alternative ways of formulating a robust control problem. Chapter 16 uses a Lagrangian formulation and invariant subspace methods to construct robust decision rules for controlling forward-looking models. As already indicated in chapter 2, the optimal linear regulator can be induced to do all of the hard work in computing a robust rule for such models.

---

[17] This algorithm is a slight generalization of the doubling algorithm for Lyapunov equations discussed in Anderson and Moore (1979). A Lyapunov equation is a Sylvester equation in which $S = T'$.

Chapter 5
The Kalman filter

... we are always searching for something hidden or merely potential or hypothetical, following its traces whenever they appear on the surface.
— *Italo Calvino, Six Memos for the Next Millennium, 1996*

5.1. Introduction

The Kalman filter is a recursive method for computing linear least squares estimates of sequences of random vectors comprising hidden states and future observables. The states and observables are described by a *known* linear state-space system that is perturbed by Gaussian shocks with zero mean and known covariances.

Remarkably, the Kalman filter formulas are identical with those for an optimal linear regulator, a fact that reflects the duality of filtering and control, the subject of this chapter. Following Whittle (1990, 1996), we formulate a filtering problem in terms of a Lagrangian. After performing minimizations and maximizations in a particular order, an optimal linear regulator problem emerges with the flow of time reversed. We therefore say that the linear regulator problem is *dual* to the Kalman filter, and vice versa.

The Kalman filter is a powerful tool in economics and econometrics because it accomplishes many tasks, including the following: (1) it efficiently computes the Wold and autoregressive representations associated with an economic model whose equilibrium can be represented as a linear state-space system;[1] (2) by recovering an autoregressive representation, it enables computing the likelihood function of a linear model recursively; (3) by building upon (2), it can be used to infer the econometric implications of aggregation over time; and (4) it is the basic tool for estimating and forecasting hidden factors in linear models. Items (1)–(4) make the Kalman filter an essential tool in deducing the observable implications for an important class of models whose equilibria occur, or can be well approximated, in the form of a linear state-space system.[2]

---

[1] A common practice in the real business cycle literature is to approximate an equilibrium as a linear state-space system in logarithms of state variables. That enables the application of the Kalman filter to obtain the vector autoregressive representation and the likelihood. For examples, see Schorfheide (2000) and Otrok (2001a).

[2] So far as first and second moments are concerned, those implications are characterized by a vector autoregression. Using the Kalman filter is the easiest way to obtain the autoregressive representation. See Hansen and Sargent (2008, chapter 9).

Before getting into the details, we first state the Kalman filtering problem and its solution, then assert the associated optimal linear regulator problem for which it is the dual. The remaining sections of the chapter fill in the details required to prove the duality of the filtering and control problems.

We assume throughout this chapter that the state-space model is true, so that issues of model approximation are not in play. Chapters 17 and 18 will formulate filtering problems in settings where the decision maker suspects model misspecification and therefore wants a robust filter.

5.2. Review of Kalman filter and preview of main result

Throughout this chapter, we let x_t denote a state vector at time t and y_t a vector of possibly noise-ridden observations on linear combinations of x_{t-1}. This section uses a convention for indexing time that differs from the one used in the remainder of the chapter. We temporarily use this timing convention because we shall use it again in chapter 17 and because it leads to a dual control problem in which the direction of time matches the one we used in chapters 2 and 4. To attain that familiar representation for the control problem, for the filtering problem we have to let larger indexes t recede further into the past. We begin with a simple and famous example.

5.2.1. Muth's problem

John F. Muth (1960) applied classical filtering methods to discover a stochastic process for income for which Milton Friedman's (1956) adaptive expectations scheme would be an optimal estimator of permanent income. Muth's problem can be formulated recursively using the Kalman filter. Where x_{-t} is a scalar state variable and y_{-t} is a scalar observed variable at time $-t, t \geq 0$, consider the state-space system

$$x_{-t} = ax_{-t-1} + \begin{bmatrix} c & 0 \end{bmatrix} \epsilon_{-t} \tag{5.2.1a}$$

$$y_{-t} = gx_{-t-1} + \begin{bmatrix} 0 & d \end{bmatrix} \epsilon_{-t} \tag{5.2.1b}$$

where a, g, c, d are scalars and ϵ_{-t} is an i.i.d. (2×1) vector of Gaussian random variables with mean zero and covariance matrix I. To analyze Milton Friedman's concept of permanent income, Muth set $a = 1, g = 1$ and $c > 0, d > 0$. He regarded x_{-t} as a permanent component of income and $d\epsilon_{2,-t}$ as transitory income, while y_{-t} is measured income at $-t$. A consumer facing an income process with this structure wants to estimate his permanent income. Thus, he wants to compute $\hat{x}_{-t} \equiv E\left[x_{-t}|y^{-t}\right]$ where y^{-t} denotes the infinite history of $[y_{-t}, y_{-t-1}, \ldots]$. That is, the consumer wants to form an estimator $\hat{x}_{-t}$ that is a measurable function of the infinite history y^{-t} and that minimizes $E\left[(x_{-t} - \hat{x}_{-t})^2 | y^{-t}\right]$.

The Kalman filter attains Muth's solution of this problem.[3] The solution for the optimal estimator takes the recursive form $\hat{x}_{-t} = (a - Kg)\hat{x}_{-t-1} + Ky_{-t}$, which can also be represented as

$$\hat{x}_{-t} = K \sum_{j=0}^{\infty} (a - Kg)^j y_{-t-j} \qquad (5.2.2)$$

where K is the Kalman gain. Equation (5.2.2) expresses the consumer's estimate of the permanent component of his income as a geometric weighted sum of past income levels. The conditional variance of this estimator is $\Sigma = E\left[x_{-t} - \hat{x}_{-t} | y^{-t}\right]^2$. The Kalman filter gives a way to compute Σ and K.

5.2.2. The dual to Muth's filtering problem

The *dual* to Muth's filtering problem is the optimal linear regulator

$$-\Sigma \lambda_0^2 \equiv \max_{\{\mu_t\}} - \sum_{t=0}^{\infty} \left(c^2 \lambda_t^2 + d^2 \mu_t^2\right) \qquad (5.2.3)$$

where the maximization is subject to the law of motion

$$\lambda_{t+1} = a\lambda_t + g\mu_t, \qquad (5.2.4)$$

with λ_0 given, and where a, g, c, d take the same values as in Muth's problem. Problem (5.2.3), (5.2.4) has a solution in the form of a feedback rule

$$\mu_t = -K\lambda_t \qquad (5.2.5)$$

where K is the *same* scalar that emerges from the Kalman filter, and the matrix Σ in the value function $-\Sigma \lambda_0^2$ is the state covariance matrix that emerges from the Kalman filter. In this chapter, we shall interpret the λ's as Lagrange multipliers associated with the Kalman filtering problem.

For particular values of a, g, c, d, we invite the reader to use the Matlab program `olrp.m` to solve the regulator problem and `kfilter.m` to solve the Kalman filtering problem, and thereby to verify numerically the duality that we have asserted. In the next section, we verify duality analytically and in the process tell why the adjective "dual" is appropriate, in the sense of mathematical programming. But first we state more general versions of the filtering and dual optimal linear regulator problems.

---

[3] Muth solved the problem using classical (i.e., non-recursive) methods.

5.2.3. The filtering problem

Consider the following optimal filtering problem that generalizes Muth's problem. For $t \geq 0$, a state vector x_{-t} and an observation vector y_{-t} satisfy [4]

$$x_{-t} = Ax_{-t-1} + C\epsilon_{-t} \qquad (5.2.6a)$$

$$y_{-t} = Gx_{-t-1} + D\epsilon_{-t} \qquad (5.2.6b)$$

where ϵ_{-t} is an i.i.d. Gaussian vector with mean zero and covariance matrix I. We want a recursive way to compute the projections $\hat{x}_{-t} = E\left[x_{-t}|y^{-t}\right], \hat{y}_{-t} = E\left[y_{-t}|y^{-t-1}\right]$ where $y^{-t} \equiv [y_{-t}, y_{-t-1}, \ldots]$. [5] Let Σ be the covariance matrix of the state-reconstruction errors $e_{-t} = x_{-t} - \hat{x}_{-t}$, conditional on y^{-t}. The maximum-likelihood estimator $\hat{x}_{-t}$ maximizes $-e'_{-t}\Sigma^{-1}e_{-t}$. The Kalman filter constructs Σ and gives a recursive way of computing $\hat{x}_{-t}$ as a function of the infinite history y^{-t}. In particular, the Kalman filter attains the representation

$$\hat{x}_{-t} = A\hat{x}_{-t-1} + K\left(y_{-t} - \hat{y}_{-t}\right) \qquad (5.2.7a)$$

$$\hat{y}_{-t} = G\hat{x}_{-t-1} \qquad (5.2.7b)$$

where K is the Kalman gain. Equations $(5.2.6)$, $(5.2.7)$ imply that the prediction errors satisfy $y_{-t} - \hat{y}_{-t} = G(x_{-t-1} - \hat{x}_{-t-1}) + D\epsilon_{-t}$. Define the error in estimating x_{-t} as $e_{-t} = x_{-t} - \hat{x}_{-t}$. Substitute $(5.2.7)$ into $(5.2.6)$ to deduce

$$e_{-t} = (A - KG)\,e_{-t-1} + (C - KD)\,\epsilon_{-t}. \qquad (5.2.8)$$

Define the error covariance matrix $\Sigma_{-t} = Ee_{-t}e'_{-t}$. Then for a fixed, not necessarily optimal K, $(5.2.8)$ implies

$$\Sigma_{-t} = (A - KG)\,\Sigma_{-t-1}\,(A - KG)' + (C - KD)\,(C - KD)'. \qquad (5.2.9)$$

If iterations on $(5.2.9)$ converge, the limit satisfies [6]

$$\Sigma = (A - KG)\,\Sigma\,(A - KG)' + (C - KD)\,(C - KD)'. \qquad (5.2.10)$$

---

[4] The text of this section assumes an infinite history y^t. Alternatively, let s denote a finite horizon. Then for the filtering problem with the timing convention of this section, we would have an initial condition stating that e_{-s} has a Gaussian distribution with mean zero and covariance matrix Σ_0. This corresponds to setting a terminal value function for the dual control problem with the quadratic form $\lambda'_s\Sigma_0\lambda_s$. Under the different convention about time indexes that we shall use in section 5.3 and the rest of this chapter, for the horizon s version of the problem, the initial condition for the filtering problem is stated in terms of a quadratic form $e'_0\Sigma_0^{-1}e_0$. That corresponds to a terminal condition stated in terms of $\lambda'_0\Sigma_0\lambda_0$. It is a terminal condition because the flow of time is reversed.

[5] Note the different conditioning information denoted by $\hat{x}_{-t}$ and $\hat{y}_{-t}$.

[6] Conditions for convergence are dual versions of the detectability and stabilizability conditions of chapter 4.

The value of K that minimizes Σ in $(5.2.10)$ satisfies

$$K = (CD' + A\Sigma G')(DD' + G\Sigma G')^{-1}. \tag{5.2.11}$$

Formulas $(5.2.10)$, $(5.2.11)$ implement the steady-state Kalman filter. For later use in chapter 17, it is useful to define two operators associated with $(5.2.9)$ and $(5.2.11)$

$$\mathcal{K}(\Sigma) = (CD' + A\Sigma G')(DD' + G\Sigma G')^{-1} \tag{5.2.12a}$$

$$T^*(\Sigma) = (A - \mathcal{K}(\Sigma)G)\Sigma(A - \mathcal{K}(\Sigma)G)'$$
$$+ (C - \mathcal{K}(\Sigma)D)(C - \mathcal{K}(\Sigma)D)'. \tag{5.2.12b}$$

An efficient algorithm for computing (K, Σ) iterates on $(5.2.12)$, starting from the initial value $\Sigma = 0$. This is a version of the Howard policy improvement algorithm.

Equations $(5.2.11)$, $(5.2.10)$ also implement the policy improvement algorithm for solving a particular optimal linear regulator that is defined in terms of a state vector λ_t and a control vector μ_t. Given the initial value of the state, λ_0, the dual problem is

$$\max_{\{\mu_t\}}\left\{-.5\sum_{t=0}^{\infty}\tilde{z}_t'\tilde{z}_t\right\} \tag{5.2.13}$$

where the maximization is subject to λ_0 given and

$$\tilde{z}_t = C'\lambda_t + D'\mu_t \tag{5.2.14a}$$

$$\lambda_{t+1} = A'\lambda_t + G'\mu_t. \tag{5.2.14b}$$

Equation $(5.2.14a)$ defines the objective function. The solution of the optimal linear regulator is a policy rule

$$\mu_t = -K'\lambda_t \tag{5.2.15}$$

that attains the optimal value function

$$v(\lambda_0) = -.5\lambda_0'\Sigma\lambda_0. \tag{5.2.16}$$

We shall show that $\lambda_0 = \Sigma^{-1}e_0$ and that therefore the optimized value $-.5\lambda_0'\Sigma\lambda_0$ in $(5.2.13)$ equals the quadratic term $-.5e_0'\Sigma^{-1}e_0$ in a log-likelihood function.

The key practical insight of these findings is that we can compute the pair (Σ, K) for the filtering problem by solving the associated optimal linear regulator $(5.2.13)$, $(5.2.15)$. The reversal in time and the transposition of matrices as we move from the filtering problem to the optimal linear regulator problem are manifestations of duality, as subsequent sections show.

The duality of optimal filtering and control brings substantial insights and computational advantages. In chapters 17 and 18, we shall use these insights again to pose and solve robust filtering problems.

The remainder of this chapter substantiates our claims about duality. The reader who is willing to accept the preceding assertions about duality on faith can proceed immediately to subsequent chapters. Though it can be skipped, we think that the following arguments convey some of the magic associated with the duality of filtering and control.

5.3. Sequence version of primal and dual problems

This section substantiates various assertions in the previous section. We show how the Kalman filtering problem leads to an augmented optimal linear regulator problem in terms of dual variables. We now let the time index t flow forward. This has the consequence that a reversal of time will occur in the dual problem. We consider the state-space system for $t \geq 1$

$$x_t = Ax_{t-1} + C\epsilon_t \qquad\qquad (5.3.1a)$$

$$y_t = Gx_{t-1} + D\epsilon_t. \qquad\qquad (5.3.1b)$$

Here ϵ_t, $t \geq 1$, is an i.i.d. Gaussian disturbance vector with mean zero and covariance matrix I. We take the initial condition x_0 to be unknown with prior distribution described by

$$x_0 = \hat{x}_0 + e_0 \qquad\qquad (5.3.2)$$

where e_0 is a Gaussian vector with mean zero and covariance matrix $Ee_0e_0' = \Sigma_0$. We assume that e_0 is distributed independently of the ϵ_t's for $t \geq 0$. For any variable z, let z^s be the vector of observations on $\{z_t, t = 1, \ldots, s\}$. The joint density of (y^s, x^s) is Gaussian. Therefore, it can be represented

$$f(x^s, y^s) \propto \exp(-\mathcal{D}_s),$$

where

$$\mathcal{D}_s = \frac{1}{2}e_0'\Sigma_0^{-1}e_0 + \frac{1}{2}\sum_{t=1}^{s}\epsilon_t'\epsilon_t. \qquad\qquad (5.3.3)$$

Whittle (1990, 1996) calls $\mathcal{D}_s$ the "discrepancy." To see that the time t contribution to $\mathcal{D}_s$ is $(1/2)\epsilon_t'\epsilon_t$, note that by (5.3.1)

$$\begin{bmatrix} x_t \\ y_t \end{bmatrix} = \begin{bmatrix} A \\ G \end{bmatrix} x_{t-1} + C^*\epsilon_t,$$

where $C^* = \begin{bmatrix} C \\ D \end{bmatrix}$. The covariance matrix of $C^* \epsilon_t$ is $C^* C^{*\prime}$. Then the time t contribution to the discrepancy is[7]

$$\frac{1}{2} \epsilon_t' C^{*\prime} (C^* C^{*\prime})^{-1} C^* \epsilon_t = \frac{1}{2} \epsilon_t' \epsilon_t.$$

5.3.1. Sequence version of Kalman filtering problem

Given y^s, we seek estimators of the hidden state x_t for $t = 1, \ldots, s - 1$. We observe y^s and estimate the hidden states by maximizing the log-likelihood $-\mathcal{D}_s$ with respect to the unobserved states and shocks ϵ_s. In particular, we seek values of $e_0, \{\epsilon_t, x_{t-1}\}_{t=1}^s$ that minimize (5.3.3) subject to (5.3.1), (5.3.2). Following Whittle (1990, 1996), we formulate this minimization problem in terms of a Lagrangian. Letting $\{\lambda_t, \mu_{t+1}\}_{t=0}^s$ be sequences of vectors of Lagrange multipliers, we form

$$
\begin{aligned}
J_1 = {} & \frac{1}{2} e_0' \Sigma_0^{-1} e_0 + \frac{1}{2} \sum_{t=1}^s \epsilon_t' \epsilon_t + \lambda_0' (x_0 - \hat{x}_0 - e_0) \\
& + \sum_{t=1}^s \lambda_t' (x_t - A x_{t-1} - C \epsilon_t) + \sum_{t=1}^s \mu_t' (y_t - G x_{t-1} - D \epsilon_t).
\end{aligned}
\tag{5.3.4}
$$

5.3.2. Sequence version of dual problem

We want to *minimize* J_1 with respect to e_0, ϵ_t for $t = 1, \ldots, s$, and x_t for $t = 0, \ldots, s - 1$ and to *maximize* with respect to $\lambda_t, t = 0, \ldots, s$, and $\mu_t, t = 1, \ldots, s$. To illuminate how the Kalman filter is the dual of a linear regulator, we optimize in a particular order, thereby eventually arriving at a reduced Lagrangian that takes the form of an augmented linear regulator problem.

5.3.2.1. Minimizing over e_0, ϵ_t

Following Whittle (1990, 1996), we first minimize with respect to $e_0, \epsilon_t, t = 1, \ldots, s$. The first-order conditions with respect to ϵ_t and e_0 can be written

$$\epsilon_t = C' \lambda_t + D' \mu_t \tag{5.3.5a}$$

$$e_0 = \Sigma_0 \lambda_0. \tag{5.3.5b}$$

Condition (5.3.5a) implies that

$$\epsilon_t' \epsilon_t = \begin{bmatrix} \lambda_t \\ \mu_t \end{bmatrix}' \begin{bmatrix} CC' & CD' \\ DC' & DD' \end{bmatrix} \begin{bmatrix} \lambda_t \\ \mu_t \end{bmatrix}. \tag{5.3.6}$$

---

[7] The matrix $(C^* C^{*\prime})^{-1} C^*$ is the Moore-Penrose generalized inverse of $C^{*\prime}$.

A quick calculation also shows that

$$\lambda_t' C\epsilon_t + \mu_t' D\epsilon_t = \begin{bmatrix} \lambda_t \\ \mu_t \end{bmatrix}' \begin{bmatrix} CC' & CD' \\ DC' & DD' \end{bmatrix} \begin{bmatrix} \lambda_t \\ \mu_t \end{bmatrix}. \tag{5.3.7}$$

Condition (5.3.5*b*) implies that

$$e_0' \Sigma_0^{-1} e_0 = \lambda_0' \Sigma_0 \lambda_0 \tag{5.3.8}$$

and that

$$\lambda_0' (x_0 - \hat{x}_0 - e_0) = \lambda_0' (x_0 - \hat{x}_0 - \Sigma_0 \lambda_0). \tag{5.3.9}$$

Note the presence of Σ_0 rather than Σ_0^{-1} on the right side of (5.3.8). Substituting (5.3.6), (5.3.7), (5.3.8), and (5.3.9) into (5.3.4) gives $J_1 = J_2$ where

$$J_2 = -\frac{1}{2}\lambda_0' \Sigma_0 \lambda_0 - \frac{1}{2}\sum_{t=1}^{s} \begin{bmatrix} \lambda_t \\ \mu_t \end{bmatrix}' \begin{bmatrix} CC' & CD' \\ DC' & DD' \end{bmatrix} \begin{bmatrix} \lambda_t \\ \mu_t \end{bmatrix} + \lambda_0' (x_0 - \hat{x}_0)$$

$$+ \sum_{t=1}^{s} \lambda_t' (x_t - Ax_{t-1}) + \sum_{t=1}^{s} \mu_t' (y_t - Gx_{t-1}). \tag{5.3.10}$$

By expressing the objective in terms of the dual variables (i.e., the multipliers μ_t, λ_t), through equation (5.3.8) the objective function in (5.3.10) involves a quadratic form in Σ_0 rather than Σ_0^{-1}. This feature is important for understanding the duality of filtering and control.

5.3.2.2. Extremizing over $\lambda_t, \mu_t; x_t$

We want to *maximize* J_2 with respect to $\lambda_t, t = 0, \ldots, s$ and $\mu_t, t = 1, \ldots, s$, and to *minimize* it with respect to $x_t, t = 0, \ldots, s - 1$. Minimizing (5.3.10) with respect to $x_t, t = 0, \ldots, s - 1$ yields the first-order condition

$$\lambda_{t-1} = A'\lambda_t + G'\mu_t. \tag{5.3.11}$$

Having minimized out the x_t's, we are left with the problem of choosing $\lambda_t, t = 0, \ldots, s$ and $\mu_t, t = 1, \ldots, s$ to maximize

$$J_3 = -\frac{1}{2}\lambda_0' \Sigma_0 \lambda_0 - \frac{1}{2}\sum_{t=1}^{s} \begin{bmatrix} \lambda_t \\ \mu_t \end{bmatrix}' \begin{bmatrix} CC' & CD' \\ DC' & DD' \end{bmatrix} \begin{bmatrix} \lambda_t \\ \mu_t \end{bmatrix}$$

$$- \lambda_0' \hat{x}_0 + \sum_{t=1}^{s} \mu_t' y_t \tag{5.3.12}$$

subject to (5.3.11) and the boundary conditions $\lambda_t = 0, \mu_t = 0$ for $t > s$. Here $J_3 = J_2$. Notice how this resembles a finite-horizon augmented linear regulator problem (see page 68) with state vector λ_t and control vector μ_t.

However, the direction of time is reversed. The term $-\frac{1}{2}(\lambda_0'\Sigma_0\lambda_0 + 2\lambda_0'\hat{x}_0)$ plays the role of a terminal value function once time is reversed. The optimal control takes the form of a feedback rule

$$\mu_t = -K_t'\lambda_t + g_t y_t + f_t \hat{x}_0, \tag{5.3.13}$$

where K_t is a version of the Kalman gain, as we shall see in detail below.

5.4. Digression: reversing the direction of time

We briefly return to a formulation of the filtering problem in which time recedes into the past with increases in t, as in section 5.2. Supposing that $s > 0$ and letting $t = 0, \ldots, s$, the state-space system is (5.2.6) where the initial condition at time $-s-1$ is

$$x_{-s-1} = \hat{x}_{-s-1} + e_{-s-1}$$

where e_{-s-1} is a Gaussian random vector with mean zero and covariance matrix Σ_{-s-1}. Define the discrepancy at horizon s as

$$\mathcal{D}_s = \frac{1}{2}e_{-s-1}'\Sigma_{-s-1}^{-1}e_{-s-1} + \frac{1}{2}\sum_{t=0}^{s}\epsilon_{-t}'\epsilon_{-t}. \tag{5.4.1}$$

We could follow the steps in the previous section to derive the dual problem with these timing conventions. In the limit as $s \to +\infty$, the dual problem would assume the form of the optimal linear regulator (5.2.13), (5.2.15).

For the remainder of this chapter, we shall use the timing conventions of section 5.3. However, in chapter 17, we shall again use the timing convention of section 5.2.

5.5. Recursive version of dual problem

We are sometimes interested in versions of problem (5.3.12) that condition on infinite histories of observations, in which case there is a recursive formulation of the problem. We seek a time-invariant K, which we attain by studying the problem as $s \to \infty$ and then taking the limit of K_t as $t \to \infty$. The recursive version of problem (5.3.12) is associated with the Bellman equation

$$-\frac{1}{2}\lambda'\Sigma\lambda - \lambda'\hat{x} - \iota = \max_{\mu,\lambda^*}\left\{-\frac{1}{2}\lambda^{*'}\Sigma^*\lambda^* - \frac{1}{2}\begin{bmatrix}\lambda\\\mu\end{bmatrix}'\begin{bmatrix}CC' & CD'\\DC' & DD'\end{bmatrix}\begin{bmatrix}\lambda\\\mu\end{bmatrix}\right.$$
$$\left. + \mu'y - \lambda^{*'}\hat{x}_0\right\} \tag{5.5.1}$$

where the maximization on the right is subject to the law of motion

$$\lambda^* = A'\lambda + G'\mu \tag{5.5.2}$$

and where λ^* now denotes *last* period's value of λ, and Σ^* is last period's value of Σ. The term ι is a constant that we'll explain later. This Bellman equation induces a mapping from Σ^* to Σ. The unique positive semidefinite matrix fixed point Σ and the matrix K associated with the optimal feedback rule supply the ingredients (Σ, K) that solve the infinite-history Kalman filtering problem.

Letting ψ be a vector of Lagrange multipliers on (5.5.2), the first-order conditions with respect to λ^*, μ for maximizing (5.5.1) subject to (5.5.2) are

$$0 = -\Sigma^*\lambda^* - \hat{x}_0 - \psi$$
$$0 = -DC'\lambda + y + G\psi - DD'\mu.$$

Eliminate ψ and rearrange to get the feedback rule

$$\mu = -K'\lambda + (G\Sigma^*G' + DD')^{-1}(y - G\hat{x}_0), \tag{5.5.3}$$

where

$$K = (CD' + A\Sigma^*G')(DD' + G\Sigma^*G')^{-1}. \tag{5.5.4}$$

The matrix K is the Kalman gain. When (5.5.4) is evaluated at the stationary solution $\Sigma = \Sigma^*$ of the Riccati equation implied by the Bellman equation (5.5.1), (5.5.3) solves the infinite-history, time-invariant filtering problem. We now indicate how (5.5.1) implies a Riccati equation mapping Σ^* into Σ.

Use (5.5.2) and (5.5.3) to express λ^* as

$$\lambda^* = (A - KG)'\lambda + G'(G\Sigma^*G' + DD')^{-1}(y - G\hat{x}_0). \tag{5.5.5}$$

Using (5.5.3) and (5.5.5) to evaluate the quadratic forms in λ^* on the first line of the right side of (5.5.1) shows

$$\left\{\lambda^{*\prime}\Sigma^*\lambda^* + \begin{bmatrix} \lambda \\ \mu \end{bmatrix}' \begin{bmatrix} CC' & CD' \\ DC' & DD' \end{bmatrix} \begin{bmatrix} \lambda \\ \mu \end{bmatrix}\right\} = \lambda'\Sigma\lambda + \text{terms in } (y - G\hat{x}_0)$$

where

$$\Sigma = (A - KG)\Sigma^*(A - KG)' + (C - KD)(C - KD)'. \tag{5.5.6}$$

Formula (5.5.6) in conjunction with formula (5.5.4) is one form of the Riccati equation for the conditional covariance matrix Σ for the hidden state next period.

For the next step of the argument, we temporarily ignore the term in $y - G\hat{x}_0$ appearing in (5.5.3). Then, using (5.5.5) and $\mu = -K'\lambda$, we can calculate that

$$\mu'y - \lambda^{*\prime}\hat{x}_0 = -\lambda'(A\hat{x}_0 + K(y - G\hat{x}_0)) \equiv -\lambda'\hat{x} \qquad (5.5.7)$$

where

$$\hat{x} = A\hat{x}_0 + K(y - G\hat{x}_0) \qquad (5.5.8)$$

is the estimator of the state for next period. Formulas (5.5.8) and (5.5.4), evaluated at the fixed point of (5.5.6), are the standard time-invariant Kalman filtering formulas.

Finally, we have to complete and collect the terms coming from $(G\Sigma^*G' + DD')^{-1}(y - G\hat{x}_0)$ in (5.5.3). Tedious algebra verifies that they contribute the term

$$\iota = (y - G\hat{x}_0)'(G\Sigma^*G' + DD')^{-1}(y - G\hat{x}_0)$$

that appears on the left side of (5.5.1). The matrix $G\Sigma^*G' + DD'$ is the covariance matrix of the innovations $y - G\hat{x}_0$.

5.6. Recursive version of Kalman filtering problem

For some of our future work, it is convenient to study a recursive version of the filtering problem using the dual variables again but to embrace a somewhat different perspective.

We return to the original problem. In a recursive spirit, we formulate a one-period filtering problem and seek a recursion in an optimized value function. The state-space system is

$$x = Ax_0 + C\epsilon \qquad (5.6.1a)$$

$$y = Gx_0 + D\epsilon \qquad (5.6.1b)$$

$$x_0 = \hat{x}_0 + e_0, \qquad (5.6.1c)$$

where ϵ is a Gaussian random vector with mean zero and identity covariance matrix and e_0 is a Gaussian random vector distributed independently of ϵ with mean 0 and covariance matrix Σ_0. The joint density of (x, y) is

$$f(x, y) \propto \exp(-\mathcal{D})$$

where

$$\mathcal{D} = \frac{1}{2}\left(e_0'\Sigma_0^{-1}e_0 + \epsilon'\epsilon\right). \qquad (5.6.2)$$

Given $y, \hat{x}_0$, we want to choose (ϵ, x) to maximize the log-likelihood or, equivalently, to minimize discrepancy $\mathcal{D}$ subject to (5.6.1). We will show that the optimized value of the discrepancy (5.6.2) takes the form

$$\frac{1}{2} e_1' \Sigma_1^{-1} e_1 + \frac{1}{2} \iota \qquad (5.6.3)$$

where $e_1 = x - \hat{x}_1$, $\hat{x}_1 = A\hat{x}_0 + K(y - G\hat{x}_0)$, K is the Kalman gain, Σ_1 is related to Σ_0 by a matrix Riccati difference equation, and ι, defined in our discussion of (5.5.1), is the contribution to the log-likelihood function (entropy) that cannot be influenced by the filter. Thus, we have the Bellman equation

$$\frac{1}{2} e_1' \Sigma_1^{-1} e_1 + \frac{1}{2} \iota = \min_{\epsilon, x} .5 \left\{ e_0' \Sigma_0^{-1} e_0 + \epsilon' \epsilon \right\} \qquad \cdot \qquad (5.6.4)$$

where the minimization is subject to (5.6.1). Further, the quadratic form $e_1' \Sigma_1^{-1} e_1$ on the left equals the quadratic form $\lambda_1' \Sigma_1 \lambda_1$ that appears on the left side of the Bellman equation for the dual problem (5.5.1).

To solve the filtering problem for an additional period, we would use Σ_1 to update the criterion (5.6.2) to be $\frac{1}{2} \left(e_1' \Sigma_1^{-1} e_1 + \epsilon' \epsilon \right)$ and continue as before with next period's observation on y and $e_1 = x - \hat{x}_1$.

It is useful to solve the recursive version of the filtering problem using Lagrangian methods. Form the Lagrangian

$$J = \frac{1}{2} \left(e_0' \Sigma_0^{-1} e_0 + \epsilon' \epsilon \right) + \lambda_0' \left(x_0 - \hat{x}_0 - e_0 \right)$$
$$+ \lambda' \left(x - Ax_0 - C\epsilon \right) + \mu' \left(y - Gx_0 - D\epsilon \right).$$

The first-order conditions for minimizing J with respect to (ϵ, e_0) imply

$$\epsilon = C'\lambda + D'\mu \qquad (5.6.5a)$$
$$e_0 = \Sigma_0 \left(A'\lambda + G'\mu \right), \qquad (5.6.5b)$$

where we are using the first-order condition with respect to x_0, namely $\lambda_0 = A'\lambda + G'\mu$, to get (5.6.5b).

The equality $e_0 = x_0 - \hat{x}_0$ and (5.6.1) imply

$$x - A\hat{x}_0 = C\epsilon + Ae_0 \qquad (5.6.6a)$$
$$y - G\hat{x}_0 = D\epsilon + Ge_0. \qquad (5.6.6b)$$

Substitute (5.6.5) into (5.6.6) and rearrange to get

$$\begin{bmatrix} y - G\hat{x}_0 \\ x - A\hat{x}_0 \end{bmatrix} = \Lambda \begin{bmatrix} \mu \\ \lambda \end{bmatrix}, \qquad (5.6.7)$$

where

$$\Lambda = \begin{bmatrix} G\Sigma_0 G' + DD' & DC' + G\Sigma_0 A' \\ CD' + A\Sigma_0 G' & A\Sigma_0 A' + CC' \end{bmatrix}. \tag{5.6.8}$$

Then

$$\begin{bmatrix} \mu \\ \lambda \end{bmatrix} = \Lambda^{-1} \begin{bmatrix} y - G\hat{x}_0 \\ x - A\hat{x}_0 \end{bmatrix}.$$

For reasons to be explained in chapter 18, we call the optimized value of $\epsilon'\epsilon + e_0'\Sigma_0^{-1}e_0$ the conditional entropy of (y, x) and denote it $\text{ent}(y, x)$. It is the maximized value of the log-likelihood function. Using (5.6.5), we can evaluate $\text{ent}(y, x)$ to be

$$\text{ent}\,(y, x) \equiv \epsilon'\epsilon + e_0'\Sigma_0^{-1}e_0 = \begin{bmatrix} \mu \\ \lambda \end{bmatrix}' \Lambda \begin{bmatrix} \mu \\ \lambda \end{bmatrix}$$

$$= \begin{bmatrix} y - G\hat{x}_0 \\ x - A\hat{x}_0 \end{bmatrix}' \Lambda^{-1} \begin{bmatrix} y - G\hat{x}_0 \\ x - A\hat{x}_0 \end{bmatrix}. \tag{5.6.9}$$

Let

$$L = \begin{bmatrix} I & 0 \\ -K & I \end{bmatrix}$$

where

$$K = \Lambda_{21}\Lambda_{11}^{-1} \equiv (A\Sigma_0 G' + CD')(DD' + G\Sigma_0 G')^{-1}. \tag{5.6.10}$$

We recognize K to be the Kalman gain. It can be verified that

$$LAL' = \begin{bmatrix} \Lambda_{11} & 0 \\ 0 & \Lambda_{22} - \Lambda_{21}\Lambda_{11}^{-1}\Lambda_{21}' \end{bmatrix}, \tag{5.6.11}$$

where

$$\Sigma_1 \equiv \Lambda_{22} - \Lambda_{21}\Lambda_{11}^{-1}\Lambda_{21}'$$
$$= CC' + A\Sigma_0 A' - (A\Sigma_0 G' + CD')(DD' + G\Sigma_0 G')^{-1}(A\Sigma_0 G' + CD')'. \tag{5.6.12}$$

It turns out that Λ_{11} is the covariance matrix of the innovations $y - G\hat{x}_0$ and $\Lambda_{22} - \Lambda_{21}\Lambda_{11}^{-1}\Lambda_{21}'$ is the covariance matrix of $x - \hat{x}_1$ where $\hat{x}_1$ is the estimator of the state x. In particular, notice that

$$L \begin{bmatrix} y - G\hat{x}_0 \\ x - A\hat{x}_0 \end{bmatrix} = \begin{bmatrix} y - G\hat{x}_0 \\ x - A\hat{x}_0 - K(y - G\hat{x}_0) \end{bmatrix} = \begin{bmatrix} y - G\hat{x}_0 \\ x - \hat{x}_1 \end{bmatrix}$$

where

$$\hat{x}_1 = A\hat{x}_0 + K(y - G\hat{x}_0). \tag{5.6.13}$$

Here $\hat{x}_1$ is the estimate of the state next period, based on the observed value of y. Thus, returning to (5.6.9), we have

$$
\begin{aligned}
\operatorname{ent}(y,x) &= \begin{bmatrix} y - G\hat{x}_0 \\ x - A\hat{x}_0 \end{bmatrix}' L' \left(L\Lambda L'\right)^{-1} L \begin{bmatrix} y - G\hat{x}_0 \\ x - A\hat{x}_0 \end{bmatrix} \\
&= \begin{bmatrix} y - G\hat{x}_0 \\ x - \hat{x}_1 \end{bmatrix}' \begin{bmatrix} \Lambda_{11} & 0 \\ 0 & \Lambda_{22} - \Lambda_{21}\Lambda_{11}^{-1}\Lambda_{21}' \end{bmatrix}^{-1} \begin{bmatrix} y - G\hat{x}_0 \\ x - \hat{x}_1 \end{bmatrix} \quad (5.6.14) \\
&= (y - G\hat{x}_0)' \Lambda_{11}^{-1} (y - G\hat{x}_0) \\
&\quad + (x - \hat{x}_1)' \left(\Lambda_{22} - \Lambda_{21}\Lambda_{11}^{-1}\Lambda_{21}'\right)^{-1} (x - \hat{x}_1) \\
&= (y - G\hat{x}_0)' \Lambda_{11}^{-1} (y - G\hat{x}_0) + e_1' \Sigma_1^{-1} e_1.
\end{aligned}
$$

Formula (5.6.14) inspires the updating formula (5.6.12) for the covariance matrix of $x - \hat{x}_1$. The entropy-minimizing choice of x is evidently $\hat{x}_1$; the value of y is observed, and the value $\hat{x}_0$ is given, so the first term on the last line of (5.6.14) cannot be influenced by the filter. It contributes ι in (5.6.3).

5.7. Concluding remarks

In the filtering and control problems of this chapter, the decision maker assumes that his state-space model is correctly specified. Later chapters extend the duality between filtering and control to filtering problems in which the decision maker fears that the model (5.2.6) is misspecified. Chapters 7 and 8 formulate and solve a robust control problem. Chapter 17 then exploits duality to discover a corresponding robust filtering problem. Effectively, that chapter works backwards from a robust version of the optimal linear regulator problem (5.2.13), (5.2.15) to get a corresponding filtering problem. Not surprisingly in view of the time reversal between the dual and original problems, the objective function of the decision maker in the dual problem is backward-looking. While interesting, that is not always the most natural formulation for economic problems. Therefore, in chapter 18 we alter the objective function of the decision maker to be forward looking. That leads us to another robust filtering problem.

Part III

Robust control

Chapter 6
Static multiplier and constraint games

There's always a hole in theories somewhere if you look close enough.
— *Mark Twain*

6.1. Introduction

To highlight some conceptual issues, this chapter strips off all dynamics and focuses on two types of interrelated static two-player zero-sum games whose equilibria induce robust decisions for the maximizing player within a one-period setting. We call them a multiplier game and a constraint game. We take up dynamic versions of both of these games in subsequent chapters.

We begin with a simple static Phillips curve example in section 6.2. Subsequent sections then focus on another simple example with the aim of exposing the role of technical assumptions that reconcile outcomes from alternative games.

We consider two classes of possible misspecifications to a static Gaussian approximating model. The more restricted setting allows misspecifications only in the mean of a Gaussian random variable. The more generous setting allows for misspecifications in the form of arbitrary alternative distributions that are absolutely continuous with respect to the approximating model. For a Gaussian approximating model, the worst-case model from this class remains Gaussian, but it has distortions to both the mean and the variance.[1]

6.2. Phillips curve example

To illustrate basic ideas, this section adapts Kydland and Prescott's (1977) model of a policy maker who sets inflation in view of an expectational Phillips curve. We modify Kydland and Prescott's framework[2] by assuming that the policy maker views his model as an approximation. The policy maker solves a *multiplier game* as a way to compute a decision that is robust to model misspecification. Let U, π, π_e be the unemployment rate, the inflation rate, and the public's expected rate of inflation, respectively. The government's approximating model is

$$U = U^* - \gamma (\pi - \pi_e) + \hat{\epsilon} \tag{6.2.1}$$

---

[1] Chapters 2 and 3 described two such distortions for dynamic models.

[2] We are building on Sargent's (1999) rendition of Kydland and Prescott's model in the style of Stokey (1989).

where $\gamma > 0$ and $\hat{\epsilon}$ is $\mathcal{N}(0,1)$. Here U^* is the natural rate of unemployment, the unemployment rate that on average prevails when $\pi = \pi_e$. The government sets π, the public sets π_e, and nature draws $\hat{\epsilon}$. The government views $(6.2.1)$ as an approximation in the sense that it suspects that U might actually be governed by

$$U = U^* - \gamma(\pi - \pi_e) + \epsilon, \qquad (6.2.2)$$

where $\epsilon = \hat{\epsilon} + w$ is distributed as $\mathcal{N}(w,1)$ and w is an unknown distortion to the mean ϵ.[3] Thus, the government suspects that the natural unemployment rate might be $U^* + w$ for some unknown w. The government does know that

$$w^2 \leq \eta. \qquad (6.2.3)$$

Later we will allow for more general distortions to the distribution for ϵ and show that doing so has modest consequences.

6.2.1. The government's problem

The government values outcomes (U, π) according to the utility function assigned by Kydland and Prescott, namely,

$$-E\left(U^2 + \pi^2\right) \qquad (6.2.4)$$

where E denotes the mathematical expectation. Because it does not trust the approximating model, the government cares about the mathematical expectation over multiple models indexed by w's that satisfy $(6.2.3)$.

We proceed in the spirit of Stokey's (1989) analysis of credible government policies. We derive the government's robust best response to the private sector's setting of π_e. The appendix then uses that robust best response function to formulate a rational expectations equilibrium. The government's best response function takes π_e as fixed. Given π_e, the government wants to set π so that it attains satisfactory outcomes for all $w^2 \leq \eta$. The government therefore sets π equal to the equilibrium π-component of the following two-player zero-sum *multiplier game*

$$\max_{\pi} \min_{w} -E\left(U^2 + \pi^2\right) + \theta w^2 \qquad (6.2.5)$$

where both the minimization and maximization are subject to $(6.2.2)$ and $\theta > 1$ is a penalty parameter. We shall soon explain how the penalty parameter

---

[3] To bring the setup closer to that used in dynamic settings in chapters 2 and 7, we could have added a parameter c and expressed $(6.2.2)$ as $U = U^* - \gamma(\pi - \pi_e) + c\epsilon$, where c is used to scale the volatility of the noise ϵ and $\epsilon = \hat{\epsilon} + w$ for some number w implying that ϵ is distributed $\mathcal{N}(w,1)$. We have set $c = 1$ to simplify some formulas in this chapter.

θ relates to η in (6.2.3) and why we impose $\theta > 1$. We shall also discuss conditions that let us interchange the order of maximization and minimization in (6.2.5). The first-order conditions for π and w, respectively, for problem (6.2.5) are

$$\left(1 + \gamma^2\right) \pi - \gamma^2 \pi_e - \gamma \left(U^* + w\right) = 0 \tag{6.2.6a}$$

$$U^* - \gamma\pi + \gamma\pi_e + w \left(1 - \theta\right) = 0. \tag{6.2.6b}$$

Solving these equations jointly for π, w as functions of π_e gives

$$\pi\left(\theta\right) = \left(\frac{\gamma\theta}{\theta - 1 + \gamma^2\theta}\right) \left(U^* + \gamma\pi_e\right) \tag{6.2.7}$$

$$w\left(\theta\right) = \left(\frac{1}{\theta - 1 + \gamma^2\theta}\right) \left(U^* + \gamma\pi_e\right). \tag{6.2.8}$$

Here $\pi(\theta)$ gives the government's (robust) best response function for setting π as a function of π_e, while $w(\theta)$ determines the worst-case model, given π_e and the government's setting $\pi(\theta)$.

Note that when $\theta = +\infty$, so that there is no concern about model misspecification,

$$\pi\left(\infty\right) = \left(\frac{\gamma}{1 + \gamma^2}\right) \left(U^* + \gamma\pi_e\right) \tag{6.2.9}$$

$$w\left(\infty\right) = 0. \tag{6.2.10}$$

Note also that (6.2.6a) says that $\pi(\theta)$ satisfies

$$\pi\left(\theta\right) = \left(\frac{\gamma}{1 + \gamma^2}\right) \left(\left[U^* + w\left(\theta\right)\right] + \gamma\pi_e\right).$$

This equation defines a function

$$\pi\left(\theta\right) = B\left(\pi_e; \theta\right), \tag{6.2.11}$$

which is the government's robust best response function to the state of expectations π^e. Evidently the robust rule can be obtained by replacing the estimate of the natural unemployment rate U^* under the approximating model in (6.2.9) with the worst-case estimate of the natural rate $U^* + w(\theta)$. Thus, one way to achieve robustness is to distort estimates of exogenous variables in a pessimistic way relative to the approximating model, then to proceed with ordinary decision-making procedures.[4] A related characterization of robust decision making procedures will prevail in the dynamic settings to be studied

---

[4] See the citation attributed to Fellner on page 38 of chapter 2.

in subsequent chapters. However, because the models there are dynamic, the distortions become more interesting and involve misspecifications in the way state vectors feed back on their own histories.

It is useful to compute the limiting decision $\pi(\theta)$ and worst-case distortion $w(\theta)$ as $\theta \searrow 1$ [5]

$$\pi(1) = \gamma^{-1}U^* + \pi_e \tag{6.2.12}$$

$$w(1) = \gamma^{-2}(U^* + \gamma\pi_e). \tag{6.2.13}$$

In the appendix to this chapter we show how the unit slope of the government's best response to π_e in (6.2.12) will cause a rational expectations equilibrium inflation rate to approach $+\infty$ as $\theta \searrow 1$. That rational expectations inflation rate satisfies $\pi = \pi_e$. At the same time, π is a government's robust best government response to π_e.

Given π_e, we can now tell how the penalty parameter θ is related to the constraint η. We will motivate the multiplier game by using θ as a Lagrange multiplier on the specification-error constraint in the closely related *constraint game*

$$\sup_{\pi} \inf_{|w|^2 \leq \eta} -E\left(U^2 + \pi^2\right).$$

For $\theta > 1$ there is an associated constraint η given by

$$\eta = w(\theta)^2 = \left(\frac{1}{\theta - 1 + \gamma^2\theta}\right)^2 (U^* + \gamma\pi_e)^2 \tag{6.2.14}$$

where we have used formula (6.2.8). Equation (6.2.14) shows values of η that are implicitly associated with alternative choices of θ. A larger penalty θ is associated with a smaller η. As described by equation (6.2.14), the parameter θ thus measures the set of alternative models over which the decision maker seeks satisfactory outcomes. Formula (6.2.14) generates values of η less than an *upper* bound as θ varies while exceeding the *lower* bound we have imposed on it.

We shall discuss the connection between the constraint game and the multiplier game further in the following sections. Before that, we briefly describe the sense in which (6.2.7) gives a decision for π that is robust to model misspecification.

---

[5] The value $\theta = 1$ is the breakdown point to be discussed later. In the generalization of the model where $c(\epsilon + w)$ replaces $(\epsilon + w)$, the breakdown point is $\theta = c^2$.

6.2.2. Robustness of robust decisions

For convenience, we define $\sigma = -\theta^{-1}$; σ is the risk-sensitivity parameter of Jacobson (1973) and Whittle (1990). Figure 6.2.1 illustrates the sense in which a robust decision for π is robust. Let $J(\sigma_1, \sigma_2)$ be the value of $-E(U^2 + \pi^2)$ associated with setting $\pi = \pi(\sigma_1)$ when $w = w(\sigma_2)$. Assuming $\gamma = 1, U^* = 5$, for three settings of inflation $\pi(\sigma_1)$, figure 6.2.1 plots $J(\sigma_1, \cdot)$ as a function of σ_2, where the worst-case $w = w(\sigma_2)$ varies along the ordinate axis. Notice how the three payoff functions $J(\sigma_1, \cdot)$ cross. The $\sigma = \sigma_1 = 0$ rule gives the highest value for the government's objective when there is no specification error (i.e., $\sigma_2 = 0$ implies that $w = 0$), but its performance deteriorates more quickly than the robust ($\sigma_1 = -.25, \sigma_1 = -.5$) rules as $|w|$ increases as σ_2 decreases. The robust rules sacrifice performance when the approximating model is correct. However, they experience lower rates of deterioration in the objective J as the specification error increases.

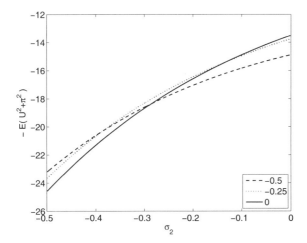

Figure 6.2.1: Values of $J(\sigma_1, \sigma_2) = -E(U^2 + \pi^2)$ for three decision rules $\pi(\sigma_1)$ for $\sigma_1 = 0, -.25, -.5$ for the worst-case $w(\sigma_2)$ for values of σ_2 on the ordinate axis. The $\sigma_1 = 0$ rule works best when $w = 0$, but its performance deteriorates more rapidly as $|w|$ increases (i.e., toward $|w(\sigma_2 = -.5)|$) than do the robust rules.

Because our principal focus in this chapter is single-agent robust control theory, we have taken π_e as given. To complete the analysis of the Kydland-Prescott model, we should describe how π_e is set. Appendix A applies the notion of a rational expectations equilibrium to make π_e equal to the $\pi(\sigma)$

chosen by the robust monetary authority. We postpone that material to the appendix because it involves issues that would interrupt our main line of argument. We now turn to important technical details about our single-agent decision model.

6.3. Basic setup with a correct model

This section uses a very simple static model to describe in more detail the relationship between a static constraint game and a static multiplier game. Let x be an endogenous state variable and u a scalar control variable. The variables u and x are linked by the approximating model

$$x = u + \hat{\epsilon} \tag{6.3.1}$$

where $\hat{\epsilon}$ is a random variable with mean zero and variance 1. Letting E denote the mathematical expectation operator and b be a scalar, a decision maker wants (u, x) to maximize

$$-\frac{u^2}{2} - \frac{1}{2} E \left(x - b \right)^2 \tag{6.3.2}$$

or

$$-\frac{u^2}{2} - \frac{\left(u - b \right)^2}{2} - \frac{1}{2}. \tag{6.3.3}$$

The maximizing choice is $u = \frac{b}{2}$.

We want to think about the situation where the decision maker treats the model $(6.3.1)$ not as true but as an approximation. To represent specification error, the decision maker replaces the approximating model $(6.3.1)$ with the distorted model where $\hat{\epsilon}$, which has a standard normal distribution function, is replaced by $\epsilon = \hat{\epsilon} + w$. The decision maker formulates the idea that his model is a good approximation by assuming that $|w|^2 \leq \eta$ where $\eta > 0$. Substituting

$$x = u + \epsilon = u + \hat{\epsilon} + w$$

into $(6.3.2)$, the criterion function becomes

$$-\frac{u^2}{2} - \frac{\left(u + w - b \right)^2}{2} - \frac{1}{2}. \tag{6.3.4}$$

The decision maker seeks u that works well for any $w^2 \leq \eta$. Since the variance equals 1, we can replace $(6.3.4)$ with

$$-\frac{u^2}{2} - \frac{\left(u + w - b \right)^2}{2}. \tag{6.3.5}$$

Within this simple setting, we consider two types of two-person zero-sum games that can be used to choose u that is robust to misspecifications that take the form of alternative values of w. The two games are: (1) a constraint game that constrains the choices of u, v in $(6.3.5)$ by $w^2 \leq \eta$; and (2) a multiplier game that appends to the right side of $(6.3.5)$ a penalty term $\frac{\theta}{2}(w^2 - \eta)$.

6.4. The constraint game with $b = 0$

This section considers a pathological case in which variations in the decision maker's concern about robustness, as measured by the penalty parameter θ, has no effect on his decision u. We temporarily set $b = 0$. To induce a robust decision u we formulate a constraint game[6]

$$\max_{u} \min_{|w|^2 \leq \eta} -\frac{u^2}{2} - \frac{(u+w)^2}{2}. \qquad (6.4.1)$$

Notice that the objective is concave and not convex in w (this is also true when $b \neq 0$). Also notice the timing protocol implicit in the order of maximization and minimization in $(6.4.1)$: the maximizing player chooses first, the minimizing player second.

The equilibrium of this two-person zero-sum game can be computed by considering three possible sets of values for u. If $u = 0$, $w = \pm\sqrt{\eta}$ solves the inner minimization problem, with a minimized value of $-\frac{\eta}{2}$. If $u > 0$, the solution of the inner problem is to set $w = \sqrt{\eta}$, which makes the objective smaller than $-\frac{\eta}{2}$. Similarly, if $u \leq 0$, the solution of the inner problem is to set $w = -\sqrt{\eta}$, and the objective $(6.4.1)$ is again smaller than $-\frac{\eta}{2}$. Thus, the robust decision is to set u to zero; this decision is supported by the maximizing player's belief that w will respond to u by the rule $w = \frac{u}{|u|}\sqrt{\eta}$ for $u \neq 0$ and $w = \pm\sqrt{\eta}$ when u is zero. The value of the game (the value of the objective at the solution) is $-\eta/2$.

A strange feature of $(6.4.1)$ is that a preference for robustness to model misspecification has no effect on the decision u. The equilibrium outcome for u is 0, independently of the value of η.

For various reasons that we explain below, we would like to be able to interchange the order of minimization and maximization in $(6.4.1)$. If we interchange orders, the maximizing agent sets $u = -w/2$ and $w = \pm\sqrt{\eta}$. The value of this game is $-\eta/4$ and the equilibrium outcome for u is $\mp\sqrt{\eta}$. Thus, another peculiarity of $(6.4.1)$ is that we cannot interchange orders of the minimization and maximization operations without altering the value of

---

[6] We thank Dirk Bergemann for suggesting this example and its consequences.

the game. Moreover, there is no pure strategy Nash equilibrium. We will compute mixed strategy equilibria later.

6.5. Multiplier game with $b = 0$

We want to understand the connection between the constraint game $(6.4.1)$ and an associated "multiplier game." To do so, in this section we study a Lagrangian formulation of the constraint game. The standard sufficient conditions for the Lagrange multiplier theorem do not hold here. While the constraint set for w is convex, the objective is concave in w. As we will now illustrate and will discuss extensively in chapter 7, a modified version of Lagrange multiplier theorem does apply. This will eventually lead us to a multiplier game.

We reformulate the constraint in $(6.4.1)$ as $w^2 \leq \eta$ and form a Lagrangian

$$\sup_{u} \inf_{w} \sup_{\theta \geq 0} -\frac{u^2}{2} - \frac{(u+w)^2}{2} + \frac{\theta}{2}\left(w^2 - \eta\right). \tag{6.5.1}$$

Our first inclination might be to change orders of optimization by studying

$$\sup_{u} \sup_{\theta \geq 0} \inf_{w} -\frac{u^2}{2} - \frac{(u+w)^2}{2} + \frac{\theta}{2}\left(w^2 - \eta\right). \tag{6.5.2}$$

To interchange orders of optimization in this way while preserving the value of the resulting game requires that we impose some additional restrictions.

The inner maximization in problem $(6.5.1)$ has a degenerate solution that makes θ and hence the objective arbitrarily large when $w^2 > \eta$. Thus, to enforce the constraint we must allow for large values of θ. When $w^2 < \eta$, maximizing choice for θ is $\theta = 0$. In comparison consider the inner minimization problem of $(6.5.2)$, holding θ and u fixed. Suppose $\theta \leq 1$. Then the objective is concave in w (it is affine for $\theta = 1$), and the infimum over w makes $|w|$ arbitrarily large and the value of the game $-\infty$. Therefore, we are led to consider only $\theta > 1$

$$\sup_{u} \sup_{\theta > 1} \inf_{w} -\frac{u^2}{2} - \frac{(u+w)^2}{2} + \frac{\theta}{2}\left(w^2 - \eta\right). \tag{6.5.3}$$

The objective is concave in the pair (u, θ) for each choice of w and hence remains concave after minimization. (The infimum of concave functions is concave.) Thus, the order of maximization is inconsequential to equilibrium outcomes and we are free to postpone maximization over θ until the last step and first study [7]

$$\sup_{u} \inf_{w} -\frac{u^2}{2} - \frac{(u+w)^2}{2} + \frac{\theta}{2}\left(w^2 - \eta\right). \tag{6.5.4}$$

---

[7] Maximization over θ at the last step may lead us to choose $\theta = 1$ or $\theta = \infty$.

for each choice of $\theta > 1$. Game (6.5.4) is a special case of what we call a multiplier game.

What problems can the lower bound on θ cause? The constraint may be slack when in fact we would like it to bind. We will have to check for this in the calculations that follow.

For a fixed $\theta > 1$ and u, the first-order condition for w is

$$(\theta - 1)\, w - u = 0,$$

or

$$w = \frac{u}{\theta - 1}.$$

After substituting this solution for w into the objective function

$$L\left(u, \theta\right) = - \left[\frac{2\theta - 1}{2\left(\theta - 1\right)}\right] u^2 - \frac{\theta}{2}\eta. \qquad (6.5.5)$$

We now investigate the behavior of the worst case w for alternative choices of u and θ. In maximizing L in (6.5.5), we can proceed in sequence or simultaneously. The order of maximization carries revealing insights about the role of w.

First, consider maximizing objective (6.5.5) with respect to u given θ. Notice that if we set $\theta = 1$, u drops out of the objective, so we set $\theta > 1$. Provided that $\theta > 1$, the maximizing solution for a fixed θ is $u = 0$, which attains a value for the objective of $-\frac{\theta\eta}{2}$. Associated with $u = 0$, an implied solution for w is $w = 0$. The objective function is decreasing in θ and the limiting objective as θ declines to unity is $-\eta/2$. Thus, we recover the $u = 0$ solution from the constraint game and the correct objective function as θ declines to one. However, we fail to approximate the outcome for w that emerges from the constraint game.

Next consider maximizing (6.5.5) by choice of θ for a fixed $u \neq 0$. There is an interior maximum for θ in the domain $(1, +\infty)$ because the objective tends to $-\infty$ at both endpoints of this interval. Moreover, the maximum is attained by setting θ so that the constraint is satisfied. Thus,

$$\theta = 1 + \frac{|u|}{\sqrt{\eta}}$$

and

$$w = \frac{u}{|u|}\sqrt{\eta}.$$

At this value of θ, the objective (6.5.5) (or equivalently (6.5.3)) becomes

$$\bar{L}\left(u\right) = -u^2 - \frac{\eta}{2} - \sqrt{\eta}|u|.$$

By making u arbitrarily close to zero, the objective approximates its least upper bound of $-\eta/2$.

To summarize, choices of w at the boundary of the constraint remain important in assessing alternative choices for u different from the solution $u = 0$. For every $u \neq 0$, the constraint can be made binding by a suitable choice of θ. Either maximization order approximates the correct value of the objective of the constraint game (6.4.1) under the original order of moves. Moreover, $u = 0$ is the correct robust action for that game. By maximizing first with respect to θ for a given $u \neq 0$, we may approximate the solutions $w = \pm\sqrt{\eta}$ of the constraint game. If we fix w at one of these limiting solutions, however, $u = 0$ will not be the maximizing solution of the objective

$$-\frac{u^2}{2} - \frac{(u+w)^2}{2}. \tag{6.5.6}$$

Later we will avoid some of these complications by expanding the choice set used in minimization. We do this because the approach that we will primarily rely on fixes $\theta > 1$ and solves

$$\sup_u \inf_w -\frac{u^2}{2} - \frac{(u+w)^2}{2} + \frac{\theta}{2}w^2. \tag{6.5.7}$$

Actually, sometimes we shall take the lower threshold for θ to differ from unity. Instead, it will depend on the details of the decision problem. Problem (6.5.7) is the same as (6.5.4) except that we have dropped the term η, a term that is inconsequential when θ is fixed and can easily be included when we want to optimize over θ. As we have argued, the objective in (6.5.4) is concave in (u, θ) and convex in w. This will remain true of our dynamic counterparts to (6.5.4). It can be verified directly that the order of maximization and minimization does not matter, and that the Nash equilibrium of the game defined by (6.5.4) can be obtained by stacking and solving first-order conditions for the minimizing and maximizing players.[8]

Problems (6.4.1) and (6.5.4) are pathological because neither η in the constraint game nor θ in the multiplier problem (6.5.4) affects the equilibrium decision u. The decision u makes the magnitude of $|w|$ inconsequential. We show below how this pathology occurs because $b^2 < \eta$.[9]

---

[8] This is a version of von Neumann's minimax theorem. For example, see Dantzig (1998, pp. 286–287).

[9] A related pathology underlies the H_∞ limiting control problems that we study in chapter 8.

6.6. The model with $b \neq 0$

By setting $b \neq 0$, we can alter the outcome that variations in the multiplier θ in (6.5.3) do not change the action u. We alter (6.4.1) to

$$\max_{u} \min_{|w|^2 \leq \eta} -\frac{u^2}{2} - \frac{(u + w - b)^2}{2}. \tag{6.6.1}$$

We consider the multiplier problem

$$L^*(\theta) = \sup_{u} \inf_{w} -\frac{u^2}{2} - \frac{(u + w - b)^2}{2} + \frac{\theta w^2}{2} \tag{6.6.2}$$

for $\theta > 1$. We restrict θ because it is again true that for $\theta < 1$, the innermost minimization problem has a criterion equal to $-\infty$ for any u. Thus, $\theta = 1$ remains a breakdown point. For fixed θ, there is no need to include the term $-\theta \eta$ in the construction of L^* because this term is pertinent only when we maximize over θ. The function L^* is increasing and concave in θ, and the first-order condition for maximizing $L^*(\theta) - \theta \eta$ is

$$\frac{d}{d\theta} L^*(\theta) = \eta,$$

which determines θ as a function of η.

Consider first the equilibrium of the multiplier game for a fixed $\theta > 1$. Variations of θ for $\theta > 1$ will now affect the choice of u and thereby capture how θ expresses concerns about robustness. The first-order conditions are

$$u + (u + w - b) = 0$$
$$(u + w - b) - \theta w = 0.$$

The equilibrium outcomes are

$$u = \frac{\theta b}{2\theta - 1}$$
$$w = \frac{-b}{2\theta - 1}. \tag{6.6.3}$$

Recall that our lower bound on θ may not induce the constraint to bind. When we check this, we obtain the following result.

Theorem 6.6.1. *For $\sqrt{\eta}$ in the interval $(0, |b|)$ we can find a value of $\theta > 1$ for which the solution to the multiplier game (6.6.2) is the same as that of the constraint game (6.6.1) and conversely.*

Proof. Notice from (6.6.3) that $|w|$ decreases with θ and, in particular, is $|b|$ for $\theta = 1$. Provided that $|b| > \sqrt{\eta}$, the maximization over θ is equivalent to finding a θ for which the constraint is satisfied at equality. Alternatively, it can be shown that the derivative $\frac{d}{d\theta}L^*(\theta)$ is equal to b^2 at the lower boundary $\theta = 1$. ∎

Theorem 6.6.1 gives a mapping from θ to η

$$\eta = \left(\frac{b}{2\theta - 1}\right)^2.$$

Changing the penalty parameter or multiplier θ is equivalent to enforcing alternative constraints. This mapping, however, only applies for $\theta > 1$, which rules out large values of η. For each w of the form (6.6.3) associated with a $\theta > 1$, the corresponding u solves

$$\sup_u -\frac{u^2}{2} - \frac{(u + w - b)^2}{2}.$$

Notice that $u = \frac{b}{2}$ for the limiting $\theta = +\infty$ case, and that u converges to b as θ declines to one. As we will now show, $u = b$ remains the solution to the constraint game (6.4.1) for values of η that exceed b^2. Increasing η reduces the objective without altering the solution for u.

To verify this, form two quadratic functions

$$p_-(u) = -\frac{u^2}{2} - \frac{\left(u - \sqrt{\eta} - b\right)^2}{2}$$

$$p_+(u) = -\frac{u^2}{2} - \frac{\left(u + \sqrt{\eta} - b\right)^2}{2}.$$

The robust choice of u solves

$$\max_u \min\{p_-(u), p_+(u)\}.$$

Notice that $p_-(b) = p_+(b)$. Moreover, $dp_-(0)/du = b + \sqrt{\eta}$ and $dp_+(0)/du = b - \sqrt{\eta}$. Because $\sqrt{\eta} > |b|$, these derivatives have opposite signs, implying that $u = b$ remains the robust solution.

Figures 6.6.1 and 6.6.2 depict the two cases $\sqrt{\eta} > |b|$ and $\sqrt{\eta} < |b|$. Figure 6.6.1 plots the function $\min\{p_-(u), p_+(u)\}$ for $\sqrt{\eta} = .3, b = 0$ while figure 6.6.2, in turn, plots it for $\sqrt{\eta} = .3, b = .5$. In figure 6.6.1, which corresponds to a pathological case in which $\sqrt{\eta} > |b|$, the function $\min\{p_-(u), p_+(u)\}$ is nondifferentiable at the maximizer $u = b = 0$, a point at the intersection of the $p_-(u)$ and $p_+(u)$. In figure 6.6.2, for which $\sqrt{\eta} < |b|$, the maximum of $\min\{p_-(u), p_+(u)\}$ occurs at $u = \frac{\sqrt{\eta} + b}{2} = .4$, a point where the function is differentiable. Here u depends on η, reflecting a concern for robustness that was absent in the pathological $\sqrt{\eta} > |b|$ case.

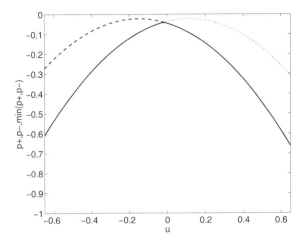

Figure 6.6.1: The functions $p_-(u), p_+(u), \min\{p_-(u), p_+(u)\}$ for $\sqrt{\eta} = .3, b = 0$. The maximum of $\min\{p_-(u), p_+(u)\}$ occurs at $u = b = 0$, a kink point of the function.

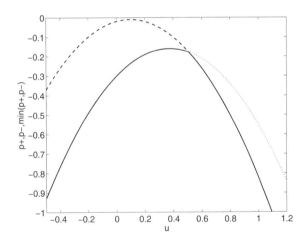

Figure 6.6.2: The functions $p_-(u), p_+(u), \min\{p_-(u), p_+(u)\}$ for $\sqrt{\eta} = .3, b = .5$. The maximum of $\min\{p_-(u), p_+(u)\}$ occurs at $u = \frac{b + \sqrt{\eta}}{2} = .4$, where the function is differentiable.

6.7. Probabilistic formulation ($b = 0$)

We now alter game (6.4.1) by enlarging the class of allowable perturbations to include more than just mean shifts by considering random perturbations to the approximating model. The approximating model is

$$x = u + \epsilon$$

where $\epsilon \sim f_o(\epsilon)$ and f_o is the standard normal density. The distorted models have $\epsilon \sim f(\epsilon)$ for some density $f \neq f_o$. Corresponding to the $b = 0$ case above, we let the objective in our two-player zero-sum games be

$$-\frac{u^2}{2} - \frac{\int (u + \epsilon)^2 f(\epsilon) \, d\epsilon}{2}. \tag{6.7.1}$$

To measure model misspecification we use relative entropy, which is defined to be the expected log-likelihood ratio, where the expectation is evaluated at the distorted model

$$\mathcal{I}(f) = \int [\log f(\epsilon) - \log f_o(\epsilon)] f(\epsilon) \, d\epsilon. \tag{6.7.2}$$

This entropy measure is convex in f. We study the game

$$\max_u \min_{f, \mathcal{I}(f) \leq \xi, \int f = 1} -\frac{u^2}{2} - \frac{\int (u + \epsilon)^2 f(\epsilon) \, d\epsilon}{2} \tag{6.7.3}$$

where $\xi \geq 0$ measures set of perturbed densities. The objective in $(6.7.3)$ is linear in the density f and the constraint set is convex. Therefore, Lagrangian methods apply.

6.7.1. Gaussian perturbations

Before relating game $(6.7.3)$ to game $(6.4.1)$, we calculate the entropy measure $(6.7.2)$ where f is a normal density with mean w and variance σ^2. Then[10]

$$\mathcal{I}(f) = \frac{w^2}{2} + \frac{\sigma^2 - 1}{2} - \frac{\log \sigma^2}{2}. \tag{6.7.4}$$

Thus, entropy decomposes into a part $\frac{w^2}{2}$ due to a mean distortion and a part $\frac{\sigma^2 - 1}{2} - \frac{\log \sigma^2}{2}$ due to a variance distortion. Because the logarithm is a concave function, the variance distortion is nonnegative

$$\frac{\sigma^2 - 1}{2} - \frac{\log \sigma^2}{2} \geq 0.$$

To understand how game $(6.7.3)$ is related to game $(6.4.1)$, consider a perturbed density f that is normal with mean w and unit variance $\sigma^2 = 1$

---

[10] Simple calculations show that $\mathcal{I}(f)$ is the expectation of $\log(\sigma^{-1}) - (2\sigma^2)^{-1}(\epsilon - w)^2 + (2)^{-1}\epsilon^2$ evaluated with respect to $f(\epsilon)$.

so that the distortion consists solely of a mean shift. Then $\mathcal{I}(f) = \frac{w^2}{2}$ and the objective (6.7.1) becomes

$$-\frac{u^2}{2} - \frac{(u+w)^2 + 1}{2},$$

which matches (6.3.4) when $b = 0$. With the Gaussian $f(\epsilon)$, we can view (6.7.3) as extending (6.4.1) to a larger set of perturbations. In effect, (6.4.1) admits only perturbations that are equivalent to mean shifts in a standard normal distribution. The η in (6.4.1) relates to the parameter ξ in (6.7.3) through the formula

$$\xi = \frac{\eta}{2}. \tag{6.7.5}$$

In shifting the distortions from numbers w to densities f, we have made the objective function linear in the distortion. The family of normal distributions with a unit variance and mean w is not convex, however.[11]

6.7.2. Letting the minimizing agent choose random perturbations when $b = 0$

By appropriately choosing f, which is the counterpart to w in (6.4.1), the minimizing player can in effect implement a mixed strategy. This changes the solution to the problem in a substantial way.

The Lagrange saddle-point problem is

$$\max_u \ \min_{f, \int f = 1} \ \sup_{\theta \geq 0} -\frac{u^2}{2} - \frac{\int (u+\epsilon)^2 f(\epsilon)\, d\epsilon}{2} + \theta\left[\mathcal{I}(f) - \xi\right]$$

or

$$\max_u \max_{\theta \geq 0} \ \inf_{f, \int f = 1} -\frac{u^2}{2} - \frac{\int (u+\epsilon)^2 f(\epsilon)\, d\epsilon}{2} + \theta\left[\mathcal{I}(f) - \xi\right]. \tag{6.7.6}$$

The first-order conditions for the innermost minimization problem of (6.7.6) are

$$\theta\left[\log f(\epsilon) - \log f_o(\epsilon) + 1\right] + \kappa = \frac{(u+\epsilon)^2}{2} \tag{6.7.7}$$

where κ is a constant introduced by the constraint $\int f = 1$. The solution to this problem is

$$f_\theta(\epsilon) \propto \exp\left[\frac{(u+\epsilon)^2}{2\theta}\right] f_o(\epsilon) \tag{6.7.8}$$

---

[11] An approach that we might have taken would be to mix w actions by allowing finite mixtures of normal distributions. Rather than doing that, we allow arbitrary densities. These arbitrary densities cannot necessarily be represented as mixtures over a finite number of normal densities. We constrain their relative entropies, which effectively restricts them to be absolutely continuous with respect to f_o.

where the constant of proportionality is chosen so that $f_\theta(\epsilon)$ integrates to unity. Such a constant will exist only when

$$\int \exp\left[\frac{(u+\epsilon)^2}{2\theta}\right] f_o\left(\epsilon\right) d\epsilon < \infty.$$

The integral is finite provided that $\theta > 1$. When $\theta > 1$, the density f_θ defined by (6.7.8) is normal since it is the product of exponentials with quadratic terms in ϵ. It is easy to verify that the density f_θ is proportional to the exponential of the term

$$\frac{(u+\epsilon)^2}{2\theta} - \frac{\epsilon^2}{2} = -\frac{(\theta-1)\,\epsilon^2}{2\theta} + \frac{u\epsilon}{\theta} + \frac{u^2}{2\theta}$$

$$= -\frac{(\epsilon-\mu_\theta)^2}{2\sigma_\theta^2} + c$$

where c does not depend on ϵ and where

$$\mu_\theta = \frac{u}{\theta-1}$$

$$\sigma_\theta^2 = \frac{\theta}{\theta-1}.$$

Thus, f_θ is normal with mean μ_θ and variance σ_θ^2. Notice that the variance σ_θ^2 becomes arbitrarily large as θ approaches unity. As a consequence, the relative entropy associated with a θ that approaches unity becomes arbitrarily large. For instance, when $u = 0$ (6.7.4) implies

$$\mathcal{I}\left(f_\theta\right) = \frac{\sigma_\theta^2 - 1}{2} - \frac{\log \sigma_\theta^2}{2}.$$

A multiplier θ is associated with each positive $\xi = 2\eta$ defined in (6.7.5). The optimized choice of u remains zero in this example, and the worst-case distribution f has an increased variance (relative to the standard normal distribution) that depends on ξ. Thus, in contrast to the deterministic game, values of $\theta > 1$ correspond to specific values of ξ. Moreover, every value of ξ is associated with a multiplier θ that is greater than one. Finally, we can interchange the order of the min and max, which implies that $u = 0, f = f_\theta$ is a Nash equilibrium as well, where θ is chosen to satisfy the entropy constraint for a given value of ξ. Moreover, u solves

$$\max_u -\frac{u^2}{2} - \frac{\int (u+\epsilon)^2 f\left(\epsilon\right) d\epsilon}{2} \qquad (6.7.9)$$

for the minimized choice of f. If at the outset we had endowed the decision maker with this f, the choice of u, the robust u is also the optimal u for the problem with no uncertainty about the density.

Thus, by expanding the set of admissible perturbations from mean shifts to arbitrary (absolutely continuous) density shifts, we have been able to avoid some of the complications of game (6.4.1). But we continue to be led to study limiting decision rules as θ decreases to some critical value, namely, $\theta = 1$ in this example. The breakdown point for θ will no longer be associated with a finite value of ξ. The limiting solution as $\theta \searrow 1$ corresponds to the H_∞ control in chapter 8.

Introducing a translation term b into the objective as in

$$-\frac{u^2}{2} - \frac{\int (u - b + \epsilon)^2 f(\epsilon) \, d\epsilon}{2}$$

will cause the worst-case distribution to have a nonzero mean, but there will still be a variance enhancement. The quadratic objective makes the worst-case distribution remain normal. The enhanced variance will not alter the decision for u. Thus, the multiplier solution for u in (6.5.2) also solves the stochastic game (6.7.3). However, the implied variance enhancement is needed to match multipliers and constraints for the stochastic game.

6.8. Constraint and multiplier preferences

In dynamic settings, Hansen, Sargent, Turmuhambetova, and Williams (2006) have described constraint and multiplier preferences associated with dynamic versions of the two games that we have studied in this chapter. Our static games are convenient settings for describing the relationship between these preferences.[12] Consider a two-state case and a risk-neutral consumer who without fear of model mispecification orders consumption pairs c_1, c_2 according to their expected utility

$$\pi c_1 + (1 - \pi) c_2$$

where π is the probability of state 1 and c_i is consumption in state i. Multiplier preferences over (c_1, c_2) are ordered by[13]

$$W(c_1, c_2, \theta) = -\theta \log \left[\pi \exp(-c_1/\theta) + (1 - \pi) \exp(-c_2/\theta) \right]. \qquad (6.8.1)$$

---

[12] See Maccheroni, Marinacci, and Rustichini (2006a) for a more extensive treatment.

[13] $W(c_1, c_2, \theta)$ is the indirect utility function of the problem

$$\min_{\mu \in [0,1]} \left\{ \mu c_1 + (1 - \mu) c_2 + \theta \left(\mu \log(\mu/\pi) + (1 - \mu) \log[(1 - \mu)/(1 - \pi)] \right) \right\}.$$

Constraint preferences are ordered by

$$J(c_1, c_2, \eta) = \min_{\mu \in [0,1]} \mu c_1 + (1 - \mu) c_2 \qquad (6.8.2)$$

where the minimization is subject to the constraint on entropy

$$\mu \log (\mu/\pi) + (1 - \mu) \log [(1 - \mu) / (1 - \pi)] \leq \eta. \qquad (6.8.3)$$

Figure 6.8.1 plots indifference curves for the two preference orderings both of which are drawn tangent to a budget line that depicts a situation in which c_1 is cheaper than c_2. Noteworthy features of the figure are: (1) the indifference curve for the constraint preferences (6.8.2) has a kink at the 45 degree certainty line while the multiplier preferences indifference curve is smooth there; (2) we have made the indifference curves for the two preference orderings tangent to the budget line at the same point by adjusting η to make the Lagrange multiplier associated with the entropy constraint (6.8.3) equal to the θ used to define the multiplier preferences; (3) the indifference curves for the two preference orderings differ away from that tangency point. In chapter 7, an analogous outcome will characterize constraint and multiplier preferences in dynamic settings in the sense that while they imply identical choices along equilibrium paths for the respective two-player zero-sum games, they imply different orderings off the equilibrium paths.

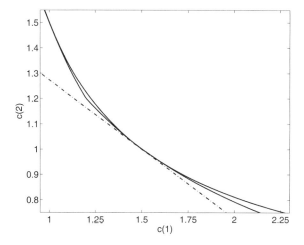

Figure 6.8.1: Budget line (dashed-dotted) and level curves for constraint preferences $J(c_1, c_2, \eta)$ (kinked at 45 degree line) and multiplier preferences $W(c_1, c_2, \theta)$ (smooth at 45 degree line).

6.9. Concluding remarks

This chapter has displayed two types of two-player zero-sum games that induce decisions that are robust to model misspecification. Each game has a
malevolent nature choose a model misspecification to hurt the decision maker.
The *constraint game* directly constrains the distortions to the approximating
model that the malevolent agent can make. The *multiplier game* penalizes
those distortions. The two games are equivalent under conditions that allow us
to invoke the Lagrange multiplier theorem. For our simple static example, we
displayed conditions under which the two games are equivalent and explored
conditions under which they capture concerns about model misspecification.

Our examples showed how randomization by the minimizing agent altered
outcomes. Randomization can be interpreted as allowing the minimizing agent
to distort entire densities, not just means, subject to an entropy penalty or
constraint. For our quadratic problems with normally distributed shocks, the
minimizing agent chooses to distort means and variances while preserving
the normal density. Interestingly, for θ above a lower bound (one in our
examples) the mean distortions as a function of θ remain the same. Thus,
the main consequence of allowing distortions to higher moments of the density
is that the mapping from the multiplier θ to the constraint must be altered
to account for the variance distortion associated with each value of θ.

In the static setting of this chapter, for the first class of mean misspecifications only, misspecification is confined to not knowing the mean of a random
shock or a constant term in a linear equation. Subsequent chapters take up
models where the decision maker fears misspecified *dynamics*. He expresses
those fears by allowing a distortion w to be the conditional mean of a shock
vector. By allowing that conditional mean to feed back on the history of the
state, a variety of misspecifications can be modeled. The consequences of
randomization are analogous. Shock variances will be enhanced, but we can
compute the mean distortions without simultaneously computing the covariance distortions for alternative choices of the penalty parameter θ.

In continuous-time models with Brownian motion information structures,
Hansen, Sargent, Turmuhambetova, and Williams (2006) show that the worst-
case model distorts the drifts of the underlying Brownian motions, but not
their volatilities. In the the continuous-time two-player zero-sum games of
Hansen, Sargent, Turmuhambetova, and Williams, the derivative $\frac{d}{d\theta}L^*(\theta)$
becomes infinite at the breakdown point for θ. This contrasts with outcomes
in the examples in this section and allows a finite entropy constraint to be
associated with an appropriate choice of θ.

The following two chapters take up dynamic games that can be used
to design robust decision rules. But the conceptual issues connecting the

constraint game and the multiplier game that we have considered in the static context of this chapter will carry over to the richer setting of chapters 7 and 8.

A. Rational expectations equilibrium

The Phillips curve example of section 6.2 took π_e as given. This appendix constructs a rational expectations version of the model and shows how to compute a time-consistent or Nash equilibrium rate of inflation. We proceed by adapting some concepts of Stokey (1989) to this example. Thus, we define a Nash equilibrium (with robustness) for the model as follows:

Definition 6.A.1. Given multiplier $\theta > 1$, a *Nash equilibrium* is a pair (π, π_e) such that (a) $\pi = B(\pi_e; \theta)$, and (b) $\pi = \pi_e$. Here B is the government's best response map (6.2.11).

Condition (a) says that given π_e, the government is choosing a robust rule associated with multiplier θ. Condition (b) imposes rational expectations. It is easy to compute a rational expectations equilibrium by solving (6.2.7) and $\pi = \pi_e$ for π_e:

$$\pi_e(\theta) = \frac{\theta}{\theta - 1} U^* \gamma. \tag{6.A.1}$$

Notice that $\pi_e'(\theta) < 0$, $\lim_{\theta \nearrow \infty} \pi_e(\theta) = U^* \gamma$, and $\lim_{\theta \searrow 1} \pi_e(\theta) = +\infty$. If the approximating model is true, so that the government's concern about misspecification is ungrounded, the government's ignorance of the model causes it to set inflation higher than if it knew the model for sure.

Notice that Definition 6.A.1 imputes a concern for model misspecification to the government, but not to the private forecasters, who are assumed to know the π chosen by the government. In chapter 16 we shall return to discuss an alternative version of rational expectations that imposes more symmetry between the government and private agents.

Chapter 7
Time domain games for attaining robustness

... a disposition among the doubters to dig in and face confusion along a new line of defense.
— *Frederick Allen Lewis, Only Yesterday, 1931*

7.1. Alternative time domain formulations

This chapter generalizes the static constraint and multiplier games of chapter 6 to a dynamic setting. We study two-player zero-sum dynamic games in which a minimizing player helps a maximizing player design a decision rule that is robust to misspecification of a dynamic model that links controls today to state variables tomorrow. We represent misspecification by allowing shocks to feed back on the history of the state in ways that an approximating model excludes. Constraint and multiplier games differ in how they parameterize a set of alternative specifications that surround an approximating model. The constraint games require that the discounted entropy of each alternative model relative to the approximating model not exceed a nonnegative parameter η. The multiplier games restrict discounted entropy implicitly via a penalty parameter θ. If the parameters η and θ are appropriately related, the constraint and multiplier games have equivalent outcomes.

We devote most of this chapter to studying four multiplier games that have identical players, payoffs, and actions, but different timing protocols. The games are (1) an effectively static Stackelberg multiplier game in which a maximizing player at time 0 chooses a history-dependent sequence of controls after a minimizing player at time 0 chooses a history-dependent sequence of distortions to transition densities for the state; (2) an effectively static Stackelberg multiplier game in history-contingent sequences in which the minimizing player chooses first at time 0; (3) a Markov perfect multiplier game in which both players choose sequentially and the maximizing player chooses first each period $t \geq 0$; and (4) a Markov perfect multiplier game in which both players choose sequentially and the minimizing player chooses first each period $t \geq 0$. We use games 3 and 4 to generate candidates that we verify are equilibria of games 1 and 2.

Games with different timing protocols usually have different outcomes, but because the two players' preferences are perfectly *mis*aligned, our games have identical outcomes. We devote much of this chapter to verifying the equivalence of outcomes and equilibrium representations of multiplier games for our different timing protocols. After that, in section 7.8, we show how the equilibrium of a multiplier game can be used to construct an equilibrium of a constraint game by setting θ and η appropriately. We link the penalty parameter θ in a multiplier game to the Lagrange multiplier on a discounted entropy constraint and to the derivative of the value function with respect to continuation in a constraint game.

In the economic applications in subsequent chapters, we shall exploit the equivalence of outcomes of multiplier games across different timing protocols, for example, in the equilibrium in a model with a Ramsey planner that we propose in chapter 16. While some of the proofs in this chapter involve lengthy arguments, they justify simple algorithms and appealing ways of interpreting robust decision rules. We summarize these algorithms compactly in section 7.4.3 and appendix C.

7.2. The setting

A decision maker has a unique explicitly specified approximating model but concedes that the data might actually be generated by an unknown member of a set of models that surround the approximating model. One parameter, either θ or η, measures a set of perturbations to the approximating model. Three models within the set are especially important: the decision maker's approximating model; an unknown model that generates the data; and a worst-case model that emerges from a robust decision making procedure. Each model specifies that an $n \times 1$ state vector evolves according to

$$x_{t+1} = Ax_t + Bu_t + C\epsilon_{t+1} \qquad (7.2.1)$$

where x_0 is given and u_t is a vector of controls. The approximating model assumes that $\{\epsilon_{t+1} : t = 0, 1, \ldots\}$ is an i.i.d. sequence of multivariate standard normally distributed random vectors. The pair $(\sqrt{\beta}A, B)$ is *stabilizable*, where $\beta \in (0,1)$ is a discount factor. The pair $(\sqrt{\beta}A, B)$ is said to be stabilizable if there exists a matrix $\tilde{F}$ for which $A - B\tilde{F}$ has all of its eigenvalues strictly less than $\frac{1}{\sqrt{\beta}}$. See chapter 4, page 69 for more about stabilizability.[1]

The decision maker observes current and past values of the shock ϵ_t. The control u_t is constrained to be in the set U_t of all (Borel measurable) functions from $(x_0, \epsilon_1, \ldots, \epsilon_{t+1})$ to a space $\mathbf{R}^k$ of admissible values for the k-dimensional control vector. The maximizing agent chooses a sequence $u = \{u_t : t = 0, 1, \ldots\}$, where $u_t \in U_t$ for all $t \geq 0$. Call this space of control processes $\mathcal{U}$.

---

[1] We can rewrite the system $x_{t+1} = Ax_t + Bu_t$ as $x_{t+1} = (A - B\tilde{F})x_t + B\tilde{u}_t$, where $u_t = -\tilde{F}x_t + \tilde{u}_t$, and then proceed to view $\tilde{u}_t$ as the control.

Our formulation of the choices open to the minimizing agent follows Petersen, James and Dupuis (2000) and Hansen, Sargent, Turmuhambetova, and Williams (2006).[2] The minimizing agent chooses densities for the shock ϵ_{t+1} conditioned on $(x_0, \epsilon_1, \ldots, \epsilon_t)$. The date $t+1$ density $f_{t+1}(\epsilon^* | x_0, \epsilon_1, \ldots, \epsilon_t)$ must be nonnegative and integrate to unity. The minimizing agent chooses a sequence of densities $\{f_{t+1} : t = 0, 1, \ldots\}$ that are used to compute discounted expected utilities.

Our analysis in chapter 3 indicated that a mathematically equivalent way to pose the minimizing agent's choice of actions is to use a convenient change of measure by introducing a sequence of likelihood ratios M_t. Let $M_0 = 1$ and form

$$M_{t+1} = M_t m_{t+1}$$

where m_{t+1} is a scalar, nonnegative Borel measurable function of $(x_0, \epsilon_1, \ldots, \epsilon_{t+1})$ such that $E(m_{t+1} | x_0, \epsilon_1, \ldots, \epsilon_t) = 1$. In this formulation, the expectation operator is computed using the i.i.d. standard normal density for ϵ_{t+1}. The process $\{M_{t+1} : t = 0, 1, \ldots\}$ is a nonnegative martingale with expectation equal to unity for each t. The functional dependence of m_{t+1} on ϵ_{t+1} determines the density f_{t+1} conditioned on $(x_0, \epsilon_1, \ldots, \epsilon_t)$ relative to the standard normal density.

To complete the specification of preferences, define a target vector

$$z_t = H x_t + J u_t. \tag{7.2.2}$$

The objective is

$$E\left[\sum_{t=0}^{\infty} \beta^t M_t \left(-\frac{z_t \cdot z_t}{2} + \beta \theta m_{t+1} \log m_{t+1} \right) \Big| x_0 \right].$$

The likelihood ratio M_t acts like a preference shock. Let $\mathcal{M}$ be the space of admissible multiplicative martingale increments $\{m_{t+1} : t = 0, 1, \ldots\}$. Discounted relative entropy is

$$E\left[\sum_{t=0}^{\infty} \beta^t M_t m_{t+1} \log m_{t+1} | x_0 \right].$$

In section 7.8, we add a constraint on discounted entropy to the constraints forming a two-player zero-sum Stackelberg game in sequences. In the next section, we adopt the alternative approach of simply penalizing the date t contribution to discounted entropy with a penalty parameter θ.

---

[2] Petersen, James and Dupuis (2000) and Hansen, Sargent, Turmuhambetova, and Williams (2006) formulate robust control problems in the context of an approximating model that is possibly nonlinear and explicitly stochastic.

7.3. Two Stackelberg games

In our Stackelberg games, at time 0, the maximizing player chooses a sequence of controls $u = \{u_t : t = 0, 1, \ldots\}$, where $u_t \in U_t$ for all $t \geq 0$, while the minimizing player chooses a sequence of densities for the shock ϵ_{t+1} conditioned on $(x_0, \epsilon_1, \ldots, \epsilon_t)$. We study two Stackelberg games that are distinguished by which player is the leader in the sense of choosing first. The maximizing player chooses first in the following Stackelberg game

$$\sup_{u \in \mathcal{U}} \inf_{m \in \mathcal{M}} E \left[\sum_{t=0}^{\infty} \beta^t M_t \left(-\frac{z_t \cdot z_t}{2} + \beta \theta m_{t+1} \log m_{t+1} \right) | x_0 \right] \qquad (7.3.1)$$

where the optimization of both players is subject to

$$\begin{aligned} x_{t+1} &= A x_t + B u_t + C \epsilon_{t+1} \\ M_{t+1} &= M_t m_{t+1} \\ z_t &= H x_t + J u_t \end{aligned} \qquad (7.3.2)$$

where x_0 is given and $M_0 = 1$. In our second Stackelberg game, the minimizing player chooses first

$$\inf_{m \in \mathcal{M}} \sup_{u \in \mathcal{U}} E \left[\sum_{t=0}^{\infty} \beta^t M_t \left(-\frac{z_t \cdot z_t}{2} + \beta \theta m_{t+1} \log m_{t+1} \right) | x_0 \right]. \qquad (7.3.3)$$

subject again to constraints $(7.3.2)$. Notice that the inner problem, i.e., the maximization problem, in $(7.3.3)$ is a standard linear-quadratic control problem with a distorted expectation that is determined by the sequence of likelihood ratios M_t. When this game has a solution, the worst-case sequence m defines a probability distribution under which the stochastic control process u is optimal. We will eventually use this fact to provide an *ex post* Bayesian interpretation of a robust decision rule.

We shall show that these two Stackelberg games have the same value, a fact called the Bellman-Isaacs condition, whose important ramifications we explore below. The control from the first Stackelberg game $(7.3.1)$ is the robust control process and the distortion process from the second game $(7.3.3)$ defines the worst-case probability distribution.

7.4. Two Markov perfect equilibria

The Stackelberg games in sequences are, in effect, static games subject to information constraints. Rather than solving them directly, it is more convenient to find Markov perfect equilibria of two related games that can be solved by applying dynamic programming, and then to use the solutions from these other games to construct guesses for the equilibria of the static games (7.3.1) and (7.3.3), then finally to verify those solutions.

7.4.1. Markov perfect equilibrium: definition

We say that Stackelberg games are static because the players once and for all choose processes $\{u_t\}$ and $\{m_{t+1}\}$. In contrast, in Markov perfect equilibria, players choose sequentially. A Markov perfect equilibrium is defined in terms of a sequence of time t continuation values

$$
E\left[\sum_{j=0}^{\infty} \beta^j M_{t+j}\left(-\frac{z_{t+j} \cdot z_{t+j}}{2} + \beta\theta m_{t+j+1}\log m_{t+j+1}\right)\Big| x_t, M_t\right] \quad (7.4.1)
$$

for $t \geq 0$.

Definition 7.4.1. A sequence of decision rules for $t \geq 0$ mapping (x_t, M_t) into $u_t \in \mathbf{R^k}$ and (x_t, M_t) into a perturbation of a time $t+1$ conditional density $m(\epsilon_{t+1}|x_t, M_t)$ is said to be a *Markov perfect equilibrium* if for every $t \geq 0$, (a) given the decision rules of the maximizing u-setting player for $s \geq t$ and the decision rules for the minimizing m-setting player for $s > t$, the time t decision rule for m_{t+1} minimizes (7.4.1); and (b) given the decision rules of the maximizing u-setting player for $s > t$ and the decision rules for the minimizing m-setting player for $s \geq t$, the time t decision rule for u_t maximizes (7.4.1).

Thus, in a Markov perfect equilibrium, the players choose u_t and m_{t+1} period by period, setting u_t as a function of the state (x_t, M_t) at date t and m_{t+1} as a function of the state (x_t, M_t) and the shock ϵ_{t+1}. (As we shall show, they actually choose not to make their decisions be functions only of M_t.)

REMARK: In a Markov perfect equilibrium, the continuation value function (7.4.1) is

$$
W(x_t, M_t) = E\left[\sum_{j=0}^{\infty} \beta^j M_{t+j}\left(-\frac{z_{t+j} \cdot z_{t+j}}{2} + \beta\theta m_{t+j+1}\log m_{t+j+1}\right)\Big| x_t, M_t\right].
$$

Below, we shall show that the value function has the form $W(x_t, M_t) = M_t(-x_t'P^*x_t - k^*)$.

Our definition of a Markov perfect equilibrium leaves open which of the two players we imagine to choose first each period. We shall study two Markov perfect equilibria, one that has the maximizing player choosing first, the other that lets the minimizing player choose first. The value functions are identical for these two timing protocols.

7.4.2. Markov perfect equilibria: value functions

The value functions of our Markov perfect equilibria are quadratic. Furthermore, it turns out that we can avoid carrying along an additional state variable M_t because the value function scales linearly in M. Thus, guess a value function of the form

$$-\frac{1}{2} M_{t+1} \left(x_{t+1}{}' P_{t+1} x_{t+1} + k_{t+1} \right)$$

and consider the recursion

$$\max_{u_t} \min_{m_{t+1}} - M_t \left(\frac{z_t \cdot z_t}{2} \right)$$
$$+ \beta E M_{t+1} \left(\frac{- \left(x_{t+1}' P_{t+1} x_{t+1} + k_{t+1} \right)}{2} + \theta \log m_{t+1} \right) \bigg|_{(x_t, M_t)} \tag{7.4.2}$$

where the optimization is subject to

$$x_{t+1} = A x_t + B u_t + C \epsilon_{t+1}$$
$$M_{t+1} = M_t m_{t+1} \tag{7.4.3}$$
$$z_t = H x_t + J u_t,$$

where m_{t+1} is allowed to depend on ϵ_{t+1} but is constrained to satisfy $E(m_{t+1} | x_t, M_t) = 1$ for all $t \geq 0$. Recursion $(7.4.2)$ defines one of our two Markov perfect equilibria. Soon we shall describe another game in which the within period order of maximization and minimization is interchanged.

Substituting from $(7.4.3)$ for M_{t+1} and noticing that the objective scales in M_t implies that u_t and m_{t+1} can be chosen independently of M_t and can be expressed as functions of x_t alone. The objective in $(7.4.2)$ is convex in m_{t+1} and concave in u_t so long as $\theta > \underline{\theta}$, a breakdown value that we shall discuss in section 7.9.1 and more extensively in chapter 8, where we give a frequency domain interpretation of it.

7.4.3. Useful recursions

We will construct Markov perfect equilibria via recursions that are defined in terms of the following operators[3]

$$T(P) = H'H - H'J (J'J)^{-1} J'H + \beta \left[A' - H'J (J'J)^{-1} B' \right]$$

---

[3] Appendix C describes versions of these formulas that are consistent with the notation of chapter 2.

$$\left[P - \beta PB \left(J'J + \beta B'PB \right)^{-1} B'P \right]$$

$$\left[A - B \left(J'J \right)^{-1} J'H \right] \qquad (7.4.4a)$$

or

$$T(P) = H'H + \beta A'PA - \left(\beta B'PA + H'J \right)$$
$$\times \left(J'J + \beta B'PB \right)^{-1} \left(\beta B'PA + J'H \right) \qquad (7.4.4b)$$

$$\mathcal{D}(P) = P + PC \left(\theta I - C'PC \right)^{-1} C'P \qquad (7.4.4c)$$

$$\mathcal{F}(P) = \left(J'J + \beta B'PB \right)^{-1} \left(\beta B'PA + J'H \right) \qquad (7.4.4d)$$

$$\mathcal{K}(P) = \left(\theta I - C'PC \right)^{-1} C'P \left(A - B\mathcal{F} \left(\mathcal{D}(P) \right) \right) \qquad (7.4.4e)$$

$$\mathcal{S}(P) = H'_F H_F + \beta A'_F \mathcal{D}(P) A_F, \qquad (7.4.4f)$$

where $A_F = A - BF$ and $H_F = H - JF$.

As we shall see, formulas (7.4.4) provide simple algorithms for solving all of our games and for computing a robust decision rule. We will use these operators in subsequent sections to justify the equivalence of outcomes from distinct two-player zero-sum dynamic games, namely, our two Stackelberg and two Markov perfect games. We shall say more about the $\mathcal{S}$ operator in subsection 7.9.2 when we describe a policy improvement algorithm.

7.5. Computing a Markov perfect equilibrium: the recursion

We compute a Markov perfect equilibrium by working backwards on an appropriate set of Bellman equations that solve a two-period game with a given terminal value function. To compute an infinite horizon Markov perfect equilibrium, we iterate to convergence on those Bellman equations. We solve the two-period game in this section. We first consider the minimization with respect to m_{t+1} in the two-period game (7.4.2). It it convenient and revealing to accomplish this minimization in two steps.

7.5.1. Step one: distorting the covariance matrix

Initially we impose the constraint that

$$E \left(m_{t+1} \epsilon_{t+1} | x_t, M_t \right) = w_{t+1}. \qquad (7.5.1)$$

We promise to investigate the choice of w_{t+1} in the second step.

Theorem 7.5.1. *Suppose that* $(\theta I - C'P_{t+1}C)$ *is positive definite, and that* *constraint (7.5.1) is satisfied.* Then

$$m_{t+1} = \exp\left[-(1/2)(\epsilon_{t+1} - w_{t+1})'\left(I - \frac{1}{\theta}C'P_{t+1}C\right)(\epsilon_{t+1} - w_{t+1})\right]$$

$$\times \exp\left[(1/2)\epsilon_{t+1} \cdot \epsilon_{t+1}\right]$$

$$\times \det\left(I - \frac{1}{\theta}C'P_{t+1}C\right)^{1/2}$$

The corresponding density f_{t+1} is normal with conditional mean w_{t+1} and covariance matrix $(I - \frac{1}{\theta}C'P_{t+1}C)^{-1}$. Moreover,

$$E\left(m_{t+1}\log m_{t+1}|x_t, M_t\right) = \frac{1}{2}\log\det\left(I - \frac{1}{\theta}C'P_{t+1}C\right) + \frac{1}{2\theta}w_{t+1} \cdot w_{t+1}.$$

Proof. The first-order conditions for m_{t+1} are

$$\theta\log m_{t+1} = -\frac{1}{2}(\epsilon_{t+1})'C'P_{t+1}C\epsilon_{t+1} + \lambda_{t+1} \cdot \epsilon_{t+1} + \xi_{t+1}$$

where λ_{t+1} is a vector and ξ_{t+1} is a scalar, both of which can depend on x_t and M_t. They are chosen to assure that constraint (7.5.1) is satisfied and that $E(m_{t+1}|M_t, x_t) = 1$. The conclusion follows from a complete-the-square argument (see appendix D) in conjunction with the functional form of the multivariate normal distribution. ∎

The term $\log\det(I - \frac{1}{\theta}C'P_{t+1}C)$ contributes to the constant term of the date t value function. This constant term is given by

$$k_t = \beta k_{t+1} + \beta\theta\log\det\left(I - \frac{1}{\theta}C'P_{t+1}C\right) + \beta\text{trace}\left[P_{t+1}\left(I - \frac{1}{\theta}C'P_{t+1}C\right)^{-1}\right]$$

The choice of control u_t has no impact on the covariance distortion implied by m_{t+1} and hence on the constant of the date t value function.

7.5.2. Step two: distorting the mean

After computing conditional expectations and removing the constant term, we are led to solve

$$\max_{u_t}\min_{w_{t+1}} -\frac{1}{2}z_t \cdot z_t - \frac{\beta}{2}\bar{x}'_{t+1}P_{t+1}\bar{x}_{t+1} + \frac{\beta\theta}{2}w_{t+1} \cdot w_{t+1}$$

subject to

$$\bar{x}_{t+1} = Ax_t + Bu_t + Cw_{t+1}$$

$$z_t = Hx_t + Ju_t$$

where $\bar{x}_{t+1}$ is the conditional mean of x_{t+1} under the distortion associated with m_{t+1}. Conditioning on x_t eliminates all uncertainty. The effects of uncertainty are completely absorbed in a constant term k_t. Uncertainty has no impact on the choice of either u_t or w_{t+1} conditioned on x_t.

Theorem 7.5.2. *Suppose that* $(\theta I - C'P_{t+1}C)$ *is positive definite. Then*

$$
\max_{u_t} \min_{w_{t+1}} -\frac{1}{2} z_t \cdot z_t - \frac{\beta}{2} \bar{x}'_{t+1} P_{t+1} \bar{x}_{t+1} + \frac{\beta\theta}{2} w_{t+1} \cdot w_{t+1}
$$

$$
= \min_{w_{t+1}} \max_{u_t} -\frac{1}{2} z_t \cdot z_t - \frac{\beta}{2} \bar{x}'_{t+1} P_{t+1} \bar{x}_{t+1} + \frac{\beta\theta}{2} w_{t+1} \cdot w_{t+1}
$$

and the Markov perfect equilibrium decision rules for u_t *and* w_{t+1} *as a function of* x_t *are*

$$
u_t = -\mathcal{F}\left(\mathcal{D}\left(P_{t+1}\right)\right)
$$

$$
w_{t+1} = (\theta I - C'P_{t+1}C)^{-1} C'P_{t+1}\left(A - Bu_t\right) = \mathcal{K}\left(P_{t+1}\right) x_t
$$

where $\mathcal{F}$ *and* $\mathcal{K}$ *are given by (7.4.4c) and (7.4.4d). Moreover, the value of the game is* $-\frac{1}{2} x_t' T(\mathcal{D}(P_{t+1})) x_t$ *where* T *is given by (7.4.4a) or (7.4.4b).*

The operator $\mathcal{D}$ comes from updating the value function after optimizing with respect to w_{t+1} conditioned on a given choice of u_t. The conditional value function (ignoring uncertainty) is

$$
-\frac{\beta}{2} \left(Ax_t + Bu_t\right)' \mathcal{D}\left(P_{t+1}\right) \left(Ax_t + Bu_t\right)
$$

The operator T is derived by optimizing with respect to u_t.

7.5.3. Another Markov perfect equilibrium and a Bellman-Isaacs condition

At this point, we show that the value function for a two-period game does not depend on whether the maximizing or minimizing player chooses first. Thus, we verify that we would have obtained the same value function for our two-period problem had we allowed the choice of m_{t+1} given $E(m_{t+1}\epsilon_{t+1}|x_t, M_t) = w_{t+1}$ to be made last. We have already shown that when the minimization over m_{t+1} given $E(m_{t+1}\epsilon_{t+1}|x_t, M_t) = w_{t+1}$ occurs first, the solution depends on neither u_t nor w_{t+1}.

Theorem 7.5.3. *Suppose that* $\theta I - C'P_{t+1}C$ *is positive definite. Then*

$$
-\frac{1}{2} M_t \left[(x_t)' P_t x_t + k_t \right] \tag{7.5.2}
$$

$$
= \max_{u_t} \min_{m_{t+1}} -\frac{1}{2} M_t \left(z_t \cdot z_t \right) - \frac{\beta}{2} E\big(M_{t+1}\big[(x_{t+1})' P_{t+1} x_{t+1} + k_{t+1}
$$

$$
- \theta \log m_{t+1}\big]\big|x_t, M_t\big)
$$

$$
= \min_{m_{t+1}} \max_{u_t} -\frac{1}{2} M_t \left(z_t \cdot z_t \right) - \frac{\beta}{2} E\big(M_{t+1}\big[(x_{t+1})' P_{t+1} x_{t+1} + k_{t+1}
$$

$$
- \theta \log m_{t+1}\big]\big|x_t, M_t\big)
$$

subject to

$$x_{t+1} = Ax_t + Bu_t + C\epsilon_{t+1}$$

$$M_{t+1} = M_t m_{t+1}$$

$$z_t = Hx_t + Ju_t$$

where m_{t+1} can depend on ϵ_{t+1} but is restricted to satisfy $E(m_{t+1}|x_t, M_t) = 1$. The matrix in the value function is given by $P_t = T(\mathcal{D}(P_{t+1}))$ and the constant term by

$$k_t = \beta k_{t+1} + \beta\theta \log\det\left(I - \frac{1}{\theta}C'P_{t+1}C\right) + \beta\operatorname{trace}\left[P_{t+1}\left(I - \frac{1}{\theta}C'P_{t+1}C\right)^{-1}\right].$$

The freedom to interchange the role of minimization and maximization asserted in this theorem is referred to as the Bellman-Isaacs condition for zero-sum dynamic games.

7.5.4. Taking inventory

In formulating and solving game (7.4.2) eventually to obtain (7.5.2), we exploited the Markov structure of the reward and the evolution equation. As in ordinary single-agent linear-quadratic problems in which a certainty equivalence result prevails, the randomness in ϵ_{t+1} leads to adjustments only in the constant terms of value functions. The decision rules in our stochastic Markov perfect equilibrium can be computed by solving the corresponding zero-sum game without randomness given in Theorem 7.5.2. These decision rules do not depend on M_t and the value function for the game is linear in M_t. The effect of randomness is to enlarge the covariance matrix for ϵ_{t+1} in the worst-case model relative to what it is in the benchmark model. Our next task is to construct infinite horizon Markov perfect equilibria.

7.6. Markov perfect equilibrium of infinite horizon game

So far we have considered only a two-period game. We now consider an infinite horizon game. The ability to interchange minimization and maximization allows us to proceed by stacking first order conditions. To compute the Markov perfect equilibrium, we take advantage of the remarks about certainty equivalence in the previous subsection and temporarily abstract from uncertainty. Then we aim to compute a value function of the form $-\frac{1}{2}x'P^*x$ and equilibrium decision rules of the forms $u_t = -F^*x_t$ and $w_{t+1} = K^*x_t$. We study the deterministic two-player zero-sum game

$$-\frac{1}{2}(x_t)' P^* x_t = \max_{u_t} \min_{w_{t+1}} -\frac{1}{2} z_t \cdot z_t - \frac{\beta}{2}(x_{t+1})' P^* x_{t+1} + \frac{\beta\theta}{2} w_{t+1} \cdot w_{t+1}$$

$$= \min_{w_{t+1}} \max_{u_t} -\frac{1}{2} z_t \cdot z_t - \frac{\beta}{2}(x_{t+1})' P^* x_{t+1} + \frac{\beta\theta}{2} w_{t+1} \cdot w_{t+1}$$

where the optimization is subject to

$$x_{t+1} = A x_t + B u_t + C w_{t+1}$$
$$z_t = H x_t + J u_t.$$

To generate a candidate equilibrium, let $\mu_t = P^* x_t$. After substituting in the constraints, first-order conditions for u_t, w_{t+1}, x_{t+1}, respectively, are

$$J' J u_t + J' H x_t + \beta B' \mu_{t+1} = 0$$
$$-\theta w_{t+1} + C' \mu_{t+1} = 0$$
$$\beta A' \mu_{t+1} + H' H x_t + H' J u_t - \mu_t = 0. \tag{7.6.1}$$

For the second equation, we use the envelope theorem in computing μ_t. This allows us to ignore the consequences of differentiation with respect to x_t on u_t and w_{t+1}. Assume that $J'J$ is nonsingular and solve for u_t and w_{t+1}

$$u_t = -(J'J)^{-1} J' H x_t - \beta (J'J)^{-1} B' \mu_{t+1} \tag{7.6.2}$$

$$w_{t+1} = \frac{1}{\theta} C' \mu_{t+1}. \tag{7.6.3}$$

Substitute these expressions for u_t and w_{t+1} into the state equation to get

$$x_{t+1} = \left[A - B (J'J)^{-1} J' H \right] x_t - \left[\beta B (J'J)^{-1} B' - \frac{1}{\theta} CC' \right] \mu_{t+1}.$$

Substituting the same expressions into (7.6.1) gives

$$\beta \left[A' - H' J (J'J)^{-1} B' \right] \mu_{t+1} + \left[H'H - H' J (J'J)^{-1} J' H \right] x_t - \mu_t = 0.$$

Write the system as

$$L \begin{bmatrix} x_{t+1} \\ \mu_{t+1} \end{bmatrix} = N \begin{bmatrix} x_t \\ \mu_t \end{bmatrix} \tag{7.6.4}$$

where

$$L = \begin{pmatrix} I & \left[\beta B (J'J)^{-1} B' - \frac{1}{\theta} CC' \right] \\ 0 & \beta \left[A' - H' J (J'J)^{-1} B' \right] \end{pmatrix}$$

and

$$N = \begin{pmatrix} \left[A - B (J'J)^{-1} J' H \right] & 0 \\ -\left[H'H - H' J (J'J)^{-1} J' H \right] & I \end{pmatrix}.$$

It can be verified that the matrix pencil $(\frac{\lambda}{\sqrt{\beta}} L - N)$ is symplectic.[4] It follows that the generalized eigenvalues of (L, N) come in $\sqrt{\beta}$-symmetric pairs: for every eigenvalue λ_i, there is another eigenvalue λ_{-i} such that $\lambda_i \lambda_{-i} = \beta^{-1}$.

---

[4] See chapter 4 for the definition and properties of symplectic pencils.

We use the following

Definition 7.6.1. A matrix A is said to be $\sqrt{\beta}$-stable if all of its eigenvalues are strictly less than $\frac{1}{\sqrt{\beta}}$.

To assure existence of a candidate equilibrium, we rule out generalized eigenvalues of (L, N) on the circle $\Gamma = \{\zeta : |\zeta| = \frac{1}{\sqrt{\beta}}\}$, so that half of the generalized eigenvalues are inside the circle Γ and the other half are outside of this circle in the complex plane. The generalized eigenvectors associated with the eigenvalues inside Γ generate stable deflating subspace, where here stable means that the pertinent eigenvalues are less than $\frac{1}{\sqrt{2}}$ in modulus. The dimension of this subspace equals the number of entries in the state vector x_t.

Assume that there exists a positive semidefinite matrix P^* such that the stable deflating subspace can be represented as $\begin{pmatrix} I \\ P^* \end{pmatrix} x$. Then we can construct a candidate equilibrium with $\mu_t = P^* x_t$ and a state vector sequence that satisfies

$$L \begin{pmatrix} I \\ P^* \end{pmatrix} x_{t+1} = N \begin{pmatrix} I \\ P^* \end{pmatrix} x_t. \tag{7.6.5}$$

Thus, we now consider a finite horizon game and construct a terminal value of the form

$$-\frac{1}{2} M_T \left[(x_T)' P^* x_T + k^* \right]$$

at date T, such that the value function for the Markov perfect equilibria is time invariant. That is, the date t value function is

$$-\frac{1}{2} M_t \left[(x_t)' P^* x_t + k^* \right].$$

As a consequence, we can make the date T arbitrarily large without changing the equilibrium outcomes in the initial dates. We verify this construction under the conditions summarized in the following theorem.

Theorem 7.6.1. *Suppose that*

(i) $(\sqrt{\beta} A, B)$ *is stabilizable.*

(ii) $J'J$ *is nonsingular.*

(iii) (L, N) *has no generalized eigenvalues on* Γ.

(iv) an element of the $(\sqrt{\beta})$*-stable deflating subspace of* (L, N) *can be represented as* $\begin{pmatrix} I \\ P^* \end{pmatrix} x$ *for some vector* x *and a given positive semidefinite matrix* P^*.

(v) $\theta I - C' P^* C$ *is positive definite.*

Then there exist K^* and F^* for which a Markov perfect equilibrium is $u_t = -F^* x_t$ and $w_{t+1} = K^* x_t$. All eigenvalues of the matrix $A - BF^* + CK^*$ are inside Γ. The matrix P^* is necessarily symmetric and the date t value of the game is $-\frac{1}{2} x_t' P^* x_t$. Also, $F^* = (J'J)^{-1}(J'H + \beta B' P^* A^*)$, $K^* = \frac{1}{\theta} C' P^* A^*$.

Proof. We have already computed a candidate equilibrium by stacking the state-costate equations of the two players to get the linear difference equation system (7.6.5). The candidate equilibrium is a $\sqrt{\beta}$ stable sequence of state vectors that satisfies (7.6.5). Given conditions (iii) and (iv), from the first partition of (7.6.5), we see that

$$\left(I + \left[\beta B \left(J'J \right)^{-1} B' - \frac{1}{\theta} CC' \right] P^* \right) x_{t+1} = \left[A - B \left(J'J \right)^{-1} J'H \right] x_t.$$

(7.6.6)

It follows from Theorem 21.7 and Remark 21.2 of Zhou, Doyle, and Glover (1996) that P^* is symmetric and that the matrix on the left side of (7.6.6) is nonsingular. Hence, we have the state evolution

$$x_{t+1} = A^* x_t$$

where

$$A^* = \left(I + \left[\beta B \left(J'J \right)^{-1} B' - \frac{1}{\theta} CC' \right] P^* \right)^{-1} \left[A - B \left(J'J \right)^{-1} J'H \right].$$

By using the same partitioned inverse reasoning that led to equation (4.3.9), it can be shown that

$$\left(I + \left[\beta B \left(J'J \right)^{-1} B' - \frac{1}{\theta} CC' \right] P^* \right)^{-1}$$

$$= I - \beta (B \quad C) \begin{pmatrix} J'J + \beta B' P^* B & \beta B' P^* C \\ \beta C' P^* B & -\beta \theta I + \beta C' P^* C \end{pmatrix}^{-1} \begin{pmatrix} B' P^* \\ C' P^* \end{pmatrix}.$$

Therefore,

$$A^* = A - BF^* + CK^*$$

where F^* and K^* satisfy

$$F^* = (J'J)^{-1} (J'H + \beta B' P^* A^*)$$

$$K^* = \frac{1}{\theta} C' P^* A^*.$$

(7.6.7)

By (iv), A^* has eigenvalues that are inside the circle Γ. Moreover, the first-order conditions (7.6.1) imply $w_{t+1} = K^* x_t$ and $u_t = -F^* x_t$. ∎

Conditions (i) and (ii) occur in the standard control theory summarized in chapter 4 and assure the existence of an optimal control that stabilizes the state in the absence of concerns about misspecification. Condition (iv) can be viewed as an equilibrium selection device in cases in which there are multiple choices of P^* that satisfy the Riccati equation $P = T[\mathcal{D}(P)]$. Condition (v) guarantees that the objective is strictly convex in w_{t+1}.

Suppose next that $(H, \sqrt{\beta}A)$ is detectable.[5] When $\theta = \infty$, by adding the restriction we are guaranteed a unique positive, semidefinite matrix P^* of the Ricatti equation

$$P = T(P) \tag{7.6.8}$$

because it is optimal to stabilize the state vector process. For more general values of θ, Başar and Bernhard (1995) show that when multiple positive semidefinite solutions P^* exist to the Riccati equation

$$P = T[\mathcal{D}(P)] \tag{7.6.9}$$

and $(H, \sqrt{\beta}A)$ is detectable, it is the smallest such solution that corresponds to one given in Theorem 7.6.1. In this case, the Markov perfect equilibrium can be approximated by a sequence of finite games in which the terminal value function is identically zero. (See Theorem 3.7 of Başar and Bernhard (1995).[6])

7.7. Recursive representations of Stackelberg games

7.7.1. Markov perfect equilibria as candidate Stackelberg equilibria

Markov perfect equilibria are of interest *per se*, but they also give a convenient way to construct solutions for our two Stackelberg games. In the same way that dynamic programming gives a recursive way to solve a date zero decision problem involving choice of infinite sequences, our Markov perfect equilibria can be used to construct representations of the equilibria of the date zero Stackelberg games. The Bellman-Isaacs condition established in Theorem 7.5.3 allows us to use the Markov perfect equilibrium to produce recursive representations of the Stackelberg games (7.3.1) and (7.3.3) and to argue that they have identical values. Consequently, which player chooses first does not affect the value of the game.[7]

---

[5] Or, equivalently, $(\sqrt{\beta}A', H')$ is stabilizable.

[6] Başar and Bernhard (1995) have an extension that shows when the solution of Theorem 7.6.1 is the smallest solution to (7.6.9) that is larger than the largest solution to (7.6.8). (See their Theorem 3.8'.) In this case, $\sqrt{\beta}$-stability is imposed as an additional constraint on the decision problem.

[7] A Markov perfect equilibrium *cannot* be computed by stacking and solving the Euler

7.7.2. Maximizing player chooses first

Recall Stackelberg game (7.3.1). Our candidate equilibrium has the maximizing player choose

$$u_t = -F^* x_t$$

where

$$x_{t+1} = (A - BF^*) x_t + C\epsilon_{t+1}$$

and x_0 is given. By repeated substitution, we obtain the following history-contingent rule for setting u_t

$$u_t = -F^* \left[\sum_{j=0}^{t-1} (A - BF^*)^j C\epsilon_{t-j} + (A - BF^*)^t x_0 \right]. \qquad (7.7.1)$$

Given (7.7.1), the minimizing agent selects worst-case distributions for the shocks represented using $\{m_{t+1}\}$. The minimizing process $\{m_{t+1}\}$ conditioned on the maximizing u-choice (7.7.1) implies that the minimizing conditional shock distributions are

$$\epsilon_{t+1} \sim \mathcal{N}(w_{t+1}, \Sigma)$$

for $t = 0, 1, \ldots$ where

$$w_{t+1} = K^* \left[\sum_{j=0}^{t-1} (A - BF^*)^j C\epsilon_{t-j} + (A - BF^*)^t x_0 \right]$$

and

$$\Sigma = \left(I - \frac{1}{\theta} C' P^* C \right)^{-1}. \qquad (7.7.2)$$

The implied mean for ϵ_{t+1} conditioned only on x_0 given this distorted probability is

$$K^* (A - BF^* + CK^*)^t x_0.$$

---

equations for the two players. Doing so would produce a candidate equilibrium that would not be subgame perfect. But the Bellman-Isaacs condition that pertains to two-player *zero-sum* games implies that a Markov perfect equilibrium *can* be computed by stacking and solving the Euler equations. See Başar and Bernhard (1995, chapter 2) for more discussion. Technically, the irrelevance of timing protocols for zero-sum two-player dynamic games is related to Chari, Kehoe, and Prescott's (1989, pp. 269–272) remark that time inconsistency in macroeconomics occurs only in situations in which there is *conflict* between a society's objective and those of the agents within it. Chari, Kehoe, and Prescott note that the existence of a single value function for both players makes the order of maximization irrelevant. Comparing their result to the Bellman-Isaacs condition for two-player zero-sum dynamic games reveals that to avoid time inconsistency requires only that the objective functions of different decision makers be completely *aligned*, a condition that holds when there is perfect conflict just as well as when there is perfect agreement.

Similarly, we may infer the implied distorted distribution for $\epsilon_{t+\ell}$ conditioned on date t information for $\ell > 1$.

It follows from the structure of Stackelberg game (7.3.1) that

$$\inf_{m \in \mathcal{M}} E \left[\sum_{t=0}^{\infty} \beta^t M_t \left(-\frac{z_t \cdot z_t}{2} + \beta \theta m_{t+1} \log m_{t+1} \right) | x_0 \right] \leq -E \left[\sum_{t=0}^{\infty} \beta^t \frac{z_t \cdot z_t}{2} | x_0 \right]$$

where

$$x_{t+1} = A x_t - B F^* x_t + C \epsilon_{t+1}$$
$$M_{t+1} = m_{t+1} M_t$$
$$z_t = (H - J F^*) x_t$$

and $M_0 = 1$. The bound on the right side is attained by setting $m_{t+1} = 1$ for all $t \geq 0$, which implies that $m_{t+1} \log m_{t+1} = 0$ for all $t \geq 0$. Thus, provided that the original Stackelberg game (7.3.1) has a finite value, the objective has a finite value when there is no probability distortion.

Corollary 7.7.1.   *Under the assumptions of Theorem 7.6.1, all eigenvalues of $A - B F^*$ are strictly less than $\sqrt{\beta}$ in absolute value.*

Proof. It follows from Theorem 7.6.1 and the Bellman-Issacs condition that the game has a finite value when $u_t = -F^* x_t$. The conclusion follows from the assumptions that (i) $(\sqrt{\beta} A, B)$ is stabilizable and (ii) (H, A) is detectable. As a consequence, it is feasible to $\sqrt{\beta}$-stabilize the state vector process with a time invariant control law. Also, the only way to attain a finite objective is to have the eigenvalues of $A - B F^*$ all be less that $\sqrt{\beta}$ in modulus.   ∎

This corollary allows us, *ex ante*, to limit the choice of control laws to ones that $\sqrt{\beta}$-stabilize the state. In chapter 8, we suppose that the maximizing agent submits a decision rule $u_t = -F x_t$ and, given this decision rule, the minimizing agent chooses a sequence of unconditional mean distortions for $\{\epsilon_{t+1} : t = 0, 1, ...\}$. For convenience, we ignore randomness in the investigation that we carry out in chapter 8.

7.7.3. Minimizing player chooses first

Consider next Stackelberg game (7.3.3) in which at date zero the maximizing player chooses control process given the probability distortion. We represent the equilibrium recursively by introducing a state vector process $\{\hat{x}_t\}$ that evolves as

$$\hat{x}_{t+1} = (A - B F^*) \hat{x}_t + C \epsilon_{t+1}$$

and another state vector process

$$x_{t+1} = A x_t + B u_t + C \epsilon_{t+1}$$

where $x_0 = \hat{x}_0$. Notice that no endogenous state variables are included in $\{\hat{x}_t\}$. That is, the control process cannot influence this state vector process.

The process $\{\epsilon_{t+1}\}$ is distorted as

$$\epsilon_{t+1} \sim \mathcal{N}\left(K^*\hat{x}_t, \Sigma\right)$$

where Σ is again given by (7.7.2). Therefore, we can write

$$\hat{\epsilon}_{t+1} = \epsilon_{t+1} - K^*\hat{x}_t.$$

so that $\hat{\epsilon}_{t+1}$ has conditional mean zero. Then the state variable evolution can be expressed as

$$x_{t+1} = Ax_t + CK^*\hat{x}_t + Bu_t + C\hat{\epsilon}_{t+1}$$
$$\hat{x}_{t+1} = \left(A - BF^* + CK^*\right)\hat{x}_t + C\hat{\epsilon}_{t+1}.$$

The maximizing player chooses a control process subject to this state evolution. Notice that u_t influences subsequent positions of x_t but not of $\hat{x}_t$ and therefore not subsequent values of w_{t+1}. This is a version of the Big K, little k trick mentioned earlier, where $\hat{x}$ plays the role of Big K.

Our next theorem characterizes a recursive solution of this maximization problem. It exploits the insight that the problem takes the form of what Anderson, Hansen, McGrattan, and Sargent (1996) and chapter 4 call an *augmented regulator problem*. This allows us to break it into subproblems, the first of which is simply the non-robust $(\theta = +\infty)$ version of the u-player's decision problem with $u_t = -\bar{F}x_t$ being the decision rule. This decision rule is augmented with an adjustment that is based solely on the uncontrollable state vector $\hat{x}_t$.

Theorem 7.7.1. *Consider an ordinary (non-robust) optimal linear regulator with current period objective*

$$-\frac{1}{2}\left(Hx_t + Ju_t\right)'\left(Hx_t + Ju_t\right) + \frac{\beta\theta}{2}\left(K^*\hat{x}_t\right) \cdot \left(K^*\hat{x}_t\right) \tag{7.7.3}$$

subject to the law of motion

$$\begin{pmatrix} x_{t+1} \\ \hat{x}_{t+1} \end{pmatrix} = \begin{pmatrix} A & \hat{A} \\ 0 & A^* \end{pmatrix}\begin{pmatrix} x_t \\ \hat{x}_t \end{pmatrix} + \begin{pmatrix} B \\ 0 \end{pmatrix}u_t \tag{7.7.4}$$

where $\hat{A} = CK^*$ and $A^* = A - BF^* + CK^*$. Then the optimal value function is

$$-\frac{1}{2}\left(\begin{pmatrix} x_t \\ \hat{x}_t \end{pmatrix}'\begin{pmatrix} \bar{P} & \hat{P} \\ \hat{P} & \tilde{P} \end{pmatrix}\begin{pmatrix} x_t \\ \hat{x}_t \end{pmatrix} + k^*\right)$$

where

$$\hat{P} = P^* - \bar{P}$$
$$\tilde{P} = \bar{P} - P^*$$

and where $\bar{P}$ is the stabilizing solution to the Riccati equation for the ordinary (non-robust) control problem and P^* is the stabilizing solution to the Riccati equation for the robust control problem. The constant k^* is

$$k^* = \frac{\beta}{1-\beta} \text{trace}\,(P^* C \Sigma C')$$

where $\Sigma = (I - \frac{1}{\theta} C' P^* C)^{-1}$

   The optimal control law is

$$u_t = -\bar{F} x_t - \hat{F} \hat{x}_t$$

where

$$\bar{F} = \left(J'J + \beta B' \bar{P} B \right)^{-1} \left(\beta B' \bar{P} A + J'H \right)$$
$$\hat{F} = \left(J'J + \beta B' \bar{P} B \right)^{-1} \left(\beta B' \bar{P} \hat{A} + \beta B' P^* A^* \right).$$

Moreover, $u_t = -\bar{F} x_t$ is the control law for the ordinary (non-robust) problem and $\hat{F} + \bar{F} = F^*$ where $u_t = -F^* x_t$ is the control law for the robust control problem.

Proof. The matrices $\bar{P}$ and P^* are fixed points for the Riccati equations for the ordinary and robust linear regulators, respectively, so that $\bar{P} = T(\bar{P})$ and $P^* = T \circ \mathcal{D}(P^*)$. The proof proceeds by solving the augmented linear regulator defined by problem $(7.7.3)$, $(7.7.4)$, which leads us to compute $\bar{P}, \hat{P}, \tilde{P}$ recursively, and then by verifying that these matrices solve the following equations $\bar{P} = T(\bar{P})$, $\bar{P} + \hat{P} = T \circ \mathcal{D}(\bar{P} + \hat{P})$, $\tilde{P} - \bar{P} = T \circ \mathcal{D}(\tilde{P} - \bar{P})$.

   Because the optimization problem $(7.7.3)$, $(7.7.4)$ is an augmented linear regulator problem (see chapter 4), we can solve it in three steps. In the first step, we set $\hat{x}_0 = 0$. This makes the sequence $\hat{x}_t$ disappear from the problem. Let $\bar{P}$ denote the matrix that stabilizes the corresponding deflating subspace so that $\bar{P}$ solves the algebraic Riccati equation $\bar{P} = T(\bar{P})$ or

$$P = \beta \left[A' - H'J \left(J'J \right)^{-1} B' \right] \left[P - \beta P B \left(J'J + \beta B'PB \right)^{-1} B'P \right]$$
$$\left[A - B \left(J'J \right)^{-1} J'H \right] + H'H - H'J \left(J'J \right)^{-1} J'H.$$

Let $\bar{F}$ denote the control law for the ordinary (non-robust) control problem given by

$$\bar{F} = \left(J'J + \beta B' \bar{P} B \right)^{-1} \left(\beta B' \bar{P} A + J'H \right).$$

Define $\bar{A} = A - B\bar{F}$. The matrix $\bar{P}$ also solves the Sylvester equation

$$P = \left(H - J\bar{F}\right)' \left(H - J\bar{F}\right) + \beta\bar{A}'P\bar{A}.$$

In the second step, we activate the uncontrollable state $\hat{x}_t$ and compute $\hat{P}$. The optimal control law is

$$u_t = -\bar{F}x_t - \hat{F}\hat{x}_t$$

and $P = \hat{P}$ solves the Sylvester equation

$$\beta\left(A - B\bar{F}\right)'\left(\bar{P}\hat{A} + PA^*\right) = P.$$

Equivalently, $P = \hat{P}$ solves

$$\beta\left[A' - H'J\left(J'J\right)^{-1}B'\right]\left[\bar{P} - \beta\bar{P}B\left(J'J + \beta B'\bar{P}B\right)^{-1}B'\bar{P}\right]\hat{A}$$
$$+ \beta\left[A' - H'J\left(J'J\right)^{-1}B'\right]\left[P - \beta\bar{P}B\left(J'J + \beta B'\bar{P}B\right)^{-1}B'P\right]A^* = P.$$

The matrix $\hat{P}$ that solves this Sylvester equation equals $\hat{P} = P^* - \bar{P}$, where P^* solves the Riccati equation $P^* = T \circ \mathcal{D}(P^*)$ that is associated with the robust control problem, which is

$$P^* = \beta\left[A' - H'J(J'J)^{-1}B'\right]$$
$$\left[P^* - \beta P^*\left(B \quad C\right)\begin{pmatrix} J'J + \beta B'P^*B & \beta B'P^*C \\ \beta C'P^*B & -\beta\theta I + \beta C'P^*C \end{pmatrix}^{-1}\begin{pmatrix} B' \\ C' \end{pmatrix}P^*\right]$$
$$\left[A - BJ(J'J)^{-1}J'H\right] + H'H - H'J(J'J)^{-1}J'H.$$

In appendix A, we verify that $\hat{P} = P^* - \bar{P}$. The portion of the control law that feeds back onto $\hat{x}$ is

$$\hat{F} = \left(J'J + \beta B'\bar{P}B\right)^{-1}\left(\beta B'\bar{P}\hat{A} + \beta B'\hat{P}A^*\right).$$

In the third step, we compute $\tilde{P}$, which solves the Sylvester equation

$$P = -\theta K^{*'}K^* + \beta A^{*'}PA^* + \beta\hat{A}'\left[\bar{P} - \beta\bar{P}B(J'J + \beta B'\bar{P}B)^{-1}B'\bar{P}\right]\hat{A}$$
$$+ \beta A^{*'}\left[\hat{P} - \beta\hat{P}B(J'J + \beta B'\bar{P}B)^{-1}B'\bar{P}\right]\hat{A}$$
$$+ \beta\hat{A}'\left[\hat{P} - \bar{P}B(J'J + \beta B'\bar{P}B)^{-1}B'\hat{P}\right]A^*.$$

The constant term k^* solves the fixed point equation

$$k = \beta k + \beta\text{trace}\left[\begin{pmatrix} \bar{P} & \hat{P} \\ \hat{P} & \tilde{P} \end{pmatrix}\begin{pmatrix} C \\ C \end{pmatrix}\Sigma\left(C' \quad C'\right)\right] = \beta k + \beta\text{trace}\left(P^*C\Sigma C'\right),$$

where P^* is the matrix used to represent the robust value function. ∎

The optimization problem studied in Theorem 7.7.1 gives a decision rule $u_t = -\begin{bmatrix} \bar{F} & \hat{F} \end{bmatrix} \begin{bmatrix} x_t \\ \hat{x}_t \end{bmatrix}$ where $F^* = \bar{F} + \hat{F}$. Thus, the theorem shows that the adjustment $\hat{F} = F^* - \bar{F}$ in the decision needed to accommodate misspecification can be viewed as the optimal response to a stochastic evolution with an additional exogenous state vector. The term $\hat{F}$ is the so-called feedforward adjustment for exogenous state dynamics. When $x_0 = \hat{x}_0$, $x_t = \hat{x}_t$ as an equilibrium outcome. Thus, in this equilibrium,

$$u_t = -\bar{F}x_t - \hat{F}\hat{x}_t = -F^*x_t$$

where the right-hand side is the robust control law from the Markov perfect equilibrium.

7.7.4. Bayesian interpretation of robust decision rule

Since $\hat{x}_t$ cannot be influenced by the control u_t, we would have computed the same optimal control law if we had used

$$-\frac{1}{2}z_t \cdot z_t = -\frac{1}{2}\left(Hx_t + Ju_t\right)'\left(Hx_t + Ju_t\right)$$

as the period utility function instead of the one maintained in Theorem 7.7.1. This change will alter the value function, but not the optimal control law. Thus, an outcome of Theorem 7.7.1 is an alternative stochastic specification for $\{\epsilon_{t+1}\}$ for which a robust control law (appropriately decomposed) is optimal. Under this alternative specification, the process $\{\epsilon_{t+1}\}$ is no longer i.i.d. Instead, it is predictable and has a larger conditional covariance matrix. When this choice of an alternative probability distribution for $\{\epsilon_{t+1}\}$ is viewed as an alternative "prior" to our benchmark specification, the decision rule of Theorem 7.7.1 is the resulting Bayesian decision rule. This *ex post* Bayesian construction is familiar from the statistical decision theory developed in Blackwell and Girschik (1954) and Ferguson (1967). They use such a construction to establish the *admissibility* of a decision rule, which requires that the decision rule cannot be dominated over a family of possible probability distributions.

Appendix B links the *ex post* Bayesian interpretation to a version of certainty equivalence that Hansen and Sargent (2005a) also discussed.

7.8. Relation between multiplier and constraint Stackelberg problems

In this section, we relate the equilibrium outcome from the multiplier game (7.3.1) to the equilibrium of the following two-player zero-sum game defined in

Definition 7.8.1. A Stackelberg *constraint* game is

$$\sup_{u \in \mathcal{U}} \inf_{m \in \mathcal{M}} E\left[\sum_{t=0}^{\infty} \beta^t M_t \left(-\frac{z_t \cdot z_t}{2}\right)\right] \tag{7.8.1}$$

where the optimization of both players is subject to

$$x_{t+1} = Ax_t + Bu_t + C\epsilon_{t+1}$$
$$M_{t+1} = M_t m_{t+1}$$
$$z_t = Hx_t + Ju_t \tag{7.8.2}$$
$$\eta \geq E\left[\sum_{t=0}^{\infty} \beta^{t+1} M_t m_{t+1} \log m_{t+1} | x_0\right].$$

The last inequality in (7.8.2) is a constraint on discounted entropy. It replaces the θ parameter penalty on the time t increment to entropy in the corresponding Stackelberg multiplier game (7.8.1). By interchanging the order of maximization and minimization, we can obtain another constraint game that corresponds to the multiplier Stackelberg game (7.3.3).

To relate the equilibrium of the multiplier game (7.8.1) to the constraint game defined in Definition 7.8.1, we begin by considering the equilibrium solution $\{m_{t+1}^* : t = 0, 1, ...\}$ associated with the probability distortions for a given choice of $\theta > \underline{\theta}$ in the multiplier game. Construct a corresponding measure of discounted entropy by

$$\eta = E\left[\sum_{t=0}^{\infty} \beta^{t+1} M_t^* m_{t+1}^* \log m_{t+1}^*\right] | x_0$$

where $M_{t+1}^* = m_{t+1}^* M_t^*$ and $M_0^* = 1$. Define

$$\mathcal{M}(\eta) = \left\{m \in \mathcal{M} : E\left[\sum_{t=0}^{\infty} \beta^{t+1} M_t^* m_{t+1}^* \log m_{t+1}^* \Big| x_0\right] \leq \eta\right\}.$$

In this way, we can find an entropy constraint that gives a ball of specification errors associated with each admissible value of θ. Chapter 8 develops this connection in more detail in the context of a frequency domain specification of Stackelberg multiplier and constraint games.

The two-player game in Definition 7.8.1 is a version of the max-min expected utility model for expressing ambiguity aversion that Gilboa and Schmeidler (1989) axiomatized.[8]

7.8.1. Dynamic consistency

The dynamic consistency of the multiplier games follows directly once we have verified the Bellman-Isaacs condition. It takes a different argument to present a sense in which the equilibrium of the constraint game is dynamically consistent. We do so by constructing an additional state variable, continuation entropy, and by describing its law of motion. The remainder of this subsection describes a recursive formulation of the constraint problem stated in Definition 7.8.1.[9] Define a time t version of *continuation entropy* (7.8.3) as

$$R_t = E \left[\sum_{\tau=1}^{\infty} \beta^\tau \frac{M_{t+\tau-1}}{M_t} m_{t+\tau} \log m_{t+\tau} | \epsilon_t, \epsilon_{t-1}, ..., \epsilon_1, x_0 \right]. \qquad (7.8.3)$$

Evidently,

$$R_t = \beta E \left(m_{t+1} \left[\log \left(m_{t+1} \right) + R_{t+1} \right] | \epsilon_t, \epsilon_{t-1}, ..., \epsilon_1, x_0 \right).$$

For the recursive formulation, we follow Hansen, Sargent, Turmuhambetova and Williams (2006)

$$MV(x, R) = \sup_u \inf_{\check{m}, \check{R}} M \left(-\frac{1}{2} z' z + \beta E \left[\check{m} \left[\log \check{m} + V \left(\check{x}, \check{R} \right) \right] \right] \right) \qquad (7.8.4)$$

subject to

$$R = \beta E \left(\check{m} \left[\log \left(\check{m} \right) + \check{R} \right] \right). \qquad (7.8.5)$$

and counterparts to the remaining constraints in (7.8.2), where $\check{m}$ can be a function of ϵ but must have expectation equal to unity. Equation (7.8.5) is a "promise keeping" constraint on the allocation of entropy R between distortion $\check{m}$ to the next period transition density and the allowable distortion from tomorrow on $\check{R}$. The minimizing agent can allocate continuation entropy over time, but must respect constraint (7.8.5). In this construction, $V_R(x, R)$ equals minus θ, interpreted as the Lagrange multiplier on the last constraint in (7.8.5). Hansen, Sargent, Turmuhambetova and Williams (2006) show that the multiplier Markov perfect equilibrium also solve this recursive game where θ equals minus $V_R(x, R)$ and is interpreted as the Lagrange multiplier on the last constraint in (7.8.5).

---

[8] Maccheroni, Marinacci, and Rustichini (2006a) have axiomatized preferences expressing ambiguity aversion that can be represented as versions of Stackelberg game (7.8.1).

[9] See Hansen, Sargent, Turmuhambetova, and Williams (2006) for an extended discussion about the subject of this section.

7.9. Miscellaneous details

7.9.1. Checking for the breakdown point

In section 7.4, we mentioned the breakdown point $\underline{\theta}$, a lower bound on θ that is required to keep the objective of the two-person zero-sum game convex in m_{t+1} and concave in u_t. The breakdown point will play an important role in arguments that we develop in chapter 8. Here we briefly indicate a check that $\theta > \underline{\theta}$. If we take a fixed point $P^* = T \circ \mathcal{D}(P^*)$, we can verify that $\theta > \underline{\theta}$ by checking whether

$$\log \det (\theta I - C'P^*C) > -\infty \tag{7.9.1}$$

or, equivalently, whether the eigenvalues of $(\theta I - C'P^*C)$ are all positive. This follows from Theorem 8.8.2. Of course, this check requires that we can compute a fixed point of $T \circ \mathcal{D}$, which might not be possible for $\theta < \underline{\theta}$. An alternative and, in a sense, more practical way to assure that $\theta > \underline{\theta}$ is to check the condition

$$\log \det (\theta I - C'P_j C) > -\infty \tag{7.9.2}$$

for each iterate $P_j, j \geq 1$, where P_j is computed as $P_{j+1} = T \circ \mathcal{D}(P_j)$ starting from $P_0 = 0$.

The $T \circ \mathcal{D}$ operator can be calculated in one step as

$$\begin{aligned}
T \circ \mathcal{D}(P) = H'H - H'J(J'J)^{-1}J'H + \beta \left[A' - H'J(J'J)^{-1}B' \right] \\
\times \left[P - \beta P (B \quad C) \begin{pmatrix} J'J + \beta P'BP & \beta B'PC \\ \beta C'PB & -\beta \theta I + \beta C'PC \end{pmatrix}^{-1} \right. \\
\left. \begin{pmatrix} B' \\ C' \end{pmatrix} P \right] [A - B(J'J)^{-1}J'H].
\end{aligned} \tag{7.9.3}$$

7.9.2. Policy improvement algorithm

For a given θ, a policy improvement algorithm for computing a robust decision rule iterates on the operators $\mathcal{S}$ and $\mathcal{F}$

1. For a fixed decision rule F, define the associated operator $\mathcal{S}$, and compute the fixed point $P = \mathcal{S}(P)$.

2. Compute a new decision rule $F = \mathcal{F}(P)$.

3. Iterate to convergence on steps 1 and 2.

Step 1 computes a value function attained by using a fixed decision rule F forever, where the 'distortion operator' $\mathcal{D}$ evaluates future utilities. Step 2 finds an F that solves a two-period optimum problem, with $\mathcal{D}(P)$ being used to form the continuation value function. This is an efficient algorithm for computing a robust rule.[10] The operator $\mathcal{S}$ is known as a risk-sensitivity operator.[11]

7.10. Concluding remarks

In addition to justifying convenient algorithms for computing robust decision rules that we had mentioned earlier in chapter 2, we have shown that multiplier games with different timing protocols have identical outcomes and identical recursive representations of equilibrium decision rules. In section 7.8, we have also shown how η and θ can be chosen to make outcomes of multiplier and constraint games equivalent.

These relationships are useful for interpreting robust decision problems. Different games are useful for representing various interesting features. For example, the Stackelberg constraint game defined in Definition 7.8.1 is linked directly to theories of ambiguity aversion featured in the max-min expected utility theory of Gilboa and Schmeidler (1989) and the Stackelberg multiplier game (7.8.1) is linked to the multiplier preferences axiomatized by Maccheroni, Marinacci, and Rustichini (2006a). As another example, the Stackelberg game (7.3.3) in which the minimizing player chooses first provides an *ex post* Bayesian interpretation of a robust decision rule by displaying a 'prior' for which a robust decision rule is optimal. Consequently, a robust decision rule is admissible in the sense of statistical decision theory, as mentioned in subsection 7.7.4.

We shall also use game (7.3.3) when we interpret a form of precautionary savings that a concern for robustness imparts to a permanent income consumer and when we study asset pricing in an economy where a representative agent is concerned about model misspecification.[12] We shall use the equivalence of outcomes from alternative games in chapter 16 when we formulate a robust version of a two-player game in which one of the players is worried about possible model misspecification.

It is advisable to bear in mind the equivalence relationships that we have established here when we move on to study frequency domain representations of robust decision rules in the next chapter. There we will focus almost exclusively on Stackelberg multiplier games as we seek frequency domain rep-

---

[10] Other efficient algorithms use a doubling algorithm to compute the fixed point of $T \circ \mathcal{D}$. See chapter 4.

[11] It will recur as the $\mathcal{R}$ operator of chapter 14.

[12] Also see Barillas, Hansen, and Sargent (2007).

resentations of objective functions and of worst-case models. We accomplish this by adopting two simplifications that the analysis of this chapter justifies. First, we restrict the maximizing agent to choose a time invariant control law as a function of the state, and, second, we restrict the minimizing agent to choose only sequences of means of the shocks $\{\epsilon_{t+1}\}$ conditioned on date zero information when evaluating the objective at date zero using a candidate control law. Restricting the choice of the minimizing player in this way is simpler than letting him choose distortions to the conditional densities, but he ends up choosing the same robust control law derived in this chapter under the more general choice set. This allows us to pose the game as a deterministic one and to use Fourier transform methods to characterize worst-case sequences for alternative decision rules. This lets us construct frequency domain characterizations of robustness to misspecification.

A. Details of a proof of Theorem 7.7.1

This appendix verifies a key assertion made in the proof of Theorem 7.7.1.[13] To verify that $\hat{P} = P^* - \bar{P}$, we make use of the following identities that characterize $\hat{P}, P^*$, and $\bar{P}$.

1. The matrix $\hat{P}$ solves

$$
\beta \left(A' - H'J \left(J'J \right)^{-1} B' \right) \left(\bar{P} - \beta \bar{P}B \left(J'J + \beta B'\bar{P}B \right)^{-1} B'\bar{P} \right) \hat{A}
$$
$$
+ \beta \left(A' - H'J \left(J'J \right)^{-1} B' \right) \left(\hat{P} - \beta \bar{P}B \left(J'J + \beta B'\bar{P}B \right)^{-1} B'\hat{P} \right) A^* = \hat{P}
$$

where

$$
A^* = \left(I + \left[\beta B \left(J'J \right)^{-1} B' - \frac{1}{\theta}CC' \right] P^* \right)^{-1} \left[A - B \left(J'J \right)^{-1} J'H \right]
$$

$$
\hat{A} = \frac{1}{\theta}CC'P^*A^*.
$$

Therefore, the matrix $\hat{P}$ solves

$$
\beta \left(A' - H'J \left(J'J \right)^{-1} B' \right) \left[\bar{P}\frac{1}{\theta}CC'P^* - \beta \bar{P}B \left(J'J + \beta B'\bar{P}B \right)^{-1} B'\bar{P}\frac{1}{\theta}CC'P^*
$$
$$
+ \hat{P} - \beta \bar{P}B \left(J'J + \beta B'\bar{P}B \right)^{-1} B'\hat{P} \right] A^* = \hat{P}
$$

which yields

$$
\beta(A' - H'J(J'J)^{-1}B')
$$
$$
\left[\bar{P}\frac{1}{\theta}CC'P^* - \beta\bar{P}B(J'J + \beta B'\bar{P}B)^{-1}B'\bar{P}\frac{1}{\theta}CC'P^* + \hat{P}
$$
$$
- \beta\bar{P}B(J'J + \beta B'\bar{P}B)^{-1}B'\hat{P} \right] \left(I + \left[\beta B(J'J)^{-1}B' - \frac{1}{\theta}CC' \right] P^* \right)^{-1} \quad (7.\text{A}.1)
$$
$$
\times \left[A - B(J'J)^{-1}J'H \right] = \hat{P}.
$$

---

[13] We are very grateful to Tomasz Piskorski for his help in verifying these equalities.

2. The matrix P^* solves

$$\beta\left[A' - H'J(J'J)^{-1}B'\right]P^*\left(I + \left[\beta B(J'J)^{-1}B' - \frac{1}{\theta}CC'\right]P^*\right)^{-1}$$
$$\left[A - B(J'J)^{-1}J'H\right] \tag{7.A.2}$$
$$+ H'H - H'J(J'J)^{-1}J'H = P^*.$$

where

$$\left(I + \left[\beta B\left(J'J\right)^{-1}B' - \frac{1}{\theta}CC'\right]P^*\right)^{-1} =$$
$$\left[I - \beta\left(\begin{bmatrix} B & C \end{bmatrix}\right)\left(\begin{bmatrix} JJ' + \beta B'P^*B & \beta B'P^*C \\ \beta C'P^*B & -\beta\theta I + \beta C'P^*C \end{bmatrix}\right)^{-1}\left(\begin{bmatrix} B' \\ C' \end{bmatrix}\right)P^*\right].$$

3. The matrix $\bar{P}$ solves

$$\beta\left(A' - H'J\left(J'J\right)^{-1}B'\right)\left(\bar{P} - \beta\bar{P}B\left(J'J + \beta B'\bar{P}B\right)^{-1}B'\bar{P}\right)$$
$$\times \left(A - B\left(J'J\right)^{-1}J'H\right) + H'H - H'J\left(J'J\right)^{-1}J'H = \bar{P}. \tag{7.A.3}$$

We weave together these three facts to compose the following

Proof. Subtracting (7.A.3) from (7.A.2) yields

$$\beta\left[A' - H'J\left(J'J\right)^{-1}B'\right]\left(P^*\left(I + \left[\beta B\left(J'J\right)^{-1}B' - \frac{1}{\theta}CC'\right]P^*\right)^{-1}\right.$$
$$\left. - \left(\bar{P} - \beta\bar{P}B\left(J'J + \beta B'\bar{P}B\right)^{-1}B'\bar{P}\right)\right)\left[A - B\left(J'J\right)^{-1}J'H\right] = P^* - \bar{P}$$

which is equivalent to

$$\beta\left[A' - H'J(J'J)^{-1}B'\right]$$
$$\times \left(P^* - \left(\bar{P} - \beta\bar{P}B(J'J + \beta B'\bar{P}B)^{-1}B'\bar{P}\right)\right.$$
$$\times \left(I + \left[\beta B(J'J)^{-1}B' - \frac{1}{\theta}CC'\right]P^*\right))$$
$$\times \left(I + \left[\beta B(J'J)^{-1}B' - \frac{1}{\theta}CC'\right]P^*\right)^{-1}\left[A - B(J'J)^{-1}J'H\right] = P^* - \bar{P}$$

or

$$\beta\left[A' - H'J(J'J)^{-1}B'\right]Y$$
$$\times \left(I + \left[\beta B(J'J)^{-1}B' - \frac{1}{\theta}CC'\right]P^*\right)^{-1}\left[A - B(J'J)^{-1}J'H\right] = P^* - \bar{P} \tag{7.A.4}$$

where

$$Y = P^* - \left(\bar{P} - \beta\bar{P}B(J'J + \beta B'\bar{P}B)^{-1}B'\bar{P}\right)\left(I + \left[\beta B(J'J)^{-1}B' - \frac{1}{\theta}CC'\right]P^*\right).$$

Note that

$$
\begin{aligned}
Y &= P^* - \left(\bar{P} - \beta\bar{P}B(J'J + \beta B'\bar{P}B)^{-1}B'\bar{P}\right)\left(I + \left[\beta B(J'J)^{-1}B' - \frac{1}{\theta}CC'\right]P^*\right)\\
&= \left(P^* - \bar{P}\right) - \bar{P}\beta B(J'J)^{-1}B'P^* + \bar{P}\frac{1}{\theta}CC'P^* + \beta\bar{P}B(J'J + \beta B'\bar{P}B)^{-1}B'\bar{P}\\
&\quad + \beta\bar{P}B(J'J + \beta B'\bar{P}B)^{-1}B'\bar{P}\beta B(J'J)^{-1}B'P^*\\
&\quad - \beta\bar{P}B(J'J + \beta B'\bar{P}B)^{-1}B'\bar{P}\frac{1}{\theta}CC'P^*\\
&= \bar{P}\frac{1}{\theta}CC'P^* - \beta\bar{P}B(J'J + \beta B'\bar{P}B)^{-1}B'\bar{P}\frac{1}{\theta}CC'P^* + \left(P^* - \bar{P}\right)\\
&\quad + \beta\bar{P}B(J'J + \beta B'\bar{P}B)^{-1}B'\bar{P} + \beta\bar{P}B(J'J + \beta B'\bar{P}B)^{-1}B'\bar{P}\beta B(J'J)^{-1}B'\\
&\quad - \bar{P}\beta B(J'J)^{-1}B'P^*.
\end{aligned}
$$

Thus, we have

$$
\begin{aligned}
Y &= \bar{P}\frac{1}{\theta}CC'P^* - \beta\bar{P}B(J'J + \beta B'\bar{P}B)^{-1}B'\bar{P}\frac{1}{\theta}CC'P^*\\
&\quad + \left(P^* - \bar{P}\right) + Z
\end{aligned}
\tag{7.A.5}
$$

where

$$
\begin{aligned}
Z &= \beta\bar{P}B(J'J + \beta B'\bar{P}B)^{-1}B'\bar{P} + \beta\bar{P}B(J'J + \beta B'\bar{P}B)^{-1}B'\bar{P}\beta B(J'J)^{-1}B'\\
&\quad - \bar{P}\beta B(J'J)^{-1}B'P^*.
\end{aligned}
$$

Now note

$$
\begin{aligned}
Z &= \beta\bar{P}B(J'J + \beta B'\bar{P}B)^{-1}B'\bar{P} + \beta\bar{P}B(J'J + \beta B'\bar{P}B)^{-1}B'\bar{P}\beta B(J'J)^{-1}B'\\
&\quad - \bar{P}\beta B(J'J)^{-1}B'P^* = -\beta\bar{P}B(J'J + \beta B'\bar{P}B)^{-1}B'(P^* - \bar{P})\\
&\quad + \beta\bar{P}B(J'J + \beta B'\bar{P}B)^{-1}B'P^* + \beta\bar{P}B(J'J + \beta B'\bar{P}B)^{-1}B'\bar{P}\beta B(J'J)^{-1}B'P^*\\
&\quad - \bar{P}\beta B(J'J)^{-1}B'P^* = -\beta\bar{P}B(J'J + \beta B'\bar{P}B)^{-1}B'(P^* - \bar{P})\\
&\quad + \left[\beta\bar{P}B(J'J + \beta B'\bar{P}B)^{-1}(I + \beta B'\bar{P}B(J'J)^{-1}) - \beta\bar{P}B(J'J)^{-1}\right]B'P^*.
\end{aligned}
\tag{7.A.6}
$$

Using the fact that $I + \beta B'\bar{P}B(J'J)^{-1} = (J'J + \beta B'\bar{P}B)(J'J)^{-1}$ gives us

$$
\begin{aligned}
&\left[\beta\bar{P}B(J'J + \beta B'\bar{P}B)^{-1}(I + \beta B'\bar{P}B(J'J)^{-1}) - \beta\bar{P}B(J'J)^{-1}\right]B'P^*\\
&= \left[\beta\bar{P}B(J'J + \beta B'\bar{P}B)^{-1}(J'J + \beta B'\bar{P}B)(J'J)^{-1} - \beta\bar{P}B(J'J)^{-1}\right]B'P^*\\
&= \left(\beta\bar{P}B(J'J)^{-1} - \beta\bar{P}B(J'J)^{-1}\right)P^* = 0.
\end{aligned}
\tag{7.A.7}
$$

Substituting $(7.A.7)$ back to $(7.A.6)$ yields

$$
Z = -\beta\bar{P}B(J'J + \beta B'\bar{P}B)^{-1}B'(P^* - \bar{P}).
\tag{7.A.8}
$$

Substituting $(7.A.8)$ into $(7.A.5)$ yields

$$
\begin{aligned}
Y &\bar{P}\frac{1}{\theta}CC'P^* - \beta\bar{P}B(J'J + \beta B'\bar{P}B)^{-1}B'\bar{P}\frac{1}{\theta}CC'P^* + \left(P^* - \bar{P}\right)\\
&\quad - \beta\bar{P}B(J'J + \beta B'\bar{P}B)^{-1}B'(P^* - \bar{P}).
\end{aligned}
\tag{7.A.9}
$$

Finally, substituting $(7.A.9)$ into $(7.A.4)$ yields

$$
\beta \left[A' - H'J(J'J)^{-1}B' \right]
$$
$$
\times \left[\bar{P}\frac{1}{\theta}CC'P^* - \beta\bar{P}B(J'J + \beta B'\bar{P}B)^{-1}B'\bar{P}\frac{1}{\theta}CC'P^* + \left(P^* - \bar{P} \right) \right.
$$
$$
\left. - \beta\bar{P}B(J'J + \beta B'\bar{P}B)^{-1}B'(P^* - \bar{P}) \right] \qquad (7.A.10)
$$
$$
\times \left(I + \left[\beta B(J'J)^{-1}B' - \frac{1}{\theta}CC' \right] P^* \right)^{-1} \left[A - B(J'J)^{-1}J'H \right]
$$
$$
= P^* - \bar{P}.
$$

But this is just Riccati equation $(7.A.1)$ with $\hat{P} = P^* - \bar{P}$, therefore $(P^* - \bar{P})$ solves the Riccati equation for $\hat{P}$, so $\hat{P} = P^* - \bar{P}$. ∎

B. Certainty equivalence

A certainty equivalence result utilized by Hansen and Sargent (2005a) has a very similar structure to Theorem 7.7.1. A wide class of decision problems in macroeconomics automatically takes the form of a discounted augmented linear regulator where the objective function can be expressed as

$$
- \begin{bmatrix} x_{10} \\ x_{20} \end{bmatrix}' \begin{bmatrix} P_{11} & P_{12} \\ P_{21} & P_{22} \end{bmatrix} \begin{bmatrix} x_{10} \\ x_{20} \end{bmatrix} - \rho
$$
$$
= E_0 \sum_{t=0}^{\infty} \beta^t \left\{ - \begin{bmatrix} x_{1t} \\ x_{2t} \end{bmatrix}' \begin{bmatrix} R_{11} & R_{12} \\ R_{21} & R_{22} \end{bmatrix} \begin{bmatrix} x_{1t} \\ x_{2t} \end{bmatrix} - u_t Q u_t \right\} \qquad (7.B.1)
$$

and the transition law is

$$
\begin{bmatrix} x_{1t+1} \\ x_{2t+1} \end{bmatrix} = \begin{bmatrix} A_{11} & A_{12} \\ 0 & A_{22} \end{bmatrix} \begin{bmatrix} x_{1t} \\ x_{2t} \end{bmatrix} + \begin{bmatrix} B_1 \\ 0 \end{bmatrix} u_t + \begin{bmatrix} 0 \\ C_2 \end{bmatrix} \epsilon_{t+1} \qquad (7.B.2)
$$

where ϵ_{t+1} is an i.i.d. random vector with mean zero and identity covariance matrix. The optimal (non-robust) decision rule is

$$
u_t = -F_1 x_{1t} - F_2 x_{2t} \qquad (7.B.3)
$$

where F_1 and F_2 can be computed recursively as in the augmented linear regulator in chapter 4; F_1 is the feedback part and F_2 is the feedforward part.

For a given $\theta \in (\underline{\theta}, \infty)$, we can solve a robust linear regulator and obtain another decision rule

$$
u_t = -\tilde{F}_1 x_{1t} - \tilde{F}_2 x_{2t} \qquad (7.B.4)
$$

of the form $(7.B.3)$ where now $\tilde{F}_1$ and $\tilde{F}_2$ depend on θ and C_2. Let $w_{t+1} = \begin{bmatrix} \tilde{K}_1 & \tilde{K}_2 \end{bmatrix} \begin{bmatrix} x_{1t} \\ x_{2t} \end{bmatrix}$ be the associated worst-case shock. We can apply the method used in Theorem 7.7.1 to construct a law of motion that is distorted relative to the approximating model $(7.B.2)$ and for which an ordinary (non-robust) decision rule matches the robust rule $(7.B.4)$ for a given θ. Form the law of motion for the synthetic variable

$$\begin{bmatrix} \hat{x}_{1t+1} \\ \hat{x}_{2t+1} \end{bmatrix} = \begin{bmatrix} A_{11} - B_1 F_1 & A_{12} - B_1 F_2 \\ C_2 K_1 & A_{22} + C_2 K_2 \end{bmatrix} \begin{bmatrix} \hat{x}_{1t} \\ \hat{x}_{2t} \end{bmatrix}. \tag{7.B.5}$$

Now alter the law of motion for x_1 in problem $(7.B.1)$-$(7.B.2)$ to be

$$x_{1t+1} = A_{11} x_{1t} + A_{12} \hat{x}_{2t} + B_1 u_t \tag{7.B.6}$$

and use $\hat{x}_{2t}$ to replace x_{2t} in the objective $(7.B.1)$. Solve the ordinary control problem with $(7.B.5)$, $(7.B.6)$ replacing $(7.B.2)$. This again is a discounted augmented linear regulator problem. The decision rule is

$$u_t = -F_1 x_{1t} - \hat{F}_{21} \hat{x}_{1t} - \hat{F}_{22} \hat{x}_{2t}. \tag{7.B.7}$$

Equating $\hat{x}_t$ to x_t, we obtain

$$u_t = -\left(F_1 + \hat{F}_{21}\right) x_{1t} - \hat{F}_{22} x_{2t}. \tag{7.B.8}$$

Then

$$\tilde{F}_1 = F_1 + \hat{F}_{21}, \tilde{F}_2 = \hat{F}_{22}. \tag{7.B.9}$$

The distortion of the law of motion for the x_{2t} component, which enters through the $\hat{F}_{2i}, i = 1, 2$ terms, promotes robustness.

C. Useful formulas

This appendix provides two sets of convenient formulas for computing decision rules that solve the game

$$-x' P^* x = \max_u \min_w \left[-(Hx + Ju)'(Hx + Ju) + \beta \theta w' w - \beta y' P^* y \right] \tag{7.C.1}$$

where the maximization is subject to

$$y = Ax + Bu + Cw.$$

For the purpose of displaying these formulas, notice that the one-period loss function in $(7.C.1)$ can be represented as

$$\begin{aligned} r(x, u) &\equiv (Hx + Ju)'(Hx + Ju) \\ &= \begin{bmatrix} x \\ u \end{bmatrix}' \begin{bmatrix} H'H & H'J \\ J'H & J'J \end{bmatrix} \begin{bmatrix} x \\ u \end{bmatrix} \\ &\equiv \begin{bmatrix} x \\ u \end{bmatrix}' \begin{bmatrix} \overline{Q} & W \\ W' & R \end{bmatrix} \begin{bmatrix} x \\ u \end{bmatrix}, \end{aligned}$$

where $\overline{Q} = H'H, W = H'J, R = J'J$. As in chapter 4, we transform the problem to one that eliminates cross-products between states and controls. Define

$$\begin{aligned} Q &= \overline{Q} - WR^{-1}W' \\ \tilde{A} &= A - BR^{-1}W' \\ \tilde{u}_t &= u_t + R^{-1}W' x_t. \end{aligned} \tag{7.C.2}$$

Then

$$x_{t+1} = \tilde{A}x_t + B\tilde{u}_t + Cw_{t+1} \tag{7.C.3}$$

and

$$\tilde{r}(x,\tilde{u}) = r(x,u) = \begin{bmatrix} x \\ \tilde{u} \end{bmatrix}' \begin{bmatrix} Q & 0 \\ 0 & R \end{bmatrix} \begin{bmatrix} x \\ \tilde{u} \end{bmatrix}. \tag{7.C.4}$$

The Bellman equation (7.C.1) is equivalent to

$$-x'Px = \max_{\tilde{u}} \min_w \left\{ -\tilde{r}(x,\tilde{u}) + \beta\theta w'w - \beta y'Py \right\} \tag{7.C.5}$$

where

$$y = \tilde{A}x + B\tilde{u} + Cw. \tag{7.C.6}$$

In the problem on the right of (7.C.5), the minimizing agent moves second, taking as given the feedback rule $\tilde{u} = -Fx$ chosen by the maximizing agent. By working backwards, we break the problem on the right of (7.C.5) into these two parts

1. The problem for the minimizing agent reduces to

$$\mathcal{J} = \min_w \left[\theta w'w - y'Py \right] \tag{7.C.7}$$

   subject to

$$y = \check{A}x + Cw \tag{7.C.8}$$

   where $\check{A} = \tilde{A} - BF$ and F is to be chosen in the problem in part 2. The minimizing w is

$$w = \theta^{-1}\left(I - \theta^{-1}C'PC\right)^{-1}C'P\check{A}x. \tag{7.C.9}$$

   Let

$$\mathcal{D}(P) = P + PC\left(\theta I - C'PC\right)^{-1}C'P. \tag{7.C.10}$$

   The minimized value of the problem can be expressed as

$$\mathcal{J} = -x'\check{A}'\mathcal{D}(P)\check{A}x$$

   or as

$$\mathcal{J} = -y'\mathcal{D}(P)y \tag{7.C.11}$$

   where in (7.C.11), y is to be evaluated under the approximating model $y = Ax$, *not* under the distorted model (7.C.8). Under the approximating model, (7.C.11) is a conservative continuation value for the problem of the maximizing agent.

2. Part 2 of the problem hands this conservative valuation function and the approximating model to the maximizing agent. Working backwards, the problem of the maximizing agent can be expressed as

$$\max_{\tilde{u}} \left[-x'Qx - \tilde{u}'R\tilde{u} - \beta y'\mathcal{D}(P)y \right] \tag{7.C.12}$$

   subject to

$$y = \tilde{A}x + B\tilde{u}. \tag{7.C.13}$$

Notice that (7.C.13) is the approximating model and that allowance for distortions occurs only through the presence of $\mathcal{D}(P)$ on the right side of (7.C.12). The solution to this problem is found by taking one step on the usual Riccati equation, with $\mathcal{D}(P)$ as the terminal value function. Thus, define the operators

$$\mathcal{F}\left(\Omega\right) = \beta\left[R + \beta B'\Omega B\right]^{-1}B'\Omega\tilde{A} \qquad (7.C.14)$$

$$T\left(P\right) = Q + \beta\tilde{A}'\left(P - \beta PB\left(R + \beta B'PB\right)^{-1}B'P\right)\tilde{A}. \qquad (7.C.15)$$

Substituting in the definitions of Q and R, T can also be expressed as

$$T\left(P\right) = H'H - H'J\left(J'J\right)^{-1}J'H + \beta\left(A - B\left(J'J\right)^{-1}J'H\right)'$$
$$\times\left(P - \beta PB\left(J'J + \beta B'PB\right)^{-1}B'P\right)\left(A - B\left(J'J\right)^{-1}J'H\right).$$
$$(7.C.16)$$

Then the solution of problem (7.C.12) is $\tilde{u} = -Fx$ where $F = \mathcal{F}\circ\mathcal{D}(P)$. The maximized value of (7.C.12) is $-x'T\circ\mathcal{D}(P)x$. Notice that $u_t = \tilde{u}_t - R^{-1}Wx_t = -(F + (J'J)^{-1}J'H)x_t$.

We can iterate on these two subproblems to find the solution to (7.C.5).[14] Let P be the fixed point of iterations on $T\circ\mathcal{D}$

$$P = T\circ\mathcal{D}\left(\mathcal{P}\right). \qquad (7.C.17)$$

Then the solution of (7.C.5), (7.C.6) is

$$\tilde{u} = -Fx \qquad (7.C.18)$$
$$w = Kx, \qquad (7.C.19)$$

where

$$F = \mathcal{F}\circ\mathcal{D}\left(P\right) \qquad (7.C.20)$$
$$K = \theta^{-1}\left(I - \theta^{-1}C'PC\right)^{-1}C'P\left[\tilde{A} - BF\right]. \qquad (7.C.21)$$

Here T is the usual operator associated with taking one-step on the Bellman equation without a preference for robustness; it represents optimization with respect to u. The operator $\mathcal{D}$ reflects minimization with respect to w. When $\theta = +\infty$, $\mathcal{D}(P) = P$, and we get the usual optimal rule for a linear-quadratic dynamic program. When $\underline{\theta} \leq \theta < \infty$, we get a robust decision rule, where $\underline{\theta}$ is a lower bound on admissible parameters θ. We shall give a formula for $\underline{\theta}$ in equation (8.4.8) on page 180.

---

[14] In chapter 8, we show how the two operators are related to the discounted risk-sensitivity criterion of Hansen and Sargent (1995).

7.C.1. A single Riccati equation

A robust decision rule can also be computed simply by solving an optimal linear regulator problem.[15] This can be established in the following way.

By writing iterations $P_{k+1} = T \circ \mathcal{D}(P_k)$ and rearranging, the matrix P in the value function $-x'Px$ can be expressed as the fixed point of iterations on the Riccati equation[16]

$$P_{k+1} = \tilde{A}' \left((\beta P_k)^{-1} + BR^{-1}B' - \theta^{-1}\beta^{-1}CC' \right) \tilde{A} + Q. \tag{7.C.22}$$

This equation can also be represented as

$$P_{k+1} = Q + \tilde{A}^{*\prime} \left(P_k^{-1} + \tilde{J} \right)^{-1} \tilde{A}^*, \tag{7.C.23}$$

where $\tilde{J} = B^* R^{-1} B^{*\prime} - \theta^{-1} CC', B^* = \beta^{.5} B, \tilde{A}^* = \beta^{.5} \tilde{A}$. Equation $(7.C.23)$ is in a form to which the *doubling algorithm* described in chapter 4 applies.[17] Notice that $(7.C.22)$ is the Riccati equation associated with an ordinary optimal linear regulator problem with controls $\begin{bmatrix} u \\ w \end{bmatrix}$ and penalty matrix on those controls appearing in the criterion function of $\begin{bmatrix} R & 0 \\ 0 & -\beta\theta I \end{bmatrix}$. Therefore, the robust rules for u_t and the associated worst-case shock can be computed directly from the associated ordinary linear regulator problem. It can be checked that the right side of $(7.C.22)$ implements one step on $T \circ \mathcal{D}$. The Riccati equation $(7.C.22)$ is the one associated with the modified linear regulator used in chapter 2 on page 43 to compute a robust rule and the worst-case shock.

7.C.2. Robustness bound

The inner problem $(7.C.7)$ implies a robustness bound for continuation values. Thus, $(7.C.7)$ implies

$$-x'A'\mathcal{D}(P)Ax = \min_w \left[\theta w'w - y'Py \right] \leq \theta w'w - y'Py \tag{7.C.24}$$

where y is evaluated under the distorted model $y = Ax + Cw$. Inequalities $(7.C.24)$ imply

$$-y'Py \geq -x'A'\mathcal{D}(P)Ax - \theta w'w. \tag{7.C.25}$$

The left side is evaluated under a distorted model $y = Ax + Cw$ while the quadratic form in x on the right is a conservative estimate of the continuation value of the state y under the approximating model $y = Ax$.[18] Inequality $(7.C.25)$ states that the continuation value is at least as great as a conservative estimate of the continuation value under the approximating $(w = 0)$ model, minus θ times the measure of model misspecification $w'w$. The parameter θ influences the conservative-adjustment operator $\mathcal{D}$ and also determines the rate at which the bound deteriorates with misspecification. Lowering θ lowers the rate at which the bound deteriorates with misspecification. Thus, $(7.C.25)$ provides a sense in which lower values of θ provide more conservative and also more robust estimates of continuation utility.

---

[15] See chapter 2, page 43.
[16] See Hansen and Sargent (2008).
[17] The Matlab program `doublex9.m` computes the solution using the doubling algorithm.
[18] That is, when $w = 0$, $-y'\mathcal{D}(P)y$ understates the continuation value.

7.C.3. A pure forecasting problem

Here is an example of a pure forecasting problem in which the absence of a control eliminates the maximization part of (7.C.5). The following state-space system governs consumption and bliss consumption

$$
\begin{aligned}
x_{t+1} &= Ax_t + Cw_{t+1} \\
c_t &= H_c x_t \\
b_t &= H_b x_t
\end{aligned}
\tag{7.C.26}
$$

where c_t is an exogenous scalar consumption process, b_t is a bliss level of consumption, and w_{t+1} is a specification error sequence. To attain a conservative way of evaluating $-\sum_{t=0}^{\infty} \beta^t (c_t - b_t)^2$, we compute

$$
-x_0' P x_0 = \min_{\{w_{t+1}\}} -\sum_{t=0}^{\infty} \beta^t \left[x_t' H' H x_t - \beta \theta w_{t+1}' w_{t+1} \right]
\tag{7.C.27}
$$

subject to (7.C.26), where $H = H_c - H_b$. For this special case, the absence of a control causes the operator T defined in (7.C.15) to simplify to

$$
T(P) = H'H + \beta A' P A.
\tag{7.C.28}
$$

The matrix P in (7.C.27) is the fixed point of iterations on $T \circ \mathcal{D}$. The minimizer of (7.C.27) is given by (7.C.9), or $w = Kx$, where K is defined implicitly by (7.C.9). It follows from our earlier characterizations of K and $P = T \circ \mathcal{D}(P)$ that

$$
-x_0' P x_0 = -\sum_{t=0}^{\infty} \beta^t x_t' H' H x_t
$$

where the right side is computed using the distorted law of motion

$$
x_{t+1} = (A + KC) x_t.
$$

D. Completing the square

We use the following calculation repeatedly. Suppose that

$$
x^* = Ax + C\epsilon^*
\tag{7.D.1}
$$

where ϵ^* is a multivariate standard normally distributed random vector distributed independently from x. Our aim is to compute

$$
E \left[\exp \left(\frac{1}{2} x^{*\prime} V x^* \right) | x \right]
\tag{7.D.2}
$$

where the matrix V is positive semidefinite and the expectation is taken with respect to the distribution of ϵ^*. To guarantee this conditional expectation is finite, restrict $I \geq C'VC$.

Substitute for ϵ^*. The normal density is proportional to

$$\exp\left(-\frac{1}{2}e'e\right)$$

where e is dummy variable used to depict the density. To perform the required integration we express the objective as a function ϵ^* and multiply the resulting expression by the normal density. Taking logarithms, this gives

$$L\left(e\right) = \frac{1}{2}x'A'VAx + \frac{1}{2}e'C'VCe + x'A'VCe - \frac{1}{2}e'e \qquad (7.D.3)$$

where e is stand in for the alternative realized values of ϵ^*. Next represent $(7.D.3)$ as an alternative quadratic form by completing the square

$$\begin{aligned}
L\left(e\right) = &-\frac{1}{2}e'\left(I - C'VC\right)e + e'\left(I - C'VC\right)\left(I - C'VC\right)^{-1}C'VAx \\
&-\frac{1}{2}x'A'VC\left(I - C'VC\right)^{-1}C'VAx \qquad (7.D.4) \\
&+\frac{1}{2}x'A'\left(VC\left(I - C'VC\right)^{-1}C'V + V\right)Ax.
\end{aligned}$$

The exponential of first two lines of term $(7.D.4)$ is the same as the exponential term of a normal density with mean $(I - C'VC)^{-1}C'VAx$ and covariance matrix $(I - C'VC)^{-1}$. We use this insight to evaluate $(7.D.2)$ because a normal density integrates to one by construction. As a consequence,

$$E\left[\exp\left(\frac{1}{2}x^{*'}Vx^*\right)|x\right] = \exp\left[\frac{1}{2}x'A'\left(VC\left(I - C'VC\right)^{-1}C'V + V\right)Ax\right]$$

$$\times\left[\det\left(I - C'VC\right)\right]^{1/2}.$$

The determinant is included because of the required scaling for normal density with covariance matrix $(I - C'VC)^{-1}$. This formula is easily modified when Ax is replaced by $Ax + Bu$ in the evolution equation $(7.D.1)$.

Chapter 8
Frequency domain games and criteria for robustness

> *Machines take me by surprise with great frequency.*
> — Alan Turing, "Computing, Machinery and Intelligence," 1950

8.1. Robustness in the frequency domain

Frequency domain decompositions of variances (spectral densities) are useful for analyzing covariance-stationary time series. Whiteman (1985, 1986) and Otrok (2001b) have used frequency domain decompositions of inner products that represent objective functions of linear-quadratic dynamic optimization problems. In this chapter, we use frequency domain decompositions of objective functions to help design a robust decision rule. A frequency domain approach provides interesting insights about dimensions along which a decision rule is particularly fragile by displaying both the objective function and a worst-case shock process in the frequency domain. Brock and Durlauf (2005), Brock, Durlauf, and Rondina (2006), and Brock, Durlauf, Nason, and Rondina (2006) have also studied robustness from the perspective of the frequency domain.[1]

In the two-player zero-sum games of chapter 7, a minimizing player helps a maximizing player analyze the fragility of a decision rule $u_t = -Fx_t$. In this chapter, we take the fruitful point of view that the indirect utility function of the minimizing player forms an intertemporal valuation function that, when used by the maximizing player, produces a robust decision rule. We use frequency domain decompositions to express two such objective functions that the maximizing player can use to attain a robust decision rule, namely, the so-called entropy criterion and the H_∞ criterion. We explain how each of these relates to the multiplier parameter θ.

We require the maximizing player to choose a time-invariant policy rule $u_t = -Fx_t$. However, our frequency domain calculations allow the minimizing player to choose a sequence of distortions w in an appropriate space $\mathcal{W}$ to be defined in subsection 8.4. This puts us into the framework of the Stackelberg game of chapter 7. In this chapter, the only distortions allowed are to means conditioned on date zero information. We ignore randomness and conditioning information that arrives after the initial date. We are free to do so for reasons

---

[1] Tornell (1998) is an early study using H_∞ control to study asset pricing.

given in chapter 7. We focus on frequency domain characterizations of the distortions.

For alternative settings of an initial condition x_0 and a constraint η on the size of the specification error, minimizing over distorted mean sequences w leads to different indirect utility functions with representations in the frequency domain. These become three different frequency domain criteria that the maximizing agent can use to evaluate alternative time-invariant F's. The first criterion forswears robustness by setting $\eta = 0$ and is a discounted version of the so-called H_2 criterion, the maximization of which leads to an algebraic Riccati equation associated with the steady state of a time-invariant infinite-horizon optimal linear regulator problem. Other assumptions about x_0 and η lead to discounted versions of what are known as the H_∞ criterion and an entropy criterion. Each of these promotes robust decision rules. The entropy criterion is indexed by a single parameter θ that is tightly linked to the parameter with the same name that played such a key role in the multiplier game of chapter 7. Indeed, for the same fixed admissible θ, maximizing the entropy criterion leads to the same decision rule F associated with the robust version of the linear regulator that we obtained in chapter 7.

The frequency domain provides an interesting perspective on fear of model misspecification. By analyzing the entropy criterion, we show that activating a concern about misspecification of the approximating model generates a preference for smoothness across frequencies. This looks like risk aversion across frequencies. The H_∞ criterion can be viewed as a limiting version of the entropy criterion that emerges when the multiplier θ approaches the critical breakdown point $\underline{\theta}$ that we mentioned in chapter 7. The H_∞ criterion is expressed in terms of the largest eigenvalue across frequencies of that same frequency domain decomposition of discounted utility and embodies an extreme preference for smoothness across frequencies.[2]

Undiscounted versions of both the H_∞ and the entropy criteria exist in the control literature. Our analysis of discounting is an innovative part of this chapter. Accommodating discounting requires that, relative to arguments in the control literature, we must pay special attention to initial conditions.[3]

Key findings of this chapter are the following: (1) the H_2 criterion gives rise to the optimal linear regulator without robustness; (2) for a given $\theta > \underline{\theta}$, the entropy criterion leads to an infinite-horizon time-invariant discounted robust linear regulator with a value function matrix P associated with the

---

[2] The examples in section 8.7 indicate that in some contexts it is possible to satisfy an extreme preference for smoothing losses across frequencies, while in others it is not.

[3] Our derivation of the entropy criterion will also provide a link to the discounted risk-sensitivity criterion of Hansen and Sargent (1995).

limit of iterations on the composite operator $T \circ \mathcal{D}$ described in chapter 7; (3) the breakdown value $\underline{\theta}$ equals the squared value of the H_∞ criterion.

8.2. Stackelberg game in time domain

Throughout this chapter we adopt a timing protocol associated with the Stackelberg robust multiplier problem from chapter 7. After recalling this game in the time domain, we shall describe a frequency domain version.

The game requires the maximizing player to choose a time-invariant decision rule of the form $u_t = -Fx_t$. To attain representations that build in $u_t = -Fx_t$, we substitute this decision rule into (7.2.1) to get the closed-loop law of motion for the state

$$x_{t+1} = A_F x_t + C w_{t+1}, \tag{8.2.1}$$

where

$$A_F = A - BF. \tag{8.2.2}$$

Under $u_t = -Fx_t$, the target becomes

$$z_t = H_F x_t$$

where $H_F = H - JF$.

In formulating the Stackelberg game, we use the spaces

$$W = \{w : \sum_{t=1}^{\infty} \beta^t w_t' w_t < +\infty\}$$

$$\widetilde{\mathcal{F}} = \{F : A - BF \text{ has eigenvalues with moduli strictly less than } 1/\sqrt{\beta}\}.$$

Corollary 7.7.1 prompts us to impose the stability requirement in constructing $\widetilde{\mathcal{F}}$.

Definition 8.2.1. The *Stackelberg robust constraint problem* is to find $(F, \{w_t\}_{t=1}^{\infty})$ that attain

$$\max_{F \in \widetilde{\mathcal{F}}} \inf_{w \in W} -\sum_{t=0}^{\infty} \beta^t z_t' z_t \tag{8.2.3}$$

subject to (8.2.1) and

$$\sum_{t=0}^{\infty} \beta^t w_t' w_t \leq \eta + w_0' w_0 \tag{8.2.4a}$$

$$x_0 = C w_0. \tag{8.2.4b}$$

This game is indexed by two parameters (w_0, η). In contrast to the time domain formulations in chapter 7, we restrict ourselves to considering initial values for the state vector x_0 that can be expressed as $C w_0$ for some w_0. This facilitates using frequency domain methods. The parameter η governs the magnitude of the allowable shock sequences after netting out the contribution of w_0.

Two versions of the Stackelberg robust constraint problem are convenient benchmarks and correspond to different settings of η, w_0:

1. The H_2 problem: set $\eta = 0$, with arbitrary w_0.

2. The H_∞ problem: set $w_0 = 0$, but let $\eta > 0$ be arbitrary.

The first version makes the inf part trivial, turns the game into a standard single-person linear-quadratic optimum problem, and leads to the so-called H_2 criterion in the frequency domain. The second can be regarded as emerging from a limiting process that yields a decision rule that performs adequately over a largest possible set of perturbed models surrounding the approximating model. In this H_∞ case, the decision rule is invariant to the choice of η because $w_0 = 0$ is zero.

8.3. Fourier transforms

To formulate the Stackelberg game in the frequency domain, we use Fourier transforms. We define the following one-sided Fourier transforms

$$X(\zeta) \equiv \sum_{t=0}^{\infty} x_t \zeta^t,$$

$$W(\zeta) \equiv \sum_{t=0}^{\infty} w_t \zeta^t, \qquad (8.3.1)$$

$$Z(\zeta) \equiv \sum_{t=0}^{\infty} z_t \zeta^t,$$

where ζ is a complex variable. Then $(8.2.1)$ and $(8.3.1)$ imply that $\zeta^{-1}[X(\zeta) - x_0] = A_F X(\zeta) + \zeta^{-1} C [W(\zeta) - w_0]$. Using $(8.2.4b)$ and solving for $X(\zeta)$ gives $X(\zeta) = (I - \zeta A_F)^{-1} C W(\zeta)$, and hence

$$Z(\zeta) = G_F(\zeta) W(\zeta) \qquad (8.3.2)$$

where

$$G_F(\zeta) \equiv H_F (I - \zeta A_F)^{-1} C$$

is the transfer function from shocks to targets.

Applying Parseval's equality to (8.3.2) gives the following representation:

$$\sum_{t=0}^{\infty} \beta^{t} z_{t}' z_{t} = \int_{\Gamma} W\left(\zeta\right)' G_{F}\left(\zeta\right)' G_{F}\left(\zeta\right) W\left(\zeta\right) d\lambda\left(\zeta\right), \qquad (8.3.3)$$

where the operation $'$ denotes both matrix transposition and complex conjugation. The measure λ has density

$$d\lambda\left(\zeta\right) \equiv \frac{1}{2\pi i \sqrt{\beta}\zeta} d\zeta,$$

and where the region of integration is the following circle in the complex plane:

$$\Gamma \equiv \{\zeta : |\zeta| = \sqrt{\beta}\}.$$

The region Γ can be parameterized conveniently in terms of $\zeta = \sqrt{\beta}\exp(i\omega)$ for ω in the interval $(-\pi, \pi]$. Here the measure λ satisfies

$$d\lambda\left(\zeta\right) = \frac{1}{2\pi} d\omega.$$

Thus, the contour integral on the right side of (8.3.3) can be expressed as

$$\int_{\Gamma} W(\zeta)' G_{F}(\zeta)' G_{F}(\zeta) W(\zeta) d\lambda(\zeta)$$
$$= \frac{1}{2\pi} \int_{-\pi}^{\pi} W(\sqrt{\beta}\exp(i\omega))' \left\{ G_{F}[\sqrt{\beta}\exp(i\omega)]' G_{F}[\sqrt{\beta}\exp(i\omega)] \right\} \qquad (8.3.4)$$
$$W(\sqrt{\beta}\exp(i\omega)) d\omega.$$

We use the contour integral on the left of (8.3.4) to simplify notation.

Parseval's equality also implies

$$\sum_{t=0}^{\infty} \beta^{t} w_{t}' w_{t} = \int_{\Gamma} W\left(\zeta\right)' W\left(\zeta\right) d\lambda\left(\zeta\right). \qquad (8.3.5)$$

8.4. Stackelberg constraint game in frequency domain

To represent the Stackelberg game in the frequency domain, we define the following two sets of admissible $W(\zeta)$'s

$$\mathcal{W}^{a} = \{W\left(\zeta\right) : W\left(\zeta\right) \text{ is analytic on the interior of } \Gamma \text{ with coefficients}$$
$$w_{t} \text{ that are vectors of real numbers and } W\left(0\right) = w_{0}\}$$

$$\mathcal{W} = \{W\left(\zeta\right) \in \mathcal{W}^{a} : \sum_{t=0}^{\infty} \beta^{t} w_{t}' w_{t} < \infty\}.$$

Below, we shall encounter situations in which a worst-case model w is in $\mathcal{W}^a$ but not in $\mathcal{W}$.

We use (8.3.3) and (8.3.5) to represent the time-domain Stackelberg robust constraint problem of Definition 8.2.1 as

Definition 8.4.1. A *Stackelberg constraint game in the frequency domain* finds $(F, W(\zeta))$ that attain

$$\max_{\widetilde{\mathcal{F}}} \inf_{\mathcal{W}} - \int_{\Gamma} W(\zeta)' G_F(\zeta)' G_F(\zeta) W(\zeta) \, d\lambda(\zeta) \qquad (8.4.1)$$

subject to

$$\int_{\Gamma} W(\zeta)' W(\zeta) \, d\lambda(\zeta) \leq \eta + w_0' w_0. \qquad (8.4.2)$$

As we remarked earlier, two limiting versions of the Stackelberg constraint game are

1. H_2: set $\eta = 0$, with $W(0) = w_0$ arbitrary.
2. H_∞: set arbitrary $\eta > 0$ but $W(0) = w_0 = 0$

where we now view w_0 as a constraint on the function W.

8.4.1. Version 1: H_2 criterion

When $\eta = 0$ in (8.2.4a), $W(\zeta) = w_0$ and

$$-\sum_{t=0}^{\infty} \beta^t z_t' z_t = -w_0' \left[\int_{\Gamma} G_F(\zeta)' G_F(\zeta) \, d\lambda(\zeta) \right] w_0.$$

For an arbitrary w_0, the H_2 problem is to maximize this expression by choosing a feedback rule F. The H_2 criterion can be expressed as

$$H_2 \equiv -\int_{\Gamma} \operatorname{trace} \left[G_F(\zeta)' G_F(\zeta) \right] d\lambda(\zeta). \qquad (8.4.3)$$

The F that maximizes H_2 is also the stabilizing solution of the standard optimal linear regulator problem. Thus, the H_2 criterion gives a frequency domain expression to the preferences embodied in the optimal linear regulator. We turn next to frequency domain criteria that express a concern about model misspecification.

8.4.2. Version 2: the H_∞ criterion

Version 2 of the Stackelberg game in the frequency domain imposes the side condition that $W(0) = 0$, but otherwise leaves $W(\zeta)$ free.

Let $\rho(\zeta)$ denote the eigenvalues of $G_F(\zeta)'G_F(\zeta)$. The following theorem tells how version 2 of the game leads to the H_∞ criterion:

$$H_\infty \equiv -\sup_{\zeta \in \Gamma} \left[\rho(\zeta) \right]^{1/2}. \tag{8.4.4}$$

Theorem 8.4.1.   For any $F \in \widetilde{\mathcal{F}}$,

$$\inf_{W} - \int_\Gamma W(\zeta)' G_F(\zeta)' G_F(\zeta) W(\zeta) d\lambda(\zeta) = -(H_\infty)^2 \eta \tag{8.4.5}$$

where the infimization is subject to (8.4.2).

Proof. Given $G_F(\zeta)$, for each $\zeta = \sqrt{\beta} \exp(i\omega)$ solve the following eigenvalue problem:[4]

$$G_F(\zeta)' G_F(\zeta) v = \rho(\zeta) v$$

for the largest eigenvalue $\rho(\zeta)$. This problem has a well defined solution with eigenvalue $\rho(\omega)$ for each $\zeta = \sqrt{\beta} \exp(i\omega)$. Then

$$\int_\Gamma W(\zeta)' G_F(\zeta)' G_F(\zeta) W(\zeta) d\lambda(\zeta) \leq \int_\Gamma \rho(\zeta) W(\zeta)' W(\zeta) d\lambda(\zeta)$$

$$\leq \sup_{\zeta \in \Gamma} \rho(\zeta) \int_\Gamma W(\zeta)' W(\zeta) d\lambda(\zeta)$$

$$\leq \sup_{\zeta \in \Gamma} \rho(\zeta)\eta.$$

---

[4]   It may be useful to remind the reader of the principal components problem. Let a be an $(n \times 1)$ random vector with covariance matrix V. The first *principal component* of a is a scalar $b = p'a$ where p is an $(n \times 1)$ vector with unit norm (i.e., $p'p = 1$) for which the variance of b is maximal. Thus, the first principal component solves the problem

$$\max_{p} \; p'Vp$$

subject to

$$p'p = 1.$$

Putting a Lagrange multiplier λ on the constraint, the first-order conditions for this problem are

$$(V - \lambda I) p = 0, \tag{8.4.6}$$

with the value of the variance of $p'b$ evident from (8.4.6)

$$p'Vp = \lambda p'p = \lambda. \tag{8.4.7}$$

Thus, (8.4.6) and (8.4.7) indicate that p is the eigenvector of V associated with the largest eigenvalue and that the variance of b equals the largest eigenvalue λ.

The bound on the right side is attained by the limit of a sequence of approximating W functions described in appendix A. Associated with each such function is a sequence $\{w_t\}$. ∎

Thus, the H_∞ criterion looks at worst-case performance across all frequencies. For technical reasons described in appendix A, the infimum in $(8.4.5)$ is not necessarily attained by an analytic function $W \in \mathcal{W}$.

The square of the optimized H_∞ criterion equals the lower bound on the set of admissible θ's alluded to in condition $(7.9.1)$ in chapters 6 and 7:

$$\underline{\theta} = \left(\inf_{\widetilde{\mathcal{F}}} H_\infty (F) \right)^2 . \tag{8.4.8}$$

The lower bound $\underline{\theta}$ is called the breakdown value of θ.[5]

The maximizer F of version 2 maximizes $(8.4.4)$. We can drop η from the performance criterion $(8.4.4)$ because it becomes a positive scale factor that is independent of the control law F. This feature emerges from imposing the initial condition $w_0 = 0$.

8.5. Stackelberg multiplier game in frequency domain

The H_2 criterion emerged from ignoring possible model misspecification by setting $\eta = 0$. Under discounting, the H_∞ control problem came from allowing model misspecification while setting w_0 to zero. We now consider an intermediate case that allows misspecification but also constrains the malevolent agent to respect the initial condition $x_0 = C w_0$. When the initial w_0 is distinct from zero, the value of η matters, in contrast to its irrelevance in the H_∞ case.

To analyze this case, we formulate the multiplier version of the Stackelberg game in the frequency domain. We let θ penalize large choices of W, and obtain

Definition 8.5.1. A *Stackelberg multiplier game in the frequency domain* finds $(\theta, F, W(\zeta))$ that attain

$$L(\theta, w_0) = \sup_{\widetilde{\mathcal{F}}} \inf_{\mathcal{W}} \left[\int_\Gamma W' (\theta I - G'_F G_F) W \, d\lambda \right] \tag{8.5.1}$$

for $\theta > \underline{\theta}$.[6]

---

[5] Whittle (1990) calls $\underline{\theta}$ the point of "utter psychotic despair." In section 8.7, we analyze worst-case models and decision rules as θ approaches the breakdown point. At Whittle's point of utter psychotic despair, the objective function that the malevolent player seeks to minimize threatens not to be convex in the malevolent player's control. At $\underline{\theta}$, convexity is lost even by slightly reducing θ.

[6] We have already studied the $\eta = 0, \theta = \infty$ (H_2) and $w_0 = 0, \theta = \underline{\theta}$ (H_∞) cases.

Notice that we modified the H_∞ objective by adding θI.

Consider the family of multiplier games parameterized by θ, where $F(\theta)$ and W_θ are the equilibrium solutions to the multiplier game. We use this family to produce a corresponding family of solutions to the constraint game, as we now verify. With this in mind, construct the following set for the minimizing agent in the constraint game:

$$\mathcal{W}(\eta) = \{W \in \mathcal{W} : \int_\Gamma W_\theta'W_\theta d\lambda \leq \eta + w_0 \cdot w_0\}.$$

Our candidate constraint parameter is

$$\eta(\theta) = \int_\Gamma W_\theta'W_\theta d\lambda - w_0 \cdot w_0.$$

Throughout the remainder of this chapter, we assume that the parameterization satisfies:

ASSUMPTION T:
(a) $\lim_{\theta \downarrow \underline{\theta}} F(\theta) = F(\underline{\theta})$ where $F(\underline{\theta}) \in \widetilde{\mathcal{F}}$.
(b) $\lim_{\theta \to \infty} F(\theta) = F(\infty)$ where $F(\infty) \in \widetilde{\mathcal{F}}$.
(c) $\int_\Gamma W_\theta'W_\theta d\lambda < \infty$ for all $\theta > \underline{\theta}$ and all w_0.

We will eventually show that $F(\infty)$ solves the H_2 and that $F(\underline{\theta})$ solves the H_∞ problem, respectively. We will also justify a frequency domain objective parameterized by θ for intermediate settings of θ. First we establish a connection between the multiplier game and a corresponding constraint game.

Theorem 8.5.1. *Suppose that $\theta > \underline{\theta}$ and $\eta(\theta) > 0$. The equilibrium for the multiplier game is an equilibrium for the corresponding constraint game.*

Proof. The fact that $F(\theta)$ is the θ solution implies

$$\int_\Gamma W_\theta'W_\theta d\lambda \geq L(\theta, w_0) - \theta \int_\Gamma W'W d\lambda$$

$$= L(\theta, w_0) - \theta(\eta + w_0 \cdot w_0) - \theta\left[\int_\Gamma W'W d\lambda - \eta - w_0 \cdot w_0\right].$$

Thus, $L(\theta, w_0) - \theta(\eta + w_0 \cdot w_0)$ is a lower bound on

$$-\int_\Gamma WG_{F(\theta)}'G_{F(\theta)}W d\lambda$$

unless

$$\int_\Gamma W'W d\lambda > \eta + w_0 \cdot w_0.$$

By virtue of a Bellman-Isaacs condition[7]

$$\int_\Gamma W_\theta{}' [\theta I - G_F' G_F] W_\theta d\lambda \le \int_\Gamma W_\theta{}' \left[\theta I - G_{F(\theta)}' G_{F(\theta)}\right] W_\theta d\lambda,$$

which implies that

$$\inf_{W \in \mathcal{W}[\eta(\theta)]} -\int_\Gamma W G_F{}' G_F W d\lambda \le -\int_\Gamma W_\theta G_F{}' G_F W_\theta d\lambda$$

$$\le -\int_\Gamma W_\theta G_{F(\theta)}{}' G_{F(\theta)} W_\theta d\lambda$$

$$= \inf_{W \in \mathcal{W}[\eta(\theta)]} -\int_\Gamma W' G_{F(\theta)}{}' G_{F(\theta)} W d\lambda.$$

Thus, the solution for a multiplier game for a given θ also gives the solution for the constraint game for $\eta(\theta)$. ∎

Proofs of the following two lemmas appear in appendix C. The first lemma asserts that making θ larger causes the constraint set to decrease.

Lemma 8.5.1. *$\eta(\theta)$ is decreasing in θ for $\theta > \underline{\theta}$.*

The next lemma asserts that by making θ arbitrarily large, we make η in the constraint game arbitrarily small.

Lemma 8.5.2. *$\lim_{\theta \to \infty} \eta(\theta) = 0$.*

8.6. A multiplier problem

To study the $\inf_{\mathcal{W}}$ part of game (8.5.1), we take θ, F, and therefore G_F as given.[8] We refer to the resulting optimization problem as the *multiplier problem* and state it as

$$L^* (\theta, w_0, F) = \inf_{\mathcal{W}, W(0) = w_0} \int_\Gamma W(\zeta)' [\theta I - G_F(\zeta)' G_F(\zeta)] W(\zeta) d\lambda(\zeta).$$
(8.6.1)

For this problem to have an optimized value that exceeds $-\infty$, we require that $\theta I - G_F' G_F$ be positive semidefinite.

---

[7]   See the discussion in footnote 7 of chapter 7. See Hansen, Sargent, Turmuhambetova, and Williams (2006) for a discussion of the Bellman-Isaacs condition in a continuous time setting.

[8]   Recall that $G_F \equiv H_F(I - \zeta(A - BF))^{-1} C$.

8.6.1. Robustness bound

For a given decision rule F, the multiplier problem yields an inequality that bounds the rate at which the criterion function deteriorates as specification errors increase. Using the objective (8.6.1) for the multiplier problem,

$$- \int_\Gamma W' G'_F G_F W d\lambda \geq L^* (\theta, w_0, F) - \theta \int_\Gamma W' W d\lambda. \qquad (8.6.2)$$

Inequality (8.6.2) shows that in the absence of specification errors, $L^*(\theta, w_0, F)$ understates the performance of the policy. It also shows how θ sets the rate at which the objective function $- \int_\Gamma W' G'_F G_F W d\lambda$ deteriorates with model misspecification as measured by $\int W' W d\lambda$. Note how *lowering* θ gives more robustness as reflected by less sensitivity of the objective function to misspecifications W. By maximizing over F we obtain the best bound for a given amount of sensitivity to misspecification as measured by θ.

8.6.2. Breakdown point reconsidered

Consider next the family of control laws $F(\theta)$ and the corresponding misspecifications W_θ for $\theta > \underline{\theta}$. Recall that

$$\lim_{\theta \downarrow \underline{\theta}} F(\theta) = F(\underline{\theta}).$$

We use the robustness inequality to show:

Lemma 8.6.1. *The limiting control law $F(\underline{\theta})$ is a solution to the H_∞ control problem.*

Proof. The family of value functions constructed by applying the limiting control is increasing in θ, nonnegative, and has a nonnegative right limit

$$\lim_{\theta \downarrow \underline{\theta}} L(\theta, w_0) = L^* [\underline{\theta}, F(\underline{\theta}), w_0] < \infty.$$

The robustness inequality (8.6.2) now applies in the limit

$$- \int_\Gamma W' G'_{F(\underline{\theta})} G_{F(\underline{\theta})} W d\lambda \geq L^* [\underline{\theta}, w_0, F(\underline{\theta})] - \underline{\theta} \int_\Gamma W' W d\lambda.$$

Consider any W such that

$$\int_\Gamma W' W d\lambda = 1,$$

and scale this W by $\sqrt{\eta}$. By the robustness inequality (8.6.2),

$$- \eta \int_\Gamma W' G'_{F(\underline{\theta})} G_{F(\underline{\theta})} W d\lambda \geq \underline{L} [\underline{\theta}, w_0, F(\underline{\theta})] - \eta \underline{\theta}.$$

Divide by η and take limits as η gets arbitrarily large. It follows that

$$- \int_\Gamma W' G'_{F(\underline{\theta})} G_{F(\underline{\theta})} W d\lambda \geq -\underline{\theta}$$

or, equivalently, that

$$\int_\Gamma W' G'_{F(\underline{\theta})} G_{F(\underline{\theta})} W d\lambda \leq \underline{\theta}$$

for all W such that $\int_\Gamma W' W d\lambda = 1$. Therefore, Theorem 8.4.1 and formula (8.4.8) imply that the control law $F(\underline{\theta})$ must necessarily be the H_∞ control law. ∎

Since L is increasing in θ and nonnegative for $\theta > \underline{\theta}$, its right limit at the breakdown point must be finite:

$$\lim_{\theta \downarrow \underline{\theta}} L(\theta, w_0) = L(\underline{\theta}, w_0) < \infty.$$

What can be said about the right limit of W_θ at $\underline{\theta}$? We consider two possible outcomes. One possibility is that

$$\lim_{\theta \downarrow \underline{\theta}} \int_\Gamma W_\theta' W_\theta d\lambda = \infty.$$

Equivalently, $\bar{\eta} = \eta(\underline{\theta}) = \infty$. Later we will provide sufficient conditions for this case. Another possibility is that there exists a $W_{\underline{\theta}} \in \mathcal{W}$ such that

$$\lim_{\theta \downarrow \underline{\theta}} \int_\Gamma |W_\theta - W_{\underline{\theta}}|^2 d\lambda = 0.$$

Thus, W_θ is right continuous at the breakdown point $\underline{\theta}$. We do not claim that these two cases are exhaustive.

In the second case,

$$\bar{\eta} = \int_\Gamma W_{\underline{\theta}}' W_{\underline{\theta}} d\lambda < \infty.$$

For any $W \in \mathcal{W}(\bar{\eta})$, by the right continuity in θ,

$$- \int_\Gamma W' G_{F(\underline{\theta})}' G_{F(\underline{\theta})} W d\lambda \leq L(\underline{\theta}, w_0) - \underline{\theta}\bar{\eta}.$$

Also, by right continuity, the bound is attained when $W = W(\underline{\theta})$ and hence

$$\inf_{W \in \mathcal{W}(\bar{\eta})} - \int_\Gamma W' G_{F(\underline{\theta})}' G_{F(\underline{\theta})} W d\lambda = L(\underline{\theta}, w_0) - \underline{\theta}\bar{\eta}.$$

For any other F, right continuity of W_θ implies that

$$-\int_\Gamma W_{\underline{\theta}}{}' G_F{}' G_F W_{\underline{\theta}} d\lambda \le L(\underline{\theta}, w_0) - \underline{\theta}\bar{\eta}.$$

Thus,

$$\inf_{W \in \mathcal{W}(\bar{\eta})} - \int_\Gamma W_{\underline{\theta}}{}' G_F{}' G_F W_{\underline{\theta}} d\lambda \le L(\underline{\theta}, w_0) - \underline{\theta}\bar{\eta}.$$

It follows that $F(\underline{\theta})$ and $W(\underline{\theta})$ solve the constraint game for $\eta = \bar{\eta}$. Moreover, $W(\underline{\theta})$ gives a worst-case distortion under which $F(\underline{\theta})$ is the optimal control law. In this second case, the limiting solution to the multiplier game solves the constraint game and is optimal against the limiting form of misspecification. This second case is the dynamic extension of the $b \ne 0$ example in section 6.6 of chapter 6.

8.6.3. *Computing the worst-case misspecification*

To obtain further characterizations of the multiplier problem, we now compute the implied worst-case W. For this purpose, we rewrite the problem as

$$\inf_{W(\zeta) \in \mathcal{W}} \int_\Gamma W(\zeta)' \left[\theta I - G_F(\zeta)' G_F(\zeta)\right] W(\zeta) \, d\lambda(\zeta) \qquad (8.6.3)$$

subject to

$$\int_\Gamma W(\zeta) \, d\lambda(\zeta) = w_0 \ne 0 \qquad (8.6.4)$$

and

$$\int_\Gamma W(\zeta) \zeta^j d\lambda(\zeta) = 0, \qquad (8.6.5)$$

for $j = 1, 2, \dots$. Constraint $(8.6.4)$ can be restated as $W(0) = w_0$. Constraint $(8.6.5)$ states that $w_j = 0$ for $j < 0$. From the definition of $\mathcal{W}$, the infimum in $(8.6.3)$ is over $W(\zeta)$ that have coefficients such that $\sum_{t=-\infty}^\infty \beta^t w_t' w_t < \infty$.

Our next result imposes the following restriction on a frequency domain characterization of entropy

$$\int_\Gamma \log \det \left(\theta I - G_F{}' G_F\right) d\lambda(\zeta) > -\infty. \qquad (8.6.6)$$

We shall explain the appellation "entropy" in section 8.9.

Theorem 8.6.1. *Assume that F and θ are such that $\int_\Gamma \log \det(\theta I - G_F' G_F) d\lambda > -\infty$. Then multiplier problem $(8.6.1)$ has an optimized value function $w_0' D(0)' D(0) w_0$, where $D(0)$ is nonsingular and independent of w_0. The minimized value is attained if $\theta I - G_F' G_F$ is nonsingular on Γ.*

Proof. The solution to the multiplier problem can be found using techniques from linear prediction theory (e.g., see Rozanov (1967) and Whittle (1983)).[9] We must factor a spectral-density-like matrix

$$\left[\theta I - G_F\left(\zeta\right)' G_F\left(\zeta\right)\right] = D\left(\zeta\right)' D\left(\zeta\right) \qquad (8.6.7)$$

where D is rational in ζ, has no poles inside or on the circle Γ, is invertible inside Γ, and has matrix coefficients of its power series expansion inside Γ that can be chosen to be real. The matrix analytic function D is unique only up to premultiplication by an orthogonal matrix but can be chosen to be independent of w_0. The existence of this factorization follows from results about the linear extrapolation of covariance stationary stochastic processes. In particular, it is known from Theorems 4.2, 6.2, and 6.3 of Rozanov (1967) that the infimum of the objective is

$$w_0' D\left(0\right)' D\left(0\right) w_0. \qquad (8.6.8)$$

When $\theta I - G_F' G_F$ is nonsingular on Γ, the infimum is attained. To verify this, write the first-order conditions for maximizing (8.6.3) subject to (8.6.4) and (8.6.5) as

$$\left[\theta I - G_F\left(\zeta\right)' G_F\left(\zeta\right)\right] W\left(\zeta\right) = \mathcal{L}\left(\zeta\right)', \qquad (8.6.9)$$

where $\mathcal{L}$ is the Lagrange multiplier on (8.6.4) and (8.6.5). Then the matrix D in the factorization (8.6.7) is nonsingular with an inverse that is rational and well defined on and inside the circle Γ. Substituting the factorization (8.6.7) into (8.6.9) gives

$$D\left(\zeta\right)' D\left(\zeta\right) W\left(\zeta\right) = \mathcal{L}\left(\zeta\right)', \qquad (8.6.10)$$

where $D(\zeta), W(\zeta)$, being analytic inside Γ, have expansions in nonnegative powers of ζ, and $D(\zeta)'$ and $\mathcal{L}(\zeta)'$ have expansions in nonpositive powers of ζ in the interior of Γ. If $D(\zeta)'$ is invertible, then following Whittle (1983, p. 100), $W(\zeta)$ satisfies

$$D\left(\zeta\right) W\left(\zeta\right) = \left[D\left(\zeta\right)'^{-1} \mathcal{L}\left(\zeta\right)'\right]_+,$$

where $[\cdot]_+$ is the annihilation operator that sets negative powers of ζ to zero. Because $D(\zeta)'^{-1}$ and $\mathcal{L}(\zeta)'$ are both one-sided in nonpositive powers of ζ, $[D(\zeta)'^{-1}\mathcal{L}(\zeta)']_+ = D(0)'^{-1}\mathcal{L}(0)'$. Therefore, the solution is

$$D\left(\zeta\right) W\left(\zeta\right) = D\left(0\right)'^{-1} \mathcal{L}\left(0\right)'. \qquad (8.6.11)$$

---

[9] Appendix B displays a linear prediction problem that leads to the spectral factorization problem here.

Then from $(8.6.10)$, $\mathcal{L}(0)' = D(0)'D(0)W(0)$. Substituting into $(8.6.11)$ gives

$$D(\zeta)W(\zeta) = D(0)w_0. \tag{8.6.12}$$

In addition, the infimum is attained by [10]

$$W^*(\zeta) = D(\zeta)^{-1}D(0)w_0. \tag{8.6.13}$$

Substituting into $(8.6.3)$ confirms that the minimized solution is $(8.6.8)$. ∎

As is evident from the proof, the infimum in $(8.6.3)$ may not be attained when $\theta I - G_F'G_F$ is singular somewhere on Γ. But this problem can be remedied by enlarging the space from $\mathcal{W}$ to $\mathcal{W}^a$.

Corollary 8.6.1. *Assume that F is such that $\int_\Gamma \log \det(\theta I - G_F'G_F)d\lambda > -\infty$. Then the multiplier problem $(8.6.1)$ has a solution in the space $\mathcal{W}^a$ with the same minimized value $w_0'D(0)'D(0)w_0$.*

Proof. Solution $(8.6.13)$ is in $\mathcal{W}^a$ even when $\theta I - G_F'G_F$ is singular somewhere on Γ. ∎

Corollary 8.6.1 shows that a solution exists for the multiplier problem, provided that the entropy restriction $(8.6.6)$ is satisfied. But unless the matrix $(\theta I - G_F'G_F)$ is nonsingular at all frequencies, the minimizing misspecification will fail to satisfy

$$\int_\Gamma W'W d\lambda < \infty$$

for all choices of the initial condition w_0. For some choices of w_0, this integral could be finite even though $\int_\Gamma \log \det(\theta I - G_F'G_F)d\lambda > -\infty$. Problems occur when $W^*(\zeta) = D(\zeta)^{-1}D(0)w_0$ has a pole on Γ or, equivalently, when $D(\zeta)^{-1}$ has a pole on Γ that is not annihilated by $D(0)w_0$.

Consider in particular the control law $F(\theta)$. Under Assumption T.c, it is necessarily true that $(\theta I - G_F'G_F)$ is nonsingular at all frequencies. As a consequence,

Lemma 8.6.2. *For any $\theta > \underline{\theta}$,*

$$\lim_{\tilde{\theta}\downarrow\theta} \int_\Gamma |W_{\tilde{\theta}} - W_\theta|^2 d\lambda = 0.$$

---

[10] The factorization is also the key for calculating the projection of y_t on the semi-infinite history x_s for $s \leq t$ where $\{y_t, x_t\}$ is a covariance stationary process (see Whittle (1983, pp. 99–100)). Condition $(8.6.10)$ corresponds to the solution of Whittle's projection problem where $D(\zeta)'D(\zeta)$ is interpreted as the spectral density of x and $\mathcal{L}(\zeta)$ is interpreted as the cross-spectral density between y and x.

Therefore, the function η is continuous from the right on the domain $\theta > \underline{\theta}$.

We present a proof in appendix C.

Consider next the breakdown limit control law $F(\underline{\theta})$. By the construction of the breakdown point $\underline{\theta}$,

$$\underline{\theta} I - G'_{F(\underline{\theta})} G_{F(\underline{\theta})}$$

is singular somewhere on the boundary of Γ. When

$$\int_{\Gamma} \log \det \left[\underline{\theta} I - G'_{F(\underline{\theta})} G_{F(\underline{\theta})} \right] d\lambda < \infty$$

we can construct a worst-case limit $W(\theta)$. This limit will be in $\mathcal{W}^a$ but not in $\mathcal{W}$ for some initializations w_0. For some special choices of w_0, the problematic poles of $D(\zeta)$ can be annihilated, but this will not be possible for general choice of w_0. Thus, when the frequency domain measure of entropy is finite at the breakdown point, we expect $\bar{\eta} = \infty$ except possibly for some special initializations of w_0.

In contrast, in section 8.7, we shall give examples of models in which $\underline{\theta} I - G'_{F(\underline{\theta})} G_{F(\underline{\theta})}$ is flat at the breakdown point and there is a limiting $W(\theta)$ in $\mathcal{W}$. For examples in which the limiting $G'_{F(\underline{\theta})} G_{F(\underline{\theta})}$ is flat, entropy is infinite at the breakdown point

$$\lim_{\theta \downarrow \underline{\theta}} \int_{\Gamma} \log \det \left[\theta I - G'_{F(\theta)} G_{F(\theta)} \right] d\lambda = +\infty.$$

8.7. Three examples of frequency response smoothing

This section considers three simple examples that illustrate how activating a concern about robustness affects the frequency response $G_F(\exp(-i\omega))$. The examples also illustrate how to find the breakdown point by solving a sequence of problems, each of which is a multiplier control problem from chapter 7.[11] In examples 1 and 2, $G'_{F(\underline{\theta})} G_{F(\underline{\theta})}$ is flat. In example 3, it is not. For convenience, we set $\beta = 1$, but there are equivalent interpretations of our examples in which discounting is present. As we have seen, for purposes of computation, a $\beta < 1$ control problem can be solved by changing the diagonal entries of A.

---

[11] To solve the control problems of this section, we used the Matlab program `olrprobust.m`.

Table 8.7.1: Outcomes for example 1

θ	F	K	P
1000	.6181	0.0001	1.6181
5	.7247	0.1449	1.7247
3	.8229	0.2743	1.8229
2	1	.5	2

8.7.1. Example 1

Take a scalar x_t and scalar u_t and set $A = B = C = 1$, $H = [1 \quad 0]$, and $J = [0 \quad 1]$.[12] These settings capture the objective function $-\sum_{t=0}^{\infty}(x_t^2+u_t^2)$, where the transition law is $x_{t+1} = x_t+u_t+w_{t+1}$. For values of $\theta = 10000, 5, 3$, and 2.0005, the top panel of figure 8.7.1 displays values of $|G_F(e^{-i\omega})|^2$ and the bottom panel displays $\theta - |G_F(e^{-i\omega})|^2$. The dotted line in the top panel shows $|G_F(e^{-i\omega})|^2$ under the rule with no robustness, which we approximate by taking $\theta = 1000$. Table 8.7.1 displays values of F, K, and P for our four settings of θ. At the breakdown point $\theta = 2$, $F = 1$, which makes $A - BF = 0$ and so perfectly flattens $|G_F(\exp(-i\omega))|^2$ as a function of frequency ω in figure 8.7.1. Thus, the robust rule associated with the breakdown point $\theta = 2$ is $u_t = -x_t$, which undoes the dynamics under the approximating model. Notice that P also equals 2 at the breakdown point $\theta = 2$. Let $A_o = A - BF(\underline{\theta}) + CK(\underline{\theta})$. The limiting worst-case choice of w_{t+1} is $w_{t+1} = K(\underline{\theta})A_o^t Cw_0, t \geq 0$. The limiting worst-case W is $W[\exp(-i\omega)] = w_0 + \exp(-i\omega)K[I - A_o\exp(-i\omega)]Cw_0$. For the present example, $w_{t+1} = .5^{t+1}w_0$ for $t \geq -1$. We will consider a more general analysis of worst-case models later in this chapter.

8.7.2. Example 2

Figure 8.7.2 shows corresponding objects for the following example. The objective function is $-\sum_{t=0}^{\infty}[(k_t - b_t)^2 + u_t^2]$, where $k_{t+1} = \delta k_t + u_t$ and $b_{t+1} = \rho b_t + w_{t+1}$. Here k_t is a scalar endogenous state variable, b_t is a scalar exogenous state variable that plays the role of a bliss or target for the endogenous state, u_t is a scalar control, and w_{t+1} is a scalar specification error. We set $\delta = .95, \rho = .9$. To capture this example, we set $x_t = \begin{bmatrix} k_t \\ b_t \end{bmatrix}$, $\beta = 1$, $H = \begin{bmatrix} 1 & -1 \\ 0 & 0 \end{bmatrix}$, $J = \begin{bmatrix} 0 \\ 1 \end{bmatrix}$, $A = \begin{bmatrix} \delta & 0 \\ 0 & \rho \end{bmatrix}$, $B = \begin{bmatrix} 1 \\ 0 \end{bmatrix}$, $C = \begin{bmatrix} 0 \\ 1 \end{bmatrix}$.

---

[12] In this example, A, B, H, J are such that when $\theta = +\infty$, F and P satisfy the golden ratio.

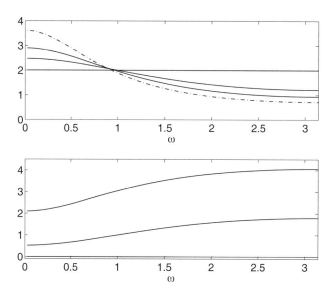

Figure 8.7.1: Example 1. Top: $|G_F(e^{-i\omega})|^2$ for $\theta = 10000, 5, 3, 2.0005$, respectively. The flatter curves are for lower θ. Bottom: $\theta - |G_F(e^{-i\omega})|^2$ for $\theta = 5, 3, 2.0005$, respectively. The curve for $\theta = 2.0005$ is nearly zero.

We have checked for whether θ is above the breakdown point by verifying that

1. $-J'J - B'PB$ is negative definite, and

2. $\theta I - C'PC$ is positive definite.

As we lower θ toward the breakdown point, we find that $\theta I - C'PC$ approaches zero from above.[13] Figure 8.7.2 indicates that a policy associated with a θ slightly above the breakdown point $\theta = 1.777546728$ flattens the frequency response $G_F(\exp(-i\omega))'G_F(\exp(-i\omega))$ completely. We used many digits in our choice of θ in order to approximate the limiting frequency response for a robust control law numerically. Under the $\underline{\theta}$ policy, F is approximately $\begin{bmatrix} 0.95 & -0.8740 \end{bmatrix}$ and $A - BF$ is approximately $\begin{bmatrix} 0 & 0.8740 \\ 0 & 0.9000 \end{bmatrix}$. K is $\begin{bmatrix} -0.5190 & 0.4860 \end{bmatrix}$, and $A - BF + CK$ is approximately $\begin{bmatrix} 0 & 0.8740 \\ -0.5190 & 1.3860 \end{bmatrix}$, which is a stable matrix.

---

[13] Actually, we can solve our Riccati equations even at values of θ below the breakdown point, provided that they are not too far below. The reason is that the Riccati equations embody first-order conditions only. When we pass through $\underline{\theta}$, it is the second order condition for minimization with respect to w_{t+1} that is violated.

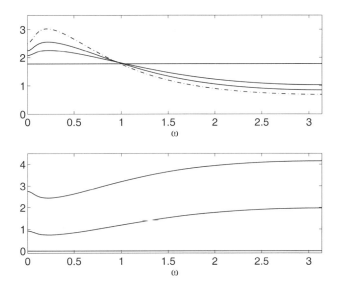

Figure 8.7.2: Example 2. Top: $G_F(e^{-i\omega})'G_F(e^{-i\omega})$ for $\theta = 10000, 5, 3, 1.777546728$, respectively. The flatter curves are for lower θ. Bottom: $\theta - G_F(e^{-i\omega})'G_F(e^{-i\omega})$ for $\theta = 5, 3, 1.777546728$, respectively. For $\theta = 1.777546728$, the curve is nearly zero.

8.7.3. Example 3

Figure 8.7.3 shows outcomes for example 3, which alters example 2 in a way that makes it impossible for the H_∞ control law completely to flatten the frequency response. The law of motion for the state is as in example 2, but now we specify an objective function as $H = \begin{bmatrix} 1 & -1 \\ 0 & -.01 \end{bmatrix}$, $J = \begin{bmatrix} 0 \\ 1 \end{bmatrix}$. We continue to assume that $A = \begin{bmatrix} \delta & 0 \\ 0 & \rho \end{bmatrix}$, $B = \begin{bmatrix} 1 \\ 0 \end{bmatrix}$, $C = \begin{bmatrix} 0 \\ 1 \end{bmatrix}$ where $\delta = .95, \rho = .9$.

In example 3, $A - BF + CK$ acquires an eigenvalue with a unit absolute value as θ approaches the breakdown point. Consistent with this outcome, the implied value of η becomes arbitrarily large as θ approaches the breakdown point for nonzero values of w_0.

8.8. Entropy is the indirect utility function of the multiplier game

In stating the multiplier problem, we imposed the initial condition $W(0) = w_0$. We now show that for a given θ, the control law that solves the multiplier game does not depend on the choice of initial condition w_0 and that

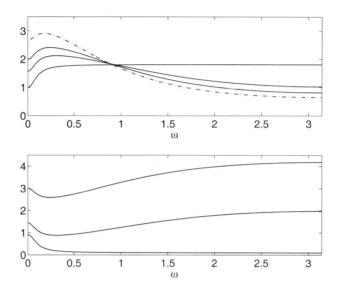

Figure 8.7.3: Example 3. Top: $G_F(e^{-i\omega})'G_F(e^{-i\omega})$ for $\theta = 10000, 5, 3, 1.90532584149715$, respectively. The flatter curves are for lower θ. Bottom: $\theta - G_F(e^{-i\omega})'G_F(e^{-i\omega})$ for $\theta = 5, 3, 1.777546728$, respectively. The curve for $\theta = 1.90532584149715$, which is very close to the breakdown value for θ, is not flat.

it also equals the control law that solves an entropy control problem. As a consequence, we can replace the multiplier problem by an entropy criterion in the frequency domain that does not depend on the initial condition. The entropy criterion is motivated by the representation described in the following theorem:

Theorem 8.8.1. *Assume that θ and F are such that $\int_\Gamma \log \det(\theta I - G_F'G_F)d\lambda > -\infty$. The criterion $\log \det[D(0)'D(0)]$ can be represented as*

$$\log \det \left[D\left(0\right)' D\left(0\right) \right] = \int_\Gamma \log \det \left[\theta I - G_F\left(\zeta\right)' G_F\left(\zeta\right) \right] d\lambda\left(\zeta\right). \qquad (8.8.1)$$

Proof. $D(0)'D(0)$ can be regarded as a one-step prediction error covariance matrix for a vector process $D(L)\epsilon_t$, where L is the lag operator and ϵ_t is an i.i.d. random process with mean zero and identity contemporaneous covariance matrix, and $D(\zeta)$ originates in the spectral factorization (8.6.7). We can use a result from linear prediction theory to verify the representation (8.8.1). See Theorem 6.2 of Rozanov (1967, p. 76). ∎

Theorem 8.6.1 and Theorem 8.8.1 both require that $\int_\Gamma \log \det(\theta I - G_F' G_F) d\lambda > -\infty$ but permit $\theta I - G_F' G_F$ to be singular at isolated points in Γ.

Evaluating the right-hand side of (8.8.1) requires no spectral factorization, just integration over frequencies. The contour integral on the right side of (8.8.1) is the entropy criterion. In the undiscounted case, it coincides with the measure of entropy used by Mustafa and Glover (1990).[14] When $\beta = 1$, the F that maximizes (8.8.1) is often motivated as an approximation of the F that maximizes the H_∞ criterion, one that maintains analyticity of W.

Next we give a representation for the coefficients of the minimizing W. Recall that these coefficients are the time domain values of the minimizing misspecification w_{t+1} for $t = 0, 1, \ldots$.

Theorem 8.8.2. *Assume θ and F are such that $\theta I - G_F' G_F$ is nonsingular on Γ. Then the solution to the multiplier problem is*

$$w_{t+1} = K \left(A_F + CK \right)^t C w_0 \tag{8.8.2}$$

where

$$K = \left(\theta I - C'PC \right)^{-1} C'PA_F, \tag{8.8.3}$$

and P^* is the positive semidefinite solution to the Riccati equation

$$P = H_F' H_F + \beta A_F' P A_F + \beta A_F' P C \left(\theta I - C'PC \right)^{-1} C'PA_F \tag{8.8.4}$$

for which $A_F + CK$ has eigenvalues that are inside the circle Γ. Moreover,

$$\int_\Gamma \log \det \left(\theta I - G_F' G_F \right) d\lambda = \log \det \left(\theta I - C'P^*C \right). \tag{8.8.5}$$

Proof. We use a recursive formulation and solution of the spectral factorization problem (8.6.7) to prove the theorem. To compute D in the spectral factorization $I\theta - G_F' G_F = D'D$, we apply the factorization result given by Zhou, Doyle, and Glover (1996). Recall that $G_F = H_F (I - \zeta A_F)^{-1} C$. The spectral density matrix to be factored is

$\theta I - G_F' G_F$

$= \theta I - C' \left[I - \sqrt{\beta} \exp\left(-i\omega\right) A_F' \right]^{-1} H_F' H_F \left[I - \sqrt{\beta} \exp\left(i\omega\right) A_F \right]^{-1} C$

$= \theta I - C' \left[\exp\left(i\omega\right) I - \sqrt{\beta} A_F' \right]^{-1} H_F' H_F \left[\exp\left(-i\omega\right) I - \sqrt{\beta} A_F \right]^{-1} C,$

---

[14] It coincides with their measure of entropy at $s_0 = \infty$, in their notation.

where we have used the parameterization $\zeta = \sqrt{\beta}\exp(i\omega)$. From Theorem 21.26 of Zhou, Doyle, and Glover (1996, p. 555), we obtain the factorization

$$
\begin{aligned}
\theta I - & C'[\exp(i\omega)I - \sqrt{\beta}A_F']^{-1}H_F'H_F[\exp(-i\omega)I - \sqrt{\beta}A_F]^{-1}C \\
= & (I - C'[\exp(i\omega)I - \sqrt{\beta}A_F']^{-1}\sqrt{\beta}K') \\
& R(I - \sqrt{\beta}K[\exp(-i\omega)I - \sqrt{\beta}A_F]^{-1}C) \\
= & (I - \zeta'C'[I - \zeta'A_F']^{-1}K')R(I - \zeta K[I - \zeta A_F]^{-1}C)
\end{aligned}
\tag{8.8.6}
$$

where

$$
R = \theta I - C'PC,
\tag{8.8.7}
$$

$$
K = R^{-1}C'PA_F,
\tag{8.8.8}
$$

and $P \geq 0$ is the stabilizing solution of the Riccati equation

$$
\beta A_F'P\left(I - \frac{1}{\theta}CC'P\right)^{-1}A_F - P + H_F'H_F = 0.
\tag{8.8.9}
$$

We establish that formula (8.8.9) is equivalent with (8.8.4) by showing that

$$
\left(I - \frac{1}{\theta}CC'P\right)^{-1} = I + C\left(\theta I - C'PC\right)^{-1}C'P.
$$

We verify this result by postmultiplying the matrix $I - \frac{1}{\theta}CC'P$ by the matrix $I + C(\theta I - C'PC)^{-1}C'P$

$$
\begin{aligned}
\left(I - \frac{1}{\theta}CC'P\right) & \left[I + C\left(\theta I - C'PC\right)^{-1}C'P\right] \\
& = I - \frac{1}{\theta}CC'P + C\left(I - \frac{1}{\theta}C'PC\right)(\theta I - C'PC)^{-1}C'P \\
& = I - \frac{1}{\theta}CC'P + \frac{1}{\theta}CC'P \\
& = I.
\end{aligned}
$$

For the stabilizing solution, K from (8.8.8) is such that $I - \zeta\sqrt{\beta}K[I - \sqrt{\beta}\zeta A_F]^{-1}C$ has zeros outside the unit circle of the complex plane (Zhou, Doyle, and Glover (1996)). As a consequence, $I - \zeta K[I - \zeta A_F]^{-1}C$ has zeros outside of the circle Γ. Therefore, (8.8.6) and (8.6.7) imply that

$$
D^*(\zeta) = R^{1/2}\left(I - \zeta K[I - \zeta A_F]^{-1}C\right)
\tag{8.8.10}
$$

has zeros outside Γ, and

$$
\theta I - G_F'G_F = D^{*\prime}D^*.
$$

Furthermore,
$$D^* (0)' D^* (0) = R = \theta I - C' P^* C.$$

Thus, $\log \det[D^*(0)'D^*(0)]$ can be represented as $\log \det(\theta I - C'P^*C)$.

From formula (8.6.12), the solution for $W(\zeta)$ can be represented as
$$D^* (\zeta) W (\zeta) = D^* (0) w_0.$$

Notice that $D^*(0) = R^{1/2}$. Formula (8.8.10) gives
$$\left(I - \zeta K \left[I - \zeta A_F \right]^{-1} C \right) W (\zeta) = w_0.$$

To solve this equation, we first construct a two-equation system by including
$$\bar{X} (\zeta) = [I - \zeta A_F]^{-1} C W (\zeta). \tag{8.8.11}$$

Thus,
$$[I - \zeta A_F] \bar{X} (\zeta) = C W (\zeta) \tag{8.8.12}$$

and hence from equation (8.8.11) we have
$$W (\zeta) - \zeta K \bar{X} (\zeta) = w_0. \tag{8.8.13}$$

Adding the equation (8.8.12) to (8.8.12) premultiplied by C gives
$$[I - \zeta A_F - \zeta C K] \bar{X} (\zeta) = C w_0.$$

Thus,
$$\bar{X} (\zeta) = \sum_{j=0}^{\infty} \zeta^j (A + CK)^j C w_0.$$

From the second equation
$$W (\zeta) = \sum_{j=1}^{\infty} \zeta^j K (A + CK)^{j-1} C w_0 + w_0.$$

The coefficient on ζ^j in this power series is the implied value of w_j.   ∎

Theorem 8.8.2 can be extended to allow for isolated singularities by considering solutions in the larger space $\mathcal{W}^a$. In appendix E, we show that the entropy formula (8.8.5) of Theorem 8.8.2 continues to hold if $\theta I - G'_F G_F$ is positive semidefinite and nonsingular at either $\sqrt{\beta}$ or $-\sqrt{\beta}$.

Formula (8.8.4) can also be written $P = H'_F H_F + A'_F \mathcal{D}(P) A_F = S(P)$ where the operators $\mathcal{D}$ and S are defined in (7.4.4c) and (7.4.4f) on page 144. Note also that (8.8.3) matches (7.4.4e).

Readers may notice that Theorem 8.8.2 and its extension overlap with Theorem 8.5.1 of chapter 7. Theorem 8.5.1 characterizes outcomes in the time domain within the equilibrium of the same Stackelberg game analyzed in this chapter. The time-domain representation of the worst-case sequence $\{w_{t+1} : t = 0, 1, ...\}$ in Theorem 8.5.1 coincides with the distorted means for the shock process $\{\epsilon_{t+1}\}$ from Theorem 8.8.2 conditioned only on date zero information when evaluated at the equilibrium F.

We have constructed a frequency domain criterion for the robust control law at the breakdown point (H_∞) and a frequency domain criterion for $\theta = \infty$. Theorem 8.8.2 motivates an alternative objective function that can be used to fashion a robust control law, which is why we do not restrict attention to the equilibrium outcome. We now show that the Stackelberg multiplier game can be restated by using entropy defined as

$$\int_\Gamma \log \det \left(\theta I - G_F{}' G_F \right) d\lambda \tag{8.8.14}$$

to rank control laws instead of the solution to the multiplier problem. The multiplier criterion (8.6.8) depends on w_0, while (8.8.14) does not. But Theorem 8.5.1 showed that the F that solves the two-player zero-sum game stated in equation (8.5.1) is independent of w_0. Therefore, we will attain the same decision rule F by maximizing a criterion defined in terms of $D(0)'D(0)$ alone, ignoring w_0. Thus, let $w_0'\hat{D}(0)'\hat{D}(0)w_0$ denote criterion (8.6.8) for another control law, say $\hat{F}$. If

$$w_0' D\left(0 \right)' D\left(0 \right) w_0 \geq w_0' \hat{D}\left(0 \right)' \hat{D}\left(0 \right) w_0$$

for all w_0, then

$$D\left(0 \right)' D\left(0 \right) \geq \hat{D}\left(0 \right)' \hat{D}\left(0 \right)$$

where $\geq$ is the standard partial ordering of positive semidefinite matrices. As a consequence,

$$\log \det \left[D\left(0 \right)' D\left(0 \right) \right] \geq \log \det \left[\hat{D}\left(0 \right)' \hat{D}\left(0 \right) \right].$$

Thus, instead of taking the minimized objective of the multiplier problem for a given w_0 as our criterion to rank control laws, we take our criterion to be

$$\log \det D\left(0 \right)' D\left(0 \right).$$

Theorem 8.8.1 shows that this is the entropy criterion used to define (8.8.14).

Consider now the limiting behavior of entropy as θ becomes arbitrarily large. For a fixed θ, we can subtract a constant term from the instantaneous objective without changing the ranking. We have to subtract a constant to prevent the limiting intertemporal objective function from becoming infinite. It can be shown that

$$\lim_{\theta \uparrow +\infty} \int_\Gamma \left[\log \det \left(\theta I - G_F{}' G_F \right) - \log \det \left(\theta I \right) \right] d\lambda$$

$$= \int_\Gamma \left[\log \det \left(I - \frac{1}{\theta} G_F{}' G_F \right) \right] d\lambda = 0$$

for any $F \in \widetilde{\mathcal{F}}$. Although the criterion is degenerate for every control law F, the derivative with respect to $\frac{1}{\theta}$ evaluated at zero will *not* be degenerate. The derivative is

$$- \int_\Gamma \text{trace} \left(G_F{}' G_F \right) d\lambda - H_2 \left(F \right).$$

Thus, an appropriate limit of the entropy criterion is the H_2 criterion. Moreover, since $F(\theta)$ as a well defined limit $F(\infty)$, it is necessarily true that this limiting control law is the solution to the H_2 problem.

To summarize, we have constructed a family of entropy objectives indexed by θ and a family of associated control laws $F(\theta)$. For a given initial condition and a given value of $\theta > \underline{\theta}$, there is a corresponding Stackelberg multiplier game for which $F(\theta)$ and W_θ are equilibrium outcomes. In particular, W_θ is a power series representation of a worst-case specification error sequence. An associated Stackelberg constraint game also yields the same equilibrium outcomes. Thus, we have three alternative ways to justify the control law $F(\theta)$. The limiting control laws $F(\underline{\theta})$ and $F(\infty)$ are the solutions to the H_∞ and H_2 problems, respectively.

8.9. Meaning of entropy

The criterion (8.8.14) acquires the name "entropy" via formula (8.8.1), which links (8.8.14) to the log det of a one-step ahead prediction error covariance matrix for a process with moving average representation $D(L)\varepsilon_t$, where ε_t is an i.i.d. process with mean zero and identity covariance matrix. For an ordinary (non-robust) filtering problem, we have also applied the term entropy to a closely related criterion that appears in (5.6.9) and (5.6.14) on pages 115 and 116, respectively. There the connection to a prediction problem was immediate, but here it is only indirect via the link revealed in formula (8.8.1) and the arguments in the proof of Theorem 8.6.1.[15] Our notion of entropy

---

[15] Also, the presence of discounting compels us to use the change of measure associated with λ to reveal the connection to the log det of what looks like a prediction error covariance matrix.

here is a relative one that compares $G_F{}'G_F$ to a constant frequency matrix θI.

8.10. Risk aversion across frequencies

This section discusses how the entropy criterion adjusts the H_2 criterion to express a concern about model misspecification by putting additional concavity into a utility function. We thereby develop a sense in which the entropy criterion represents model misspecification by inducing *risk aversion* across frequencies.

The H_2 criterion is

$$H_2 = - \int_\Gamma \text{trace} \left[G_F \left(\zeta \right)' G_F \left(\zeta \right) \right] d\lambda \left(\zeta \right),$$

and the entropy criterion is

$$\text{ent} = \int_\Gamma \log \det \left[\theta I - G_F \left(\zeta \right)' G_F \left(\zeta \right) \right] d\lambda \left(\zeta \right).$$

Take a symmetric negative semidefinite matrix V with eigenvalues $-\delta_1, \ldots, -\delta_n$ Let $\theta > \max_i -\delta_i$. Then $\text{trace}(V) = \sum_j -\delta_j$ and

$$\log \det \left(\theta I + V \right) = \sum_j \log \left(\theta - \delta_j \right).$$

Note that $\log(\theta - \delta)$ is a concave function of $-\delta$.

Associated with each ζ is a set of eigenvalues of $G_F(\zeta)'G_F(\zeta)$ that we denote $\delta_1(\zeta), \ldots, \delta_n(\zeta)$. Let them be ordered according to their magnitude. Then we can write the H_2 criterion as

$$H_2 = \sum_j \int_\Gamma -\delta_j \left(\zeta \right) d\lambda \left(\zeta \right).$$

The entropy criterion is formed from H_2 by putting a concave transformation inside the integration:

$$\text{ent} = \sum_j \int_\Gamma \log \left[\theta - \delta_j \left(\zeta \right) \right] d\lambda \left(\zeta \right). \tag{8.10.1}$$

Thus, the entropy criterion puts more curvature into the return function. These effects could also be represented as enhanced risk aversion. Notice that here the "risk aversion" is across frequencies: in (8.10.1) we average over eigenvalues and frequencies instead of states of nature. Big eigenvalues have relatively more weight in the entropy criterion because of the concavity of the logarithm function.

8.11. Concluding remarks

The decision maker's approximating model asserts that the Fourier transform of a target vector $Z(\zeta)$ is

$$Z(\zeta) = G_F(\zeta) w_0$$

where $G_F(\zeta)$ is the transfer function $G_F(\zeta) = H_F(I - (A - BF)\zeta)^{-1}C$ and F is the decision maker's feedback rule. The approximating model sets $W(\zeta) = w_0$, but the misspecified models assert that

$$Z(\zeta) = G_F(\zeta) W(\zeta).$$

Deviations of $W(\zeta)$ from w_0 represent the approximating model's misspecification of the temporal properties of the shock process.[16]

Without fear of model misspecification, the decision maker would choose F to maximize H_2 defined in equation $(8.4.3)$. A concern about robustness to model misspecification can be expressed by having the decision maker replace H_2 by either H_∞ or an entropy criterion. The H_∞ criterion induces a robust decision rule via the following thought process. The decision maker considers perturbations to the temporal properties of the shocks and wants decisions that will work well across a broad set of such perturbations. To promote robustness, the decision maker investigates the consequences of a candidate decision rule under a worst-case shock process. But what is worst depends on his decision rule. Given his decision rule, the *worst* serial correlation pattern focuses spectral power at the frequency that attains the highest weight in the frequency domain representation of $Z(\zeta)'Z(\zeta)$. The contribution of that frequency to discounted costs is measured by the maximal eigenvalue of $G_F(\zeta)'G_F(\zeta)$. The decision maker achieves a robust rule by optimizing against that worst serial correlation pattern, in particular, by selecting the feedback rule that minimizes the maximum eigenvalue across all frequencies. Under the entropy criterion, when $\theta > \underline{\theta}$, the decision maker responds in a similar but less severe way by flattening the response $G_F(\zeta)$ across ζ's. We study an example of such behavior in chapter 10, where we use insights from the frequency domain to interpret how a form of precautionary savings is called for by a robust decision rule for a permanent income model.

---

[16] See appendix F for an interpretation of $W(\zeta)$ in terms of the spectral density matrix of a random vector of shocks.

A. Infimization of H_∞

To verify that we have found the infimum of version 2 of $(8.4.1)$-$(8.4.2)$, let ω^* be the frequency associated with the maximum value of ρ and let $v(\omega^*)$ denote the corresponding eigenvector. This eigenvector can be complex. We can find a $W^*(\zeta)$ with all real coefficients, with an initial coefficient zero that coincides with $v(\omega^*)$ for $\zeta = \sqrt{\beta}\exp(i\omega^*)$. We accomplish this while setting all values of w_t to zero except possibly those for w_1 and w_2. In particular, that the coefficients of $W^*(\zeta)$ be real requires symmetry, i.e., $W^*(\sqrt{\beta}\exp(i\omega))' = W^*(\sqrt{\beta}\exp(-i\omega))^\top$, where $^\top$ denotes transposition. This leads to two equations of the form $W^*(\zeta^*) = w_1\zeta^* + w_2\zeta^{*2}$, $W^*(\zeta^{*'}) = w_1\zeta^{*'} + w_2\zeta^{*'2}$, where here $'$ denotes the complex conjugate, and $\zeta^* = \sqrt{\beta}\exp(i\omega)$. These two equations determine real-valued vectors w_1, w_2. To form the infimizing $W(\zeta)$, we shall construct an approximating sequence of "distributed lags" of $W^*(\zeta)$ that converge to it. To get distributed lags of the desired form, create a sequence of continuous positive scalar functions $\{g_n\}$ such that

(i) $g_n(\omega) = g_n(-\omega)$;
(ii) $\frac{1}{2\pi}\int_{-\pi}^{\pi} g_n(\omega)d\omega = 1$;
(iii) $\{g_n(\omega^*)\}$ diverges;
(iv) $\{g_n\}$ converges uniformly to zero outside any open interval containing ω^*;
(v) $\int_{-\pi}^{\pi} \log g_n(\omega)d\omega > 0$.

Then associated with each g_n is a real scalar (one-sided) sequence with transform $b_n(\zeta)$ such that $b_n(\zeta)^* b_n(\zeta) = g_n(\omega)$ for $\zeta = \sqrt{\beta}\exp(i\omega)$.

Construct $W_n(\zeta) \propto b_n(\zeta)W^*(\zeta)$, where the constant of proportionality makes the resulting W_n satisfy constraint $(8.4.2)$. We have designed the sequence $\{W_n\}$ to approximate the direction $v(\omega^*)$. The sequence of transforms $\{g_n\}$ converges to a generalized function, namely a Dirac delta function with mass concentrated at frequency ω^*. It is straightforward to show that

$$\lim_{n\to\infty} \int_\Gamma W_n(\zeta)' G_F(\zeta)' G_F(\zeta) W_n(\zeta)\, d\lambda(\zeta) = \eta(H_\infty)^2.$$

B. A dual prediction problem

A prediction problem is dual to maximizing $(8.6.3)$ subject to $(8.6.4)$-$(8.6.5)$. Let $[\theta I - G_F(\zeta)' G_F(\zeta)]$ for $\zeta = \sqrt{\beta}\exp(i\omega)$ denote a spectral density matrix for a covariance-stationary process $\{y_t\}$. The purpose is to predict $(w_0)'y_t$ linearly from past values of y_t. A candidate forecast rule of the form

$$-\sum_{j=1}^{\infty} (w_j)' y_{t-j} \tag{8.B.1}$$

has forecast error

$$\sum_{j=0}^{\infty} (w_j)' y_{t-j}.$$

Then criterion $(8.6.3)$ is interpretable as the forecast-error variance associated with this prediction problem. The constraints $(8.6.5)$ prevent the forecast from depending on y_{t+j} for $j \geq 1$.

C. Proofs of three lemmas

Proof of Lemma 8.5.1:

Proof. Suppose that $\tilde{\theta} > \theta$. Write

$$
(\tilde{\theta} - \theta) \int_\Gamma W_{\tilde{\theta}}{}' W_{\tilde{\theta}} d\lambda = \int_\Gamma W_{\tilde{\theta}}{}' \left[\tilde{\theta} I - G_{F(\theta)}{}' G_{F(\theta)} \right] W_{\tilde{\theta}} d\lambda
$$
$$
- \int_\Gamma W_{\tilde{\theta}}{}' \left[\theta I - G_{F(\theta)}{}' G_{F(\theta)} \right] W_{\tilde{\theta}} d\lambda. \tag{8.C.1}
$$

Since W_θ is a minimizer given $F(\theta)$,

$$
- \int_\Gamma W_{\tilde{\theta}}{}' \left[\theta I - G_{F(\theta)}{}' G_{F(\theta)} \right] W_{\tilde{\theta}} d\lambda \leq - \int_\Gamma W_\theta{}' \left[\theta I - G_{F(\theta)}{}' G_{F(\theta)} \right] W_\theta d\lambda
$$

and since $F(\theta)$ is a maximizer given W_θ,

$$
- \int_\Gamma W_\theta{}' \left[\theta I - G_{F(\theta)}{}' G_{F(\theta)} \right] W_\theta d\lambda \leq - \int_\Gamma W_\theta{}' \left[\theta I - G_{F(\tilde{\theta})}{}' G_{F(\tilde{\theta})} \right] W_\theta d\lambda.
$$

Taken together, these two inequalities imply that

$$
- \int_\Gamma W_{\tilde{\theta}}{}' \left[\theta I - G_{F(\theta)}{}' G_{F(\theta)} \right] W_{\tilde{\theta}} d\lambda \leq - \int_\Gamma W_\theta{}' \left[\theta I - G_{F(\tilde{\theta})}{}' G_{F(\tilde{\theta})} \right] W_\theta d\lambda. \tag{8.C.2}
$$

Since $F(\tilde{\theta})$ is a maximizer given $W_{\tilde{\theta}}$,

$$
\int_\Gamma W_{\tilde{\theta}}{}' \left[\tilde{\theta} I - G'_{F(\theta)} G_{F(\theta)} \right] W_{\tilde{\theta}} d\lambda \leq \int_\Gamma W_{\tilde{\theta}}{}' \left[\tilde{\theta} I - G'_{F(\tilde{\theta})} G_{F(\tilde{\theta})} \right] W_{\tilde{\theta}} d\lambda.
$$

and since $W_{\tilde{\theta}}$ is a minimizer given $F(\tilde{\theta})$:

$$
\int_\Gamma W'_{\tilde{\theta}} \left[\tilde{\theta} I - G'_{F(\tilde{\theta})} G_{F(\tilde{\theta})} \right] W_{\tilde{\theta}} d\lambda \leq \int_\Gamma W_\theta{}' \left[\tilde{\theta} I - G'_{F(\tilde{\theta})} G_{F(\tilde{\theta})} \right] W_\theta d\lambda.
$$

Taken together, these two inequalities imply that

$$
\int_\Gamma W_{\tilde{\theta}}{}' \left[\tilde{\theta} I - G'_{F(\theta)} G_{F(\theta)} \right] W_{\tilde{\theta}} d\lambda \leq \int_\Gamma W_\theta{}' \left[\tilde{\theta} I - G'_{F(\tilde{\theta})} G_{F(\tilde{\theta})} \right] W_\theta d\lambda. \tag{8.C.3}
$$

Substituting (8.C.2) and (8.C.3) into the right-hand side of (8.C.1) proves that

$$
(\tilde{\theta} - \theta) \int_\Gamma W_{\tilde{\theta}}{}' W_{\tilde{\theta}} d\lambda \leq (\tilde{\theta} - \theta) \int_\Gamma W_\theta{}' W_\theta d\lambda.
$$

Since $\tilde{\theta} > \theta$, the conclusion follows. ∎

Proof of Lemma 8.5.2:

Proof. For any $\theta > \underline{\theta}$,

$$\int_\Gamma W' \left(I - \frac{1}{\theta} G_{F(\theta)}' G_{F(\theta)} \right) W \lambda \geq \int_\Gamma W_\theta' \left(I - \frac{1}{\theta} G_{F(\theta)}' G_{F(\theta)} \right) W_\theta d\lambda \tag{8.C.4}$$

$$\geq \int_\Gamma \left(1 - \frac{1}{\theta} \operatorname{trace} \left[G_{F(\theta)}' G_{F(\theta)} \right] \right) W_\theta' W_\theta d\lambda.$$

The functions $\operatorname{trace}[G_{F(\theta)}' G_{F(\theta)}]$ converge uniformly on Γ to

$$\operatorname{trace} \left[G_{F(\infty)}' G_{F(\infty)} \right],$$

and, hence, $(1 - \frac{1}{\theta} \operatorname{trace}[G_{F(\theta)}' G_{F(\theta)}])$ converges uniformly to one. Therefore, taking limits as $\theta \to \infty$

$$\limsup_{\theta \to \infty} \int_\Gamma W' W d\lambda \geq \limsup_{\theta \to \infty} \int_\Gamma W_\theta' W_\theta d\lambda.$$

Minimizing the left-hand side with respect to W, given the constraint that $W(0) = w_0$, implies that

$$w_0 \cdot w_0 \geq \limsup_{\theta \to \infty} \int_\Gamma W_\theta' W_\theta d\lambda \geq w_0 \cdot w_0$$

since $W_\theta(0) = w_0$. The conclusion follows. ∎

Proof of Lemma 8.6.2:

Proof. The objective function $L(\theta, w_0)$ is concave in θ and hence continuous on the domain $\theta > \underline{\theta}$. Suppose $\tilde{\theta} > \theta$. Then

$$L\left(\tilde{\theta}, w_0\right) = \int_\Gamma W_{\tilde{\theta}}' \left[\tilde{\theta} I - G_{F(\tilde{\theta})}' G_{F(\tilde{\theta})} \right] W_{\tilde{\theta}} d\lambda \geq \int_\Gamma W_{\tilde{\theta}}' \left[\tilde{\theta} I - G_{F(\theta)}' G_{F(\theta)} \right] W_{\tilde{\theta}} d\lambda$$

$$\geq \int_\Gamma W_{\tilde{\theta}}' \left[\theta I - G_{F(\theta)}' G_{F(\theta)} \right] W_{\tilde{\theta}} d\lambda$$

$$\geq \int_\Gamma W_\theta' \left[\theta I - G_{F(\theta)}' G_{F(\theta)} \right] W_\theta d\lambda$$

$$= L\left(\theta, w_0\right).$$

The first inequality follows because $F(\tilde{\theta})$ solves the maximization part of the $\tilde{\theta}$ game, the second inequality follows because $\tilde{\theta} > \theta$, and the third inequality follows because W_θ solves the minimization part of the θ game. Since $L(\tilde{\theta}, w_0) - L(\theta, w_0)$ can be made arbitrarily small by choice of θ, it follows that

$$\int_\Gamma W_{\tilde{\theta}}' \left[\theta I - G_{F(\theta)}' G_{F(\theta)} \right] W_{\tilde{\theta}} d\lambda - \int_\Gamma W_\theta' \left[\theta I - G_{F(\theta)}' G_{F(\theta)} \right] W_\theta d\lambda$$

can be made arbitrarily small. By convexity of positive definite quadratic forms,

$$\frac{1}{4} \left[W_{\tilde{\theta}} + W_\theta \right]' \left[\theta I - G_{F(\theta)}' G_{F(\theta)} \right] \left[W_{\tilde{\theta}} + W_\theta \right] \geq \frac{1}{2} W_{\tilde{\theta}}' \left[\theta I - G_{F(\theta)}' G_{F(\theta)} \right] W_{\tilde{\theta}}$$

$$+ \frac{1}{2} W_\theta' \left[\theta I - G_{F(\theta)}' G_{F(\theta)} \right] W_\theta.$$

Therefore,

$$\frac{1}{4} \int_\Gamma \left[W_{\tilde\theta} + W_\theta \right]' \left[\theta I - G_{F(\theta)}{}' G_{F(\theta)} \right] \left[W_{\tilde\theta} + W_\theta \right] d\lambda$$

$$- \int_\Gamma W_\theta{}' \left[\theta I - G_{F(\theta)}{}' G_{F(\theta)} \right] W_\theta d\lambda$$

can be made arbitrarily small by choice of $\tilde\theta$, as can

$$- \int_\Gamma \left[W_{\tilde\theta} + W_\theta \right]' \left[\theta I - G_{F(\theta)}{}' G_{F(\theta)} \right] \left[W_{\tilde\theta} + W_\theta \right] d\lambda$$

$$+ 2 \int_\Gamma W_{\tilde\theta}{}' \left[\theta I - G_{F(\theta)}{}' G_{F(\theta)} \right] W_{\tilde\theta} d\lambda$$

$$+ 2 \int_\Gamma W_\theta{}' \left[\theta I - G_{F(\theta)}{}' G_{F(\theta)} \right] W_\theta d\lambda.$$

By the *parallelogram law* this expression simplifies to

$$\int_\Gamma \left[W_{\tilde\theta} - W_\theta \right]' \left[\theta I - G_{F(\theta)}{}' G_{F(\theta)} \right] \left[W_{\tilde\theta} - W_\theta \right] d\lambda,$$

which therefore converges to zero as $\tilde\theta$ declines to θ. Since

$$\theta I - G_{F(\theta)}{}' G_{F(\theta)} \geq \epsilon I$$

on Γ for some positive ϵ, it follows that

$$\lim_{\tilde\theta \downarrow \theta} \int_\Gamma \left[W_{\tilde\theta} - W_\theta \right]' \left[W_{\tilde\theta} - W_\theta \right] d\lambda = 0,$$

and hence $\lim_{\tilde\theta \downarrow \theta} \int_\Gamma W_{\tilde\theta}{}' W_{\tilde\theta} d\lambda = \int_\Gamma W_\theta{}' W_\theta d\lambda.$ ∎

D. Duality

In the text, we showed the link between a constraint game and a multiplier game and how to go from one to the other. In this appendix we study a simpler problem of evaluating a fixed control law using either a Lagrange multiplier or a constraint. We show how to apply standard duality methods except for an extra restriction on the magnitude of the multiplier. We also explore some consequences when the frequency domain entropy for the control law is not finite.

8.D.1. Evaluating a given control law

For a given control law F form the corresponding G_F and define

$$\theta_F = \left(H_\infty \left(F \right) \right)^2.$$

It follows that for all $W(\zeta)$

$$\theta_F \int_\Gamma W' W d\lambda \geq \int_\Gamma W' G_F' G_F W d\lambda.$$

Therefore, for all $\theta \geq \theta_F$, $\int_\Gamma W' \left[\theta I - G_F' G_F \right] W d\lambda$ is well defined for all $\theta \geq \theta_F$ but not for $\theta < \theta_F$.

For fixed F, consider the infimization part of the game defined in (8.4.1):

Worst-case minimization problem with a constraint:

Problem 1
$$\inf_W - \int_\Gamma W' G_F' G_F W d\lambda$$

subject to

$$\int_\Gamma W' W d\lambda \leq w_0' w_0 + \eta.$$

This problem minimizes a concave function subject to a convex constraint set, so standard duality theory does not apply. Therefore, we study the following alternative problem:

A related constrained problem

Problem 2
$$\inf_W \int_\Gamma W' \left(\theta_F I - G_F' G_F \right) W d\lambda$$

subject to

$$\int_\Gamma W' W d\lambda \leq \eta + {w_0}' w_0.$$

This problem is to minimize a convex function subject to a convex constraint set, so duality theory applies. We shall first show that a solution of Problem 2 with binding constraint also solves Problem 1. Then we shall apply standard duality theory to Problem 2.

Theorem 8.D.1. *A solution to Problem 2 with binding constraint solves Problem 1.*

Proof. Let W^* solve Problem 2 with the magnitude constraint binding

$$\int_\Gamma W^{*'} W^* d\lambda = \eta + w_0' w_0$$

and

$$W^* (0) = w_0.$$

Consider any other W such that

$$\int_\Gamma W' W d\lambda \leq \eta + w_0' w_0.$$

and

$$W (0) = w_0.$$

Then

$$\int_\Gamma W' \left(\theta_F I - G_F' G_F \right) W d\lambda \geq \int_\Gamma W^{*'} \left(\theta_F I - G_F' G_F \right) W^* d\lambda$$

and

$$\theta_F \int_\Gamma W'W\,d\lambda \le \theta_F \int_\Gamma W^{*\prime}W^*\,d\lambda.$$

Therefore

$$-\int_\Gamma W'G_F'G_FW\,d\lambda \ge -\int_\Gamma W^{*\prime}G_F'G_FW^*\,d\lambda,$$

which implies that W^* also solves Problem 1. ∎

Thus, a way to solve Problem 1 is to solve Problem 2 and verify the solution satisfies the magnitude constraint with equality.

We now apply duality theory to Problem 2 by forming

Saddle point version of problem 2:

$$\inf_W \sup_{\theta \ge \theta_F} \left[\int_\Gamma W' \left(\theta I - G_F'G_F \right) W\,d\lambda - (\theta - \theta_F)\left(\eta + w_0'w_0\right) \right].$$

We interpret $\theta - \theta_F$ as the Lagrange multiplier for Problem 2 and θ as the Lagrange multiplier for Problem 1. Because Problem 2 entails minimizing a convex function subject to a convex constraint set, standard duality theory applies to it. The conjugate problem is obtained by switching the order of the infimum and supremum operations

$$\sup_{\theta \ge \theta_F} \inf_W \left[\int_\Gamma W' \left(\theta I - G_F'G_F \right) W\,d\lambda - (\theta - \theta_F)\left(\eta + w_0'w_0\right) \right]. \qquad (8.D.1)$$

We can use this problem to construct the Lagrange multiplier θ for each $\eta > 0$.

By construction the saddle-point value for the conjugate problem coincides with the optimized value for Problem 2. When the specification-error constraint is binding for Problem 2, we can obtain the optimized value for Problem 1 by subtracting the constant $\theta_F(\eta + w_0'w_0)$ from $(8.D.1)$. The resulting conjugate problem is

$$\sup_{\theta \ge \theta_F} \inf_W \left[\int_\Gamma W' \left(\theta I - G_F'G_F \right) W\,d\lambda - \theta\left(\eta + w_0'w_0\right) \right]. \qquad (8.D.2)$$

Thus, we have eliminated the influence of θ_F on the objective of the saddle-point problem. But θ_F still affects the constraint set limiting the choice of θ (through the appearance of θ_F under the sup operator). This dependence can also be removed by virtue of the following theorem.

Theorem 8.D.2. *If the value of $(8.D.2)$ is finite, then $\theta \ge \theta_F$.*

Proof. Suppose that $\theta < \theta_F$, and consider the inner infimum part of the saddle-point problem $(8.D.2)$

$$\inf_W \int_\Gamma W' \left(\theta I - G_F'G_F \right) W\,d\lambda. \qquad (8.D.3)$$

Given the construction of θ_F, $(\theta I - G_F'G_F)$ has negative eigenvalues for some $|\zeta^*| = \sqrt{\beta}$. Parameterize Γ by forming $\zeta = \sqrt{\beta}\exp(i\omega)$, and let ω^* be the frequency associated with ζ^*. Thus, there exists a complex vector v such that

$$v' \left(\theta I - G_F'G_F \right) v < 0$$

on a nondegenerate interval of ω's containing ω^*. Imitating the argument in appendix A, we can form a $W^*(\zeta) = w_1\zeta + w_2\zeta$ such that $W^*(\zeta^*) = v$. We can then use the appendix A construction to form $W_n(\zeta) \sim b_n(\zeta)W^*(\zeta)$. Then it is straightforward to show that

$$\lim_{n\to\infty} \int_\Gamma W_n' \left(\theta I - G_F' G_F\right) W_n d\lambda = v' \left[\theta I - G_F\left(\zeta^*\right)' G_F\left(\zeta^*\right)\right] v < 0.$$

By construction $W_n(0) = 0$ and hence fails to satisfy the constraint for problem $(8.D.3)$. Also problem $(8.D.3)$ does not constrain the magnitude of W. We now form the sequence

$$\tilde{W}_n = nW_n + w_0,$$

which by construction satisfies $\tilde{W}_n(0) = w_0$. Given our multiplication of W_n by n, it clearly follows that

$$\lim_{n\to\infty} \int_\Gamma W_n' \left(\theta I - G_F' G_F\right) W_n d\lambda = -\infty.$$

Therefore, the optimized value of problem $(8.D.3)$ is $-\infty$ whenever $\theta < \theta_F$.　▪

Given what the theorem establishes about the behavior of the inner infimum part of saddle-point problem $(8.D.2)$ when $\theta < \theta_F$, we can state that $(8.D.2)$ corresponds to $(8.D.3)$, defined as

Conjugate saddle point version of problem 1

$$\sup_\theta \inf_W \left[\int_\Gamma W' \left(\theta I - G_F' G_F\right) W d\lambda - \theta \left(\eta + w_0' w_0\right)\right]. \qquad (8.D.4)$$

Whenever this problem has a solution for W that satisfies the specification-error constraint with equality, the resulting W also solves Problem 1 and the value of the conjugate saddle-point problem coincides with that of Problem 1. This conjugate problem provides the Lagrange multiplier $\theta \geq \theta_F$ associated with Problem 1. Armed with this multiplier, consider the inner infimum problem, which we call the *multiplier problem*

Problem　3　　　　　$\inf_W \left[\int_\Gamma W' \left(\theta I - G_F' G_F\right) W d\lambda\right].$

The solution of Problem 3 coincides with that of the prediction problem described in appendix B and analyzed in the text.

Given any η, we have just shown how to find the multiplier θ. We now suppose that the multiplier $\theta \geq \theta_F$ is given and want to deduce the corresponding value of η. Thus, suppose that we have a solution of the multiplier problem (Problem 3). It is sufficient for this problem to have a solution with $\theta > \theta_F$. (Later we shall discuss the case in which $\theta = \theta_F$.) We assume that

$$\int \log \det \left(\theta_F I - G_F' G_F\right) d\lambda > -\infty. \qquad (8.D.5)$$

Later we will describe what happens when this condition is violated.

Theorem 8.D.3. *Suppose that* $\theta > \theta_F$ *and that* $W(\zeta)$ *solves the multiplier Problem 3. Then there exists* $\eta > 0$ *such that* $W(\zeta)$ *solves Problem 1.*

Proof. From the dual prediction problem of appendix B, we know that when $\theta > \theta_F$, the solution to the multiplier problem is

$$W(\zeta) = D(\zeta)^{-1} D(0) w_0 \qquad (8.D.6)$$

where

$$D'D = \left(\theta I - G_F' G_F\right)$$

and D is continuous and nonsingular on the region $|\zeta| \leq \sqrt{\beta}$. Notice that D depends implicitly on θ. The resulting objective function is $w_0' D(0)' D(0) w_0$. The η corresponding to this choice of θ satisfies

$$\eta = \int w_0' D(0)' \left(\theta I - G_F' G_F\right)^{-1} D(0) w_0 d\lambda - w_0' w_0. \qquad (8.D.7)$$

∎

8.D.2. When $\theta = \theta_F$

We now study the multiplier problem in some special cases. For fixed control law F, suppose that θ is equal to the lower threshold value θ_F. Condition (8.D.5) implies that we can still obtain the factorization

$$D'D = \theta_F I - G_F' G_F,$$

where D is nonsingular on the region $|\zeta| < \sqrt{\beta}$, but now it is singular at some points $|\zeta| = \sqrt{\beta}$. Thus, the candidate solution for W given by (8.D.6) may not be well defined, and the infimum in the multiplier Problem 3 may not be attained. Nevertheless, the infimum is still given by the quadratic form: $w_0' D(0)' D(0) w_0$ and the implied η_F satisfies (8.D.7), and it will typically be infinite.

When $\eta_F = \infty$, we can find a $\theta > \theta_F$ that yields any positive η. Sometimes η_F is finite for a small (Lebesgue measure zero) set of initializations w_0. When this happens, we may only find $\theta \geq \theta_F$ for values of $\eta \leq \eta_F$.

8.D.3. Failure of entropy condition

Finally, we consider what happens when

$$\int \log \det \left(\theta_F I - G_F' G_F\right) d\lambda = -\infty.$$

Since G_F is a rational function of ζ with no poles in the region $|\zeta| \leq \sqrt{\beta}$, $\theta_F I - G_F' G_F$ is singular for all $|\zeta| = \sqrt{\beta}$. Factorizations still exist and are now of the form

$$D'D = \theta_F I - G_F' G_F$$

where D has fewer rows than columns and has full rank on the region $|\zeta| < \sqrt{\beta}$ (see Rozanov (1967, pp. 43–50)). This makes it possible to have a variety of solutions to Problem 2, including solutions for which the specification error constraint is slack.

To understand the multiplicity better, note that it is now possible to find $\tilde{W}$ such that

$$D\tilde{W} = 0 \qquad (8.D.8)$$

and for which $\tilde{W}(0) = 0$. Given any solution W^* to Problem 2, we may form $W^* + r\tilde{W}$ for any real number r without altering the objective of Problem 2. The value of r is restrained by the specification-error constraint, but it is possible for this range to be nondegenerate.

When the specification-error constraint for Problem 2 can be slack at the optimum, the Lagrange multiplier, $\theta - \theta_F$, is zero or, equivalently, $\theta = \theta_F$. Problem 2 will then have solutions in which the specification-error constraint is binding (but with a zero multiplier), and it is *only* these solutions that also solve Problem 1. As a consequence, solving the multiplier problem (Problem 3) for choices of θ greater than θ_F may not correspond to fixing an η for Problem 1. We illustrate this possibility in the following example.

Exceptional example

In this example, we construct $\tilde{W}$ satisfying (8.D.8) and $\tilde{W} > 0$ $\forall \zeta \in \Gamma$. Suppose that $A - BF = 0$ and hence $G_F = H_F C$, which is constant across frequencies. Then θ_F is the largest eigenvalue of the symmetric matrix $C'H'_F H_F C$, and $\det[\theta_F I - G'_F G_F] = 0$ for all $\zeta \in \Gamma$. Let μ be an eigenvector associated with θ_F with norm one. Solutions W^* to Problem 2 are given by

$$w_0^* = w_0$$

$$w_t^* = \alpha_t \mu$$

for $t > 0$ and the real numbers α_t chosen so that the magnitude constraint is satisfied. The resulting objective for Problem 2 is

$$w_0{}' \left(\theta_F I - C'H'_F H_F C \right) w_0.$$

Provided that $\eta > 0$, the magnitude constraint can be made slack (say by letting α_t be zero).

A solution to Problem 1 is obtained by setting α_t to make the magnitude constraint be satisfied with equality. Then the objective for Problem 1 is

$$-\theta_F \eta - w_0{}' C'H'_F H_F C w_0.$$

Finally, the Lagrange multiplier obtained from the conjugate problem is given by its lower threshold θ_F.

E. Proof of Theorem 8.8.2

This appendix restates a version of Theorem 8.8.2 under weaker assumptions about the nonsingularity of $[\theta I - G_F(\zeta)'G_F(\zeta)]$.

Theorem 8.E.1. *Suppose that*
 (i) A_F has eigenvalues that are inside the circle Γ;
 (ii) $\theta I - G'_F G_F \geq 0$ on Γ;
 (iii) Either $\theta I - G_F(-\sqrt{\beta})'G_F(-\sqrt{\beta})$ or $\theta I - G_F(\sqrt{\beta})'G_F(\sqrt{\beta})$ is nonsingular.

Then the entropy criterion can be represented as

$$\log \det D(0)' D(0) = \log \det \left(\theta I - C'PC \right)$$

where P is defined implicitly by (8.E.3) below.

Proof. We prove this theorem by referring to results from Zhou, Doyle, and Glover (1996). We outline the proof in four steps.

Step one: Transform the discrete-time discounted formulation into a continuous-time undiscounted formulation. Suppose that $\theta I - G_F(-\sqrt{\beta})' G_F(-\sqrt{\beta})$ is nonsingular. Define the linear fractional transformation

$$\zeta = -\sqrt{\beta} \left(\frac{s + \sqrt{\beta}}{s - \sqrt{\beta}} \right). \tag{8.E.1}$$

This transformation maps $s = -\sqrt{\beta}$ into $\zeta = 0$, $s = 0$ into $\sqrt{\beta}$, $s = \infty$ into $-\sqrt{\beta}$. The transformation maps the imaginary axis into the circle Γ and points on the left side of the complex plane into points inside the circle.

    Note also that

$$\beta \zeta^{-1} = -\sqrt{\beta} \left(\frac{-s + \sqrt{\beta}}{-s - \sqrt{\beta}} \right).$$

    In the case that $\theta I - G_F(\sqrt{\beta})' G_F(\sqrt{\beta})$ is singular, we replace linear fractional transformation (8.E.1) with

$$\zeta = \sqrt{\beta} \left(\frac{s + \sqrt{\beta}}{s - \sqrt{\beta}} \right). \tag{8.E.2}$$

In what follows we will use (8.E.1) but the argument for (8.E.2) is entirely similar.

Step two: Use parameterization (8.E.1) to write

$$
\begin{aligned}
G_F(\zeta) &= \left(s - \sqrt{\beta} \right) H_F \left[\left(s - \sqrt{\beta} \right) I + \left(s + \sqrt{\beta} \right) \sqrt{\beta} A_F \right]^{-1} C \\
&= \left(s - \sqrt{\beta} \right) H_F \left[s \left(I + \sqrt{\beta} A_F \right) - \sqrt{\beta} \left(I - \sqrt{\beta} A_F \right) \right]^{-1} C \\
&= \left(s - \sqrt{\beta} \right) H_F \left(sI - \hat{A} \right)^{-1} \hat{C} \\
&= \hat{G}_F(s)
\end{aligned}
$$

where

$$\hat{A} = \sqrt{\beta} \left(I + \sqrt{\beta} A_F \right)^{-1} \left(I - \sqrt{\beta} A_F \right)$$

$$\hat{C} = \left(I + \sqrt{\beta} A_F \right)^{-1} C.$$

Rewrite $\hat{G}_F$ as

$$
\begin{aligned}
\hat{G}_F(s) &= s H_F \left(sI - \hat{A} \right)^{-1} \hat{C} - \sqrt{\beta} H_F \left(sI - \hat{A} \right)^{-1} \hat{C} \\
&= H_F \left(sI - \hat{A} \right) \left(sI - \hat{A} \right)^{-1} \hat{C} + H_F \hat{A} \left(sI - \hat{A} \right)^{-1} \hat{C} - \sqrt{\beta} H_F \left(sI - \hat{A} \right)^{-1} \hat{C} \\
&= H_F \hat{C} - \hat{H}_F \left(sI - \hat{A} \right)^{-1} \hat{C},
\end{aligned}
$$

where

$$\hat{H}_F = H_F \left(\sqrt{\beta} I - \hat{A} \right).$$

Notice that

$$H_F \hat{C} = H_F \left(I + \sqrt{\beta} A_F \right)^{-1} C = \hat{G}_F \left(\infty \right) = G_F \left(-\sqrt{\beta} \right).$$

Step three: Write for s imaginary

$$\theta I - \hat{G}_F' \hat{G}_F = \left(\hat{C}' \left(-sI - \hat{A}' \right)^{-1} \quad I \right) \begin{pmatrix} -\hat{H}_F' \hat{H}_F & \hat{H}_F' H_F \hat{C} \\ \hat{C}' H_F' \hat{H}_F & \theta I - \hat{C}' H_F' H_F \hat{C} \end{pmatrix}$$
$$\begin{pmatrix} \left(sI - \hat{A} \right)^{-1} \hat{C} \\ I \end{pmatrix}.$$

Notice that

$$\theta I - \hat{C}' H_F' H_F \hat{C} = \theta I - G_F \left(-\sqrt{\beta} \right)' G_F \left(-\sqrt{\beta} \right)$$

is nonsingular and, in fact, positive definite.

Step four: Apply Corollary 13.20 of Zhou, Glover, and Doyle (1996) to conclude that there exists a matrix F such that

$$\theta I - \hat{G}_F' \hat{G}_F = \left[I - \hat{C}' \left(-sI - \hat{A}' \right)^{-1} F' \right] \left(\theta I - \hat{C}' H_F' H_F \hat{C} \right) \left[I - F \left(sI - \hat{A} \right)^{-1} \hat{C} \right].$$

Now inverse transform from s to ζ. The following are useful formulas for carrying out this transformation. First

$$\hat{A} = \sqrt{\beta} \left(I + \sqrt{\beta} A_F \right)^{-1} \left(I - \sqrt{\beta} A_F \right).$$

Invert this relation to find that

$$\left(I + \sqrt{\beta} A_F \right) \hat{A} = \sqrt{\beta} I - \beta A_F$$

or

$$\sqrt{\beta} \left(\hat{A} + \sqrt{\beta} I \right) A_F = - \left(\hat{A} - \sqrt{\beta} I \right)$$

or

$$A_F = \frac{1}{\sqrt{\beta}} \left(\sqrt{\beta} I + \hat{A} \right)^{-1} \left(\sqrt{\beta} I - \hat{A} \right).$$

Similarly,

$$\left(s - \sqrt{\beta} \right) \zeta = -\sqrt{\beta} \left(s + \sqrt{\beta} \right)$$

or

$$\left(\zeta + \sqrt{\beta} \right) s = \sqrt{\beta} \left(\zeta - \sqrt{\beta} \right)$$

or

$$s = \sqrt{\beta} \left(\frac{\zeta - \sqrt{\beta}}{\zeta + \sqrt{\beta}} \right).$$

Write

$$I - F\left(sI - \hat{A}\right)^{-1}\hat{C} = I - \left(\zeta + \sqrt{\beta}\right)F\left[\sqrt{\beta}\left(\zeta - \sqrt{\beta}\right)I - \left(\zeta + \sqrt{\beta}\right)\hat{A}\right]^{-1}\hat{C}$$

$$= I - \left(\zeta + \sqrt{\beta}\right)F\left[\zeta\left(\sqrt{\beta}I - \hat{A}\right) - \sqrt{\beta}\left(\sqrt{\beta}I + \hat{A}\right)\right]^{-1}\hat{C}$$

$$= I + \left(\zeta + \sqrt{\beta}\right)F\left(I - \zeta A_F\right)^{-1}\frac{1}{\sqrt{\beta}}\left(\sqrt{\beta}I + \hat{A}\right)^{-1}\hat{C}$$

$$= I + \frac{\left(\zeta + \sqrt{\beta}\right)}{2\sqrt{\beta}}F\left(I - \zeta A_F\right)^{-1}C$$

$$= \tilde{G}_F\left(\zeta\right).$$

Note that

$$I + \frac{\left(\zeta + \sqrt{\beta}\right)}{2\sqrt{\beta}}F\left(I - \zeta A_F\right)^{-1}C = I + \frac{1}{2}FC + \frac{\zeta}{2\sqrt{\beta}}F\left(I + \sqrt{\beta}A_F\right)\left(I - \zeta A\right)^{-1}C.$$

Define P implicitly by

$$\theta I - C'PC = \left(I + \frac{1}{2}C'F'\right)\left[\theta I - C'\left(I + \sqrt{\beta}A_F'\right)^{-1}H_F'H_F\left(I + \sqrt{\beta}A_F\right)^{-1}C\right]$$

$$\times \left(I + \frac{1}{2}FC\right).$$

$$(8.E.3)$$

■

F. Stochastic interpretation of H_2

This appendix displays another game that implies H_2 where the shocks w_t are permitted to be nonzero for $t > 0$. Recall that w_t is $m \times 1$, where m is the number of shocks. We continue to assume that $w_t = 0$ for all $t < 0$. We state

Game Sa: Choose $(F, \{w_t\})$ to attain

$$\max_{\widetilde{\mathcal{F}}} \inf_{\{w_t\}} -\sum_{t=0}^{\infty}\beta^t z_t'z_t \qquad (8.F.1)$$

subject to

$$x_0 = Cw_0 \qquad (8.F.2a)$$

$$\sum_{t=0}^{\infty}\beta^t w_t w_t' = \sigma^2 I \qquad (8.F.2b)$$

$$\sum_{t=0}^{\infty}\left(\beta^{\frac{t}{2}}w_t\right)\left(\beta^{\frac{t-j}{2}}w_{t-j}\right)' = 0 \ \forall j \neq 0 \qquad (8.F.2c)$$

$$\sigma^2 \leq \eta \qquad (8.F.2d)$$

Equations $(8.F.2b)$, $(8.F.2c)$ imply that

$$W\left(\zeta\right)W\left(\zeta\right)' = \sigma^2 I, \quad |\zeta| = \sqrt{\beta}. \tag{8.F.3}$$

Further, $(8.F.3)$ implies $(8.F.2b)$, $(8.F.2c)$.

Game Sa has the following counterpart in the frequency domain

Game Sb: Find $\left(F, \sigma^2\right)$ that attain

$$\max_{F} \inf_{\sigma^2} -\sigma^2 \int_{\Gamma} \text{trace}\left[G_F\left(\zeta\right)' G_F\left(\zeta\right)\right] d\lambda\left(\zeta\right), \tag{8.F.4}$$

subject to

$$\sigma^2 \leq \eta. \tag{8.F.5}$$

We substituted $(8.F.3)$ into $(8.4.1)$ to obtain $(8.F.4)$. The solution of game Sb sets σ^2 at its upper bound η and sets F to maximize the H_2 criterion $(8.4.3)$.

8.F.1. Stochastic counterpart

Criterion $(8.4.3)$ emerges when the shock process $\{w_t\}_{t=1}^{\infty}$ is taken to be a martingale difference sequence adapted to J_t, the sigma algebra generated by x_0 and the history of w, where $E w_{t+1} w'_{t+1} | J_t = I$. The martingale difference specification implies

$$E \sum_{t=0}^{\infty} \left(\beta^{\frac{t}{2}} w_t\right) \left(\beta^{\frac{t-j}{2}} w_{t-j}\right)' = \begin{cases} \sigma^2 \left(1 - \beta\right)^{-1} I & \text{if } j = 0; \\ 0 & \text{otherwise.} \end{cases} \tag{8.F.6}$$

Equation $(8.F.6)$ is equivalent with $E[W(\zeta)W(\zeta)]' = \sigma^2(1-\beta)^{-1}I$ for $\zeta \in \Gamma$. With this representation, $(8.4.3)$ is proportional to $-(1 - \beta)^{-1} E \sum_{t=0}^{\infty} \beta^t z_t z'_t$.[17]

---

[17] See Whiteman (1985b).

Chapter 9
Calibrating misspecification fears with detection error probabilities

> *The temptation to form premature theories upon insufficient data is the bane of our profession.*
> — *Sherlock Holmes, in Sir Arthur Conan Doyle, The Valley of Fear, 1915*

9.1. Introduction

This chapter proposes a strategy for calibrating the robustness parameter θ for some macroeconomic applications of multiplier robust control problems. Our procedure is to set θ so that, given the finite amount of data at his disposal, a decision maker would find it difficult statistically to distinguish members of a set of alternative models against which he seeks robustness (i.e., the models on and inside the entropy ball depicted in figure 1.7.1). We have in mind that, relative to the rate at which new data arrive, the decision maker's discount factor makes him sufficiently impatient that he cannot wait for those new data to resolve his model misspecification fears for him.

In chapter 14, we apply the approach of this chapter to calibrate an asset pricing example. There we demonstrate what we find to be a fascinating connection between the statistical detection error probabilities of this chapter and an object that is conventionally interpreted as the market price of risk, but that we suggest should instead be regarded as the market price of model uncertainty.

9.2. Entropy and detection error probabilities

Random disturbances in the transition law conceal the distortion of a perturbed model relative to the approximating model and can make the distortion difficult to detect statistically.[1] In this chapter, we illustrate how unconditional entropy governs statistics for distinguishing two models using moderate amounts of data. We use a statistical theory of model selection[2] to define a mapping from the parameter θ to a detection error probability for discriminating between the approximating model and an endogenous worst-case model associated with that θ. We use that detection error probability

---

[1] See chapter 3 for a formulation with stochastic shocks to the transition law.
[2] For example, see Burnham and Anderson (1998).

to determine a context-specific θ that is associated with a set of alternative models against which it is reasonable to seek robustness.[3]

9.2.1. The context-specific nature of θ

An outcome of the analysis in this chapter is a proposal to calibrate θ in a preliminary analysis the inputs of which include (1) a decision maker's approximating model, and (2) the decision maker's intertemporal objective function. In the course of describing detection error probabilities, we hope to clarify a mental experiment in which the decision maker is confronted with a model selection problem that differs markedly from the mental experiment involving *known* models with which Pratt (1964) confronted a decision maker when he wanted to extract measures of the decision maker's risk aversion. Chapter 14 draws out the differing natures of these mental experiments in the context of asset pricing.

9.2.2. Approximating and distorting models

For a given decision rule $u_t = -Fx_t$, we assume that the approximating model makes the state evolve according to the stochastic difference equation

$$x_{t+1} = A_o x_t + C \check{\epsilon}_{t+1}, \tag{9.2.1}$$

where now $\check{\epsilon}_{t+1}$ is an i.i.d. sequence of Gaussian disturbances with mean zero and identity contemporaneous covariance matrix. In turn, we will represent a distorted model as

$$\begin{aligned}
x_{t+1} &= A_o x_t + C \left(\epsilon_{t+1} + w_{t+1} \right) \\
&= \hat{A} x_t + C \epsilon_{t+1}
\end{aligned} \tag{9.2.2}$$

where $\hat{A} = A_o + C\kappa(\theta)$, $w_{t+1} = \kappa(\theta)x_t$, and ϵ_{t+1} is another i.i.d. Gaussian vector with mean 0 and identity covariance matrix. The transition densities associated with models (9.2.1) and (9.2.2) are absolutely continuous with respect to each other, i.e., they put positive probabilities on the same events.[4] Models that are not absolutely continuous with respect to each other are easy to distinguish empirically.

---

[3] For continuous-time models, Anderson, Hansen, and Sargent (2003) relate the penalty parameter and entropy to a bound on detection error probabilities as well as to alterations of market prices for risk associated with a concern about robustness.

[4] The two models (i.e., the two infinite-horizon stochastic processes) are absolutely continuous over finite intervals, a concept whose definition is reported by Hansen, Sargent, Turmuhambetova, and Williams (2006). The stochastic processes are not mutually absolutely continuous (over infinite intervals).

9.3. Detection error probabilities

Detection error probabilities can be calculated using likelihood ratio tests. Thus, consider two alternative models. Model A is the approximating model (9.2.1), and model B is the distorted model (9.2.2) associated with the context specific worst-case shock implied by θ. Consider a fixed sample of observations on the n-dimensional state vector x_t for $t = 0, \ldots, T - 1$. Let L_i be the likelihood of that sample for model i. Form the log-likelihood ratio

$$\log \frac{L_A}{L_B}.$$

A likelihood ratio test selects model A when $\log \frac{L_A}{L_B} > 0$ and model B when $\log \frac{L_A}{L_B} < 0$. When model A generates the data, the probability of a model detection error is

$$p_A = \text{Prob} \left(\log \frac{L_A}{L_B} < 0 \Big| A \right).$$

In turn when model B generates the data, the probability of a model detection error is

$$p_B = \text{Prob} \left(\log \frac{L_A}{L_B} > 0 \Big| B \right).$$

Form the probability of a detection error by averaging p_A and p_B with prior probabilities over models A and B of .5:

$$p(\theta) = \frac{1}{2} \left(p_A + p_B \right).$$

Here, θ is the robustness parameter used to generate a particular model B by taking the associated worst-case perturbation of model A in light of a particular objective function for a decision maker. The following section shows in detail how to estimate the detection error probability by means of simulations. In a given context, we propose to set $p(\theta)$ to a reasonable number, then invert $p(\theta)$ to find a plausible value of θ.

9.4. Details

We now describe how to estimate detection error probabilities.

9.4.1. Likelihood ratio under the approximating model

Define w^A as the mean of the worst-case shock assuming that the actual data generating process is the approximating model, i.e., $w^A = \kappa x^A$ where x^A is generated under (9.2.1). Define $\hat{A} = A_o + C\kappa$. Then we can express the innovation under the worst-case model as

$$
\begin{aligned}
\epsilon_{t+1} &= (C'C)^{-1} C' \left(x_{t+1} - \hat{A}x_t \right) \\
&= \check{\epsilon}_{t+1} - \kappa x_t \\
&= \check{\epsilon}_{t+1} - w_{t+1}^A.
\end{aligned}
\tag{9.4.1}
$$

The log-likelihood function under the approximating model is

$$
\log L_A = -\frac{1}{T} \sum_{t=0}^{T-1} \{ n \log \sqrt{2\pi} + \frac{1}{2} (\check{\epsilon}_{t+1} \cdot \check{\epsilon}_{t+1}) \}
$$

The log-likelihood function for the distorted model is

$$
\begin{aligned}
\log L_B &= -\frac{1}{T} \sum_{t=0}^{T-1} \{ n \log \sqrt{2\pi} + \frac{1}{2} (\epsilon_{t+1} \cdot \epsilon_{t+1}) \} \\
&= -\frac{1}{T} \sum_{t=0}^{T-1} \{ n \log \sqrt{2\pi} + \frac{1}{2} (\check{\epsilon}_{t+1} - w_{t+1}^A)' (\check{\epsilon}_{t+1} - w_{t+1}^A) \}.
\end{aligned}
\tag{9.4.2}
$$

The log-likelihood ratio is therefore

$$
r|A = \frac{1}{T} \sum_{t=0}^{T-1} \{ \frac{1}{2} w_{t+1}^{A\prime} w_{t+1}^A - w_{t+1}^{A\prime} \check{\epsilon}_{t+1} \},
\tag{9.4.3}
$$

assuming that the approximating model is the data generating process. The second term in the above expression will vanish as $T \to \infty$, so that the log-likelihood ratio converges to the unconditional average value of $.5 w_{t+1}^{A\prime} w_{t+1}^A$, the measure of model discrepancy used throughout chapter 2, for example.

We can estimate the detection error probability conditional on model A by simulating a large number for x_t of length T under model A and counting the fraction of realizations for which $r|A$ computed as in (9.4.3) is negative.

9.4.2. Likelihood ratio under the distorted model

Now suppose that the data generating process is actually the distorted model (9.2.2). The innovations in the approximating model are linked to those in the distorted model by $\check{\epsilon}_{t+1} = \epsilon_{t+1} + w_{t+1}^B$, where $w_{t+1}^B = \kappa x_t^B$ and x_t^B is generated under (9.2.2).

Assuming that the distorted model generates the data, the log-likelihood function $\log L_B$ for the distorted model is

$$
\log L_B = -\frac{1}{T} \sum_{t=0}^{T-1} \{ n \log \sqrt{2\pi} + \frac{1}{2} (\epsilon_{t+1} \cdot \epsilon_{t+1}) \}.
\tag{9.4.4}
$$

The log-likelihood function $\log L_A$ for the approximating model is

$$
\begin{aligned}
\log L_A &= -\frac{1}{T} \sum_{t=0}^{T-1} \{ n \log \sqrt{2\pi} + \frac{1}{2} (\check{\epsilon}_{t+1} \cdot \check{\epsilon}_{t+1}) \} \\
&= -\frac{1}{T} \sum_{t=0}^{T-1} \{ n \log \sqrt{2\pi} + \frac{1}{2} (\epsilon_{t+1} + w_{t+1}^B)' (\epsilon_{t+1} + w_{t+1}^B) \}.
\end{aligned}
\tag{9.4.5}
$$

Hence, assuming that the distorted model B is the data-generating process, the log-likelihood ratio is

$$
r|B = \frac{1}{T} \sum_{t=0}^{T-1} \{ \frac{1}{2} w_{t+1}^{B'} w_{t+1}^B + w_{t+1}^{B'} \epsilon_{t+1} \}.
\tag{9.4.6}
$$

As $T \to \infty$, $r|B$ converges to the unconditional average value of one-period entropy $.5 w_{t+1}^{B'} w_{t+1}^B$. Again, we can estimate p_B, the detection error probability conditioned on model B, by simulating a large number of paths of length T under model B and counting the fraction of realizations for which $r|B$ is positive.

9.4.3. The detection error probability

If we attach equal prior weights to models A and B, the overall detection error probability is

$$
p(\theta) = \frac{1}{2} (p_A + p_B),
\tag{9.4.7}
$$

where $p_i = \text{freq}(r|i \leq 0)$ for $i = A, B$. [5]

9.4.4. Breakdown point examples revisited

Figures 9.4.1 and 9.4.2 display estimated detection error probabilities for examples 2 and 3 from section 8.7, where we studied the effects of driving θ downwards toward the breakdown point $\underline{\theta}$. The figures record detection error probabilities for samples of length $T = 50$ and $T = 200$. We estimated the detection error probabilities for each value of $\sigma = -\theta^{-1}$ by averaging detection error rates over 100,000 simulations of length T.

The figures indicate that for $T = 200$, the detection error probability for θ near the breakdown point is essentially zero for both examples. But a sample size of $T = 50$ is small enough to leave the detection error probabilities as high as .05 near the breakdown point.

---

[5] The Matlab program `detection2.m` computes detection error probabilities.

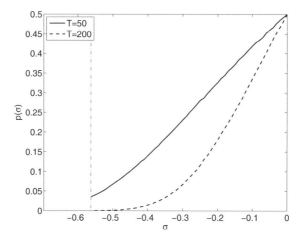

Figure 9.4.1: Detection error probability as a function of $\sigma = -\theta^{-1}$ for example 2 of section 8.7. The dotted vertical line denotes the breakdown point.

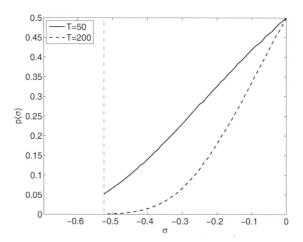

Figure 9.4.2: Detection error probability as a function of $\sigma = -\theta^{-1}$ for example 3 of section 8.7. The dotted vertical line denotes the breakdown point

9.5.   Ball's model

We illustrate the use of detection error probabilities to discipline the choice of θ in the context of the simple dynamic model that Ball (1999) designed to study alternative rules by which a monetary policy authority might set an interest rate.[6] The model is

$$y_t = -\beta r_{t-1} - \delta e_{t-1} + \epsilon_t \tag{9.5.1}$$

$$\pi_t = \pi_{t-1} + \alpha y_{t-1} - \gamma \left(e_{t-1} - e_{t-2} \right) + \eta_t \tag{9.5.2}$$

$$e_t = \theta r_t + \nu_t, \tag{9.5.3}$$

where y is the log of real output, r is the real interest rate, e is the log of the real exchange rate, π is the inflation rate, and ϵ, η, ν are serially uncorrelated and mutually orthogonal disturbances. Ball assumed that the monetary authority wants to maximize

$$C - - E \left(\pi_t^2 + y_t^2 \right).$$

The government sets the interest rate r_t as a function of the current state at t, which Ball shows can be reduced to y_t, e_t.

Ball motivates $(9.5.1)$ as an open-economy IS curve and $(9.5.2)$ as an open-economy Phillips curve. He uses $(9.5.3)$ to capture effects of the interest rate on the exchange rate. Ball set the parameters $\gamma, \theta, \beta, \delta$ at the values $.2, 2, .6, .2$. Following Ball, we set the standard deviation of the innovation equal to $1, 1, \sqrt{2}$.

To discipline the choice of the parameter expressing a concern about robustness, we calculated the detection error probabilities for distinguishing Ball's model from the worst-case models associated with various values of $\sigma \equiv -\theta^{-1}$. We calculated these taking Ball's parameter values as the approximating model and assuming that $T = 142$ observations are available, which corresponds to 35.5 years of annual data for Ball's quarterly model. Figure 9.5.1 shows these detection error probabilities $p(\sigma)$ as a function of σ. Notice that the detection error probability is .5 for $\sigma = 0$, which verifies that the approximating model and the worst-case model are identical. The detection error probability falls to .1 for $\sigma \approx -.085$. If we think that a reasonable concern about robustness is to want rules that work well for alternative models whose detection error probabilities are .1 or greater, then $\sigma = -.085$ is a reasonable choice of this parameter.

We can use Ball's model to illustrate the robustness attained by alternative settings of the parameter θ. In particular, we compute a robust decision rule for Ball's model with $\sigma = -.085$ and compare its performance to the $\sigma = 0$ rule. For Ball's model, figure 9.5.2 shows that while robust rules do worse when the approximating model actually generates the data, their

---

[6] See Sargent (1999b) for further discussion of Ball's model from the perspective of robust decision theory.

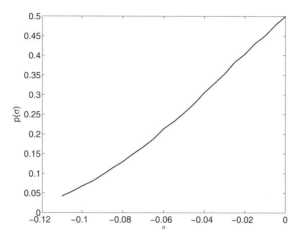

Figure 9.5.1: Detection error probability (coordinate axis) as a function of $\sigma \equiv -\theta^{-1}$ for Ball's model.

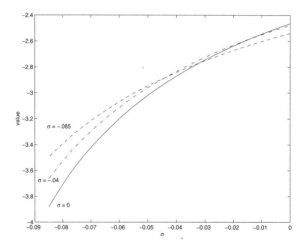

Figure 9.5.2: Value of criterion function $C = -E(\pi^2 + y^2)$ for three decision rules when the data are generated by the worst-case model associated with the value of σ on the horizontal axis: $\sigma = 0$ rule (solid line), $\sigma = -.04$ rule (dashed-dotted line), $\sigma = -.085$ (dashed) line.

performance deteriorates more slowly with departures of the data-generating mechanism from the approximating model.

Figure 9.5.2 plots the value $C = -E(\pi^2 + y^2)$ attained by three rules under the alternative data-generating model associated with the worst-case model for the value of σ on the ordinate axis. The rules correspond to values $\sigma = 0, -.04, -.085$, respectively. Recall how the detection error probabilities computed above associate a value of $\sigma = -.085$ with a detection error probability of about .1. Notice how the robust rules (those computed with robustness parameter $\sigma = -.04$ or $-.085$) yield criterion values that deteriorate at a lower rate with model misspecification (they are flatter). Notice that the rule for $\sigma = -.085$ does worse than the $\sigma = 0$ or $\sigma = -.04$ rules when $\sigma = 0$, but is more robust in the sense that it deteriorates less when the model becomes more misspecified.

9.6. Concluding remarks

We shall use detection error probabilities to discipline the choice of θ again when we study a permanent income model of Hansen, Sargent, and Tallarini (1999) in chapter 10 and an asset pricing model of Tallarini (2000) in chapter 14.[7]

---

[7] Anderson, Hansen, and Sargent (2003) and Hansen (2007) analyzed some mathematical connections among entropy, market prices of model uncertainty, and bounds on detection error probabilities.

Chapter 10
A permanent income model

If you would be wealthy, think of saving as well as getting.
— *Benjamin Franklin*

10.1. Introduction

The permanent income model is a good laboratory for exploring the consequences of a consumer's fears about misspecification of the stochastic process
governing his labor income. We shall see that a consumer who distrusts his
specification of the labor income or endowment process engages in a kind of
precautionary savings that comes from his worst-case slanting of the probability law for the endowment process.[1] We use the Stackelberg multiplier game
of chapter 7 to help us interpret how this probability slanting manifests itself
in the permanent income model.

The permanent income model is also a good vehicle for gathering intuition from the frequency domain approach of chapter 8. A permanent income
consumer is patient enough to smooth high-frequency fluctuations in income.
That means that he automatically acquires robustness with respect to misspecification of the high-frequency details of the stochastic process for his
labor income. But he is not patient enough to smooth low-frequency (i.e.,
very persistent) income fluctuations. Recognizing that the latter fluctuations
cause the consumer the most trouble, the minimizing agent makes the worst-
case shocks more persistent, an outcome that informs the consumer that his
decision rule is most fragile with respect to low-frequency misspecifications
of his income process. The robust permanent income consumer responds to
those more persistent worst-case shocks by saving more than he would if he
had no doubts about his endowment process. Thus, he engages in a form of
precautionary savings that prevails even when he has quadratic preferences,
which distinguishes this from the conventional form of precautionary savings
that emerges for preferences that have convex marginal utilities.[2]

We apply the label "precautionary" because the effect increases with the
volatility of innovations to endowments under the consumer's approximating model and because it also depends on the parameter θ that indexes his
concern about robustness. Our model of precautionary savings exhibits the

---

[1] We can regard this context-specific slanting as corresponding to that mentioned by
Fellner in the passage cited on page 38 of chapter 1.

[2] Leland (1968) and Miller (1974) are classic references on precautionary savings. See
footnote 21 in this chapter.

usual feature that it modifies the certainty equivalence present in the linear-quadratic permanent income model. However, the model keeps the marginal propensity to save out of financial wealth equal to that out of human wealth, in contrast to models like those of Caballero (1990), where precautionary saving makes the marginal propensity to save out of human wealth exceed that out of financial wealth.[3]

To explore these issues, this chapter uses an equilibrium version of a permanent income model that Hansen, Sargent, and Tallarini (1999) (HST) estimated for U.S. consumption and investment data.[4] We restate (and extend in appendix B) an observational equivalence result of HST, who showed that activating a concern about robustness increases savings in the same way that increasing the discount factor would: the discount factor can be changed to offset the effect of a change in the robustness parameter θ on consumption and investment. HST thereby established that consumption and investment data alone are insufficient to identify both the robustness parameter θ and the subjective discount factor β.[5] We use the Stackelberg multiplier game from chapter 7 to shed more light on this observational equivalence proposition and the impact on decision rules of distortions in the conditional expectations under the worst-case model. We state another observational equivalence result for a new baseline model and use it to show that activating a concern about robustness still equalizes the marginal propensities to save out of human and nonhuman wealth.[6]

In addition, this chapter illustrates how the detection error probabilities described in chapter 9 can discipline plausible choices of θ and provides some numerical examples of how much robustness can be achieved by rules designed

---

[3] See Wang (2003) for a treatment of how precautionary savings without robustness separates the marginal propensities to consume out of financial and nonfinancial wealth.

[4] Hall (1978), Campbell (1987), Heaton (1993), and Hansen, Roberds, and Sargent (1991) applied versions of this model to aggregate U.S. time series data on consumption and investment.

[5] Despite their failure to affect the consumption allocation, HST showed that such variations in (σ, β) do affect the relevant stochastic discount factor and therefore the valuation of risky assets. We shall take up asset pricing implications of the robust permanent income model in chapter 13.

[6] Kasa (1999) constructs an observational equivalence result for the optimal linear regulator problem and its robust counterpart for the single-state, single-control case. He shows that for a given H_∞ decision rule there is a strictly convex function relating values of the H_∞ norm to the variable summarizing the relative cost of state versus control variability. Orlik (2006) establishes a general observational equivalence result between the standard optimal control and robust control problems. In an example application of the result, she shows that the same interest rate will be set by the policy maker who fully trusts his model as well as by the robust central banker provided that the preferences of the latter one with respect to inflation-output gap stabilization are appropriately specified.

with various settings of θ. In chapter 12, we describe how to decentralize the allocation chosen by the planner in the economy of this chapter. Then in chapter 13, we use that decentralized economy as a laboratory for studying ways to represent the effects on asset prices of a concern about robustness.

10.2. A robust permanent income theory

HST's model features a planner with preferences over consumption streams $\{c_t\}_{t=0}^{\infty}$, intermediated through service streams $\{s_t\}_{t=0}^{\infty}$.[7] Let b be a preference shifter in the form of a utility bliss point. The Bellman equation for the robust planner is

$$-x'Px - p = \sup_c \inf_w \left\{ -(s-b)^2 + \beta\left(\theta w^{*\prime} w^* - E x^{*\prime} P x^* - p\right) \right\} \quad (10.2.1)$$

where the maximization is subject to

$$s = (1+\lambda)c - \lambda h \qquad (10.2.2a)$$

$$h^* = \delta_h h + (1-\delta_h)c \qquad (10.2.2b)$$

$$k^* = \delta_k k + i \qquad (10.2.2c)$$

$$c + i = \gamma k + d \qquad (10.2.2d)$$

$$\begin{bmatrix} d \\ b \end{bmatrix} = Uz \qquad (10.2.2e)$$

$$z^* = A_{22}z + C_2(\epsilon^* + w^*) \qquad (10.2.2f)$$

$$x' = \begin{bmatrix} h' & k' & z' \end{bmatrix}. \qquad (10.2.2g)$$

Here $*$ denotes next period's value, $'$ denotes transpose, $\epsilon^* \sim \mathcal{N}(0, I)$, E is the expectation operator, c is consumption, s denotes a scalar service measure, and the law of motion mapping this period's state x into next period's state will be defined below. As before, the penalty parameter $\theta > 0$ governs concern about robustness to misspecification of the endowment process d and the preference shock process b embedded in $(10.2.2e)$ and $(10.2.2f)$. HST assumed that the eigenvalues of A_{22} are bounded in modulus by unity. We transform θ to the risk-sensitivity parameter $\sigma = -\theta^{-1}$. In $(10.2.1)$, a scalar household service s_t is produced by the scalar consumption c_t via the household technology $(10.2.2a)$ and $(10.2.2b)$ where $\lambda > 0$ and $\delta_h \in (0,1)$. The household technology $(10.2.2a),(10.2.2b)$ accommodates habit persistence or durability as in Ryder and Heal (1973), Becker and Murphy (1988), Sundaresan (1989), Constantinides (1990), and Heaton (1993). By construction, h_t is

---

[7] The model fits within the framework described in chapter 11. See page 257 for an additional stability condition that must be imposed.

a geometric weighted average of current and past consumption. Setting $\lambda > 0$ induces intertemporal complementarities. Consumption services depend positively on current consumption, but negatively on a weighted average of past consumption, a reflection of habit persistence.

There is a linear production technology ($10.2.2d$) where the capital stock k^* at the end of period t evolves according to ($10.2.2c$), where i is time t gross investment, and $\{d_t\}$ is an exogenously specified endowment process. The parameter γ is the (constant) marginal product of capital, and δ_k is the depreciation factor for capital. HST specified a bivariate ("two-factor") stochastic endowment process: $d_t = \mu_d + \tilde{d}_t + \hat{d}_t$.[8] They assumed that the two endowment processes are orthogonal and that both obey second-order autoregressions

$$(1 - \phi_1 L)(1 - \phi_2 L)\tilde{d}_t = c_{\tilde{d}}\left(\epsilon_t^{\tilde{d}} + w_t^{\tilde{d}}\right)$$

$$(1 - \alpha_1 L)(1 - \alpha_2 L)\hat{d}_t = c_{\hat{d}}\left(\epsilon_t^{\hat{d}} + w_t^{\hat{d}}\right)$$

where the vector ϵ_t is i.i.d. Gaussian with mean zero and identity covariance matrix, and $w_t^{\tilde{d}}, w_t^{\hat{d}}$ are distortions to the means of $\epsilon_t^{\tilde{d}}, \epsilon_t^{\hat{d}}$. HST estimated values of the ϕ_j's and α_j's that imply that the $\tilde{d}_t$ process is more persistent than the $\hat{d}_t$ process, as we see below.

Solving the capital evolution equation for investment and substituting into the linear production technology gives

$$c_t + k_t = Rk_{t-1} + d_t, \tag{10.2.3}$$

where

$$R \equiv \delta_k + \gamma,$$

which is the physical gross return on capital, taking into account that capital depreciates over time.[9]

Let the state vector be $x_t' = \begin{bmatrix} h_{t-1}' & k_{t-1}' & d_{t-1} & 1 & d_t & \tilde{d}_t & \tilde{d}_{t-1} \end{bmatrix}$ (see Hansen, Sargent, and Wang (2002)). There is a set of state transition equations indexed by a $\{w_{t+1}\}$ process:

$$x_{t+1} = Ax_t + Bu_t + C(w_{t+1} + \epsilon_{t+1}) \tag{10.2.4}$$

where $u_t = c_t$ and $w_{t+1}' = [\, w_{t+1}^{\tilde{d}} \quad w_{t+1}^{\hat{d}} \,]'$ is the distortion to the conditional mean of ϵ_{t+1}. Let J_t be the sigma algebra induced by $\{x_0, \epsilon_s, 0 \le s \le t\}$.

---

[8] For two observed time series (c_t, i_t), HST's econometric specification needed at least two shock processes to avoid stochastic singularity.

[9] For HST's decentralized economy, R coincided with the gross return on a risk-free asset.

We require that the components of the solution for $\{c_t, h_t, k_t\}$ belong to L_0^2, the space of stochastic processes $\{y_t\}$ defined as

$$L_0^2 = \{y : y_t \text{ is in } J_t \text{ for } t = 0, 1, \ldots \text{ and } E \sum_{t=0}^{\infty} R^{-t} (y_t)^2 \mid J_0 < +\infty\}.$$

Given x_0, the planner chooses a process $\{c_t, k_t\}$ with components in L_0^2 to solve the Bellman equation $(10.2.1)$ subject to versions of $(10.2.2a)$-$(10.2.2d)$ and $(10.2.3)$.[10] In what follows we shall discuss HST's parameter values and some properties of their numerical solution. But first we show that in terms of its effects on consumption and investment, more concern about robustness works, *ceteris paribus*, like an increase in the discount factor.[11]

10.3. Solution when $\sigma = 0$

We apply results from chapter 7 to show that the robust decision rule for $\sigma < 0$ also solves a $\sigma = 0$ version of the model in which the maximizing agent in $(10.2.1)$ replaces the approximating model with a particular distorted model for $[d_t' \quad b_t']$. We shall eventually use that insight to study the identification of σ and β. To begin, this section solves the $\sigma = 0$ model.

10.3.1. The $\sigma = 0$ benchmark case

This subsection computes a solution of the planning problem in the $\sigma = 0$ case. Though we shall soon focus on the case when $\beta R = 1$, we also want the solution when $\beta R \neq 1$. Thus, for now we allow $\beta R \neq 1$. When $\sigma = 0$, the decision maker's objective reduces to

$$E_0 \sum_{t=0}^{\infty} \beta^t \{-(s_t - b_t)^2\}. \tag{10.3.1}$$

Formulate the planning problem as a Lagrangian by putting random Lagrange multiplier processes $2\beta^t \mu_{st}$ on $(10.2.2a)$, $2\beta^t \mu_{ht}$ on $(10.2.2b)$, and $2\beta^t \mu_{ct}$ on $(10.2.3)$. First-order necessary conditions are

$$\mu_{st} = b_t - s_t \tag{10.3.2a}$$

---

[10] We can convert this problem into a special case of the control problem posed in chapter 7 as follows. Form a composite state vector x_t as described above, and let the control be given by $s_t - b_t$. Solve $(10.2.2a)$ for c_t as a function of $s_t - b_t$, b_t, and h_{t-1} and substitute into equations $(10.2.2b)$ and $(10.2.3)$. Stack the resulting two equations along with the state evolution equation for z_t to form the evolution equation for x_{t+1}.

[11] However, in chapter 13, we shall show that (σ, β) pairs that imply observationally equivalent consumption and investment plans nevertheless imply different prices for risky assets. This finding is the basis of what Lucas (2003, p. 7) calls Tallarini's (2000) finding of "an astonishing separation of quantity and asset price determination."

$$\mu_{ct} = (1 + \lambda)\,\mu_{st} + (1 - \delta_h)\,\mu_{ht} \qquad (10.3.2b)$$

$$\mu_{ht} = \beta E_t\left[\delta_h \mu_{ht+1} - \lambda \mu_{st+1}\right] \qquad (10.3.2c)$$

$$\mu_{ct} = \beta R E_t \mu_{ct+1} \qquad (10.3.2d)$$

and also $(10.2.2a)$-$(10.2.2b)$ and $(10.2.3)$. Equation $(10.3.2d)$ implies that $E_t\mu_{ct+1} = (\beta R)^{-1}\mu_{ct}$. Then $(10.3.2b)$ and $(10.3.2c)$ solved forward imply that μ_{st}, μ_{ht} must satisfy $E_t\mu_{st+1} = (\beta R)^{-1}\mu_{st}$ and $E_t\mu_{ht+1} = (\beta R)^{-1}\mu_{ht}$. Therefore, μ_{st} has the representation

$$\mu_{st} = (\beta R)^{-1}\,\mu_{st-1} + \nu'\epsilon_t \qquad (10.3.3)$$

for some vector ν. The endogenous volatility vector ν will play an important role below, and we shall soon tell how to compute it. The effects of the endogenous state variables h_{t-1}, k_{t-1} on consumption and investment are intermediated through the one-dimensional endogenous state vector μ_{st}, the marginal valuation of services.

Use $(10.3.2a)$ to write $s_t = b_t - \mu_{st}$, substitute this into the household technology $(10.2.2a)$-$(10.2.2b)$, and rearrange to get the system

$$c_t = \frac{1}{1 + \lambda}\,(b_t - \mu_{st}) + \frac{\lambda}{1 + \lambda}h_{t-1} \qquad (10.3.4a)$$

$$h_t = \tilde{\delta}_h h_{t-1} + \left(1 - \tilde{\delta}_h\right)(b_t - \mu_{st}) \qquad (10.3.4b)$$

where $\tilde{\delta}_h = \frac{\delta_h + \lambda}{1 + \lambda}$. Equation $(10.3.4a)$ shows that knowledge of μ_{st}, b_t, h_{t-1} allows us to compute c_t, so that μ_{st} plays the role of the essential scalar endogenous state variable in the model. Equation $(10.3.4b)$ can be used to compute

$$E_t \sum_{j=0}^{\infty} R^{-j} h_{t+j-1} = \left(1 - R^{-1}\tilde{\delta}_h\right)^{-1} h_{t-1}$$

$$+ \frac{R^{-1}\left(1 - \tilde{\delta}_h\right)}{\left(1 - R^{-1}\tilde{\delta}_h\right)} E_t \sum_{j=0}^{\infty} R^{-j}(b_{t+j} - \mu_{st+j}). \qquad (10.3.5)$$

For the purpose of solving the first-order conditions $(10.3.2)$, $(10.2.2a)$, $(10.2.2b)$, $(10.2.3)$ subject to the side condition that $\{c_t, k_t\} \in L_0^2$, treat the technology $(10.2.3)$ as a difference equation in $\{k_t\}$, solve forward, and take conditional expectations on both sides to get

$$k_{t-1} = \sum_{j=0}^{\infty} R^{-(j+1)} E_t\,(c_{t+j} - d_{t+j}). \qquad (10.3.6)$$

Use $(10.3.4a)$ to eliminate $\{c_{t+j}\}$ from $(10.3.6)$, then use $(10.3.3)$ and $(10.3.5)$. Solve the resulting system for μ_{st} to get

$$\mu_{st} = \Psi_1 k_{t-1} + \Psi_2 h_{t-1} + \Psi_3 \sum_{j=0}^{\infty} R^{-j} E_t b_{t+j} + \Psi_4 \sum_{j=0}^{\infty} R^{-j} E_t d_{t+j}, \quad (10.3.7)$$

where

$$\Psi_1 = -(1+\lambda) R \left(1 - R^{-2}\beta^{-1}\right) \left[\frac{1 - R^{-1}\tilde{\delta}_h}{1 - R^{-1}\tilde{\delta}_h + \lambda \left(1 - \tilde{\delta}_h\right)} \right]$$

$$\Psi_2 = \frac{\lambda \left(1 - R^{-2}\beta^{-1}\right)}{1 - R^{-1}\tilde{\delta}_h + \lambda \left(1 - \tilde{\delta}_h\right)} \qquad (10.3.8)$$

$$\Psi_3 = \left(1 - R^{-2}\beta^{-1}\right)$$

$$\Psi_4 = R^{-1}\Psi_1.$$

Equations $(10.3.7)$, $(10.3.4)$, and $(10.2.3)$ represent the solution of the planning problem when $\sigma = 0$.[12]

To compute ν in $(10.3.3)$, it is useful to notice that formula $(10.3.7)$ can be rewritten as

$$\mu_{st} = (\beta R)^{-1} \mu_{st-1} + \Phi_3 \sum_{j=0}^{\infty} R^{-j} \left(E_t b_{t+j} - E_{t-1} b_{t+j}\right)$$

$$+ \Phi_4 \sum_{j=0}^{\infty} R^{-j} \left(E_t d_{t+j} - E_{t-1} d_{t+j}\right) \qquad (10.3.9)$$

where

$$\mu_{st-1} = \Phi_1 k_{t-1} + \Phi_2 h_{t-1} + \Phi_3 \sum_{j=0}^{\infty} R^{-j} E_{t-1} b_{t+j} + \Phi_4 \sum_{j=0}^{\infty} R^{-j} E_{t-1} d_{t+j}.$$

The third and fourth terms of equation $(10.3.9)$ are scalars Ψ_3 and Ψ_4 multiplied by the innovations at t in the present values of b_t and d_t, respectively. Let the moving average representations for b_t and d_t be

$$b_t = \zeta_b(L) \epsilon_t \qquad (10.3.10)$$

$$d_t = \zeta_d(L) \epsilon_t, \qquad (10.3.11)$$

---

[12] When $\beta R = 1$, $(10.3.7)$ makes μ_{st} depend on a geometric average of current and future values of b_t. Therefore, both the optimal consumption service process and optimal consumption depend on the difference between b_t and a geometric average of current and expected future values of b. So there is no "level effect" of the preference shock on the optimal decision rules for consumption and investment. However, the level of b_t will affect equilibrium asset prices.

where $\zeta_b(L) = U_b(I - A_{22}L)^{-1}C_2$ and $\zeta_d(L) = U_d(I - A_{22}L)^{-1}C_2$ from $(10.2.2e)$.

By applying a formula of Hansen and Sargent (1980), it is easy to show that the innovations in the present values of b_t and d_t, respectively, equal the present values of the coefficients in these moving average representations.[13] Therefore, representation $(10.3.9)$ can be rewritten as

$$\mu_{st} = (\beta R)^{-1} \mu_{st-1} + \left[\Psi_3 \zeta_b \left(R^{-1} \right) + \Psi_4 \zeta_d \left(R^{-1} \right) \right] \epsilon_t. \qquad (10.3.12)$$

Comparing this with $(10.3.3)$, we see that

$$\nu' = \Psi_3 \zeta_b \left(R^{-1} \right) + \Psi_4 \zeta_d \left(R^{-1} \right). \qquad (10.3.13)$$

An equivalent way to compute ν is to note that formula $(10.3.7)$ for μ_{st} can be represented in matrix notation as

$$\mu_{st} = M_s x_t \qquad (10.3.14)$$
$$x_t = A_o x_{t-1} + C\epsilon_t \qquad (10.3.15)$$

where x_t is the state vector k_{t-1}, h_{t-1}, z_t, where $z_t = \begin{bmatrix} d_{t-1} & 1 & d_t & \tilde{d}_t & \tilde{d}_{t-1} \end{bmatrix}'$ the matrix M_s is determined by equation $(10.3.7)$ and A_o, C and the laws of motion for b_t, d_t determine the law of motion for the entire state under the optimal rule for c_t.[14] It follows that $\mu_{st} = M_s A_o x_{t-1} + M_s C\epsilon_t$, which must agree with $(10.3.3)$, so that $\mu_{s,t-1} \equiv M_s A_o x_{t-1}$ and

$$\nu' \equiv M_s C. \qquad (10.3.16)$$

The scalar $\alpha = \sqrt{\nu'\nu}$ plays an important role in the argument below. It obeys

$$\alpha = \sqrt{M_s C C' M_s'}. \qquad (10.3.17)$$

In the widely studied special case that $\lambda = \delta_h = 0$, so that $s_t = c_t$ and $\mu_{st} = b_t - c_t$, $(10.3.7)$, $(10.3.8)$ imply that the marginal propensity to consume out of "non-human wealth" Rk_{t-1} and the marginal propensity to consume out of "human wealth" $\sum_{j=0}^{\infty} R^{-j} E_t d_{t+j}$ both equal $-\Psi_1$. It is a well-known feature of the linear-quadratic model that these marginal propensities to consume are equal. Notice that human wealth is formed by discounting expected future endowments at the risk-free rate.

---

[13] The present value of the moving average coefficients plays an important role in linear-quadratic permanent income models. See Flavin (1981), Campbell (1987), and Hansen, Roberds, and Sargent (1991).

[14] Here C is the matrix that appears in $(10.2.4)$ above. See Hansen and Sargent (2008, chapter 10) for fast ways to compute A_o, M_s, C for a class of models that includes that of this chapter.

10.3.2. Observational equivalence for quantities of $\sigma = 0$ and $\sigma \neq 0$

In the $\sigma = 0$ case, HST followed Hall (1978) and imposed that $\beta R = 1$. HST then showed that for fixed values of all other parameters, there is a set of (β, σ) pairs that leave the consumption-investment plan unaltered. In particular, if as we vary σ we also vary β according to[15]

$$\hat{\beta}(\sigma) = \frac{1}{R} + \frac{\sigma \alpha^2}{R-1}, \tag{10.3.18}$$

then we leave unaltered the decision rules for (c_t, i_t). Here $\alpha^2 = \nu' \nu$, where ν, as defined in (10.3.13), is a vector in the following martingale representation for the marginal utility of services μ_{st} that prevails as a special case of (10.3.3) when $\sigma = 0$ and $\beta R = 1$:

$$\mu_{st} = \mu_{st-1} + \nu' \epsilon_t.$$

(Also see equation (10.3.12).) The following subsection explains how HST constructed the locus identified by (10.3.18).

10.3.3. Observational equivalence: intuition

Here is the basic idea underlying the observational equivalence proposition. As already mentioned, a single factor μ_{st} summarizes the endogenous state variables h_{t-1}, k_{t-1}. When $\beta R = 1$ and $\sigma = 0$, it has the law of motion

$$\mu_{st} = \mu_{st-1} + \nu' \epsilon_t,$$

which can also be represented as

$$\mu_{st} = \mu_{st-1} + \alpha \tilde{\epsilon}_t \tag{10.3.19}$$

where $\tilde{\epsilon}_t$ is a scalar i.i.d. process with zero mean and unit variance and where $\alpha = \sqrt{\nu' \nu}$ verifies $\alpha \tilde{\epsilon}_t = \nu' \epsilon_t$. We generate our observational equivalence result by reverse engineering. We activate a concern about robustness by setting $\sigma < 0$, but insist that (10.3.19) continue to describe μ_{st} under the approximating model in order to make sure that the (c_t, i_t) allocation remains the same when $\sigma < 0$. For $\sigma < 0$ and a new value $\hat{\beta}$ that is to be determined, the worst-case model for μ_{st} is

$$\mu_{st} = \mu_{st-1} + \alpha (\tilde{\epsilon}_t + \tilde{w}_t) \tag{10.3.20}$$

---

[15] See footnote 23 of this chapter.

or

$$\mu_{st} = \left(1 + \alpha K\left(\sigma, \hat{\beta}\right)\right)\mu_{st-1} + \alpha \tilde{\epsilon}_t \tag{10.3.21}$$

where $\tilde{w}_t = K(\sigma, \hat{\beta})\mu_{st-1}$. Evidently, (10.3.21) implies that $\hat{E}_t \mu_{st+1} = (1 + \alpha K(\sigma, \hat{\beta}))\mu_{st}$, where $\hat{E}$ is the mathematical expectation with respect to the distorted model. Notice that we once again use the modified certainty equivalence principle. With a concern about robustness, the decision maker's choices conform to the following version of the Euler equation (10.3.3):

$$\hat{E}_t \mu_{st+1} = \left(\hat{\beta}R\right)^{-1}\mu_{st},$$

where $\hat{E}_t$ is evaluated with respect to the worst-case model (10.3.21) and $\hat{\beta}$ is a new value for β that we design to offset the effects of setting $\sigma < 0$. That is, if possible, we want to choose $\hat{\beta}$ to compensate for using the worst-case distribution to evaluate expectations in the above Euler equation. And we want the distorted model to be associated with the same approximating model (10.3.19) that generates the original c_t, i_t allocation. But according to (10.3.21), if the approximating model is to be (10.3.19), then $\hat{E}_t \mu_{st+1} = (1 + K(\sigma, \hat{\beta})\alpha)\mu_{st}$. Thus, for a given $\sigma < 0$, we want to find a replacement $\hat{\beta}$ for β that enables us to verify $(\hat{\beta}R)^{-1} = (1 + \alpha K(\sigma, \hat{\beta}))$, where $K(\sigma, \hat{\beta})$ solves the minimization problem that gives rise to the worst-case shock. In summary, we want to solve $1 = (\hat{\beta}R)(1 + \alpha K(\sigma, \hat{\beta}))$ for $\hat{\beta}$ as a function of σ. The proof of our observational equivalence Theorem 10.3.1 shows that a solution for $\hat{\beta}$ exists, that it is unique, and that it satisfies (10.3.18).

10.3.4. Observational equivalence: formal argument

Following HST, we begin by assuming that $\beta R = 1$ when $\sigma = 0$. We state

Theorem 10.3.1. (*Observational Equivalence, I*)   *Fix all parameters, including R, except (σ, β). Suppose $\beta R = 1$ when $\sigma = 0$. There exists a $\underline{\sigma} < 0$ such that for any $\sigma \in (\underline{\sigma}, 0)$, the optimal consumption-investment plan for $(0, \beta)$ is also chosen by a robust decision maker when parameter values are $(\sigma, \hat{\beta}(\sigma))$ and where $\hat{\beta}(\sigma) < \beta$ satisfies (10.3.18).*

Proof. The proof is constructive. Begin with an allocation $\{\bar{s}_t, \bar{c}_t, \bar{k}_t, \bar{h}_t\}$ for a benchmark $\sigma = 0, \beta R = 1$ economy, then form a comparison economy with a $\sigma \in [\underline{\sigma}, 0]$, where $\underline{\sigma}$ is the lowest value for which the solution of (10.3.25) reported below is real. The comparison economy fixes all parameters except (σ, β) at their values for the benchmark economy. We then construct a discount factor $\hat{\beta} < \beta$ for which $\{\bar{s}_t, \bar{c}_t, \bar{k}_t, \bar{h}_t\}$ is also the allocation for the $\sigma < 0$ economy.

When $\beta R = 1$, $(10.3.3)$ becomes

$$\mu_{st} = \mu_{st-1} + \nu' \epsilon_t. \tag{10.3.22}$$

The optimality of the allocation under the original $(0, \beta)$ implies that $(10.3.22)$ is satisfied, which in turn implies that $E_t \mu_{st+1} = \mu_{st}$ and $(10.3.7)$ are satisfied where E_t is the expectation operator under the approximating model. We seek a new value $\sigma < 0$ and an associated value $\hat{\beta}(\sigma)$ for which: (1) $(10.3.22)$ remains satisfied under the approximating model; (2) the robust decision maker chooses the $(\cdot)$ allocation, which requires that $\hat{\beta} R \hat{E}_t \mu_{st+1} = \mu_{st}$, where $\hat{E}$ is the expectation with respect to the worst-case model associated with $(\sigma, \hat{\beta})$ when the approximating model obeys $(10.3.22)$. However, when the approximating model satisfies $(10.3.22)$, the worst-case model associated with $(\sigma, \hat{\beta})$ implies that $\hat{E}_t \mu_{st+1} = \hat{\zeta}(\hat{\beta}) \mu_{st}$, where $\hat{\zeta}(\hat{\beta}) = (1 + \alpha K(\sigma, \hat{\beta})) > 1$ can be found by solving the pure forecasting problem[16] associated with law of motion $\mu_{st} = \mu_{st-1} + \nu'(\epsilon_t + w_t)$, $(10.3.22)$, one-period return function $-\mu_{st}^2 = -(b_t - s_t)^2$, and discount factor $\hat{\beta}$. If the σ-robust decision maker is to choose a decision rule that sustains $(10.3.22)$ under the approximating model, so that (1) and (2) both prevail, $\hat{\beta}$ must verify

$$\hat{\beta} R \hat{\zeta}\left(\hat{\beta}\right) = 1. \tag{10.3.23}$$

To complete the argument, we compute $\hat{\zeta}(\hat{\beta})$ by solving a pure forecasting problem to find the distorted expectation operator $\hat{E}_t$. We use the recipe given in formulas $(7.C.10)$ on page 168 and $(7.C.26)$ and $(7.C.27)$ on page 171. Taking $(10.3.22)$ as given under the approximating model and noting that $\mu_{st}^2 = (b_t - s_t)^2$, the evil agent in the pure forecasting problem seeks to minimize $-\sum_{t=0}^{\infty} \hat{\beta}^t (\mu_{st}^2 + \hat{\beta} \frac{1}{\sigma} w_{t+1}^2)$ under the distorted law $\mu_{st} = \mu_{st-1} + \alpha w_t$, where $\alpha = \sqrt{\nu' \nu}$ (see $(10.3.22)$). Taking μ_s as the state, the evil agent's Bellman equation $(7.C.27)$ is[17]

$$-P\mu_s^2 = -\mu_s^2 + \hat{\beta} \min_w \left(-\frac{1}{\sigma} w^2 - P\left(\mu_s + \alpha w\right)^2 \right). \tag{10.3.24}$$

The scalar P that solves $(10.3.24)$ is

$$-P\left(\hat{\beta}\right) = \frac{\hat{\beta} - 1 + \sigma \alpha^2 + \sqrt{\left(\hat{\beta} - 1 + \sigma \alpha^2\right)^2 + 4\sigma \alpha^2}}{-2\sigma \alpha^2}. \tag{10.3.25}$$

---

[16] See page 171 for the definition of a pure forecasting problem.

[17] We exploit a version of certainty equivalence and ignore the stochastic parts of the Bellman equation and the law of motion for μ_s.

Let $\hat{\zeta}(\hat{\beta}) = A + CK(\sigma,\hat{\beta}) = 1 + \alpha K(\sigma,\hat{\beta})$, where $w = K(\sigma,\hat{\beta})\mu_s$ is the formula for the worst-case shock and $A + CK$ is the state transition matrix for the distorted law of motion as in chapter 7. Applying formula (7.C.21) for $K(\sigma,\hat{\beta})$ in chapter 7 to the current problem gives

$$\hat{E}_t\mu_{st+1} = \hat{\zeta}\mu_{st} \tag{10.3.26}$$

where

$$\hat{\zeta} = \hat{\zeta}\left(\hat{\beta}\right) = 1 + \frac{\sigma\alpha^2 P\left(\hat{\beta}\right)}{1 - \sigma\alpha^2 P\left(\hat{\beta}\right)} = \frac{1}{1 - \sigma\alpha^2 P\left(\hat{\beta}\right)}. \tag{10.3.27}$$

Hansen, Sargent, and Wang (2002) solve (10.3.23), (10.3.25), and (10.3.27) to obtain

$$\hat{\beta}\left(\sigma\right) = \frac{1}{R} + \frac{\sigma\alpha^2}{R-1}. \tag{10.3.28}$$

For $\sigma \in [\underline{\sigma},0]$, equation (10.3.28) defines a locus of $(\sigma,\hat{\beta})$'s, each point of which is observationally equivalent to $(0,\beta)$ for observations on (c_t,k_t) because each supports the benchmark ($\sigma = 0$) allocation.   ▮

This proposition means that with the appropriate adjustments in β given by $\hat{\beta}(\sigma)$, the robust decision maker chooses precisely the same quantities $\{c_t,k_t\}$ as a decision maker without a concern for robustness. Thus, as far as these quantity observations are concerned, the robust ($\sigma < 0, \hat{\beta}(\sigma)$) version of the permanent income model is observationally equivalent to the benchmark ($\sigma = 0, \beta$) version.[18] However, as we shall see in chapter 13, (σ,β) pairs that imply equivalent allocations because they satisfy (10.3.28) do *not* imply the same asset prices. The reason is that as we alter (σ,β) within this observationally equivalent set, we alter continuation valuations by altering $\mathcal{D}(P)$.

---

[18] The asset pricing theory developed by HST, which is encoded in (10.3.23), implies that the price of a sure claim on consumption one period ahead is R^{-1} for all t and for all $(\sigma,\hat{\beta})$ in the locus (10.3.18). Therefore, these different parameter pairs are also observationally equivalent with respect to the risk-free rate. In this model, the technology (10.2.3) ties down the risk-free rate. For a version of the model with quadratic costs of adjusting capital, the risk-free rate comes to depend on σ, even though the observations on quantities are approximately independent of σ. See Hansen and Sargent (2008).

10.3.5. *Precautionary savings interpretation*

The consumer's concern about model misspecification activates a particular kind of precautionary savings motive that underlies our observational equivalence proposition. A concern about robustness inspires the consumer to save *more*. Decreasing his discount factor induces the consumer to save *less*. The observational equivalence proposition asserts that these two effects can be arranged to offset each other.

The following experiment highlights the precautionary motive for savings. Take the base model with $\sigma = 0$ used in our proof of Theorem 10.3.1. Then activate a concern about robustness by setting $\sigma < 0$, but offset its effect on consumption by setting β equal to $\hat{\beta}(\sigma)$. Notice from (10.3.28) that $\hat{\beta}(\sigma)$ depends on the volatility parameter α. Consider a $(\sigma, \hat{\beta}(\sigma))$ pair corresponding to a given $\alpha > 0$. The innovation volatility associated with a positive α means that future endowments are forecast with error. If future endowments and preference shifters *could* be forecast perfectly, then at the value $\beta = \hat{\beta}(\sigma)$, the consumer would choose to make his capital stock, and therefore also his consumption, drift downward because discounting is large relative to the marginal productivity of capital. Investment would be sufficiently unattractive that the optimal linear rule would eventually send both consumption and capital below zero.[19],[20] However, when randomness is activated (i.e., the innovation variances are positive), this downward drift is arrested or even completely offset, as it is in our observational equivalence proposition. Thus, our robust control interpretation of the permanent-income decision rule delivers a form of precautionary savings.

The precautionary savings coming from a concern about robustness differs in structure from another, perhaps more familiar, kind of precautionary savings motive that has attracted much attention in the macroeconomics literature and that emerges when a positive variance of the innovations to the endowment process interacts with a convex derivative of the marginal utility of consumption.[21] In contrast, the precautionary savings induced by a con-

---

[19] Introducing nonnegativity constraints in capital and/or consumption would induce nonlinearities into the consumption and savings rules, especially near zero capital. But investment would remain unattractive in the presence of those constraints for experiments like the one we are describing here. See Deaton (1992) for a critical survey and quantitative assessment of consumption models with binding borrowing constraints.

[20] As emphasized by Carroll (1992), even when the discount factor is small relative to the interest rate, precautionary savings can emerge when there is a severe utility cost for zero consumption. Such a utility cost is absent in our formulation.

[21] Take the Euler equation $E_t \beta R u'(c_{t+1}) = u'(c_t)$ and assume that $\beta R = 1$ so that $E_t u'(c_{t+1}) = u'(c_t)$. If u' is a convex function, then applying Jensen's inequality implies $E_t c_{t+1} > c_t$, so that consumption is expected to grow when the conditional distribution of

cern about robustness emerges because the consumer wants to protect himself against mistakes in specifying conditional *means* of shocks to the endowment. Thus, a concern for robustness inspires precautionary savings because of how fears of misspecification are expressed in conditional *first* moments of shocks. This type of precautionary saving does not require that the marginal utility of consumption be convex and occurs even in models with quadratic preferences, as we have shown.

A concern about robustness affects consumption by slanting probabilities in the way Fellner described in the passage cited on page 38 of this book. The household saves more for a given β because it makes pessimistic forecasts of future endowments. Precisely how pessimism manifests itself depends on the detailed structure of the permanent income model and the temporal properties of the endowment process, as we shall discuss in the next section.

10.4. Observational equivalence and distorted expectations

In this section, we use insights from a Stackelberg multiplier game to interpret Theorem 10.3.1. In the Stackelberg multiplier game, decisions for the maximizing player can be computed by solving his Euler equations using a particular distorted law of motion to form conditional expectations of the shocks.[22]

In the benchmark $\sigma = 0, \beta R = 1$ case that is contemplated in Theorem 10.3.1, the solution of the planning problem is determined by equations $(10.3.4)$, $(10.2.3)$, and $(10.3.7)$, where the Ψ_j's satisfy $(10.3.8)$ with $\beta R = 1$. For a $\sigma \in [\underline{\sigma}, 0)$ and a $\hat\beta = \hat\beta(\sigma)$, the decision rule for the robust planner is characterized by equations $(10.3.4)$, $(10.2.3)$, and the following modified version of $(10.3.7)$:

$$\mu_{st} = \hat\Psi_1 k_{t-1} + \hat\Psi_2 h_{t-1} + \hat\Psi_3 \sum_{j=0}^{\infty} R^{-j} \hat E_t b_{t+j} + \hat\Psi_4 \sum_{j=0}^{\infty} R^{-j} \hat E_t d_{t+j}, \quad (10.4.1)$$

where $\hat\Psi_j$ are determined by $(10.3.8)$ with $\beta = \hat\beta(\sigma)$; and $\hat E_t$ is the conditional expectation operator with respect to the distorted law of motion for the state x_t. The observational equivalence Theorem 10.3.1 implies that $(10.4.1)$

---

c_{t+1} is not concentrated at a point. Such consumption growth reflects precautionary savings. See Ljungqvist and Sargent (2004, chapter 16) for an analysis of these precautionary savings models.

[22] While the timing protocol for the Stackelberg multiplier game differs from the Markov perfect timing embedded in game $(10.2.1)$, chapter 7 showed that identical equilibrium outcomes and recursive representations of equilibria prevail under these different timing protocols.

and (10.3.7) are identical solutions for μ_{st}. By substituting for the terms in expected future values, the solutions (10.3.7) and (10.4.1) can also be expressed as $\mu_{st} = M_s x_t$ and $\mu_{st} = \hat{M}_s x_t$. Observational equivalence requires that $M_s = \hat{M}_s$. This requires that the $\hat{\Psi}_j$'s and $\hat{E}$ mutually adjust to keep M_s fixed.[23]

To expand on this point, consider the special case that $\lambda = \delta_h = 0$, so that we need not retain h_{t-1} as a state variable. Also, assume for simplicity that $b_t = b$, so that the preference shock is constant. Shutting down the volatility of b prevents distortions in it from affecting the robust decision rule. Then equating the right sides of (10.3.7) and (10.4.1) gives

$$
\begin{aligned}
0 = \left(\Psi_4 - \hat{\Psi}_4\right) R k_{t-1} &+ \left(\Psi_3 - \hat{\Psi}_3\right)\left(1 - R^{-1}\right)^{-1} b \\
&+ \Psi_4 \sum_{j=0}^{\infty} R^{-j} E_t d_{t+j} - \hat{\Psi}_4 \sum_{j=0}^{\infty} R^{-j} \hat{E}_t d_{t+j}
\end{aligned}
\tag{10.4.2}
$$

where Ψ_j without hats denotes values of Ψ_j that satisfy (10.3.8) and those with hats satisfy (10.3.8) evaluated at $\beta = \hat{\beta}(\sigma)$. Equation (10.4.2) shows how the observational equivalence result asserts offsetting alterations in the coefficients Ψ_j and the distorted expectations operator $\hat{E}_t$ used to form the expected sum of discounted future endowments that defines human wealth.

The distorted expectations operator is to be interpreted in terms of the recursive formulation of the maximizing player's problem in a Stackelberg multiplier game of chapter 7. The Euler equation approach used to derive (10.3.7) or (10.4.1) presumes the following timing protocol. *After* the minimizing player has committed to an entire path for the w_{t+1} process, the maximizing agent faces the following recursive representation of the motion for the endowment and preference shocks:

$$
X_{t+1} = \left(A - BF\left(\sigma, \hat{\beta}\right) + CK\left(\sigma, \hat{\beta}\right)\right) X_t + C\tilde{\epsilon}_{t+1}
\tag{10.4.3a}
$$

$$
\begin{bmatrix} b_t \\ d_t \end{bmatrix} = S X_t
\tag{10.4.3b}
$$

where $\tilde{\epsilon}_{t+1}$ is an i.i.d. shock identical in distribution to that of ϵ_{t+1}.[24] Because the minimizing player has committed himself to a stochastic process for $\{w_{t+1}\}$ that implies the recursive representation (10.4.3) of the endowment and preference shock processes, the maximizing player takes the X_t

---

[23] Note from formula (10.3.17) that M_s determines α, a key parameter defining the observational equivalence locus (10.3.18). Thus, because M_s remains fixed, so does α so long as $(\sigma, \hat{\beta})$ obey (10.3.18).

[24] In (10.4.3), X_t is used to attain a recursive representation of the worst-case endowment and preference shock processes that keeps them exogenous to the maximizer's decisions.

process as exogenous and uses the forecasting rule $\hat{E}_t X_{t+j} = (A - BF(\sigma, \hat{\beta}) + CK(\sigma, \hat{\beta}))^j X_t$ to form forecasts of (b_{t+j}, d_{t+j}) in $(10.4.1)$. These forecasts, together with $(10.4.1)$, $(10.3.4)$, and $(10.2.3)$ can be solved to yield a decision rule $c_t = -\mathcal{F} \begin{bmatrix} x_t \\ X_t \end{bmatrix}$ as in chapter 7. After computing the decision rule as a function of x_t, X_t, we equate $x_t = X_t$; that gives the maximizing agent's decision rule in the form $c_t = -F x_t$.[25]

10.4.1. Distorted endowment process

Figures 10.4.1 and 10.4.2 illustrate the probability slanting that leads to precautionary savings. The figures assume HST's parameter values that are reported in appendix A and record impulse response functions for the total endowment d_t under the approximating model and a worst-case model associated with $\sigma = -.0001$, where β is adjusted according to $(10.3.18)$ as required under our observational equivalence proposition in order to preserve the same decision rule $F(\sigma, \hat{\beta})$ for different σ's.[26]

For the approximating and the worst-case models with $\sigma = -.0001$, the figures report the response of the total endowment d_t to innovations ϵ_t^* and $\hat{\epsilon}_t$ in the relatively permanent and transitory components of the endowment, $\tilde{d}_t$, $\hat{d}_t$, respectively. Under the distorted model, the impulse response functions diverge and the eigenvalue of $A - BF(\sigma, \hat{\beta}) + CK(\sigma, \hat{\beta})$ that has maximum modulus increases from its value of unity under the approximating model to 1.0016.

The distorted endowment processes respond to innovations with more persistence than they do under the approximating model. With a fixed β, the increased persistence makes the agent save more than under the approximating model, which the observational equivalence proposition offsets by decreasing the household's patience via $(10.3.18)$.

Figures 10.5.1 and 10.5.2 record impulse response functions for the total endowment d_t under the approximating model and a worst-case model associated with $\sigma = -.0001$, *where β is held fixed at HST's benchmark value.* Because these figures do not adjust the discount factor according to $(10.3.18)$ as it was done for figures 10.4.1 and 10.4.2, the distorted impulse response functions deviate from those of the approximating model even more than those of these earlier figures. The reduction in β from $(10.3.18)$ works through two channels to make the $\sigma < 0$ decision rule equal to that for a $\sigma = 0$ rule: (1) it brings the distorted impulse response functions closer to those of the

---

[25] The procedure of first optimizing, then setting $x_t = X_t$ to eliminate X_t is a common way of formulating rational expectations equilibria in macroeconomics, where it is sometimes called the "Big K, little k" method.

[26] The observational equivalence proposition makes the decision rules equivalent under the approximating model.

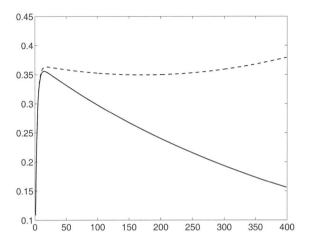

Figure 10.4.1: Response of total endowment d_t to innovation in 'permanent' component $\tilde{d}_t$ under the approximating model (dotted line) and the distorted model associated with the worst-case shock (dashed line) for the $\sigma = -.0001$, $\beta = \beta(\sigma)$ model.

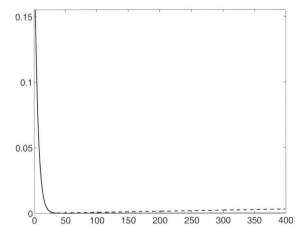

Figure 10.4.2: Response of total endowment d_t to innovation in 'transitory' component $\hat{d}_t$ under the approximating model (solid line) and the distorted model associated with the worst-case shock (dotted line) for the $\sigma = -.0001, \beta = \beta(\sigma)$ model.

approximating model, and (2) more impatience combats the precautionary savings motive.

10.5. Another view of precautionary savings

To interpret the precautionary savings motive inherent in our model, appendix B asserts another observational equivalence proposition. Theorem 10.B.1 takes a baseline case where $\beta R = 1$ and shows that in its effects on (c, i), activating a concern for robustness operates just like an *increase* in the discount factor. This result is useful because the $\beta R = 1$ case forms a benchmark in the permanent income literature (for example, see Hall (1978)). Theorem 10.B.1 shows that the effects of activating concerns about robustness by putting $\sigma < 0$ are replicated by keeping $\sigma = 0$ and raising β so that $\beta R > 1$.

To use this result to shed more light on how the precautionary motive manifests itself in the decision rule for consumption, we consider the important special case that $\delta = \lambda = \tilde{\delta} = 0$. Then $\mu_{st} = \mu_{ct} = b - c_t$ and the consumption Euler equation $(10.3.2d)$ without a concern about robustness becomes

$$b - c_t = E_t \left[(\beta R) (b - c_{t+1}) \right].$$

If $\beta R > 1$, this equation implies that $b - c_t > E_t(b - c_{t+1})$, or

$$c_t < E_t c_{t+1}, \tag{10.5.1}$$

so that the optimal policy is to make consumption grow on average.

Theorem 10.B.1 shows that when $\beta R = 1$, a concern about robustness $(\sigma < 0)$ has the same effect on c_t, i_t as setting $\sigma = 0$ and setting a particular β for which $\beta R > 1$. Therefore, when $\beta R = 1$, the precautionary savings that occurs when $\sigma < 0$ follows from $(10.5.1)$. Activating a concern about robustness imparts an upward drift to the expected consumption profile.

We can also use Theorem 10.B.1 to discuss some facts about the decision rule for consumption in our special case that $\lambda = \delta = \tilde{\delta} = 0$. The solution $(10.3.8)$ for $\sigma = 0$ implies the consumption rule

$$c_t = \left(1 - R^{-2} \beta^{-1} \right) \left[R k_{t-1} + E_t \sum_{j=0}^{\infty} R^{-j} d_{t+j} \right] + \left(\frac{(R\beta)^{-1} - 1}{R - 1} \right) b. \tag{10.5.2}$$

Notice that the marginal propensity to consume out of financial wealth $R k_{t-1}$ equals that out of human wealth $E_t \sum_{j=0}^{\infty} R^{-j} d_{t+j}$.[27] Further, an increase in β *decreases* the constant $\left(\frac{(R\beta)^{-1} - 1}{R - 1} \right) b$ and *increases* the marginal propensity

---

[27] This implication of precautionary savings coming from robustness differs from that coming from convex marginal utility functions, where precautionary savings reduces the marginal propensity to consume out of endowment income relative to that from financial wealth. See Wang (2003).

to consume $1 - R^{-2}\beta$. Relative to the baseline $\beta R = 1$ case, raising β raises the marginal propensity to consume out of wealth by $R^{-1}(\dot{1} - (R\beta)^{-1})$. This increase in the marginal propensity to consume still allows wealth to have an upward trajectory because of the reduction in the second term $\frac{(R\beta)^{-1}-1}{R-1}b$.

The permanent income model of consumption has an interpretation in terms of the frequency domain that is familiar to macroeconomists. It is that his concave one-period utility function makes the permanent income consumer dislike high-frequency volatility in consumption and therefore adjust his asset holdings in a way that protects his consumption from high-frequency fluctuations in income. The following section views the precautionary savings that are inspired by fears of model misspecification from the vantage point of the frequency domain.

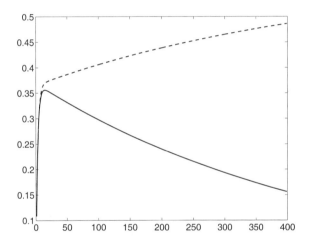

Figure 10.5.1: Response of total endowment d_t to innovation in "permanent" component $\tilde{d}_t$ under the approximating model (solid line) and the distorted model associated with the worst-case shock (dotted line) for $\sigma = -.0001$, with β at benchmark value.

10.6. Frequency domain representation

This section uses HST's estimated permanent income model to illustrate features of the frequency domain decompositions of the consumer's objective function and of the worst-case shocks for different values of σ.

Importing some notation from chapter 8, denote the transfer function from shocks ϵ_t to the "target" $s_t - b_t$ as $G(\zeta)$. For the baseline model with

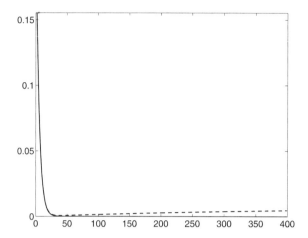

Figure 10.5.2: Response of total endowment d_t to innovation in "permanent" component $\tilde{d}_t$ under the approximating model (solid line) and the distorted model associated with the worst-case shock (dotted line) for $\sigma = -.0001$ with β at benchmark value.

habit persistence, recall formula (8.4.3) for the frequency decomposition of H_2:

$$H_2 = -\frac{1}{2\pi} \int_{-\pi}^{\pi} \text{trace}\left[G\left(\sqrt{\beta} \exp\left(i\omega\right)\right)' G\left(\sqrt{\beta} \exp\left(i\omega\right)\right) \right] d\omega.$$

A reinterpretation of formula (8.3.5) also gives us the frequency domain representation

$$E \sum_{t=0}^{\infty} \beta^t w_t' w_t = \frac{1}{2\pi} \int_{-\pi}^{\pi} W\left(\sqrt{\beta} \exp\left(i\omega\right)\right)' W\left(\sqrt{\beta} \exp\left(i\omega\right)\right) d\omega.$$

Figure 10.6.1 shows $G(\sqrt{\beta}\exp(i\omega))'G(\sqrt{\beta}\exp(i\omega))$ for the baseline ($\sigma = 0$) line as a function of frequency ω; $G'G$ is larger at lower frequencies. Remember that $G(\zeta) = (I - (A_o - BF)\zeta)^{-1}C$ embodies the consumer's optimal decision rule F. The noise process ϵ_t upon which $G(\zeta)$ operates is i.i.d. under the approximating model, so that the spectral density matrix of ϵ_t is constant across frequencies. But seeing that the consumer's policy makes him most vulnerable to the low-frequency components of ϵ_t, the minimizing player makes the conditional mean of the worst-case shock w_{t+1} highly serially correlated. For two values of σ, figure 10.6.2 shows frequency decompositions of trace $W(\zeta)'W(\zeta)$ for $\zeta = \sqrt{\beta}\exp(i\omega)$. Notice how most of the power is at the lowest frequencies. As we varied σ from zero to the two values in figure

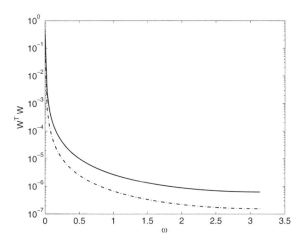

Figure 10.6.2: Frequency decomposition of volatility of worst-case shocks for $-\theta^{-1} = \sigma = -.0001$ (solid line) and $\sigma = -.00005$ (dotted line); $\text{trace}[W(\zeta)'W(\zeta)]$ plotted as a function of ω where $\zeta = \sqrt{\beta}\exp(i\omega)$.

10.6.2, we adjusted $\beta = \hat{\beta}$ according to (10.3.18), which keeps the robust $\sigma < 0$ decision rule for consumption equal to that for the baseline no robustness ($\sigma = 0$) model. Notice that $[\text{trace } W(\zeta)'W(\zeta)]$ varies directly with the absolute value of σ.

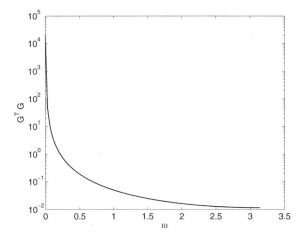

Figure 10.6.1: Frequency decomposition of criterion function; $G(\zeta)'G(\zeta)$ plotted as a function of ω where $\zeta = \sqrt{\beta}\exp(i\omega)$.

10.7. Detection error probabilities

For HST's parameter values, figure 10.7.1 reports detection error probabilities associated with various values of σ, adjusting β according to $(10.3.18)$ so as to keep the decision rule fixed. These detection error probabilities were calculated by the method of chapter 9 for a sample of the same length that HST used to estimate their model and for HST's initial conditions. To calculate the detection error probabilities, all other parameter values were frozen at the values from table 10.A.1. Then the formula for the worst-case distortions $w_{t+1} = K(\sigma, \hat{\beta}) x_t$ was used to compute an alternative law of motion for the endowment process.

For different values of σ, figure 10.7.1 records the detection error probabilities for distinguishing an approximating model from a worst-case model associated with that value of σ. The approximating model is

$$x_{t+1} = (A - BF(0, \beta)) x_t + C\epsilon_{t+1}$$

while the distorted model associated with σ is

$$x_{t+1} = \left(A - BF(0, \beta) + CK\left(\sigma, \hat{\beta}\right)\right) x_t + C\tilde{\epsilon}_{t+1}$$

where both ϵ_t and $\tilde{\epsilon}_t$ are i.i.d. processes with mean zero and identity covariance matrix, and where $F(0, \beta) = F(\sigma, \hat{\beta})$ by the observational equivalence proposition.

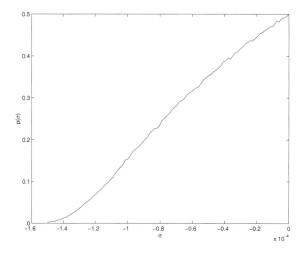

Figure 10.7.1: Detection error probabilities as a function of σ.

The detection error probability equals .5 for $\sigma = 0$ because then the models are identical and, hence, cannot be distinguished. The detection error probability falls with σ because the two models differ more from one another. In the following section, we use figure 10.7.1 to guide a choice of σ as measuring the size of a set of models against which it is plausible for the consumer to seek robustness.

10.8. Robustness of decision rules

For $\sigma = -\theta^{-1}$, express the equilibrium decision rules of game $(10.2.1)$ as

$$c_t = -F(\sigma)x_t \qquad (10.8.1a)$$

$$w_{t+1} = K(\sigma)x_t \qquad (10.8.1b)$$

and express $s_t - b$ as $H(\sigma)x_t$. For possibly different values σ_1, σ_2, consider the law of motion of the state under the consumption plan $F(\sigma_2)x_t$ and the worst-case shock process $K(\sigma_1)x_t$:

$$x_{t+1} = (A - BF(\sigma_2) + CK(\sigma_1))x_t + C\epsilon_{t+1}. \qquad (10.8.2)$$

For x_0 given, we evaluate the expected payoff

$$\pi(\sigma_1; \sigma_2) = -E_{0,\sigma_1} \sum_{t=0}^{\infty} \beta^t x_t' H(\sigma_2)' H(\sigma_2)x_t \qquad (10.8.3)$$

under the law of motion $(10.8.2)$. That is, we want to evaluate the performance of the rule designed by setting σ_2 when the data are generated by the distorted model associated with σ_1. For three values of σ_2, figure 10.8.1 plots $\pi(\sigma_1; \sigma_2)$ as a function of the parameter σ_1 that indexes the magnitude of the distortion in the model generating the data. By construction, the $\sigma_2 = 0$ decision rule does better than the other rules when $\sigma_1 = 0$. But its performance deteriorates faster with decreases in σ_1 below zero than do the more robust $\sigma_1 = -.00004, \sigma_1 = -.00008$ rules.

From figure 10.8.1, $\sigma = -.00004$ is associated with a detection error probability of over .3, and $\sigma = -.00008$ with a detection error probability about .2. It is plausible for the consumer to want decisions that are robust against alternative models that are as close as the worst-case models associated with those values of σ.

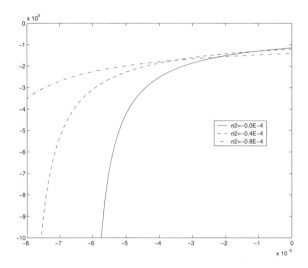

Figure 10.8.1: Payoff

$$\pi(\sigma_1; \sigma_2) = -E_{0,\sigma_1} \sum_{t=0}^{\infty} \beta^t x_t' H(\sigma_2)' H(\sigma_2) x_t$$

as a function of σ_1 on the ordinate axis for decision rules $F(\sigma_2)$ associated with three values of σ_2.

10.9. Concluding remarks

Different observationally equivalent (σ, β) pairs identified by Theorem 10.3.1 have different implications concerning (1) pricing risky assets; (2) the amounts required to compensate the planner for confronting different amounts of risk; (3) the amount of model misspecification used to justify the planner's decisions if risk sensitivity is reinterpreted as reflecting concerns about model misspecification. Hansen, Sargent, and Tallarini (1999) and Hansen, Sargent, and Wang (2002) have analyzed the asset pricing implications of the model in this chapter. They show that although movements along the observational equivalence locus described by (10.3.18) do not affect consumption and investment, they put an adjustment for fear of model misspecification into asset prices and boost what macroeconomists typically measure as market prices of risk. In chapter 13, we shall describe how standard asset pricing formulas are altered when a representative consumer is concerned about robustness. There we shall describe an asset pricing theory under a concern about robustness in the context of a class of general equilibrium models. The model from this chapter can be viewed as a special case of this class of models.

Table 10.A.1: HST's parameter estimates

Object	Habit Persistence	No Habit Persistence
Risk Free Rate	.025	.025
β	.997	.997
δ_h	.682	
λ	2.443	0
α_1	.813	.900
α_2	.189	.241
ϕ_1	.998	.995
ϕ_2	.704	.450
μ_d	13.710	13.594
$c_{\hat{d}}$	.155	.173
$c_{\tilde{d}}$	.108	.098
$2 \times \text{LogLikel}$	779.05	762.55

A. Parameter values

HST calibrated a $\sigma = 0$ version of their permanent income model by maximizing a likelihood function conditioned only on U.S. quarterly consumption and investment data. They used U.S. quarterly data on consumption and investment for the period 1970I–1996III. They measured consumption by nondurables plus services and investment by the sum of durable consumption and gross private investment.[28] They estimated the model from data on (c_t, i_t), setting $\sigma = 0$, then deduced pairs (σ, β) that are observationally equivalent, using formula (10.3.18).

The forcing processes are governed by seven free parameters: $(\alpha_1, \alpha_2, c_{\hat{d}}, \phi_1, \phi_2, c_{\tilde{d}}, \mu_d)$. The parameter μ_b sets a bliss point. While μ_b alters the marginal utilities, it does not influence the decision rules for consumption and investment. HST fixed μ_b at an arbitrary number, namely 32, for estimation.

Four parameters govern the endogenous dynamics: $(\gamma, \delta_h, \beta, \lambda)$. HST set $\delta_k = .975$, and imposed the permanent-income restriction, $\beta R = 1$. The restrictions that $\beta R = 1, \delta_k = .975$ pin down γ once β is estimated. HST imposed $\beta = .9971$, which after adjustment for the effects of the geometric growth factor of 1.0033 implies an annual real interest rate of 2.5%.

Table 10.A.1 reports HST's estimates for the parameters governing the endogenous and exogenous dynamics. Figures 10.A.1 and 10.A.2 report impulse response functions for consumption and investment to innovations in both components of the endowment process. For comparison, table 10.A.1 reports estimates from a no habit persistence ($\lambda = 0$) model as well.

Notice that the persistent endowment shock process contributes much more to consumption and investment fluctuations than does the transitory endowment shock process.

---

[28] They estimated the model from data that had been scaled through multiplication by 1.0033^{-t}.

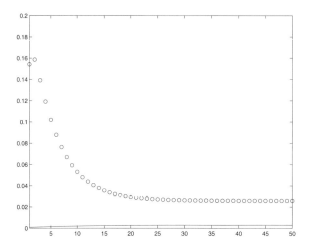

Figure 10.A.1: Impulse response functions of investment (circles) and consumption (solid line) to innovation in transitory endowment process $(\hat{d})$, at maximum likelihood estimate of habit persistence.

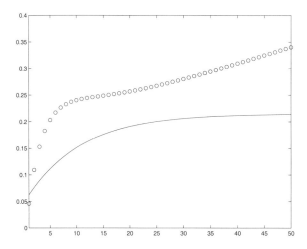

Figure 10.A.2: Impulse response functions of investment (circles) and consumption (solid line) to innovation in persistent shock $(\tilde{d})$, at maximum likelihood estimate of habit persistence.

B. Another observational equivalence result

To shed more light on the form of precautionary savings, we state another observational equivalence result that takes as its benchmark an initial allocation associated with parameter settings $\beta R = 1$ and $\sigma < 0$. Then we find another value of β that implies the same decisions for c_t, i_t as the base model when $\sigma = 0$, so that the decision maker fears model misspecification. This entails working backwards from the worst-case model that is reflected in the $\sigma < 0$ decision rule to the associated approximating model.

Theorem 10.B.1. *(Observational Equivalence, II)* *Fix all parameters except (σ, β). Consider a consumption-investment allocation for $(\hat{\sigma}, \hat{\beta})$ where $\hat{\beta}$ satisfies $\hat{\beta}R = 1$ and $\hat{\sigma} < 0$ and $\underline{\sigma} < \hat{\sigma}$. Then there exists a $\tilde{\beta} > \hat{\beta}$ such that the $(\hat{\sigma}, \hat{\beta})$ allocation also solves the $(0, \tilde{\beta})$ problem.*

Proof. We suppose that $\hat{\sigma} < 0$, so that the worst-case model differs from the approximating model. We want to find the approximating model and a value $\tilde{\beta}$ of β for which a $\sigma = 0$ decision maker would choose the $(\hat{\sigma}, \hat{\beta})$ allocation. Under the model with $\hat{\sigma} < 0$, where $\hat{E}_t$ denotes a conditional expectation under the worst-case model, we have

$$\hat{E}_t \mu_{c,t+1} = \mu_{c,t} \tag{10.B.1}$$

because $\hat{\beta}R = 1$. Let

$$\hat{E}_l \mu_{s,l+1} - \xi\left(\tilde{\beta}\right)\mu_{s,l}. \tag{10.B.2}$$

Equation $(10.B.1)$ implies that we want

$$1 = \xi\left(\tilde{\beta}\right) \tag{10.B.3}$$

where the projection coefficient $\xi(\tilde{\beta})$ emerges from the multiplier problem for the evil agent for $\hat{\sigma} < 0$, which can be cast as

$$\min_{\{w_{t+1}\}} \left[-\sum_{t=0}^{\infty} \hat{\beta}^t \{\mu_{st}^2 + \hat{\beta}\frac{1}{\hat{\sigma}}w_{t+1}^2\} \right]$$

subject to the law of motion

$$\mu_{st} = \delta\left(\tilde{\beta}\right)\mu_{s,t-1} + \alpha w_t \tag{10.B.4}$$

where $\delta(\tilde{\beta}) = \frac{1}{\tilde{\beta}R}$ and α is given by $(10.3.17)$, $(10.3.14)$, $(10.3.15)$ under the $(\hat{\sigma}, \hat{\beta})$ model. (Remember that the decision rule for c_t and therefore the law for μ_{st} will be the same under our two observationally equivalent (σ, β) pairs, so we can use the benchmark case to compute α.) We freeze all parameters except σ, β. The approximating model would be $\mu_{st} = \delta\mu_{s,t-1} + \alpha\epsilon_t$, so that $(10.B.4)$ adds a perturbation αw_t to the law of motion of μ_{st} under a deterministic version of the approximating model. The Bellman equation for the minimizing agent is evidently

$$-P\mu_s^2 = -\mu_s^2 + \hat{\beta}\min_w\left[-\frac{1}{\hat{\sigma}}w^2 - P\left(\delta\mu_s + \alpha w\right)^2\right]. \tag{10.B.5}$$

Notice the presence of both $\hat{\beta}$ and $\tilde{\beta}$, via δ and α. The first-order condition is

$$w = K\mu_s,$$

where

$$K = -\frac{\alpha\delta\hat{\sigma}P}{1 + \alpha^2\hat{\sigma}P}.$$

Notice that

$$\xi\left(\tilde{\beta}\right) = A + KC = \delta + K\alpha = 1,$$

which implies that

$$1 = \xi\left(\tilde{\beta}\right) = \delta + K\alpha = \frac{\delta}{1 + \alpha^2 \hat{\sigma} P}.$$

Therefore,

$$\delta = 1 + \hat{\sigma}\alpha^2 P < 1. \qquad (10.B.6)$$

Equation $(10.B.5)$ implies that

$$-P = -1 + \hat{\beta}\left[-\frac{1}{\hat{\sigma}}K^2 - P\left(\delta + K\alpha\right)^2\right].$$

Simplifying the above identity leaves

$$P = \frac{1}{1 - \hat{\beta}}\left[1 + \frac{\hat{\beta}}{\hat{\sigma}}\left(\frac{1 - \delta}{\alpha}\right)^2\right]. \qquad (10.B.7)$$

Equations $(10.B.6)$ and $(10.B.7)$ together imply that

$$0 = \hat{\beta}\left(1 - \delta\left(\tilde{\beta}\right)\right)^2 + \left(1 - \hat{\beta}\right)\left(1 - \delta\left(\tilde{\beta}\right)\right) + \alpha\left(\tilde{\beta}\right)^2\hat{\sigma}.$$

A solution of this equation determines $\tilde{\beta}$. The solution of this quadratic equation is

$$\delta = 1 - \frac{-\left(1 - \hat{\beta}\right) \pm \sqrt{\left(1 - \hat{\beta}\right)^2 - 4\hat{\beta}\sigma\alpha^2}}{2\hat{\beta}}.$$

If $\sigma = 0$, this equation implies $\delta = 1$. When $\sigma < 0$, the appropriate root is

$$\delta = 1 - \frac{-\left(1 - \hat{\beta}\right) + \sqrt{\left(1 - \hat{\beta}\right)^2 - 4\hat{\beta}\sigma\alpha^2}}{2\hat{\beta}}.$$

Using $\hat{\beta}R = 1$, this is equivalent to

$$\tilde{\beta}\left(\sigma\right) = \frac{\hat{\beta}\left(1 + \hat{\beta}\right)}{2\left(1 + \sigma\alpha^2\right)}\left[1 + \sqrt{1 - 4\hat{\beta}\frac{1 + \sigma\alpha^2}{\left(1 + \hat{\beta}\right)^2}}\right]. \qquad (10.B.8)$$

Part IV
Multi-agent problems

Chapter 11
Competitive equilibria without robustness

11.1. Introduction

The next four chapters study prices and quantities in dynamic competitive equilibrium models. This chapter sets the stage by describing competitive equilibria when the representative agent has no concern about model misspecification. It introduces the basic objects and equilibrium representations of prices and quantities that we will modify when we add concerns about model missspecification in chapters 12, 13, and 14.

11.2. Pricing risky claims

In an economy with complete markets, history-date prices equal intertemporal marginal rates of substitution times conditional probabilities evaluated at an equilibrium allocation. Complete markets assure that intertemporal rates of substitution are equated across all consumers, making it possible to speak unambiguously of *the* intertemporal rate of substitution and thereby allowing us to synthesize a representative agent.[1]

In a pure endowment economy with a representative consumer, like Lucas's (1978), it is trivial to compute the equilibrium history-date prices. They equal the representative consumer's intertemporal marginal rates of substitution, evaluated at the respective endowments, times the exogenous conditional probabilities. These prices can be used to evaluate risky claims that consist of bundles of history-date contingent commodities.

Brock (1982) extended this pricing strategy to representative household economies that have endogenous state variables like capital stocks that help to produce goods and household services. Household capital stocks can be used to represent non-separabilities over time in the household's preferences. Brock's procedure for pricing risky claims consists of the following steps:

1. Compute optimal allocations by solving a planning problem. The optimal allocations can be represented recursively as functions of a state vector, the endogenous components of which are influenced by the planner.

---

[1] Hansen and Sargent (2008) extend methods for calculating a representative household in a heterogenous agent economy to situations where households can have different dynamic technologies for transforming consumption goods into household services (e.g., different degrees of habit persistence).

2. Compute shadow prices of the history-date contingent consumption goods as conditional probabilities times intertemporal marginal rates of substitution evaluated at the optimal allocation. Take the shadow prices to be the history-date contingent prices.

3. Represent a security as a stochastic process of payouts, i.e., as a sequence of measurable functions of the economy's history of shocks.

4. Price a security by multiplying the history-date pay outs by the history-date prices computed in step (2), then sum across histories and over time.

Chapter 13 relies heavily on the four-step strategy (1)-(4) for pricing assets. Here and in chapter 12, we lay out alternative decentralizations of our planning problem. The four-step strategy is powerful partly because it allows us to price assets using the state vector x_t for the planning problem. However, to express the idea that the household is a price taker in a recursive competitive equilibrium, we have to augment the state x_t with additional components X_t that are comparable in dimension to x_t; X_t becomes a part of the state vector that the household takes as exogenous and in terms of which we express prices.[2] In a competitive equilibrium, we impose $X_t = x_t$, but only *after* the household has optimized while taking X_t as beyond its control. Setting $X_t = x_t$ after optimization makes the representative household be representative. After we have set $X_t = x_t$, we can cast asset pricing formulas solely in terms of the state x_t in the planning problem, provided that we adopt the assumption of time-zero trading that is embedded in the standard Arrow-Debreu model of competitive equilibrium. The Arrow-Debreu timing is contained in one of the three types of competitive equilibrium models to be described in this chapter.

11.3. Types of competitive equilibria

We study a class of economic environments that fit the optimal linear regulator.[3] Three types of competitive equilibria share common specifications of information, preferences, and technologies; yield identical allocations; but have different market structures. They are (1) an "Arrow-Debreu equilibrium" with trades at time 0 in a complete set of state-contingent dated commodities; (2) an "equilibrium with Arrow securities" that has a sequence of complete markets in current period commodities and one-period-ahead state-contingent

---

[2] In related contexts, this idea was used by Lucas and Prescott (1971) and Prescott and Mehra (1980).

[3] Hansen (1987) and Hansen and Sargent (2008) have studied such economies.

claims; and (3) a "partial equilibrium" model in which a competitive representative firm acts as a price taker and prices lie along a system of demand equations perturbed by shocks. The three types of competitive equilibria provide alternative decentralized ways of attaining the same allocation by confronting households and firms with different price systems and trading opportunities. For applications, it is useful to know how to transform one type of equilibrium into another.

11.4. Information, preferences, and technology

11.4.1. Information

An exogenous information vector z_t is governed by

$$z_{t+1} = A_{22}z_t + C_2\epsilon_{t+1}, \qquad (11.4.1)$$

where $\{\epsilon_t\}$ is an i.i.d. Gaussian vector with mean 0 and covariance matrix I, and the eigenvalues of $\tilde{A}_{22} \equiv \sqrt{\beta}A_{22}$ are bounded by unity in modulus. The vector z_t determines a time t preference shock b_t and a time t endowment shock d_t via

$$\begin{aligned} d_t &= U_d\, z_t \\ b_t &= U_b\, z_t. \end{aligned} \qquad (11.4.2)$$

To account for the flow of information in the economy, we define the space $J_t = [\epsilon^t, x_0]$, where $J_0 = [x_0]$ and $\epsilon^t = [\epsilon_t, \epsilon_{t-1}, \ldots, \epsilon_1]$. We say that a stochastic process is adapted to J_t if its time t component is a measurable function of J_t.

11.4.2. Preferences

A representative household has preferences ordered by

$$-\left(\frac{1}{2}\right) E\left(\sum_{t=0}^{\infty} \beta^t \left(|s_t - b_t|^2 + \ell_t^2\right) \,\bigg|\, J_0\right), \qquad (11.4.3)$$

where ℓ_t is a scalar process that constrains a vector g_t of intermediate activities (designed to capture generalized adjustment costs) in equation (11.4.6) below, and s_t is a vector of household services produced at time t via the household technology

$$\begin{aligned} s_t &= \Lambda h_{t-1} + \Pi c_t \\ h_t &= \Delta_h h_{t-1} + \Theta_h c_t. \end{aligned} \qquad (11.4.4)$$

Sometimes we interpret ℓ_t in (11.4.3) as labor input. In (11.4.4), h_t is a vector of stocks of household durable goods at t, c_t is a vector of consumption flows, and Λ, Π, Δ_h, Θ_h are matrices.

11.4.3. Technology

There is a constant returns to scale production technology

$$\Phi_c c_t + \Phi_i i_t + \Phi_g g_t = \Gamma k_{t-1} + d_t$$

$$k_t = \Delta_k k_{t-1} + \Theta_k i_t,$$

(11.4.5)

where k_t is a vector of capital goods used in production, i_t is a vector of investment goods, Δ_k is a matrix, and g_t is constrained by[4]

$$g_t \cdot g_t \leq \ell_t^2.$$

(11.4.6)

11.4.4. Planning problem

The planning problem is to maximize (11.4.3) over choices of processes for $\{s_t, c_t, i_t, g_t, k_t, h_t\}_{t=0}^\infty$ that are adapted to J_t subject to (11.4.1), (11.4.2), (11.4.4), and (11.4.5) with given initial conditions for (z_0, h_{-1}, k_{-1}). The planning problem takes the form of an optimal linear regulator. Let

$$x_t \equiv \begin{bmatrix} h_{t-1} \\ k_{t-1} \\ z_t \end{bmatrix}.$$

The two components h and k of the state vector are *endogenous* and z is *exogenous*. If the matrix $\Phi \equiv [\,\Phi_c \quad \Phi_g\,]$ is nonsingular, the control vector u_t can be chosen to be investment i_t because[5]

$$\begin{bmatrix} c_t \\ g_t \end{bmatrix} = \Phi^{-1} \left(\Gamma k_{t-1} + U_d z_t - \Phi_i i_t \right).$$

(11.4.7)

Using this relation, the constraints (11.4.4) and (11.4.5) can be rewritten

$$x_{t+1} = Ax_t + Bu_t + C\epsilon_{t+1}$$

(11.4.8)

for appropriately chosen matrices A, B, C. The matrix A is block triangular and the bottom row block of B is zero as required for the discounted stochastic linear regulator problem (see page 71). Moreover, using (11.4.7) and (11.4.4), the time t terms $|s_t - b_t|^2$ and $|g_t|^2$ in the objective function (11.4.3) of the planner can both be expressed as quadratic forms in the control $u_t = i_t$ and the augmented state x_t.

The planner's optimal decision rule is $u_t = -Fx_t$. Under this rule, the state evolves according to

$$x_{t+1} = A^o x_t + C\epsilon_{t+1},$$

(11.4.9)

where $A^o = A - BF$.

---

[4] Under the constant returns to scale interpretation, d_t is taken as an additional input available in fixed supply.

[5] The matrix Φ can usually be rendered nonsingular by augmenting the control vector to include some components of consumption or the labor-intensive intermediate activities.

11.4.5. Imposing stability

In permanent income economies, optimality does not automatically imply stability of the state vector process. For example, the economy of chapter 10 has a single consumption good, a single capital good, and no labor-intensive intermediate activities g_t. The counterpart to equation (11.4.7) is

$$c_t = \Gamma k_{t-1} + U_d z_t - i_t.$$

The chapter 10 model constrains the subjective discount factor to be the reciprocal of the physical return to capital: $\beta = \frac{1}{\Gamma + \Delta_k}$. Without imposing stability as an additional constraint, the optimal sequence of capital stocks diverges to minus infinity at a rate that is not dominated by $\frac{1}{\sqrt{\beta}}$. We want to impose stability because solutions that require x_t not to explode at a rate exceeding $\frac{1}{\sqrt{\beta}}$ are much better approximations to models that impose debt limits or various non-negativity constraints. We therefore impose stability as an additional constraint, with the consequence that the solution of the resulting infinite-horizon control problem equals the limit of a sequence of solutions to the corresponding finite-horizon problems, each of which imposes a zero terminal capital stock.

We now describe competitive equilibria with three different types of trading structures, each of which supports an allocation that solves the planning problem.

11.5. Arrow-Debreu

11.5.1. The price system at time 0

An Arrow-Debreu equilibrium has complete markets at time 0 in claims to history-contingent dated commodities. We follow Harrison and Kreps (1979) and Hansen and Sargent (2008) in rescaling the Arrow-Debreu prices. The rescaled prices are the ordinary Arrow-Debreu history-date prices divided by probabilities times discount factors. Using the scaled prices converts present values into expected discounted geometric sums of quadratic forms that are easy to compute by solving Sylvester equations (see chapter 4).

We use a price system with components $\{p_{ct}^0, \, p_{it}^0, \, p_{\ell t}^0, \, p_{dt}^0, \, p_{rt}^0\}_{t=0}^{\infty}$, each element of which resides in a space L_0^2 defined by

$$L_0^2 = \left[\{y_t\}_{t=0}^{\infty} \colon y_t \text{ is a random variable in } J_t \text{ for } t \geq 0, \right.$$

$$\left. \text{and } E\left[\sum_{t=0}^{\infty} \beta^t \, y_t^2 \mid J_0\right] < +\infty \right].$$

That "y_t is in J_t" means that y_t can be expressed as a measurable function of J_t. The square summability requirement, $E[\sum_{t=0}^{\infty} \beta^t y_t^2 \mid J_0] < \infty$, imposes that y_t not grow too fast in absolute value.

Our price system contains the following prices: p_{ct}^0 is an $n_c \times 1$ stochastic process that prices the consumption process c_t; $p_{\ell t}^0$ is a scalar stochastic process that prices ℓ_t; p_{dt}^0 is a vector stochastic process that prices the process $\{d_t\}$; p_{it}^0 is an $n_k \times 1$ vector stochastic process that prices new investment goods; and p_{rt}^0 is an $n_k \times 1$ vector stochastic process of capital rental rates. A time t component of the price system is a random vector that is a function of J_t. The *price system* is a *sequence* of vector-valued measurable functions of the time t histories J_t.

Prices and quantities are stochastic processes. We require the stochastic processes for both prices and quantities to reside in L_0^2. By virtue of a Cauchy-Schwarz inequality, this makes the conditional inner products to be used in the budget constraints and objective functions below well defined and finite in equilibrium. Later it will be convenient to obtain recursive representations for both prices and quantities.

We now describe the choice problems faced by a household and a firm within a competitive equilibrium in which all trades occur at time 0. The household and firm act as price takers. The allocations chosen by the household and the firm must be "realizable" in the sense that time t decisions depend only on information available at time t, i.e., they must reside in L_0^2.

11.5.2. The household

We let E denote the mathematical expectation evaluated with respect to the joint probability distribution of $[\epsilon^t, x_0]$. We also let E_t denote $E(\cdot \mid J_t)$. The household chooses stochastic processes for $\{c_t, s_t, h_t, \ell_t, i_t, k_t\}_{t=0}^{\infty}$, each element of which is in L_0^2, to maximize

$$-\frac{1}{2} E_0 \sum_{t=0}^{\infty} \beta^t \left[(s_t - b_t) \cdot (s_t - b_t) + \ell_t^2 \right] \tag{11.5.1}$$

subject to

$$E \sum_{t=0}^{\infty} \beta^t \left(p_{ct}^0 \cdot c_t + p_{it}^0 \cdot i_t \right) \mid J_0$$

$$= E \sum_{t=0}^{\infty} \beta^t \left(p_{\ell t}^0 \ell_t + p_{rt}^0 \cdot k_{t-1} + p_{dt}^0 \cdot d_t \right) \mid J_0 \tag{11.5.2a}$$

$$s_t = \Lambda h_{t-1} + \Pi c_t \tag{11.5.2b}$$

$$h_t = \Delta_h h_{t-1} + \Theta_h c_t \tag{11.5.2c}$$

$$k_t = \Delta_k k_{t-1} + \Theta_k i_t \tag{11.5.2d}$$

$$b_t = U_b z_t \tag{11.5.2e}$$

$$d_t = U_d z_t \tag{11.5.2f}$$

$$z_{t+1} = A_{22} z_t + C_2 \epsilon_{t+1} \tag{11.5.2g}$$

with h_{-1}, k_{-1}, z_0 given.

11.5.3. The firm

A firm rents capital and labor and buys the realization of the endowment process d_t. It uses these inputs to produce consumption goods and investment goods that it sells to the household. The firm chooses stochastic processes for $\{c_t, i_t, k_t, \ell_t, g_t, d_t\}$, each element of which is in L_0^2, to maximize

$$E_0 \sum_{t=0}^{\infty} \beta^t \left(p_{ct}^0 \cdot c_t + p_{it}^0 \cdot i_t - p_{rt}^0 \cdot k_{t-1} - p_{\ell t}^0 \ell_t - p_{dt}^0 \cdot d_t \right) \tag{11.5.3}$$

subject to

$$\Phi_c c_t + \Phi_g g_t + \Phi_i i_t = \Gamma k_{t-1} + d_t \tag{11.5.4}$$

$$-\ell_t^2 + g_t \cdot g_t = 0. \tag{11.5.5}$$

11.5.4. Competitive equilibrium with time-0 trading

A competitive equilibrium has all trades being made at time 0.

Definition 11.5.1. A *competitive equilibrium* is a price system $\{p_{ct}^0, p_{\ell t}^0, p_{dt}^0, p_{it}^0, p_{rt}^0\}_{t=0}^{\infty}$ and an allocation $\{c_t, i_t, s_t, k_t, h_t, \ell_t, g_t\}_{t=0}^{\infty}$ that satisfy the following conditions:

(1) The allocation and each component of the price system reside in the space L_0^2.

(2) Given the price system, the allocation solves the problems of the household and firm.

11.5.5. Equilibrium computation

A strategy for computing an equilibrium is first to solve the planning problem for equilibrium quantities, then to compute shadow prices that we transform into equilibrium prices.

The optimal linear regulator can be used to solve a planning problem. The optimal law of motion for the state x_t and the value function for the planning problem contain enough information to compute competitive equilibrium prices. Let $V(x) = -x'Px - p$ be the optimal value of the planning problem starting from initial state $x = [h' \quad k' \quad z']'$. The Bellman equation for the planning problem is

$$-x'Px - p = \max_{c,i,g} \left\{ -.5\left[(s-b)\cdot(s-b) + g\cdot g\right] + \beta E\left(-x^{*\prime}Px^* - p\right)\right\}$$
(11.5.6)

subject to the linear constraints

$$\Phi_c c + \Phi_g g + \Phi_i i = \Gamma k + d$$
$$k^* = \Delta_k k + \Theta_k i$$
$$h^* = \Delta_h h + \Theta_h c$$
$$s = \Lambda h + \Pi c \tag{11.5.7}$$
$$z^* = A_{22} z + C_2 \epsilon^*$$
$$b = U_b z$$
$$d = U_d z,$$

where $*$ denotes a next-period value. The time-invariant character of the planning problem makes the optimal decision rules time invariant. Time t decision rules are linear in the state vector x_t. We denote these rules $c_t = S_c x_t$, $g_t = S_g x_t$, $h_t = S_h x_t$, $i_t = S_i x_t$, $k_t = S_k x_t$, $s_t = S_s x_t$.

The law of motion for the state vector is linear

$$x_{t+1} = A^o x_t + C\epsilon_{t+1} \tag{11.5.8}$$

where

$$A^o \equiv \begin{bmatrix} A_{11}^o & A_{12}^o \\ 0 & A_{22} \end{bmatrix}, \ C \equiv \begin{bmatrix} 0 \\ C_2 \end{bmatrix}. \tag{11.5.9}$$

The partitioning of the A^o and C matrices is according to the endogenous state vector $[h'_{t-1} \quad k'_{t-1}]'$ and the exogenous state vector z_t. The zero restriction on the (2,1) partition of A^o reflects the fact that the exogenous component of the state vector at time $t+1$ does not depend on the endogenous state vector at time t. The zero restriction on the first rows in the partition of C reflects the fact that the endogenous state vector at time $t+1$ is predetermined (i.e., depends only on time t information). The contingency plans for h_t and k_t are embedded in the part of (11.5.9) that determines the endogenous state vector as a function of x_t. In particular,

$$\begin{bmatrix} S_h \\ S_k \end{bmatrix} = [\, A_{11}^o \quad A_{12}^o \,]. \tag{11.5.10}$$

The planner's decision rules are recursive in the sense that the time t decision depends on the state vector at time t, which in turn depends on the state vector at time $t-1$.

11.5.6. *Shadow prices*

Equilibrium prices can be found by appropriately reinterpreting shadow prices as prices. Formulas for shadow prices corresponding to the elements of the price system $\{p_{ct}^0, p_{\ell t}^0, p_{dt}^0, p_{it}^0, p_{rt}^0\}_{t=0}^\infty$ can be extracted from A^o and the matrix P in the quadratic form in the value function. Evaluating these shadow prices at the equilibrium allocation recovers prices.

The time t component of these shadow prices are linear functions of x_t. In particular, the vector of shadow prices p_{ct}^0 for c_t is given by[6]

$$p_{ct}^0 = M_c x_t$$

where

$$M_c = \Theta'_h M_h + \Pi' M_s. \tag{11.5.11}$$

Here $M_h x_t$ is the shadow price of consumer durables and $M_s x_t$ is the shadow price of household services. These shadow prices satisfy

$$M_h x_t = E\left[\sum_{\tau=1}^\infty \beta^\tau (\Delta'_h)^{\tau-1} \Lambda' M_s x_{t+\tau} | J_t\right] \tag{11.5.12}$$

$$M_s x_t = (s_t - b_t), \tag{11.5.13}$$

where the mathematical expectation is evaluated with respect to the model (11.5.8) and where $b_t = S_b x_t$ and $s_t = S_s x_t$ is the planner's solution for s_t as a function of x_t. Also, let the planner's solution for intermediate inputs g_t be $g_t = S_g x_t$. Hansen and Sargent (2008) show that these other components of the shadow price system have representations[7]

$$
\begin{aligned}
p_{ct}^0 &= M_c x_t \\
p_{it}^0 &= M_i x_t \\
p_{rt}^0 &= \Gamma' M_d x_t \\
p_{dt}^0 &= M_d x_t \\
p_{\ell t}^0 &= |M_\ell x_t|,
\end{aligned}
\tag{11.5.14}
$$

where Hansen and Sargent give the following formulas for the M_j's in terms of P and A^o:

$$M_k = 2\beta \begin{bmatrix} 0 & I & 0 \end{bmatrix} P A^o$$

$$M_h = 2\beta \begin{bmatrix} I & 0 & 0 \end{bmatrix} P A^o$$

$$M_s = (S_b - S_s)$$

---

[6] The objects $M_j x_t$ emerge from derivatives of the planner's value function and are measured in units of marginal utility.

[7] Hansen and Sargent also compute a shadow price of capital, $p_{kt}^0 = (\Gamma' M_d + \Delta'_k M_k) x_t$.

$$M_d = \begin{bmatrix} \Phi'_c \\ \Phi'_g \end{bmatrix}^{-1} \begin{bmatrix} \Theta'_h M_h + \Pi' M_s \\ -S_g \end{bmatrix}$$

$$M_c = \Theta'_h M_h + \Pi' M_s$$

$$M_i = \Theta'_k M_k \tag{11.5.15}$$

$$M_\ell = S_g.$$

Here the partitions $[0 \ I \ 0]$ and $[I \ 0 \ 0]$ are conformable with the partition $[h'_{t-1}, k'_{t-1}, z_t]'$ of x_t.

11.5.7. Recursive representation of time 0 prices

Formulas (11.5.8) and (11.5.14) imply that we can regard the price system as consisting of sequences of measurable functions of the histories $J_t = [\epsilon^t, x_0]$. Equations (11.5.8) and (11.5.14) give a recursive representation of this price system in terms of the planner's state vector x_t. Although this representation of the price system turns out to be very convenient for asset pricing, it is not an appropriate representation for posing a recursive version of the household's optimization problem in a competitive equilibrium. We can obtain a recursive representation of the price system that will serve this purpose by introducing an additional state vector designed to keep track of the histories J_t for $t \geq 0$. In particular, define a new state vector X_t with components H_{t-1}, K_{t-1} that have the same dimensions as h_{t-1}, k_{t-1}, respectively:

$$X_t = \begin{bmatrix} H_{t-1} \\ K_{t-1} \\ z_t \end{bmatrix}.$$

The exogenous state vector z_t is a common component of x_t and of X_t. Impose an initial condition

$$X_0 = \begin{bmatrix} H_{-1} \\ K_{-1} \\ z_0 \end{bmatrix} = \begin{bmatrix} h_{-1} \\ k_{-1} \\ z_0 \end{bmatrix} = x_0.$$

Take the law of motion for X to be

$$X_{t+1} = A^o X_t + C\epsilon_{t+1} \tag{11.5.16a}$$

where A^o is the *same* matrix that appears in the representation (11.4.9) for the evolution of x_t under the planner's optimal control. Then we can represent the shadow price system as

$$p_t^0 = M X_t. \tag{11.5.16b}$$

What is the purpose of this "big X" representation for prices?[8] First, note that by setting $X_0 = x_0$, we assure that (11.5.16) reproduces the planner's shadow prices. But by expressing them in terms of X_t rather than x_t, we make these prices depend only on a state variable that is beyond the control of the household. The role of X_t is to account for the history $J_t = [\epsilon^t, x_0]$. In a competitive equilibrium, we want households and firms to influence the evolution of h_t and k_t, the endogenous components of x_t, but still to be price takers. Therefore, in expressing the choices facing households and firms in a competitive equilibrium, we use X_t to provide a recursive representation of prices.

11.5.8. *Recursive representation of household's problem*

The household chooses an allocation to maximize (11.5.1) subject to (11.5.2) and the price system (11.5.16a), (11.5.16b), which the household regards as exogenous. Thus the household maximizes

$$E_0 \sum_{t=0}^{\infty} \beta^t \left\{ -.5 \left[(s_t - b_t) \cdot (s_t - b_t) + \ell_t^2 \right] \right\} \tag{11.5.17}$$

subject to

$$E \sum_{t=0}^{\infty} \beta^t \left(p_{ct}^0 \cdot c_t + p_{it}^0 \cdot i_t \right) \mid J_0$$

$$= E \sum_{t=0}^{\infty} \beta^t \left(p_{\ell t}^0 \ell_t + p_{rt}^0 \cdot k_{t-1} + p_{dt}^0 \cdot d_t \right) \mid J_0 \tag{11.5.18a}$$

$$s_t = \Lambda h_{t-1} + \Pi c_t \tag{11.5.18b}$$

$$h_t = \Delta_h h_{t-1} + \Theta_h c_t \tag{11.5.18c}$$

$$k_t = \Delta_k k_{t-1} + \Theta_k i_t \tag{11.5.18d}$$

$$b_t = U_b z_t \tag{11.5.18e}$$

$$d_t = U_d z_t \tag{11.5.18f}$$

$$p_t^0 = M_0 X_t \tag{11.5.18g}$$

$$X_{t+1} = A^0 X_t + C \epsilon_{t+1} \tag{11.5.18h}$$

with h_{-1}, k_{-1}, z_0 given. For a given Lagrange multiplier μ_0^w attached to (11.5.18a), problem (11.5.17), (11.5.18) takes the form of an optimal linear

---

[8] In their concept of a recursive competitive equilibrium, Prescott and Mehra (1980) distinguished between the market-wide level of capital $\underline{k}$ and the level chosen by an individual k in order to represent price-taking behavior. Our purpose is somewhat different from theirs, which was not to get a recursive representation of time 0 Arrow-Debreu prices.

regulator. (See section 12.4 for details and also for a way to compute μ_0^w from the solution of the planning problem.)

The maximizing choice of the household makes the time t component of $a_t = \begin{bmatrix} c_t & i_t & \ell_t \end{bmatrix}'$ a function of the composite state $\begin{bmatrix} h_{t-1} \\ k_{t-1} \\ X_t \end{bmatrix}$, namely,

$$a_t = -\begin{bmatrix} f_1 & f_2 & f_3 \end{bmatrix} \begin{bmatrix} h_{t-1} \\ k_{t-1} \\ X_t \end{bmatrix}. \tag{11.5.19}$$

The solution of the planning problem makes a_t a function of the state X_t, namely,

$$a_t = -FX_t. \tag{11.5.20}$$

In an equilibrium, $x_t = X_t$ in (11.5.19), so that the following equality prevails for all $x_t = X_t$: $-\begin{bmatrix} f_1 & f_2 & f_3 \end{bmatrix} \begin{bmatrix} h_{t-1} \\ k_{t-1} \\ X_t \end{bmatrix} = -FX_t$.

11.5.9. *Units of prices and reopening markets*

Prices have the units of time 0 marginal utilities of the representative agent. We can choose a numeraire to express prices in terms of one of the consumption goods. In particular, denote the time t marginal utility of the first consumption good $e_1 u_{c,t}$ and assume that $e_1 u_{c,t} \neq 0$ with probability one for all t. This assumption makes the first consumption good at time t a legitimate numeraire. We choose to express the price system at time 0 in units of the first consumption good. Therefore, we set

$$p_t^0 = \frac{M x_t}{e_1 u_{c,0}}. \tag{11.5.21}$$

More generally, for $t \geq \tau$ where $\tau \geq 0$, we could define a time τ price system[9]

$$p_t^\tau = \frac{M x_t}{e_1 u_{c,\tau}}. \tag{11.5.22}$$

To convert the tail of the time 0 price system for $t \geq 1$ to the time 1 price system we can use

$$p_{ct}^1 = p_{ct}^0 \frac{e_1 u_{c,0}}{e_1 u_{c,1}},$$

and so on.

---

[9] This time τ price system would prevail if we were to reopen markets at time τ, subject to appropriate initial conditions being inherited from earlier trading at time 0 prices.

11.6. Sequential markets with Arrow securities

We noted in section 11.5.7 that the time 0 prices for an Arrow-Debreu time 0 competitive equilibrium have a recursive representation based on $(11.5.16a)$, $(11.5.16b)$. This fact makes it easy to construct equilibrium prices for trading in a sequence of one-period markets. Following Arrow (1964), we can use $(11.5.16)$ to form competitive equilibrium prices with sequential trading of all current dated commodities and one-period state-contingent claims to a composite commodity called wealth. In this setting, the decision problem of the household is recursive and that of the firm is static. Though the trading arrangement differs, the equilibrium allocation is the same as the one attained in the equilibrium of the Arrow-Debreu model with time 0 trading of all history-contingent commodities for all dates.

11.6.1. Arrow securities

To explain why it is natural to move from an equilibrium with time 0 trading to an equilibrium with sequential trading, represent the consumer's budget constraint $(11.5.2)$ as

$$E_0 \sum_{t=1}^{\infty} \beta^t \left(p_{ct}^0 \cdot c_t + p_{it}^0 \cdot i_t - p_{\ell t}^0 \ell_t - p_{rt}^0 \cdot k_{t-1} - p_{dt}^0 \cdot d_t \right) + p_{c0}^0 \cdot c_0 + p_{i0}^0 \cdot i_0$$
$$= p_{\ell 0}^0 \ell_0 + p_{r0}^0 \cdot k_{-1} + p_{d0}^0 \cdot d_0.$$

Express the expected discounted sum on the left side as

$$E_0 \beta \left(\frac{e_1 u_{c,1}}{e_1 u_{c,0}} \right) \sum_{t=1}^{\infty} \beta^{t-1} \left(p_{ct}^1 \cdot c_t + p_{it}^1 \cdot i_t - p_{\ell t}^1 \ell_t - p_{rt}^1 \cdot k_{t-1} - p_{dt}^1 \cdot d_t \right)$$
$$\equiv E_0 \beta \left(\frac{e_1 u_{c,1}}{e_1 u_{c,0}} \right) a_1 (X_1) = \int q(X_1|X_0) a_1 (X_1) \, d X_1,$$

$$(11.6.1)$$

where $a_1 = a_1(X_1)$ measures wealth at time 1 in state X_1 in units of the time 1 consumption good, and the one-step-ahead pricing kernel $q(X_1|X_0) \equiv \beta \frac{e_1 u_{c,1}}{e_1 u_{c,0}} f(X_1|X_0)$. Here $f(X_1|X_0)$ is the transition density of X defined by $(11.5.16a)$. Use $(11.6.1)$ to express the budget constraint as

$$\int q(X_1|X_0) a_1 (X_1) \, d X_1 + p_{c0}^0 \cdot c_0 + p_{i0}^0 \cdot i_0$$
$$= p_{\ell 0}^0 \ell_0 + p_{d0}^0 \cdot d_0 + p_{r0}^0 \cdot k_{-1} + a_0 (X_0)$$

$$(11.6.2)$$

where $a_0(X_0)$ is the value of the household's initial wealth, namely, the capital stock k_{-1}. More generally, take prices without superscripts to be denominated in units of time t consumption of the first good and write

$$\int q(X_{t+1}|X_t) a_{t+1} (X_{t+1}) \, d X_{t+1} + p_{ct} \cdot c_t + p_{it} \cdot i_t$$
$$= p_{\ell t} \ell_t + p_{dt} \cdot d_t + p_{rt} \cdot k_{t-1} + a_t (X_t)$$

$$(11.6.3)$$

where

$$q\left(X_{t+1}|X_t\right) = \beta \frac{e_1 u_{c,t+1}}{e_1 u_{c,t}} f\left(X_{t+1}|X_t\right) \qquad (11.6.4)$$

is the kernel for pricing claims of the first consumption good at time $t+1$ in terms of time t consumption of the first good.

The spot prices $p_{\cdot t}$ are given by the appropriate time t components of our original time 0 prices defined in (11.5.16). Together with the pricing kernel defined as (11.6.4), they allow us to support the solution of the planning problem by a competitive equilibrium with sequential markets. Within that equilibrium, the problem of the household is recursive and the problem of the firm is static, as we now proceed to show.

11.6.2. The household's problem in the sequential equilibrium

The household's Bellman equation is

$$W\left(a_t, h_{t-1}, k_{t-1}, X_t\right) = \max_{c_t, i_t, \ell_t, a(X_{t+1})} \left\{ -\left(|s_t - b_t|^2 + \ell_t^2\right) \right.$$
$$\left. + \beta \int W\left(a\left(X_{t+1}\right), h_t, k_t, X_{t+1}\right) f\left(X_{t+1}|X_t\right) d X_{t+1} \right\} \qquad (11.6.5)$$

where the maximization is subject to [10]

$$s_t = \Lambda h_{t-1} + \Pi c_t \qquad (11.6.7a)$$

$$h_t = \Delta_h h_{t-1} + \Theta_h c_t \qquad (11.6.7b)$$

$$k_t = \Delta_k k_{t-1} + \Theta_k i_t \qquad (11.6.7c)$$

$$X_{t+1} = A^o X_t + C \epsilon_{t+1} \qquad (11.6.7d)$$

---

[10] In settings with Arrow securities and non-negativity constraints on c_t, i_t, one needs to constrain the household's choice of $-a(x_{t+1})$ to be no less than the amount that it is feasible for the household to repay in state x_{t+1}. These are sometimes called the natural borrowing limits. See Ljungqvist and Sargent (2004, chapter 8) for a discussion of these limits. Because we do not require that c_t, i_t be non-negative, it is not appropriate for us to impose such conditions here. We instead impose that the $\{c_t, i_t\}$ sequence that is implied by the solution of the household's problem imply that the following additional constraints on the two endogenous state vectors h_t and k_t are satisfied:

$$E \sum_{t=0}^{\infty} \beta^t h_t \cdot h_t \mid J_0 < \infty \quad \text{and} \quad E \sum_{t=0}^{\infty} \beta^t k_t \cdot k_t \mid J_0 < \infty. \qquad (11.6.6)$$

We can accomplish this by taking the limit of a sequence of finite-horizon versions of problem (11.6.5)-(11.6.7) with zero-value terminal value functions. We can express (11.6.6) by saying that we require that each component of h_t and each component of k_t belongs to L_0^2 where we define the space $L_0^2 = [\{y_t\} : y_t$ is a random variable in J_t and $E \sum_{t=0}^{\infty} \beta^t y_t^2 \mid J_0 < +\infty]$. Here J_t is the information set generated by $x_t, x_{t-1}, \ldots, x_0$.

$$p_t = MX_t \tag{11.6.7e}$$

$$b_t = S_b X_t \tag{11.6.7f}$$

$$d_t = S_d X_t \tag{11.6.7g}$$

$$\int a\left(X_{t+1}\right) q\left(X_{t+1}|X_t\right) d\, X_{t+1} = a_t + p_{\ell t} \ell_t + p_{dt} \cdot d_t + p_{rt} \cdot k_{t-1} \\ - p_{ct} \cdot c_t - p_{it} \cdot i_t \tag{11.6.7h}$$

and $b_t = S_b X_t \equiv U_b z_t$. The optimal policy functions express c_t, i_t, ℓ_t, and $a(X_{t+1})$ each as a function of $(a_t, h_{t-1}, k_{t-1}, X_t)$.

11.6.3. The firm

The problem of a firm is static:

$$\max_{c_t, i_t, \ell_t, g_t, d_t, k_{t-1}} \left(p_{ct} \cdot c_t + p_{it} \cdot i_t - p_{rt} \cdot k_{t-1} - p_{dt} \cdot d_t - p_{\ell t} \ell_t\right) \tag{11.6.8}$$

subject to the technology $(11.5.4)$, $(11.5.5)$.

11.6.4. Recursive competitive equilibrium

We call a competitive equilibrium with Arrow securities a *recursive competitive equilibrium*. In a recursive competitive equilibrium, the household takes the law of motion for X_t as given. However, the household and the firm choose elements h_s, k_s of the state x_{s+1} that correspond to the elements H_s, K_s of X_{s+1}. A recursive competitive equilibrium requires that $X_t = x_t$ for $t \geq 1$, starting from $X_0 = x_0$, which means that the laws of motion chosen by firms and the household must be consistent with the law of motion $(11.5.16)$ that inspires the household's decisions.

It can be verified that the quantities that solve the planning problem are recursive competitive equilibrium quantities at the candidate prices described above.

11.7. Asset pricing in a nutshell

It is a significant practical convenience that we can dispense with X_t as a state variable when we actually compute asset prices. After we have computed the equilibrium quantities and prices, for the purpose of computing asset prices, it is sufficient to express streams of payouts and prices both as functions of the state vector x_t that appears in the planning problem.[11] As an example,

---

[11] We view this as a manifestation of Brock's (1982) idea of evaluating history-date prices by multiplying the relevant conditional probabilities by the representative consumer's

let an endowment shock be a linear function of the exogenous component z_t, and let the endogenous component h_{t-1} track movements in the intertemporal rate of substitution that drives the prices. Let $\{y_t\}_{t=0}^{\infty}$ be a stochastic process of "dividends," i.e., claims on the vector of consumption goods with representation $y_t = S_c x_t$. In units of the first time t consumption good, let a_{yt} denote the price at time t of a claim on the tail of the dividend process $\{y_s\}_{s=t}^{\infty}$. The price a_{yt} of a claim on the dividend stream from t onward can be represented as

$$x_{t+1} = A^o x_t + C\epsilon_{t+1} \qquad (11.7.1a)$$

$$y_t = S_c x_t \qquad (11.7.1b)$$

$$p_{cs} = (e_1 M_c x_t)^{-1} M_c x_s \qquad (11.7.1c)$$

$$a_{yt} = E_t \sum_{t=0}^{\infty} \beta^t p_{ct+j} \cdot y_{t+j}. \qquad (11.7.1d)$$

Equation $(11.7.1d)$ can be evaluated by solving a Sylvester equation.

Equations $(11.7.1)$ capture the spirit of Brock's (1982) extension of Lucas's asset pricing formulas in which equilibrium history-date prices are the pertinent probabilities times the intertemporal marginal rate of substitution evaluated at the equilibrium allocation. The single state vector x_t tracks both the history-date prices and the dividend process.

11.8. Partial equilibrium interpretation

Another decentralization of the planning problem makes contact with partial equilibrium models in the style of Lucas and Prescott (1971), Rosen, Murphy, and Scheinkman (1994), Rosen and Topel (1988), Ryoo and Rosen (2004), and Sargent (1987, chapter XIV). These models have a representative firm that acts as a price taker within an industry that faces a stochastically shifting linear demand schedule.

Within the environment of this chapter, consider a representative firm that chooses stochastic processes $\{c_t, g_t\}$ to maximize

$$E_0 \sum_{t=0}^{\infty} \beta^t \{p_t \cdot c_t - g_t \cdot g_t\} \qquad (11.8.1)$$

marginal rates of substitution evaluated at the allocation that solves the planning problem. Incidentally, another perspective on Brock's insight is Mehra and Prescott's (1985) observation that the cross-equation restrictions between asset prices and consumption are not affected by whether consumption is regarded as exogenous or endogenous. Making consumption endogenous adds restrictions across consumption and yet other processes.

subject to the constraints

$$k_t = \Delta_k k_{t-1} + \Theta_k i_t \tag{11.8.2a}$$

$$\Phi_c c_t + \Phi_g g_t + \Phi_i i_t = \Gamma k_{t-1} + d_t \tag{11.8.2b}$$

$$X_{t+1} = A^o X_t + C\epsilon_{t+1} \tag{11.8.2c}$$

$$d_t = U_d X_t \tag{11.8.2d}$$

$$p_t = M_c X_t. \tag{11.8.2e}$$

Here $(11.8.2c)$, $(11.8.2e)$ are used to represent a dynamic demand curve, where M_c and the state X_t are defined as above. The H_t component of X_t can express high-order dynamics in demand.[12] The Bellman equation is

$$V(k_{t-1}, X_t) = \max_{c_t, k_t, i_t, g_t} \{p_t \cdot c_t - g_t \cdot g_t + \beta EV(k_t, X_{t+1})\} \tag{11.8.3}$$

where the maximization is subject to $(11.8.2)$. The optimal decision rule expresses c_t, g_t as functions of k_{t-1}, X_t, so that the firm chooses to make k_t follow a law that can be expressed as

$$k_t = k(k_{t-1}, X_t) = k(k_{t-1}, H_{t-1}, K_{t-1}, z_t). \tag{11.8.4}$$

Embedded in $(11.8.2c)$ is the firm's perceived law of motion for K_t, namely,

$$K_t = K(X_t) = K(H_{t-1}, K_{t-1}, z_t). \tag{11.8.5}$$

A competitive equilibrium requires that $k_s \equiv K_s$ for all s and all z_s, or

$$k(K_{t-1}, H_{t-1}, K_{t-1}, z_t) = K(H_{t-1}, K_{t-1}, z_t). \tag{11.8.6}$$

The left side of $(11.8.6)$ is the actual law of motion for K that emerges from *optimization* (this is the content of the function $k(\cdot)$) and *equilibrium* (this is the content of the condition $k = K$ that makes the representative firm representative). The right side of $(11.8.6)$ is the representative firm's perceived law of motion for K. Thus, $(11.8.6)$ requires equality between the perceived law of motion for K and the actual law of motion implied by those perceptions. Equality between these two laws imposes rational expectations and respects the price taking behavior of the firm.[13]

---

[12] See Hansen and Sargent (2008) for an analysis.

[13] Marcet and Sargent (1989) and Evans and Honkapohja (2001) extensively exploit the definition of a rational expectations equilibrium as the fixed point of a mapping from a perceived to an actual law of motion.

11.9. Concluding remarks

This chapter has set forth a class of dynamic linear-quadratic economies and described three types of competitive equilibria. We have made the standard rational expectations assumption that a planner and the agents all trust their common model. The next chapter alters that assumption by instilling in both the household and a planner the same degree of preference for robustness of decision rules with respect to deviations of the actual data-generation mechanism from a common approximating model. Thus, the next chapter will contain modifications of the Bellman equation $(11.5.6)$, $(11.5.7)$ for the planner and the Bellman equation $(11.6.5)$, $(11.6.7)$ for the household trading Arrow securities. With a preference for robustness, these will be replaced by Bellman equations for two-player zero-sum games. Decentralizing the robust planning problem will then require checking that the choices of both the maximizing and the minimizing players for the planning problem and the household within a competitive equilibrium, respectively, are mutually consistent. Here agents choose an allocation as well as worst-case shocks. To decentralize the economy, we shall require that these worst-case shocks be appropriately aligned with those chosen by the planner.

Chapter 12
Competitive equilibria with robustness

Believe those who are seeking the truth. Doubt those who find it.
— *Andre Gide*

12.1. Introduction

This chapter puts fear of model misspecification into the mind of the representative household from the model of chapter 11. The analysis parallels that of chapter 11 except that we replace Bellman equations for the maximizing agents in chapter 11 with equations that pertain to two-player zero-sum games. In each game, a minimizing player helps the decision maker explore the fragility of a decision rule with respect to various difficult-to-detect perturbations of the approximating model. To decentralize an allocation that solves the planning problem, we specify two-player zero-sum games for the representative household in a decentralized economy and describe how at the equilibrium prices both the allocation and the worst-case model chosen by the household are aligned with counterparts that are chosen by the planner. Equilibrium quantities solve a robust planning problem. Competitive equilibrium prices are shadow prices for the robust planning problem. As an example, we study versions of a partial equilibrium occupational choice model of Ryoo and Rosen (2004). Chapter 13 uses these prices to value assets when agents fear model misspecification. Appendix A describes a partial equilibrium decentralization of a robust planning problem with adjustment costs.

Before describing competitive equilibria with the more general household and production technologies of chapter 11, we begin with a pure endowment economy.

12.2. A pure endowment economy

12.2.1. The planning problem

We consider a nonstochastic pure endowment economy described by

$$x_{t+1} = Ax_t + Cw_{t+1} \qquad (12.2.1a)$$

$$b_t = U_b x_t \qquad (12.2.1b)$$

$$d_t = U_d x_t. \qquad (12.2.1c)$$

Here x_t, b_t, d_t, w_t are vectors; d_t is an exogenous endowment and b_t is an exogenous preference shock sequence; w_{t+1} is a distortion to the state x_t

that determines the endowment and preference shock processes. A representative household receives consumption $c_t = d_t$. Because the endowment is exogenous, the robust planning problem becomes

$$-x_0' P x_0 = \min_{\{w_{t+1}\}} \sum_{t=0}^{\infty} \beta^t \left\{ -|c_t - b_t|^2 + \beta\theta w_{t+1}' w_{t+1} \right\} \qquad (12.2.2)$$

where $\theta \in (\underline{\theta}, +\infty]$ measures the planner's fear that $(12.2.1a)$ is misspecified. The planner minimizes criterion $(12.2.2)$ subject to $(12.2.1)$ and $c_t = d_t$. The planning problem is an optimal linear regulator. Let $R = (U_d - U_b)'(U_d - U_b)$. The Bellman equation for the planning problem is

$$-x' P x = \min_{w} \left\{ -x' R x + w' (\beta\theta I) w - y' P y \right\} \qquad (12.2.3a)$$

where the minimization is subject to

$$y = Ax + Cw. \qquad (12.2.3b)$$

The solution of the planning problem is a feedback rule

$$w = Kx. \qquad (12.2.4)$$

The law of motion for the state x under the worst-case rule is

$$x_{t+1} = (A + KC) x_t$$

and the worst-case endowment and preference sequences can be represented

$$c_t = U_d (A + CK)^t x_0 \qquad (12.2.5a)$$
$$b_t = U_b (A + CK)^t x_0. \qquad (12.2.5b)$$

The worst-case processes in $(12.2.5)$ generate a shadow price sequence $q_t = \beta^t p_t$ associated with the robust planning problem, where

$$p_t = M x_t \qquad (12.2.6)$$

and where $M = 2(U_b - U_d)$ or

$$p_t = 2 (U_b - U_d) (A + CK)^t x_0. \qquad (12.2.7)$$

12.2.2. Household problem

We confront the representative household with the sequence of scaled (Harrison and Kreps (1979)) prices $\{p_t\}_{t=0}^{\infty}$ from (12.2.7). It is convenient to represent the price system recursively as

$$X_{t+1} = (A + CK) X_t \tag{12.2.8a}$$

$$p_t = M X_t \tag{12.2.8b}$$

where $X_0 = x_0$. The household's problem is

$$\min_{\{w_{t+1}\}_{t=0}^{\infty}} \max_{\{c_t\}_{t=0}^{\infty}} \sum_{t=0}^{\infty} \beta^t \{-|c_t - b_t|^2 + \beta\theta w_{t+1}'w_{t+1}\} \tag{12.2.9}$$

subject to (12.2.1) and the budget constraint

$$\sum_{t=0}^{\infty} \beta^t \left[p_t \cdot d_t - p_t \cdot c_t \right] = 0. \tag{12.2.10}$$

To solve this problem, we formulate a Lagrangian

$$\begin{aligned} L = \sum_{t=0}^{\infty} \beta^t \{ &-|c_t - b_t|^2 + \beta\theta w_{t+1}'w_{t+1} \\ &+ \mu_0^w [p_t \cdot d_t - p_t \cdot c_t] \} \end{aligned} \tag{12.2.11}$$

where μ_0^w is a Lagrange multiplier on (12.2.10). Formula (12.4.11) below implies that $\mu_0^w = 1$. We are to maximize (12.2.11) with respect to c_t and minimize it with respect to w_{t+1}. The first-order condition with respect to c_t is static:

$$\mu_0^w p_t = 2(b_t - c_t) \tag{12.2.12}$$

which using $\mu_0^2 = 1$ leads to the demand curve

$$c_t = b_t - .5p_t. \tag{12.2.13}$$

Using (12.2.12) or (12.2.13) and (12.2.8b), we deduce that $-|c_t - b_t|^2 = -.25X_t'M'MX_t$, $p_t \cdot d_t = X_t'M'U_d x_t$, and $p_t \cdot c_t = X_t'M'U_b x_t - .5X_t'M'MX_t$. Therefore, the current-period term in the objective (12.2.11) becomes $-.25X_t'M'MX_t + w_{t+1}'(\beta\theta I)w_{t+1} + X_t'M'(U_d - U_b)x_t$. Note that $M'(U_d - U_b) = -.5M'M$. Thus, we have that the Bellman equation for the household's problem reduces to

$$\begin{aligned} -\begin{bmatrix} X \\ x \end{bmatrix}' \begin{bmatrix} P_{11} & P_{12} \\ P_{21} & P_{22} \end{bmatrix} \begin{bmatrix} X \\ x \end{bmatrix} = \min_w &\left\{ \begin{bmatrix} X \\ x \end{bmatrix}' \begin{bmatrix} -.25M'M & -.25M'M \\ -.25M'M & 0 \end{bmatrix} \begin{bmatrix} X \\ x \end{bmatrix} \right. \\ &\left. + w'(\beta\theta I)w - \beta \begin{bmatrix} Y \\ y \end{bmatrix}' \begin{bmatrix} P_{11} & P_{12} \\ P_{21} & P_{22} \end{bmatrix} \begin{bmatrix} Y \\ y \end{bmatrix} \right\} \end{aligned} \tag{12.2.14}$$

where the minimization is subject to

$$
\begin{bmatrix} Y \\ y \end{bmatrix} = \begin{bmatrix} A + CK & 0 \\ 0 & A \end{bmatrix} \begin{bmatrix} X \\ x \end{bmatrix} + \begin{bmatrix} 0 \\ C \end{bmatrix} w. \tag{12.2.15}
$$

The solution of the robust household's Bellman equation $(12.2.14)$, $(12.2.15)$ is attained by a policy rule

$$
w = \begin{bmatrix} \tilde{K}_1 & \tilde{K}_2 \end{bmatrix} \begin{bmatrix} X \\ x \end{bmatrix}. \tag{12.2.16}
$$

For the worst-case shock chosen by the household to be aligned with the one chosen by the planner requires that

$$
\tilde{K}_1 + \tilde{K}_2 = K. \tag{12.2.17}
$$

It can be proved that this equality holds, and furthermore that in this simple example $\tilde{K}_2 = 0$, so that the worst-case shock feeds back only on the part of the aggregate state that drives the scaled price process p_t.

As an example, set $\beta = .99$, $\theta = .001^{-1}$, $d_t - .7 d_{t-1} = (1 - .7)5 + .05 w_t$, $b_t = 30$. Let the state be $x_t = \begin{bmatrix} 1 \\ d_t \end{bmatrix}$. We computed that $\tilde{K}_1 = K = \begin{bmatrix} -0.0044 & 0.0001 \end{bmatrix}$ and $\tilde{K}_2 = 0$.[1]

12.3. A robust planning problem

We now turn from the simple endowment economy just analyzed to the more general production economy studied without robustness in chapter 11. When the representative consumer fears model misspecification, the planning problem takes the form of a robust linear regulator problem. Let $V(x) = -x'Px - p$ be the value of the robust planning problem starting from initial state x. The Bellman equation is

$$
\begin{aligned}
-x'Px - p = \min_{w^*} \max_{c,i,g} \Big\{ &-.5[(s - b) \cdot (s - b) + g \cdot g] \\
&+ \beta \theta w^{*\prime} w^* + \beta E \left(-x^{*\prime} P x^* - p \right) \Big\}
\end{aligned} \tag{12.3.1}
$$

where the extremization is subject to the linear constraints

$$
\begin{aligned}
\Phi_c c + \Phi_g g + \Phi_i i &= \Gamma k + d && (12.3.2a) \\
k^* &= \Delta_k k + \Theta_k i && (12.3.2b) \\
h^* &= \Delta_h h + \Theta_h c && (12.3.2c) \\
s &= \Lambda h + \Pi c && (12.3.2d) \\
z^* &= A_{22} z + C_2(\epsilon^* + w^*) && (12.3.2e) \\
b &= U_b z && (12.3.2f) \\
d &= U_d z, && (12.3.2g)
\end{aligned}
$$

---

[1] The Matlab program `decentr.m` computes an example.

where * denotes a next period value. Problem $(12.3.1)$, $(12.3.2)$ differs from $(11.5.6)$, $(11.5.7)$ in the following respects: (1) the addition of the distortion $C_2 w^*$ to the law of motion for z, (2) the appearance of $\beta \theta w^{*\prime} w^*$ in the continuation value function in $(12.3.1)$, and (3) the minimization over w^*. As usual, $\theta > 0$ is a robustness parameter.

A Markov perfect equilibrium of the two-player zero-sum game $(12.3.1)$, $(12.3.2)$ is a pair of decision rules $u = -F(\theta)x$, $w^* = K(\theta)x$. The equilibrium determines two laws of motion for the state, namely,

$$x_{t+1} = A^o x_t + C\epsilon_{t+1} \tag{12.3.3}$$

and

$$x_{t+1} = (A^o + CK(\theta))x_t + C\epsilon_{t+1}, \tag{12.3.4}$$

where $A^o = A - BF(\theta)$. Equation $(12.3.3)$ is the approximating model under the robust rule, while $(12.3.4)$ is the worst-case model under the robust rule. In chapter 13, we show that both of these models can be used to price assets by appropriately adjusting the stochastic discount factor.

12.4. Max-min representation of household problem

As in chapter 11, the value function and the robust law of motion for the state x_t contain information about competitive equilibrium prices (see formulas $(11.5.14)$ and $(11.5.21)$). To decentralize the solution of the robust planning problem, we must verify that when the robust representative household faces those prices as a price taker, he chooses the allocation that solves the planning problem. In checking that claim, we also verify that the representative household chooses a worst-case model that is aligned with the planner's worst-case model.

An Arrow-Debreu setting makes it natural to formulate the household's problem as a game in which the maximizing and minimizing players both commit to sequences, as in the sequence games of chapter 7. We find it convenient to embrace a recursive representation of each player's problem. The maximizing player chooses an allocation, taking as given the law of motion for X chosen by the minimizing player. We use a guess-and-verify strategy. First, we take up the problem of the maximizing player, having guessed that the minimizing player has chosen as the law of motion for X the same worst-case law that is chosen by the robust planner. Second, setting the allocation equal to the one chosen by the planner, we verify that the minimizing player chooses the same distorted law of motion as the planner.

12.4.1. Sequence problem of maximizing player

We first pose the problem of the maximizing player in a sequence formulation of the household's robust decision problem. As in chapter 11, we use a recursive representation of prices in the Arrow-Debreu equilibrium. This enables us to give a recursive representation of the maximizing player's decision problem. The maximizing player in the robust household chooses stochastic processes for $\{c_t, i_t, s_t, h_t, k_t, \ell_t\}_{t=0}^\infty$, each element of which is in L_0^2, to maximize

$$E_0 \sum_{t=0}^\infty \beta^t \left\{-.5 \left[(s_t - b_t) \cdot (s_t - b_t) + \ell_t^2\right] + \beta \theta X_{t+1}' K' K X_{t+1}\right\} \qquad (12.4.1)$$

subject to

$$E_0 \sum_{t=0}^\infty \beta^t \left(p_{ct}^0 \cdot c_t + p_{it}^0 \cdot i_t\right) \mid J_0$$

$$= E_0 \sum_{t=0}^\infty \beta^t \left(p_{\ell t}^0 \ell_t + p_{rt}^0 \cdot k_{t-1} + p_{dt}^0 \cdot d_t\right) \mid J_0 \qquad (12.4.2a)$$

$$s_t = \Lambda h_{t-1} + \Pi c_t \qquad (12.4.2b)$$

$$h_t = \Delta_h h_{t-1} + \Theta_h c_t \qquad (12.4.2c)$$

$$k_t = \Delta_k k_{t-1} + \Theta_k i_t \qquad (12.4.2d)$$

$$b_t = U_b z_t \qquad (12.4.2e)$$

$$d_t = U_d z_t \qquad (12.4.2f)$$

$$p_t^0 = M X_t \qquad (12.4.2g)$$

$$X_{t+1} = (A^o + CK)X_t + C\epsilon_{t+1} \qquad (12.4.2h)$$

with h_{-1}, k_{-1}, z_0 given, and where the mathematical expectation is evaluated with respect to the distribution over histories ϵ^t. In $(12.4.2h)$, $K = K(\theta)$ is the matrix that defines the decision rule for the worst-case shock in the robust planning problem. To compute the pricing matrix M in $(12.4.2g)$, we use the counterparts to formulas $(11.5.14)$, $(11.5.21)$ in which A^o is now the matrix $A - BF$ that solves the robust planning problem and P is the matrix in the value function for the robust planning problem that appears in $(12.3.1)$. In the household's problem $(12.4.1)$, $(12.4.2)$, E_0 denotes the expectation evaluated with respect to the ϵ_t's that together with the distorted law of motion $(12.4.2h)$ for the state X_{t+1} generate the distribution used to evaluate the present values in the budget constraint as well as the component of the state z_t that drives the preference shock b_t and the endowment process d_t. A convenient feature of problem $(12.4.1)$, $(12.4.2)$ is that the *same* distribution is used to evaluate future prospects both in the objective function $(12.4.1)$ and in the budget constraint $(12.4.2a)$. Putting a multiplier μ_0^w on the household's budget constraint, we can combine $(12.4.1)$ and $(12.4.2a)$ into a Lagrangian

$$
\begin{aligned}
L = E_0 \sum_{t=0}^{\infty} \beta^t \Big\{ &-.5 \left[(s_t - b_t) \cdot (s_t - b_t) + \ell_t^2 \right] + \beta \theta X_{t+1}' K' K X_{t+1} \\
&+ \mu_0^w (p_{\ell t}^0 \ell_t + p_{rt}^0 \cdot k_{t-1} + p_{dt}^0 \cdot d_t - p_{ct}^0 \cdot c_t - p_{it}^0 \cdot i_t) \Big\}
\end{aligned}
\tag{12.4.3}
$$

The household's problem is to choose an allocation to maximize $(12.4.3)$ and a multiplier μ_0^w to minimize it, subject to $(12.4.2b)$–$(12.4.2c)$. For a given μ_0^w, this problem takes the form of an optimal linear regulator. In the following subsection 12.4.2, we give a formula that allows us to compute μ_0^w in advance directly from the allocation that solves the robust planning problem and the price system $(12.4.2g)$, $(12.4.2h)$. Since we consider a linear regulator problem, it follows that the solution of the maximizing player's problem is a decision rule that can be expressed

$$
\begin{bmatrix} c_t \\ i_t \\ \ell_t \end{bmatrix} = \overline{S} \begin{bmatrix} h_{t-1} \\ k_{t-1} \\ X_t \end{bmatrix}.
\tag{12.4.4}
$$

For $(12.4.4)$ to confirm the solution of the planning problem it must be true that

$$
\overline{S} \begin{bmatrix} h_{t-1} \\ k_{t-1} \\ X_t \end{bmatrix} \equiv SX_t,
\tag{12.4.5}
$$

when we set $h_{t-1} = H_{t-1}$ and $k_{t-1} = K_{t-1}$, where SX_t is the decision rule that solves the planning problem. Equality $(12.4.5)$ assures that the robust household in the competitive equilibrium chooses the allocation that solves the planning problem.

The role of the pair $(12.4.2g)$ and $(12.4.2h)$ is to provide a recursive representation of the prices that appear in the household's budget constraint $(12.4.2a)$. In particular, notice how $(12.4.2h)$ makes sure that in $(12.4.2a)$ the conditional expectation is taken with respect to the "twisted" or worst-case distribution that emerges from the robust planning problem.[2] Equality $(12.4.5)$ assures that the allocation that solves the planning problem satisfies the household's budget constraint $(12.4.2a)$.

Another role of $(12.4.2h)$ is to force the household to accept the twisted probability distribution chosen by the robust planner in evaluating conditional expectations of the shocks b_t and d_t. This streamlines the problem because it

---

[2] Recall also that the A^o, P that are used in forming the prices via formulas $(11.5.14)$, $(11.5.21)$ pertain to the solution of the robust planning problem.

allows us to use a common distribution to express the conditional expectations E_0 that appear both in the objective function (12.4.1) and in the Harrison-Kreps (1979) representation of the budget constraint (12.4.2a).

12.4.2. Digression about computing μ_0^w

To solve problem (12.4.1), (12.4.2), it is useful to have a formula for the Lagrange multiplier μ_0^w on the household's budget constraint (12.4.2a) in a competitive equilibrium.[3] Hansen and Sargent (2008) derive the following convenient formula for μ_0^w. They define the implicit price of consumption services as

$$\rho_t^0 \equiv \Pi^{-1\prime}\left[p_{ct}^0 - \Theta_h' E_t \sum_{\tau=1}^{\infty} \beta^\tau (\Delta_h' - \Lambda'\Pi^{-1\prime}\Theta_h')^{\tau-1}\Lambda'\Pi^{-1\prime}p_{c,t+\tau}^0\right]. \quad (12.4.6)$$

To compute μ_0^w, Hansen and Sargent partition household capital and service sequences into two components. One is a service sequence obtained from the *initial* endowment of household capital h_{-1}. The other is the service sequence obtained from *market purchases* of consumption goods. The service sequence obtained from the initial endowment of household capital $\{s_{i,t}\}$ evolves according to

$$s_{i,t} = \Lambda h_{i,t-1}$$
$$h_{i,t} = \Delta_h h_{i,t-1} \quad (12.4.7)$$

where $h_{i,-1} = h_{-1}$. The service sequence $\{s_{m,t}\}$ obtained from purchases of consumption satisfies

$$s_{m,t} = b_t - s_{i,t} - \mu_0^w \rho_t^0. \quad (12.4.8)$$

There are two ways to compute the time-zero cost of the sequence $\{s_{m,t}\}$. One is to compute the time-zero cost of the consumption sequence $\{c_t\}$ needed to support the demand for services using the price sequence $\{p_{ct}^0\}$. Another is to use the implicit rental sequence $\{\rho_t^0\}$ directly to compute the time-zero costs of $\{s_{m,t}\}$. Hansen and Sargent verify that the two measures of costs agree:

$$E_0 \sum_{t=0}^{\infty} \beta^t \rho_t^0 \cdot s_{m,t} = E_0 \sum_{t=0}^{\infty} \beta^t p_t^0 \cdot c_t. \quad (12.4.9)$$

It follows from (12.4.8) that

$$E_0 \sum_{t=0}^{\infty} \beta^t \rho_t^0 \cdot s_{m,t} = E_0 \sum_{t=0}^{\infty} \beta^t \rho_t^0 \cdot (b_t - s_{i,t}) - \mu_0^w E_0 \sum_{t=0}^{\infty} \beta^t \rho_t^0 \cdot \rho_t^0. \quad (12.4.10)$$

---

[3] Counterparts of the same formulas would work for computing μ_0^w of the chapter 11 models without fear of model misspecification.

Substitute (12.4.9) and (12.4.10) into the consumer's budget constraint, and solve for the time zero marginal utility of wealth μ_0^w:

$$\mu_0^w = \frac{E_0 \sum_{t=0}^{\infty} \beta^t \rho_t^0 \cdot (b_t - s_{i,t}) - W_0}{E_0 \sum_{t=0}^{\infty} \beta^t \rho_t^0 \cdot \rho_t^0}, \qquad (12.4.11)$$

where W_0 denotes initial-period wealth given by

$$W_0 = E_0 \sum_{t=0}^{\infty} \beta^t (p_{\ell t}^0 \ell_t + p_{rt}^0 \cdot k_{t-1} + p_{dt}^0 \cdot d_t). \qquad (12.4.12)$$

The geometric sums in (12.4.10) and (12.4.12) can be computed by solving Sylvester equations.

12.4.3. Sequence problem of minimizing player

Our next task is to pose the problem of the minimizing player in a sequence version of the representative household's problem. We freeze the allocation chosen by the maximizing player at the one found in the last section, namely, the one that would be chosen by a robust planner. As pointed out in the previous subsection, this guarantees that the allocation satisfies the household's budget constraint (12.4.2a). We have to verify that the household chooses the same twisted law of motion that the robust planner did.

The preceding argument allows us to drop the consumer's budget constraint because we know that it is satisfied at the allocation that solves the robust planning problem. This simplifies our calculations. The minimizing player within the household chooses a sequence $\{w_{t+1}\}_{t=0}^{\infty}$ to minimize

$$E_0 \sum_{t=0}^{\infty} \beta^t \left\{ -.5[(s_t - b_t) \cdot (s_t - b_t) + \ell_t^2] + \beta \theta w_{t+1} \cdot w_{t+1} \right\} \qquad (12.4.13)$$

subject to

$$s_t = \Lambda h_{t-1} + \Pi c_t \qquad (12.4.14a)$$

$$h_t = \Delta_h h_{t-1} + \Theta_h c_t \qquad (12.4.14b)$$

$$k_t = \Delta_k k_{t-1} + \Theta_k i_t \qquad (12.4.14c)$$

$$[c_t' \quad i_t' \quad \ell_t']' = S\tilde{X}_t \qquad (12.4.14d)$$

$$\tilde{X}_{t+1} = (A^o + CK)\tilde{X}_t + C\epsilon_{t+1} \qquad (12.4.14e)$$

$$b_t = U_b z_t \qquad (12.4.14f)$$

$$d_t = U_d z_t \qquad (12.4.14g)$$

$$z_{t+1} = A_{22} z_t + C_2(\epsilon_{t+1} + w_{t+1}). \qquad (12.4.14h)$$

Here $\tilde{X}_t$ is a state vector with components comparable to those in x_t, $A^o = A - BF(\theta)$ is the decision rule that the robust planner would choose, and we impose the initial condition $\tilde{X}_0 = x_0$. Also, the conditional expectation is evaluated with respect to the distribution of future values of the joint state $h, k, z, \tilde{X}$ that is generated by the distribution for the ϵ_{t+1}'s together with the given laws of motion for the state variables. The role of (12.4.14d) and (12.4.14e) is to freeze the household's allocation at the solution of the planning problem. The solution of the minimizing player's problem is a decision rule of the form

$$w_{t+1} = \tilde{K} \begin{bmatrix} \tilde{X}_t \\ x_t \end{bmatrix}. \tag{12.4.15}$$

We want to verify that

$$\tilde{K} \begin{bmatrix} \tilde{X}_t \\ x_t \end{bmatrix} = K\tilde{X}_t \tag{12.4.16}$$

when $x_t = \tilde{X}_t$. But notice that problem (12.4.13), (12.4.14) is a recursive representation of a Stackelberg game in sequences version of the minimizing part of the robust planner's problem. Thus, (12.4.16) follows directly from results in chapter 7.

12.5. A decentralization with Arrow securities

12.5.1. A robust consumer trading Arrow securities

This section adapts the equilibrium with sequential trading of one-period Arrow securities, as in section 11.6, to the situation where the representative household is concerned about model misspecification.

As a price taker, the household faces the one-step-ahead pricing kernel $q(X_{t+1}, X_t)$ that obeys the following version of (11.6.4)

$$q(X_{t+1}|X_t) = \beta \frac{e_1 u_{c,t+1}}{e_1 u_{c,t}} \hat{f}(X_{t+1}|X_t) \tag{12.5.1a}$$

where the conditional density $\hat{f}(X_{t+1}|X_t)$ is induced by the difference equation

$$X_{t+1} = (A^o + CK)X_t + C\epsilon_{t+1} \tag{12.5.1b}$$

where $\epsilon_{t+1} \sim \mathcal{N}(0, I)$, $A^o = A - BF(\theta)$, and where $A^o + CK$ is the worst-case transition matrix for the autonomous law of motion for x_t that emerges from the robust planning problem for a given θ.[4]

---

[4] Notice that $\hat{f}(X_{t+1}|X_t)$ is the transition density under the planner's worst-case model and the robust rule. See chapter 13 for representations of pricing functions in terms of the approximating model.

We obtain the household's Bellman equation by replacing $(11.6.5)$, $(11.6.7)$ with a two-player zero-sum game. We generate a recursion in a value function $W(a_t, h_{t-1}, k_{t-1}, X_t)$ by posing an *inner problem* in which a maximizing player chooses c_t, i_t, ℓ_t, $a(X_t)$, taking as given the feedback rule for w_{t+1}; and an *outer problem* in which a minimizing player who chooses w_{t+1} takes as given the decision rule for c_t, i_t, ℓ_t, $a(X_t)$ chosen by the maximizing player.

12.5.2. The inner problem

The maximizing player solves

$$
\max_{c_t, i_t, \ell_t, a(X_{t+1})} \left\{ -.5(|s_t - b_t|^2 + \ell_t^2) + \beta\theta w'_{t+1} w_{t+1} \right.
$$
$$
\left. + \beta E_t \int W(a(X_{t+1}), h_t, k_t, X_{t+1}) \right\}
$$
$$(12.5.2)$$

where the maximization is subject to

$$
s_t = \Lambda h_{t-1} + \Pi c_t \tag{12.5.3a}
$$
$$
h_t = \Delta_h h_{t-1} + \Theta_h c_t \tag{12.5.3b}
$$
$$
k_t = \Delta_k k_{t-1} + \Theta_k i_t \tag{12.5.3c}
$$
$$
X_{t+1} = A^o X_t + C(\epsilon_{t+1} + w_{t+1}) \tag{12.5.3d}
$$
$$
w_{t+1} = K X_t \tag{12.5.3e}
$$
$$
p_t = M X_t \tag{12.5.3f}
$$
$$
b_t = S_b X_t \tag{12.5.3g}
$$
$$
d_t = S_d X_t \tag{12.5.3h}
$$
$$
\int a(X_{t+1}) q(X_{t+1}|X_t) d X_{t+1} = a_t + p_{\ell t}\ell_t + p_{rt} \cdot k_{t-1}
$$
$$
+ p_{dt} \cdot d_t - p_{ct} \cdot c_t - p_{it} \cdot i_t. \tag{12.5.3i}
$$

Here E_t denotes the mathematical expectation generated with respect to $(12.5.3d)$, $(12.5.3e)$. In $(12.5.2)$, $(12.5.3)$, the maximizing player takes for granted that w_{t+1} conforms to the decision rule chosen by the robust planner, namely,

$$
w_{t+1} = K X_t \tag{12.5.4}
$$

and chooses a decision rule of the form

$$
[\, c_t \quad i_t \quad \ell_t \quad a(X_t) \,] = S \begin{bmatrix} h_{t-1} \\ k_{t-1} \\ X_t \end{bmatrix}. \tag{12.5.5}
$$

12.5.3. The outer problem

The problem of the minimizing player is

$$W(a_t, h_{t-1}, k_{t-1}, X_t) = \min_{w_{t+1}} \Big\{ -.5(|s_t - b_t|^2 + \ell_t^2) + \beta\theta w'_{t+1}w_{t+1}$$
$$+ \beta E_t \int W(a(X_{t+1}), h_t, k_t, X_{t+1}) \Big\} \tag{12.5.6}$$

where the maximization is subject to equation (12.5.5) and

$$s_t = \Lambda h_{t-1} + \Pi c_t \tag{12.5.7a}$$
$$h_t = \Delta_h h_{t-1} + \Theta_h c_t \tag{12.5.7b}$$
$$k_t = \Delta_k k_{t-1} + \Theta_k i_t \tag{12.5.7c}$$
$$X_{t+1} = A^o X_t + C(\epsilon_{t+1} + w_{t+1}) \tag{12.5.7d}$$
$$b_t = S_b X_t. \tag{12.5.7e}$$

The minimizing player also takes as given the decision rule (12.5.5) emerging from the inner problem and chooses the following decision rule for w_{t+1}:

$$w_{t+1} = \tilde{K} \begin{bmatrix} h_{t-1} \\ k_{t-1} \\ X_t \end{bmatrix}.$$

We have not included the budget constraint (12.5.3h) in the outer problem because we know that it is satisfied from the way the inner problem has constructed decision rule (12.5.5). The optimal decision rule of the minimizing player has the form $w_{t+1} = \tilde{K} \begin{bmatrix} h_{t-1} \\ k_{t-1} \\ X_t \end{bmatrix}$. This structure can be shown to affirm the identity $\tilde{K} \begin{bmatrix} h_{t-1} \\ k_{t-1} \\ X_t \end{bmatrix} \equiv KX_t$, which aligns the worst-case shock in a recursive competitive equilibrium with that emerging from a robust planning problem.

12.6. A Bayesian planning problem

There is also an *ex post* Bayesian version of the planning problem like the one described in chapter 7. It endows the planner with a belief about the law of motion that is distorted relative to his approximating model in just such a way that he attains a robust rule by solving an ordinary Bellman equation without a concern for robustness.

We can apply an idea of chapter 7 to confront the planner with a distorted law of motion for z that will inspire him to choose a robust decision rule. This leads to what is known as an *ex post* Bayesian problem because the robust rule cannot be dominated in the sense of statistical decision theory. Rather than assigning the approximating model to the planner, we endow him with a model that has been adjusted to promote robustness. Taking that model as given, the planner then behaves as an ordinary planner without concern about misspecification.

To formulate this *ex post* Bayesian problem, we can augment the state variable x by a vector X of the same dimension. The Bellman equation is

$$-x'Px - p = \max_{c,i,g} \left\{ -.5[(s-b) \cdot (s-b) + g \cdot g] \right.$$
$$\left. + \beta E\left(-x^{*\prime}Px^* - p\right) \right\} \tag{12.6.1}$$

subject to the linear constraints formed by $(12.3.2)$ and the following additional exogenous law of motion for w:

$$X^* = A^o X + C(\epsilon^* + w) \tag{12.6.2a}$$

$$w = KX. \tag{12.6.2b}$$

Three features are noteworthy relative to equations $(12.3.2)$. First, $(12.6.1)$ is an ordinary (non-robust) dynamic programming problem. Second, through equation $(12.3.2e)$, the w determined by equation $(12.6.2)$ feeds back on the z process that governs the shocks impinging on the consumer's preference and endowment shock processes, (b, d). Third, we have augmented the state by "big X" in order to have the *ex post* Bayesian planner take $\dot{w}$ as exogenous and beyond his control. Where u_t is the control, the planner chooses a decision rule $u = -\tilde{F}\begin{bmatrix} x \\ X \end{bmatrix}$. Chapter 7 shows how, after equating $X = x$, this decision rule satisfies

$$-\tilde{F}\begin{bmatrix} x \\ x \end{bmatrix} = -Fx$$

where $u = -Fx$ solves the robust planning problem $(12.3.1)$, $(12.3.2)$.

12.6.1. Practical remarks

The direct way of solving the robust planning problem is obviously the more useful one computationally, not only because it has a lower dimensional state vector (x as compared with (x, X)), but also because in order to find the distorted model $(12.6.2)$, we have to solve a robust planning problem first. Nevertheless, the *ex post* Bayesian method is a useful reinterpretation of the allocation associated with the robust planning problem, one that we shall use when we turn to asset pricing.

12.7. A model of occupational choice and pay

Siow (1984) and Ryoo and Rosen (2004) have used pure time-to-build structures to represent price and quantity cycles in markets for occupations under rational expectations. In their models, prospective new entrants into an occupation respond to optimal forecasts of the present value of a stream of wages that will begin accruing only after a period of schooling. We want to study how in equilibrium those forecasts and workers' decisions would behave under a concern for model misspecification.

Siow and Ryoo and Rosen used partial equilibrium models cast in terms of dynamic supply and demand curves. To analyze how a concern for model misspecification affects demand and supply, we first consider the problem of a representative agent whose preferences induce the demand curve and the technology that generates the supply curve. It is straightforward to cast Ryoo and Rosen's model within the class of general equilibrium models of Chapter 11. We can then use the methods of this chapter to construct a version of the model in which the representative agent has a concern about model misspecification indexed by $\theta \in (\underline{\theta}, \infty]$.

12.7.1. A one-occupation model

For concreteness, let the occupation be called engineering. Ryoo and Rosen's (2004) model determines the stock of engineers N_t; the number of new entrants into engineering school n_t; and the wage W_t of engineers. It takes k periods of schooling to become an engineer. We'll set $k = 4$ in our example. Ryoo and Rosen's model consists of the following equations: first, an inverse demand curve for engineers

$$W_t = \eta_d - \alpha_d N_t + u_{dt} \ , \ \alpha_d > 0; \tag{12.7.1}$$

second, a description of the education process as a time-to-build structure

$$N_{t+k} = \delta_N N_{t+k-1} + n_t \ , \ 0 < \delta_N < 1; \tag{12.7.2}$$

third, a definition of the expected present value of each new engineering student

$$v_t = \beta^k E_t \sum_{j=0}^{\infty} (\beta \delta_N)^j W_{t+k+j}; \tag{12.7.3}$$

and fourth, a supply curve of new students as a function of v_t

$$n_t = \eta_s + \alpha_s v_t + u_{st} \, , \ \alpha_s > 0. \tag{12.7.4}$$

Here $u_t = \begin{bmatrix} u_{dt} & u_{st} \end{bmatrix}'$ is a stochastic process of labor demand and supply shocks. Under a potentially distorted model indexed by w_{t+1}, the shocks u_{st}, u_{dt} are given by

$$u_{st} = U_s z_t$$
$$u_{dt} = U_{d1} z_t \tag{12.7.5}$$

where

$$z_{t+1} = A_{22} z_t + C_2(\epsilon_{t+1} + w_{t+1}) \tag{12.7.6}$$

the eigenvalues of A_{22} are bounded in modulus by $\frac{1}{\sqrt{\beta}}$, U_s, U_{d1} are selector vectors, ϵ_{t+1} is an i.i.d. vector stochastic process with mean zero and covariance matrix I, and w_{t+1} is a vector of perturbations to the conditional means of the innovations to the approximating model. As usual, the approximating model assumes that $w_{t+1} \equiv 0$. Specification $(12.7.5)$–$(12.7.6)$ allows the demand and supply shocks to be serially correlated.

We use the following

Definition 12.7.1. A *rational expectations equilibrium* without a fear of model misspecification is a stochastic process $\{W_t, N_t, v_t, n_t\}_{t=0}^\infty$ satisfying $(12.7.1)$, $(12.7.2)$, $(12.7.3)$, $(12.7.4)$, $(12.7.5)$, and $(12.7.6)$, $w_{t+1} \equiv 0$, the stability condition $E_0 \sum_{t=0}^\infty \beta^t N_t^2 < +\infty$, and the initial conditions for $N_{-1}, n_{-s}, s = 1, \ldots, -k+1$.

12.7.2. Equilibrium with no concern about robustness

In the model in which the representative agent is not concerned about robustness, E_t in $(12.7.3)$ is the mathematical expectation evaluated with respect to the distribution under the approximating $(w_{t+1} \equiv 0)$ model. With a concern about robustness, the mathematical expectation under the distorted model $\hat{E}_t$ replaces E_t in $(12.7.3)$. But the distorted model is endogenous. Discovering it requires knowing the common preferences of the malevolent agent and the representative agent. To put a fear of misspecification into Ryoo and Rosen's model, it is thus necessary first to map the model without a fear of misspecification into the equilibrium framework of chapter 11. This will identify the preferences of a representative agent that the malevolent agent uses to formulate perturbations that promote robustness.

In terms of the class of general equilibrium models of chapter 11, we represent Ryoo and Rosen's model by sweeping the time-to-build structure into the household technology and the demand for engineers into the preference specification, while putting the supply of new engineers into the technology for producing goods. We explain the procedure in what follows. Take the household technology to be

$$s_t = \begin{bmatrix} \alpha_d & 0 & 0 & 0 \end{bmatrix} \begin{bmatrix} N_t \\ n_{t-1} \\ n_{t-2} \\ n_{t-3} \end{bmatrix} + 0 n_t$$

$$\begin{bmatrix} N_{t+1} \\ n_t \\ n_{t-1} \\ n_{t-2} \end{bmatrix} = \begin{bmatrix} \delta_N & 0 & 0 & 1 \\ 0 & 0 & 0 & 0 \\ 0 & 1 & 0 & 0 \\ 0 & 0 & 1 & 0 \end{bmatrix} \begin{bmatrix} N_t \\ n_{t-1} \\ n_{t-2} \\ n_{t-3} \end{bmatrix} + \begin{bmatrix} 0 \\ 1 \\ 0 \\ 0 \end{bmatrix} n_t .$$

In the notation of chapter 11, these equations can be represented as[5]

$$\begin{aligned} s_t &= \Lambda h_{t-1} + \Pi c_t \\ h_t &= \Delta_h h_{t-1} + \Theta_h c_t, \end{aligned} \tag{12.7.7}$$

where we have set n_t in Ryoo and Rosen's model to c_t and to h_{t-1} in the model of chapter 11 to $\begin{bmatrix} N_t & n_{t-1} & n_{t-2} & n_{t-3} \end{bmatrix}'$. To complete the representation of $(12.7.1)$, we set the preference shock $b_t = \eta_d + u_{dt}$.

We represent the supply of entering students by using the technology side of the model. In particular, we assume

$$\begin{bmatrix} 1 \\ 0 \end{bmatrix} c_t + \begin{bmatrix} -1 \\ \alpha_s^{-1} \end{bmatrix} i_t + \begin{bmatrix} 0 \\ -1 \end{bmatrix} g_t = \begin{bmatrix} 0 \\ 0 \end{bmatrix} k_{t-1} + \begin{bmatrix} u_{st} \\ 0 \end{bmatrix} .$$

This equation matches the representation of technology in chapter 11

$$\Phi_c c_t + \Phi_i i_t + \Phi_g g_t = \Gamma k_{t-1} + d_t .$$

Associated with this model is a representative agent who has preferences over c_t paths that are ordered by

$$-E_0 \sum_{t=0}^{\infty} \beta^t \left\{ .5(s_t - b_t) \cdot (s_t - b_t) + .5 g_t \cdot g_t \right\}, \tag{12.7.8}$$

where the mathematical expectation is taken with respect to the approximating model. Hansen and Sargent use the shadow prices from a planning

---

[5] In the language of Hansen and Sargent (2008), this preference representation is not *canonical*. Hansen and Sargent tell how to transform it into another representation that they call canonical and that is more convenient for deducing dynamic demand functions.

problem to construct a competitive equilibrium, as described in chapter 11. The shadow prices $\mathcal{M}_t^s$, $\mathcal{M}_t^h$, $\mathcal{M}_t^c$ for s_t, h_t, c_t, respectively, satisfy

$$\mathcal{M}_t^s = b_t - s_t \tag{12.7.9a}$$

$$\mathcal{M}_t^h = E_t \sum_{\tau=1}^{\infty} \beta^\tau (\Delta_h')^{\tau-1} \Lambda' \mathcal{M}_t^s \tag{12.7.9b}$$

$$\mathcal{M}_t^c = \Theta_h' \mathcal{M}_t^h + \Pi' \mathcal{M}_t^s. \tag{12.7.9c}$$

Since $\Pi = 0$ for the present example, we have

$$\mathcal{M}_t^c = \Theta_h' E_t \sum_{\tau=1}^{\infty} \beta^\tau (\Delta_h')^{\tau-1} \Lambda' \mathcal{M}_t^s. \tag{12.7.10}$$

It can be verified that the wage W_t in Ryoo and Rosen's model matches the shadow price $\mathcal{M}_t^s$ and that the present value v_t matches $\alpha_d^{-1} \mathcal{M}_t^c$ (compare (12.7.3) with (12.7.10)). Where x_t is the state,[6] Hansen and Sargent show that $\mathcal{M}_t^c = M_c x_t$ and $\mathcal{M}_t^s = M_s x_t$ and give formulas for the matrices M_c, M_s. We can use these objects to compute the equilibrium values of $W_t = M_s x_t, v_t = M_c x_t$ in Ryoo and Rosen's model. The solutions for the quantities can be determined from the representation for the equilibrium in the state-space form

$$x_{t+1} = A^o x_t + C \epsilon_{t+1}.$$

The next section computes examples of equilibria of the model both with and without a fear of misspecification. Appendix B solves the model by hand and describes some of its analytical features.

12.7.3. Numerical example of Ryoo-Rosen model

A version of the model with a fear of misspecification replaces (12.7.3) by

$$v_t = \beta^k \hat{E}_t \sum_{j=0}^{\infty} (\beta \delta_N)^j W_{t+k+j}, \tag{12.7.11}$$

where $\hat{E}_t$ is the mathematical expectation with respect to the distorted model. Representation (13.4.8) in chapter 13 implies that an equivalent representation of v_t in the model with a fear of misspecification is

$$v_t = \beta^k E_t \sum_{j=0}^{\infty} (\beta \delta_N)^j m_{t,t+k+j}^u W_{t+k+j} \tag{12.7.12}$$

---

[6] The state x_t equals $\begin{bmatrix} N_t & n_{t-1} & n_{t-2} & 1 & z_{st} & z_{dt} \end{bmatrix}'$, where z_s is the supply shock and z_d is the demand shock. The presence of z_s and z_d means that we can accommodate demand and supply shocks that are first-order autoregressive processes.

where $m_{t,\tau}^u$ is the Radon-Nikodym derivative defined in $(13.4.9)$. In $(12.7.12)$, the expectation is evaluated under the approximating model. A fear of misspecification puts an adjustment for model uncertainty into v_t, as shown in equation $(12.7.12)$. That adjustment manifests itself in the behavior of N_t, n_t, W_t in ways that the following example illustrates.

For alternative versions of the same model without a concern for robustness (the solid lines) and with a concern for robustness with $-\theta^{-1} = -.5$ (the dotted lines), figure 12.7.1 shows impulse responses to an i.i.d. supply shock where the inverse demand shock is also i.i.d. Both of these impulse responses are evaluated under the approximating model.[7] We set the covariance matrices of the two shocks to be I and the remaining parameter values at $\delta_N = .95, \alpha_s = 1, \alpha_d = .1, \eta_s = 10, \eta_d = 30, \beta = 1/1.05$.[8]

The effects of a fear of misspecification operate through the forecasting equation $(12.7.11)$. The bottom left panel of figure 12.7.1 shows that when there is fear of misspecification, the initial adverse effect on v_t of a supply shock is greater in absolute value (more negative) than when there is no concern for robustness. The top right panel shows how, because of its more adverse implications for v_t, the supply shock causes a lower entry rate under a fear of misspecification. This means that under the approximating model, the wage actually declines less in response to a supply shock under a fear of misspecification (see the top left panel). The top left panel shows wages declining less while the bottom left panel shows the expected present value declining *more* under a fear of misspecification. This discrepancy reflects the pessimistic forecasts that emanate from the worker's use of the distorted model to form $\hat{E}_t$. Wages decline less under a fear of misspecification because the lower entry rate induced by the pessimistic forecast v_t causes the actual stock of engineers N_t to increase less under a fear of misspecification (see the bottom right panel).[9]

12.8. Two asset pricing strategies

Under a preference for robustness, there are two counterparts to the strategy described in section 11.7 that express asset prices in terms of the state vec-

---

[7] Thus, for the robust version of the model the agents inside the model are basing their decisions on the distorted model, but we are assuming that the data are actually generated by the approximating model.

[8] See appendix B for a description of the role of the ratio $\alpha_s \alpha_d$ of the slopes of inverse demand and supply function in influencing the solution, and for under the i.i.d. specification an inverse demand shock has no persistent effects on any variable in the model.

[9] Appendix B gives analytical expressions that help provide more intuition about the shapes of the impulse response functions and the relations among them.

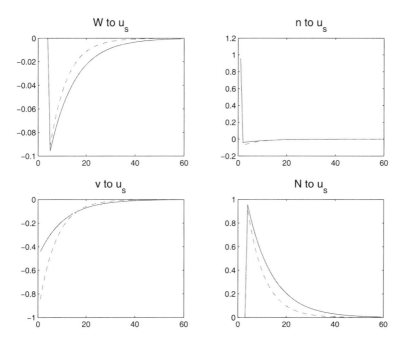

Figure 12.7.1: Impulse responses to supply shock without a fear of misspecification (solid lines) and with a fear of misspecification with $\sigma = -.5$.

tor x_t of the planner. The first uses the robust planning problem (12.3.1), (12.3.2), and the second uses the *ex post* Bayesian planning problem (12.6.1), (12.6.2).

12.8.1. Pricing from the robust planning problem

Hansen, Sargent, and Tallarini (1999) used the following three-step method to compute asset prices:

1. Solve the robust planning problem.

2. Obtain representations for the planner's shadow prices, based on marginal utilities of consumption evaluated at the allocation that solves the planning problem.

3. Use the appropriate shadow prices to price assets as conditional expectations of inner products of (scaled) history-date prices, computing the conditional expectation by taking the distorted law of motion cast in terms of little x that emerges from the robust planning problem and the corresponding sequence of information J_t.

This method leads to a representation for asset prices corresponding to (11.7.1) of the following form:

$$x_{t+1} = \hat{A}^o x_t + C\epsilon_{t+1} \qquad (12.8.1a)$$

$$y_t = S_y x_t \qquad (12.8.1b)$$

$$p_{cs}^t = (e_1 M_c x_t)^{-1} M_c x_s \qquad (12.8.1c)$$

$$a_{yt} = E_t \sum_{t=0}^{\infty} \beta^t p_{ct+j}^t \cdot y_{t+j}, \qquad (12.8.1d)$$

where E is the expectation evaluated with respect to $\hat{A}^o = A^o + CK$, the transition matrix for the worst-case transition law under the robust decision rule F, where $A^o = A - BF$; and M_c also incorporates the worst-case transition law through the presence of $A^o + CK$ in (11.5.12), (11.5.11) (also see formulas (11.5.14) and (11.5.21)).

12.8.2. *Pricing from the* ex post *Bayesian planning problem*

An alternative strategy is based on the following four-step procedure:

1. Solve a robust planning problem.

2. Obtain a representation of the worst-case shock process in terms of the new state variable X_t as on page 262.

3. Solve the *ordinary* (i.e., non-robust) planning problem with the distorted law of motion for the augmented state $\begin{bmatrix} x_t \\ X_t \end{bmatrix}$ as in (12.6.1), (12.6.2).

4. Use either of the complete-market decentralizations presented in chapter 11 for our economies *without* robustness and price assets using the standard (non-robust) asset pricing formulas.

12.9. Concluding remarks

Chapter 11 showed that without a preference for robustness, the pricing kernel for Arrow securities has the representation

$$q(X_{t+1}|X_t) = \beta \frac{e_1 u_{c,t+1}}{e_1 u_{c,t}} f(X_{t+1}|X_t)$$

where $f(X_{t+1}|X_t)$ is the transition density under the approximating model. In this chapter, we have shown that a representative consumer's fear that the approximating model is misspecified makes the pricing kernel for one-period Arrow securities become

$$q(X_{t+1}|X_t) = \beta \frac{e_1 u_{c,t+1}}{e_1 u_{c,t}} \hat{f}(X_{t+1}|X_t)$$

where $\hat{f}(X_{t+1}|X_t)$ is the planner's worst-case model. The price of Arrow securities under a preference for robustness can also be written as

$$q(X_{t+1}|X_t) = \beta \frac{e_1 u_{c,t+1}}{e_1 u_{c,t}} \left(\frac{\hat{f}(X_{t+1}|X_t)}{f(X_{t+1}|X_t)} \right) f(X_{t+1}|X_t). \tag{12.9.1}$$

In chapter 13, we shall use representations like (12.9.1) to price assets under the approximating model. The term $\left(\frac{\hat{f}(X_{t+1}|X_t)}{f(X_{t+1}|X_t)} \right)$ can be viewed as a multiplicative adjustment to the usual stochastic discount factor $\beta \frac{e_1 u_{c,t+1}}{e_1 u_{c,t}}$ that comes from the representative household's concern about model misspecification.[10] When the likelihood ratio $\left(\frac{\hat{f}(X_{t+1}|X_t)}{f(X_{t+1}|X_t)} \right)$ is volatile under the approximating model, it serves to boost the market price of macroeconomic risk.

A. Decentralization of partial equilibrium

For a partial equilibrium model with adjustment costs, this appendix studies a recursive competitive equilibrium in which the representative firm has a preference for robust decisions. We show that the standard trick of computing an equilibrium by solving the fictitious planning problem of maximizing a discounted sum of consumer plus producer surplus extends to a setting where the firm wants robustness. In this case, the planning problem becomes a robust planning problem in which the planner extremizes over decision, model distortion pairs.

Consider an adaptation for robustness of Sargent's (1987, chapter XVI) version of Lucas and Prescott's (1971) model of investment under uncertainty. Demand for a single good is governed by an inverse demand function

$$p_t = A_0 - A_1 \bar{q}_t + v_t \tag{12.A.1}$$

where

$$v_{t+1} = \rho v_t + C_v w_{t+1}. \tag{12.A.2}$$

A representative firm has one-period quadratic cost function $\sigma(q_t, q_{t+1})$ and one-period profits $\pi_t = p_t q_t - \sigma(q_t, q_{t+1})$. The firm acts as a price taker and wants to extremize $\sum_{t=0}^{\infty} \beta^t (p_t q_t - \sigma(q_t, q_{t+1}))$ with respect to sequences for $\{q_{t+1}, w_{t+1}\}_{t=0}^{\infty}$. The firm believes that the law of motion for aggregate output is

$$\bar{q}_{t+1} = \ell_q(\bar{q}_t, v_t) \tag{12.A.3}$$

where ℓ_q is a linear function. The representative firm solves the two-player zero-sum game

$$\min_{\{w_{t+1}\}} \max_{\{q_{t+1}\}} \sum_{t=0}^{\infty} \beta^t \{p_t q_t - \sigma(q_t, q_{t+1}) + \beta \theta w_{t+1}^2\} \tag{12.A.4}$$

---

[10] The likelihood ratio $\left(\hat{f}/f \right)$ that adjusts the stochastic discount factor for robustness also occurs in formulas that describe bounds on the detection error probability statistics described in chapter 9. See chapter 13 and Anderson, Hansen, and Sargent (2003) for more about the connection between detection error statistics and theoretical values of market prices of risk.

where the extremization is subject to $(12.A.1)$, $(12.A.2)$, $(12.A.3)$. An equilibrium of the representative agent's two-player zero-sum game is a pair of decision rules

$$q_{t+1} = \phi_q(q_t, v_t, \bar{q}_t) \tag{12.A.5a}$$

$$w_{t+1} = \phi_w(q_t, v_t, \bar{q}_t). \tag{12.A.5b}$$

The representative agent's extremization problem induces a mapping from ℓ_q in $(12.A.3)$ to (ϕ_q, ϕ_w). When the representative firm perceives the law of motion for $\bar{q}_t$ to be $(12.A.3)$, it acts to make the actual law of motion to be $\bar{q}_{t+1} = \phi_q(\bar{q}_t, v_t, \bar{q}_t)$. A *competitive equilibrium under robustness* is a fixed point of the mapping from $\ell_q(\bar{q}, v)$ to $\phi_q(\bar{q}, v, \bar{q})$. That is, for the representative firm to be representative, it must be true that ℓ_q satisfies

$$\phi_q(\bar{q}_t, v_t, \bar{q}_t) = \ell_q(\bar{q}_t, v_t). \tag{12.A.6}$$

Fortunately, by extending lines of argument of Lucas and Prescott (1971) and Sargent (1987), it is not necessary to attack this fixed-point problem directly. In particular, we can compute ℓ_q and an associated ℓ_w directly by solving a fictitious robust planning problem. The fictitious planning problem is

$$\min_{\{w_{t+1}\}} \max_{\{\bar{q}_{t+1}\}} \sum_{t=0}^{\infty} \beta^t \{S(\bar{q}_t, v_t) - \sigma(\bar{q}_t, \bar{q}_{t+1}) + \beta\theta w'_{t+1} w_{t+1}\} \tag{12.A.7}$$

where $S(\bar{q}, v)$ is consumer surplus defined as

$$S(\bar{q}, v) = \int_0^{\bar{q}} (A_0 - A_1 x + v) dx$$

$$= A_0 \bar{q} - \frac{A_1}{2} \bar{q}^2 + \bar{q}v.$$

The state of the market is $\bar{q}_t, v_t$. A solution of this two-player zero-sum game is

$$\bar{q}_{t+1} = \ell_q(\bar{q}_t, v_t) \tag{12.A.8a}$$

$$w_{t+1} = \ell_w(\bar{q}_t, v_t) \tag{12.A.8b}$$

It turns out that $\ell_j(\bar{q}, v) = \phi_j(\bar{q}, v, \bar{q})$ for $j = q, w$. This assertion can be proved by extending the proof in Sargent (1987, chapter XIV). The proof strategy is to obtain the Euler equations for extremizing $(12.A.4)$, then to use the demand curve $(12.A.1)$ to eliminate price, rearrange, and note that these Euler equations-cum equilibrium conditions match the Euler equations for extremizing the fictitious planning criterion $(12.A.7)$.

B. Solving Ryoo and Rosen's model by hand

Using methods described by Sargent (1987), we can solve Ryoo and Rosen's model by hand and thereby discover a reduced description of the state. Substituting equations $(12.7.1)$, $(12.7.3)$, and $(12.7.4)$ into $(12.7.2)$ and rearranging yields

$$\left(1 + \beta\delta_N^2 + \alpha_s\alpha_d\beta^k - \delta_N L - \beta\delta_N L^{-1}\right) N_{t+k}$$
$$= E_t \left[(1 - \beta\delta_N L^{-1})(\eta_s + u_{st}) + \alpha_s\beta^k(\eta_d + u_{d,t+k})\right], \tag{12.B.1}$$

where L is the backward shift operator. Notice the appearance in the characteristic polynomial of $\alpha_d \alpha_s = \frac{\alpha_d}{\alpha_s}$, the ratio of the slope of the inverse demand schedule to the slope of the inverse supply schedule. The polynomial in L on the left side evidently can be factored as $f_0 f(\beta L^{-1}) f(L)$ where $f(L) = (1 - \psi L)$ and $|\psi| < 1$. Then the stabilizing solution of $(12.B.1)$ is

$$N_{t+k} = \psi N_{t+k-1} + E_t\left\{\left(\frac{f_0^{-1}}{1 - \psi\beta L^{-1}}\right)[(1 - \beta\delta_N L^{-1})(\eta_s + u_{st})\right.$$
$$\left. + \alpha_s\beta^k(\eta_d + u_{d,t+k})]\right\}. \tag{12.B.2}$$

It follows from $(12.B.2)$ that N_{t+k-1} is a complete description of the endogenous part of the state vector at the beginning of time t. We could have guessed this from $(12.7.2)$ because N_{t+k-1} is independent of decisions or shocks that occur before time t.

When u_{st}, u_{dt} are i.i.d., $(12.B.2)$ simplifies to

$$N_{t+k} = \psi N_{t+k-1} + \eta_s + \alpha_s\beta^k + u_{st}. \tag{12.B.3}$$

In the i.i.d. case, it follows from $(12.7.2)$ and $(12.B.3)$ that the decision rule for n_t is

$$n_t = (\psi - \delta_N)N_{t+k-1} + \eta_s + \alpha_s\beta^k + u_{st}. \tag{12.B.4}$$

Chapter 13
Asset pricing

Doubt is not a pleasant condition, but certainty is absurd.
— *Voltaire*

13.1. Introduction

This chapter explores how a fear of model misspecification affects prices of risky securities.[1] Without fear of misspecification, the price of a claim to a random future payoff equals the conditional expectation of the inner product of a stochastic discount factor and the random future payoff, evaluated using the representative agent's model.[2] When the representative agent fears misspecification of his approximating model, two such inner-product representations of asset prices are available. They differ in what they take as the model with respect to which the conditional expectation is evaluated. In the first one, the conditional expectation is evaluated with respect to the representative agent's worst-case model, a model that depends on the parameter θ that calibrates his fear of misspecification. A second representation of the same prices exists because the approximating model and the worst-case model put positive probabilities on the same events. This second representation evaluates the conditional expectation with respect to the approximating model. The first representation captures a concern about robustness by adjusting the probability distribution relative to the approximating model, while the second representation instead adjusts the stochastic discount factor (a.k.a. pricing kernel). In particular, to represent asset prices in terms of conditional expectations under the approximating model, the second representation multiplies the ordinary stochastic discount factor without fear of misspecification by the likelihood ratio, or Radon-Nikodym derivative, of the endogenous worst-case distorted model relative to the approximating model. When evaluated with respect to the worst-case probability distribution, the expected value of the logarithm of that likelihood ratio is the entropy measure that we used in chapter 2 to measure the proximity of models. It is also closely related to another entropy concept that describes bounds on the detection error probabilities of chapter 9 (see Anderson, Hansen, and Sargent (2003)).

---

[1] Studies of asset pricing under some form of model ambiguity include Dow and Werlang (1992), Epstein and Wang (1994), Chen and Epstein (2002), Maenhout (2004), Rigotti and Shannon (2005), and Hansen, Sargent, and Tallarini (1999).

[2] Without fear about misspecification, an agent can discard the adjective "approximating."

After reviewing asset pricing formulas in a standard model without a fear of misspecification, this chapter modifies those formulas to express a representative agent's fear of misspecification. As an example, we study asset pricing in the permanent income economy of chapter 10.

13.2. Approximating and distorted models

Chapters 11 and 12 describe planning problems and competitive equilibria for a class of linear-quadratic models. The consumption smoothing model of chapter 10 and the occupational choice model of section 12.7 are special cases of these models. The environment of chapter 11 is arranged so that without a fear of misspecification, the planning problem fits into the optimal linear regulator problem. Chapter 12 then uses a robust linear regulator to create a model in which the representative household's fear of misspecification is indexed by parameter $\theta > 0$. Equilibrium representations for prices and quantities can be determined from the solution of the robust linear regulator.

Chapter 11 describes matrices that portray the preferences, technology, and information structure of the economy. These can be assembled into matrices that define the robust linear regulator for a planning problem. The solution of the planning problem determines competitive equilibrium prices and quantities. Associated with the robust planning problem is the Bellman equation

$$-x'Px - p = \max_u \min_w \{r(x, u) + \theta\beta w'w + \beta E(-x^{*\prime}Px^* - p)\} \qquad (13.2.1)$$

where the extremization is subject to

$$x^* = Ax + Bu + C(\epsilon + w), \qquad (13.2.2)$$

where $\epsilon \sim \mathcal{N}(0, I)$ and $\theta \in (\underline{\theta}, +\infty]$. A Markov perfect equilibrium of this two-player zero-sum game is a pair of decision rules $u = -F(\theta)x, w = K(\theta)x$. The equilibrium determines the following two laws of motion for the state:

$$x_{t+1} = A^o x_t + C\epsilon_{t+1} \qquad (13.2.3)$$

and

$$x_{t+1} = (A^o + CK(\theta))x_t + C\epsilon_{t+1}, \qquad (13.2.4)$$

where $A^o = A - BF(\theta)$. For a given $\theta \in [\underline{\theta}, \infty)$, (13.2.3) is the approximating model under the robust rule for u, while (13.2.4) is the distorted worst-case model under the robust rule.

Where there is no fear of misspecification, $\theta = +\infty$. Chapter 11 describes a class of economies whose equilibria can be presented in the form (13.2.4) together with selector matrices that determine equilibrium prices and quantities as functions of the state x_t. In particular, quantities Q_t and scaled state-contingent prices p_t are linear functions of the state:

$$Q_t = S_Q x_t \qquad (13.2.5a)$$

$$p_t = p_Q x_t. \qquad (13.2.5b)$$

We shall soon remind the reader what we mean by scaled prices. We showed how to compute these in chapter 11 (see formulas (11.5.14), (11.5.21)).

To determine equilibria under a fear of misspecification, we simply set $\theta < +\infty$ in (13.2.1). Formulas for equilibrium prices and quantities from chapter 11 (i.e., the S_Q, M_Q in (13.2.5)) apply directly. Associated with an equilibrium under a fear of misspecification are the approximating transition law (13.2.3) and the distorted transition law (13.2.4) for the state x_t, as well as auxiliary equations for prices and quantities of the form (13.2.5).

The approximating and distorted equilibrium laws of motion (13.2.3) and (13.2.4) induce Gaussian transition densities[3]

$$f(x_{t+1}|x_t) \sim \mathcal{N}(A^o x_t, CC') \qquad (13.2.6a)$$

$$\hat{f}(x_{t+1}|x_t) \sim \mathcal{N}((A^o + CK)x_t, CC'), \qquad (13.2.6b)$$

where we use f without a $(\hat{\cdot})$ to denote a transition density under the approximating model and f with a $(\hat{\cdot})$ to denote a probability associated with the distorted model (13.2.4). These transition densities induce joint densities $f^{(t)}(x^t)$ on histories $x^t = [x_t, x_{t-1}, \dots, x_0]$ via

$$f^{(t)}(x^t) = f(x_t|x_{t-1})f(x_{t-1}|x_{t-2}) \dots f(x_1|x_0)f(x_0),$$

and similarly for $\hat{f}^{(t)}(x^t)$. Let $f_t(x_t|x_0)$ denote the t-step transition densities

$$f_t(x_t|x_0) \sim \mathcal{N}(A^{ot}x_0, V_t) \qquad (13.2.7a)$$

$$\hat{f}_t(x_t|x_0) \sim \mathcal{N}((A^o + CK)^t x_0, \hat{V}_t), \qquad (13.2.7b)$$

where V_t satisfies the recursion $V_t = A^{o\prime} V_{t-1} A_o + CC'$ initialized from $V_1 = CC'$, and $\hat{V}_t$ satisfies the recursion $\hat{V}_t = (A^o + CK)'\hat{V}_{t-1}(A_o + CK) + CC'$ initialized from $\hat{V}_1 = CC'$.

---

[3] An alternative formulation in chapter 3 allows for a broader set of perturbations of a Gaussian approximating model by letting the minimizing agent choose an arbitrary density. Under that formulation, the minimizing agent would still choose a Gaussian transition density with the same conditional mean as (13.2.6b) but with conditional covariance $\hat{C}\hat{C}' = C(I - \theta^{-1}C'PC)^{-1}C'$.

13.3. Asset pricing without robustness

In section 11.7, we explained how the value of claims on risky streams of returns can be represented as the inner product of price and payout processes, where both the price and payout are expressed as functions of the planner's state vector x_t. In portraying the household's problem in a recursive competitive equilibrium, we needed to distinguish between the individual household's x_t and its "market wide" counterpart X_t that drives prices. Nevertheless, we showed that for the purpose of computing asset prices, we can exclude X_t from the state vector and simply use x_t as the state vector. Accordingly, in the remainder of this chapter, we express prices in terms of x_t and histories x^t.[4]

When $\theta = +\infty$, there is no discrepancy between the distorted and worst-case models and the following standard representative agent asset pricing theory applies. Let c_t denote a vector of time-t consumption goods. The price of a unit vector of consumption goods in period t contingent on the history x^t is[5]

$$q^{(t)}(x^t|x_0) = \beta^t \frac{u'(c_t(x^t))}{e_1 \cdot u'(c_0(x_0))} f^{(t)}(x^t|x_0), \qquad (13.3.1)$$

where $c_t(x^t)$ is a possibly history-dependent state-contingent consumption process, $u'(c)$ is the vector of marginal utilities of consumption, and e_1 is a selector vector that pulls off the first consumption good, the time-zero value of which we take as numeraire. To make ($13.3.1$) well defined, we assume that $e_1 \cdot u'(c_0(x_0)) \neq 0$ with probability one. If we assume that the consumption allocation is not history-dependent, so that $c_t(x^t) = c(x_t)$, as it is true in the models that occupy us, then we can use the t-step pricing kernel

$$q_t(x_t|x_0) = \beta^t \frac{u'(c(x_t))}{e_1 \cdot u'(c(x_0))} f_t(x_t|x_0). \qquad (13.3.2)$$

Let the owner of an asset be entitled to $\{y(x_t)\}_{t=0}^{\infty}$, a stream of a vector of consumption goods whose state-contingent price is given by ($13.3.2$). The time-zero price of the asset is

$$a_0 = \sum_{t=0}^{\infty} \int_{x_t} q_t(x_t|x_0) \cdot y(x_t) d\,x_t$$

---

[4] The household in a competitive economy would face prices that are the same functions of X_t and X^t.

[5] We denote by $u'(c_t)$ the vector of marginal utilities of the consumption vector c_t. In our model, $u'(c_t) = M_c x_t$.

or

$$a_0 = \sum_{t=0}^{\infty} \int_{x_t} \beta^t \frac{u'(c(x_t))}{e_1 \cdot u'(c(x_0))} y(x_t) f_t(x_t|x_0) d\, x_t. \qquad (13.3.3)$$

We can represent $(13.3.3)$ as

$$a_0 = \frac{E_0 \sum_{t=0}^{\infty} \beta^t u'(c(x_t)) \cdot y(x_t)}{e_1 \cdot u'(c(x_0))}. \qquad (13.3.4)$$

In linear-quadratic general equilibrium models, $u'(c(x_t))$ and $y(x_t)$ are both linear functions of the state. This means that the price of an asset is the conditional expectation of a geometric sum of a quadratic form, as portrayed in $(13.3.4)$. Equation $(13.3.4)$ implies a Sylvester equation (see page 97). Thus, let

$$p_c(x_t) = \frac{u'(c(x_t))}{e_1 \cdot u'(c(x_0))}.$$

Then the asset price can be represented as

$$a_0 = E_0 \sum_{t=0}^{\infty} \beta^t p_c(x_t) \cdot y(x_t). \qquad (13.3.5)$$

We can regard p_c as a scaled Arrow-Debreu price. We scale the Arrow-Debreu state price by dividing it by β^t times the pertinent conditional probability. Scaling the price system in this way facilitates computation of asset prices as conditional expectations of an inner product of state prices and payouts. Often $\beta^t p_c(x_t)$ is called a t-period *stochastic discount factor*. Below we shall also denote the stochastic discount factor as $m_{0,t} \equiv \beta^t p_c(x_t)$, so that $(13.3.5)$ becomes

$$a_0 = E_0 \sum_{t=0}^{\infty} m_{0,t} \cdot y(x_t).$$

Hansen and Sargent (2008) provide a more complete treatment of asset pricing within linear-quadratic general equilibrium models. They show that (1) equilibrium scaled Arrow-Debreu prices and quantities have representations $(13.2.5)$; (2) the information required to form the matrix S_Q is embedded in F, A, B from the optimal linear regulator problem; and (3) the matrices M_p that pin down the scaled Arrow-Debreu prices can be extracted from the matrix P in the value function $-x'Px - p$ and the matrix $A^o = A - BF$ that emerge from the planner's problem (see formulas $(11.5.14)$, $(11.5.21)$). Thus, in such models

$$p_c(x_t) = M_c x_t / e_1 M_c x_0. \qquad (13.3.6)$$

See $(11.5.11)$, $(11.5.13)$ in chapter 11 for a formula for M_c and more details.

13.4. Asset pricing with robustness

We activate a fear of misspecification by setting $\theta < +\infty$, which causes the transition densities (13.2.6a), (13.2.6b) under the approximating and distorted models to disagree. In addition, the formulas for S_Q and M_Q in (13.2.5) respond to the setting for θ, via the dependence of S_Q on $F(\theta)$ and the dependence of M_Q on the P that solves the Bellman equation (13.2.1). Again, see (11.5.14), (11.5.21). We give an example in section 12.7.

The price system that supports a competitive equilibrium can be represented in the forms (13.3.1) and (13.3.2), with the distorted densities $\hat{f}^{(t)}$ and $\hat{f}_t$ replacing the corresponding densities for the approximating model in (13.3.1) and (13.3.2). Thus, with a fear of misspecification, the time 0 price of the asset corresponding to (13.3.3) is

$$a_0 = \sum_{t=0}^{\infty} \int_{x_t} \beta^t p_c(x_t) \cdot y(x_t) \hat{f}_t(x_t | x_0) d\, x_t. \qquad (13.4.1)$$

We can represent (13.4.1) as

$$a_0 = \hat{E}_0 \sum_{t=0}^{\infty} \beta^t p_c(x_t) \cdot y_t \qquad (13.4.2)$$

where $\hat{E}$ denotes mathematical expectation using the distorted model (13.2.4), and $u'(c(x_t))$ must be computed using the M_Q in representation (13.2.5b) associated with θ.

13.4.1. Adjustment of stochastic discount factor for fear of model misspecification

Formula (13.4.2) represents the asset price in terms of the distorted measure that the planner uses to evaluate future utilities in the Bellman equation (13.2.1). To compute asset prices using this formula, we must solve a Sylvester equation using transition matrix $A^o + CK(\theta)$ from equation (13.2.4) to reflect that we are evaluating the expectation using the *distorted* transition law. We can also evaluate asset prices by computing expectations under the *approximating* model, but this requires that we adjust the stochastic discount factor to make the asset price satisfy (13.4.1). By dividing and multiplying by $f_t(x_t | x_0)$, we can represent (13.4.1) as

$$a_0 = \sum_{t=0}^{\infty} \int_{x_t} \beta^t p_c(x_t) \left(\frac{\hat{f}_t(x_t | x_0)}{f_t(x_t | x_0)} \right) \cdot y(x_t) f_t(x_t | x_0) d\, x_t \qquad (13.4.3)$$

or

$$a_0 = E_0 \sum_{t=0}^{\infty} \beta^t p_c(x_t) \left(\frac{\hat{f}_t(x_t | x_0)}{f_t(x_t | x_0)} \right) \cdot y(x_t), \qquad (13.4.4)$$

where the absence of a $(\hat{\cdot})$ from E denotes that the expectation is evaluated with respect to the approximating model (13.2.3).[6]

In summary, with a fear of misspecification, if we want to evaluate asset prices under the approximating model, we have to adjust the ordinary t-period stochastic discount factor $m_{0,t} = \beta^t p_c(x_t)$ for a concern about model misspecification and to use the modified stochastic discount factor[7]

$$m_{0,t} \left(\frac{\hat{f}_t(x_t|x_0)}{f_t(x_t|x_0)} \right).$$

For our linear-quadratic-Gaussian setting, the likelihood ratio is

$$L_t = \frac{\hat{f}_t(x_t|x_0)}{f_t(x_t|x_0)} = \exp\left[\sum_{s=1}^{t} \{\epsilon'_s w_s - .5 w'_s w_s\} \right].$$

13.4.2. Reopening markets

This section describes how to extend our asset pricing formulas to allow us to price "tail assets" that are traded at time t and that pay vectors of consumption $\{y_\tau\}_{\tau=t}^{\infty}$ for $t > 0$. We want the price to be stated in time-t units of the numeraire good.

Letting the t-step discount factor at time 0 be $m_{0,t} \equiv \beta^t p_c(x_t)$, (13.4.2) can be portrayed as

$$a_0 = \hat{E}_0 \sum_{t=0}^{\infty} m_{0,t} \cdot y_t \tag{13.4.5}$$

where $m_{0,t}$ is a vector of time-0 stochastic discount factors for pricing a vector of time-t payoffs. Define $m_{t,\tau}$ as the vector of corresponding time-t stochastic discount factors for pricing time $\tau \geq t$ payoffs[8]

$$m_{t,\tau} = \beta^{\tau-t} p_c(x_\tau)/e_1 p_c(x_t). \tag{13.4.6}$$

Then in time t units of the numeraire consumption good, the vector of payoffs $\{y_\tau\}_{\tau=0}^{\infty}$ is

$$a_t = \hat{E}_t \sum_{\tau=t}^{\infty} m_{t,\tau} y_\tau. \tag{13.4.7}$$

---

[6] Notice the appearance of the same likelihood ratio in (13.4.4) used to define entropy in chapters 2 and 3 and to describe detection error probabilities in chapter 9.

[7] Such a multiplicative adjustment to the stochastic discount factor $m_{0,t}$ carries over to nonlinear models.

[8] We assume that $e_1 p_c(x_t) \neq 0$ with probability 1.

Equation (13.4.7) is equivalent to

$$a_t = E_t \sum_{\tau=t}^{\infty} (m_{t,\tau} m_{t,\tau}^u) \cdot y_\tau, \tag{13.4.8}$$

where the appropriate multiplicative adjustment $m_{t,\tau}^u$ to the stochastic discount factor is the likelihood ratio

$$m_{t,\tau}^u = \frac{\hat{f}_{\tau-t}(x_\tau | x_t)}{f_{\tau-t}(x_\tau | x_t)}$$
$$= \exp\left[\sum_{s=t}^{\tau} \{\epsilon_s' w_s - .5 w_s' w_s\}\right]. \tag{13.4.9}$$

13.5. Pricing single-period payoffs

We now use the permanent income model of chapter 10 to shed light on the implications of a fear of misspecification for the equity premium. Let consumption be a scalar process and y_{t+1} be a scalar random payoff at time $t + 1$. Without a fear of misspecification, the price at time t of a time $t + 1$ payout is

$$a_t = E_t m_{t,t+1} y_{t+1}. \tag{13.5.1}$$

We follow Hansen and Jagannathan (1991) by applying the definition of a conditional covariance to (13.5.1) and using the Cauchy-Schwarz inequality to obtain

$$\left(\frac{a_t}{E_t m_{t,t+1}}\right) \geq E_t y_{t+1} - \left(\frac{\sigma_t(m_{t,t+1})}{E_t m_{t,t+1}}\right) \sigma_t(y_{t+1}). \tag{13.5.2}$$

The bound is attained by payoffs on the efficient frontier. The left side is the price of the risky asset relative to the price $E_t m_{t,t+1}$ of a risk-free asset that pays out 1 for sure next period. The term $\left(\frac{\sigma_t(m_{t,t+1})}{E_t m_{t,t+1}}\right)$ is the "market price of risk": it indicates the rate at which the price ratio $a_t / E_t m_{t,t+1}$ deteriorates with increases in the conditional standard deviation of the payout y_{t+1}.

Without imposing any theory about $m_{t,t+1}$, various studies have estimated the market price of risk $\left(\frac{\sigma_t(m_{t,t+1})}{E_t m_{t,t+1}}\right)$ from data on (a_t, y_{t+1}). For post World War II quarterly data, estimates of the market price of risk hover around .25. Hansen and Jagannathan's (1991) characterization of the equity premium puzzle is that .25 is much higher than would be implied by many theories that explicitly link $m_{t,t+1}$ to aggregate consumption. A standard benchmark is the theory $m_{t,t+1} = \beta u'(c_{t+1})/u'(c_t)$, where $u(\cdot)$ is a power utility function with power γ. That specification makes $m_{t,t+1} = \beta \left(\frac{c_{t+1}}{c_t}\right)^\gamma$. But aggregate consumption is a smooth series, so that the growth rate of consumption has a standard deviation so small that unless γ is implausibly large, the market price of risk implied by this theory of the stochastic discount factor $m_{t,t+1}$ remains far below the observed value of .25. Similarly, the permanent income model of chapter 10 that sets $m_{t,t+1} = M_c x_{t+1}/M_x x_t$ also implies too low a value of the market price of risk, again because the volatility of consumption growth is too small.[9]

How does imputing a concern about robustness to the representative agent impinge on these calculations? When the representative household is concerned about robustness, we have

$$a_t = E_t(m_{t,t+1} m^u_{t,t+1})y_{t+1} \tag{13.5.3}$$

where from (13.4.9)

$$m^u_{t,t+1} = \exp\left[\epsilon'_{t+1} w_{t+1} - .5 w'_{t+1} w_{t+1}\right]. \tag{13.5.4}$$

By construction, $E_t m^u_{t,t+1} = 1$. Hansen, Sargent, and Tallarini (1999) (HST) computed that $E_t(m^u_{t,t+1})^2 = \exp(w'_{t+1} w_{t+1})$ so that

$$\sigma_t(m^u_{t,t+1}) = \sqrt{\exp(w'_{t+1} w_{t+1} - 1)} \approx |w'_{t+1} w_{t+1}|. \tag{13.5.5}$$

HST refer to $\sigma_t(m^u_{t,t+1})$ as the one-period market price of model uncertainty. Similarly, the $(\tau - t)$-period market price of model uncertainty is the conditional standard deviation of $m^u_{t,\tau}$ defined by (13.4.9). A fear of misspecification can boost the market price of risk by increasing these multiplicative adjustments to stochastic discount factors.

13.5.1. Calibrated market prices of model uncertainty

At this point, it might be useful for the reader to review the observational equivalence result in chapter 10. There we discussed the fact that there is a locus of (σ, β) pairs, all of which imply the same equilibrium quantities, i.e., the same consumption, investment, and output.[10] As in chapter 10, we follow HST and use the parameterization $\sigma \equiv -\theta^{-1}$. HST computed one-period market prices of risk for a calibrated version of the permanent income model described in chapter 10. In particular, they proceeded as follows:

---

[9] We return to these issues in chapter 14.

[10] Such observational equivalence seems also to be an excellent approximation in the non LQ model of Tallarini (2000).

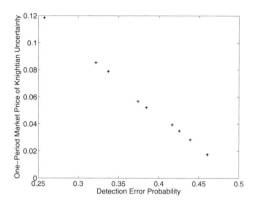

Figure 13.5.1: Market price of model uncertainty for one-period securities $\sigma_t(m_{t,t+1})^u$ as a function of detection error probability in the HST model.

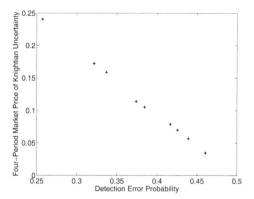

Figure 13.5.2: Market price of model uncertainty for four-period securities $\sigma_t(m_{t,t+4})^u$ as a function of detection error probability in the HST model.

1. Setting $\sigma = 0$ and $\beta R = 1$, HST used the method of maximum likelihood to estimate the remaining free parameters of the permanent income model of chapter 10.

2. HST used those maximum likelihood parameter estimates as the approximating model of the endowment processes $d_t^*, \hat{d}_t$ for a representative agent whose continuation values they used to price risky assets. Thus, HST took a stand on how the representative agent created his approximating model, something that robust control theory is silent about.

3. To study the effects of a fear of misspecification on asset prices while leav-

ing the consumption-investment allocation (c_t, i_t) intact, HST lowered σ below zero, but adjusted the discount factor according to the relation $\beta = \hat{\beta}(\sigma)$ given by equation (10.3.18), which defines a locus of (σ, β) pairs that freeze $\{c_t, i_t\}$. For each (σ, β) thereby selected, HST calculated market prices of model uncertainty and the detection error probabilities associated with distinguishing the approximating model from the worst-case model associated with σ. Figure 10.7.1 in chapter 10 reports those detection error probabilities as a function of σ. We are interested in the relation between the detection error probabilities and the j-period market prices of model uncertainty.

4. For one- and four-period horizons, figures 13.5.1 and 13.5.2 report the calculated market prices of model uncertainty plotted against the detection error probabilities. These graphs reveal two salient features. First, there appear to be approximately linear relationships between the detection error probabilities and the market prices of model uncertainty. For a continuous-time diffusion specification, Anderson, Hansen, and Sargent (2003) establish an exact linear relationship between the market price of risk and a bound on the detection error probabilities. To the extent that their bound is informative, their finding explains the striking pattern in these figures. Second, the market price of model uncertainty is substantial even for values of the detection error probability sufficiently high that it seems plausible to seek robustness against models that close to the approximating model. Thus, a detection error probability of .3 leads to a one-period market price of uncertainty of about .15, which can explain about half of the observed equity premium.

13.6. Concluding remarks

The asset pricing example of HST indicates how a little bit of concern about model misspecification can potentially substitute for a substantial amount of risk aversion when it comes to boosting theoretical values of market prices of risk. The boost in the market price of risk emerges from pessimism relative to the representative agent's approximating model. The form that the pessimism takes is endogenous, depending both on the transition law and the representative agent's discount factor and one-period return function. Pessimism has been proposed by several researchers as an explanation of asset pricing puzzles, e.g., Reitz (1988) and Abel (2002). The contribution of the robustness framework is to discipline the appeal to pessimism by restricting the direction in which the approximating model is twisted, and by how much, through the detection probability statistics that we use to restrict θ.

Chapter 14
Risk sensitivity, model uncertainty, and asset pricing

No one has found risk aversion parameters of 50 or 100 in the diversi-
fication of individual portfolios, in the level of insurance deductibles, in
the wage premiums associated with occupations with high earnings risk,
or in the revenues raised by state-operated lotteries. It would be good to
have the equity premium resolved, but I think we need to look beyond high
estimates of risk aversion to do it.
— Robert Lucas, Jr., "Macroeconomic Priorities," 2003

14.1. Introduction

This chapter gives an affirmative answer to the following question: in terms of
their implications for asset prices and real quantities, can plausible amounts of
concern about robustness to model misspecification substitute for the implausibly large values of risk aversion that Lucas and many other macroeconomists
do not like?[1] Our answer is based on how we reinterpret an elegant graph of
Tallarini (2000) that partly inspired Lucas's words. We use a value function
recursion of Hansen and Sargent (1995, 2007a) to transform Tallarini's CRRA
risk-aversion parameter γ into a parameter that measures a set of probability models for consumption growth that are difficult to distinguish from one
another and over which the consumer seeks a robust valuation.[2]

As advocated by Anderson, Hansen, and Sargent (2003), instead of using
a mental experiment of Pratt (1964)[3] to solicit an individual's aversion to taking random draws from a *known* probability distribution, we use a detection
error probability for comparing alternative probability distributions to restrict
γ. When we recast Tallarini's key diagram in terms of model detection error
probabilities, there emerges a link between model detection probabilities and
what is usually interpreted as the market price of risk, but that Anderson et
al. interpret as the market price of model uncertainty.

---

[1] This chapter is based on ideas and computations that are pursued more extensively
in Barillas, Hansen, and Sargent (2007).

[2] What we call γ, Tallarini called χ.

[3] Cochrane (1997) describes how mental experiments using Pratt's (1964) calculations
provide most economists' intuition that γ should be small.

14.1.1. Organization

The remainder of this chapter is organized as follows. Section 14.2 reviews Hansen and Jagannathan's characterization of asset pricing puzzles in models with time-separable CRRA preferences (e.g., equity premium and risk-free rate puzzles). Section 14.3 describes how Tallarini (2000) used Kreps and Porteus (1978) preferences and two alternative models of log consumption to find sets of values of γ, one set for a random walk model, another set for a trend stationary model, that can explain the risk-free rate puzzle of Weil (1990), albeit values so high that they provoked Lucas's skeptical remark. Section 14.4 uses Tallarini's formulas for the risk-free rate and the market price of risk under the two models of consumption growth to prepare an updated version of Tallarini's figure. Section 14.5 defines a concern about robustness in terms of the martingale perturbations that Hansen and Sargent (2005b, 2007a) and chapter 3 and 7 used to represent alternative specifications that are statistically near the approximating model. We then reinterpret Tallarini's utility recursion in terms of a max-min expected utility formulation in which the minimization operator expresses the agent's concerns about his stochastic specification. Section 14.6 uses detection error probabilities to select different context-specific γ's for the random walk and trend stationary models, then modifies Tallarini's figure to exhibit a link between detection probabilities and what we interpret as market prices of model uncertainty. The figure reveals a link between the market price of model uncertainty and detection error probability that transcends differences in the stochastic specification of the representative consumer's approximating model for consumption growth, an outcome that could be anticipated from the tight relationship between the market price of model uncertainty and a large deviation bound on detection error probabilities described in Anderson, Hansen, and Sargent (2003). An appendix describes how to compute worst-case probability distributions that are important ingredients for calculating detection error probabilities.

14.2. Equity premium and risk-free rate puzzles

Along with Tallarini (2000), we begin with a characterization of the risk-free rate and equity premium puzzles by Hansen and Jagannathan (1991). The random variable $m_{t,t+1}$ is said to be a stochastic discount factor if it confirms the following basic equation for the price p_t of an asset with one-period payoff x_{t+1}:

$$p_t = E_t \left(m_{t,t+1} x_{t+1} \right),$$

where E_t denotes the mathematical expectation over the joint probability distribution of $m_{t,t+1}$ and x_{t+1}. For time-separable CRRA preferences with discount factor β, $m_{t,t+1}$ is simply the marginal rate of substitution:

$$m_{t,t+1} = \beta \left(\frac{C_{t+1}}{C_t} \right)^{-\gamma} \qquad (14.2.1)$$

where γ is the coefficient of relative risk aversion and C_t is consumption. The risk-free rate is

$$\frac{1}{r_t^f} = E_t \left[m_{t,t+1} \right] = E_t \left[\beta \left(\frac{C_{t+1}}{C_t} \right)^{-\gamma} \right]. \qquad (14.2.2)$$

Let ξ be the one-period excess return on any security or portfolio of securities. Using the definition of a conditional covariance and a Cauchy-Schwarz inequality, Hansen and Jagannathan (1991) establish the following bound:

$$\frac{|E[\xi]|}{\sigma(\xi)} \le \frac{\sigma(m)}{E[m]}.$$

The ratio $\frac{\sigma(m)}{E[m]}$ is commonly called the market price of risk. The market price of risk is the slope of the mean-standard deviation frontier. It is the increase in the expected rate of return needed to compensate an investor for bearing a unit increase in the standard deviation of return along the efficient frontier.[4] Hansen and Jagannathan's statement of the equity premium puzzle is that reconciling formula (14.2.1) with measures of the market price of risk extracted from data on asset returns and prices, like those in table 14.2.1, requires a value of γ so high that it elicits doubts like those expressed by Lucas in the epigraph starting this chapter.

But another failure isolated by figure 14.2.1 motivated Tallarini (2000). The figure plots the Hansen and Jagannathan bound (the parabola) as well as the locus of pairs of the reciprocal of the risk-free rate $1/r^f$ and market price of risk $\frac{\sigma(m)}{E[m]}$ implied by equations (14.2.1) and (14.2.2) for different values of γ.[5] The figure addresses the question of whether such a value of γ can be found for which the associated $\left(1/r^f, \frac{\sigma(m)}{E[m]} \right)$ pair is inside the Hansen and Jagannathan bounds. The figure shows that while high values of γ deliver high market prices of risk, high values of γ also push the reciprocal of the

---

[4] A Sharpe ratio measures the excess return relative to the standard deviation. The market price of risk is the maximal Sharpe ratio.

[5] Formulas for $E(m)$ and $\sigma(m)/E(m)$ for the random walk and trend stationary specifications are for the random walk model $E[m] = \beta \exp \left[\gamma \left(-\mu + \frac{\sigma_\varepsilon^2 \gamma}{2} \right) \right]$ and $\frac{\sigma(m)}{E[m]} = \left\{ \exp \left[\sigma_\varepsilon^2 \gamma^2 \right] - 1 \right\}^{\frac{1}{2}}$ and $E[m] = \beta \exp \left[\gamma \left(-\mu + \frac{\sigma_\varepsilon^2 \gamma}{2} \left(1 + \frac{1-\rho}{1+\rho} \right) \right) \right]$, and $\frac{\sigma(m)}{E[m]} = \left\{ \exp \left[\sigma_\varepsilon^2 \gamma^2 \left(1 + \frac{1-\rho}{1+\rho} \right) \right] - 1 \right\}^{\frac{1}{2}}$ for the trend stationary model.

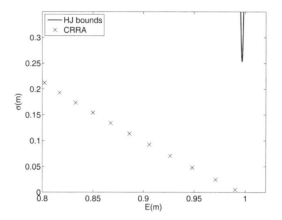

Figure 14.2.1: Solid line: Hansen-Jagannathan volatility bounds for quarterly returns on the value-weighted NYSE and Treasury Bill, 1948-2005. Crosses: Mean and standard deviation for intertemporal marginal rate of substitution for CRRA time separable preferences. The coefficient of relative risk aversion, γ takes on the values 1, 5, 10, 15, 20, 25, 30, 35, 40, 45, 50 and the discount factor β=0.995.

risk-free rate down and away from the Hansen and Jagannathan bounds. This is the risk-free rate puzzle of Weil (1990).[6]

Next we recount how, by adopting a recursive preference specification, Tallarini (2000) could claim success by finding a value of γ that pushed the $1/r^f, \frac{\sigma(m)}{E[m]}$ pair inside the Hansen and Jagannathan bounds. However, the values of γ that work are still so high that they provoked Lucas's skeptical remark.

14.2.1. Shocks and consumption plans

We let $c_t = \log C_t$, x_0 be an initial state vector, and ε_{t+1} for $t \geq 1$ be a sequence of random shocks with conditional densities $\pi(\varepsilon_{t+1}|\varepsilon^t, x_0)$ and an implied joint density $\pi(\varepsilon^\infty|x_0)$. Let $\mathcal{C}$ be a set of consumption plans whose time t element c_t is a measurable function of (ε^t, x_0). We further restrict

---

[6] Kocherlakota (1990) pointed out that by adjusting (β, γ) pairs suitably, it is possible to attain the Hansen-Jagannathan bounds for the random walk model of log consumption and CRRA time-separable preferences, thus explaining both the equity premium and the risk-free rate. Doing so requires a high γ and $\beta > 1$.

Table 14.2.1: Asset Market data: Sample moments from quarterly U.S. data 1948:II-2005:IV, r^e is the return on the value-weighted NYSE portfolio and r^f is the return on the three-month Treasury bill. Returns are measured in percent per quarter.

Return	Mean	Std. dev.
r^e	2.27	7.68
r^f	0.32	0.61
$r^e - r^f$	1.95	7.67
Market price of risk:	0.2542	

ourselves to consumption plans with the following recursive representation:

$$x_{t+1} = Ax_t + B\varepsilon_{t+1}$$
$$c_t = Hx_t \tag{14.2.3}$$

where x_t is an $n \times 1$ state vector, ε_{t+1} is an $m \times 1$ shock, and the eigenvalues of A are bounded in modulus by $\frac{1}{\sqrt{\beta}}$. Representation $(14.2.3)$ implies that the time t element of the consumption plan can be expressed as the following function of x_0 and the history of shocks:

$$c_t = H(B\varepsilon_t + AB\varepsilon_{t-1} + \cdots + A^{t-1}B\varepsilon_1) + HA^t x_0. \tag{14.2.4}$$

Throughout this chapter, we will work extensively with one of the following two consumption plans that work well in fitting post WWII U.S. per capita consumption.

geometric random walk:

$$c_t = c_0 + t\mu + \sigma_\varepsilon(\varepsilon_t + \varepsilon_{t-1} + \cdots + \varepsilon_1), \ t \geq 1 \tag{14.2.5}$$

where $\varepsilon_t \sim \pi(\varepsilon_t) \sim \mathcal{N}(0,1)$.

geometric trend stationary:

$$c_t = \rho^t c_0 + t\mu + \sigma_\varepsilon(\varepsilon_t + \rho\varepsilon_{t-1} + \cdots + \rho^{t-1}\varepsilon_1), \ t \geq 1 \tag{14.2.6}$$

where $\varepsilon_t \sim \pi(\varepsilon_t) \sim \mathcal{N}(0,1)$.

Tallarini used these two models of consumption due to the fact that they both fit the data well and because they are difficult to distinguish because unit root tests lack power when a series is as serially correlated as consumption.

We estimated both processes using quarterly U.S. data 1948:2–2005:4. The maximum likelihood point estimates are summarized in table 14.4.1. We shall use these point estimates as inputs into the calculations below.

14.3. Recursive preferences

Tallarini assumed preferences that can be described by a recursive non-expected utility function à la Kreps and Porteus (1978), Epstein and Zin (1989), and Weil (1990), namely, [7]

$$V_t = W\left(C_t, \mu\left(V_{t+1}\right)\right)$$

where W is an aggregator function, $\mu\left(\cdot\right)$ is a certainty equivalent function

$$\mu\left(V_{t+1}\right) = f^{-1}\left(E_t f\left(V_{t+1}\right)\right),$$

f is a function that determines attitudes toward atemporal risk,

$$f\left(z\right) = z^{1-\gamma} \quad \text{if } 0 < \gamma \neq 1$$

$$f\left(z\right) = \log z \quad \text{if } \gamma = 1,$$

and γ is the coefficient of relative risk aversion

Following Epstein and Zin (1991), it is common to use the CES aggregator W

$$W\left(C, \mu\right) = \left[\left(1 - \beta\right) C^{1-\eta} + \beta \mu^{1-\eta}\right]^{\frac{1}{1-\eta}} \quad \text{for } 0 < \eta \neq 1$$

or

$$\lim_{\eta \to 1} W\left(C, \mu\right) = C^{1-\beta} \mu^{\beta}$$

where $\frac{1}{\eta}$ is the intertemporal elasticity of substitution. When $\gamma = \eta$, we get the case of additive expected power utility with discount factor β.

Following many authors in the real business cycle literature, Tallarini (2000) set $\eta = 1$, which leads to log preferences under certainty

$$W\left(C, W^*\right) = C^{1-\beta} W^{*\beta}$$

where $\cdot^*$ denotes a next-period value. Tallarini used a power certainty equivalent function to get the following recursive utility under uncertainty

$$V_t = C_t^{1-\beta} \left[\left(E_t \left(V_{t+1}^{1-\gamma}\right)\right)^{\frac{1}{1-\gamma}}\right]^{\beta}.$$

Taking logs gives

$$\log V_t = \left(1 - \beta\right) c_t + \frac{\beta}{1 - \gamma} \log E_t \left(V_{t+1}^{1-\gamma}\right)$$

---

[7] Obstfeld (1994) and Dolmas (1998) used recursive preferences to study costs of consumption fluctuations.

or

$$\frac{\log V_t}{(1-\beta)} = c_t + \frac{\beta}{(1-\gamma)(1-\beta)} \log E_t \left(V_{t+1}^{1-\gamma}\right). \tag{14.3.1}$$

Define $U_t \equiv \log V_t/(1-\beta)$ and

$$\theta = \frac{-1}{(1-\beta)(1-\gamma)}. \tag{14.3.2}$$

Then

$$U_t = c_t - \beta\theta \log E_t \left[\exp\left(\frac{-U_{t+1}}{\theta}\right)\right]. \tag{14.3.3}$$

This is the risk-sensitive recursion of Hansen and Sargent (1995).[8] In the special case that $\gamma = 1$ (or $\theta = +\infty$), recursion (14.3.3) becomes the standard discounted expected utility recursion

$$U_t = c_t + \beta E_t U_{t+1}.$$

For the set of consumption processes $\mathcal{C}$ associated with different specifications of (A, B, H) in (14.2.3), recursion (14.3.3) implies the following Bellman equation:

$$U(x) = c - \beta\theta \log E \exp\left(\frac{-U(Ax + B\varepsilon)}{\theta}\right). \tag{14.3.4}$$

For the random walk specification, the value function that solves (14.3.4) is

$$U_t = \frac{\beta}{(1-\beta)^2} \left[\mu - \frac{\sigma_\varepsilon^2}{2\theta(1-\beta)}\right] + \frac{1}{1-\beta}c_t. \tag{14.3.5}$$

For the trend stationary model the value function is:

$$U_t = \frac{\beta\mu}{(1-\beta)^2} - \frac{\sigma_\varepsilon^2 \beta}{2\theta(1-\beta)(1-\beta\rho)^2} + \frac{\mu\beta(1-\rho)}{(1-\beta\rho)(1-\beta)}t + \frac{1}{1-\beta\rho}c_t. \tag{14.3.6}$$

14.3.1. Stochastic discount factor for risk-sensitive preferences

With risk-sensitive preferences, the stochastic discount factor is

$$m_{t,t+1} = \left(\beta\frac{C_t}{C_{t+1}}\right)\left(\frac{\exp\left((1-\beta)(1-\gamma)U_{t+1}\right)}{E_t\left[\exp\left((1-\beta)(1-\gamma)U_{t+1}\right)\right]}\right), \tag{14.3.7}$$

---

[8] Tallarini defined $\sigma = 2(1-\beta)(1-\gamma)$ in order to interpret his recursion in terms of the risk-sensitivity parameter σ of Hansen and Sargent (1995), who regarded negative values of σ as enhancing risk aversion.

so that the price of a one-period risk-free claim to one unit of consumption at date $t + 1$ is

$$\frac{1}{r_t^f} = E_t \left[m_{t,t+1} \right] = E_t \left[\left(\beta \frac{C_t}{C_{t+1}} \right) \left(\frac{\exp \left((1 - \beta)(1 - \gamma) U_{t+1} \right)}{E_t \left[\exp \left((1 - \beta)(1 - \gamma) U_{t+1} \right) \right]} \right) \right].$$
(14.3.8)

Below, we will reinterpret the forward-looking term $\frac{\exp((1-\beta)(1-\gamma)U_{t+1})}{E_t[\exp((1-\beta)(1-\gamma)U_{t+1})]}$ that multiplies the ordinary logarithmic stochastic discount factor $\beta \frac{C_t}{C_{t+1}}$ as an adjustment that reflects a consumer's concerns about model misspecification.

14.4. Risk-sensitive preferences let Tallarini attain the Hansen-Jagannathan bounds

For the random walk and trend stationary consumption processes, Tallarini computed the following formulas for the risk-free rate and market price of risk under his risk-sensitive specification of preferences.

Random walk:

$$r^f = \frac{1}{\beta} \exp \left[\mu - \frac{\sigma_\varepsilon^2}{2} (2\gamma - 1) \right]$$
(14.4.1)

$$\frac{\sigma(m)}{E[m]} = \left\{ \exp \left[\sigma_\varepsilon^2 \gamma^2 \right] - 1 \right\}^{\frac{1}{2}}.$$
(14.4.2)

Trend stationary:

$$r^f = \frac{1}{\beta} \exp \left[\mu - \frac{\sigma_\varepsilon^2}{2} \left(1 - \frac{2(1 - \beta)(1 - \gamma)}{1 - \beta\rho} + \frac{1 - \rho}{1 + \rho} \right) \right]$$
(14.4.3)

$$\frac{\sigma(m)}{E[m]} = \left\{ \exp \left[\sigma_\varepsilon^2 \left(\left\{ \frac{(1 - \beta)(1 - \gamma)}{1 - \beta\rho} - 1 \right\}^2 + \frac{1 - \rho}{1 + \rho} \right) \right] - 1 \right\}^{\frac{1}{2}}$$
(14.4.4)

Figure 14.4.1 is our version of Tallarini's (2000) decisive figure. It uses the above formulas to plot loci of $(E(m), \sigma(m))$ pairs for different values of the risk-aversion parameter γ. This figure chalks up a striking success for Tallarini when it is compared to the corresponding figure 14.2.1 for time separable CRRA preferences. Notice how for both specifications of the endowment process, increasing γ pushes the volatility of the stochastic discount factor upward toward the Hansen-Jagannathan bounds while leaving $E(m)$ unaffected, thus avoiding the risk-free rate puzzle of Weil (1990). However, there is a cloud in every silver lining, because approaching the Hansen-Jagannathan bounds requires that Tallarini set the risk-aversion parameter γ to such a high value that it provoked the skeptical remarks in the quotation from Lucas (2003).

Table 14.4.1: Estimates from quarterly U.S. data 1948:2-2005:4.

Parameter	Random Walk	Trend Stationary
μ	0.004952	0.004947
σ_ε	0.005050	0.005058
ρ	-	0.99747

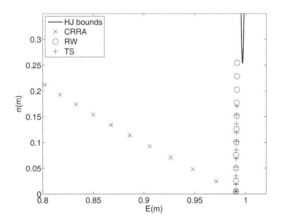

Figure 14.4.1: Solid line: Hansen-Jagannathan volatility bounds for quarterly returns on the value-weighted NYSE and Treasury bill, 1948–2005. Circles: Mean and standard deviation for intertemporal marginal rate of substitution generated by Epstein-Zin preferences with random walk consumption. Pluses: Mean and standard deviation for stochastic discount factor generated by Epstein-Zin preferences with trend stationary consumption. Crosses: Mean and standard deviation for intertemporal marginal rate of substitution for CRRA time separable preferences. The coefficient of relative risk aversion γ takes on the values 1, 5, 10, 15, 20, 25, 30, 35, 40, 45, 50 and the discount factor $\beta = 0.995$.

14.5. Reinterpretation of the utility recursion

To confront Lucas's reluctance to use Tallarini's findings as a source of evidence about the representative consumer's attitude about consumption fluctuations, in the remainder of this chapter, we reinterpret γ as a parameter that expresses model specification doubts rather than risk aversion.

14.5.1. Using martingales to represent probability distortions

We use the framework of chapter 3 to represent sets of perturbations to an approximating model. Let the agent's information set be $\mathcal{X}_t$, which in our context will be the history of log consumption growth rates up to date t. Hansen and Sargent (2005b) and chapters 3 and 7 use a nonnegative $\mathcal{X}_t$-measurable function G_t with $EG_t = 1$ to create a distorted probability measure that is absolutely continuous with respect to the probability measure over $\mathcal{X}_t$ generated by our approximating model for log consumption growth.[9] The random variable G_t is a martingale under this probability measure. Using G_t as a Radon-Nikodym derivative generates a distorted measure under which the expectation of a bounded $\mathcal{X}_t$-measurable random variable W_t is $\tilde{E}W_t \equiv EG_tW_t$. The *entropy* of the distortion at time t conditioned on date zero information is $E\left(G_t \log G_t | \mathcal{X}_0\right)$.

14.5.2. Recursive representations of distortions

Following Hansen and Sargent (2005b), recall how we often factor a joint density F_{t+1} for an $\mathcal{X}_{t+1}$-measurable random vector as $F_{t+1} = f_{t+1}F_t$, where f_{t+1} is a one-step-ahead density conditioned on $\mathcal{X}_t$. It is also useful to factor G_t. Thus, take a nonnegative martingale $\{G_t : t \geq 0\}$ and form

$$
g_{t+1} = \begin{cases} \frac{G_{t+1}}{G_t} & \text{if } G_t > 0 \\ 1 & \text{if } G_t = 0. \end{cases}
$$

Then $G_{t+1} = g_{t+1}G_t$ and

$$
G_t = G_0 \prod_{j=1}^{t} g_j. \tag{14.5.1}
$$

The random variable G_0 has unconditional expectation equal to unity. By construction, g_{t+1} has date t conditional expectation equal to unity. For a bounded random variable W_{t+1} that is $\mathcal{X}_{t+1}$-measurable, the distorted conditional expectation implied by the martingale $\{G_t : t \geq 0\}$ is

$$
\frac{E(G_{t+1}W_{t+1}|\mathcal{X}_t)}{E(G_{t+1}|\mathcal{X}_t)} = \frac{E(G_{t+1}W_{t+1}|\mathcal{X}_t)}{G_t} = E\left(g_{t+1}W_{t+1}|\mathcal{X}_t\right)
$$

provided that $G_t > 0$. We use g_{t+1} to represent distortions of the conditional probability distribution for $\mathcal{X}_{t+1}$ given $\mathcal{X}_t$. For each $t \geq 0$, construct the space $\mathcal{G}_{t+1}$ of all nonnegative, $\mathcal{X}_{t+1}$-measurable random variables g_{t+1} for which $E(g_{t+1}|\mathcal{X}_t) = 1$. In the next subsection, we shall use the nonnegative

---

[9] See Hansen, Sargent, Turnuhambetova, and Williams (2006) for a corresponding continuous time formulation.

random variable g statistically to perturb the one-step ahead conditional distribution of consumption growth that is associated with the representative consumer's approximating model.

14.5.3. Ambiguity averse multiplier preferences

In the spirit of chapter 7, an agent is said to have *multiplier preferences* if his preference ordering over $c \in \mathcal{C}$ is described by [10]

$$W(x_0) = \min_{\{g_{t+1}\}} \sum_{t=0}^{\infty} E\left\{\beta^t G_t \left[c_t + \beta\theta E(g_{t+1}\log g_{t+1}|\varepsilon^t, x_0)\right]\Big|x_0\right\} \quad (14.5.2)$$

subject to

$$x_{t+1} = Ax_t + B\varepsilon_{t+1}$$

$$c_t = Hx_t, \quad x_0 \text{ given} \quad (14.5.3)$$

$$G_{t+1} = g_{t+1}G_t, \quad E[g_{t+1}|\varepsilon^t, x_0] = 1, g_{t+1} \geq 0, G_0 = 1.$$

The value function associated with these preferences solves the following Bellman equation:

$$GW(x) = \min_{g(\varepsilon)\geq 0} G\left(c + \beta \int \Big(g(\varepsilon)W(Ax + B\varepsilon) + \theta g(\varepsilon)\log g(\varepsilon)\Big)\pi(\varepsilon)d\varepsilon\right).$$

Dividing by G gives

$$W(x) = c + \min_{g(\varepsilon)\geq 0} \left(\beta \int \Big(g(\varepsilon)W(Ax + B\varepsilon) + \theta g(\varepsilon)\log g(\varepsilon)\Big)\pi(\varepsilon)d\varepsilon\right)$$

where the minimization is subject to $Eg = 1$. Substituting the minimizer into the above equation once again gives the risk-sensitive recursion of Hansen and Sargent (1995):

$$W(x) = c - \beta\theta \log E \exp\left(\frac{-W(Ax + B\varepsilon)}{\theta}\right). \quad (14.5.4)$$

The minimizing martingale increment is

$$\hat{g}_{t+1} = \left(\frac{\exp\left(-W(Ax_t + B\varepsilon_{t+1})/\theta\right)}{E_t\left[\exp\left(-W(Ax_t + B\varepsilon_{t+1})/\theta\right)\right]}\right). \quad (14.5.5)$$

While (14.5.4) is identical with (14.3.4), the interpretation of the parameter θ is different. In (14.5.4), θ is a penalty parameter attached to entropy and it measures the size of the set of models about which the decision maker is ambiguous. In (14.3.4), θ is interpreted as a measure of risk aversion.

---

[10] Hansen and Sargent (2001) and Hansen, Sargent, Turnuhambetova, and Williams (2006) describe multiplier preferences and how they are related to constraint preferences that can be viewed as a version of Gilboa and Schmeidler's multiple priors model.

14.5.4. Observational equivalence? Yes and no

The identity of recursions (14.5.4) and (14.3.4) means that so far as choices among consumption plans indexed by A, B, H are concerned, the risk-sensitive representative consumer of Tallarini (2000) is observationally equivalent to our representative consumer who is concerned about model misspecification. But the motivations behind their choices differ and that would allow us to distinguish them if we were able to confront them with choices between gambles with known distributions and gambles with unknown distributions.

Thus, while Tallarini interprets γ or θ as a parameter measuring aversion to atemporal gambles, under robustness γ or θ measures the consumer's concern about model misspecification. The quote from Lucas (2003) and the reasoning of Cochrane (1997), who applied the ideas of Pratt (1964), explain why economists think that only small positive values of γ are plausible when it is interpreted as a risk-aversion parameter. Pratt's experiments confront a decision maker with choices between gambles with *known* probability distributions. How should we think about plausible values of γ (or θ) when it is instead interpreted as encoding responses to gambles that involve *unknown* probability distributions? Our answer will be based on the detection error probabilities introduced in chapter 9. They lead us to argue that it is not appropriate to regard γ or θ as a parameter that remains fixed when we vary the stochastic process for consumption under the consumer's approximating model. As a step in completing that argument, in the next subsection, we describe the worst-case densities $\hat{\pi}$ of ε_t that emerge under the random walk and trend stationary consumption models.

14.5.5. Worst-case random walk and trend stationary models

In appendix A, we show that the worst-case density for the innovation ε under the random walk model is

$$\hat{\pi}\left(\varepsilon_{t+1}\right) \propto \exp\left(\frac{-\left(\varepsilon_{t+1} + \frac{\sigma_\varepsilon \varepsilon_{t+1}}{(1-\beta)\theta}\right)^2}{2}\right),$$

while under the trend stationary model it is

$$\hat{\pi}\left(\varepsilon_{t+1}\right) \propto \exp\left(\frac{-\left(\varepsilon_{t+1} + \frac{\sigma_\varepsilon \varepsilon_{t+1}}{(1-\rho\beta)\theta}\right)^2}{2}\right).$$

Thus, the worst-case distributions shift the mean of ε_{t+1} from 0 to $w_{t+1} = -\frac{\sigma_\varepsilon}{(1-\beta)\theta}$ under the random walk model and to $w_{t+1} = -\frac{\sigma_\varepsilon}{(1-\rho\beta)\theta}$ under the trend stationary model. Note that the worst-case models do not perturb the variances of ϵ_{t+1}, a consequence of the fact that the value functions are linear under Tallarini's log preference specification.

14.5.6. Market prices of risk and model uncertainty

Hansen, Sargent, and Tallarini (1999) and Hansen, Sargent, and Wang (2002) note that the conditional standard deviation of the Radon-Nikodym derivative $g(\epsilon)$ is

$$\mathrm{std}_t(g) = [\exp(w'_{t+1}w_{t+1}) - 1]^{\frac{1}{2}} \approx |w_{t+1}|. \tag{14.5.6}$$

By construction $E_t g = 1$. We call $\mathrm{std}_t(g)$ the market price of model uncertainty. It can be verified that for both the random walk and the trend stationary models, $|w_{t+1}|$ given by the above formulas comprises the lion's share of what Tallarini interpreted as the market price of risk given by formulas (14.4.2) and (14.4.4). This is because the first difference in the log of consumption has a small conditional coefficient of variation in our data, the heart of the equity premium puzzle. Thus, formula (14.5.6) is a good approximation to Tallarini's formulas (14.4.2) and (14.4.4).

14.6. Calibrating γ using detection error probabilities

This section uses the Bayesian detection error probabilities described in chapter 9 to calibrate a plausible value for γ or θ when it is interpreted as a parameter measuring the consumer's concern about model misspecification. Our idea is that it is plausible for agents to be concerned about models that are statistically difficult to distinguish from one another with data sets of moderate size. We implement this idea by focusing on distinguishing the approximating model (call it model A) from a worst-case model associated with a particular θ (call it model B), calculated as in section 14.5.5. Thus, as in chapter 9, we imagine that before seeing any data, the agent had assigned probability .5 to both the approximating model and the worst-case model associated with θ. After seeing T observations, the agent performs a likelihood ratio test for distinguishing model A from model B. If model A were correct, the likelihood ratio could be expected falsely to claim that model B generated the data p_A percent of the time. Similarly, if model B were correct, the likelihood ratio could be expected falsely to claim that model A generated the data p_B percent of the time. We weight these detection error probabilities p_A, p_B by the prior probabilities .5 to obtain what we call the overall detection error probability:

$$p(\gamma) = \frac{1}{2}(p_A + p_B). \tag{14.6.1}$$

It is a function of γ (or θ) because the worst-case model depends on γ. When $\gamma = 1$ ((or $\theta = +\infty$); see equation (14.3.2)), it is easy to see that $p(\gamma) = .5$ because then the two models are equivalent. As we raise γ above one (i.e., lower θ below $+\infty$), $p(\gamma)$ falls below .5. Introspection instructs us about plausible values of $p(\gamma)$ as a measure of concern about model misspecification. Thus, we think it is sensible for a decision maker to want to guard against possible misspecifications whose detection error probabilities are .2 or more.

As a function of γ, $p(\gamma)$ will change as we vary the specification of the approximating model, in particular, when we switch from the trend stationary to the random walk model of log consumption. When comparing outcomes across different approximating models, we advocate comparing outcomes for the *same* detection error probabilities $p(\gamma)$ and adjusting the γ's appropriately across models. We shall do that for our version of Tallarini's model and will recast his figure 14.4.1 in terms of loci that record $E(m), \sigma(m)/E(m)$ pairs as we vary the detection error probability.

14.6.1. Recasting Tallarini's graph

Figure 14.6.1 describes the detection probability $p(\gamma)$ for the random walk (dashed line) and trend stationary (solid line) models. We simulated the approximating and the worst-case models 500,000 times and followed the procedure outlined in section 14.5.5 to compute the detection error probabilities for a given γ. The simulations were done for $T = 231$ periods, which is the sample size of available consumption data.

Figure 14.6.1 reveals that for the random walk and the trend stationary models, a given detection error probability $p(\gamma)$ is associated with different values of γ. Therefore, if we want to compute $E(m), \sigma(m)/E(m)$ pairs for the same detection error probabilities, we have to use different values of γ for our two models. We shall use figure 14.6.1 to read off these different values of γ associated with a given detection error probability, then redraw Tallarini's figure in terms of detection probabilities.

Thus, to prepare figure 14.6.2, our counterpart to figure 14.4.1, which is our updated version of Tallarini's figure, we invert the detection error probability functions $p(\gamma)$ in figure 14.6.1 to get γ as a function of $p(\gamma)$ for each model, then use this γ either in formulas (14.4.1), (14.4.2) or in formulas (14.4.3), (14.4.4) to compute the $\frac{1}{r^f}$, market price of risk pairs to plot à la Tallarini. We present the results in figure 14.6.2.

We invite the reader to compare our figure 14.6.2 with figure 14.4.1. The calculations summarized in figure 14.4.1 taught Tallarini that with the random walk model for log consumption, the $\frac{1}{r^f}$, market price of risk pairs approach the Hansen and Jagannathan bound when γ is around 50, whereas

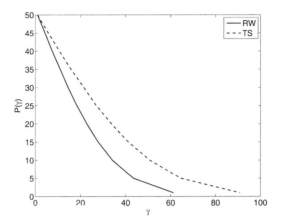

Figure 14.6.1: Detection probabilities versus γ for the random walk (dashed line) and trend stationary (solid line) models.

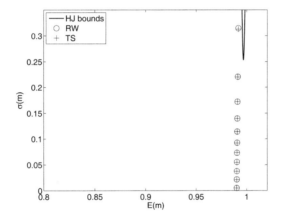

Figure 14.6.2: Reciprocal of risk-free rate, market price of risk pairs for the random walk ($\circ$) and trend stationary ($+$) models for values of $p(\gamma)$ of 50, 45, 40, 35, 30, 25, 20, 15, 10, 5 and 1 percent.

under the trend stationary model we need γ to be 250 in order to approach the bound. Figure 14.6.2 simply restates those results by using the detection error probabilities $p(\gamma)$ that we computed in figure 14.6.1 to trace out loci of $\frac{1}{r^f}$, market price of risk pairs as we vary the detection error probability.

Figure 14.6.2 reveals the striking pattern that varying the detection error probabilities traces out nearly the same loci for the random walk and the trend stationary models of consumption. This outcome faithfully reflects a pattern that holds exactly for large deviation bounds on the detection error probabilities that were studied by Anderson, Hansen, and Sargent (2003), who showed a tight link between those bounds and the market price of model uncertainty that transcends details of the stochastic specification for the representative consumer's approximating model.

In terms of the issue raised by Lucas (2003), figure 14.6.2 reveals that regardless of the stochastic specification for consumption, plausible detection error probabilities in the vicinity of .15 or .2 take us half of the way toward the Hansen and Jagannathan bounds. Figure 14.6.2 alters our sense of what plausible settings of γ are and warns us not to keep γ constant when moving across different specifications for the representative consumer's approximating model. Regardless of the details of the specification of the approximating model, we come close to attaining the Hansen and Jagannathan bounds with a detection error probability of 5 percent. A representative consumer who sets a detection error probability of 5 percent might seem a little timid, but not as timid as one who sets a CRRA coefficient as high as 50 or 250.

14.7. Concluding remarks

Tallarini (2000) calibrated a risk-aversion parameter γ high enough to move $E(m)$ and $\sigma(m)/E(m)$ close to values that approach the Hansen-Jagannathan bounds. Then he used γ to reevaluate the costs of business cycles in the way that Lucas (2003) did. Tallarini found that γ's that approach the Hansen-Jagannathan bounds imply much higher costs of business cycles than Lucas had computed. Tallarini's finding helped prompt the epigraph by Lucas cited at the beginning of this chapter.

Barillas, Hansen, and Sargent (2007) extend the findings of this chapter to calculate how much a representative consumer would be willing to pay to eliminate amounts of model uncertainty that are associated with values of γ that nearly attain the Hansen-Jagannathan bounds. Because they eliminate model uncertainty, not risk, those calculations conduct a mental experiment that differs conceptually from the aggregate risk-elimination experiment that concerned Lucas (1987, 2003). That response to Lucas's (2003) opinion that "... we need to look beyond high estimates of risk aversion [to explain the equity premium]" severs the link between asset prices and measures of the welfare costs of business cycles advocated by Alvarez and Jermann (2004).

A. Value function and worst-case process

14.A.1. The value function

We begin with the random-walk-with-drift consumption process. We want to solve

$$U(c_t) = c_t - \beta\theta \log E_t\left[\exp\left(\frac{-U(c_{t+1})}{\theta}\right)\right]$$

$$c_{t+1} = c_t + \left(\mu - \frac{1}{2}\sigma_\varepsilon^2\right) + \varepsilon_{t+1}$$

for a value function $U(c_t)$. We guess that $U(c_t) = A + Bc_t$. Then

$$U(c_t) = c_t - \beta\theta \log E_t\left[\exp\left(\frac{-\left(A + B\left(c_t + \mu - \frac{1}{2}\sigma_\varepsilon^2\right)\right)}{\theta}\right)\exp\left(\frac{-B\varepsilon_{t+1}}{\theta}\right)\right]$$

which simplifies to

$$U(c_t) = c_t + \beta\left(A + B\left(c_t + \mu - \frac{1}{2}\sigma_\varepsilon^2\right)\right) - \beta\theta \log E_t\left[\exp\left(\frac{-B\varepsilon_{t+1}}{\theta}\right)\right].$$

Recall that if $\log x \sim N\left(\mu, \sigma^2\right)$, then $\log E(x) = \mu + \sigma^2/2$. Using this fact we get that

$$U(c_t) = c_t + \beta A + \beta B\left(c_t + \mu - \frac{1}{2}\sigma_\varepsilon^2\right) - \beta\theta\frac{B^2\sigma_\varepsilon^2}{2\theta^2},$$

so that now we can match coefficients in

$$A + Bc_t = c_t + \beta\left[A + Bc_t + B\mu - B\frac{\sigma_\varepsilon^2}{2}\left(1 + \frac{B}{\theta}\right)\right].$$

This implies

$$B = \frac{1}{1-\beta}$$

$$A = \frac{\beta}{1-\beta}\left[\frac{\mu}{1-\beta} - \frac{\sigma_\varepsilon^2}{2(1-\beta)}\left(1 + \frac{1}{(1-\beta)\theta}\right)\right].$$

Now recall that $\gamma = 1 + \frac{1}{(1-\beta)\theta}$ and so

$$A = \frac{\beta}{(1-\beta)^2}\left[\mu - \frac{\sigma_\varepsilon^2}{2}\gamma\right].$$

Therefore, we have found that the value function is

$$U(c_t) = \frac{\beta}{(1-\beta)^2}\left[\mu - \frac{\sigma_\varepsilon^2}{2}\gamma\right] + \frac{1}{1-\beta}c_t.$$

14.A.2. The distortion

Now that we have the value function, we can compute the distortion g_{t+1} for the random walk model:

$$g_{t+1} = \frac{\exp\left(\frac{-U(c_{t+1})}{\theta}\right)}{E_t\left[\exp\left(\frac{-U(c_{t+1})}{\theta}\right)\right]}.$$

The denominator of this expression is

$$E_t\left[\exp\left(\frac{-U\left(c_{t+1}\right)}{\theta}\right)\right]$$

$$= E_t\left[\exp\left(\frac{-\left(A + B\left(c_{t+1} + \mu - \frac{1}{2}\sigma_\varepsilon^2\right)\right)}{\theta}\right)\exp\left(\frac{-B\varepsilon_{t+1}}{\theta}\right)\right]$$

$$= \exp\left(D\right)\exp\left(\frac{B^2\sigma_\varepsilon^2}{2}\theta^2\right).$$

Similarly, the numerator is simply

$$\exp\left(\frac{-U\left(c_{t+1}^*\right)}{\theta}\right) = \exp\left(D\right)\exp\left(\frac{-B\varepsilon_{t+1}}{\theta}\right)$$

and therefore

$$g_{t+1} = \frac{\exp\left(\frac{-U\left(c_{t+1}^*\right)}{\theta}\right)}{E_t\left[\exp\left(\frac{-U\left(c_{t+1}^*\right)}{\theta}\right)\right]} = \frac{\exp\left(\frac{-B\varepsilon_{t+1}}{\theta}\right)}{\exp\left(\frac{B^2\sigma_\varepsilon^2}{2\theta^2}\right)} \propto \exp\left(\frac{-\sigma_\varepsilon\varepsilon_{t+1}}{(1-\beta)\theta}\right).$$

To get the distorted distribution, we need to multiply by the density of the approximating model, which is

$$\pi\left(\varepsilon_{t+1}\right) \sim \mathcal{N}\left(0,1\right) \propto \exp\left(\frac{-\varepsilon_{t+1}^2}{2}\right)$$

and so the distorted distribution is

$$\hat{\pi}\left(\varepsilon_{t+1}\right) \propto \exp\left(\frac{-\varepsilon_{t+1}^2}{2}\right)\exp\left(\frac{-\sigma_\varepsilon\varepsilon_{t+1}}{(1-\beta)\theta}\right).$$

Completing the square, we get

$$\hat{\pi}\left(\varepsilon_{t+1}\right) \propto \exp\left(\frac{-\left(\varepsilon_{t+1} + \frac{\sigma_\varepsilon\varepsilon_{t+1}}{(1-\beta)\theta}\right)^2}{2}\right),$$

which is

$$\mathcal{N}\left(\frac{-\sigma_\varepsilon}{(1-\beta)\theta},1\right). \tag{14.A.1}$$

14.A.3. An alternative computation

Here is an easier way to compute the distorted distribution. Note that

$$g_{t+1} = \frac{\exp\left(v\varepsilon_{t+1}\right)}{\exp\left(\frac{1}{2}v^2\right)}$$

$$v = \frac{-\sigma_\varepsilon}{\left(1 - \beta\right)\theta}.$$

Now compute conditional entropy

$$E_t g_{t+1} \log g_{+1} = E_t \left[\frac{\exp\left(v\varepsilon_{t+1}\right)}{\exp\left(\frac{1}{2}v^2\right)} \left(v\varepsilon_{t+1} - \frac{1}{2}v^2\right)\right].$$

We know that the effect of multiplying a random variable by g_{t+1} is to distort the distribution $N\left(0, 1\right)$ to $N\left(v, 1\right)$. So this results in

$$\tilde{E}_t \left(v\varepsilon_{t+1} - \frac{1}{2}v^2\right) = v^2 - \frac{v^2}{2} = \frac{v^2}{2},$$

and so we have that

$$E_t g_{t+1} \log g_{+1} = \frac{v^2}{2},$$

which leads us to pose the problem in the equivalent way

$$\min_{\{w_{t+1}\}} E_0 \sum_{t=0}^{\infty} \beta^t \left\{c_t + \beta\theta \frac{w'_{t+1} w_{t+1}}{2}\right\}$$

$$s.t. \quad c_{t+1} = c_t + \mu - \frac{1}{2}\sigma_\varepsilon^2 + \sigma_\varepsilon \left(\varepsilon_{t+1} + w_{t+1}\right).$$

The Lagrangian of this problem is

$$L = \beta^t \left\{c_t + \beta\theta \frac{w'_{t+1} w_{t+1}}{2} + \lambda_t \left(c_t + \mu - \frac{1}{2}\sigma_\varepsilon^2 + \sigma_\varepsilon \left(\varepsilon_{t+1} + w_{t+1}\right) - c_{t+1}\right)\right\}$$

and the first-order conditions are

$$w_{t+1} : \beta\theta w_{t+1} + \lambda_t \sigma_\varepsilon = 0$$
$$c_t : 1 + \lambda_t - \beta^{-1}\lambda_{t-1} = 0.$$

Therefore, $\lambda = \beta/\left(1 - \beta\right)$ and $w_{t+1} = \frac{-\sigma_\varepsilon}{(1-\beta)\theta}$.

14.A.4. The trend stationary model

We also computed the distortion for the trend stationary model, which is

$$w_{t+1}^{TS} = \frac{-\sigma_\varepsilon}{\left(1 - \rho\beta\right)\theta}. \tag{14.A.2}$$

Chapter 15
Markov perfect equilibria with robustness

The Fed presents what they think is the most likely outlook for the economy, while the bond market prices in the risk of a different result. There is no difference of opinion between the Fed and the bond market, they just operate from different perspectives.
— *Dominic Konstam, head of interest rate strategy at Credit Suisse, Financial Times, March 31, 2007*

15.1. Introduction

This chapter and the next describe equilibria in which several decision makers share an approximating model and at least one of them is concerned about model misspecification. We impute a common approximating model to the agents because we want to preserve as much as possible of the structure and empirical power of rational expectations. When they have different objective functions, the context-specific worst-case models of different decision makers will differ. We thus have a highly structured way of modeling what *ex post* seem to be heterogeneous beliefs, a point we discuss further in subsection 15.2.3.

In the present chapter, we study dynamic games between two players, each of whom distrusts a common approximating model. Each of these two players himself uses an "internal" two-player zero-sum game to construct a robust decision rule. There are thus *two* two-player zero-sum games *inside* the original dynamic game.[1] We adapt the concept of Markov perfect equilibrium to incorporate concerns about robustness to model misspecification. Here the timing protocol is that both players choose sequentially. In chapter 16, we study another timing protocol in which a Stackelberg leader chooses once and for all at time 0, while Stackelberg followers choose sequentially.[2]

15.2. Markov perfect equilibria with robustness

The decisions of two agents affect the motion of a state vector that impinges on the return functions of both agents. Without concerns about robustness, a Markov perfect equilibrium can be computed by working backwards on pairs of

---

[1] The two zero-sum two-player games describe a civil war that rages within the soul of each player in the original game.

[2] See Rigotti and Shannon (2005) and Strzalecki (2007) for formulations of multi-agent models that characterize restrictions on preferences that lead to trade.

Bellman functions and some equations that express decision rules as functions of continuation value functions.[3] We shall show how similar procedures apply when we impute concerns about robustness to both decision makers. For each agent, the approximating model incorporates the robust decision rule used by the other agent.

The model is

$$x_{t+1} = Ax_t + B_1 u_{1t} + B_2 u_{2t} + C\epsilon_{t+1} \qquad (15.2.1)$$

where u_{it} is a control vector chosen by agent i as a function of the state x_t, and ϵ_{t+1} is an i.i.d. Gaussian random vector with mean zero and identity covariance matrix. Agent i acknowledges model misspecification by thinking that the actual data generating mechanism comes from a set of perturbations to $(15.2.1)$ of the form

$$x_{it+1} = Ax_t + B_1 u_{1t} + B_2 u_{2t} + C(\epsilon_{t+1} + w_{it+1}) \qquad (15.2.2)$$

where w_{it+1} represents misspecified dynamic components that depend on the history of x_s up to time t. We shall soon explain why x_{it+1} is on the left side while x_t is on the right side. Agent i wants to maximize

$$E_0 \sum_{t=0}^{\infty} \beta^t r_i(x_t, u_{it}) \qquad (15.2.3)$$

where $\beta \in (0,1)$ and $r_i(x_t, u_{it}) = -[x_t' R_i x_t + u_{it}' Q_i u_{it} + 2u_{it}' H_i x_t]$.

We will pose a pair of extremum problems that express each decision maker's doubts about (1) the transition law $(15.2.2)$, and (2) the decision rule that is used by the other player. We appeal to the version of certainty equivalence cited on page 33 to allow us to drop the ϵ_{t+1} term from $(15.2.2)$ and the conditional expectation E from $(15.2.3)$ and proceed to solve nonstochastic versions of both players' extremum problems.

We define a Nash equilibrium with robust decision makers and a common approximating model. In equilibrium, player i selects a robust decision rule of the form

$$u_{it} = -F_{it} x_t. \qquad (15.2.4)$$

Though in the limit we will seek a time-invariant rule F_i, to accommodate backward induction we begin by allowing time-varying rules. The set of laws of motion confronting agent i has the form

$$x_{it+1} = (A - B_{-i} F_{-it})x_t + B_i u_{it} + C w_{it+1} \qquad (15.2.5)$$

---

[3] See Ljungqvist and Sargent (2004, chapter 7).

where x_{it+1} is the value of x_{t+1} forecast by player i under the w_{it+1}-distortion and a subscript $-i$ refers to the other player. Notice that (15.2.5) incorporates the robust rule F_{-it} of the other player and that each player has his own distortion process w_{it+1}. Player i solves a multiplier robust control problem with multiplier θ_i.

15.2.1. Explanation of x_{it+1}, x_t notation

Notice that (15.2.5) has an x_t on the right side that is common to both players $i = 1, 2$, but values of x_{t+1} that are specific to player i on the left side. Writing the laws of motion under the distorted models for players $i = 1, 2$ in this way accommodates two features of the problem: (1) because the state x_t is observed by both players at time t, they agree on x_t; (2) because their perturbed models of the transition dynamics differ when $w_{1t+1} \neq w_{2t+1}$, at time t the two players' forecasts of x_{t+1} differ. Please notice how we build this feature into the Bellman equation (15.2.6)-(15.2.7).

Definition 15.2.1. A *Markov perfect equilibrium with concerns about robustness* consists of pairs of value functions $V_i(x)$, decision rules $u_i = -F_i x_i$, and rules for worst-case shocks $w_i^* = K_i x_i$ such that the decision rules for u_i, w_i^* attain $V_i(x)$ and the value functions V_i satisfy the Bellman equations

$$V_i(x) = \max_{u_i} \min_{w_i^*} \{r_i(x, u_i) + \beta\theta_i w_i^{*'} w_i^* + \beta V_i(x_i^*)\} \tag{15.2.6}$$

where $*$ denotes next period's value and the extremization is subject to

$$x_i^* = (A - B_{-i}F_{-i})x + B_i u_i + C w_i^*. \tag{15.2.7}$$

The value functions assume the forms

$$V_i(x) = -x' P_i x,$$

where $P_i = T_i \circ \mathcal{D}_i(P_i)$ is a fixed point defined in terms of the composition of modified versions of two familiar operators

$$\begin{aligned}
T_i(P_i) = {} & Q_i + \beta(A - B_{-i}F_{-i})' P_i (A - B_{-i}F_{-i}) \\
& - (\beta(A - B_{-i}F_{-i})' P_i B_i + H_i')(R_i + \beta B_i' P_i B_i)^{-1} \\
& \times (\beta B_i' P_i (A - B_{-i}F_{-i}) + H_i) \tag{15.2.8}
\end{aligned}$$

$$\mathcal{D}_i(P_i) = P_i + \theta_i^{-1} P_i C (I - \theta_i^{-1} C' P_i C)^{-1} C' P_i. \tag{15.2.9}$$

The T_i operator is associated with the maximization part of the problem on the right side of (15.2.6), while the $\mathcal{D}_i$ operator is associated with the minimization part.

In the next subsection, we describe a recursive algorithm for computing a Markov perfect equilibrium with concerns about robustness.

15.2.2. *Computational algorithm: iterating on stacked Bellman equations*

Define the iterations

$$F_{it} = (R_i + \beta B'_i \mathcal{D}_i(P_{it+1})B_i)^{-1}$$
$$(\beta B'_i \mathcal{D}(P_{it+1})(A - B_{-i}F_{-it}) + H) \tag{15.2.10}$$
$$P_{it} = T_i \circ \mathcal{D}_i(P_{it+1}). \tag{15.2.11}$$

We propose to use these iterations to find fixed points F_i, P_i for $i = 1, 2$ that satisfy

$$F_i = (R_i + \beta B'_i \mathcal{D}_i(P_i)B_i)^{-1}(\beta B'_i \mathcal{D}(P_i)(A - B_{-i}F_{-i}) + H) \tag{15.2.12}$$
$$P_i = T_i \circ \mathcal{D}_i(P_i). \tag{15.2.13}$$

Suppose that control vector u_i has k_i entries. Then F_i is a k_i by n matrix. Given P_{1t+1}, P_{2t+1}, equations $(15.2.10)$ for $i = 1, 2$ form $(k_1 + k_2) \times n$ linear equations in the same number of variables, namely, F_{1t}, F_{2t}. To compute an equilibrium, start with zero terminal value matrices P_{1T}, P_{2T}, solve $(15.2.10)$ for F_{1T}, F_{2T}, then iterate backwards on $(15.2.10),(15.2.11)$ until, hopefully, the F_{it}, P_{it} sequences converge. If they converge, we say that asymptotically there is a time-invariant equilibrium law of motion.[4]

When both players use time-invariant robust rules, the approximating model becomes

$$x_{t+1} = A^o x_t + C\epsilon_{t+1} \tag{15.2.14}$$

where $A^o = A - B_1 F_1 - B_2 F_2$ and where we have reactivated the Gaussian disturbance. The two agents share this approximating model but in general have different worst-case models. The worst-case model for agent i is

$$x_{t+1} = A^o x_t + C(\epsilon_{t+1} + w_{it+1})$$
$$w_{it+1} = K_i x_t$$

where

$$K_i = \theta_i^{-1}(I - \theta_i^{-1} C' P_i C)^{-1} C' P_i A^o. \tag{15.2.15}$$

Another expression for the worst-case model of player i is

$$x_{t+1} = (A^o + CK_i)x_t + C\epsilon_{t+1}. \tag{15.2.16}$$

---

[4] We do not know conditions that guarantee convergence. Notice that the algorithm produces a well-defined equilibrium for finite horizons.

15.2.3. *Bayesian interpretation and belief heterogeneity*

A version of our usual "*ex post* Bayesian interpretation" of each player's robust rule applies. After we have computed an equilibrium and know the different worst-case shocks $w_{it+1} = K_i x_t$ of the two players, each player i can be regarded as solving an ordinary control problem, using its own twisted law of motion (15.2.16) and taking as given the decision rule $u_{-i,t} = -F_{-i} x_t$ of the other player. Notice how this builds in complete knowledge about the other player's decision rule, a counterpart to a rational expectations assumption.

Thus, we have a disciplined way of generating what appear *ex post* to be heterogeneous beliefs. That Bellman equations for the two-player zero-sum game solved by each player are the sources of those heterogeneous beliefs implies cross-equation restrictions that are very similar to those that come from rational expectations models (e.g., see Hansen and Sargent (1980, 1981)).

15.2.4. *Heterogeneous worst-case beliefs*

We have seen that while the approximating model is $x_{t+1} = A^o x_t$ and time 0 conditional forecasts from the approximating model are $x^t = (A^o)^t x_0$, the worst-case model of agent i is $x_{t+1} = A_i^o x_t$, where $A_i^o = A^o + C K_i$, and time 0 conditional forecasts from these worst-case models are $x_{it} = (A_i^o)^t x_0$. Thus, player i's time 0 conditional forecasts of player $-i$'s time t actions are $u_{-i,t}^i = -F_{-i}(A_i^o)^t x_0$, which in general differ from player $-i$'s forecasts of his own actions, $u_{-i,t}^{-i} = -F_{-i}(A_{-i}^o)^t x_0$.

As a function of the current state, these worst case models give beliefs about next period's state that support each agent's robust control. We allow these worst-case beliefs to differ even though next period's state will in fact be the same for each player. In our recursive representation, the beliefs of the two players have the same structure at each calendar date. We have not constructed another possible representation that implements an *ex-post* Bayesian Markov perfect equilibrium, nor have we even shown that such an equilibrium exists. As in the homogeneous agent problem, such a construction would require that we eliminate the endogenous states from the implied evolution of the exogenous shocks via yet another application of the macroeconomist's Big K, little k trick.

15.3. Concluding remarks

We have proposed an equilibrium concept in which all participants in a dynamic game share a common approximating model but are concerned that it is misspecified. Their disparate motives imply that their worst-case beliefs come from twisting the approximating model in different ways. We have shown how this kind of equilibrium can be computed by adapting existing methods for computing Markov perfect equilibria without concerns about robustness. In the next chapter, we apply a similar equilibrium concept to a setting with a timing protocol that requires one agent to commit and the other agents to choose sequentially.

Chapter 16
Robustness in forward-looking models

The whole problem with the world is that fools and fanatics are always so certain of themselves, but wiser people so full of doubts.
— *Bertrand Russell*

16.1. Introduction

This chapter continues the chapter 15 enterprise of studying situations in which agents who have possibly different objective functions nevertheless share a common approximating model and at least one of them wants a robust decision rule.[1] We alter the timing protocols from those in chapter 15. A "Stackelberg leader" commits to future contingency plans at time 0, while "followers" choose sequentially. To simplify the problem, we impute concerns about misspecification to the Stackelberg leader only. At time 0, the leader chooses a sequence of actions, taking into account how followers' decisions at each date will respond to their forecasts of the leader's future actions. The leader's policy instruments appear as forcing variables in the followers' Euler equations. Those Euler equations describe how followers' decisions depend on the leader's action sequence.

Without concerns about robustness, a first-order approach to solving Stackelberg problems is to use the followers' Euler equations to summarize their best responses to the leader's decisions, then to form a Lagrangian for the leader with a sequence of multipliers adhering to the followers' Euler equations. The followers' Euler equations are implementability constraints that require the leader's time t decision to confirm forecasts on which the followers had based their earlier decisions. The Lagrange multipliers on the implementability constraints encode how the leader's actions depend on the

---

[1] This chapter builds on and corrects aspects of Hansen and Sargent (2003). For recent work on related problems, see Woodford (2005) and Karantounias, Hansen, and Sargent (2007). Woodford analyzes a monetary policy problem under commitment in which the government trusts its model of the economy, the representative agents in the private sector trust their model, but the government does not trust its model of the way the private sector forms expectations. Karantounias, Hansen, and Sargent focus mostly on a problem in which the representative private agent distrusts its model while the government has complete confidence in its model. One of the ways that the government can manipulate equilibrium prices in their model is to manipulate martingale increments that distort the worst-case model of the representative private agent. Both Woodford and Karantounias, Hansen, and Sargent exploit a martingale representation of distortions of the type mentioned in chapter 3 and Hansen and Sargent (2005b, 2007a).

history of outcomes and allow a recursive representation of the leader's decision problem and decision rule. This chapter shows how to extend this method to handle situations in which the leader is concerned about model misspecification, but the followers are not. To do this, we devise an iterative algorithm for determining the volatility loading on the followers' Lagrange multipliers, something that we do not have to worry about when the Stackelberg leader is not concerned about model misspecification. In what seems to be a natural counterpart of rational expectations, we assume that the leader and followers share a common approximating model.

The computational algorithm proposed in this chapter relies on iterating over a coefficient that measures the exposure of a Lagrange multiplier to a shock. This shock exposure governs channels by which concerns about robustness influence the actions of the Stackelberg leader. For problems such as those studied in this chapter, we do not see how to apply certainty equivalent type arguments, like those used in previous chapters, that avoid simultaneously computing shock exposures and equilibrium decision rules. At this juncture, we want to point out that we have not established conditions that describe when our scheme for iterating over the shock exposure converges, nor have we proved that, when it does converge, it necessarily converges to the Stackelberg equilibrium that prevails in a corresponding stochastic environment. We only suspect that it might work. Thus, the findings in this chapter remain conjectural. We put them on the table to stimulate further thought about what we think is an interesting problem.

The remainder of this chapter is organized as follows. Section 16.2 states a problem in which a Stackelberg leader fears model misspecification. Section 16.3 describes how to solve the robust Stackelberg problem by, first, rearranging and reinterpreting some state variables and some Lagrange multipliers from the solution to a robust linear regulator problem and then using an iterative algorithm to compute the volatility loadings on those multipliers. As an example, section 16.4 describes a dynamic model of a monopolist facing a competitive fringe. Section 16.5 uses the robust Stackelberg plan to describe a recursive version of the representative firm's problem. Section 16.6 gives a numerical example. Section 16.7 concludes. Appendix A describes how the invariant subspace methods of chapter 4 can also be used to compute robust Ramsey plans. Appendix B studies the Riccati equation that solves the robust Ramsey problem. Appendix C describes the connection of our work to a Bellman equation that Marcet and Marimon (2000) used to solve problems with implementability constraints like ours.

16.1.1. Related literature

Hurwicz (1951) advocated zero-sum games when a decision maker could not specify a unique model. Brunner and Meltzer (1969) and von zur Muehlen (1982) were early advocates of using two-person zero-sum games to represent model uncertainty and to design macroeconomic rules. Stock (1999), Sargent (1999b), and Onatski and Stock (2002) have used versions of robust control theory to study robustness of purely backward-looking macroeconomic models. They focused on whether a concern for robustness would make policy rules more or less aggressive in response to shocks. Vaughan (1970), Blanchard and Khan (1980), Whiteman (1983), and Anderson and Moore (1985) were early sources on solving control problems with forward-looking private sectors.[2] Without concerns for robustness, Kydland and Prescott (1980), Hansen, Epple, and Roberds (1985), Miller and Salmon (1985a, 1985b), Backus and Driffill (1986), Sargent (1987), Currie, and Levine (1987), Pearlman, Currie, and Levine (1986), Pearlman (1992), Woodford (1999), King and Wolman (1999), and Marcet and Marimon (2000) have solved Stackelberg or Ramsey problems using Lagrangian formulations. Pearlman, Currie, and Levine (1986), Pearlman (1992) and Svensson and Woodford (2000) studied the control of forward-looking models where part of the state is unknown and must be filtered. DeJong, Ingram, and Whiteman (1996), Otrok (2001a), and others studied the Bayesian estimation of forward-looking models. They summarize the econometrician's doubts about parameter values with a prior distribution, meanwhile attributing no doubts about parameter values to the private agents in their models. Giannoni (2002) studied robustness in a forward-looking macro model. He modeled the policy maker as knowing all parameters except two, for each of which he knows only bounds. The policy maker then computes the policy rule. Kasa (2002) also studied robust policy in a forward-looking model. Onatski (2001) designed simple (not history dependent) robust policy rules for a forward-looking monetary model. Christiano and Gust (1999) studied robustness from the viewpoint of the determinacy and stability of rules under nearby parameters. They adopted a perspective of robust control theorists like Başar and Bernhard (1995) and Zhou, Doyle, and Glover (1996), who were interested in finding rules that stabilize a system under the largest possible set of departures from a reference model. Tetlow and von zur Muehlen (2004) study robustness in the context of recurrent escapes from a self-confirming equilibrium in a macro model of inflation-unemployment dynamics. Kocherlakota and Phelan (2007) study a robust mechanism design problem in which a planner distrusts the joint probability distribution

---

[2] Chapter 4 describes efficient computational algorithms for such models.

of private agents' publicly observed decisions and their wealth, which is not observed by the planner.

We follow the papers that we have just cited by attributing model uncertainty to the leader (a.k.a. the government) while assuming that the followers have no doubts about the model.[3]

16.2. The robust Stackelberg problem

A Stackelberg leader is concerned about model misspecification. In macroeconomic problems, the Stackelberg leader is often a government and the Stackelberg follower is a representative agent within a private sector. In section 16.4, we present a microeconomic application with a monopolist and a competitive fringe.

Let z_t be an $n_z \times 1$ vector of natural state variables, x_t an $n_x \times 1$ vector of endogenous variables that are free to jump at t, and U_t a vector of the leader's controls. The z_t vector is inherited from the past. The model determines the "jump variables" x_t at time t. Included in x_t are prices and quantities that adjust to clear markets at time t; x_t can instead or in addition include costate variables in the followers' optimal control problems. Let $y_t = \begin{bmatrix} z_t \\ x_t \end{bmatrix}$. Define the Stackelberg leader's one-period loss function[4]

$$r(y, U) = y'Qy + U'RU. \tag{16.2.1}$$

Where $\check{E}_0$ is the mathematical expectation with respect to the leader's perturbed model, the leader wants to maximize

$$-\check{E}_0 \sum_{t=0}^{\infty} \beta^t r(y_t, U_t). \tag{16.2.2}$$

The leader makes policy in light of a set of models indexed by a vector of specification errors W_{t+1} around its approximating model

$$\begin{bmatrix} I & 0 \\ G_{21} & G_{22} \end{bmatrix} \begin{bmatrix} z_{t+1} \\ x_{t+1} \end{bmatrix} = \begin{bmatrix} \hat{A}_{11} & \hat{A}_{12} \\ \hat{A}_{21} & \hat{A}_{22} \end{bmatrix} \begin{bmatrix} z_t \\ x_t \end{bmatrix} + \hat{B}U_t + \hat{C}(W_{t+1} + \check{\epsilon}_{t+1}), \tag{16.2.3}$$

---

[3] As mention in footnote 1, Woodford (2005) studied a setting in which a monetary authority fully trusts its own model of the economy and agents in the private sector also fully trust theirs, but in which the monetary authority does not trust its views about how the private sector forms expectations about its own future actions.

[4] The problem assumes that there are no cross-products between states and controls in the return function. A simple transformation converts a problem whose return function has cross-products into an equivalent problem that has no cross-products. See chapter 4, page 72.

where $\check{\epsilon}_{t+1}$ is an i.i.d. $\mathcal{N}(0, I)$ process under the leader's perturbed model. We assume that the matrix on the left is invertible, so that[5]

$$\begin{bmatrix} z_{t+1} \\ x_{t+1} \end{bmatrix} = \begin{bmatrix} A_{11} & A_{12} \\ A_{21} & A_{22} \end{bmatrix} \begin{bmatrix} z_t \\ x_t \end{bmatrix} + BU_t + C(W_{t+1} + \check{\epsilon}_{t+1}) \qquad (16.2.4)$$

or

$$y_{t+1} = Ay_t + BU_t + C(W_{t+1} + \check{\epsilon}_{t+1}). \qquad (16.2.5)$$

The followers' behavior is summarized by the second block of equations of (16.2.3) or (16.2.4). These typically include the first-order conditions of private agents' optimization problems (i.e., their Euler equations). These equations summarize the forward-looking aspects of the followers' behavior. In section 16.4, we analyze an example.

Returning to (16.2.3) or (16.2.4), we allow the vector W_{t+1} of unknown specification errors to feed back, possibly nonlinearly, on the history y^t, which lets the W_{t+1} sequence represent misspecified dynamics in the leader's approximating model. The leader regards its approximating model (which asserts that $W_{t+1} = 0$) as a *good* approximation to the unknown true model in the sense that the unknown W_{t+1} sequence satisfies

$$\check{E}_0 \sum_{t=0}^{\infty} \beta^{t+1} W_{t+1}' W_{t+1} \leq \eta \qquad (16.2.6)$$

where $\eta > 0$. As we shall see, a careful application of the certainty equivalence principle stated on page 33 allows us to work with non-stochastic approximating and distorted models.

Let X^t denote the history of X from 0 to t. Kydland and Prescott (1980), Miller and Salmon (1985a, 1985b), Hansen, Epple, and Roberds (1985), Pearlman, Currie, and Levine (1986), Sargent (1987), Pearlman (1992), and others have studied non-robust (i.e., $\eta = 0$) versions of the following problem

Definition 16.2.1. For $\eta > 0$, the *constraint version of the Stackelberg or Ramsey problem* is to extremize (16.2.2) subject to (16.2.3) or (16.2.5) by finding a sequence of decision rules expressing U_t and W_{t+1} as sequences of functions mapping the time t history of the state z^t into the time t decision. The leader chooses these decision rules at time 0 and commits to them forever.

Definition 16.2.2. When $\eta > 0$, a sequence of decision rules for U_t that solves the Stackelberg problem is called a robust *Stackelberg plan* or robust *Ramsey plan*.

---

[5] We have assumed that the matrix on the left of (16.2.3) is invertible for ease of presentation. However, by appropriately using the invariant subspace methods described in chapter 4 and appendix A, it is straightforward to adapt the computational method when this assumption is violated.

Note that the decision rules are designed to depend on $z_t, z_{t-1}, \ldots, z_0$. For a non-robust version of the problem, the aforementioned authors show that the optimal rule is history-dependent, which in our context means that U_t, W_{t+1} depend not only on z_t but also on its lags. The sources of history dependence are (1) the leader's ability to commit to a sequence of state-contingent actions at time 0,[6] and (2) the forward-looking behavior of the followers that is embedded in the second block of equations in (16.2.3) or (16.2.4).

Fortunately, there is a recursive way of expressing this history dependence by having decisions U_t, W_{t+1} depend linearly on the current value z_t and on μ_{xt}, a vector of Lagrange multipliers on the last n_x equations of (16.2.3) or (16.2.4), i.e., the implementability conditions. A solution of the problem in Definition 16.2.2 implies a law of motion that expresses μ_{xt+1} as an *exact* linear function of (z_t, μ_{xt}), i.e., one containing no additive random term. We will exploit this property of the equilibrium dynamics for μ_{xt+1}, especially in section 16.4.8. The dynamics of μ_{xt} help capture the history dependence of the leader's plan. These multipliers track the current cost to the leader of confirming the private sector's past expectations about current and future settings of U. If at time 0 there are no past expectations to confirm, it is appropriate for the leader to initialize the multipliers to zero because this maximizes the leader's criterion function. The multipliers take nonzero values thereafter, reflecting subsequent costs to the leader of adhering to its time 0 plans.

16.2.1. Multiplier version of the robust Stackelberg problem

In chapters 7 and 8, we showed that it is usually more convenient to solve a multiplier game than a constraint game. Accordingly, we use

Definition 16.2.3. The *multiplier version of the robust Stackelberg problem* is the two-player zero-sum game

$$\max_{\{U_t\}_{t=0}^{\infty}} \min_{\{W_{t+1}\}_{t=0}^{\infty}} -\sum_{t=0}^{\infty} \beta^t \left\{ r(y_t, U_t) - \beta \Theta W'_{t+1} W_{t+1} \right\} \tag{16.2.7}$$

where the extremization is subject to (16.2.5) and $\underline{\Theta} < \Theta < \infty$.

---

[6] The leader would make different choices if he were to choose sequentially, that is, if he were to set U_t at time t rather than at time 0.

16.3. Solving the robust Stackelberg problem

This section describes a three-step algorithm for solving a multiplier version of a robust Stackelberg problem.

16.3.1. Step 1: Solve a robust linear regulator

Step 1 temporarily disregards the forward-looking aspect of the problem (step 3 will take account of that) and notes that the multiplier version of the robust Stackelberg problem (16.2.7), (16.2.5) has the form of a robust linear regulator problem. Mechanically, we can solve this artificial robust linear regulator by noting that associated with problem (16.2.7) is the Bellman equation[7]

$$v(y) = \max_{u} \min_{W} \left\{ -r(y, u) + \beta \Theta W' W + \beta v(y^*) \right\}, \tag{16.3.1}$$

where y^* denotes next period's value of the state and the extremization is subject to the transition law $y^* = Ay + Bu + CW$. The value function that satisfies (16.3.1) has the form $v(y) = -y'Py$, where P is a fixed point of the operator $T \circ \mathcal{D}$ defined in chapters 2 and 7, namely,

$$T(P) = Q + \beta A'PA - \beta^2 A'PB(R + \beta B'PB)^{-1}B'PA \tag{16.3.2}$$

$$\mathcal{D}(P) = P + \Theta^{-1}PC(I - \Theta^{-1}C'PC)^{-1}C'P. \tag{16.3.3}$$

Thus, the Bellman equation (16.3.1) leads to the Riccati equation

$$P = T \circ \mathcal{D}(P). \tag{16.3.4}$$

The T operator emerges from maximization over U on the right side of (16.3.1), while the $\mathcal{D}$ operator emerges from minimization over W. The extremizing decision rules are given by $U_t = -Fy_t$, where

$$F = \beta(R + \beta B'\mathcal{D}(P)B)^{-1}B'\mathcal{D}(P)A \tag{16.3.5}$$

and $W_{t+1} = Ky_t$, where

$$K = \Theta^{-1}(I - \Theta^{-1}C'PC)^{-1}C'P(A - BF). \tag{16.3.6}$$

(See page 35.) All of the information that we need to solve the robust Stackelberg problem is encoded in the triple (P, F, K), where $P = T \circ \mathcal{D}(P)$.

---

[7] By following the approaches of Kydland and Prescott (1980) and Marcet and Marimon (2000), appendix C describes a closely related Bellman equation that can be used to compute a robust Ramsey plan.

16.3.2. Step 2: Use the stabilizing properties of shadow price Py_t

We use P to describe how shadow prices on the transition law relate to the artificial state vector $y_t = [z'_t \quad x'_t]'$. (We say "artificial" because x_t is a vector of jump variables.) The Lagrangian methods used in chapters 4 and 7 provide another way to solve the multiplier version of the robust Stackelberg problem (16.2.7), (16.2.5), namely, by forming the Lagrangian

$$\mathcal{L} = -\sum_{t=0}^{\infty} \beta^t \Big[y'_t Q y_t + U'_t R U_t + 2\beta \mu'_{t+1}(A y_t + B U_t + C W_{t+1} - y_{t+1})$$
$$- \beta \Theta W'_{t+1} W_{t+1} \Big].$$
(16.3.7)

We want to maximize (16.3.7) with respect to sequences for U_t and y_t and minimize it with respect to a sequence for W_{t+1}. The first-order conditions with respect to U_t, y_t, W_{t+1}, respectively, are

$$0 = R U_t + \beta B' \mu_{t+1} \qquad\qquad (16.3.8a)$$

$$\mu_t = Q y_t + \beta A' \mu_{t+1} \qquad\qquad (16.3.8b)$$

$$0 = \beta \Theta W_{t+1} - \beta C' \mu_{t+1}. \qquad\qquad (16.3.8c)$$

Solving (16.3.8a) and (16.3.8c) for U_t and W_{t+1} and substituting into (16.2.5) gives

$$y_{t+1} = A y_t - \beta(B R^{-1} B' - \beta^{-1} \Theta^{-1} C C') \mu_{t+1}. \qquad (16.3.9)$$

Write (16.3.9) as

$$y_{t+1} = A y_t - \beta \tilde{B} \tilde{R}^{-1} \tilde{B}' \mu_{t+1}. \qquad\qquad (16.3.10)$$

We can represent the system formed by (16.3.10) and (16.3.8b) as

$$\begin{bmatrix} I & \beta \tilde{B} \tilde{R}^{-1} \tilde{B}' \\ 0 & \beta A' \end{bmatrix} \begin{bmatrix} y_{t+1} \\ \mu_{t+1} \end{bmatrix} = \begin{bmatrix} A & 0 \\ -Q & I \end{bmatrix} \begin{bmatrix} y_t \\ \mu_t \end{bmatrix} \qquad (16.3.11)$$

or

$$L^* \begin{bmatrix} y_{t+1} \\ \mu_{t+1} \end{bmatrix} = N \begin{bmatrix} y_t \\ \mu_t \end{bmatrix}. \qquad\qquad (16.3.12)$$

We want to find a stabilizing solution of (16.3.12), i.e., one that satisfies

$$\sum_{t=0}^{\infty} \beta^t y'_t y_t < +\infty.$$

The stabilizing solution is obtained by setting $\mu_0 = P y_0$, where P solves the matrix Riccati equation $P = T \circ \mathcal{D}(P)$. The solution $\mu_0 = P y_0$ replicates itself over time in the sense that

$$\mu_t = P y_t. \qquad\qquad (16.3.13)$$

16.3.3. Step 3: Convert implementation multipliers into state variables

In a typical robust linear regulator problem, y_0 is a state vector inherited from the past; the multiplier μ_0 jumps at $t = 0$ to satisfy $\mu_0 = Py_0$. See chapter 4. But in the Stackelberg problem, pertinent components of *both* y_0 and μ_0 must adjust to satisfy $\mu_0 = Py_0$, as shown in step 2. Partition μ_t conformably with the partition of y_t into $[\,z_t'\ \ x_t'\,]'$ [8]

$$\mu_t = \begin{bmatrix} \mu_{zt} \\ \mu_{xt} \end{bmatrix}.$$

For the robust Stackelberg problem, only the first n_z elements z_t of $y_t = [\,z_t'\ \ x_t'\,]'$ are predetermined and the remaining x_t components are free. And while the first n_z elements μ_{zt} of μ_t are free to jump at t, the remaining components μ_{xt} are not. The third step completes the solution of the robust Stackelberg problem by taking account of these facts. We convert the last n_x Lagrange multipliers μ_{xt} into state variables by using the following procedure *after* we have performed the key step of computing P that solves the Riccati equation $P = T \circ \mathcal{D}(P)$.

Write the last n_x equations of (16.3.13) as

$$\mu_{xt} = P_{21}z_t + P_{22}x_t. \tag{16.3.14}$$

The vector μ_{xt} becomes part of the state at t, while x_t is free to jump at t. Therefore, solve (16.3.13) for x_t in terms of (z_t, μ_{xt})

$$x_t = -P_{22}^{-1}P_{21}z_t + P_{22}^{-1}\mu_{xt}. \tag{16.3.15}$$

Then we can write

$$y_t \equiv \begin{bmatrix} z_t \\ x_t \end{bmatrix} = \begin{bmatrix} I & 0 \\ -P_{22}^{-1}P_{21} & P_{22}^{-1} \end{bmatrix} \begin{bmatrix} z_t \\ \mu_{xt} \end{bmatrix}. \tag{16.3.16}$$

Using (16.3.16), the solutions for the control and worst-case shock are

$$\begin{bmatrix} U_t \\ W_{t+1} \end{bmatrix} = \begin{bmatrix} -F \\ K \end{bmatrix} \begin{bmatrix} I & 0 \\ -P_{22}^{-1}P_{21} & P_{22}^{-1} \end{bmatrix} \begin{bmatrix} z_t \\ \mu_{xt} \end{bmatrix}. \tag{16.3.17}$$

---

[8] This argument adapts one in Pearlman (1992). The Lagrangian associated with the robust Stackelberg problem remains (16.3.7). Then the logic of section 16.3.2 implies that the stabilizing solution must satisfy (16.3.13). It is only in how we impose (16.3.13) that the solution diverges from that for the linear regulator.

16.3.4. Law of motion under robust Ramsey plan

The law of motion for y_{t+1} under the leader's perturbed model is

$$y_{t+1} = Ay_t + BU_t + C(W_{t+1} + \check{\epsilon}_{t+1})$$

where $\check{\epsilon}_{t+1}$ is an i.i.d. $\mathcal{N}(0, I)$ process, while under the approximating model

$$y_{t+1} = Ay_t + BU_t + C\epsilon_{t+1}$$

where ϵ_{t+1} is an i.i.d. $\mathcal{N}(0, I)$ process. Thus, the approximating model asserts that $\check{\epsilon}_{t+1} + W_{t+1}$, and not $\check{\epsilon}_{t+1}$ is i.i.d. $\mathcal{N}(0, I)$. Therefore, under the approximating model, the law of motion for $\begin{bmatrix} z_t \\ \mu_{xt} \end{bmatrix}$ is

$$\begin{bmatrix} z_{t+1} \\ \mu_{xt+1} \end{bmatrix} = \mathcal{M} \begin{bmatrix} z_t \\ \mu_{xt} \end{bmatrix} + \begin{bmatrix} I & 0 \\ P_{21} & P_{22} \end{bmatrix} C\epsilon_{t+1}$$

or

$$\begin{bmatrix} z_{t+1} \\ \mu_{xt+1} \end{bmatrix} = \mathcal{M} \begin{bmatrix} z_t \\ \mu_{xt} \end{bmatrix} + C_M \epsilon_{t+1} \qquad (16.3.18)$$

where

$$\mathcal{M} = \begin{bmatrix} I & 0 \\ P_{21} & P_{22} \end{bmatrix} (A - BF) \begin{bmatrix} I & 0 \\ -P_{22}^{-1}P_{21} & P_{22}^{-1} \end{bmatrix} \qquad (16.3.19)$$

and

$$C_M = \begin{bmatrix} I & 0 \\ P_{21} & P_{22} \end{bmatrix} C. \qquad (16.3.20)$$

Recalling (16.3.15), we can express x_{t+1} as

$$x_{t+1} = \hat{\mathcal{M}} \begin{bmatrix} z_t \\ \mu_{xt} \end{bmatrix} + [\, -P_{22}^{-1}P_{21} \quad P_{22}^{-1} \,] \begin{bmatrix} I & 0 \\ P_{21} & P_{22} \end{bmatrix} C\epsilon_{t+1}$$

where $\hat{\mathcal{M}} = [\, -P_{22}^{-1}P_{21} \quad P_{22}^{-1} \,]\mathcal{M}$. Equivalently, we can write the above equation as

$$x_{t+1} = \hat{\mathcal{M}} \begin{bmatrix} z_t \\ \mu_{xt} \end{bmatrix} + C_x \epsilon_{t+1}$$

where $[\, 0 \quad I \,] C = C_x$. The matrix C_x is one of the objects to be determined in designing a robust Stackelberg plan. In the application in section 16.4, x_t will be a Lagrange multiplier describing the followers' best responses. The multiplier's exposure to shock volatility is encoded in C_x. In section 16.4.10 we describe an iterative algorithm for determining C_x.

16.4. A monopolist with a competitive fringe

As an example, this section studies an industry with a large firm that acts as a Stackelberg leader with respect to a competitive fringe. The industry produces a single nonstorable homogeneous good. One large firm called the monopolist produces Q_t and a representative firm in a competitive fringe produces q_t. We use q_t to denote the quantity chosen by the individual competitive firm and $\bar{q}_t$ to denote the equilibrium quantity. In equilibrium, $q_t = \bar{q}_t$, but in posing the optimum problem of the representative competitive firm, it is necessary to distinguish q_t from $\bar{q}_t$. The representative firm in the competitive fringe takes Q_t and $\bar{q}_t$ as exogenous and chooses sequentially. The monopolist commits to a policy at time 0, taking into account its own ability to manipulate the price sequence through its quantity choices. Subject to the competitive fringe's best response, the monopolist views itself as choosing $\bar{q}_{t+1}$ *and* Q_{t+1} for $t \geq 0$.

Costs of production are $C_t = eQ_t + .5gQ_t^2 + .5c(Q_{t+1} - Q_t)^2$ for the monopolist and $s_t = dq_t + .5hq_t^2 + .5c(q_{t+1} - q_t)^2$ for a representative competitive firm, where $d > 0, e > 0, c > 0, g > 0, h > 0$ are cost parameters.

16.4.1. The approximating and distorted models

There is a linear inverse demand curve

$$p_t = a_0 - a_1(Q_t + \bar{q}_t) + v_t, \qquad (16.4.1)$$

where a_0, a_1 are both positive and v_t is a disturbance to demand governed by

$$v_{t+1} = \rho v_t + C_\epsilon \epsilon_{t+1} \qquad (16.4.2a)$$

where $|\rho| < 1$ and

$$\epsilon_{t+1} \sim \mathcal{N}(0, 1). \qquad (16.4.2b)$$

The monopolist and the competitive firm share specification $(16.4.2)$ as their approximating model for the demand shock. The representative competitive firm fully trusts this model but the monopolist does not. The monopolist wants a decision rule that is robust to alternative specifications of the process for the demand shock. The monopolist considers the class of perturbations

$$v_{t+1} = \rho v_t + C_\epsilon(\check{\epsilon}_{t+1} + W_{t+1}) \qquad (16.4.3a)$$

$$\check{\epsilon}_{t+1} \sim \mathcal{N}(0, 1). \qquad (16.4.3b)$$

Evidently, the approximating model asserts that

$$\epsilon_{t+1} = \check{\epsilon}_{t+1} + W_{t+1} \qquad (16.4.4)$$

is distributed i.i.d. $\mathcal{N}(0,1)$. We let E_t and $\breve{E}_t$ denote expectations under the approximating model and the monopolist's perturbed model, respectively.

Here W_{t+1} represents the specification errors feared by the monopolist. The distortion W_{t+1} can feed back on the history of the state of the market, namely, $(\bar{q}, Q, v)$.

16.4.2. The problem of a firm in the competitive fringe

The representative competitive firm regards $\{Q_t, \bar{q}_t\}_{t=0}^{\infty}$ as given stochastic processes and chooses an output plan $\{q_{t+1}\}_{t=0}^{\infty}$ to maximize

$$E_0 \sum_{t=0}^{\infty} \beta^t \{p_t q_t - s_t\}, \quad \beta \in (0,1) \tag{16.4.5}$$

subject to q_0 given, where E_t is the mathematical expectation based on time t information evaluated with respect to the approximating model. Let $u_t = q_{t+1} - q_t$. We take u_t as the representative competitive firm's control variable at t. The Lagrange multiplier λ_t^q to be computed in $(16.5.8)$ and an associated noise loading σ_q to be described shortly will play a prominent role in the Lagrangian featured in this section. We begin by supposing that σ_q is known, but will ultimately describe an iterative algorithm to compute it. To pose the maximization problem of a firm in the competitive fringe, form the Lagrangian

$$\begin{aligned} L = E_0 \sum_{t=0}^{\infty} \beta^t \Big\{ & [a_0 - a_1(Q_t + \bar{q}_t) + v_t]q_t \\ & - [dq_t + .5hq_t^2 + .5cu_t^2] \\ & + \beta\lambda_{t+1}^q[q_t + u_t - q_{t+1}] \Big\}. \end{aligned}$$

It is very important to note that while q_{t+1} and u_t will be exact functions of time t information, the marginal value λ_{t+1}^q of q_{t+1} actually realized will depend on information that will become available only at time $t + 1$. To verify this, please see formula $(16.5.8)$ below, which expresses λ_{t+1}^q and other time $t + 1$ multipliers as linear functions of the information that a firm in the competitive fringe possesses at time $t + 1$. First-order conditions for maximizing with respect to u_t, q_t for $t \geq 0$, respectively, are[9]

$$u_t = c^{-1}\beta E_t \lambda_{t+1}^q \tag{16.4.6a}$$

$$E_t \lambda_{t+1}^q = \beta^{-1}\Big\{ \lambda_t^q - [a_0 - a_1(Q_t + \bar{q}_t) + v_t] + d + hq_t \Big\}. \tag{16.4.6b}$$

---

[9] For $t \geq 1$, equation $(16.4.6b)$ is the first-order condition for q_t; for $t = 0$, it determines the marginal value of exogenous variations in the initial condition q_0.

Solving for u_t, we obtain

$$u_t = c^{-1} \left\{ \lambda_t^q - [a_0 - a_1(Q_t + \bar{q}_t) + v_t] + d + hq_t \right\}. \qquad (16.4.7)$$

Once we know λ_t^q as a function of the state, we can solve for a decision rule for u_t. We do that in the next subsection.

16.4.3. Changes of measure

We want to assemble the competitive firm's first-order conditions $(16.4.6)$ into a set of implementability conditions that confront the monopolist under his distorted model. To accomplish this, we transform them into stochastic difference equations that are driven by the shock in the monopolist's perturbed model. We begin by positing that

$$\lambda_{t+1}^q = E_t \lambda_{t+1}^q + \sigma_q \epsilon_{t+1}, \qquad (16.4.8)$$

where we have assumed that ϵ_{t+1} is i.i.d. $\mathcal{N}(0,1)$ under the approximating model that the representative firm in the competitive fringe believes in fully, but the monopolist does not.

16.4.4. Euler equation for λ^q under the approximating model

To represent the Euler equations under the approximating model, we substitute $(16.4.8)$ into the Euler equations $(16.4.6b)$ to get

$$\lambda_{t+1}^q = \beta^{-1} \left\{ \lambda_t^q - [a_0 - a_1(Q_t + \bar{q}_t) + v_t] + d + h\bar{q}_t \right\} + \sigma_q \epsilon_{t+1}. \qquad (16.4.9)$$

16.4.5. Euler equation for λ^q under the monopolist's perturbed model

To find the Euler equations under the monopolist's perturbed model, use $(16.4.4)$ to justify replacing ϵ_{t+1} with $\check{\epsilon}_{t+1} + W_{t+1}$ in $(16.4.9)$

$$\lambda_{t+1}^q = \beta^{-1} \left\{ \lambda_t^q - [a_0 - a_1(Q_t + \bar{q}_t) + v_t] + d + h\bar{q}_t \right\}$$
$$+ \sigma_q(\check{\epsilon}_{t+1} + W_{t+1}). \qquad (16.4.10)$$

We will include conditional expectations of these first-order conditions under the monopolist's perturbed model.

16.4.6. The monopolist's transition equations

Assembling all of the transition equations that the monopolist faces under his perturbed measure, we have

$$\bar{q}_{t+1} = \bar{q}_t + c^{-1}\big\{\lambda_t^q - [a_0 - a_1(Q_t + \bar{q}_t) + v_t]$$
$$+ d + h\bar{q}_t\big\} \tag{16.4.11a}$$

$$v_{t+1} = \rho v_t + C_\epsilon(\check{\epsilon}_{t+1} + W_{t+1}) \tag{16.4.11b}$$

$$Q_{t+1} = Q_t + U_t \tag{16.4.11c}$$

$$\lambda_{t+1}^q = \beta^{-1}\big\{\lambda_t^q - [a_0 - a_1(Q_t + \bar{q}_t) + v_t] + d + h\bar{q}_t\big\}$$
$$+ \sigma_q(\check{\epsilon}_{t+1} + W_{t+1}). \tag{16.4.11d}$$

Under the monopolist's perturbed model, $\check{\epsilon}_{t+1}$ is i.i.d. $\mathcal{N}(0,1)$. We use certainty equivalence under the monopolist's perturbed model to set $\check{E}_t\check{\epsilon}_{t+1} = 0$ and thereby express these in terms of the matrix transition equation that we shall take as a counterpart to (16.2.5):

$$
\begin{bmatrix} 1 \\ v_{t+1} \\ Q_{t+1} \\ \bar{q}_{t+1} \\ \lambda_{t+1}^q \end{bmatrix}
=
\begin{bmatrix}
1 & 0 & 0 & 0 & 0 \\
0 & \rho & 0 & 0 & 0 \\
0 & 0 & 1 & 0 & 0 \\
\frac{(d-a_0)}{c} & -\frac{1}{c} & \frac{a_1}{c} & \frac{(a_1+h)}{c}+1 & \frac{1}{c} \\
\frac{(-a_0+d)}{\beta} & -\frac{1}{\beta} & \frac{a_1}{\beta} & \frac{a_1+h}{\beta} & \beta^{-1}
\end{bmatrix}
\begin{bmatrix} 1 \\ v_t \\ Q_t \\ \bar{q}_t \\ \lambda_t^q \end{bmatrix}
$$
$$
+ \begin{bmatrix} 0 \\ 0 \\ 1 \\ 0 \\ 0 \end{bmatrix} U_t
+ \begin{bmatrix} 0 \\ C_\epsilon \\ 0 \\ 0 \\ \sigma_q \end{bmatrix} W_{t+1}. \tag{16.4.12}
$$

Notice that when the volatility loading σ_q is not zero, the motion of the representative firm's costate λ^q is exposed to misspecification $\sigma_q W_{t+1}$. Part of our problem is to determine the endogenous volatility loading σ_q. For now, we take it as given.

16.4.7. The monopolist's problem

Represent the monopolist's transition law (16.4.12) as

$$y_{t+1} = Ay_t + BU_t + CW_{t+1}. \tag{16.4.13}$$

Although we have included λ_t^q as a component of the "state" y_t, λ_t^q is actually a "jump" variable that corresponds to x_t in section 16.3. The analysis in section 16.3 implies that information needed to solve the monopolist's problem is encoded in the Riccati equation associated with a robust linear regulator that takes $(16.4.13)$ as the transition law.

To capture the setup of section 16.3, we partition y_t as $y_t' = [z_t' \quad x_t']$ where $z_t' = [1 \quad v_t \quad Q_t \quad \bar{q}_t]$, $x_t = \lambda_t^q$, and let $\mu_{xt} = \mu_{qt}$ be the multiplier associated with the Euler equation for λ_t^q. The monopolist's artificial optimal linear regulator problem can be expressed

$$-\begin{bmatrix} z_t \\ x_t \end{bmatrix}' P \begin{bmatrix} z_t \\ x_t \end{bmatrix} = \max_{\{U_t\}} \min_{\{W_{t+1}\}} \left\{ p_t Q_t - C_t + \beta \Theta W_{t+1}' W_{t+1} \right.$$

$$\left. - \beta \begin{bmatrix} z_{t+1} \\ x_{t+1} \end{bmatrix}' P \begin{bmatrix} z_{t+1} \\ x_{t+1} \end{bmatrix} \right\}$$

or

$$-\begin{bmatrix} z_t \\ x_t \end{bmatrix}' P \begin{bmatrix} z_t \\ x_t \end{bmatrix} = \max_{\{U_t\}} \min_{\{W_{t+1}\}} \left\{ (a_0 - a_1(\bar{q}_t + Q_t) + v_t)Q_t - eQ_t \right.$$

$$\left. - .5gQ_t^2 - .5cU_t^2 + \beta \Theta W_{t+1}^2 - \beta \begin{bmatrix} z_{t+1} \\ x_{t+1} \end{bmatrix}' P \begin{bmatrix} z_{t+1} \\ x_{t+1} \end{bmatrix} \right\}$$
$$(16.4.14)$$

subject to $(16.4.13)$. Thus, the monopolist's problem can be written

$$\max_{\{U_t\}} \min_{\{W_{t+1}\}} - \left\{ y_t' Q y_t + U_t' R U_t - \beta \Theta W_{t+1}^2 + \beta y_{t+1}' P y_{t+1} \right\} \qquad (16.4.15)$$

subject to $(16.4.13)$ where

$$Q = - \begin{bmatrix} 0 & 0 & \frac{a_0-e}{2} & 0 & 0 \\ 0 & 0 & \frac{1}{2} & 0 & 0 \\ \frac{a_0-e}{2} & \frac{1}{2} & -a_1 - .5g & -\frac{a_1}{2} & 0 \\ 0 & 0 & -\frac{a_1}{2} & 0 & 0 \\ 0 & 0 & 0 & 0 & 0 \end{bmatrix}$$

and $R = \frac{c}{2}$. In the notation of section 16.3, let $z_t = [1 \quad v_t \quad Q_t \quad \bar{q}_t]'$ and $\mu_{xt} = \mu_{qt}$. The results of section 16.3.4 leading to the representation $(16.3.18)$ apply, so we know that, under the approximating model, the solution of the robust Ramsey problem has the representation

$$\begin{bmatrix} z_{t+1} \\ \mu_{xt+1} \end{bmatrix} = \mathcal{M} \begin{bmatrix} z_t \\ \mu_{xt} \end{bmatrix} + C_M \epsilon_{t+1}. \qquad (16.4.16)$$

16.4.8. Computing the volatility loading on λ_t^q

In the preceding argument, we assumed that the multiplier volatility loading σ_q is known. We now offer a way to compute it.

As in section 16.3, we can represent the solution for $y_t = \begin{bmatrix} z_t \\ x_t \end{bmatrix}$ as

$$y_{t+1} = (A - BF)y_t + \begin{bmatrix} C_z \\ C_x \end{bmatrix} \epsilon_{t+1}$$

where

$$C_z = \begin{bmatrix} 0 \\ C_\epsilon \\ 0 \\ 0 \end{bmatrix}, \qquad C_x = \sigma_q.$$

Using equation (16.3.14), write

$$\mu_{xt+1} - E_t\mu_{xt+1} = \begin{bmatrix} P_{21} & P_{22} \end{bmatrix} \begin{bmatrix} C_z \\ C_x \end{bmatrix} \epsilon_{t+1}$$
$$= (P_{21}C_z + P_{22}C_x)\epsilon_{t+1}. \tag{16.4.17}$$

We can solve (16.4.17) for

$$\sigma_q = C_x = -P_{22}^{-1}P_{21}C_z. \tag{16.4.18}$$

Given an approximation to the matrix P in the value function for the monopolist, (16.4.18) allows us to compute σ_q. Equation (16.4.18) will become part of an iterative algorithm for computing a robust Ramsey or Stackelberg plan.

16.4.9. Timing subtlety

Before describing our algorithm, we pause to note a subtle aspect of the timing of the multipliers λ^q and the multiplier μ_x on the multiplier λ^q. In our application, μ_{xt+1} is the vector of multipliers on the monopolist's implementability constraint

$$E_t\lambda_{t+1}^q = \beta^{-1}\left\{\lambda_t^q - [a_0 - a_1(Q_t + \bar{q}_t) + v_t] + d + h\bar{q}_t\right\}. \tag{16.4.19}$$

To match the date on λ_{t+1}^q, we have used $t+1$ to date this μ_x "multiplier on the fringe's multiplier." But it is important to notice that the implementability constraint (16.4.19) actually constrains the mathematical expectation of λ_{t+1}^q conditioned on date t information. Therefore, it is appropriate to constrain the multiplier μ_{xt+1} to depend only on date t information, so that $\mu_{xt+1} - E_t\mu_{xt+1} = 0$.

16.4.10. An iterative algorithm

We propose the following iterative algorithm for computing robust decision rules for the monopolist and the representative firm in the competitive fringe:

1. Make an initial guess for σ_q.

2. Solve the monopolist's problem for P and representation (16.4.16).

3. Compute σ_q using (16.4.18).

4. Iterate to convergence over σ_q.

We shall apply this algorithm to compute a robust Stackelberg plan for our model of a monopolist facing a competitive fringe. But first we describe how to use a recursive formulation of the competitive firm's problem to check those calculations.

16.5. Recursive representation of a competitive firm's problem

In this section, we show how to obtain a recursive representation of the problem of a representative firm in the competitive fringe. This will involve yet another application of the Big K, little k trick that we have used often before. The calculations in this section are useful for practitioners who are interested in ways to verify that the calculations in the previous section have been executed properly on a computer.

To obtain a recursive representation of a competitive firm's problem, note that the firm confronts the law of motion (16.4.16) for components of the state that it regards as exogenous to its own decisions. It is convenient to write (16.4.16) as

$$z_{t+1} = \mathcal{M}_{11} z_t + \mathcal{M}_{12} \mu_{xt} + C_{M1} \epsilon_{t+1}$$
$$\mu_{xt+1} = \mathcal{M}_{21} z_t + \mathcal{M}_{22} \mu_{xt} + C_{M2} \epsilon_{t+1}$$

where $C_{M2} = 0$. Let $\bar{A}_{ij} = \mathcal{M}_{ij}$. The representative firm in the competitive fringe faces the law of motion

$$z_{t+1} = \bar{A}_{11} z_t + \bar{A}_{12} \mu_{xt} + C_{M1} \epsilon_{t+1}$$
$$\mu_{xt+1} = \bar{A}_{21} z_t + \bar{A}_{22} \mu_{xt}$$
$$q_{t+1} = q_t + u_t$$

or

$$X_{t+1} = \bar{A} X_t + \bar{B} u_t + \bar{C} \epsilon_{t+1} \qquad (16.5.1)$$

where $X_t = \begin{bmatrix} z_t \\ \mu_{xt} \\ q_t \end{bmatrix}$ and $\bar{C} = \begin{bmatrix} C_{M1} \\ 0 \end{bmatrix}$. Under the approximating model, the representative firm in the competitive fringe faces law of motion $(16.5.1)$ and views $Q_t, \bar{q}_t$ as exogenous processes determined by

$$
\begin{aligned}
Q_t &= e_Q X_t \\
\bar{q}_t &= e_q X_t.
\end{aligned}
\tag{16.5.2}
$$

The representative firm in the competitive fringe chooses $\{u_t, q_{t+1}\}$ sequences to maximize [10]

$$
E_0 \sum_{t=0}^{\infty} \beta^t \left\{ \left[a_0 - a_1(Q_t + \bar{q}_t) + v_t \right] q_t - s_t \right\}
\tag{16.5.3}
$$

subject to $(16.5.2)$, $(16.5.1)$, and $s_t = dq_t + .5hq_t^2 + .5c(q_{t+1} - q_t)^2$. This problem can be formulated as an ordinary (non-robust) discounted linear regulator with value function [11]

$$
v(X_0) = -X_0' P_f X_0 - p_f
\tag{16.5.4}
$$

and corresponding decision rule

$$
u_t = d_u X_t.
\tag{16.5.5}
$$

16.5.1. Multipliers

According to the approximating model, the law of motion for the state under the robust decision rules of the competitive fringe and monopolist is

$$
X_{t+1} = (\bar{A} - \bar{B}\bar{F})X_t + \bar{C}\epsilon_{t+1}
\tag{16.5.6}
$$

because $u_t = -\bar{F}X_t$. Define the multipliers in the usual way by

$$
\lambda_t = 2P_f X_t.
\tag{16.5.7}
$$

---

[10] The shadow price λ_t^q pertains to this maximization problem.

[11] The matrix in the quadratic form in the state is

$$
Q_f = - \begin{bmatrix}
0 & 0 & 0 & 0 & 0 & \frac{(a_0 - d)}{2} \\
0 & 0 & 0 & 0 & 0 & .5 \\
0 & 0 & 0 & 0 & 0 & -a_1/2 \\
0 & 0 & 0 & 0 & 0 & -a_1/2 \\
0 & 0 & 0 & 0 & 0 & 0 \\
\frac{(a_0 - d)}{2} & .5 & -a_1/2 & -a_1/2 & 0 & -.5h
\end{bmatrix}
$$

and the scalar in the quadratic form in u_t is $R_f = c/2$.

Evidently,

$$\lambda_{t+1} = 2P_f X_{t+1} = 2P_f (\bar{A} - \bar{B}\bar{F})X_t + 2P_f \bar{C}\epsilon_{t+1}$$
$$= E_t \lambda_{t+1} + \sigma \epsilon_{t+1} \qquad (16.5.8)$$

where

$$\sigma = 2P_f \bar{C}. \qquad (16.5.9)$$

We are particularly interested in the component of λ_t that corresponds to q_t, namely, λ_t^q. We can use $(16.5.9)$ as another way to compute σ_q and as a check on $(16.4.18)$.

16.5.2. Cross-checking the solution for u_t, w_{t+1}

Once we have the solution for λ_t, we know that for our problem λ_t becomes x_t in $(16.3.15)$, so that

$$\lambda_t^q = \begin{bmatrix} -P_{22}^{-1}P_{21} & P_{22}^{-1} \end{bmatrix} \begin{bmatrix} z_t \\ \mu_{xt} \end{bmatrix} \equiv G_q \begin{bmatrix} z_t \\ \mu_{xt} \end{bmatrix} \qquad (16.5.10)$$

where the natural state $z_t = \begin{bmatrix} 1 & v_t & Q_t & \bar{q}_t \end{bmatrix}'$ and μ_{xt} is the monopolist's multiplier on λ_t^q. If we substitute this formula into $(16.4.7)$, we obtain

$$u_t = c^{-1} \left\{ G_q \begin{bmatrix} z_t \\ \mu_{xt} \end{bmatrix} - [a_0 - a_1(Q_t + \bar{q}_t) + v_t] \right.$$
$$\left. + d + h\bar{q}_t \right\}. \qquad (16.5.11)$$

This decision rule should match $(16.5.5)$.

16.6. Numerical example

This section briefly describes a numerical example of the monopoly-competitive fringe model. We start without concerns about robustness, then study the effects of activating concerns about robustness for the Stackelberg leader.[12] For parameter settings $(a_0, a_1, \rho, C_\epsilon, c, d, e, g, h, \beta) = (100, 1, .8, 2, 10, 20, 20, 1, 1, .95)$. Table 16.6.1 displays steady-state values associated with two settings for Θ under the approximating model and the robust rule. The case of almost no concern about robustness corresponds to $\Theta = 10000000000 \approx +\infty$. To activate concerns about robustness, we set Θ equal to 30.

The first column of table 16.6.1 serves as a benchmark where concerns about robustness having been turned off by setting $\Theta \approx +\infty$. The next

---

[12] The calculations are performed by the Matlab programs `robust_stackelbergfn.m` and `robust_stackelbergall.m`.

Table 16.6.1: Steady-state values

Θ	∞	30
p	50	51.43
$\bar{q}$	30	31.46
Q	20	17.07
μ_q	5	4.16
W	0	-1.67

column activates a concern about robustness for the monopolist. The entries in the table show that activating the monopolist's concerns about robustness make the steady-state values of the worst-case shock W negative. The table shows that the monopolist's pessimistic forecasts about demand pushes its output down. However, when we activate the monopolist's concern about robustness, the steady-state output of the representative firm rises under the approximating model as it responds to the higher steady-state price.

16.7. Concluding remarks

This chapter has extended standard methods for solving Ramsey problems in linear-quadratic forward-looking models to include a concern for model misspecification on the part of a Stackelberg leader (e.g., a Ramsey planner or government). The government and private agents (or Stackelberg leader and followers) share an approximating model that describes the shocks and other exogenous variables hitting the economy. We add one parameter Θ to the standard rational expectations setup, a penalty parameter that measures sets of models near the approximating model over which the Stackelberg leader wants robust decision rules. We compute the Ramsey rule by forming an optimal linear regulator problem while carefully interchanging the roles of the forward-looking model's artificial state variables and the Lagrange multipliers on their laws of motion. Mechanically, robustness for the leader is achieved simply by adding another control to the regulator problem, a distortion to the conditional mean of the disturbances that is chosen by a fictitious evil agent.

For technical reasons that we are now exploring in ongoing research, the problem in which the Stackelberg leader and the followers are both concerned about model misspecification is more intricate than the problem studied in this chapter, but we anticipate that the iterative method for solving the Stackelberg problem that we have advocated in this chapter will be a useful tool for solving that more ambitious problem.

A. Invariant subspace method

Let $L = L^* \beta^{-.5}$ and transform the system $(16.3.12)$ to

$$L_\bullet \begin{bmatrix} y_{t+1}^* \\ \mu_{t+1}^* \end{bmatrix} = N \begin{bmatrix} y_t^* \\ \mu_t^* \end{bmatrix}, \tag{16.A.1}$$

where $y_t^* = \beta^{t/2} y_t, \mu_t^* = \mu_t \beta^{t/2}$. Now $\lambda L - N$ is a symplectic pencil, so that the generalized eigenvalues of L, N occur in reciprocal pairs: if λ_i is an eigenvalue, then so is λ_i^{-1}.

We can use Evan Anderson's Matlab program `schurg.m` to find a stabilizing solution of system $(16.A.1)$. The program computes the ordered real generalized Schur decomposition of the matrix pencil. Thus, `schurg.m` computes matrices $\bar{L}, \bar{N}, V$ such that $\bar{L}$ is upper triangular, $\bar{N}$ is upper block triangular, and V is the matrix of right Schur vectors such that for some orthogonal matrix W the following hold:

$$\begin{aligned} WLV &= \bar{L} \\ WNV &= \bar{N}. \end{aligned} \tag{16.A.2}$$

Let the stable eigenvalues (those less than 1) appear first. Then the stabilizing solution is

$$\mu_t^* = P y_t^* \tag{16.A.3}$$

where

$$P = V_{21} V_{11}^{-1},$$

V_{21} is the lower left block of V, and V_{11} is the upper left block.

If L is nonsingular, we can represent the solution of the system as[13]

$$\begin{bmatrix} y_{t+1}^* \\ \mu_{t+1}^* \end{bmatrix} = L^{-1} N \begin{bmatrix} I \\ P \end{bmatrix} y_t^*. \tag{16.A.4}$$

The solution is to be initiated from $(16.A.3)$. We can use the first half and then the second half of the rows of this representation to deduce the following recursive solutions for y_{t+1}^* and μ_{t+1}^*:

$$\begin{aligned} y_{t+1}^* &= A_o^* y_t^* \\ \mu_{t+1}^* &= \psi^* y_t^* \end{aligned} \tag{16.A.5}$$

---

[13] The solution method in the text assumes that L is nonsingular and well conditioned. If it is not, the following method proposed by Evan Anderson can be applied. We want to solve for a solution of the form

$$y_{t+1}^* = A_o^* y_t^*.$$

Note that with $(16.A.3)$,

$$L[I; P] y_{t+1}^* = N[I; P] y_t^*.$$

The solution A_o^* will then satisfy

$$L[I; P] A_o^* = N[I; P].$$

Thus A^{o*} can be computed via the Matlab command

$$A_o^* = (L * [I; P]) \backslash (N * [I; P]).$$

Now express this solution in terms of the original variables

$$
\begin{aligned}
y_{t+1} &= A_o y_t \\
\mu_{t+1} &= \psi y_t, \quad \bullet
\end{aligned}
\tag{16.A.6}
$$

where $A_o = A_o^* \beta^{-.5}, \psi = \psi^* \beta^{-.5}$. We also have the representation

$$
\mu_t = P y_t.
\tag{16.A.7}
$$

The matrix $A_o = A - \tilde{B}F$, where F is the matrix for the optimal decision rule.

B. The Riccati equation

The stabilizing P obeys a Riccati equation coming from the Bellman equation. Substituting $\mu_t = P y_t$ into ($16.3.10$) and ($16.3.8b$) gives

$$
(I + \beta \tilde{B} \tilde{R}^{-1} \tilde{B}' P) y_{t+1} = A y_t
\tag{16.B.1a}
$$
$$
\beta A' P y_{t+1} = -Q y_t + P y_t.
\tag{16.B.1b}
$$

A matrix inversion identity implies

$$
(I + \beta \tilde{B} \tilde{R}^{-1} \tilde{B}' P)^{-1} = I - \beta \tilde{B} (\tilde{R} + \beta \tilde{B}' P \tilde{B})^{-1} \tilde{B}' P.
\tag{16.B.2}
$$

Solving ($16.B.1a$) for y_{t+1} gives

$$
y_{t+1} = (A - \tilde{B}F) y_t
\tag{16.B.3}
$$

where

$$
F = \beta (\tilde{R} + \beta \tilde{B}' P \tilde{B})^{-1} \tilde{B}' P A.
\tag{16.B.4}
$$

Premultiplying ($16.B.3$) by $\beta A' P$ gives

$$
\beta A' P y_{t+1} = \beta (A' P A - A' P \tilde{B}F) y_t.
\tag{16.B.5}
$$

For the right side of ($16.B.5$) to agree with the right side of ($16.B.1b$) for any initial value of y_0 requires that

$$
P = Q + \beta A' P A - \beta^2 A' P \tilde{B} (\tilde{R} + \beta \tilde{B}' P \tilde{B})^{-1} \tilde{B}' P A.
\tag{16.B.6}
$$

Equation ($16.B.6$) is the algebraic matrix Riccati equation associated with the ordinary linear regulator for the system $A, \tilde{B}, Q, \tilde{R}$.

C. Another Bellman equation

We briefly indicate the connection of the preceding formulation to that of Kydland and Prescott (1980) and Marcet and Marimon (2000). For a class of problems with structures close to ours, they construct a Bellman equation in a state vector defined as (z, μ_x): these are the "natural" state variables and the vector of multipliers on the laws of motion for the "jump" variables x_t. We show how to modify that Bellman equation to include a concern about model misspecification.

Let μ_{xt} denote the sub vector of multipliers attached to the implementability constraints that summarize the Euler equations of the private sector. Then the Lagrangian for the optimum problem (16.3.7) can be written

$$\mathcal{L} = -\sum_{t=0}^{\infty} \beta^t \left\{ \begin{bmatrix} z_t \\ x_t \end{bmatrix}' Q \begin{bmatrix} z_t \\ x_t \end{bmatrix} + U_t' R U_t - \beta \theta w_{t+1}' w_{t+1} \right. $$
$$\left. + \beta \mu_{xt+1}'(A_{21} z_t + A_{22} x_t + B_2 U_t + C_2 w_{t+1} - x_{t+1}) \right\}. \tag{16.C.1}$$

This Lagrangian is to be "extremized" (i.e., maximized or minimized, as appropriate) with respect to sequences $\{z_t, x_t \, \mu_{xt}, w_{t+1}\}$ subject to $\lambda_0 = 0$ and the transition law

$$z_{t+1} = A_{11} z_t + A_{12} x_t + B_1 U_t + C_1 w_{t+1}. \tag{16.C.2}$$

Equation (16.C.1) can be rewritten

$$\mathcal{L} = -\sum_{t=0}^{\infty} \beta^t \left\{ \begin{bmatrix} z_t \\ x_t \end{bmatrix}' Q \begin{bmatrix} z_t \\ x_t \end{bmatrix} + U_t' R U_t - \beta \theta w_{t+1}' w_{t+1} \right. $$
$$\left. + (\beta \mu_{xt+1}' A_{22} - \mu_{xt}') x_t + \beta \mu_{xt+1}'(A_{21} z_t + B_2 U_t + C_2 w_{t+1}) \right\}, \tag{16.C.3}$$

which is to be extremized with respect to the same constraints (16.C.2). Define the one-period return function $-\tilde{r}(z, \mu_x, x, \mu_x^*, w) = \begin{bmatrix} z \\ x \end{bmatrix}' Q \begin{bmatrix} z \\ x \end{bmatrix} + u' R u - \beta \theta w' w +$ $(\beta \mu_x^{*'} A_{22} - \mu_x') x + \beta \mu_x^{*'}(A_{21} z + B_2 u + C_2 w)$, where * superscripts denote one-period-ahead values. Let $v(z, \mu_x)$ be the optimum value of the problem starting with augmented state (z, μ_x). Problem (16.C.3) is recursive and has the following Bellman equation:

$$v(z, \mu_x) = \max_{\{u,x\}} \min_{\{w, \mu_x^*\}} \left\{ \tilde{r}(z, \mu_x, x, \mu_x^*, w) + \beta v(z^*, \mu_x^*) \right\} \tag{16.C.4}$$

where the extremization is subject to

$$z^* = A_{11} z + A_{12} x + B_1 u + C_1 w. \tag{16.C.5}$$

The Bellman equation (16.C.4), (16.C.5) is a version of the recursive saddle-point problem described by Kydland and Prescott (1980) and Marcet and Marimon (2000). We have added a concern for robustness via the extra minimization with respect to the shock distortion w. In related contexts, Marcet and Marimon stress that while such problems are not recursive in the natural state variables z alone, they become recursive when the multipliers μ_x are included.

Although one could solve our problem by iterating to convergence on (16.C.4), (16.C.5), it is more convenient to use the method described in section 16.3 that suggests solving the Riccati equation (16.3.4) and its associated Bellman equation.

Part V

Robust estimation and filtering

Chapter 17
Robust filtering with commitment

Experience must be our only guide. Reason may mislead us.
— John Dickinson, at the Constitutional Convention, August 13, 1787

17.1. Alternative formulations

Here and in chapter 18, we study estimation and filtering problems in which a decision maker distrusts his approximating model. We formulate dynamic robust estimation in terms of max-min problems where a first player seeks to minimize and a malevolent second player seeks to maximize a measure of estimation error. In this chapter, at each date the malevolent player who *maximizes* estimation error is committed to accept distortions to the approximating model that were chosen by previous maximizing players. In our linear-quadratic-Gaussian setting, it will turn out that those prior distortions take the form of an enlarged hidden state covariance matrix that the maximizing player inherits from robust estimation problems at earlier dates. In chapter 18, we describe alternative dynamic filtering problems that eliminate the maximizing player's commitment to distortions chosen by earlier maximizing players.[1]

The robust filtering problem of this chapter is the dual of the robust optimal linear regulator that we studied extensively in chapters 2, 7, and 8. For that reason, this chapter is organized as follows. In section 17.2, we recall a version of the robust linear regulator that is to be compared with the robust filter. We begin to derive the robust filter by studying a static robust estimation problem in section 17.3. In section 17.4, we pose and solve a two-period dynamic robust estimation problem. Iterations on this problem yield a recursive version of a robust filtering problem that can be interpreted as a robust version of a Kalman filter. Section 17.5 and appendix A bring out that this robust filtering problem is the dual of the robust linear regulator from section 17.2. Duality allows us to compute a robust filter with the same software that we use to solve a robust linear regulator, a point brought out in subsection 17.6. To illuminate more of the structure of the robust filtering problem, section 17.7 displays a dynamic programming problem from which we can deduce a worst-case model with which the malevolent agent confronts the robust decision maker. In section 17.8, we use that worst-case model to

---

[1] In more general settings, Hansen and Sargent (2005b, 2007a) study robust dynamic estimation problems with the commitment protocol of this chapter and the no-commitment protocol of chapter 18.

formulate a Bayesian interpretation of the robust filter, thereby providing a counterpart to the Bayesian interpretation of the robust linear regulator that we derived in chapter 7. Section 17.9 studies a robust version of a filtering problem posed by John F. Muth (1960).

The decision maker's concerns about misspecification reduce his confidence in his estimate of a hidden state and have a simple characterization as enlarging the covariance matrix of the distribution around that estimate. In dynamic settings, that bigger covariance matrix alters the weight that he attaches to new information as it becomes available in subsequent periods. In particular, that enlarged covariance of the state estimate means that the decision maker regards current and past observations as less informative, causing him to alter future estimates of the state accordingly.

17.2. A linear regulator

We begin by describing an ordinary nonstochastic optimal linear regulator problem. The linear regulator allows cross-products between states and controls in the objective function. The problem can be stated as

$$-x_0' P x_0 = \max_{\{u_t\}_{t=0}^\infty} -\sum_{t=0}^\infty z_t' z_t \tag{17.2.1}$$

subject to x_0 given and

$$z_t = H x_t + J u_t \tag{17.2.2a}$$

$$x_{t+1} = A x_t + B u_t. \tag{17.2.2b}$$

The solution is a time-invariant decision rule $u_t = -F^* x_t$, where

$$F^* = \mathcal{F}(P_\infty) = (J'J + B'P_\infty B)^{-1}(B'P_\infty A + J'H), \tag{17.2.3}$$

and where P_∞ is the fixed point of the matrix Riccati equation $P_\infty = T(P_\infty)$ that is the limit of iterations on the operator $T(P)$ defined as

$$T(P) = [A - B\mathcal{F}(P)]' P [A - B\mathcal{F}(P)] + [H - J\mathcal{F}(P)]'[H - J\mathcal{F}(P)]. \tag{17.2.4}$$

A robust version of this control problem (abstracting from uncertainty) is

$$-x_0' P x_0 = \max_{\{u_t\}_{t=0}^\infty} \min_{\{w_{t+1}\}_{t=0}^\infty} \left\{ -z_t' z_t + \theta w_{t+1}' w_{t+1} \right\} \tag{17.2.5}$$

where the extremization is subject to $(17.2.2a)$ and

$$x_{t+1} = A x_t + B u_t + C w_{t+1}. \tag{17.2.6}$$

The solution is a time-invariant decision rule $u_t = -F^* x_t$, where F^* now satisfies

$$F^* = \mathcal{F}[\mathcal{D}(P_\infty)] \tag{17.2.7}$$

where $\mathcal{F}(P)$ is the same function as was defined in (17.2.3),

$$\mathcal{D}(P) = P + \theta^{-1} PC(I - \theta^{-1} C'PC)^{-1} C'P, \tag{17.2.8}$$

and P_∞ satisfies

$$P_\infty = T \circ \mathcal{D}(P_\infty) \tag{17.2.9}$$

We shall encounter these formulas again as ingredients for solving what at first will seem to be a very different problem, namely, a robust estimation problem.

17.3. A static robust estimation problem

Consider the following static "pure estimation" problem.[2] A decision maker has probability model $x \sim \mathcal{N}(\hat{x}, \hat{\Sigma})$ and wants to estimate $z = Hx$. Let the action a denote his estimator of Hx. Let n be a nonnegative random variable with mean 1. The decision maker forms a robust evaluation of his estimation error $a - Hx$ by solving

$$\max_{a} \min_{n \geq 0, En=1} E\left[-n(a - Hx)'(a - Hx) + \alpha n \log n \right]. \tag{17.3.1}$$

Multiplication by the nonnegative random variable n distorts the probability distribution of x_0; $\alpha = 2\theta$ is a penalty on the relative entropy of the distortion. The objective is concave in a and convex in n. To solve problem (17.3.1), we appeal to the min-max theorem to allow us to interchange the order of minimization and maximization and to study

$$\min_{n \geq 0, En=1} \max_{a} E\left[-n(a - Hx)'(a - Hx) + \alpha n \log n \right]. \tag{17.3.2}$$

In problem (17.3.2), a decision maker chooses a after the "malevolent agent" chooses n. Provided that the distorted distribution has a finite second moment, for a given n^*, the inner maximization problem has as its solution $a = HEn^* x$, where $En^* x$ is the expectation of x with respect to the distorted distribution represented by the random variable n^*.[3]

---

[2] We recommend reviewing chapter 3 before reading this section.

[3] See chapter 3 for an explanation of how multiplication by the nonnegative random variable n enables us to express a perturbation to an approximating model. Also, see Hansen and Sargent (2005b, 2007a).

In the equilibrium of the two-person zero-sum game (17.3.1), the pertinent n^* is the one associated with the worst-case distribution. The outer maximization problem entails finding a minimizing distortion n^* that satisfies

$$n^* \propto \exp\left(\frac{(En^*x - x)'H'H(En^*x - x)}{\alpha}\right).$$

The proportionality factor must be chosen so that when integrated against a normal distribution with mean $\hat{x}$ and covariance matrix $\hat{\Sigma}$, the appropriately scaled version of the right side integrates to unity. Therefore, the worst-case density is proportional to

$$\exp\left(\frac{1}{2\theta}x'H'Hx - \frac{1}{\theta}(En^*x)'H'Hx\right)\exp\left[-\frac{1}{2}(x'\hat{\Sigma}^{-1}x + x'\hat{\Sigma}^{-1}\hat{x})\right] =$$
$$\exp\left[-\frac{1}{2}x'\left(\hat{\Sigma}^{-1} - \frac{1}{\theta}HH'\right)x + x'\left(\hat{\Sigma}^{-1}\hat{x} - \frac{1}{\theta}HH'En^*x\right)\right].$$
(17.3.3)

This gives the worst-case density as a function of its mean En^*x. Evidently, the worst-case density is normal with mean $\bar{x} = En^*x$ and covariance $\bar{\Sigma}$, and so can be expressed as being proportional to

$$\exp\left[-\frac{1}{2}(x - \bar{x})'\bar{\Sigma}^{-1}(x - \bar{x})\right]$$
$$= \exp\left[-\frac{1}{2}(x'\bar{\Sigma}^{-1}x - 2\bar{x}'\bar{\Sigma}^{-1}x + \bar{x}'\bar{\Sigma}^{-1}\bar{x})\right].$$
(17.3.4)

Matching quadratic forms in x in (17.3.3) and (17.3.4) gives

$$\bar{\Sigma}^{-1} = \hat{\Sigma}^{-1} - \theta^{-1}H'H.$$
(17.3.5)

Matching cross product terms in $\bar{x}$ and x gives

$$-\frac{1}{\theta}\bar{x}'H'Hx + \hat{x}'\hat{\Sigma}^{-1}x = \bar{x}\bar{\Sigma}^{-1}x.$$

Rearranging terms gives

$$\hat{x}'\hat{\Sigma}^{-1}x = \bar{x}\hat{\Sigma}^{-1}x.$$

Since this is true for all x, $\bar{x} = \hat{x}$ as expected.

Express (17.3.5) as

$$\bar{\Sigma} = \mathcal{D}(\hat{\Sigma}) \equiv (\hat{\Sigma}^{-1} - \theta^{-1}H'H)^{-1}.$$
(17.3.6)

Setting $a = \hat{\Sigma}^{-1}, b = (1/\sqrt{\theta})H', c = (1/\sqrt{\theta})H, d^{-1} = I$ in the partitioned inverse formula $(a - bd^{-1}c)^{-1} = a^{-1} + a^{-1}b(d - ca^{-1}b)^{-1}ca^{-1}$ gives

$$\mathcal{D}(\hat{\Sigma}) = \hat{\Sigma} + \theta^{-1}\hat{\Sigma}H'(I - \theta^{-1}H\Sigma H')^{-1}H\hat{\Sigma}.$$
(17.3.7)

When $C' = H$ and $P = \hat{\Sigma}$, the operator $\mathcal{D}$ defined in $(17.3.7)$ is identical to the operator $\mathcal{D}$ defined in $(17.2.8)$ on page 360, a connection that we explore in detail in section 17.5.

To summarize, for the static problem $(17.3.2)$, starting from the initial distribution $x \sim \mathcal{N}(\hat{x}, \hat{\Sigma})$, the worst-case distribution associated with the minimizing n^* from problem $(17.3.2)$ is

$$x \sim \mathcal{N}\left(\hat{x}, \mathcal{D}(\hat{\Sigma})\right).\tag{17.3.8}$$

Relative to the initial distribution, n^* distorts the covariance matrix but not the mean of x. We can summarize this by saying that in this static problem, the mean under the original distribution *is* a robust estimator. A concern for misspecification leads the decision maker to enhance the covariance matrix of x relative to what it is in the approximating model, but leaves his estimate of x unaltered. We shall soon see that a concern for robustness will have more interesting consequences in dynamic settings. But first we note a useful property of distorted conditional expectations.

17.3.1. A digression on distorted conditional expectations

To prepare the way for solving a dynamic estimation problem under a concern about model misspecification, we state a useful result about distorted conditional expectations. Its proof is a direct application of the Law of Iterated Expectations.

Theorem 17.3.1. *Let n be a nonnegative random variable with expectation one that we use to create a distorted probability distribution for x, and let y be a conditioning random variable. Under the n-distorted probability distribution, the conditional expectation of x given y is*

$$\bar{E}(x|y) = \frac{1}{E(n|y)}E(nx|y).$$

Proof. Let $\phi(y)$ be any bounded, Borel measurable function of y. It suffices to show that the estimation error

$$e = x - \bar{E}(x|y)$$

is orthogonal to ϕ under the distorted probability measure. Apply the Law of Iterated Expectations to show

$$E\left[\frac{n}{E(n|y)}E(nx|y)\phi(y)\right] = E\left(E\left[\frac{n}{E(n|y)}E(nx|y)\phi(y)|y\right]\right)$$

$$= E\left(\frac{E(nx|y)\phi(y)}{E(n|y)}E(n|y)\right)$$

$$= E\left([E(nx|y)\phi(y)|y]\right)$$

$$= E\left[nx\phi(y)\right].$$

It follows that
$$Ene = 0.$$

∎

17.4.   A dynamic robust estimation problem

We seek a recursive representation of a two-period commitment problem. An action a_1 is taken at date one as a function of observed data y_1, and an action a_0 is taken at date zero. The objective function is

$$E\left[-n(a_1 - Hx_1)'(a_1 - Hx_1) - n(a_0 - Hx_0)'(a_0 - Hx_0) + \alpha n \log n\right]$$

where $n \geq 0$ and $En = 1$ and where the joint distribution for (x_1, y_1) is generated by

$$x_1 = Ax_0 + C\epsilon_1$$
$$y_1 = Gx_0 + D\epsilon_1$$
(17.4.1)

where x_0 is distributed as $\mathcal{N}\left(\hat{x}_0, \hat{\Sigma}_0\right)$ and ϵ_1 is distributed as $\mathcal{N}(0, I)$ and is independent of x_0.

We use the solution to the static problem to help solve this problem. Consider solving the static problem for a choice n_0 as a function of a given action a_0. We take as the static objective

$$E\left[-n_0(a_0 - Hx_0)'(a_0 - Hx_0) + \alpha n_0 \log n\right].$$

Recall that for a given action a_0, the choice of n_0 is

$$n_0 = \frac{\exp\left[\frac{1}{\alpha}(a_0 - Hx_0)'(a_0 - Hx_0)\right]}{E \exp\left[\frac{1}{\alpha}(a_0 - Hx_0)'(a_0 - Hx_0)\right]}.$$
(17.4.2)

where $\theta = \alpha/2$. The probability distribution associated with this choice of n_0 implies that x_0 remains normally distributed. The covariance matrix is $\mathcal{D}(\hat{\Sigma}_0)$. Since we have not yet optimized over a_0, the mean x_0 is also distorted and given by

$$En_0 x_0 = \mathcal{D}(\hat{\Sigma}_0)\left[-\frac{1}{\theta}H'a_0 + (\hat{\Sigma}_0)^{-1}\hat{x}_0\right]$$
(17.4.3)

where $\theta = \alpha/2$. Notice that when $a_0 = H\hat{x}_0$, the n_0 mean of x_0 is $\hat{x}_0$ as expected.

Parameterize $n = n_1 n_0$ where $E(n_1 n_0) = 1$. We follow Hansen and Sargent (2005b) by using n_0 to define a new benchmark probability model, and at date one choosing n_1 to distort probabilities relative to the probabilities implied by n_0. With this in mind, this parameterization of n gives a decomposition of relative entropy with respect to the original benchmark model

$$E(n \log n) = E(n_1 n_0 \log n_1) + E(n_1 n_0 \log n_0).$$

Also, using formula $(17.4.2)$ for n_0

$$E\left[-n_1 n_0 (a_0 - Hx_0)'(a_0 - Hx_0) + \alpha n_1 n_0 \log n_0\right]$$
$$= -\alpha \log E \exp\left[\frac{1}{\alpha}(a_0 - Hx_0)'(a_0 - Hx_0)\right],$$

which does not depend on n_1. Thus, we can rewrite the objective for the two-period problem as

$$E\left[-n(a_1 - Hx_1)'(a_1 - Hx_1) - n(a_0 - Hx_0)'(a_0 - Hx_0) + \alpha n \log n\right]$$
$$= E\left[-n_1 n_0 (a_1 - Hx_1)'(a_1 - Hx_1) + \alpha n_1 n_0 \log n_1\right]$$
$$- \alpha \log E \exp\left[-\frac{1}{\alpha}(a_0 - Hx_0)'(a_0 - Hx_0)\right]$$

$$(17.4.4)$$

Given this derived representation of the objective, we solve the two period problem sequentially. The random variable n_0 only distorts the distribution of x_0 but not the distribution of ϵ_1. Suppose that this distortion preserves normality. We solve for a_1 and n_1. The optimal action is

$$a_1 = H\frac{E(n_1 n_0 x_1 | y_1)}{E(n_1 n_0 | y_1)}$$

which simplifies to $a_1 = H\frac{E(n_0 x_1 | y_1)}{E(n_0 | y_1)}$ as in the static problem. In particular,

$$a_1 = H\frac{E(n_0 x_1 | y_1)}{E(n_0 | y_1)}$$
$$= H\left[AEn_0 x_0 + \mathcal{K}[\mathcal{D}(\hat{\Sigma}_0)](y_1 - GEn_0 x_0)\right]$$

where $E(n_0 x_0)$ is given in $(17.4.3)$ and $\mathcal{K}(\Sigma) = (CD' + A\Sigma G')(DD' + G\Sigma G')^{-1}$ is used in the ordinary Kalman filter recursion. The random variable n_1 used to represent distorted expectations at date one is

$$n_1 = \frac{\exp\left[\frac{1}{\alpha}(a_1 - Hx_1)'(a_1 - Hx_1)\right]}{E\left(n_0 \exp\left[\frac{1}{\alpha}(a_1 - Hx_1)'(a_1 - Hx_1)\right]\right)}$$

This choice of n_1 does not distort the n_0 mean of x_1 conditioned on y_1, it only enhances the conditional covariance matrix of x_1 conditioned on y_1. Substituting this choice of n_1 into the two-period objective results in

$$-\alpha \log E\left(n_0 \exp\left[\frac{1}{\alpha}(a_1 - Hx_1)'(a_1 - Hx_1)\right]\right)$$
$$- \alpha \log E \exp\left[\frac{1}{\alpha}(a_0 - Hx_0)'(a_0 - Hx_0)\right].$$

$$(17.4.5)$$

Given our solution for a_1 and n_0, objective $(17.4.5)$ can expressed in terms of a_0 alone. The second term of $(17.4.5)$ is a negative definite quadratic form in $H\hat{x}_0 - a_0$ plus a constant term that does not depend on a_0. This can be verified using a *complete-the-square* argument. To evaluate the first term of $(17.4.5)$, write the forecast error as

$$
\begin{aligned}
x_1 - E(n_1 n_0 x_1 | y_1) &= A(x_0 - E n_0 x_0) + C \epsilon_1 \\
&\quad - \mathcal{K}[\mathcal{D}(\hat{\Sigma}_0)][G(x_0 - E n_0 x_0) + D \epsilon_1] \\
&= (C - \mathcal{K}[\mathcal{D}(\hat{\Sigma}_0)]D)\epsilon_1 + (A - \mathcal{K}[\mathcal{D}(\hat{\Sigma}_0)]G)(x_0 - E n_0 x_0)
\end{aligned}
$$

By construction, n_0 does not distort ϵ_1, and as a consequence the first term in objective $(17.4.5)$ is a negative semi-definite quadratic form in $\hat{x}_0 - E n_0 x_0$ plus a constant term, which does not depend on a_0. Thus, $a_0 = H\hat{x}_0$ makes this term as small as possible, since for this choice a_0, $E n_0 x_0 = \hat{x}_0$.

While we solve this problem using backward induction, in fact the choice of a_0 is identical to that obtained by solving the single period date zero solution. This means that as in an ordinary filtering problem, we may solve this problem using forward induction. While $a_0 = H\hat{x}_0$, the resulting choice of n_0 will distort the mean of Hx_1 given y_1 and hence $a_1 \neq HE(x_1 | y_1)$. Since the covariance matrix of x_0 is enlarged under the n_0 probability, the expectation of x_1 given y_1 will be altered by n_0. A concern about robustness reduces confidence in the current state estimate, which in turn alters conditional expectations in the future. This is reflected both in the choices of n_0 and n_1.

17.4.1. Many-period filtering problem

If we iterate our two-period problem over time, we obtain the following recursions for $t \geq 1$:

$$
K_t = \mathcal{K}\left[\mathcal{D}(\hat{\Sigma}_{t-1})\right] \tag{17.4.6a}
$$

$$
\hat{\Sigma}_t = T^* \circ \mathcal{D}(\hat{\Sigma}_{t-1}) \tag{17.4.6b}
$$

$$
\hat{x}_t = A\hat{x}_{t-1} + K_t(y_t - G\hat{x}_{t-1}) \tag{17.4.6c}
$$

where

$$
T^*(\Sigma) = (A - \mathcal{K}(\Sigma)G)\Sigma(A - \mathcal{K}(\Sigma)G)' + (C - \mathcal{K}(\Sigma)D)(C - \mathcal{K}(\Sigma)D)'
$$

is defined as for the ordinary Kalman filter described in equation $(5.2.12a)$ in chapter 5. We begin the recursions from $(\hat{x}_0, \hat{\Sigma}_0)$, which express the decision maker's prior over $x_0 \sim \mathcal{N}(\hat{x}_0, \hat{\Sigma}_0)$.

Notice that in using these recursions, we change each time t benchmark model vis-à-vis the decision maker's time t approximating model

$$x_t = Ax_{t-1} + C\epsilon_t \qquad (17.4.7a)$$

$$y_t = Gx_{t-1} + D\epsilon_t \qquad (17.4.7b)$$

$$x_{t-1} \sim \mathcal{N}(\bar{x}_{t-1}, \bar{\Sigma}_{t-1}), \qquad (17.4.7c)$$

where here $(\bar{x}_{t-1}, \bar{\Sigma}_{t-1})$ are computed from iterations on the ordinary Kalman filter $\hat{\Sigma}_t = T^{*t}(\hat{\Sigma}_0)$ where the distribution for x_{t-1} is conditioned on date $t-1$ history of the y's. Under the robust filtering scheme, the time t benchmark model is $(17.4.7a)$, $(17.4.7b)$ and

$$x_{t-1} \sim \mathcal{N}(\hat{x}_{t-1}, \mathcal{D}(\hat{\Sigma}_{t-1})) \qquad (17.4.8)$$

conditioned on the date $t - 1$ history of past y's, where $(\hat{x}_{t-1}, \hat{\Sigma}_{t-1})$ are computed from iterations on $(17.4.6)$. At each iteration, the new benchmark model justifies our computation of the robust estimates. In section 17.7, we shall characterize a single worst-case dynamic model that is associated with a limiting version of iterations on $(17.4.6a)$, $(17.4.6b)$ and that authorizes a Bayesian interpretation of the associated robust filter.

Notice how the recursions defining the robust filter accumulate earlier distortions in both $\hat{x}_{t-1}$ and $\hat{\Sigma}_{t-1}$. This feature of the recursions reflects how we have built commitment to earlier distortions into the problem.[4]

In comparing the covariance matrix sequence $\{\hat{\Sigma}_t\}$ from the robust filter to $\{\bar{\Sigma}_t\}$ from the ordinary Kalman filter, we see that the robust filter enhances the covariance matrix at every iteration through application of $\mathcal{D}$. This enhancement expresses the decision maker's response to his lack of confidence in the distribution of the hidden state. Since future state estimates depend on the current state covariance matrix, the adjustment for robustness has an enduring impact.

17.5. Duality of robust filtering and control

To solve the infinite-horizon robust linear regulator problem defined in section 17.2, expressions $(17.2.3)$, $(17.2.9)$ tell us to select a matrix P by iterating to convergence on $T \circ \mathcal{D}(P)$ and to choose F as $F = F(\mathcal{D}(P))$. If we compare this outcome with the limit of recursions of $(17.4.6a)$, $(17.4.6b)$, we recognize that the infinite-horizon version of the robust filtering problem in section 17.4 is related to the robust control problem of section 17.2 via the duality relationships delineated in table 17.5.1.

---

[4] In chapter 18, we describe another robust filtering problem without commitment. In that problem, the ordinary Kalman filter is used as the time t benchmark model.

Table 17.5.1: Matching objects in robust filtering and control

Filter	A'	G'	H'	C'	D'	θ	$\hat{\Sigma}$	K'
Control	A	B	C	H	J	θ	P	F

This means that we can compute the time-invariant robust Kalman filter gain K associated with θ by solving the following robust optimal linear regulator problem: choose a sequence $\{\mu_t\}_{t=0}^{\infty}$ to maximize and a sequence $\{\phi_{t+1}\}_{t=0}^{\infty}$ to minimize

$$\frac{1}{2}\sum_{t=0}^{\infty}\left\{-\tilde{z}_t'\tilde{z}_t + \theta\phi_{t+1}'\phi_{t+1}\right\} \tag{17.5.1}$$

subject to

$$\tilde{z}_t = C'\lambda_t + D'\phi_t \tag{17.5.2a}$$

$$\lambda_{t+1} = A'\lambda_t + G'\mu_t + H'\phi_{t+1} \tag{17.5.2b}$$

subject to λ_0 given. The optimal decision rule for μ_t is

$$\mu_t = -K'\lambda_t \tag{17.5.3}$$

where K is the robust Kalman filter gain that is defined by iterations to convergence on $(17.4.6a)$, $(17.4.6b)$. We interpret the dual variables λ_t, ϕ_{t+1} in appendix A of this chapter.

17.6. Matlab programs

We can induce our Matlab program `doublex9.m` to compute T^*, $\mathcal{K}$, and $\mathcal{D}$ by exploiting the duality displayed in section 17.5. We accomplish this in the following steps.[5]

1. Input the objects A, C, G, D that form the state-space system, H in the decision maker's criterion function, and θ; A is $n \times n$, C is $n \times p$, G is $m \times n$, D is $m \times p$, and H is $r \times n$, where n is the dimension of the state, p the number of shocks, m the number of observables, and r the number of variables entering the decision maker's criterion function.

2. Prepare the robust linear regulator formulated in $(17.5.1)$ and $(17.5.2)$ by setting $Q = CC', R = DD', W = CD', A = A', B = G', D = H'$. These are the objects in a discounted robust linear regulator problem

---

[5] The Matlab program `rfilter.m` performs these steps.

with cross-products between states and controls. Therefore, if we want to use `doublex9.m`, which is meant for undiscounted problem without cross-products between states and controls, we have to use the trick described in chapter 4 on page 72 for converting to such a problem. We accomplish this in step 3.

3. Form `As` $= (A - BR^{-1}W')$, `Bs`$= B$, `Qs`$= Q - WR^{-1}W'$. The Matlab program `trick.m` accomplishes these tasks.

4. Set `sig`$= -\theta^{-1}$ and issue the Matlab command:
   `[F,K,P,Pt]=doublex9(As,Bs,D,Qs,R,sig)`
   To complete the trick begun in step 3, set $\bar{F} = F + R^{-1}W$, as described in chapter 4 on page 73.

5. Finally, set $K = F'$.

Section 17.7.2 describes how to compute the feedback rule for the distorted shock for the worst-case model affiliated with the robust filter K. Section 17.8 then describes a worst-case distorted transition law for the state. If we compute the ordinary Kalman gain for this distorted model, we obtain a robust filter.

17.7. The worst-case model

In this section, we take a gain K as given, find an associated law of motion for the resulting reconstruction errors $x_t - \hat{x}_t$, then derive a worst-case model associated with that K. We are most interested in the worst-case model for the gain K from the robust filter.

17.7.1. Law of motion for the state reconstruction error

Consider the state-space system

$$x_{t+1} = Ax_t + C\epsilon_{t+1} \tag{17.7.1a}$$

$$y_{t+1} = Gx_t + D\epsilon_{t+1} \tag{17.7.1b}$$

where $x_0 \sim \mathcal{N}(\hat{x}_0, \hat{\Sigma}_\infty)$ and

$$\hat{\Sigma}_\infty = T^* \circ \mathcal{D}(\hat{\Sigma}_\infty). \tag{17.7.2}$$

For $K = K(\hat{\Sigma}_\infty)$, consider the time-invariant robust filter constructed as in section 17.5 as

$$\hat{x}_{t+1} = A\hat{x}_t + K[y_{t+1} - G\hat{x}_t]$$
$$= A\hat{x}_t + K[Gx_t + D\epsilon_{t+1} - G\hat{x}_t]$$
$$= (A - KG)\hat{x}_t + KGx_t + KD\epsilon_{t+1}.$$

Subtracting the last equation from equation $(17.7.1a)$ gives

$$e_{t+1} = (A - KG)e_t + (C - KD)\epsilon_{t+1} \qquad (17.7.3)$$

where $e_t = x_t - \hat{x}_t$ is the reconstruction error.

17.7.2. The worst-case model associated with a time-invariant K

To construct a worst-case distribution associated with the robust Kalman filter K given by $(17.4.6a)$, we could follow the recipe in Hansen and Sargent (2005a) by forming the random variable

$$\Phi_T = \exp\left[\frac{1}{2\theta} \sum_{u=0}^{T} (He_u)'(He_u)\right] \qquad (17.7.4)$$

where e_t obeys $(17.7.3)$. A sequence of distorted probability distributions is associated with the sequence of random variables $\{\Phi_T : T = 0, 1, \ldots\}$ once they have been rescaled to have unit expectation.

In what follows we give a heuristic characterization of the corresponding limiting probability measure. This argument is heuristic because we do not give a rigorous treatment of the limit calculations.[6] Let $\mathcal{E}_t$ denote the sigma algebra generated by x_0 and the history of observations ϵ_s, $s = 0, \ldots, t$. Construct a martingale

$$M_t = \lim_{T \to \infty} \frac{E\left[\Phi_T | \mathcal{E}_t\right]}{E(\Phi_T)} \qquad (17.7.5)$$

and construct the multiplicative increment to M_t from $m_{t+1} = \frac{M_{t+1}}{M_t}$. The random variable m_{t+1} distorts the one-step ahead transition density for the error process ϵ_{t+1} in $(17.7.1)$ and the random variable M_t distorts the probabilities of $\mathcal{E}_t$-measurable events.

We can compute m_{t+1} recursively by forming an analogue of the problem studied in a chapter 3. The problem is

$$\min_{\{m_{t+1}, E(m_{t+1}|\mathcal{E}_t)=1\}_{t=0}^{\infty}} E \sum_{t=0}^{T} M_t \left\{-(He_t)'(He_t) + \alpha m_{t+1} \log m_{t+1}\right\} \qquad (17.7.6)$$

where the minimization is subject to

$$\begin{aligned} e_{t+1} &= (A - KG)e_t + (C - KD)\epsilon_{t+1} \\ M_{t+1} &= m_{t+1}M_t \end{aligned} \qquad (17.7.7)$$

and the initial conditions $M_0 = 1$ and $e_0 = 0$. We achieve time invariance by taking limits of the decision process for m_{t+1} as T gets large.

---

[6] A formal treatment would lead us to exploit some of the mathematical methods that underlie large deviation theory and the limiting behavior of Feynman-Kac probability measures.

17.7.3. A deterministic control problem for the worst-case mean

A kind of certainty equivalence argument in chapter 3 implies that we can read the solution of problem (17.7.6), (17.7.7) from the solution of the following deterministic optimal linear regulator problem:

$$e_0' P e_0 = \max_{\{w_{t+1}\}_{t=0}^\infty} \sum_{t=0}^\infty (e_t' H' H e_t - \theta w_{t+1}' w_{t+1}) \qquad (17.7.8)$$

subject to

$$e_{t+1} = (A - KG)e_t + (C - KD)w_{t+1}. \qquad (17.7.9)$$

The Bellman equation for this problem is

$$e' P e = \max_{w^*} \Big(e' H' H e - \theta w^{*\prime} w^* +$$
$$[(A - KG)e + (C - KD)w^*]' P[(A - KG)e + (C - KD)w^*] \Big).$$
$$(17.7.10)$$

The matrix P can be computed by solving an ordinary undiscounted non-stochastic optimal linear regulator problem. Given the value function, the first-order necessary condition for w^* can be expressed as

$$[\theta I - (C - KD)' P(C - KD)]w^* - (C - KD)' P(A - KG)e = 0$$

or

$$w^* = Qe \qquad (17.7.11)$$

where

$$Q = [\theta I - (C - KD)' P(C - KD)]^{-1}(C - KD)' P(A - KG). \qquad (17.7.12)$$

As in chapter 3, we can use the value function for this deterministic problem to deduce the worst-case distribution of ϵ_{t+1} in (17.7.7). From the argument in section 3.10, the precision matrix of ϵ_{t+1} is distorted to become

$$I - \frac{1}{\theta}(C - KD)' P(C - KD)$$

and the mean of ϵ_{t+1} is

$$w_{t+1} = Qe_t = [\theta I - (C - KD)' P(C - KD)]^{-1} (C - KD)' P(A - KG)e_t$$

where P is the matrix in the quadratic form for the Bellman equation for the deterministic linear regulator (17.7.10).

17.8. A Bayesian interpretation

In chapter 7, we described a Bayesian interpretation of a robust control problem. In particular, we described a law of motion for the state that is distorted relative to the approximating model and that has the property that if the decision maker were to regard that distorted model as the true one and then solve an ordinary linear regulator, he would attain the same decision rule as would a robust decision maker who solves a robust linear regulator because he distrusts the approximating model.

In this section, we perform a corresponding exercise for the robust filter by finding a distorted law of motion for the state with the property that if the decision maker completely trusts this distorted model and applies the ordinary (nonrobust) Kalman filter to it, he will attain the robust filter (17.4.6).

To form the appropriate distorted model, we use ingredients computed in section 17.7.2 and let

$$
\begin{aligned}
Q &= [\theta I - (C - KD)'P(C - KD)]^{-1} (C - KD)'P(A - KG) \\
A_1^* &= CQ \\
A_2^* &= (C - KD)Q \\
C_1^* &= CJ \\
C_2^* &= (C - KD)J \\
G^* &= DQ \\
D^* &= DJ \\
JJ' &= \left[I - \frac{1}{\theta}(C - KD)'\Sigma^{-1}(C - KD)\right]^{-1}.
\end{aligned}
\tag{17.8.1}
$$

We let ϵ_{t+1}^* be i.i.d. and normally distributed with mean zero and covariance matrix I. Consider the state-space model

$$
\begin{bmatrix} x_{t+1} \\ e_{t+1} \end{bmatrix} = \begin{bmatrix} A & A_1^* \\ 0 & (A - KG + A_2^*) \end{bmatrix} \begin{bmatrix} x_t \\ e_t \end{bmatrix} + \begin{bmatrix} C_1^* \\ C_2^* \end{bmatrix} \epsilon_{t+1}^*
$$

$$
y_{t+1} = \begin{bmatrix} G & DQ \end{bmatrix} \begin{bmatrix} x_t \\ e_t \end{bmatrix}
$$

or

$$
\begin{bmatrix} x_{t+1} \\ e_{t+1} \end{bmatrix} = \tilde{A} \begin{bmatrix} x_t \\ e_t \end{bmatrix} + \tilde{C}\epsilon_{t+1}^*
$$

$$
y_{t+1} = \tilde{G} \begin{bmatrix} x_t \\ e_t \end{bmatrix} + \tilde{D}\epsilon_{t+1}^*
\tag{17.8.2a}
$$

with initial distribution

$$
\begin{bmatrix} x_0 \\ e_0 \end{bmatrix} \sim \mathcal{N}\left(\begin{bmatrix} \hat{x}_0 \\ 0 \end{bmatrix}, \begin{bmatrix} \mathcal{D}(\Sigma_\infty) & 0 \\ 0 & G\mathcal{D}(\Sigma_\infty)G' + DD' \end{bmatrix} \right).
\tag{17.8.2b}
$$

System (17.8.2) represents the joint distribution of $\{y_{t+1}, x_{t+1}\}_{t=0}^{\infty}$ under the worst-case model associated with the robust filter $K = K(\mathcal{D}(\Sigma_{\infty}))$. Notice that the distorted state evolution for x_t in (17.8.2) feeds back on the reconstruction error e_t, a source of feedback that is absent in the approximating model (17.4.1). However, as in (17.7.3), e_t does not feed back on x_t.

Apply the *ordinary* Kalman filter to the state-space system (17.8.2) to construct the time-invariant innovations representation

$$\begin{bmatrix} \tilde{x}_{t+1} \\ \tilde{e}_{t+1} \end{bmatrix} = \tilde{A} \begin{bmatrix} \tilde{x}_t \\ \tilde{e}_t \end{bmatrix} + \tilde{K}\tilde{a}_{t+1} \tag{17.8.3a}$$

$$\tilde{y}_{t+1} = \tilde{G} \begin{bmatrix} \tilde{x}_t \\ \tilde{e}_t \end{bmatrix} + \tilde{a}_{t+1} \tag{17.8.3b}$$

where $\tilde{x}_{t+1} = \tilde{E}[x_{t+1}|y_{t+1}, \ldots, y_1]$, $\tilde{e}_{t+1} = \tilde{E}[e_{t+1}|y_{t+1}, \ldots, y_1]$, and $\tilde{a}_{t+1} = y_{t+1} - \tilde{E}[y_{t+1}|y_{t+1}, \ldots, y_1]$, where $\tilde{E}$ is an expectation with respect to the distribution associated with the distorted model (17.8.2). It is true that (1) $\hat{x}_{t+1} \equiv \tilde{x}_{t+1}$, (2) $\tilde{e}_{t+1} \equiv 0$, and (3) $Ea_t a_t' = G\mathcal{D}(\hat{\Sigma}_{\infty})G' + DD' = \tilde{E}\tilde{a}_t\tilde{a}_t' = \tilde{G}\tilde{\Sigma}\tilde{G}' + \tilde{D}\tilde{D}'$, where $\tilde{\Sigma} = E(x_{t+1} - \tilde{x}_{t+1})(x_{t+1} - \tilde{x}_{t+1})'$.

17.9. Robustifying a problem of Muth

As a simple example of the filtering problem under commitment formulated in this chapter, consider Muth's (1960) problem of estimating the position of a random walk disturbed by measurement error. We set $H = 1$ (so that the decision maker cares about the hidden state), and assume the approximating model

$$x_{t+1} = x_t + \alpha\hat{\epsilon}_{1,t+1} \tag{17.9.1a}$$

$$y_{t+1} = x_t + \hat{\epsilon}_{2,t+1} \tag{17.9.1b}$$

where α is the signal-to-noise ratio and $\hat{\epsilon}_{t+1} = \begin{bmatrix} \hat{\epsilon}_{1,t+1} & \hat{\epsilon}_{2,t+1} \end{bmatrix}'$ is an i.i.d. Gaussian process with mean zero and identity covariance matrix. The state x_t is to be estimated from current and past values of y_t. Setting $H = 1$ makes the decision maker's criterion equal to the variance of the error in reconstructing the state x from past signals y. We consider the filter

$$\hat{x}_{t+1} = \hat{x}_t + K(y_{t+1} - \hat{x}_t) \tag{17.9.2}$$

where $\hat{x}_{t+1}$ is the estimate of the state using the history of y_s through $t+1$. We want K to be robust to possible misspecification of (17.9.1).

We use the program `rfilter.m` described in section 17.6 to compute the robust K. To illuminate the perturbations to the approximating model that the decision maker is considering, we also display the following calculations.

To attain robustness, the decision maker considers a family of perturbed models

$$x_{t+1} = x_t + \alpha(\epsilon_{1,t+1} + w_{1,t+1}) \qquad (17.9.3a)$$

$$y_{t+1} = x_t + \epsilon_{2,t+1} + w_{2,t+1} \qquad (17.9.3b)$$

where $\epsilon_{t+1} = \begin{bmatrix} \epsilon_{1,t+1} & \epsilon_{2,t+1} \end{bmatrix}'$ is another i.i.d. Gaussian process with mean zero and identity covariance matrix, and $[w_{1,t+1}, w_{2,t+1}]$ are distortions to the conditional means of the two shocks $\hat{\epsilon}_{t+1}$ in $(17.9.1)$. Subtracting $(17.9.2)$ from $(17.9.3a)$ and using $(17.9.3b)$ gives

$$e_{t+1} = (1 - K)e_t + \alpha\epsilon_{1,t+1} - K\epsilon_{2,t+1} + \alpha w_{1,t+1} - K w_{2,t+1}, \qquad (17.9.4)$$

where $e_t \equiv x_t - \hat{x}_t$. Using formulas $(17.7.11), (17.7.12)$, we can represent the worst-case mean distortions as

$$\begin{aligned} w_{1,t+1} &= -Q_1 e_t \\ w_{2,t+1} &= -Q_2 e_t, \end{aligned} \qquad (17.9.5)$$

where Q_1 and Q_2 are computed using formula $(17.7.11), (17.7.12)$. Please notice that Q_1, Q_2 are functions of θ and K.

For arbitrary K and *fixed* $w_{1,t+1} = -Q_1 e_t, w_{2,t+1} = -Q_2 e_t$, the error in reconstructing the state when the model associated with (Q_1, Q_2) prevails is

$$e_{t+1} = (1 - K)e_t - \alpha Q_1 e_t + K Q_2 e_t + \alpha\epsilon_{1,t+1} - K\epsilon_{2,t+1} \qquad (17.9.6)$$

or

$$e_{t+1} = \chi e_t + \alpha\epsilon_{1,t+1} - K\epsilon_{2,t+1}, \qquad (17.9.7)$$

where

$$\chi = 1 - K - \alpha Q_1 + K Q_2. \qquad (17.9.8)$$

Equation $(17.9.7)$ gives the law of motion of the error e_t in reconstructing the state for filter K when the conditional means of the shocks are feeding back on e_t via Q_1, Q_2. Denote the variance of e_t by $\text{var}_e(K; Q_1, Q_2)$. From $(17.9.7)$ it follows directly that

$$\text{var}_e(K; Q_1, Q_2) = \frac{\alpha^2 + K^2}{1 - \chi^2}. \qquad (17.9.9)$$

The spectral density of e is

$$S_e(\omega; K, Q_1, Q_2) = g_1(\omega)g_1(-\omega) + g_2(\omega)g_2(-\omega) \qquad (17.9.10)$$

where $g_1(\omega) = \frac{\alpha}{1-\chi\exp(-i\omega)}$, $g_2(\omega) = \frac{K}{1-\chi\exp(-i\omega)}$; S_e achieves the decomposition of var_e across frequencies

$$\mathrm{var}_e = \frac{1}{2\pi} \int_{-\pi}^{\pi} S_e(\omega; K, Q_1, Q_2) d\omega.$$

Consider var_e as a function of K. Let $\hat{K}(\theta)$ be the robust filter associated with θ. When $Q_1(\theta), Q_2(\theta)$ deliver the worst-case distortions w_1 and w_2 to the conditional means of the two components of ϵ for a given θ, $\mathrm{var}_e(K; Q_1, Q_2)$ is minimized at $K = \hat{K}(\theta)$.

17.9.1. Reconstructing the ordinary Kalman filter

Let $K^* = \hat{K}(+\infty)$ denote the standard Kalman filter. If $\theta = +\infty$, then $Q_1 = Q_2 = 0$ and the variance of e_t simplifies to

$$\begin{aligned}\mathrm{var}_e(K; 0, 0) &= \frac{\alpha^2 + K^2}{1 - (1-K)^2} \\ &= \frac{\alpha^2 + K^2}{2K - K^2}.\end{aligned} \tag{17.9.11}$$

Minimizing $(17.9.11)$ with respect to K gives a formula for K that agrees with that produced by the ordinary Kalman filter $K^* = \frac{\sqrt{\alpha^4 + 4\alpha^2} - \alpha^2}{2}$.[7]

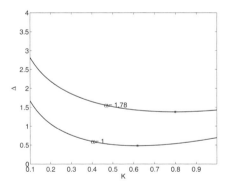

Figure 17.9.1: Variance of $e_t(K; Q_1, Q_2)$ as function of K for Q_1 and Q_2 evaluated at $\theta = 10^8$. Here the ordinary Kalman gain K^* satisfies $K^* \approx \hat{K}(\theta)$, and both K^* and $\hat{K}(\theta)$ are denoted by asterisks. The two curves are for two values of the signal-noise ratio $\alpha = 1$ and $\alpha = 1.78$.

---

[7] When $\alpha = 1$, this equals $\frac{\sqrt{5}-1}{2}$, the golden ratio.

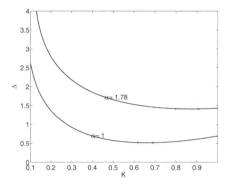

Figure 17.9.2: Variance of $e_t(K; Q_1(\theta), Q_2(\theta))$ as function of K for Q_1 and Q_2 evaluated at $\theta = 7$. Here the ordinary Kalman gain K^* satisfies $K^* < \hat{K}(\theta)$ (where $\hat{K}$ is denoted by the x and K^* by the small vertical line on the $\mathrm{var}_e(K)$ curves). The two curves are for two values of the signal-noise ratio $\alpha = 1, 1.78$.

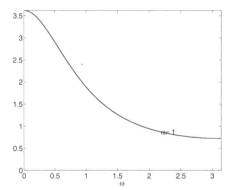

Figure 17.9.3: Frequency decomposition of the reconstruction error variance $\mathrm{var}_e(K; Q_1(\theta), Q_2(\theta))$ for $\theta = 10^8$ for $\hat{K}(\theta)$ and K^*, $\alpha = 1$. The two curves for $\hat{K}(\theta)$ and K^* approximately coincide.

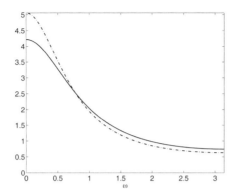

Figure 17.9.4: Frequency decomposition of the reconstruction error variance $\mathrm{var}_e(K; Q_1(\theta), Q_2(\theta))$ for $\theta = 7$ for $\hat{K}(\theta)$ and K^*, $\alpha = 1$. The solid curve is for the robust gain $\hat{K}$, the dotted one for the ordinary Kalman gain K^*. The robust gain $\hat{K}$ flattens the decomposition of variance across frequencies.

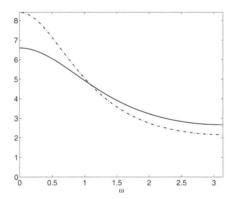

Figure 17.9.5: Frequency decomposition of the reconstruction error variance $\mathrm{var}_e(K; Q_1, Q_2)$ for $\theta = 7$ for $\hat{K}(\theta)$ and K^*, $\alpha = 1.78$. The solid curve is for the robust gain $\hat{K}$, the dotted one for the ordinary Kalman gain K^*.

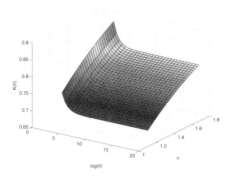

Figure 17.9.6: The robust Kalman gain $\hat{K}(\theta)$ as a function of $\log(\theta)$ and α.

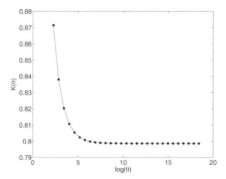

Figure 17.9.7: The robust Kalman gain $\hat{K}(\theta)$ as a function of $\log(\theta)$, given $\alpha = 1.78$.

17.9.2. Illustrations

In figure 17.9.1, we have fixed $\theta = 10^8$, and derived the associated $\hat{K}, Q_1, Q_2$ (all three are functions of θ), and plotted $\text{var}_e(K; Q_1, Q_2)$, the variance of $e_t(K)$, as a function of K. It has a minimum at $\hat{K}(\theta)$. We have also put $K^* = \hat{K}(+\infty)$ and $\hat{K}(\theta)$ on the graph. For this large value of θ, K^* is indistinguishable from $\hat{K}(\theta)$.

Figure 17.9.2 sets the value of $\theta = 7$. Now $\hat{K}(7) > K^* = K(\infty)$, though the state reconstruction error variances var_e associated with them are close.

Figure 17.9.3 displays the frequency decomposition of $\text{var}_e(K^*; 0, 0)$. Because $Q_1 = Q_2 = 0$, this is the frequency decomposition of the variance of e_t under the assumption of no specification error, using the ordinary Kalman gain K^* with $\alpha = 1$. (See (17.9.7), (17.9.8).) Figure 17.9.3 shows that the ordinary Kalman filter K^* is most vulnerable to low frequency components of e_t, which can be induced by having the worst-case conditional means feed back positively on e_t.

Figure 17.9.4 shows the frequency decomposition of $\text{var}_e(K; Q_1(7), Q_2(7))$ for two values of K, namely, K^* and $\hat{K}(7)$. Here 7 is the value of θ. Thus, the dotted line is the frequency decomposition of $\text{var}_e(K^*; Q_1(7), Q_2(7))$, while the solid line is the frequency decomposition of $\text{var}_e(\hat{K}(7); Q_1(7), Q_2(7))$. Because they are computed using (17.9.7), (17.9.8) and evaluated at $Q_1(7), Q_2(7)$, these spectral densities describe the frequency decompositions of the variances of the reconstruction errors associated with K^* and $\hat{K}(\theta)$ *under the worst-case model* associated with $\theta = 7$. Figure 17.9.4 is for $\alpha = 1$, while figure 17.9.5 is for $\alpha = 1.78$. Note that for the ordinary Kalman gain K^*, the spectral density under the approximating model in figure 17.9.3 is lower at low frequencies than is the spectral density in figure 17.9.4, which is evaluated under the worst-case model. This illustrates how the evil agent spends most of his "entropy budget" on deceiving the decision maker at low frequencies. Figure 17.9.4 shows how the robust filter responds by lowering the low frequency contributions to variance under the worst-case model. Figure 17.9.4 shows how the worst-case conditional means associated with $\theta = 7$ pump up the low frequencies of e_t, and how the robust $\hat{K}(7)$ filter achieves a lower variance $\text{var}_e(K; Q_1, Q_2)$ by flattening the spectrum, accepting higher variance at higher frequencies in exchange for lower variance at the low frequencies where the worst-case conditional means operate the strongest.

Figures 17.9.6 and 17.9.7 show the robust Kalman gain $\hat{K}$ as functions of $\log(\theta)$ and α. These figures show how increasing the preference for a robust filter (i.e., decreasing θ) raises the Kalman gain.

17.9.3. Another example

Velde (2006) considers a state-space system of the form (17.7.1) in which the first component of x_t is core inflation and remaining components describe the dynamics of a vector of relative prices. Velde is interested in minimizing $E(x_{1,t} - \hat{x}_{1,t})^2$. To get a robust Kalman filter, we would take Velde's estimates of A, C, G, D and set $H = \begin{bmatrix} 1 & 0 & \cdots & 0 \end{bmatrix}$.

17.10. A forward-looking perspective

To pave the way for the material in the next chapter, we briefly introduce a problem that takes a different view about the misspecifications that concern the decision maker when he is filtering.

Consider the situation in which the decision maker cares only about current and future values of the state. In particular, suppose that, conditional on knowing the state x, he has a value function $-x'\Omega x$, where the symmetric and positive semidefinite matrix Ω might be obtained by iterating on a Riccati equation for valuing future outcomes. Suppose further that if the decision maker knew the state, he would optimally use the decision rule $u = -Fx$. Now suppose that the state is not known and that the decision maker estimates the state using an ordinary Kalman filter. The outcome of applying the Kalman filter is that the time t state x is distributed according to a Gaussian distribution with conditional mean $\hat{x}$ and conditional covariance Σ, so that the decision maker acts as if the (partially hidden) state x obeyed $x = \hat{x} + \hat{e}$, where $\hat{e}$ is normal with mean 0 and covariance Σ. An application of a certainty equivalence argument would tell the decision maker to use the decision rule $u = -F\hat{x}$.

But now suppose that the decision maker fears that the posterior distribution emerging from the Kalman filter is misspecified, so that x instead obeys $x = \hat{x} + \hat{e} + u$ where u is a perturbation to the conditional mean. Because the decision maker wants decisions that are robust with respect to such misspecifications, he conducts a context-specific worst-case analysis that inspires him to choose the distortion u to harm the forward-looking criterion $-x'\Omega x$. To find a worst-case perturbation u, he penalizes u by entropy as measured by $u\Sigma^{-1}u$ and considers the problem

$$\min_u -(\hat{x} + u)'\Omega(\hat{x} + u) + \theta u \Sigma^{-1} u \qquad (17.10.1)$$

whose first-order necessary condition implies

$$u = -(\Omega - \theta\Sigma^{-1})^{-1}\Omega\hat{x}. \qquad (17.10.2)$$

Apply the partitioned inverse formula

$$(a - bd^{-1}c)^{-1} = a^{-1} + a^{-1}b[d - ca^{-1}b]^{-1}ca^{-1}$$

with $a = \Omega, b = \theta, d = \Sigma, c = 1$ to get

$$(\Omega - \theta\Sigma^{-1})^{-1} = \Omega^{-1} + \Omega^{-1}\theta[\Sigma - \Omega^{-1}\theta]^{-1}\Omega^{-1}.$$

Then from (17.10.2) we have

$$u = -\left(I + \Omega^{-1}[\theta^{-1}\Sigma - \Omega^{-1}]^{-1}\right)\hat{x}.$$

The worst-case x is then $\check{x} = \hat{x} + u$, or

$$\check{x} = (I - \theta^{-1}\Sigma\Omega)^{-1}\hat{x}. \tag{17.10.3}$$

The decision maker achieves robustness to doubts about the specification of the prior distribution coming from the Kalman filter by using the decision rule

$$u = -F\check{x}. \tag{17.10.4}$$

17.10.1. *Relation to a formulation from control theory literature*

Başar and Bernhard (1995) and Whittle (1990) use a decision rule of the form (17.10.4), where instead of starting with the prior for x that emerges from the Kalman filter, they begin from the distorted prior that we deduced from our robust Kalman filter. In that formulation, *past* distortions to the conditional covariance of the current value of the hidden state that are used to design the robust Kalman filter affect the decision rule through their effects on $\hat{x}$. In addition, distortions to the distribution of *future* values of the state vector affect the decision rule through the design of a robust F via the approach described in chapter 2 and 7. See Whittle (1990), Başar and Bernhard (1995), and Hansen and Sargent (2005b) for extensive discussions of this type of setup.

17.10.2. *The next chapter*

In the next chapter, we adopt a different timing protocol for the players, in particular, one that makes it impossible for the minimizing player to commit to prior distortions to the distribution of the hidden state. We shall study a "two-θ" recursive formulation of decision problems in which a decision maker is worried about two sources of possible misspecification: (1) misspecified dynamics of the entire state vector, including its hidden components, and

(2) a misspecified prior distribution for the hidden state variables. We accommodate the first type of misspecifications by allowing distortions to the conditional mean of the state and measurement errors ϵ_{t+1} to feed back on past state vectors. We accommodate the second type through a perturbation like the u in problem (17.10.1). By using different θ's to penalize the entropies associated with these two perturbations, we construct a framework that allows us to focus the decision maker's concerns more on one or the other of these sources of misspecification.

A. Dual to evil agent's problem

To help interpret the dual control problem (17.5.1), (17.5.2) that we used to compute the gain K of the robust filter, we pose the following finite-horizon version of problem (17.7.8), (17.7.9). A malevolent agent chooses a sequence of shocks w_{T-t} to maximize

$$\frac{1}{2}\sum_{t=0}^{T} e'_{T-t}e_{T-t} - \theta w'_{T-t}w_{T-t} \tag{17.A.1}$$

subject to

$$e_{T-t+1} = (A - KG)e_{T-t} + (C - KD)w_{T-t}. \tag{17.A.2}$$

Notice that $t = 0, 1, \ldots, T-1, T$ while $T - t = T, T-1, \ldots, 1, 0$. We make time run backwards in order to allow it run forward in the dual problem to be derived by analyzing the following Lagrangian for (17.A.1), (17.A.2):

$$L = \left\{ \sum_{t=0}^{T} \frac{1}{2}(z'_{t-T}z_{t-T} - \theta w'_{T-t}w_{T-t}) + \lambda_{t+1}' \big[(A - KG)e_{T-t} \right.$$
$$\left. + (C - KD)w_{T-t} - e_{T-t+1} \big] + \phi'_t(He_{T-t} - z_{T-t}) \right\}. \tag{17.A.3}$$

The first-order conditions for maximizing (17.A.3) with respect to w_{T-t}, z_{T-t}, e_{T-t} are

$$w_{T-t}: \quad -\theta w_{T-t} + (C - KD)'\lambda_t = 0 \tag{17.A.4a}$$
$$z_{T-t}: \quad z_{T-t} - \phi_t = 0 \tag{17.A.4b}$$
$$e_{T-t}: \quad -\lambda_t + (A - KG)'\lambda_{t-1} + H'\phi_t = 0, \quad t = 1, \ldots, T \tag{17.A.4c}$$
$$e_T: \quad -\lambda_0 + H'\phi_0 = 0. \tag{17.A.4d}$$

Solving (17.A.4a) and (17.A.4b) for w_{T-t} and z_{T-t} and substituting into the original objective for the evil agent gives the following dual control problem. Given K, choose a sequence ϕ_t to minimize

$$-\frac{1}{2\theta}\sum_{t=0}^{T}\left\{ \lambda'_{t-1}(C - KD)(C - KD)'\lambda_{t-1} - \theta\phi'_t\phi_t \right\} \tag{17.A.5}$$

subject to

$$\lambda_{t+1} = (A - KG)'\lambda_t + H'\phi_{t+1} \tag{17.A.6a}$$
$$\lambda_0 = H'\phi_0. \tag{17.A.6b}$$

Compare this system to (17.5.1), (17.5.2), (17.5.3).

Chapter 18
Robust filtering without commitment

In commerce bygones are forever bygones and we are always starting clear at each moment, judging the value of things with a view to future utility. Industry is essentially prospective not retrospective.
— *William Stanley Jevons, The Theory of Political Economy, 1871*

18.1. Introduction

This chapter extends ideas about control and filtering from chapters 5, 7, and 17. We study a decision maker who does not observe parts of the state that help forecast variables he cares about. We formulate a joint control and prediction problem and show how it can be represented recursively.

The filtering problem in chapter 17 took as the decision maker's approximating model a state-space representation for observables and states, then posed the problem of estimating a function of hidden states with a filter that is robust to perturbations of the approximating model. The approach in this chapter has a different starting point. We take the view that the decision maker's approximating model *includes* a recursive representation of the estimator of the hidden state that is derived by applying the *ordinary* (i.e., nonrobust) Kalman filter to the approximating state-space model for states and measurements. We include among the state variables sufficient statistics for the distribution of the hidden part of the state that come from using the ordinary Kalman filter and the history of signals to estimate the hidden part of the state. The mean and covariance of the hidden part of the state are statistics that summarize the history of signals in terms of a finite dimensional state vector whose dimension does not grow over time.[1] To obtain decision rules that are robust with respect to perturbations of the conditional distributions associated with the approximating model, the decision maker imagines a malevolent agent who perturbs the distribution of future states conditional on the entire state as well as the distribution of the hidden state conditional on the history of signals.

We use figure 18.1.1 to illustrate the two types of statistical perturbation that we have in mind, one that distorts a distribution conditional on knowledge of a hidden state, another that distorts the decision maker's prior distribution over the hidden state. Figure 18.1.1 generalizes figure 1.7.1. A hidden state takes two values that for concreteness we can think of as indexing models A and B, over which the decision maker puts prior probabilities

---

[1] Unlike the history of signals itself, whose dimension does grow with time.

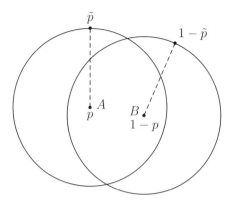

Figure 18.1.1: Two models A and B indexed by a hidden state with prior probabilities $p, 1 - p$.

$p \geq 0$ and $1 - p$, respectively.[2] Even if he were to know the hidden state, in this case submodel A or submodel B, the decision maker would distrust his model specification. Therefore, he surrounds each submodel with a set of other models specified vaguely in terms of the set of all models conditioned on the hidden state whose entropy is less than some prescribed amount. The two circles surrounding each submodel represent such clouds of models. Conditional on the hidden state (i.e., an appropriate submodel), a minimizing player chooses a worst-case model within cloud A and a worst-case model within cloud B. To achieve robustness with respect to his prior p over the hidden state, the decision maker imagines that a malevolent player distorts the distribution of the hidden state to be $\tilde{p}$. The decision maker then achieves a robust decision rule by acting as if he were maximizing with respect to the worst-case $\tilde{p}, 1 - \tilde{p}$ mixture of the worst-case submodels. In the formal analysis in this chapter, the decision maker distorts a model conditioned on the hidden state by applying an operator $\mathbf{T}^1$ and distorts a prior over models by applying an operator $\mathbf{T}^2$.

By including the sequence of distributions of the hidden state from the ordinary Kalman filter among the objects that constitute the approximating model, we assume that the time t decision maker inherits no distortions from hidden state estimation problems that were solved at earlier dates. This leads to a different dynamic estimation problem than studied in chapter 17, where

---

[2] Cogley, Colacito, Hansen, and Sargent (2007) study how concerns for robustness affect a monetary authority's incentives to design experiments that will help to tighten its prior over submodels. See Elliott, Aggoun, and Moore (1995) for an account of hidden Markov models.

such commitments constrained the time t malevolent player.[3]

18.2. A recursive control and filtering problem

In this section, we first describe the decision maker's approximating model, then define two risk-sensitivity operators that express his distrust of particular aspects of that model.

18.2.1. The decision maker's approximating model

Following Hansen and Sargent (2005b) and Hansen, Mayer, and Sargent (2007), partition a state vector as

$$x_t = \begin{bmatrix} y_t \\ z_t \end{bmatrix}$$

where y_t is observed and z_t is not observed by a decision maker whose one-period utility function is

$$U(x_t, a_t) = -.5 \begin{bmatrix} a_t' & x_t' \end{bmatrix} \begin{bmatrix} Q & P \\ P' & R \end{bmatrix} \begin{bmatrix} a_t \\ x_t \end{bmatrix}$$

where a_t is a vector of controls that influence future values of both (y, z) and a signal s that is informative about z. The decision maker ranks $\{x_t, a_t\}$ sequences according to

$$E\Big[\sum_{t=0}^{\infty} \beta^t U(x_t, a_t) \big| y_0\Big], \tag{18.2.1}$$

where E is the mathematical expectation with respect to a probability distribution that we now describe. At time $t + 1$, the decision maker observes a vector s_{t+1} that includes y_{t+1} and possibly other signals about the hidden state. The decision maker remembers past signals. The laws of motion are

$$y_{t+1} = \Pi_s s_{t+1} + \Pi_y y_t + \Pi_a a_t \tag{18.2.2a}$$

$$z_{t+1} = A_{21} y_t + A_{22} z_t + B_2 a_t + C_2 w_{t+1} \tag{18.2.2b}$$

$$s_{t+1} = D_1 y_t + D_2 z_t + H a_t + G w_{t+1} \tag{18.2.2c}$$

where $w_{t+1} \sim \mathcal{N}(0, I)$. Substituting $(18.2.2c)$ into $(18.2.2a)$ gives the following transition law for the observed state:[4]

$$y_{t+1} = A_{11} y_t + A_{12} z_t + B_1 a_t + C_1 w_{t+1}, \tag{18.2.3}$$

---

[3] This chapter draws heavily on Hansen and Sargent (2007a) and Hansen, Mayer, and Sargent (2007).

[4] Sometimes we formulate a problem directly in terms of $(18.2.3)$ without first stipulating $(18.2.2a)$.

where $A_{11} = (\Pi_s D_1 + \Pi_y), A_{12} = \Pi_s D_2, B_1 = (\Pi_s H + \Pi_a), C_1 = \Pi_s G$. Thus, we have the state-space system

$$x_{t+1} = Ax_t + Ba_t + Cw_{t+1} \tag{18.2.4a}$$

$$s_{t+1} = Dx_t + Ha_t + Gw_{t+1}. \tag{18.2.4b}$$

The decision maker believes that the distribution of the initial value of the unobserved part of the state is

$$z_0 \sim \mathcal{N}(\check{z}_0, \Delta_0). \tag{18.2.5}$$

Let $s^t = [s_t, \dots, s_0]$ denote the history of signals up to time t. Taking into account that y_t is observed and applying the ordinary Kalman filter to system (18.2.4) gives the following representation for $\check{z}_{t+1} \equiv E[z_{t+1}|s^{t+1}]$ and $\check{s}_{t+1} \equiv E[s_{t+1}|s^t]$:

$$\check{s}_{t+1} = D_1 y_t + D_2 \check{z}_t + Ha_t \tag{18.2.6a}$$

$$\check{z}_{t+1} = A_{21} y_t + A_{22} \check{z}_t + B_2 a_t + K_2(\Delta_t)(s_{t+1} - \check{s}_{t+1}) \tag{18.2.6b}$$

$$\Delta_{t+1} = A_{22}\Delta_t A_{22}' + C_2 C_2' - K_2(\Delta_t)(A_{22}\Delta_t D_2' + C_2 G')' \tag{18.2.6c}$$

$$K_2(\Delta) = (A_{22}\Delta D_2' + C_2 G')(D_2\Delta D_2' + GG')^{-1} \tag{18.2.6d}$$

where $\Delta_t = E[z_t - \check{z}_t][z_t - \check{z}_t]'$. Notice that $\check{z}_{t+1}$ conditions on s^{t+1} and that $\check{s}_{t+1}$ conditions on s^t. Under the approximating model, $z_t \sim \mathcal{N}(\check{z}_t, \Delta_t)$, and $(\check{z}_t, \Delta_t) = q_t$ is a collection of sufficient statistics for the unobserved part of the state at date t.

We regard representation (18.2.6) as a complete statement of the decision maker's approximating model. Thus, we take the laws of motion for $(\check{z}_t, \Delta_t)$ that come from applying the Kalman filter to model (18.2.4) to be parts of the decision maker's approximating model.[5] We seek a decision rule that is robust to statistical perturbations of (18.2.6). This structure isolates two random vectors whose distributions we want to perturb at date t: (1) the conditional distribution of the shock w_{t+1}, which according to the approximating model is $\mathcal{N}(0, I)$; and (2) the distribution of the hidden state z_t, which according to the approximating model is $\mathcal{N}(\check{z}_t, \Delta_t)$. A virtue of this formulation is that by taking the outcome of applying the Kalman filter to (18.2.4) as part of the approximating model, we have to solve only one Kalman filtering problem. [6]

---

[5] This contrasts with the approach in chapter 17, where the approximating model did not include the law of motion for an estimate of the hidden state induced by applying the ordinary Kalman filter.

[6] Alternative formulations can be conceived that would have the decision maker solve a separate filtering problem for each perturbation of the approximating model (18.2.4). Those would obviously be more demanding computationally. See Hansen and Sargent (2005b, 2007a) for a discussion of this issue.

Recall that to obtain a recursive solution in the filtering problem under commitment studied in chapter 17, we repeatedly modified the benchmark model. That meant that past distortions altered the current period reference model. By way of contrast, in the formulation in this chapter, each period the decision maker retains the same original benchmark model. By itself, this diminishes the impact of robust filtering. We can adjust for that diminution of the impact of robustness by allowing θ_2 to be smaller than θ_1, thereby giving the current period minimizing agent more flexibility to distort the distribution of the current hidden state.

18.2.2. Two sources of statistical perturbation

We transform representation $(18.2.6)$ in a way designed to focus our attention on perturbations to the distributions of w_{t+1} and z_t, respectively. To formulate a recursive version of our problem, let * denote a next-period value and use $(18.2.6)$ to express the evolution equation for $[\,y'_{t+1} \quad \check{z}'_{t+1} \quad \Delta_{t+1}\,]$ as

$$
\begin{bmatrix} y^* \\ \check{z}^* \\ \Delta^* \end{bmatrix} = \begin{bmatrix} A_{11} & A_{12} & 0 \\ A_{21} & A_{22} & 0 \\ 0 & 0 & 1 \end{bmatrix} \begin{bmatrix} y \\ \check{z} \\ f(\Delta) \end{bmatrix} + \begin{bmatrix} B_1 \\ B_2 \\ 0 \end{bmatrix} a + \begin{bmatrix} A_{12} \\ K_2(\Delta)D_2 \\ 0 \end{bmatrix} [z - \check{z}]
$$
$$
+ \begin{bmatrix} C_1 \\ K_2(\Delta)G \\ 0 \end{bmatrix} w^*
$$

$(18.2.7)$

where $f(\Delta) = A_{22}\Delta A'_{22} - (A_{22}\Delta D'_2 + C_2 G')(D_2 \Delta D'_2 + GG')^{-1}(A_{22}\Delta D'_2 + C_2 G')' + C_2 C'_2$, $w^* \sim \mathcal{N}(0, I)$, and $z \sim \mathcal{N}(\check{z}, \Delta)$. Notice that Δ_t evolves exogenously with respect to $(y, \check{z})$, so that given an initial condition Δ_0, a path $\{\Delta_{t+1}\}_{t=0}^{\infty}$ can be computed before observing anything else.

Two random vectors, $(z - \check{z})$ and w^*, appear in representation $(18.2.7)$. In the next subsection, we describe systematic ways of organizing context-specific perturbations to the distributions of these two random vectors. At first reading, it is possible to skim these subsections and move immediately to subsection 18.2.8, where we use a certainty equivalent problem to find the key objects needed to compute a robust decision rule.

18.2.3. Two operators

An operator $\mathbf{T}^1$ systematically perturbs the distribution of w_{t+1} conditional on $(y, \check{z}, z)$ and another operator $\mathbf{T}^2$ perturbs the distribution of z conditional on $(y, \check{z})$. Let $q = (\check{z}, \Delta)$ be our sufficient statistics for the distribution of the hidden state. Throughout this section, we let a be a measurable function of (y, q).

18.2.4. The $\mathbf{T}^1$ operator

We use the martingale representation of perturbed models that we introduced in chapter 3. Let m be a nonnegative random variable that is measurable with respect to (y^*, q^*, z^*). Assume that m has mean 1 conditional on (y, q, z, a). Hansen and Sargent (2005b, 2007a) show that m can be used to represent distortions to the joint distribution of (y^*, q^*, z^*), conditional on (y, q, z, a). In particular, m serves as a Radon-Nikodym derivative, or likelihood ratio, for transforming one distribution into another. Let $V(y, q, z, a)$ be a measurable function of (y, q, z). Then $E\left[mV(y^*, q^*, z^*, a)|y, z, q, a\right]$ equals the conditional expectation of V evaluated with respect to a distorted density formed by multiplying the original density by m. Define the entropy of m by $\varepsilon^1(m) = E(m \log m|y, q, z)$. Following Hansen and Sargent (2007a), we define the operator $\mathbf{T}^1$ by

$$\mathbf{T}^1 V(y^*, q^*, z^*, a)(y, q, z, a; \theta) = \min_{m \geq 0} E\left[mV(y^*, q^*, z^*, a)|y, z, q, a\right]$$

$$+ \theta\varepsilon^1(m) \tag{18.2.8a}$$

$$= -\theta \log \int \exp\left[\frac{-V(y^*, q^*, z^*, a)}{\theta}\right]\phi_1(w^*)dw^*, \tag{18.2.8b}$$

where ϕ_1 is the standard normal density and the minimization in $(18.2.8a)$ is subject to the law of motion $(18.2.7)$ and the restriction that $E[m|y, z, q, a] = 1$. The minimizing m is

$$m^\heartsuit \propto \exp\left[\frac{-V(y^*, q^*, z^*, a)}{\theta}\right], \tag{18.2.9}$$

where the factor of proportionality is chosen to make the mean of m conditional on (y, q, z, a) equal to 1.

18.2.5. The $\mathbf{T}^2$ operator

Let h be a nonnegative random variable that is a measurable function of (y, q, z, a) and that has mean 1 conditional on (y, q, a). Hansen and Sargent (2005b, 2007a) show that such a nonnegative random variable h can be used to represent distortions to the joint distribution of (y, q, z). Define the entropy of h as $\varepsilon^2(h) = E(h \log h|y, q, a)$. Consider a function $\check{V}(y, q, z, a)$ and define the operator

$$\mathbf{T}^2 \check{V}(y, q, z, a)(y, q, a; \theta) = \min_{h \geq 0} E\left(h\check{V}(y, q, z, a)|y, q, a\right)$$

$$+ \theta\varepsilon^2(h) \tag{18.2.10a}$$

$$= -\theta \log \int \exp\left[\frac{-\check{V}(y, q, z, a)}{\theta}\right]\phi_2(z|\check{z}, \Delta)dz \tag{18.2.10b}$$

where $\phi_2(z|\check{z}, \Delta)$ is a normal density with mean $\check{z}$ and covariance matrix Δ and the minimization is subject to $E[h|y, q, a] = 1$. The minimizing h is

$$h^{\heartsuit} \propto \exp\left[\frac{-\check{V}(y, q, z, a)}{\theta}\right], \tag{18.2.11}$$

where the factor of proportionality is chosen to make the conditional mean of h be 1.

18.2.6. Two sources of fragility

By finding a worst-case m, the operator $\mathbf{T}^1$ distorts the distribution of w^*, conditional on (y, q, z, a). It can help a decision maker explore fragility of decisions to misspecification of the distribution of (y^*, q^*, z^*) conditional on (y, q, z, a). Notice that the hidden state z is included in the conditioning set.

By finding a worst-case h, the operator $\mathbf{T}^2$ distorts the distribution of z conditional on (y, q, a). It can help a decision maker explore the fragility of a decision rule $a = a(y, \check{z})$ to misspecifications of the prior distribution for z, as represented in our linear-quadratic problem, for example, by the sufficient statistics $q = (\check{z}, \Delta)$ for the distribution of the hidden state given the history of signals. Here q keeps track of the history of signals.

18.2.7. A recursive formulation for control and estimation

By solving the following Bellman equation, the decision maker can design a decision rule that is robust to misspecifications of the conditional distribution of w^* and the distribution of the hidden state z:[7]

$$W(y, q) = \max_a \mathbf{T}^2\left[U(x, a) + \mathbf{T}^1 \beta W^*(y, q)(y, q, z, a; \theta_1)\right](y, q, a; \theta_2). \tag{18.2.12}$$

Here $\mathbf{T}^1$ integrates over w^*, conditioning on (y, q, z, a), and $\mathbf{T}^2$ integrates over z, conditioning on (y, q, a). Assigning different values to θ in the two operators lets the decision maker focus more or less on misspecifications of one or the other of the two distributions being perturbed.

By virtue of equations $(18.2.8a)$ and $(18.2.10a)$, each step in recursion $(18.2.12)$ involves maximization over a and minimization over h and m. For linear quadratic problems like the ones we are interested in here, certainty equivalence principle can be exploited to simplify the calculations. We show how to do this in the next section by first computing the means of the perturbed distributions of w^* and z, then calculating the covariance matrices later.

---

[7] Hansen, Mayer, and Sargent (2007) refer to this formulation as "Game II." Those papers also describe two other games (Game I and Game III).

18.2.8. A certainty equivalent shortcut

Let u be the mean of $z - \check{z}$ and $\tilde{v}$ the mean of w^*, both conditioned on $(y, \check{z})$. Consider the evolution equation

$$\begin{bmatrix} y^* \\ \check{z}^* \end{bmatrix} = \begin{bmatrix} A_{11} & A_{12} \\ A_{21} & A_{22} \end{bmatrix} \begin{bmatrix} y \\ \check{z} \end{bmatrix} + \begin{bmatrix} B_1 \\ B_2 \end{bmatrix} a + \begin{bmatrix} A_{12} \\ K_2(\Delta)D_2 \end{bmatrix} u + \begin{bmatrix} C_1 \\ K_2(\Delta)G \end{bmatrix} \tilde{v}$$
(18.2.13)

or

$$\tilde{x}^* = \tilde{A}\tilde{x} + \tilde{B}(\Delta)\tilde{a} \tag{18.2.14}$$

where

$$\tilde{a} = \begin{bmatrix} a \\ u \\ \tilde{v} \end{bmatrix}, \qquad \tilde{x} = \begin{bmatrix} y \\ \check{z} \end{bmatrix}. \tag{18.2.15}$$

We obtained (18.2.13) by letting $w^* = \tilde{v} + \epsilon^*$ and $z - \check{z} = u + \epsilon_u$, where ϵ^* and ϵ_u are both Gaussian random vectors with means of zero, and then dropping the terms in ϵ^* and ϵ_u from (18.2.7). Dropping these terms can be justified by a certainty equivalence argument like the one used in chapter 2. We will take account of these omitted terms later when we compute covariance matrices. The important thing to note now is that omitting these terms at this stage does not imperil our computations of u and $\tilde{v}$.[8]

We add to the utility function $U(x, a)$ the parts of two entropy terms pertinent for our deterministic problem to get the augmented return function

$$U(x, a) + \frac{\theta_1}{2}|\tilde{v}|^2 + \frac{\theta_2}{2}u'\Delta^{-1}u,$$

where θ_1 penalizes distortions v and θ_2 penalizes distortions u. Define this augmented return function as $r(\tilde{x}, \tilde{a})$ and represent it as

$$\begin{aligned} r(\tilde{x}, \tilde{a}) &= -\frac{1}{2} \begin{bmatrix} a' & y' & z' \end{bmatrix} \begin{bmatrix} Q & P_1 & P_2 \\ P_1' & R_{11} & R_{12} \\ P_2' & R_{21} & R_{22} \end{bmatrix} \begin{bmatrix} a \\ y \\ z \end{bmatrix} + \frac{\theta_1}{2}|\tilde{v}|^2 + \frac{\theta_2}{2}u'\Delta^{-1}u \\ &= -\frac{1}{2} \begin{bmatrix} \tilde{a}' & \tilde{x}' \end{bmatrix} \Pi(\Delta) \begin{bmatrix} \tilde{a} \\ \tilde{x} \end{bmatrix} \end{aligned}$$

where

$$\Pi(\Delta) = \begin{bmatrix} \Pi_{11} & \Pi_{12} \\ \Pi_{21} & \Pi_{22} \end{bmatrix}, \qquad \Pi_{11} = \begin{bmatrix} Q & P_2 & 0 \\ P_2' & R_{22} - \theta_2\Delta^{-1} & 0 \\ 0 & 0 & -\theta_1 I \end{bmatrix},$$

---

[8] This statement relies on the fact that we are solving multiplier and not constraint problems, so that we do not have to adjust the multiplier when entropies rise further after we perturb variances. See chapter 7.

$$\Pi_{12} = \begin{bmatrix} P_1 & P_2 \\ R_{21} & R_{22} \\ 0 & 0 \end{bmatrix}, \quad \Pi_{22} = \begin{bmatrix} R_{11} & R_{12} \\ R_{21} & R_{22} \end{bmatrix},$$

and $\Pi_{21} = \Pi_{12}'$. Then we can compute $(y, \check{z})$-contingent distortions to the means $(u, \tilde{v})$ and a robust decision rule for a that solve $(18.2.12)$ by solving the deterministic problem

$$\max_{\{a_t\}} \min_{\{u_t, \tilde{v}_t\}} \sum_{t=0}^{\infty} \beta^t r(\tilde{x}_t, \tilde{a}_t) \tag{18.2.16}$$

subject to

$$\tilde{x}_{t+1} = \tilde{A}\tilde{x}_t + \tilde{B}(\Delta_t)\tilde{a}_t \tag{18.2.17}$$

where Δ_t is the solution of $(18.2.6c)$, $(18.2.6d)$. The Bellman equation for problem $(18.2.16)$, $(18.2.17)$ is

$$-\frac{1}{2}\tilde{x}'\Omega(\Delta)\tilde{x} = \text{ext}_{\tilde{a}}\left\{-\frac{1}{2}\begin{bmatrix} \tilde{a}' & \tilde{x}' \end{bmatrix}\Pi(\Delta)\begin{bmatrix} \tilde{a} \\ \tilde{x} \end{bmatrix} - \frac{1}{2}\beta\tilde{x}^{*'}\Omega(\Delta^*)\tilde{x}^*\right\}, \tag{18.2.18}$$

where ext denotes extremization (i.e., maximization with respect to a and minimization with respect to u and $\tilde{v}$) and the extremization is subject to $(18.2.14)$. To be well posed, (θ_1, θ_2) must be large enough to make the matrix

$$\begin{bmatrix} \theta_2\Delta^{-1} - R_{22} & 0 \\ 0 & \theta_1 I \end{bmatrix} - \beta\begin{bmatrix} A_{12}' & D_2'K_2(\Delta)' \\ C_1' & G'K_2(\Delta)' \end{bmatrix}\Omega(\Delta^*)\begin{bmatrix} A_{12} & C_1 \\ K_2(\Delta)D_2 & K_2(\Delta)G \end{bmatrix} \tag{18.2.19}$$

be positive definite. We call $(18.2.19)$ a "no-breakdown condition."

The decision rule for $\tilde{a}$ is

$$\tilde{a} = -\left[\Pi_{11}(\Delta) + \beta\tilde{B}(\Delta)'\Omega^*(\Delta^*)\tilde{B}(\Delta)\right]^{-1}\left[\Pi_{12} + \beta\tilde{B}(\Delta)'\Omega^*(\Delta^*)\tilde{A}\right]\tilde{x} \tag{18.2.20}$$

and the recursion for $\Omega(\Delta)$ is the Riccati equation

$$\Omega(\Delta) = \Pi_{22} + \beta\tilde{A}(\Delta)'\Omega^*(\Delta^*)\tilde{A}(\Delta) - \left[\Pi_{12} + \beta\tilde{B}(\Delta)'\Omega^*(\Delta^*)\tilde{A}\right]'$$
$$\left[\Pi_{11}(\Delta) + \beta\tilde{B}(\Delta)'\Omega^*(\Delta^*)\tilde{B}(\Delta)\right]^{-1}\left[\Pi_{12} + \beta\tilde{B}(\Delta)'\Omega^*(\Delta^*)\tilde{A}\right]. \tag{18.2.21}$$

In the special case that the decision maker in effect conditions on an infinite history of signals and in which Δ_t has converged, we can set $\Delta^* = \Delta$ and exploit the observation that, as noted in chapter 2, problem $(18.2.18)$ can be solved using standard formulas for the ordinary discounted optimal linear regulator. In particular, our Matlab program `olrp.m` can be applied.

The extremizing decision rule from either (18.2.20) in the general case or `olrp.m` for the special case $\Delta_{t+1} = \Delta_0 \forall t \geq 1$ is

$$\tilde{a} \equiv \begin{bmatrix} a \\ u \\ \tilde{v} \end{bmatrix} = -\tilde{F}(\Delta)\tilde{x} = -\begin{bmatrix} \tilde{F}_1(\Delta) \\ F_2(\Delta) \\ F_3(\Delta) \end{bmatrix} \tilde{x}. \qquad (18.2.22)$$

The first block row gives the robust decision rule and the second gives the distorted mean u of $z - \check{z}$, both as functions of $\tilde{x} = \begin{bmatrix} y \\ \check{z} \end{bmatrix}$. The third block row gives the mean $\tilde{v}$ of the distorted distribution for w^*, conditional on $\tilde{x}$.

In problem (18.2.12), the distorted mean actually depends on the unobserved state z as well, since the $\mathbf{T}^1$ operator conditions on z. So while problem (18.2.16), (18.2.17) allows us to compute the decision rule a and the distortion to the mean of z that solves (18.2.12), it does not provide the mean distortion to the distribution of w^* conditioned on $(y, \check{z}, z)$ that the $\mathbf{T}^1$ operator in (18.2.12) computes. We now describe how to compute the distorted mean of w^* conditioned on the set $(y, \check{z}, z)$ that conditions $\mathbf{T}^1$. We need this conditional mean and the associated conditional covariance matrix in order to compute objects that will be of interest later.

18.2.9. Computing the $\mathbf{T}^1$ operator

Impose the robust control law for a in the law of motion (18.2.14) to get

$$\begin{bmatrix} y^* \\ \check{z}^* \end{bmatrix} = \tilde{A} \begin{bmatrix} y \\ \check{z} \end{bmatrix} - \begin{bmatrix} B_1 \\ B_2 \end{bmatrix} \tilde{F}_1(\Delta) \begin{bmatrix} y \\ \check{z} \end{bmatrix} + \begin{bmatrix} A_{12} \\ K_2(\Delta)D_2 \end{bmatrix} [z - \check{z}] + \begin{bmatrix} C \\ K_2(\Delta)G \end{bmatrix} w^*$$

or

$$\begin{bmatrix} y^* \\ \check{z}^* \end{bmatrix} = \bar{A}(\Delta) \begin{bmatrix} y \\ \check{z} \end{bmatrix} + \bar{H}(\Delta)[z - \check{z}] + \bar{C}(\Delta)w^*.$$

We already know the mean of the worst-case w^* conditioned on $(y, \check{z})$. We want to know the mean of w^* conditioned on $(y, \check{z}, z)$. An LQ control problem associated with the $\mathbf{T}^1$ operator is

$$\min_v -\frac{1}{2}\beta \begin{bmatrix} y^{*\prime} & \check{z}^{*\prime} \end{bmatrix} \Omega^*(\Delta^*) \begin{bmatrix} y^* \\ \check{z}^* \end{bmatrix} + \frac{\theta_1}{2} v'v$$

where the minimization is subject to the law of motion

$$\begin{bmatrix} y^* \\ \check{z}^* \end{bmatrix} = \bar{A}(\Delta) \begin{bmatrix} y \\ \check{z} \end{bmatrix} + \bar{H}(\Delta)[z - \check{z}] + \bar{C}(\Delta)v.$$

The first-order necessary condition for this minimum problem yields

$$v = -\beta[-\theta_1 I + \beta\bar{C}(\Delta)'\Omega^*(\Delta^*)\bar{C}(\Delta)]^{-1}\bar{C}(\Delta)'\Omega^*(\Delta^*)\left(\bar{A}(\Delta) \begin{bmatrix} y \\ \check{z} \end{bmatrix} + \bar{H}(\Delta)[z-\check{z}]\right)$$

or

$$v = -\bar{F}(\Delta) \begin{bmatrix} z - \check{z} \\ y \\ z \end{bmatrix} = -\bar{F}_1(\Delta)(z - \check{z}) - \bar{F}_2(\Delta) \begin{bmatrix} y \\ z \end{bmatrix}. \qquad (18.2.23)$$

Equation $(18.2.23)$ gives v, the worst-case mean of w^* that comes from applying the $\mathbf{T}^1$ operator. Conditional on $(y, z, \check{z})$, the covariance matrix of the worst-case distribution of w^* is

$$\Sigma(\Delta) = \left[I - \frac{\beta}{\theta_1} \bar{C}(\Delta)' \Omega^*(\Delta^*) \bar{C}(\Delta) \right]^{-1}.$$

We now compute a matrix $\bar{\Omega}(\Delta)$ in a quadratic form in $[\,(z - \check{z})' \quad y' \quad \check{z}'\,]$ that emerges from applying the $\mathbf{T}^1$ operator. First, adjust the objective for the choice of v by constructing a matrix $\bar{\Pi}(\Delta)$, whose row and column dimension equal the dimension of $[\,(z - \check{z})' \quad y' \quad \check{z}'\,]$:

$$\bar{\Pi}(\Delta) = \begin{bmatrix} 0 & -\tilde{F}_1(\Delta) \\ I & 0 & 0 \\ 0 & I & 0 \\ 0 & 0 & I \end{bmatrix}' \begin{bmatrix} Q & P_2 & P_1 & P_2 \\ P_2' & R_{22} - \theta_2 \Delta^{-1} & R_{21} & R_{22} \\ P_1' & R_{21} & R_{11} & R_{12} \\ P_2' & R_{22} & R_{21} & R_{22} \end{bmatrix}$$
$$\begin{bmatrix} 0 & -\tilde{F}_1(\Delta) \\ I & 0 & 0 \\ 0 & I & 0 \\ 0 & 0 & I \end{bmatrix}.$$

The matrix in the quadratic form in $[\,(z - \check{z})' \quad y' \quad \check{z}'\,]$ for the minimized objective function that emerges from applying the $\mathbf{T}^1$ operator is

$$\bar{\Omega}(\Delta) = \bar{\Pi}(\Delta) + \beta \begin{bmatrix} \bar{H}(\Delta)' \\ \bar{A}(\Delta)' \end{bmatrix} \Omega^*(\Delta^*) \Big\{ I +$$
$$\beta \bar{C}(\Delta) \left[\theta_1 I - \beta \bar{C}(\Omega)' \Omega^*(\Delta^*) \bar{C}(\Delta) \right]^{-1} \bar{C}(\Delta)' \Omega^*(\Delta^*) \Big\} [\,\bar{H}(\Delta) \quad \bar{A}(\Delta)\,].$$

This is a useful formula, as we see next.

18.2.10. *Worst-case distribution for $z - \check{z}$ is $\mathcal{N}(u, \Gamma(\Delta))$*

Use the partition[9]

$$\bar{\Omega}(\Delta) = \begin{bmatrix} \bar{\Omega}_{11}(\Delta) & \bar{\Omega}_{12}(\Delta) \\ \bar{\Omega}_{21}(\Delta) & \bar{\Omega}_{22}(\Delta) \end{bmatrix}$$

---

[9] Knowing $\bar{\Omega}(\Delta)$ allows us to deduce the worst-case distribution for $z - \check{z}$ conditional on $(y, \check{z})$ in another way, thereby establishing a useful cross-check on formula $(18.2.20)$ or $(18.2.22)$. See Hansen, Mayer, and Sargent (2007).

where $\bar{\Omega}_{11}(\Delta)$ has the same dimension as $z - \check{z}$ and $\bar{\Omega}_{22}(\Delta)$ has the same dimension as $\begin{bmatrix} y \\ \check{z} \end{bmatrix}$. The covariance matrix of $z - \check{z}$ is

$$\Gamma(\Delta) = - \left[\frac{1}{\theta_2} \bar{\Omega}_{11}(\Delta) \right]^{-1}, \tag{18.2.24}$$

which is positive definite when the pair of penalty parameters (θ_1, θ_2) satisfies the no-breakdown condition (18.2.19).

18.2.11. *Worst-case signal distribution*

Appendix A establishes that the distribution of the signal under the worst-case model has conditional mean and conditional covariance matrix:

$$\bar{s}^* = \bar{D}_1(\Delta)y + \bar{D}_2(\Delta)\check{z} + Ha \tag{18.2.25}$$
$$\bar{\Upsilon} = D_2\Gamma(\Delta)D_2{}' + G\Sigma(\Delta)G' \tag{18.2.26}$$

where

$$\bar{D}_1(\Delta) \doteq D_1 - D_2\tilde{F}_{21}(\Delta) - G\tilde{F}_{31}(\Delta)$$
$$\bar{D}_2(\Delta) \doteq D_2 - D_2\tilde{F}_{23}(\Delta) - G\tilde{F}_{33}(\Delta).$$

The laws of motion for $(y, \check{z})$ under the worst-case model are

$$y^* = \left[\Pi_y y + \Pi_s \bar{D}_1(\Delta) - (\Pi_s H + \Pi_a)\tilde{F}_{11}(\Delta) \right] y$$
$$+ \left[\Pi_s \bar{D}_2(\Delta) - (\Pi_s H + \Pi_a)\tilde{F}_{13}(\Delta) \right] \check{z} + \Pi_s(s^* - \bar{s}^*) \tag{18.2.27}$$
$$\check{z}^* = \left(A_{21} - B_2\tilde{F}_{11}(\Delta) + K_2(\Delta)[\bar{D}_1(\Delta) - D_1] \right) y$$
$$+ \left(A_{22} - B_2\tilde{F}_{13}(\Delta) + K_2(\Delta)[\bar{D}_2(\Delta) - D_2] \right) \check{z}$$
$$+ K_2(\Delta)(s^* - \bar{s}^*) \tag{18.2.28}$$

where the innovation $s^* - \bar{s}^*$ under the distorted model is normal with mean zero and covariance matrix $\bar{\Upsilon}$. This representation for the signal distribution depends both on the choice of the control vector and on the endogenous components of the state vector. It can applied directly in endowment economies in which asset prices are computed from the solution to a robust social planning problem. More generally, by using the version of the 'Big K, little k' trick described in chapters 2 and 7, it can be used in economies with endogenous state variables, such as stocks of physical capital, to construct worst-case models of signal distributions that do not depend on actions or endogenous states. These alternative worst-case models are then directly applicable in representing asset prices in decentralized economies.

18.3. Examples

Example 1: Jovanovic-Nyarko I

This example adds adjustment costs to a model authored by Jovanovic and Nyarko (1996). A decision maker chooses a scalar decision a_t to maximize

$$E\left[\sum_{t=0}^{\infty} \beta^t[1-(s_{t+1}-y_{2t+1})^2-da_t^2]\big|y_{20}\right] \qquad (18.3.1)$$

where

$$y_{2t+1} = y_{2t} + a_t + cw_{t+1} \qquad (18.3.2a)$$

$$s_{t+1} = z_t + gw_{t+1} \qquad (18.3.2b)$$

$$z_{t+1} = z_t \qquad (18.3.2c)$$

$$z_0 \sim \mathcal{N}(\check{z}_0, \Delta_0) \qquad (18.3.2d)$$

where w_{t+1} is an i.i.d. 2×1 Gaussian random vector with mean zero and variance I. In (18.3.1), $1-(s_{t+1}-y_{2t+1})^2$ is the decision maker's time $t+1$ output, and s_{t+1} is an "ideal" time $t+1$ action, unknown at t but observed at $t+1$, that the decision maker aspires to implement by choosing an increment a_t to a prior action y_{2t}, and da_t^2 is the adjustment cost that he pays for altering his prior action. The ideal action at time t is a noisy signal of an unknown constant mean ideal action z. The decision maker starts with a prior belief $\check{z}_0$ about the ideal action. Assume that the constant mean z of the ideal action is itself a random variable that is drawn from $\mathcal{N}(\check{z}_0, \Delta_0)$. Assume also that the initial action is $y_0 = \check{z}_0$.

To map this problem into our setting, evaluate $E[(s_{t+1}-y_{2t+1})^2] = E[z-(y_{2t}+a_t)]^2+(g-c)(g-c)'$, which implies that the time t component of the criterion function is $U(x_t,a_t) = 1-z^2-y_{2t}^2-2a_ty_{2t}-(d+1)a_t^2+2zy_{2t}+2za_t$ plus the variance $(g-c)'(g-c)$. The variance term is beyond control and can be omitted when calculating a decision rule. Let 1 be the first component of the observed part of the state y_t so that

$$\begin{bmatrix} 1 \\ y_{2t+1} \end{bmatrix} = \begin{bmatrix} 1 & 0 \\ 0 & 1 \end{bmatrix}\begin{bmatrix} 1 \\ y_{2,t} \end{bmatrix} + \begin{bmatrix} 0 \\ 1 \end{bmatrix}a_t + \begin{bmatrix} 0 \\ c \end{bmatrix}w_{t+1},$$

which is a version of (18.2.3) with $y_t = [1 \quad y_{2t}]'$, $A_{11} = I$, $B_1 = [0 \quad 1]'$, $C_1 = [0 \quad c]'$, $A_{12} = 0$. Comparing (18.3.2b) with (18.2.2c) indicates that we should set $D = [0 \quad 1]$, $H = 0$, $G = g$, and comparing (18.3.2c) with (18.2.2b) shows that we should set $A_{21} = 0$, $A_{22} = 1$, $B_2 = 0$, $C_2 = 0$. To capture the objective function, we should set $Q = (d+1)$, $P_1 = [0 \quad -1]$, $P_2 = -1$, $R_{11} = \begin{bmatrix} -1 & 0 \\ 0 & 1 \end{bmatrix}$, $R_{12} = \begin{bmatrix} 0 \\ -1 \end{bmatrix}$, $R_{22} = 1$, $R_{21} = R_{12}'$.

Figures 18.3.1 and 18.3.2 display time series $a, u, \Delta, \tilde{v}$ under the approximating model. We set the parameters at $\beta = .9, c = 1, g = 2, d = 0, z_0 = 10, \Delta_0 = 5$. The dotted line in the top left panel displays the decision a_t when $\theta_1 = \theta_2 = +\infty$. The solid lines in figure 18.3.1 show outcomes when $\theta_1 = +\infty$, $\theta_2 = 40$ while in figure 18.3.2 we show outcomes when $\theta_1 = 40, \theta_2 = +\infty$. In figure 18.3.1, concerns about robustness last only so long as there is uncertainty about the distribution of the hidden state z. Here the decision maker eventually "learns himself out of" his concern for robustness. But in figure 18.3.2 when $\theta_1 = 40$, concerns about robustness persist because we have kept the decision maker uncertain about the distribution of the disturbance w_{t+1}. In figure 18.3.2, after the decision maker has learned z, he continues to set a at a value other than 0 in order to offset the effect on the target output in $(18.3.2b)$ of his (worst-case) expectation of the mean of w_{t+1}.

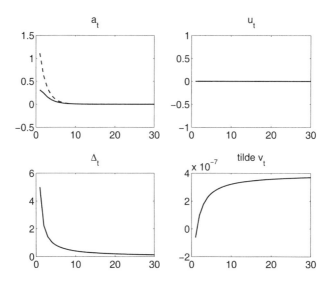

Figure 18.3.1: Jovanovic-Nyarko model with $\theta_1 = +\infty, \theta_2 = 40$; $a, u, \Delta, \tilde{v}$ are reported in successive panels.

Example 2: Jovanovic-Nyarko II

In example 1, $\lim_{t \to +\infty} \Delta_t = 0$, so that eventually learning about the hidden state is completed. This implies that $\lim_{t \to +\infty} u_t = 0$ and that the associated variance of the distorted distribution for z also converges to zero. To sustain perpetual learning about z and perpetual distortion through a nonzero setting of u, we modify the description of z_t to be

$$z_{t+1} = (1 - \rho)\mu_z + \rho z_t + c_z w_{3,t+1}$$

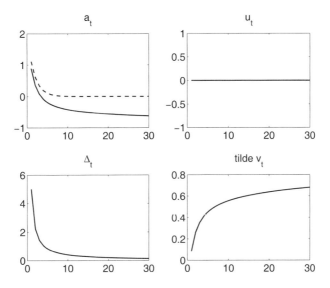

Figure 18.3.2: Jovanovic-Nyarko model with $\theta_1 = 40, \theta_2 = +\infty$; $a, u, \Delta, \tilde{v}$ are reported in successive panels.

where $w_{3,t+1} \sim \mathcal{N}(0,1)$ is a third random shock that we add to the model of example 1 and $|\rho| < 1$. The rest of the model remains the same. Now $\lim_{t \to +\infty} \Delta_t = \Delta_\infty > 0$, so that there always remains uncertainty about z. In this case, for $\theta_2 < +\infty$, u_t will not converge to zero but instead to a time-invariant linear function of $y_t, \check{z}_t$ that depends on (θ_1, θ_2).

Example 3: pure estimation of hidden state

Suppose that $B = 0$ so that the state cannot be influenced by a. The decision maker wants to estimate $-Px$. Set $Q = I$ and $R = P'P$. The decision a_t as a function of $(y_t, \check{z}_t)$ is a robust estimate of $-Px_t$.

18.4. Concluding remarks

In this chapter, we described one among three games that Hansen, Mayer, and Sargent (2007) use for robust estimation without commitment. That paper compares outcomes from these different games and how they differ from filtering problems under commitment, like the one studied in chapter 17. Cagetti, Hansen, Sargent, and Williams (2002) and Hansen, Sargent, and Wang (2002) have studied asset prices in contexts in which a representative consumer who doubts his model confronts estimation and filtering problems. They show how robust filtering affects market prices of model uncertainty. Hansen and Sargent (2007b) study how robust filtering can put time-varying uncertainty premia into asset prices. In all of those papers, a version of the worst-case signal distribution that we work out in appendix A is the key object that determines the multiplicative adjustment that the consumer's concerns about robustness puts into the stochastic discount factor.

An interesting open issue is how to extend the ideas about detection error probabilities in chapter 9 to calibrate the (θ_1, θ_2) pair that we use to parameterize specifications doubt in this chapter. We approach that problem in Hansen, Mayer, and Sargent (2007).

A. Worst-case signal distribution

In this appendix, we construct a recursive representation of the distribution of signals under the distorted probability distribution. Recall the signal evolution

$$s^* = Dx + Ha + Gw^*.$$

Under the approximating model, the signal next period is normal with mean

$$\breve{s}^* = D_1 y + D_2 \breve{z} + Ha$$

and covariance matrix

$$\breve{\Upsilon} = D_2 \Delta D_2{}' + GG'.$$

The distorted mean of the signal conditioned on the signal history is

$$\bar{s}^* = D_1 y + D_2 \breve{z} + (D_2 u + G\tilde{v}) + Ha,$$

which by virtue of the second and third blocks of rows of $(18.2.22)$ can be written

$$\bar{s}^* = \bar{D}_1(\Delta)y + \bar{D}_2(\Delta)\breve{z} + Ha \qquad (18.A.1)$$

where

$$\bar{D}_1(\Delta) \doteq D_1 - D_2 \tilde{F}_{21}(\Delta) - G\tilde{F}_{31}(\Delta)$$
$$\bar{D}_2(\Delta) \doteq D_2 - D_2 \tilde{F}_{23}(\Delta) - G\tilde{F}_{33}(\Delta).$$

The distorted covariance matrix is

$$\bar{\Upsilon} = D_2 \Gamma(\Delta) D_2{}' + G\Sigma(\Delta)G'.$$

To construct the distorted dynamics for y^*, start from the formula $y^* = \Pi_s s^* + \Pi_y y + \Pi_a a$. Substituting for the robust decision rule for a from the first row block of $(18.2.22)$ and replacing s^* with with $\bar{s}^* + (s^* - \bar{s}^*)$ from $(18.A.1)$ gives

$$y^* = [\Pi_y y + \Pi_s \bar{D}_1(\Delta) - (\Pi_s H + \Pi_a)\tilde{F}_{11}(\Delta)]y$$
$$+ [\Pi_s \bar{D}_2(\Delta) - (\Pi_s H + \Pi_a)\tilde{F}_{13}(\Delta)]\breve{z} + \Pi_s(s^* - \bar{s}^*). \qquad (18.A.2)$$

To complete a recursive representation for y^* under the worst-case distribution, we need a formula for updating $\breve{z}^*$ under the worst-case distribution. Recall the formula for $\check{z}^*$ under the approximating model from the Kalman filter ($18.2.6b$) or ($18.2.7$)

$$\check{z}^* = [A_{21} - B_2\tilde{F}_{11}(\Delta)]y + [A_{22} - B_2\tilde{F}_{13}(\Delta)]\check{z} + K_2(\Delta)(s^* - D_1y - D_2\check{z} - Ha)$$

or

$$\check{z}^* = [A_{21} - B_2\tilde{F}_{11}(\Delta)]y + [A_{22} - B_2\tilde{F}_{13}(\Delta)]\check{z} + K_2(\Delta)(s^* - \check{s}^*).$$

Using the identity

$$\begin{aligned}
s^* - \check{s}^* &= (s^* - \bar{s}^*) + (\bar{s}^* - \check{s}^*) \\
&= (s^* - \bar{s}^*) + \big([\bar{D}_1(\Delta) - D_1]y + [\bar{D}_2(\Delta) - D_2]\check{z}\big)
\end{aligned}$$

in the above equation gives

$$\begin{aligned}
\check{z}^* &= \big(A_{21} - B_2\tilde{F}_{11}(\Delta) + K_2(\Delta)[\bar{D}_1(\Delta) - D_1]\big)\, y \\
&\quad + \big(A_{22} - B_2\tilde{F}_{13}(\Delta) + K_2(\Delta)[\bar{D}_2(\Delta) - D_2]\big)\check{z} + K_2(\Delta)(s^* - \bar{s}^*).
\end{aligned} \tag{18.A.3}$$

Taken together, ($18.A.2$) and ($18.A.3$) show how to construct $\check{z}^*$ from the signal history under the distorted law of motion. The innovation $s^* - \bar{s}^*$ under the distorted model is normal with mean zero and covariance matrix $\tilde{\Upsilon}$.

Part VI
Extensions

Chapter 19
Alternative approaches

19.1. Introduction

Any theory worth its salt "sharpens the mind by narrowing it," as Justice Holmes said about the study of law.[1] By exploiting simplifications that come from using entropy to measure model discrepancies, we have given hard answers to soft questions about what to do when you do not trust your model. We cast our answers in terms familiar to economists who practice modern applied dynamics, i.e., Bellman equations, recursive competitive equilibria, Markov perfect equilibria of dynamic games, and Stackelberg and Ramsey problems. Unavoidably, we have "sharpened the mind" by imposing features that some people might find troublesome and by excluding features that other people might find essential. We conclude this book by assessing some of the limitations inherent in our approach.

In section 19.2, we confront the criticism that we allow perturbations to the approximating model that are so general that they provide too little guidance about the types of misspecification that the decision maker fears most. We describe an approach that expresses more structured misspecification fears by transforming the decision maker's objective function. Section 19.3 mentions a concept called "probabilistic sophistication," confesses that our multiplier and constraint preferences are probabilistically sophisticated, and takes up the question of whether that prevents us from capturing the kinds of behavior exhibited in experiments of Ellsberg (1961). Section 19.4 then reviews and responds to a criticism of robust control theory by Epstein and Schneider (2003a).

19.2. More structured model uncertainty

This book has focused on what people sometimes call unstructured uncertainty. The misspecifications under study are *unstructured* in the sense that they are just general specifications of the shock distributions that can feed back on the history of past states. We have apparently excluded descriptions of the set of alternative models that focus specification doubts on some particular aspects of an approximating model but that leave others unchallenged. In this section, we describe how our approach can be nudged to deal with some more focused types of model uncertainty.

---

[1] This chapter benefited from extensive discussions with Tomasz Strzalecki.

19.2.1. Model averaging

A way to focus on misspecifications with more structure would be to posit a discrete set of multiple models or even a continuously parameterized family of models, to combine them to form a single grand model by using Bayesian mixing probabilities, and then to adjust the mixing probabilities to take account of concerns that they might be misspecified. We set the stage for such a generalization of robust control and learning models in chapter 18 and explored this approach more fully in Hansen and Sargent (2005b, 2007a, 2007b). The model-mixture approach typically pushes us outside the LQG model, which means that we can no longer exploit the convenient algorithms that accompany the LQG model that are the main subject of this book.[2] Nevertheless, the approach is interesting and sometimes manageable. But there is another approach that stays within the LQG framework.

19.2.2. A shortcut

At this point, we briefly describe an approach that, by using ideas described by Petersen, James, and Dupuis (2000), allows us to incorporate unstructured model uncertainty while staying within the LQG framework.[3] Thus, consider the state equation

$$x_{t+1} = Ax_t + Bu_t + C\epsilon_{t+1},$$

and suppose for the time being that the date t state is observed. Let h be an alternative density for the shock ϵ_{t+1} conditioned on x and u. Recall that the date t conditional relative entropy is

$$\int [\log h(\epsilon|x,u) - \log f(\epsilon)]h(\epsilon|x,u)d\epsilon.$$

We append a term to capture a form of structured uncertainty and propose to replace entropy with

$$\int [\log h(\epsilon|x,u) - \log f(\epsilon)]h(\epsilon|x,u)d\epsilon - \frac{1}{2}|D_1x + D_2u|^2.$$

This penalizes our malevolent agent in a way that gives him an incentive to focus on particular kinds of perturbations to the approximating model. Those perturbations are determined by our settings of the matrices D_1 and D_2. Petersen, James, and Dupuis say that the matrices adjust "the admissible

---

[2] See Hansen and Sargent (2007b) for a setting in which, because each member of the finite set of models remains linear quadratic, we can salvage much of the convenience of the LQG framework.

[3] This short cut was suggested by Alexei Onatski when he discussed our work on robust model averaging.

perturbed noise process." In effect, we now charge the malevolent agent less for making perturbations in directions determined by the matrices D_1 and D_2. After that, the formulas described in this book apply.[4]

19.3. Probabilistic sophistication

Except in chapter 18, where we introduced hidden states, for most of this book we have specfied preference orderings in terms of either a single constraint on a measure of discounted entropy or a single convex penalization of each period's increment to entropy. These preference orderings fall within a class that Maccheroni, Marinacci, and Rustichini (2006a) studied carefully. They show that our preferences orderings express ambiguity aversion in the sense of Ghirardato and Marinacci (2002). Ghirardato and Marinacci argue that preferences are ambiguity neutral if they are expected utility preferences[5] and this gives them a benchmark for characterizing aversion to ambiguity. Maccheroni, Marinacci, and Rustichini (2006a) show that our preferences display more ambiguity aversion in the sense of Ghirardato and Marinacci when the constraint is made less restrictive or the penalization is weakened. Maccheroni, Marinacci, and Rustichini (2006a) also note that these preferences satisfy a property that Machina and Schmeidler (1992) call probabilistic sophistication. This finding sheds light on why our preferences fail to capture ambiguity in a different sense than Maccheroni, Marinacci, and Rustichini's that was defined by Epstein (1999), who identifies ambiguity neutrality with probabilistic sophistication.[6]

A decision maker can be said to be probabilistically sophisticated if at the end of the day all that matters to him are the induced distributions under the approximating model. This is a property of expected utility preferences and of our constraint and multiplier preferences as well. Thus, think of constructing a model from an underlying multivariate process for shocks. Our benchmark

---

[4] Petersen, James and Dupuis allow for states to be hidden from the decision maker, as in chapter 18 and for nonlinearity in the state evolution.

[5] See Proposition 7 of Maccheroni, Marinacci, and Rustichini (2006a).

[6] When we consider only one constraint or penalty, as we do throughout this book except in chapter 18, we can still obtain counterparts to Ellsberg's urn experiments by varying the preference parameter that governs the concern for robustness. For example, we can compare decisions, equilibrium outcomes, and welfare in two decision problems that are identical except that the agent in one problem has a concern for robustness while the one in the other problem does not. This comparison displays the implications of different perspectives on risk and uncertainty. For such a comparison, the notion of ambiguity developed by Ghirardato and Marinacci applies. See Barillas, Hansen, and Sargent (2007) for an application to interpreting measures of the costs of business cycle extracted from asset prices.

probability model posits that these shocks are independent and identically distributed with a multivariate standard normal distribution. Consider two alternative one-period utility processes, $\{u_{1,t}\}$ for $t = 0, 1, ...$ and $\{u_{2,t}\}$ for $t = 0, 1, ...$ Suppose that for each t, the distribution induced by the random variable $u_{1,t+1}$ is the same as that induced by $u_{2,t+1}$ conditioned on date t information, meaning that both have the same distribution function conditioned on date t information. For example, $u_{1,t+1}$ could depend only on the first component of the shock process and $u_{2,t+1}$ could depend only on the second component of the shock process, but their distributions are the same because they have the same functional dependence. Many other constructions would also work. Preferences that are defined by using a single constraint or penalty make the decision maker indifferent between utility processes with identical induced distributions. This situation occurs because we could have avoided distorting the shock distribution and instead just directly distorted the ultimate distributions that the shocks induce for the utility process. To see this, notice that it suffices to know the distortions to the induced distributions for evaluating discounted utility and for either checking the entropy constraint or evaluating the penalty. Thus, in comparing utility processes, all that matters are the induced distributions under the approximating model. As a consequence, the decision maker is probabilistically sophisticated.

To alter our setup to prevent our decision maker from being probabilistically sophisticated, recall how we included multiple penalty functions (e.g., two θ's) when we introduced hidden states and learning in chapter 18. Doing that prevented the associated preferences from being probabilistically sophisticated. Another way to proceed while preserving the computational tractability of our approach would be to distort the distributions of a subset of shocks.[7] Making such distinctions breaks probabilistic sophistication by positing ambiguity about some shock distributions but not others. This allows us to construct analogues to distinct Ellsberg's urns with and without ambiguity.

This way of proceeding preserves tractability but avoids probabilistic sophistication and allows us to confront the Ellsberg paradox types of behavior that interest Epstein (1999). However, it is appropriate to note that featuring a subset of shocks in this way severs the direct link between robustness and risk sensitivity that we have exploited at various points in this book. Nevertheless, it would be possible to rescue a generalized kind of risk sensitivity that distinguishes among sources of risk.

---

[7] This can be done using tricks similar to those described in section 19.2.

19.4. Time inconsistency

Because we take continuation entropy as a state variable, our constraint preferences satisfy what seems to us to be the most useful form of time consistency, namely, that a decision maker does not want to revise his plan as time passes and chances are realized. But there is another kind of time consistency that our constraint preferences lack and that other authors think of as desirable. Because continuation entropy depends on earlier distortions that the minimizing player had chosen along an equilibrium path of the two-player game, distortions that depended on the equilibrium choices of the *maximizing* player, the ranking of two plans that were *not* chosen by the maximizing player might be reversed as time passes. But this has no consequence for the temporal consistency of choices that are actually made by the maximizing player. Unchosen plans remain unchosen as time unfolds, provided that we include continuation entropy as a time t state variable in the way that we have described in chapter 7.[8]

The issue of which state variables are admissible is at the heart of discussions of dynamic consistency.[9] Any treatment of dynamic consistency has to hold *something* about past decisions fixed when comparing date 0 to date $t > 0$ preference rankings.[10] Conditioning on past choices of the maximizing agent, but not those of the minimizing agent, leads to a dynamic inconsistency characterized by Epstein and Schneider (2003a). Limiting conditioning in that way precludes our use of continuation entropy when defining the date t preferences because continuation entropy is a state variable that summarizes the history of the evil agent's actions. Not conditioning on the minimizing player's previous actions allows the minimizing agent to reassess prior choices at time t so long as they satisfy the date zero entropy constraint. Epstein and Schneider (2003a) want a property called rectangularity that can be achieved by letting the date t minimizing agent be free to revise past distortions, something that their multiple priors formulation allows but that our constraint formulation forbids.

One respectable response to Epstein and Schneider's concern is to say that once the penalty parameter θ is set, it is the multiplier formulation that

---

[8] Thus, chosen plans don't display the type of 'genuine' time inconsistency featured in the preferences with hyperbolic discounting of Phelps and Pollak (1968) and Laibson (1994, 1998).

[9] A similar issue occurs in models with internal habits as a state variable that can be constructed from a date zero initial condition and a history of past consumption choices. For a habit persistence model, past consumption was chosen by a *maximizing* agent, whereas, in our setting, continuation entropy depends on past choices made by a *minimizing* agent.

[10] Johnsen and Donaldson (1985) discuss how the same sense of time consistency that our constraint preferences satisfy is exploited in recursive models of asset prices.

depicts the underlying preferences as time passes.[11] This amounts to using the implied constraint to interpret or calibrate θ, while embracing the penalty formulation as a statement of intertemporal preferences.[12] Maccheroni, Marinacci, and Rustichini (2006a, 2006b) have axiomatized our multiplier preferences and noted that they are time consistent. In the remainder of this section, we consider aspects of these issues in more depth.[13]

19.4.1. Continuation entropy

In the stochastic formulation of chapters 3 and 14, we formulated a probability distortion as a multiplicative "preference shock" that is a non-negative martingale M_t for $t \geq 0$ with $M_0 = 1$. We can represent M_t via the factorization

$$M_{t+1} = m_{t+1} M_t, \qquad (19.4.1)$$

where m_{t+1} is a nonnegative random variable with $E_t m_{t+1} = 1$ and where we use the shorthand notation that E_t is the conditional expectation with respect to the decision maker's approximating model conditioned on the history of information known at date t. To formulate what in chapter 7 we called a constraint robust control problem, we impose a time 0 entropy constraint that can be represented as

$$\sum_{t=0}^{\infty} \beta^t E_0[M_t E_t(m_{t+1} \log m_{t+1})] \leq \eta. \qquad (19.4.2)$$

It is convenient to decompose the time 0 entropy constraint as

$$\sum_{s=0}^{t-1} \beta^s E_0[M_s E_s(m_{s+1} \log m_{s+1})] + \beta^t E M_t r_t \leq \eta, \qquad (19.4.3)$$

where r_t is continuation entropy defined as

$$r_t = E_t \left[\sum_{j=t}^{\infty} \beta^{j-t} M_j E_j(m_{j+1} \log m_{j+1}) \right].$$

---

[11] The response is possibly unsatisfactory because, after all, the constraint preferences and multiplier preferences are different mathematical objects that share equilibrium outcomes but differ off the equilibrium of the respective two-player zero-sum games.

[12] Alternatively, we can deduce the conditional entropies period by period in advance and simply have the minimizing agent explore a sequence of one-period distortions. See Hansen, Sargent, Turmuhambetova, and Williams (2006), section 9.2 for an application of this idea in a continuous-time setting.

[13] Also see Hansen and Sargent (2007c) for senses in which robust control formulations are and are not time consistent. Hansen, Sargent, Turmuhambetova, and Williams (2006) develop recursive representations in a continuous-time setting of both constraint and multiplier formulations.

REMARK 1: Throughout our analysis, we presume that, when considering decisions at future dates, for each alternative probability distribution, i.e., each choice of $\{M_t : t = 0, 1, \ldots\}$, the decision maker uses Bayes' rule to form conditional expectations. By taking continuation entropy as a state variable at date t, we limit the set of conditional distributions that can be examined at date t to a subset of the implied conditional distributions that were initially considered at date 0. Our use of continuation entropy as a state variable gives a recursive way to implement the date 0 decision problem. But it does much more by isolating the parts of his views that we allow our robust decision maker to re-assess as time unfolds.

REMARK 2: As an alternative, suppose that we were to confront the time 1 minimizing agent with the time 0 entropy constraint (19.4.2) and allow him to reallocate time 0 entropy by recomputing the distortions that he had assigned to probabilities of events that at time 1 are known *not* to have occurred. At no sacrifice in terms of his minimand, the time 1 minimizing agent could 'save entropy' by choosing not to distort those events. Allowing the decision maker to exercise this option at time 1 robs the date 0 entropy constraint of any meaningful restrictions on the minimizing agent at time 1. This is why imposing the time 0 entropy constraint repeatedly over time, in the manner suggested by Epstein and Schneider, is not a useful way to proceed restrict the set of distributions available to the minimizing agent. We expand on this argument in subsection 19.4.2.

19.4.2. Disarming the entropy constraint

In what follows we illustrate how conditioning disarms the entropy constraint. Since $M_0 = 1$, we can evidently express our time 0 entropy constraint as

$$E\left(m \log m\right) + \beta E m r \leq \eta \tag{19.4.4}$$

where r is continuation entropy and m distorts transition probabilities between date 0 and date 1. We want to study the restrictions, if any, that this constraint imposes on continuation entropy r and the associated options for the one-period future value m^* were we to allow our minimizing player to reconsider his time 0 choices by conditioning on information that will become available at time 1. We begin by considering the problem

$$\min_m [E\left(m \log m\right) + \beta E m r] \tag{19.4.5}$$

for a period 1 continuation entropy r that for the moment we take as given. The minimized value of (19.4.5) is

$$-\log E\left[\exp(-\beta r)\right].$$

As a preliminary step, consider an event A and suppose that r is zero on the complement of A. Note that

$$- \log E \left[\exp(-\beta r) \right] = - \log \left(E \left[\exp(-\beta r) | A \right] \operatorname{Prob}(A) + [1 - \operatorname{Prob}(A)] \right)$$
$$\leq - \log \left[1 - \operatorname{Prob}(A) \right].$$

First, suppose that

$$- \log \left[1 - \operatorname{Prob}(A) \right]$$

is less than η. Then *any* choice of continuation entropy $r \geq 0$ on event A satisfies the entropy constraint (19.4.4). Hence, the entropy constraint is effectively disarmed when event A is realized at time 1.

Let $\{A_j\}$ be a partitioning of the state space based on information that is realized at time 1. Suppose that

$$\sup_j - \log \left[1 - \operatorname{Prob}(A_j) \right]$$

is less than η in (19.4.4). Then conditioned on this particular partitioning of the state space, inequality (19.4.4) puts no constraint on the continuation entropy r that is assigned to any set within the partition. That is, provided that continuation entropy r can be set to zero outside of any partitioning set (19.4.4), the value of r that can be assigned to a particular partitioning is left unconstrained.

To pursue the implications of this observation, consider a partition $\{A_j\}$ for which

$$\sup_j - \log \left[1 - \operatorname{Prob}(A_j) \right]$$

can be made arbitrarily small. In our applications in which the shocks are normally distributed, such arbitrarily fine partitions always exist. In this case, conditioning on time 1 information means that (19.4.4) leaves continuation entropy unconstrained if continuation entropy can be freely reallocated at date one. Constraining the minimizing agent at date 1 by the date zero entropy constraint simply gives him so much freedom to distort future probabilities that it makes the decision problem uninteresting to us. Thus, if we condition on time 1 information, restriction (19.4.4) becomes vacuous.[14]

In formulating a recursive implementation of the constraint game that we outlined in section 7.8 of chapter 7, we avoided the vacuousness of constraint (19.4.4) conditioned on time 1 information by committing the malevolent

---

[14] This, however, is the procedure of sections 4.4 and 5 of Epstein and Schneider (2003a). This approach could be valuable in other applications, but it does not give interesting results for the problems that we investigated.

agent to his time 0 choice of continuation entropy. This leads to the recursive implementation of the constraint game that we outlined in section 7.8 of chapter 7. In that game, the allocation of continuation entropy at a given date and history is set before the realization of new information becomes available at that date.[15]

In the next subsection, we argue that it is not fruitful to substitute rectangularity for our entropy penalization or our constraints on continuation entropy.

19.4.3. Rectangularity can be taken too far

The more we separate admissible distortions to probability models across time and across shock components, the less interesting the model misspecifications that can be expressed are and the more mechanical max-min expected utility functions become. To illustrate this, suppose for simplicity that we consider a continuous-time approximating model with a shock vector that is a multivariate standard Brownian increment. To keep entropy well defined, we must restrict ourselves to perturbations that are absolutely continuous with respect to the approximating model. Absolute continuity, in turn, restricts us to consider perturbations that take the form of drift distortions only.[16]

The rectangularization procedures of Chen and Epstein (2002) and Epstein and Schneider (2003a) separate constraints over time but not necessarily over shock components within a time period. If, in the spirit of rectangularity, we impose separate restrictions on the magnitude of the drift distortions for each instant and each component, the malevolent agent's minimization problem simplifies to choosing between positive and negative mean shifts whose absolute values we have already specified. Thus, in this setting, rectangularity implies that the only things that we allow concerns about robustness to contribute to the decision problem are the separately specified magnitudes of the date-by-date and state-by-state drift distortions. After these are set, the outcome of the minimization problem can be trivial. For instance, when the shock process is univariate, the minimizing agent's decision problems reduces to the relatively trivial problem of which endpoint of an interval constraint on a mean is damaging to the maximizing agent. In a multivariate setting, rectangularity allows for tradeoffs across sources of uncertainty, but not across time.

---

[15] This is one of the recursive approaches suggested by Hansen, Sargent, Turmuhambetova, and Williams (2006). The use of such a forward-looking state variable like continuation entropy is precluded by axioms invoked by Epstein and Schneider.

[16] For an analysis of diffusion models that pursues the implication that absolute continuity restricts distortions to drift terms and leaves volatilities unaltered, see Anderson, Hansen, and Sargent (2003).

Because we want to help the decision maker guard against a bigger class of misspecified dynamics, our approach eschews imposing rectangularity and instead uses either a penalization procedure expressed in terms of our θ or an intertemporal constraint to deduce worst-case models. Such specifications of admissible perturbations to an approximating model allow intertemporal tradeoffs among distortions, so that even with Brownian motion shocks, it is interesting to characterize the worst-case distortions and their time dependence. This allows a decision maker to explore the fragility of decision rules with respect to misspecified dynamics. Calculating a worst-case model becomes an integral part of the process of finding a rule that is less fragile to dynamic misspecifications. As mentioned in different contexts in sections 19.2 and 19.3, our approach is flexible enough to allow a decision maker to focus concerns about misspecified dynamics in particular directions by using multiple θ's.

References

Abel, A. (2002). An Exploration of the Effects of Pessimism and Doubt on Asset Returns. *Journal of Economic Dynamics and Control*, Vol. 26(7-8), pp. 1075–1092.

Aiyagari, Marcet, Albert, Thomas J. Sargent, and Juha Seppälä (2002). Optimal Taxation without State-Contingent Debt. *Journal of Political Economy*, Vol. 110(6), pp. 1220–1254.

Alvarez, F. and U. J. Jermann (2004). Using Asset Prices to Measure the Cost of Business Cycles. *Journal of Political Economy*, Vol. 112(6), pp. 1223–1256.

Anderson, B. D. O. (1978). Second-Order Convergent Algorithms for the Steady-State Riccati Equation. *International Journal of Control*, Vol. 28(2), pp. 295–306.

Anderson, B. D. O. and J. B. Moore (1979). *Optimal Filtering*. Englewood Cliffs, NJ: Prentice Hall.

Anderson, E. (1995). Computing Equilibria in Linear-Quadratic Dynamic Games and Models with Distortions. Mimeo. University of Chicago.

Anderson, E. (1998). Uncertainty and the Dynamics of Pareto Optimal Allocations. Mimeo. University of Chicago Dissertation.

Anderson, E. (2005). The Dynamics of Risk-Sensitive Allocations. *Journal of Economic Theory*, Vol. 125(2), pp. 93–150.

Anderson, E., L. P. Hansen, E. R. McGrattan, and T. J. Sargent (1996). Mechanics of Forming and Estimating Dynamic Linear Economies. In H. Amman, D. A. Kendrick and J. Rust (eds.), *Handbook of Computational Economics, Vol.1*. Amsterdam: North Holland.

Anderson, E., L. P. Hansen and T. J. Sargent (2003). A Quartet of Semigroups for Model Specification, Robustness, Prices of Risk, and Model Detection. *Journal of the European Economic Association*, Vol. 1(1), pp. 68–123.

Anderson, G. and G. Moore (1985). A Linear Algebraic Procedure for Solving Linear Perfect Foresight Models. *Economics Letters*, Vol. 17(3), pp. 247–252.

Arrow, K. (1964). The Role of Securities in the Optimal Allocation of Risk-Bearing. *Review of Economic Studies*, Vol. 31(2), pp. 91–96.

Backus, D. and J. Driffill (1986). The Consistency of Optimal Policy in Stochastic Rational Expectations Models. Mimeo. CEPR Discussion Paper No. 124.

Bai, Z. and J. W. Demmel (1993). On Swapping Diagonal Blocks in Real Schur Form. *Linear Algebra and Its Applications*, Vol. 186, pp. 73–95.

Bailey, M. (1971). *National Income and the Price Level*. 2nd ed., New York: McGraw-Hill, pp. 175–186.

Ball, L. (1999). Policy Rules for Open Economies. In J. B. Taylor (ed.), *Monetary Policy Rules*. Chicago: University of Chicago Press, pp. 127–144.

Barillas, F., L. P. Hansen, and T. J. Sargent (2007). Doubts or Variability. Mimeo. New York University and University of Chicago.

Barro, R. J. (1979). On the Determination of Public Debt. *Journal of Political Economy*, Vol. 87(5), pp. 940–971.

Bartels, R. H. and G. W. Stewart (1972). Algorithm 432 Solution of the Matrix Equation $AX + XB = C$. *Communications of the ACM*, Vol. 15(9), pp. 820–826.

Başar, T. and P. Bernhard (1995). H^∞-*Optimal Control and Related Minimax Design Problems: A Dynamic Game Approach*. Boston-Basel-Berlin: Birkhäuser.

Becker, G. S. and K. M. Murphy (1988). A Theory of Rational Addiction. *Journal of Political Economy*, Vol. 96(4), pp. 675–700.

Bergemann, D. and K. Schlag (2005). Robust Monopoly Pricing: The Case of Regret. Mimeo. Yale University.

Bewley, T. F. (1986). Knightian Decision Theory: Part I. Cowles Foundation Discussion Paper No. 807.

Bewley, T. F. (1987). Knightian Decision Theory: Part II. Intertemporal Problems. Cowles Foundation Discussion Paper No. 835.

Bewley, T. F. (1988). Knightian Decision Theory and Econometric Inference. Cowles Foundation Discussion Paper No. 868.

Bierman, G. J. (1984). *Computational Aspects of the Matrix Sign Function Solution to the ARE*. Proceedings 23rd IEEE Conference on Decision Control. pp. 514–519.

Blackwell, D. and M.A. Girschik (1954). *Theory of Games and Statistical Decisions*. New York: Wiley.

Blanchard, O. J. and C. M. Kahn (1980). The Solution of Linear Difference Models under Rational Expectations. *Econometrica*, Vol. 48(5), pp. 1305–1311.

Blinder, A. S. (1998). *Central Banking in Theory and Practice*. Cambridge, MA: MIT Press.

Brainard, W. (1967). Uncertainty and the Effectiveness of Policy. *American Economic Review*, Vol. 57(2), pp. 411–425.

Bray, M. M. (1982). Learning, Estimation, and the Stability of Rational Expectations. *Journal of Economic Theory*, Vol. 26(2), pp. 318–339.

Brock, W. A. (1982). Asset Prices in a Production Economy. In J. J. McCall (ed.), *The Economics of Information and Uncertainty*. Chicago: University of Chicago Press, pp. 1–43.

Brock, W. A. and P. deFontnouvelle (2000). Expectational Diversity in Monetary Economies. *Journal of Economic Dynamics and Control*, Vol. 24(5-7), pp. 725–759.

Brock, W. A. and S. N. Durlauf (2005). Local Robustness Analysis: Theory and Application. *Journal of Economic Dynamics and Control*, Vol. 29(11), pp. 2067–2092.

Brock, W. A., S. N. Durlauf, J. M. Nason, and G. Rondina (2006). Is the Original Taylor Rule Enough? Simple versus Optimal Rules as Guides to Monetary Policy. Mimeo. University of Wisconsin, Madison.

Brock, W. A., S. N. Durlauf, and G. Rondina (2006). Design Limits and Dynamic Policy Analysis. Mimeo. University of Wisconsin, Madison.

Brock, W. A., S. N. Durlauf, and K. D. West (2003). Policy Evaluation in Uncertain Economic Environments. In W. Brainard and G. Perry (eds.), *Brookings Papers on Economic Activity*. No. 1, pp. 235–322.

Brock, W. A., S. N. Durlauf, and K. D. West (2004). Model Uncertainty and Policy Evaluation: Some Theory and Empirics. Mimeo. University of Wisconsin, SSRI Paper No. 2004-19.

Brunner, K. and A. Meltzer (1969). The Nature of the Policy Problem. In K. Bruner and A. Meltzer (eds.), *Targets and Indicators of Monetary Policy*. San Francisco: Chandler.

Bucklew, J. A. (1990). *Large Deviation Techniques in Decision, Simulation, and Estimation*. New York: John Wiley & Sons.

Burnham, K. P. and D. R. Anderson (1998). *Model Selection and Inference: A Practical Information-Theoretic Approach*. New York: Springer.

Byers, R. (1987). Solving the Algebraic Riccati Equation with the Matrix Sign Function. *Linear Algebra and Its Applications*, Vol. 85, pp. 267–279.

Caballero, R. J. (1990). Consumption Puzzles and Precautionary Saving. *Journal of Monetary Economics*, Vol. 25(1), pp. 113–136.

Cagetti, M., L. P. Hansen, T. J. Sargent, and N. Williams (2002). Robustness and Pricing with Uncertain Growth. *Review of Financial Studies*, Vol. 15(2), pp. 363–404.

Caines, P. E. (1988). *Linear Stochastic Systems*. New York: John Wiley & Sons.

Caines, P. E. and D. Q. Mayne (1970). On the Discrete Time Matrix Riccati Equation of Optimal Control. *International Journal of Control*, Vol. 12(5), pp. 785–794.

Caines, P. E. and D. Q. Mayne (1971). Correspondence: "On the Discrete Time Matrix Riccati Equation of Optimal Control - a Correction". *International Journal of Control*, Vol. 14(1), pp. 205–207.

Campbell, J. Y. (1987). Does Saving Anticipate Declining Labor Income? An Alternative Test of the Permanent Income Hypothesis. *Econometrica*, Vol. 55(6), pp. 1249–1273.

Carroll, C. D. (1992). The Buffer-Stock Theory of Saving: Some Macroeconomic Evidence. *Brookings Papers on Economic Activity*, No. 2, pp. 61–156.

Carroll, C. D. (1997). Buffer-Stock Saving and the Life Cycle/Permanent Income Hypothesis. *Quarterly Journal of Economics*, Vol. 112(1), pp. 1–55.

Chan, S. W., G. C. Goodwin, and K. S. Sin (1984). Convergence Properties of the Riccati Difference Equation in Optimal Filtering of Nonstabilizable Systems. *IEEE Transactions on Automatic Control*, Vol. AC-29(2), pp. 110–118.

Chari, V. V., P. J. Kehoe, and E. C. Prescott (1989). Time Consistency and Policy. In Robert Barro (ed.), *Modern Business Cycle Theory*. Cambridge, MA: Harvard University Press, pp. 265–305.

Chen, Z. and L. Epstein (2002). Ambiguity, Risk, and Asset Returns in Continuous Time. *Econometrica*, Vol. 70(4), pp. 1403–1443.

Chernoff, H. (1952). A Measure of Asymptotic Efficiency for Tests of a Hypothesis Based on Sums of Observations. *Annals of Mathematical Statistics*, Vol. 23(4), pp. 493–507.

Cho, I.-K. and T. J. Sargent (2007). Self-Confirming Equilibrium. Mimeo. Unpublished, to appear in *The New Palgrave Dictionary of Economics*.

Christiano, L. J. and C. J. Gust (1999). Comment. In J. B. Taylor (ed.), *Monetary Policy Rules*. Chicago: University of Chicago Press, pp. 299–316.

Cochrane, J. H. (1997). Where Is the Market Going? Uncertain Facts and Novel Theories.. *Federal Reserve Bank of Chicago Economic Perspectives*, Vol. 21(6), pp. 3–37.

Cogley, T., R. Colacito, L. P. Hansen, and T. Sargent (2007). Robustness and U.S. Monetary Policy Experimentation. Mimeo. University of California at Davis, New York University, and University of Chicago.

Constantinides, G.M. (1990). Habit Formation: A Resolution of the Equity Premium Puzzle. *Journal of Political Economy*, Vol. 98(3), pp. 519–543.

Currie, D. and P. Levine (1987). The Design of Feedback Rules in Linear Stochastic Rational Expectations Models. *Journal of Economic Dynamics and Control*, Vol. 11(1), pp. 1–28.

Dantzig, G. B. (1998). *Linear Programming and Extensions*. Princeton, NJ: Princeton University Press.

Deaton, A. (1992). *Understanding Consumption*. New York: Oxford University Press.

De Jong, D., B. Ingram, and C. Whiteman (1996). A Bayesian Approach to Calibration. *Journal of Business and Economic Statistics*, Vol. 14(1), pp. 1–9.

Dem'ianov, V. F. and V. N. Malozemov (1974). *Introduction to Minimax*. New York: Wiley.

Dempster, A. (1967). Upper and Lower Probabilities Induced by a Multivalued Mapping. *Annals of Mathematical Statistics*, Vol. 38(2), pp. 325–339.

Denman, E. D. and A. N. Beavers (1976). The Matrix Sign Function and Computations in Systems. *Applications of Mathematical Computations*, Vol. 2, pp. 63–94.

Diaconis, P. and D. Freedman (1986). On the Consistency of Bayes Estimates. *Annals of Statistics*, Vol. 14(1), pp. 1–26.

Doan, T., R. Litterman, and C. Sims (1984). Forecasting and Conditional Projection Using Realistic Prior Distributions. *Econometric Reviews*, Vol. 3(1), pp. 1–100.

Dolmas, J. (1998). Risk Preferences and the Welfare Cost of Business Cycles. *Review of Economic Dynamics*, Vol. 1(3), pp. 646–676.

Dow, J. and S. Werlang (1992). Uncertainty Aversion, Risk Aversion, and the Optimal Choice of Portfolio. *Econometrica*, Vol. 60(1), pp. 197–204.

Dow, J. and S. Werlang (1994). Learning under Knightian Uncertainty: The Law of Large Numbers for Non-Additive Probabilities. Mimeo. London Business School.

Dubra, J., F. Maccheroni, and E. Ok (2004). Expected Utility Theory without the Completeness Axiom. *Journal of Economic Theory*, Vol. 115(1), pp. 118–133.

Duffie, D. and L. G. Epstein (1992). Stochastic Differential Utility. *Econometrica*, Vol. 60(2), pp. 353–394.

Dupuis, P. and R. S. Ellis (1997). *A Weak Convergence Approach to the Theory of Large Deviations*. New York: John Wiley & Sons.

Elliott, R. J., L. Aggoun, and J. B. Moore (1995). *Hidden Markov Models. Estimation and Control*. New York: Springer-Verlag.

Ellsberg, D. (1961). Risk, Ambiguity and the Savage Axioms. *Quarterly Journal of Economics*, Vol. 75(4), pp. 643–669.

Epstein, L. G. (1999). A Definition of Uncertainty Aversion. *Review of Economic Studies*, Vol. 66(3), pp. 579–608.

Epstein, L. G. and M. Schneider (2003a). Recursive Multiple-Priors. *Journal of Economic Theory*, Vol. 113(1), pp. 1–31.

Epstein, L. G. and M. Schneider (2003b). IID: Independently and Indistinguishably Distributed. *Journal of Economic Theory*, Vol. 113(1), pp. 32–50.

Epstein, L. G. and M. Schneider (2006). Learning under Ambiguity. Mimeo. New York University.

Epstein, L. G. and T. Wang (1994). Intertemporal Asset Pricing under Knightian Uncertainty. *Econometrica*, Vol. 62(3), pp. 283–322.

Epstein, L. G. and S. E. Zin (1989). Substitution, Risk Aversion, and the Temporal Behavior of Consumption and Asset Returns: A Theoretical Framework. *Econometrica*, Vol. 57(4), pp. 937–969.

Epstein, L. G. and S. E. Zin (1991). Substitution, Risk Aversion, and the Temporal Behavior of Consumption and Asset Returns: An Empirical Analysis. *Journal of Political Economy*, Vol. 99(2), pp. 263–286.

Evans, G. and S. Honkapohja (2001). *Learning and Expectations in Macroeconomics*. Princeton, NJ: Princeton University Press.

Fellner, W. (1961). Distortion of Subjective Probabilities as a Reaction to Uncertainty. *Quarterly Journal of Economics*, Vol. 75(4), pp. 670–689.

Fellner, W. (1965). *Probability and Profit: A Study of Economic Behavior along Bayesian Lines*. Irwin Series in Economics. Homewood, IL: Richard D. Irwin

Ferguson, T.S. (1967). *Mathematical Statistics: A Decision Theoretic Approach*. New York: Academic Press.

Flavin, M. A. (1981). The Adjustment of Consumption to Changing Expectations about Future Income. *Journal of Political Economy*, Vol. 89(5), pp. 974–1009.

Fleming, W. H. and P. E. Souganidis (1989). On the Existence of Value Functions of Two-Player, Zero-Sum Stochastic Differential Games. *Indiana University Mathematics Journal*, Vol. 38(2), pp. 293–314.

Friedman, M. (1953). The Effects of a Full-Employment Policy on Economic Stability: A Formal Analysis. In M. Friedman (ed.), *Essays in Positive Economics*. Chicago: University of Chicago Press.

Friedman, M. (1956). *A Theory of the Consumption Function*. Princeton, NJ: Princeton University Press.

Friedman, M. (1959). *A Program for Monetary Stability*. New York: Fordham University Press.

Friedman, M. and L. J. Savage (1948). The Utility Analysis of Choices Involving Risk. *Journal of Political Economy*, Vol. 56(4), pp. 279–304.

Fudenberg, D. and D. M. Kreps (1995a). Learning in Extensive Games, I: Self-Confirming and Nash Equilibrium. *Games and Economic Behavior*, Vol. 8(1), pp. 20–55.

Fudenberg, D. and D. M. Kreps (1995b). Learning in Extensive Games, II: Experimentation and Nash Equilibrium. Mimeo. Harvard University.

Fudenberg, D. and D. K. Levine (1993). Self-Confirming Equilibrium. *Econometrica*, Vol. 61(3), pp. 523–545.

Fudenberg, D. and D. K. Levine (1995). Consistency and Cautious Fictitious Play. *Journal of Economic Dynamics and Control*, Vol. 19(5), pp. 1065–1089.

Fudenberg, D. and D. K. Levine (1998). *The Theory of Learning in Games*. Cambridge, MA: MIT Press.

Gardiner, J. D. and A. J. Laub (1986). A Generalization of the Matrix-Sign-Function Solution for Algebraic Riccati Equations. *International Journal of Control*, Vol. 44(3), pp. 823–832.

Gardiner, J. D., M. R. Wette, A. J. Laub, J. J. Amato, and C. B. Moler (1992). A FORTRAN-77 Software Package for Solving the Sylvester Matrix Equation $AXB^T + CXD^T = E$. *ACM Transactions on Mathematical Software*, Vol. 18(2), pp. 232–238.

Gelman, A., J. B. Carlin, H. S. Stern, and D. B. Rubin (1995). *Bayesian Data Analysis*. Boca Raton, FL: Chapman and Hall.

Georgii, H.-O. (2003). Probabilistic Aspects of Entropy. In A. Greven, G. Keller, and G. Waranecke (eds.), *Entropy*. Princeton, NJ: Princeton University Press.

Ghirardato, P. and M. Marinacci (2002). Ambiguity Made Precise: A Comparative Foundation. *Journal of Economic Theory*, Vol. 102(2), pp. 251–289.

Ghirardato, P., F. Maccheroni, and M. Marinacci (2004). Differentiating Ambiguity and Ambiguity Attitude. *Journal of Economic Theory*, Vol. 118(2), pp. 133–173.

Ghirardato, P., F. Maccheroni, M. Marinacci, and M. Siniscalchi (2003). A Subjective Spin on Roulette Wheels. *Econometrica*, Vol. 71(6), pp. 1897–1908.

Giannoni, M. P. (2002). Does Model Uncertainty Justify Caution? Robust Optimal Monetary Policy in a Forward-Looking Model. *Macroeconomic Dynamics*, Vol. 6(1), pp. 111–144.

Gilboa, I. and D. Schmeidler (1989). Maxmin Expected Utility with Non-Unique Prior. *Journal of Mathematical Economics*, Vol. 18(2), pp. 141–153.

Girsanov, I. V. (1960). On Transforming a Certain Class of Stochastic Processes by Absolutely Continuous Substitution of Measures. *Theory of Probability Applications*, Vol. 5(3), pp. 285–301.

Glover, K. and J. C. Doyle (1988). State-Space Formulae for All Stabilizing Controllers that Satisfy an H_∞-Norm Bound and Relations to Risk-Sensitivity. *System & Control Letters*, Vol. 11(1), pp. 167–172.

Golub, G. H., S. Nash, and C. Van Loan (1979). A Hessenberg-Schur Method for the Matrix Problem $AX + XB = C$. *IEEE Transactions on Automatic Control*, Vol. AC-24(6), pp. 909–913.

Golub, G. H. and C. Van Loan (1989). *Matrix Computations*. Baltimore, MD: Johns Hopkins University Press.

Golub, G. H. and J. H. Wilkinson (1976). Ill-Conditioned Eigensystems and the Computation of the Jordan Canonical Form. *SIAM Review*, Vol. 18(4), pp. 578–619.

Gudmundsson, T., C. Kenney, and A. J. Laub (1992). Scaling of the Discrete-Time Algebraic Riccati Equation to Enhance Stability of the Schur Method. *IEEE Transactions on Automatic Control*, Vol. 37(4), pp. 513–518.

Hall, R. E. (1978). Stochastic Implications of the Life Cycle-Permanent Income Hypothesis: Theory and Evidence. *Journal of Political Economy*, Vol. 86(6), pp. 971–987.

Hamilton, J. D. (1989). A New Approach to the Economic Analysis of Nonstationary Time Series and the Business Cycle. *Econometrica*, Vol. 57(2), pp. 357–384.

Hamilton, J. D. (1994). *Time Series Analysis*. Princeton, NJ: Princeton University Press.

Hammarling, S. J. (1982). Numerical Solution of the Stable Non-Negative Lyapunov Equation. *IMA Journal of Numerical Analysis*, Vol. 2(3), pp. 303–323.

Hansen, L. P. (1987). Calculating Asset Prices in Three Exchange Economies. *Advances in Econometrics, Fifth World Congress*, Cambridge, MA: Cambridge University Press.

Hansen, L. P. (2007). Beliefs, Doubts, and Learning: Valuing Macroeconomic Risk. *American Economic Review*, Vol 97(2), pp. 1–30.

Hansen, L. P., D. Epple, and W. Roberds (1985). Linear-Quadratic Duopoly Models of Resource Depletion. In T. J. Sargent (ed.), *Energy, Foresight, and Strategy*. Washington, D.C.: Resources for the Future.

Hansen, L. P., J. Heaton, and N. Li (2006). Consumption Strikes Back: Measuring Long Run Risk. Mimeo. University of Chicago.

Hansen, L. P., J. Heaton, and T. J. Sargent (1991). Faster Methods for Solving Continuous Time Recursive Linear Models of Dynamic Economies. In L. P. Hansen and T. J. Sargent (eds.), *Rational Expectations Econometrics*. Boulder, CO: Westview Press, pp. 177–208.

Hansen, L. P. and R. Jagannathan (1991). Implications of Security Market Data for Models of Dynamic Economies. *Journal of Political Economy*, Vol. 99(2), pp. 225–262.

Hansen, L. P., R. Mayer, and T. J. Sargent (2007). Robust Estimation and Control for LQ Gaussian Problems without Commitment. Mimeo. University of Chicago and New York University.

Hansen, L. P., W. T. Roberds, and T. J. Sargent (1991). Time Series Implications of Present Value Budget Balance and of Martingale Models of Consumption and Taxes. In L. P. Hansen and T. J. Sargent (eds.), *Rational Expectations and Econometric Practice*. Boulder, CO: Westview Press, pp. 121–161.

Hansen, L. P. and T. J. Sargent (1980). Formulating and Estimating Dynamic Linear Rational Expectations Models. *Journal of Economic Dynamics and Control*, Vol. 2(2) pp. 7–46.

Hansen, L. P. and T. J. Sargent (1981). Linear Rational Expectations Models for Dynamically Interrelated Models. In R. E. Lucas, Jr., and T. J. Sargent (eds.), *Rational Expectations Econometrics*. Minneapolis: University of Minnesota Press.

Hansen, L. P. and T. J. Sargent (1991). *Rational Expectations Econometrics*. Boulder, CO: Westview Press.

Hansen, L. P. and T. J. Sargent (1993). Seasonality and Approximation Errors in Rational Expectations Models. *Journal of Econometrics*, Vol. 55(1-2), pp. 21–55.

Hansen, L. P. and T. J. Sargent (1995). Discounted Linear Exponential Quadratic Gaussian Control. *IEEE Transactions on Automatic Control*, Vol. 40(5), pp. 968–971.

Hansen L. P. and T. J. Sargent (2001). Robust Control and Model Uncertainty. *American Economic Review*, Vol. 91(2), pp. 60–66.

Hansen, L. P. and T. J. Sargent (2003). Robust Control of Forward-Looking Models. *Journal of Monetary Economics*, Vol. 50(3), pp. 581–604.

Hansen, L. P. and T. J. Sargent (2005a). 'Certainty Equivalence' and 'Model Uncertainty'. In J. Faust, A. Orphanides, and D. Reifschneider (eds.), *Models and Monetary Policy: Research in the Tradition of Dale Henderson, Richard Porter, and Peter Tinsley*. Washington, D.C.: Board of Governors of the Federal Reserve System.

Hansen, L.P. and T. J. Sargent (2005b). Robust Estimation and Control under Commitment. *Journal of Economic Theory*, Vol. 124(2), pp. 258–301.

Hansen, L.P., and T.J. Sargent (2007a). Robust Estimation and Control without Commitment. *Journal of Economic Theory*, In press.

Hansen, L. P. and T. J. Sargent (2007b). Fragile Beliefs and the Price of Model Uncertainty. Mimeo. University of Chicago and New York University.

Hansen, L. P. and T. J. Sargent (2007c). Time Inconsistency of Optimal Control. Mimeo. University of Chicago and New York University.

Hansen, L. P. and T. J. Sargent (2008). *Recursive Linear Models of Dynamic Economies*. Princeton, NJ: Princeton University Press.

Hansen, L. P., T. J. Sargent, and T. Tallarini (1999). Robust Permanent Income and Pricing. *Review of Economic Studies*, Vol. 66(4), pp. 873–907.

Hansen, L. P., T. J. Sargent, G. A. Turmuhambetova, and N. Williams (2006). Robust Control, Min-Max Expected Utility, and Model Misspecification. *Journal of Economic Theory*, Vol. 128(1), pp. 45–90.

Hansen, L. P., T. J. Sargent, and N. E. Wang (2002). Robust Permanent Income and Pricing with Filtering. *Macroeconomic Dynamics*, Vol. 6(1), pp. 40–84.

Harrison, M. and D. Kreps (1979). Martingales and Arbitrage in Multiperiod Security Markets. *Journal of Economic Theory*, Vol. 20(3), pp. 381–408.

Heaton, J. (1993). The Interaction between Time-Nonseparable Preferences and Time Aggregation. *Econometrica*, Vol. 61(2), pp. 353–385.

Hitz, K. L. and B. D. O. Anderson (1972). Iterative Method of Computing the Limiting Solution of the Matrix Riccati Differential Equation. *Proc. IEE*, Vol. 119(9), pp. 1402–1406.

Hurwicz, L. (1951). Some Specification Problems and Applications to Econometric Models. *Econometrica*, Vol. 19(3), pp. 343–344.

Jacobson, D. H. (1973). Optimal Stochastic Linear Systems with Exponential Performance Criteria and their Relation to Deterministic Differential Games. *IEEE Transactions on Automatic Control*, Vol. 18(2), pp. 124–131.

James, M. R. (1992). Asymptotic Analysis of Nonlinear Stochastic Risk-Sensitive Control and Differential Games. *Mathematics of Control, Signals, and Systems*, Vol. 5(4), pp. 401–417.

James, M. R. and J. S. Baras (1996). Partially Observed Differential Games, Infinite Dimensional Hamilton-Jacobi-Isaacs Equations, and Nonlinear H_∞ Control. *SIAM Journal on Control and Optimization*, Vol. 34(4), pp. 1342–1364.

James, M. R., J. S. Baras, and R. J. Elliott (1994). Risk-Sensitive Control and Dynamic Games for Partially Observed Discrete-Time Nonlinear Systems. *SIAM Journal on Control and Optimization*, Vol. 39(4), pp. 780–791.

Johnsen, T. H. and J. B. Donaldson (1985). The Structure of Intertemporal Preferences under Uncertainty and Time Consistent Plans. *Econometrica*, Vol. 53(6), pp. 1451–1458.

Jovanovic, B. (1979). Job Matching and the Theory of Turnover. *Journal of Political Economy*, Vol. 87(5), pp. 972–990.

Jovanovic, B. (1982). Selection and the Evolution of Industry. *Econometrica*, Vol. 50(3), pp. 649–670.

Jovanovic, B. and Y. Nyarko (1995). The Transfer of Human Capital. *Journal of Economic Dynamics and Control*, Vol. 19(5-7), pp. 1033–1064.

Jovanovic, B. and Y. Nyarko (1996). Learning by Doing and the Choice of Technology. *Econometrica*, Vol. 64(6), pp. 1299–1310.

Kågström, B. and P. Poromaa (1994). Computing Eigenspaces with Specified Eigenvalues of a Regular Matrix Pair (A, B) and Condition Estimation: Theory, Algorithms and Software. LAPACK Working Note 87.

Karantounias, A., L. P. Hansen, and T. J. Sargent (2007). Optimal Fiscal Policy for an Economy without Capital and a Robust Representative Consumer. Mimeo. New York University and University of Chicago.

Kasa, K. (1999). An Observational Equivalence among H_∞ Control Policies. *Economics Letters*, Vol. 64(2), pp. 173–180.

Kasa, K. (2001). A Robust Hansen–Sargent Prediction Formula. *Economics Letters*, Vol. 71(1), pp. 43–48.

Kasa, K. (2002a). An Information Theoretic Approach to Robust Control. Mimeo. Simon Fraser University.

Kasa, K. (2002b). Model Uncertainty, Robust Policies, and the Value of Commitment. *Macroeconomic Dynamics*, Vol. 6(1), pp. 145–166.

Kasa, K. (2006). Robustness and Information Processing. *Review of Economic Dynamics*, Vol. 9(1), pp. 1–33.

Kashyap, R. L. (1970). Maximum Likelihood Identification of Stochastic Linear Systems. *IEEE Transactions on Automatic Control*, Vol. AC-15(1), pp. 25–34.

Kenney, C. S., A. J. Laub, and P. M. Papadopoulos (1993). A Newton-Squaring Algorithm for Computing the Negative Invariant Subspace of a Matrix. *IEEE Transactions on Automatic Control*, Vol. 38(8), pp. 1284–1289.

Kimura, M. (1988). Convergence of the Doubling Algorithm for the Discrete-Time Algebraic Riccati Equation. *International Journal of Systems Science*, Vol. 19(5), pp. 701–711.

Kimura, M. (1989). Doubling Algorithm for Continuous-Time Algebraic Riccati Equation. *International Journal of Systems Science*, Vol. 20(2), pp. 191–202.

King, R. G. and A. L. Wolman (1999). What Should the Monetary Authority Do When Prices are Sticky?. In J. B. Taylor (ed.), *Monetary Policy Rules*. Chicago: University of Chicago Press, pp. 349–398.

Knight, F. H. (1921). *Risk, Uncertainty and Profit*. Boston: Houghton Mifflin.

Knox, T. (2003). Foundations for Learning How to Invest When Returns Are Uncertain. Mimeo. University of Chicago Graduate School of Business.

Kocherlakota, N. (1990). ,. *Disentangling the Coefficient of Relative Risk Aversion from the Elasticity of Intertemporal Substitution: An Irrelevance Result*, Journal of Finance.Vol. 45(1), pp. 175–190

Kocherlakota, N. and C. Phelan (2007). On the Robustness of Laissez-Faire. Mimeo. Federal Reserve Bank of Minneapolis.

Kreps, D. (1988). *Notes on the Theory of Choice*. Boulder, CO: Westview Press.

Kreps, D. M. (1998). Anticipated Utility and Dynamic Choice. In D. P. Jacobs, E. Kalai, and M. I. Kamien (eds.), *Frontiers of Research in Economic Theory: The Nancy L. Schwartz Memorial Lectures, 1983-1997*. Cambridge University Press.

Kreps, D. M. and E. L. Porteus (1978). Temporal Resolution of Uncertainty and Dynamic Choice. *Econometrica*, Vol. 46(1), pp. 185–200.

Kullback, S. and R. A. Leibler (1951). On Information and Sufficiency. *Annals of Mathematical Statistics*, Vol. 22(1), pp. 79–86.

Kwakernaak, H. and R. Sivan (1972). *Linear Optimal Control Systems*. New York: Wiley–Interscience.

Kydland, F. E. and E. C. Prescott (1977). Rules Rather than Discretion: The Inconsistency of Optimal Plans.. *Journal of Political Economy*, Vol. 85(3), pp. 473–491.

Kydland, F. E. and E. C. Prescott (1980). Dynamic Optimal Taxation, Rational Expectations and Optimal Control. *Journal of Economic Dynamics and Control*, Vol. 2(1), pp. 79–91.

Kydland, F. E. and E. C. Prescott (1982). Time to Build and Aggregate Fluctuations. *Econometrica*, Vol. 50(6), pp. 1345–1370.

Laibson, D. I. (1994). Hyperbolic Discounting and Consumption. Mimeo. Massachusetts Institute of Technology.

Laibson, D. I. (1998). Life-Cycle Consumption and Hyperbolic Discount Functions. *European Economic Review*, Vol. 42(3-5), pp. 861-871.

Laub, A. J. (1979). A Schur Method for Solving Algebraic Riccati Equations. *IEEE Transactions on Automatic Control*, Vol. AC-24(6), pp. 913–921.

Laub, A. J. (1991). Invariant Subspace Methods for the Numerical Solution of Riccati Equations. In S. Bittanti, A. J. Laub, and J. C. Willems (eds.), *The Riccati Equation*. New York: Springer–Verlag.pp. 163–196

Leland, H. E. (1968). Saving and Uncertainty: The Precautionary Demand for Saving. *Quarterly Journal of Economics*, Vol. 82(3), pp. 465–473.

Levin, A., V. Wieland, and J. C. Williams (1999). Robustness of Simple Monetary Policy Rules under Model Uncertainty. In J. B. Taylor (ed.), *Monetary Policy Rules*. Chicago: University of Chicago Press, pp. 263–299.

Ljungqvist, L. and T. J. Sargent (2004). *Recursive Macroeconomic Theory, 2nd ed.*. Cambridge, MA: MIT Press.

Lopomo, G., L. Rigotti, and C. Shannon (2004). Uncertainty in Mechanism Design. Mimeo. Duke University.

Lu, L. and W. Lin (1993). An Iterative Algorithm for Solution of the Discrete-Time Algebraic Riccati Equation. *Linear Algebra and Its Applications*, Vol. 188(1), pp. 465–488.

Lucas, R. E., Jr. (1976). Econometric Policy Evaluation: A Critique. In K. Brunner and A. H. Meltzer (eds.), *The Phillips Curve and Labor Markets*. Amsterdam: North-Holland.

Lucas, R. E., Jr (1978). Asset Prices in an Exchange Economy. *Econometrica*, Vol. 46(6), pp. 1429–1445.

Lucas, R. E., Jr (1987). *Models of Business Cycles*. Yrjo Jahnsson Lectures Series. London: Blackwell.

Lucas, R. E., Jr. (2003). Macroeconomic Priorities. *American Economic Review*, Vol. 93(1), pp. 1–14.

Lucas, R. E., Jr. and E. C. Prescott (1971). Investment under Uncertainty. *Econometrica*, Vol. 39(5), pp. 659–681.

Lucas, R. E., Jr. and N. Stokey (1983). Optimal Monetary and Fiscal Policy in an Economy without Capital. *Journal of Monetary Economics*, Vol. 12(1), pp. 55–94.

Luenberger, D. G. (1969). *Optimization by Vector Space Methods*. New York: Wiley.

Maccheroni, F., M. Marinacci, and A. Rustichini (2006a). Ambiguity Aversion, Robustness, and the Variational Representation of Preferences. *Econometrica*, Vol. 74(6), pp. 1447–1498.

Maccheroni, F., M. Marinacci, and A. Rustichini (2006b). Dynamic Variational Preferences. *Journal of Economic Theory*, Vol. 128(1), pp. 4–44.

MacFarlane, A. G. J. (1963). An Eigenvector Solution of the Optimal Linear Regulator Problem. *Journal of Electronics and Control*, Vol. 14(6), pp. 643–654.

Machina, M. J. and D. Schmeidler (1992). A More Robust Definition of Subjective Probability. *Econometrica*, Vol. 60(4), pp. 745-780.

Maenhout, P. J. (2004). Robust Portfolio Rules and Asset Pricing. *Review of Financial Studies*, Vol. 17(4), pp. 951–983.

Marcet, A. and R. Marimon (1992). Communication, Commitment, and Growth. *Journal of Economic Theory*, Vol. 58(2), pp. 219–249.

Marcet, A. and R. Marimon (2000). Recursive Contracts. Mimeo. Universitat Pompeu Fabra.

Marcet, A. and T. J. Sargent (1989). Convergence of Least Squares Learning Mechanisms in Self-Referential Linear Stochastic Models. *Journal of Economic Theory*, Vol. 48(2), pp. 337–368.

Mehra, R. and E. C. Prescott (1985). The Equity Premium: A Puzzle. *Journal of Monetary Economics*, Vol. 15(2), pp. 145–162.

Miller, B. L. (1974). Optimal Consumption with a Stochastic Income Stream. *Econometrica*, Vol. 42(2), pp. 253–266.

Miller, M. and M. Salmon (1985a). Dynamic Games and the Time Inconsistency of Optimal Policy in Open Economies. *Economic Journal, Supplement*, Vol. 95, pp. 124–137.

Miller, M. and M. Salmon (1985b). Policy Coordination and Dynamic Games. In W. Buiter and R. Marston (eds.), *International Economic Policy Coordination*. Cambridge, MA: Cambridge University Press, pp. 184–213.

Milnor, J. W. (1951). Games against Nature. Mimeo. The RAND Research Memoranda Series No. RM-0679-PR.

Milnor, J. W. (1954). Games Against Nature. In R.M. Thrall, C.H. Coombs, and R.L. Davis (eds.), *Decision Processes*. New York: John Wiley & Sons, pp. 49–60.

Mustafa, D. and K. Glover (1990). *Minimum Entropy H^∞ Control*. Berlin: Springer–Verlag.

Muth, J. F. (1960). Optimal Properties of Exponentially Weighted Forecasts. *Journal of the American Statistical Association*, Vol. 55(290), pp. 299–306.

Muth, J. F. (1961). Rational Expectations and the Theory of Price Movements. *Econometrica*, Vol. 29(3), pp. 315–335.

Obstfeld, M. (1994). Evaluating Risky Consumption Paths: the Role of Intertemporal Substitutability. *European Economic Review*, Vol. 38(7), pp. 1471–1486.

Onatski, A. (2001). Robust Monetary Policy under Model Uncertainty: Incorporating Rational Expectations. Mimeo. Columbia University.

Onatski, A. and J. H. Stock (2002). Robust Monetary Policy under Model Uncertainty in a Small Model of the U.S. Economy. *Macroeconomic Dynamics*, Vol. 6(1), pp. 85–110.

Onatski, A. and N. Williams (2003). Modeling Model Uncertainty. *Journal of the European Economic Association*, Vol. 1(5), pp. 1087–1122.

Orlik, A. (2006). Rational Expectations and Robust Control: Observational Equivalence Results for Misspecified Monetary Dynamics. Mimeo. European University Institute.

Otrok, C. (2001a). On Measuring the Welfare Cost of Business Cycles. *Journal of Monetary Economics*, Vol. 47(1), pp. 61–92.

Otrok, C. (2001b). Spectral Welfare Cost Functions. *International Economic Review*, Vol. 42(2), pp. 345–367.

Pappas, T., A. J. Laub, and N. R. Sandell, Jr. (1980). On the Numerical Solution of the Discrete-Time Algebraic Riccati Equation. *IEEE Transactions on Automatic Control*, Vol. AC-25(4), pp. 631–641.

Pearlman, J. G. (1992). Reputational and Nonreputational Policies under Partial Information. *Journal of Economic Dynamics and Control*, Vol. 16(2), pp. 339–357.

Pearlman, J. G., D. A. Currie, and P. L. Levine (1986). Rational Expectations Models with Partial Information. *Economic Modeling*, Vol. 3(2), pp. 90–105.

Petersen, I. R., M. R. James, and P. Dupuis (2000). Minimax Optimal Control of Stochastic Uncertain Systems with Relative Entropy Constraints. *IEEE Transactions on Automatic Control*, Vol. 45(3), pp. 398–412.

Petkov, P. Jr., N. D. Christov, and M. M. Konstantinov (1991). *Computational Methods for Linear Control Systems*. Englewood Cliffs, NJ: Prentice Hall.

Phelps, E. S. and R. A. Pollak (1968). On Second-Best National Saving and Game-Equilibrium Growth. *Review of Economic Studies*, Vol. 35(2), pp. 185–199.

Potter, J. E. (1966). Matrix Quadratic Solutions. *SIAM Journal on Applied Mathematics*, Vol. 14(3), pp. 496–501.

Pratt, J. W. (1964). Risk Aversion in the Small and in the Large. *Econometrica*, Vol. 32(1-2), pp. 122–136.

Prescott, E. C. and R. Mehra (1980). Recursive Competitive Equilibrium: The Case of Homogeneous Households. *Econometrica*, Vol. 48(6), pp. 1365–1379.

Rabin, M. (2000). Risk Aversion and Expected-Utility Theory: A Calibration Theorem. *Econometrica*, Vol. 68(5), pp. 1281–1292.

Rigotti, L. and C. Shannon (2003). Maxmin Expected Utility and Equilibria. Mimeo. Discussion paper, University of California, Berkeley.

Rigotti, L. and C. Shannon (2005). Uncertainty and Risk in Financial Markets. *Econometrica*, Vol. 73(1), pp. 203–243.

Robert, C. (2001). *The Bayesian Choice: From Decision Theoretic Foundations to Computational Implementation*. 2nd ed. New York: Springer–Verlag.

Roberts, J. D. (1980) Linear Model Reduction and Solution of the Algebraic Equation by Use of the Sign Function. *International Journal of Control*, Vol. 32(4), pp. 677–687. (Reprint of Technical Report No. TR-13, CUED/B-Control, Cambridge University, Engineering Department, 1971)

Rosen, S., K. M. Murphy, and J. A. Scheinkman (1994). Cattle Cycles. *Journal of Political Economy*, Vol. 102(3), pp. 468–492.

Rosen, S. and R. H. Topel (1988). Housing Investment in the United States. *Journal of Political Economy*, Vol. 96(4), pp. 718–740.

Rozanov, Y. A. (1967). *Stationary Random Processes*. San Francisco: Holden-Day.

Ryder, H. E. and G. Heal (1973). Optimal Growth with Intertemporally Dependent Preferences. *Review of Economic Studies*, Vol. 40(1), pp. 1–31.

Ryoo, J. and S. Rosen (2004). The Engineering Labor Market. *Journal of Political Economy*, Vol. 112(1), pp. S110–S140.

Sargent, T. J. (1981). Interpreting Economic Time Series. *Journal of Political Economy*, Vol. 89(2), pp. 213–248.

Sargent, T. J. (1987). *Macroeconomic Theory*. 2nd ed. New York: Academic Press.

Sargent, T. J. (1999a). *The Conquest of American Inflation*. Princeton, NJ: Princeton University Press.

Sargent, T. J. (1999b). Comment. In J. B. Taylor (ed.), *Monetary Policy Rules*. Chicago: University of Chicago Press, pp. 144–154.

Savage, L. J. (1954). *The Foundations of Statistics*. New York: John Wiley & Sons.

Schmeidler, D. (1989). Subjective Probability and Expected Utility without Additivity. *Econometrica*, Vol. 57(3), pp. 571–587.

Schorfheide, F. (2000). Loss Function-Based Evaluation of DSGE Models. *Journal of Applied Econometrics*, Vol. 15(6), pp. 645–670.

Segal, U. and A. Spivak (1990). First Order versus Second Order Risk Aversion. *Journal of Economic Theory*, Vol. 51(1), pp. 111–125.

Shafer, G. (1976). *A Mathematical Theory of Evidence*. Princeton, NJ: Princeton University Press.

Sims, C. A. (1971). Distributed Lag Estimation When the Parameter Space Is Explicitly Infinite-Dimensional. *Annals of Mathematical Statistics*, Vol. 42(5), pp. 1622–1636.

Sims, C. A. (1972). The Role of Approximate Prior Restrictions in Distributed Lag Estimation. *Journal of the American Statistical Association*, Vol. 67(337), pp. 169–175.

Sims, C. A. (1974). Seasonality in Regression. *Journal of the American Statistical Association*, Vol. 69(347), pp. 618–626.

Sims, C. A. (1980). Macroeconomics and Reality. *Econometrica*, Vol. 48(1), pp. 1–48.

Sims, C. A. (1993). Rational Expectations Modeling with Seasonally Adjusted Data. *Journal of Econometrics*, Vol. 55(1-2), pp. 9–19.

Siow, A. (1984). Occupational Choice under Uncertainty. *Econometrica*, Vol. 52(3), pp. 631–645.

Stewart, G. W. (1972). On the Sensitivity of the Eigenvalue Problem $Ax = \lambda Bx$. *SIAM Journal on Numerical Analysis*, Vol. 9(4), pp. 669–686.

Stewart, G. W. (1976). Algorithm 506: HQR3 and EXCHNG: Fortran Subroutines for Calculating and Ordering the Eigenvalues of a Real Upper Hessenberg Matrix. *ACM Transactions on Mathematical Software*, Vol. 2(3), pp. 275–280.

Stock, J. H. (1999). Comment. In J. B. Taylor (ed.), *Monetary Policy Rules*. Chicago: University of Chicago Press, pp. 253–259.

Stokey, N. L. (1989). Reputation and Time Consistency. *American Economic Review*, Vol. 79(2), pp. 134–139.

Stokey, N. L. (1991). Credible Public Policy. *Journal of Economic Dynamics and Control*, Vol. 15(4), pp. 627–656.

Stokey, N. L. and R. E. Lucas, Jr. (with E. C. Prescott) 1989. *Recursive Methods in Economic Dynamics*. Cambridge, MA: Harvard University Press.

Strzalecki, T. (2007). Subjective Beliefs and Ex-Ante Agreeable Trade. Mimeo. Northwestern University.

Sundaresan, S. M. (1989). Intertemporally Dependent Preferences and the Volatility of Consumption and Wealth. *Review of Financial Studies*, Vol. 2(1), pp. 73–89.

Svensson, L. E. O. and M. Woodford (2000). Indicator Variables for Monetary Policy. Mimeo. Princeton University.

Tallarini, T. D. (2000). Risk-Sensitive Real Business Cycles. *Journal of Monetary Economics*, Vol. 45(3), pp. 507–532.

Taylor, J. B. (1999). *Monetary Policy Rules*. Chicago: University of Chicago Press.

Tetlow, R. and P. von zur Muehlen (2004). Avoiding Nash Inflation: Bayesian and Robust Responses to Model Uncertainty. *Review of Economic Dynamics*, Vol. 7(4), pp. 869–899.

Tornell, A. (1998). Excess Volatility of Asset Prices with H_∞ Forecasts. Mimeo. Harvard University.

Van Dooren, P. (1981). A Generalized Eigenvalue Approach for Solving Riccati Equations. *SIAM Journal on Scientific and Statistical Computing*, Vol. 2(2), pp. 121–135.

Van Dooren, P. (1982). Algorithm 590: DSUBSP and EXCHQZ: Fortran Subroutines for Computing Deflating Subspaces with Specified Spectrum. *ACM Transactions on Mathematical Software*, Vol. 8(4), pp. 376–382.

Vaughan, D. R. (1970). A Nonrecursive Algebraic Solution for the Discrete Riccati Equation. *IEEE Transactions on Automatic Control*, Vol. AC-15(5), pp. 597–599.

Velde, F. (2006). An Alternative Measure of Inflation. *Federal Reserve Bank of Chicago Economic Perspectives*, Vol. 30(1), pp. 55–65.

von Neumann, J. and O. Morgenstern (1944). *Theory of Games and Economic Behavior*. Princeton, NJ: Princeton University Press.

von zur Muehlen, P. (1982). Activist vs. Non-Activist Monetary Policy: Optimal Rules under Extreme Uncertainty. Mimeo. Board of Governors of the Federal Reserve Board, Washington, D.C.

Vuong, Q. H. (1989). Likelihood Ratio Tests for Model Selection and Non-Nested Hypotheses. *Econometrica*, Vol. 57(2), pp. 307–333.

Wang, N. (2003). Caballero Meets Bewley: The Permanent-Income Hypothesis in General Equilibrium. *American Economic Review*, Vol. 93(3), pp. 927–936.

Wang, N. (2004). Precautionary Saving and Partially Observed Income. *Journal of Monetary Economics*, Vol. 51(8), pp. 1645–1681.

Wang, T. (1999). Updating Rules for Non-Bayesian Preferences. Mimeo. University of British Columbia.

Ward, R. C. (1981). Balancing the Generalized Eigenvalue Problem. *SIAM Journal on Scientific and Statistical Computing*, Vol. 2(2), pp. 141–152.

Weil, P. (1989). The Equity Premium Puzzle and the Risk-Free Rate Puzzle. *Journal of Monetary Economics*, Vol. 24(3), pp. 401–421.

Weil, P. (1990). Nonexpected Utility in Macroeconomics. *Quarterly Journal of Economics*, Vol. 105(1), pp. 29–42.

Weil, P. (1993). Precautionary Savings and the Permanent Income Hypothesis. *Review of Economic Studies*, Vol. 60(2), pp. 367–383.

White, H. (1982). Maximum Likelihood Estimation of Misspecified Models. *Econometrica*, Vol. 50(1), pp. 1-25.

White, H. (1994). *Estimation, Inference, and Specification Analysis.* Econometric Society Monograph 22, Cambridge, UK: Cambridge University Press.

Whiteman, C. (1983). *Linear Rational Expectations Models: A User's Guide.* Minneapolis: University of Minnesota Press.

Whiteman, C. (1985). Spectral Utility, Wiener-Hopf Techniques, and Rational Expectations. *Journal of Economic Dynamics and Control*, Vol. 9(2), pp. 225–240.

Whiteman, C. (1986). Analytical Policy Design Under Rational Expectations. *Econometrica*, Vol. 54(6), pp. 1387–1405.

Whittle, P. (1981). Risk-Sensitive Linear/Quadratic/Gaussian Control. *Advances in Applied Probability*, Vol. 13(4), pp. 764–777.

Whittle, P. (1983). *Prediction and Regulation by Linear Least-Square Methods.* 2nd ed. Minneapolis: University of Minnesota Press.

Whittle, P (1990). *Risk-Sensitive Optimal Control.* New York: Wiley.

Whittle, P. (1996). *Optimal Control: Basics and Beyond.* New York: Wiley.

Wieland, V. (2000). Monetary policy, Parameter Uncertainty, and Optimal Learning. *Journal of Monetary Economics*, Vol. 46(1), pp. 199–228.

Wieland, V. (2005). Comment on "Certainty Equivalence and Model Uncertainty." In J. Faust, A. Orphanides, and D. Reifschneider (eds.), *Models and Monetary Policy: Research in the Tradition of Dale Henderson, Richard Porter and Peter Tinsley.* Washington, D.C.: Board of Governors of the Federal Reserve System.

Wilson, D. A. and A. Kumar (1982). Derivative Computations for the Log Likelihood Function. *IEEE Transactions on Automatic Control*, Vol. AC-27(1), pp. 230–232.

Woodford, M. (1990). Learning to Believe in Sunspots. *Econometrica*, Vol. 58(2), pp. 277–307.

Woodford, M. (1999). Optimal Monetary Policy Inertia. NBER Working Paper No. 7261.

Woodford, M. (2005). Robustly Optimal Monetary Policy with Near-Rational Expectations. Mimeo. Columbia University.

Zhou, K., J. C. Doyle, and K. Glover (1996). *Robust and Optimal Control.* London: Prentice Hall. ,

Index

absolute continuity, 31, 134, 411

admissibility

    of robust decision rule, 158, 162

admissible

    decision rule, 16

approximating model, 3, 16

    versus truth, 5

augmented regulator problem, 71

backward shift operator, 293

Bayes' Law

    updating multiple priors, 409

Bayesian interpretation

    and belief heterogeneity, 331

    of robust control, 16

    of robust filter, 360, 372

    of robust rule, 158

Bellman equation

    Kalman filter, 111

    optimal linear regulator, 28

    robust optimal linear regulator, 33–44

Bellman-Isaacs condition, 142, 153, 182

    and dynamic consistency, 160

    proved, 148

benchmark model, 367

Big K, little k, 7, 19, 37, 155, 238, 283, 331, 349, 394

breakdown point

    check for, 190

    for θ, 3, 32, 35, 129, 144, 174, 180, 217

    for θ_1, θ_2, 391

    smoothness across frequencies, 174

canonical preferences, 286

Cauchy-Schwarz inequality, 309

certainty equivalence, 32, 224, 337, 346, 380

    and *ex post* Bayesian interpretation, 158

    for problem without robustness, 29

    modified for robustness, 33

completing

    the square, 146, 171, 172, 324

concavity

    and entropy criterion, 198

constraint game

    dynamic, 169

    pathology, 130

    Stackelberg, 337

    static version, 119–136

continuous time, 82, 93

controllablity, 69

covariance-stationary, 200

cross-equation restrictions

    and robustness, 9

    rational expectations, 9

$\mathcal{D}$, 44, 147, 168, 361–366

    distortion operator, 35, 145

deflating subspace, 80

detectability, 70

detection error probabilities, 213–221, 224, 307

    and discounting, 17

    calibrate γ, 320

    in permanent income model, 244

deterministic regulator problem, 68

DGE model

    Schur algorithm, 88

    solving, 86

discounting, 6

    hyperbolic, 407

doubling algorithm, 84, 98

    Riccati equation, 84, 88–93

Sylvester equations, 100
duality, 116
    Kalman filter and linear regulator, 103
    of robust filtering and control, 359
    robust filtering and control, 367
dynamic consistency
    of constraint game, 160
    of multiplier game, 160
dynamic programming, 25

economy
    information, 253–264, 296
    preferences, 253–264, 296
    technology, 253–264, 296
entropy, 29–31, 114, 115
    criterion, 176, 198–199
    meaning, 197
    measuring model misspecification, 9
    misspecification analysis in econometrics, 9
equilibrium, 253
    competitive, 259
    Markov perfect, 142
    rational expectations, 5, 285
    self-confirming, 5, 8
equity premium, 302, 305
expected utility
    max-min, 15
extremization, 34

filtering with robustness
    with commitment, 359–380
    without commitment, 385–398
filtering without robustness, 103–116
forecasting problem, 170, 233
Fourier transform, 176
fragility, 389
frequency domain

interpretation of permanent income model, 223, 241
interpretation of robust control, 173–198
interpretation of robust filter, 379

golden ratio, 189, 375

H_2, 176, 178, 198–199, 212
H_∞, 3, 13, 135, 176, 178–180, 199
Hamiltonian matrix, 82, 93
Hansen-Jagannathan bounds
    and detection error probabilities, 322
Hessenberg decomposition, 100
Hessenberg-Schur algorithm, 98, 100
heterogeneity
    of beliefs, 7, 24, 331
    of worst-case models, 7, 331
hyperbolic discounting, 407

implementability constraint, 333, 338, 355
    multiplier on multiplier, 348, 351
incomplete preferences, 15
indirect utility function, 13, 57, 173
initial condition
    H_∞, 180
    for w, 191
    Stackelberg constraint problem, 176
invariant subspace, 21, 24, 77, 334, 337

$\mathcal{K}$, 107, 365, 366
Kalman filter, 104–116
    robust, 359–380

L_0^2, 276
    square summability, 266

Lagrange multiplier theorem, 126, 137
large deviations theory, 59, 308
Law of Iterated Expectations, 363
learning
    about model misspecification, 17, 359–381, 385–398
long-run risk, 17
Lucas critique, 9, 12, 16

marginal propensity to consume
    out of financial wealth, 240
    out of human wealth, 240
marginal propensity to save
    out of financial wealth, 224
market price
    of model uncertainty, 303, 308
        detection error probabilities, 305, 320
    of risk, 302, 307, 309
        and robustness, 303
Markov perfect equilibrium
    concerns about robustness, 329
matrix sign algorithm, 84, 93–94
misspecification
    in Ramsey problem, 338
model averaging, 404
model uncertainty
    structured, 14, 403
multiplier game
    Stackelberg, 338
    static version, 119–136

nonstochastic LQ model
    as tool for solving stochastic model, 62, 371

observability, 70
observational equivalence
    discounting and robustness, 224, 231, 248
    of quantities, 231

risk sensitivity and robustness, 318
occupational choice, 284
optimal linear regulator problem, 28, 68, 71, 72, 103, 170, 178, 256
    augmented, 68, 71–72, 94, 109, 110

parallelogram law, 203
Parseval's equality, 177
partitioned inverse formula, 75, 151, 362, 381
pencil, 79
    symplectic, 80, 83
permanent income model, 45, 51, 223–247
Phillips curve, 119
policy improvement algorithm, 107, 161
precautionary savings, 22, 47–51, 223, 234–245
    conventional versus robust, 223
    frequency domain, 241
prediction theory
    linear, 186
preference shocks
    as specification errors, 54, 408
principal components, 179
probabilistic sophistication, 403, 405
probability slanting, 9
promise keeping constraint, 160

$\mathcal{R}$, 40, 57–60
    and large deviation bound, 59
    as indirect utility, 57
Radon-Nikodym derivative, 288, 295
Ramsey problem, 335
    robust, 336, 338
rational expectations, 138
    cross-equation restrictions, 9
    econometrics, 9

rectangularity
    intertemporal distortions, 411
    multiple priors, 411
    reservations, 411
recursive
    saddle point problem, 355
regulator problem
    augmented, 71
    deterministic, 68
    discounted stochastic, 72
Riccati equation, 76–81, 169
    Kalman filter, 112
risk aversion, 307
    across frequencies, 174, 198
    versus model misspecification, 40
    versus robustness, 315
risk sensitivity, 40, 174, 313
    and probabilistic sophistication, 406
    indirect utility function, 57
    versus robustness, 315
risk-free rate puzzle, 310
robustness bound
    frequency domain, 182
    time domain, 38, 170

$\mathcal{S}$, 145, 162
Schur algorithm, 84–88
    solving DGE model, 86
Schur decomposition, 84
    generalized, 86
shadow price, 339
Sharpe ratio, 309
spectral density, 173
    factorization, 186, 193

robustness flattens, 379
square summability, 266
stabilizability, 69, 140
Stackelberg
    frequency domain, 178
    game, 335, 336
    leader
        robust, 333–352
    multiplier game, 181
        and consumption, 224, 236
    time domain, 175
stochastic discount factor, 295, 299, 308, 313
    adjustment for robustness, 291, 300
subspace
    deflating, 79
Sylvester equation, 95, 97, 98, 101, 157, 257, 268, 279, 299, 300
    efficient solution, 97–98
symplectic, 92
    matrix, 77
    pencil, 149, 340, 353

T, 44, 145, 169, 360
T^*, 107, 366
$\mathbf{T}^1$, 387, 392
$\mathbf{T}^2$, 388, 393
time inconsistency
    and conflict, 153
timidity, 322

unstructured uncertainty, 403

worst-case shock
    alternative representations, 7

Author Index

Abel, Andrew, 305
Aggoun, L., 384
Aiyagari, S. Rao, 44
Alvarez, Fernando, 322
Anderson, B.D.O., 68, 69, 83, 89, 93, 94, 101, 335
Anderson, David Raymond , 214
Anderson, Evan, 67, 68, 155, 214, 221, 295, 308, 411

Backus, David, 335
Bai, Z., 85
Bailey, Martin, 6
Ball, L., 218
Barillas, Francisco, 6, 307, 405
Barro, Robert J., 44
Bartels, R.H., 99
Başar, T., ix, 139, 335, 381
Beavers, A.N., 93
Becker, G.S., 226
Bergemann, Dirk, 13, 125
Bernhard, P., ix, 139, 335, 381
Bewley, Truman, 15
Bierman, G.J., 93
Blackwell, David, 37, 158
Blanchard, Olivier, 335
Blinder, Alan, 19
Brainard, William, 6
Brock, William A., 7, 173, 253, 267
Brunner, Karl, 335
Bucklew, James A., 59
Burnham, Kenneth P., 214
Byers, R., 93

Caballero, Ricardo, 224
Cagetti, Marco, 398
Caines, P.E., 69, 70
Calvino, Italo, 25, 103

Carlin, John B., 10
Carroll, Christopher D., 235
Chan, S. W., 70
Chen, Z., 295, 411
Cho, In-Koo, 8
Christiano, Lawrence, 335
Cochrane, John, 307
Cogley, Timothy, 19, 384
Colacito, Riccardo, 19, 384
Currie, David, 335

Dantzig, George, 128
Deaton, Angus, 235
DeFontnouvelle, Patrick, 7
DeJong, David, 335
Demmel, J.W., 85
Denman, E.D., 93
Diaconis, Percy, 15
Dickinson, John, 359
Dolmas, Jim, 312
Donaldson, John H., 407
Dow, James, 15, 295
Doyle, John C., 3, 193, 194
Driffill, John, 335
Dubra, Juan, 15
Dupuis, Paul, 405
Durlauf, Steven N., 173

Elliott, R.J., 384
Ellsberg, Daniel, 403, 405
Epple, Dennis, 335, 337
Epstein, Larry, 17, 295, 312, 403, 405, 408, 411
Evans, George, 5, 8

Fellner, W., 38, 122, 236
Ferguson, T.S., 158
Franklin, Benjamin, 223
Freedman, David, 15
Friedman, Milton, 6, 104
Fudenberg, Drew, 8, 15

Gardiner, J.D., 67, 83, 93, 100

Gelman, Andrew, 10
Ghirardato, Paolo, 15, 405
Giannoni, Marc, 335
Gilboa, Itzak, 15, 160, 162
Girschik, M.A., 37, 158
Glover, Keith, 3, 193, 194
Golub, G.H., 67, 68, 78, 85, 99, 100
Goodwin, G.C., 70
Gust, C.J., 335

Hansen, Lars Peter, 6, 9, 10, 15, 22,
        70, 135, 137, 155, 158, 182,
        214, 221, 256, 295, 302, 303,
        333, 335, 337, 385, 398, 408
Harrison, Michael, 257, 273, 278
Heal, G., 226
Heaton, John, 70, 226
Hitz, K.L., 83
Holmes, Oliver Wendell, Jr., 403
Holmes, Sherlock, 213
Honkapohja, Seppo, 5, 8
Hurwicz, Leonid, 335

Ingram, Beth, 335

Jacobson, D.J., 22, 34, 41, 44, 53,
        123
Jagannathan, Ravi, 302
James, Matthew R., 405
Jermann, Urban J., 322
Jevons, William Stanley, 383
Johnsen, Thore H., 407
Jovanovic, Boyan, 394

Kågström, B., 86
Karantounias, Anastasios, 333
Kasa, Kenneth, 224, 335
Kenney, C.S., 94
Khan, Charles, 335
Kimura, M., 79, 90, 93
King,Robert G., 335
Kocherlakota, Narayana, 310, 336
Kreps, David, 11, 257, 273, 278, 312

Kwakernaak, H., 69
Kydland, Finn, 74, 119

Laibson, David I., 407
Laub, A.J., 67, 68, 76–80, 83, 93, 94
Leland, H., 223
Levine, David, 8, 15
Levine, Paul, 335
Lewis, Frederick Allen, 139
Lin, W., 94
Ljungqvist, Lars, 328
Lopomo, G., 15
Lu, L., 94
Lucas, Robert E., Jr., 9, 16, 227,
        253, 268, 314

Maccheroni, Fabio, 15, 135, 160,
        162, 405, 408
MacFarlane, A.G.J., 78
Machina, Mark. J., 405
Maenhout, Pascal, 295
Marcet, Albert, 5, 44, 335
Marimon, Ramon, 335
Marinacci, Massimo, 15, 135, 160,
        162, 405, 408
Mayer, Ricardo, 385, 398
Mayne, D.Q., 70
McGrattan, Ellen R., 67, 68, 155
Mehra, Rajnish, 254, 267
Meltzer, Alan, 335
Miller, B.L., 223
Miller, Marcus, 335
Milnor John Willard, 12
Moore, J.B., 69, 89, 101, 335, 384
Murphy, K.M., 226, 268
Mustafa, D., 193
Muth, John F., 104, 360

Nash, S., 67, 68, 99
Nason, James M., 173
Nyarko, Yaw, 394

Obstfeld, Maurice, 312

Ok, Efe, 15
Onatski, A., 335, 404
Orlik, Anna, 224
Otrok, Christopher, 103, 173, 335

Papadopoulos, P.M., 94
Pappas, T., 67, 68, 76, 79, 80
Pearlman, J.G., 335, 337
Petersen, Ian R., 405
Phelan, Christopher, 336
Phelps, Edmund S., 407
Piskorski, Tomasz, 163
Pollak, Robert A., 407
Poromaa, P., 86
Porteus, Evan, 308, 312
Pratt, John, 214, 307
Prescott, Edward C., 74, 119, 254, 267, 268

Reitz, Thomas A., 305
Rigotti, Luca, 15, 295, 327
Roberds, William, 335, 337
Robert, Christian, 37
Roberts, J.D., 93
Rondina, Giacomo, 173
Rosen, Sherwin, 268, 284
Rozanov, Y. A., 186, 192
Rubin, Donald B., 10
Russell, Bertrand, 333
Rustichini, Aldo, 135, 160, 162, 405, 408
Ryder, H.E., 226
Ryoo, Jaewoo, 268, 284

Salmon, Mark, 335
Sandell, N.R., 67, 68, 76, 79, 80
Sargent, Thomas J., 6, 9, 10, 15, 22, 44, 70, 87, 135, 137, 155, 158, 182, 214, 218, 221, 256, 268, 295, 303, 328, 333, 398, 408
Savage, L.J., 6, 15
Scheinkman, Jose, 268

Schlag, Karl, 13
Schmeidler, David, 15, 160, 162, 405
Schneider, Martin, 17, 403, 408, 411
Schorfheide, Frank, 103
Seppälä, Juha, 44
Shakespeare, William, 15
Shannon, Chris, 15, 295, 327
Sims, Christopher A., 7, 10, 15, 16
Sin, K.S., 70
Siniscalchi, M., 15
Siow, Aloysius, 284
Sivan, R., 69
Stern, Hal S., 10
Stewart, G.W., 80, 99
Stock, J.H., 335
Stokey, Nancy, 119, 120, 138
Strzalecki, Tomasz, 15, 327, 403
Sudaresan, S.M., 226

Tallarini, Thomas D., 221, 227, 303, 307, 314
Tetlow, Robert, 335
Topel, Robert, 268
Tornell, Aaron, 173
Turing, Alan, 173
Turmuhambetova, Gauhar A., 15, 135, 137, 182, 408
Twain, Mark, 119

Van Dooren, P., 85, 86
Van Loan, C., 67, 68, 85, 99, 100
Vaughan, D.R., 78, 335
Velde, François, 380
von Neumann, John, 128
von zur Muehlen, Peter, 335
Vuong, Q.H., 10

Wang, Neng, 224, 226
Wang, Tan, 295
Weil, Phillipe, 308, 310, 312, 314
Werlang, Sergio, 15, 295
White, Halbert, 10

Whiteman, Charles, 173, 335
Whittle, Peter, ix, 22, 34, 44, 103,
	108, 109, 123, 186, 187, 381
Wilde, Oscar, 3
Wilkinson, J.H., 78

Williams, Noah, 15, 135, 137, 182,
	398, 408
Woodford, Michael, 5, 333, 335

Zhou, Kemin, 3, 193, 194
Zin, Stanley, 312

Matlab Index

bayes4.m, 52

detection2.m, 217
doublex9.m, 43, 368

olrp.m, 391

olrprobust.m, 43, 188

rfilter.m, 368
robust_stackelberg.m, 351
robust_stackelbergall.m, 351

schurg.m, 353

trick.m, 369